D1223448

DATE DUE

NOV 1 6 2004		
2-1-07 IL: 25863495		
1/2/08 IL 36593251		
APR 1 2 2010		
1/14/16 IL: 161470530		
12/10 17		

Demco, Inc. 38-293

GOVERNORS STATE UNIVERSITY LIBRARY

3 1611 00241 0444

Handbook of
School Mental Health
Advancing Practice and Research

Issues in Clinical Child Psychology

Series Editors: **Michael C. Roberts**, *University of Kansas—Lawrence, Kansas*
Lizette Peterson, *University of Missouri—Columbia, Missouri*

A Continuation Order Plan is available for this series. A continuation order will bring delivery of each new volume immediately upon publication. Volumes are billed only upon actual shipment. For further information please contact the publisher.

Handbook of
School Mental Health
Advancing Practice and Research

Edited by

Mark D. Weist, Ph.D.
University of Maryland School of Medicine
Baltimore, Maryland

Steven W. Evans, Ph.D.
James Madison University
Harrisonburg, Virginia

and

Nancy A. Lever, Ph.D.
University of Maryland School of Medicine
Baltimore, Maryland

Kluwer Academic / Plenum Publishers
New York, Boston, Dordrecht, London, Moscow

Library of Congress Cataloging-in-Publication Data

Handbook of school mental health/edited by Mark D. Weist, Steven Evans,
and Nancy Lever.
     p.   cm.
    Includes bibliographical references and index.
    ISBN 0-306-47337-2
      I. School children—Mental health services—United States—Handbooks, manuals, etc. 2.
School psychology—United States—Handbooks, manuals, etc. 3. Clinical
psychology—United States—Handbooks, manuals, etc. I. Weist, Mark D. II. Evans,
Steven, Ph.D. III. Lever, Nancy.

LB3430 .H36 2002
371.4′6—dc21

2002073083

ISBN: 0-306-47337-2

© 2003 Kluwer Academic / Plenum Publishers, New York
233 Spring Street, New York, New York 10013

http://www.wkap.nl/

10 9 8 7 6 5 4 3 2 1

A C.I.P. record for this book is available from the Library of Congress

All rights reserved

No part of this book may be reproduced, stored in a retrieval system, or transmitted in any form or
by any means, electronic, mechanical, photocopying, microfilming, recording, or otherwise,
without written permission from the Publisher, with the exception of any material supplied
specifically for the purpose of being entered and executed on a computer system, for exclusive use
by the purchaser of the work.

Printed in the United States of America

LB3430 .H36 2003
Handbook of school mental
health

Contributors

⁻ⁿⁱⁿⁱⁿⁱORS STATE UNIVERSITY
· ʲIVERSITY LIBRARY
UNIVERSITY PARK
ⁱⁱ 60466

Howard S. Adelman, UCLA Center for Mental Health in Schools, Los Angeles, California 90095-1563

Steve Adelsheim, New Mexico Department of Health, Santa Fe, New Mexico 87502

Jaleel Abdul Adil, University of Illinois at Chicago, Chicago, Illinois 60680

Melissa G. Ambrose, University of Maryland School of Medicine, Baltimore, Maryland 21201

Corinne Anderson-Ketchmark, School Social Workers Association of America, Northlake, Illinois 60164

Trina Menden Anglin, Health Resources and Services Administration, U.S. Department of Health and Human Services, Rockville, Maryland 20857

Marc S. Atkins, University of Illinois at Chicago, Chicago, Illinois 60680

Martin J. Blank, Institute for Educational Leadership, Washington, DC 20036

Eric J. Bruns, University of Maryland School of Medicine, Baltimore, Maryland 21201

Kristin V. Christodulu, State University of New York, Albany, Albany, New York 12222

Caroline Clauss-Ehlers, Rutgers University, Graduate School of Education, New Brunswick, New Jersey 08901

Shelly Cyrulik, Alliance for Children and Families, Milwaukee, Wisconsin 53224

Celene E. Domitrovich, Pennsylvania State University, University Park, Pennsylvania 16802

Kevin Dwyer, American Institutes for Research, Washington, DC 20007

Michael H. Epstein, University of Nebraska, Lincoln, Nebraska 68583

Pia Escudero, Los Angeles Unified School District Mental Health Services Unit, Van Nuys, California 91406

Steven W. Evans, James Madison University, Harrisonburg, Virginia 22807

Michael M. Faenza, National Mental Health Association, Alexandria, Virginia 22311

Michael E. Faran, Child and Adolescent Psychiatry Service, Tripler Army Medical Center, Honolulu, Hawaii 96859

Arlene Fink, University of California, Los Angeles, California 90095

Lois T. Flaherty, University of Maryland School of Medicine, Baltimore, Maryland 21201

Alicia Frank, James Madison University, Harrisonburg, Virginia 22807

Stacy L. Frazier, University of Illinois at Chicago, Chicago, Illinois 60680

Ellen Greenberg Garrison, American Psychological Association, Washington, DC 20002

Marcia Glass-Siegel, Baltimore Mental Health Systems, and Baltimore Public School Systems, Baltimore, Maryland 21202

Chandra Grabill, Dekalb County Schools, Decatur, Georgia 30032

Patricia A. Graczyk, University of Illinois at Chicago, Chicago, Illinois 60637

Mark K. Harniss, University of Washington, Seattle, Washington 98195

Susan Hill, University of Maryland School of Medicine, Baltimore, Maryland 21201

Kathy Hoganbruen, National Mental Health Association, Alexandria, Virginia 22311

Lisa Jaycox, RAND, Santa Monica, California 90407

Bjarne Kaer, Solomon Elementary School, Department of Education, Nahiawa, Hawaii 96796

Sheryl Kataoka, University of California, Los Angeles, Los Angeles, California 90095

Mary Margaret Kerr, University of Pittsburgh, Pittsburgh, Pennsylvania 15260

Hayin Kim, Children's Aid Society, New York, New York 10010

Laurel J. Kiser, University of Maryland School of Medicine, Baltimore, Maryland 21201

Michaela Kriz, University of Nebraska, Lincoln, Nebraska 68583

Joshua Langberg, James Madison University, Harrisonburg, Virginia 22807

Philip J. Leaf, Johns Hopkins University Bloomberg School of Public Health, Baltimore, Maryland 21205

Stephen S. Leff, Children's Hospital of Philadelphia, University of Pennsylvania School of Medicine, Philadelphia, Pennsylvania 19104

Heather D. Lehmkuhl, Department of Psychology, University of Cincinnati, Cincinnati, Ohio 45221

Nancy A. Lever, University of Maryland School of Medicine, Baltimore, Maryland 21201

Jennifer Axelrod Lowie, University of Maryland School of Medicine, Baltimore, Maryland 21201

Patricia H. Manz, Lehigh University College of Education, Bethlehem, Pennsylvania 18015

Jane W. McGrath, University of New Mexico School of Medicine, Albuquerque, New Mexico 87131

Matthew R. Mock, Department of Health and Human Services, Berkeley Mental Health, Family, Youth, and Children's Services, Berkeley, California 94704

Laura A. Nabors, Department of Psychology, University of Cincinnati, Cincinnati, Ohio 45221

David Nelson, National Mental Health Association, Alexandria, VA 22311

J. Ron Nelson, University of Nebraska, Lincoln, Nebraska 68182

Joseph E. Nyre, Harvard Medical School, Boston, Massachusetts 02115

David Osher, American Institutes for Research, Washington, DC 20007

Thomas J. Power, Children's Hospital of Philadelphia, University of Pennsylvania School of Medicine, Philadelphia, Pennsylvania 19104

Christine A. Prodente, Partial Hospitalization Program, Medical College of Ohio, Kobacker Center, Toledo, Ohio 43614

David B. Pruitt, University of Maryland School of Medicine, Baltimore, Maryland 21201

Jane Quinn, Children's Aid Society, New York, New York 10010

Nancy Rappaport, Teen Health Center, Cambridge Rindge and Latin School, Cambridge, Massachusetts 02139

Vestena Robbins, REACH, Louisville, Kentucky 40208

Michael C. Roberts, University of Kansas, Lawrence, Kansas 66045

Marcia Rubin, American School Health Association, Kent, Ohio 44240

Albert Y. Saito, Child and Adolescent Psychiatry Service, Tripler Army Medical Center, Honolulu, Hawaii 96859

Mark A. Sander, University of Maryland School of Medicine, Baltimore, Maryland 21201

Cindy M. Schaeffer, Johns Hopkins University Bloomberg School of Public Health, Baltimore, Maryland 21205

John Schlitt, National Assembly on School-Based Health Care, Washington, DC 20001

David Schultz, Johns Hopkins University Bloomberg School of Public Health, Baltimore, Maryland 21205

Nadine Schwab, Westport Public Schools, Westport, Connecticut 06880

Erika M. Steiger, Los Angeles Unified School District Mental Health Services Unit, Van Nuys, California 91406

Bradley D. Stein, University of Southern California, Los Angeles, California 90089

Susan B. Tager, University of Maryland School of Medicine, Baltimore, Maryland 21201

Elizabeth Talbott, Institute for Juvenile Research, Chicago, Illinois 60612

Linda Taylor, UCLA Center for Mental Health in Schools, Los Angeles, California 90095–1563

Ron Van Treuren, Seven Counties Services, Inc., Louisville, Kentucky 40220

Eric M. Vernberg, University of Kansas, Lawrence, Kansas 66045

Christine Walrath, Johns Hopkins Bloomberg School of Public Health, Baltimore, Maryland 21205

Jeffrey W. Weiser, Child and Adolescent Psychiatry Service, Tripler Army Medical Center, Honolulu, Hawaii 96859

Mark D. Weist, University of Maryland School of Medicine, Baltimore, Maryland 21201

Linda Wheeler, Alliance for Children and Families, Milwaukee, Wisconsin 53224

Jeff Williams, James Madison University, Harrisonburg, Virginia 22807

Marleen Wong, National Center for Traumatic Stress, Los Angeles, California 90095

Linda Yoshikami, Solomon Elementary School, Department of Education, Nahiawa, Hawaii 96796

Catalina Zaragoza, Los Angeles Unified School District Mental Health Services Unit, Van Nuys, California 91406

Joseph E. Zins, University of Cincinnati, Cincinnati, Ohio 45221

Foreword

It has been estimated that one in five children and adolescents experience the signs and symptoms of psychiatric disorders in any one year and that the probability of any one child or adolescent experiencing a disorder in their lifetime—prior to adulthood—approaches 33 to 50 per cent. Furthermore, aside from diagnosable disorders, the number of young people who suffer psychological problems and who are at risk for not developing into responsible and well-adjusted adults is even more staggering. The 2000 Report of the Surgeon General's Conference on Children's Mental Health asserted both the promotion of mental health in children and the treatment of mental disorders should be major public health goals. Mental health, of course, implies a positive concept and that our goal ought to be to address those factors that contribute to a state of well-being and that address how youth handle stress, relate to other people, and make decisions in their day-to-day lives. The goal is more than the treatment of disorders once they have developed. The goal is both proactive and preventative. It is also developmentally sensitive, ecologically embedded, empirically justified, and ethically defensible.

The school represents one such context in which state-of-the-art mental health services can be rendered. In this handbook, Coeditors Weist, Evans, and Lever, along with their impressive list of contributors, argue that the school setting is *the* setting that is best suited for both the promotion of mental health and the treatment of diverse mental disorders. Children and adolescents spend nearly as much waking time in school as they do with their families at home, making the school setting an appealing candidate for the provision of such services. Yet, the primary purpose of schooling—at least historically—is not mental health and the treatment of mental disorders. Its primary purpose is, of course, the education of students. Importantly, contributors to this volume argue that education and mental health are intimately enjoined and inseparable. I concur. It is difficult to imagine one without the other. Our children and adolescents do not only deserve and have a right to a good education; they also deserve, and have a right to, sound mental health and psychological well-being. To suggest or allow otherwise, would surely be a disservice to them ... and to us.

Yet, provision of such services in the school context is not easy or straightforward. Whether under the appellation of "school-based health centers," "full-service schools," "community schools," or "expanded school mental health services," considerable preparation, collaboration, and flexibility in purpose and prospect are needed. Above all else, considerable dialogue is required between and among the various partners—partnering at its best, no doubt. In this volume, the Editors have been most successful in soliciting the good work of outstanding contributors in this emerging discipline and in bringing this process to life. Five broad sections address (1) issues related to policy and advocacy; (2) strategies to enhance collaborative approaches in diverse settings; (3) delineation and advancement of effective approaches in various contexts; (4) current efforts to determine and promulgate "best practices;" and (5) cross-cutting issues that characterize the field including issues of generalization, cultural sensitivity, empirical support, and ethical and legal matters. All in all, the *Handbook* represents a formidable collection of essays and research papers that characterize initiatives aimed at "mental health in the schools." It is a volume that addresses important issues and a volume whose time has surely come.

Still, in reflecting upon the volume, one is left wondering if such a movement will address the shortcomings of school settings depicted long ago, such as that described by Shakespeare in *As You Like It* (Act II): "the whining schoolboy with his satchel and shining morning face creeping like a snail unwillingly to school." Will, or perhaps even should, they become settings in which children and adolescents willingly and in hare-like fashion clamor to attend? Of course, such idealism does not controvert the promises and prospects of school-based services. It simply articulates an aspiration, perhaps a goal for the movement to aspire toward. Schools should be fun, safe, and healthy places for our children. In pursuit of this goal, it will also be very important that this movement address the empirical status of its proposed interventions and services. Some support is presented in this volume, but more—much more—is needed. Although much is known already, much remains to be learned. What more appropriate place to advance and evaluate mental health services than in our schools?

Thomas H. Ollendick, Ph.D.
University Distinguished Professor
Virginia Polytechnic Institute and
State University
Blacksburg, Virginia

Acknowledgments

I thank my wife (Amber), children (Kylee, Jackson, Nathan, Tyler, Shannon), parents (Carole, Bob), and family (Anne, Bette, Dana, Dixie, Kara, Leah, Stan) for their love and support. My work on this book was supported by cooperative agreement U93MC00174 from the Office of Adolescent Health, Maternal and Child Health Bureau (Title V, Social Security Act), Health Resources and Services Administration, with co-funding by the Center for Mental Health Services, Substance Abuse and Mental Health Services Administration. (PHS413) MDW

I appreciate the foundation provided to me by my family (Judy, Addam, Ben, Emily, and Mom) and the guidance and teaching provided by my teachers and mentors: Bill Pelham, Jane Halonen, Betsy Short, Doug Detterman, and Toni Kring. They have all greatly influenced my ability to contribute to this book and pursue this career. Partial support for this project was provided by the Alvin V. Baird Attention and Learning Disabilities Center. SWE

Many thanks to my husband, Paul, for his encouragement and patience in the editing process and the home-cooked meals he provided at unusual hours. I would also like to thank my family, friends, and colleagues for all their guidance and support. Finally, I would like to acknowledge my coeditors for their fine work, and for offering me this wonderful opportunity. NAL

We would also like to express our appreciation to Tanya Bryant, Michael Roberts, Marcia Rubin, and Leah Rosner, who provided invaluable guidance and practical assistance in making this book a reality.

Contents

1

Introduction

Advancing Mental Health Practice and Research in Schools

MARK D. WEIST, STEVEN W. EVANS, and NANCY A. LEVER

This handbook attempts to capture the diverse and unique components of comprehensive mental health programs in schools within our nation. The roots of these programs can be found in the writings of late 19th-century educators such as John Dewey (see Sarason, 1996). Support for comprehensive school mental health ebbed and flowed throughout the 20th century (Flaherty, Weist, & Warner, 1996; Sedlak, 1997). However, it was not until the 1990s that a national movement in the United States to advance mental health in schools gained recognition.

This volume focuses on issues being confronted by *school-based* mental health programs, or those that are actually working within schools. These programs provide assessment, intervention, consultation, and/or prevention services directly in the school. They may be staffed entirely by school-employed staff (e.g., school psychologists, social workers, counselors), or may include staff from community agencies and programs (e.g., clinical, community, and counseling psychologists; clinical social workers; child and adolescent psychiatrists). A number of the chapters in the book will cite the term, "expanded school mental health," referring to programs that represent partnerships between schools and community organizations to provide a full array of services to youth in special *and* in general education (Weist, 1997). These partnerships present many advantages for both systems, for example, increased support to education and increased ability to reach youth "where they are" for mental health.

All chapters in the book are from leaders in this emerging field who are embracing the state of the art in research and practice and building bridges between

MARK D. WEIST and NANCY A. LEVER • University of Maryland School of Medicine, Baltimore, Maryland 21201.   STEVEN W. EVANS • James Madison University, Harrisonburg, Virginia 22807.

the two realms (Tashman et al., 2000). The book does not represent "clinics in schools" or "co-located" approaches to school mental health, involving providers coming into schools and operating independently in delivering services to youth with more serious problems. Instead, all chapters reflect an integrated approach, wherein staff are coming together within schools in interdisciplinary efforts that prioritize health-promoting and preventive efforts, while connecting to other programs and services in the community (see Dryfoos, 1998a; Weist et al., 2001). In such integrated approaches, mutual consultation with teachers; classroom, lunchroom, and playground observation and behavioral programming; and participation on school committees and teams are integral aspects of job descriptions of school mental health staff.

A constellation of factors has contributed to the progressive growth of comprehensive school-based mental health programs, with much of this growth occurring in the last decade. These factors include the following:

1. Increasing awareness of the considerable gap between youth who are in need of mental health services and youth who actually receive any mental health care (Burns et al., 1995; Leaf et al., 1996) and reasons for this gap (Evans, 1999; Garrison, Roy, & Azar, 1999; Knitzer, 1982; Weist, 1997).
2. The advancement of reforms in systems of child and adolescent mental health and education, such as the Child and Adolescent Service System Program (CASSP; Day & Roberts, 1991; Hodges, Nesman, & Hernandez, 1998) and revisions and improvements to the Individuals with Disabilities Education Act (Douglas, 1998; Tirozzi & Uro, 1997).
3. The important work of the Surgeon General in concert with federal and state leaders, advocates, and policymakers in dramatizing the mental health needs of youth and the need to attend to them proactively and effectively (U.S. Department of Health and Human Services, 1999; U.S. Public Health Service, 2000).
4. Systematic efforts to influence policy and expand and improve funding, technical assistance, and training at federal, state, and local levels (see Adelman et al., 1999; Adelman & Taylor, 1999).
5. The increasing focus on and support for youth development in communities (Catalano et al., 1999; National Research Council and Institute of Medicine, 2002).
6. The maturation and increasing sophistication of coalitions, especially those involving family members of youth with emotional and behavioral problems, and those focused on school-based health centers (Simpson et al., 1998; Dryfoos, 1998b).
7. Advancements in the science of child and adolescent mental health and the growth of the evidence base on effective interventions (Burns, Hoagwood, & Mrazek, 1999; Durlak & Wells, 1997, 1998; Greenberg, Domitrovich, & Bumbarger, 1999; Hibbs & Jensen, 1996; Nutbeam, 2001).
8. Emerging evaluation and outcome data documenting that school-based programs are reaching youth who are unlikely to receive care and are leading to improvements in outcomes valued by schools and communities (see Armbruster & Lichtman, 1999; Illback, Kalafat, & Sanders, 1997; Nabors & Reynolds, 2000; Weist et al., 1996).

We should note that our list reflects just some of the reasons for the increase in support and progressive growth of school-based mental health programs. The tragic events of September 11, 2001 have served to amplify attention to the significant mental health needs of communities, and of the benefits of providing care in natural settings such as schools. Indeed, schools in New York City and Washington, DC that had more comprehensive mental health programs in place prior to the tragedy were better able to respond to its multiple dimensions (Center for School Mental Health Assistance, 2001).

It should also be noted that school mental health staff represent a diverse coalition including educators, social workers, school psychologists, school counselors, nurses, clinical and counseling psychologists, licensed professional counselors, psychiatrists, nurse practitioners, pediatricians, and others. While many professional organizations have demonstrated support for school mental health, no one organization has or realistically can have full ownership. What is clear is that professional organizations focusing on the advancement of a particular discipline are not representing the school mental health field, since it is inherently interdisciplinary (Waxman, Weist, & Benson, 1999). It is also evident that efforts are needed to move people out of the status quo of discipline-specific training to participate in forums and conferences involving diverse disciplines working together, and promoting dialogue and cross training between practitioners, researchers, policymakers, and stakeholders (e.g., youth, families). Increasingly, there are venues that are doing just this, such as annual conferences of the American School Health Association, Center for School Mental Health Assistance, and National Assembly on School-Based Health Care.

In addition, there is a growing international dialogue on child and adolescent mental health- and school-based approaches. For example, World Conferences on Mental Health Promotion (led by the Clifford Beers Foundation), the International Union for Health Promotion and Education, the Society for Prevention Research, the International Congress on Behavior Therapy, and other forums are significantly enhancing the global dialogue on child and adolescent mental health. In these dialogues, it is becoming apparent that the United States is behind many other countries due to our lack of emphasis on broad efforts to promote mental health and prevent emotional and behavioral problems (see Rajala, 2001; Rowling, 2002; World Health Organization, 1995). Related to the dominance of fee-for-service reimbursement for established problems as the primary mechanism to fund health care, it must be acknowledged that in the United States we have an "illness care" versus "health care" system. However, a paradigm shift is occurring as this fact is recognized, the science base of prevention is becoming public, and the value of mental health promotion is being demonstrated (Walker & Rowling, 2002; Weist, 2001). The work of schools in this paradigm shift cannot be understated, as there is probably no better place to launch health-promoting and preventive interventions for communities (WHO, 1995).

As the nation moves to increase its attention on the learning, behavioral, and development needs of children and adolescents in schools, it is important to emphasize that this movement is still in its early stages, with considerable variability at both local and state levels (see Brener, Martindale, & Weist, 2001). Moreover, there are countless issues being addressed as school-based mental health programs confront unique challenges in all realms—in funding, training, practice, evaluation, and research. Given that school mental health is an emerging field, it is difficult to capture all of the important issues that are playing out in schools, localities, and states as the movement advances. Some of the major issues in advocacy, practice, and research that are receiving increasing attention include:

- Raising public awareness about youth mental health needs and the potential of school-based approaches to help to meet these needs.
- Advancing the breadth and impact of coalitions and advocacy groups focused on children's learning, health, and mental health, and increasing communication and coordinated activity between them.
- Influencing policy and developing new and expanding funding mechanisms to support the full continuum of mental health promotion, early intervention, and treatment in schools.
- Enhancing strategies for needs assessment and resource mapping to ensure that as resources for mental health in schools are enhanced, they are applied in a strategic manner.
- Implementing systems of early identification and screening, and doing so in ways that feed into advocacy agendas to build capacity.
- Building systems of quality assessment and improvement and developing models of best practice.
- Further building the evidence base and developing infrastructures to promote its use in schools.
- Continuing to develop and enhance systems of care by defining the work of schools and linking this work with other community programs and services.
- Developing strategies to improve family and other stakeholder involvement in program development, implementation, evaluation, and improvement.
- Improving training at all levels (preservice, graduate, postgraduate, etc.) for education, health, and mental health staff to work effectively in schools.
- Moving toward true interdisciplinary practice among staff of different educational levels and from different systems.
- Increasing opportunities for networking between practitioners, researchers stakeholders, advocates, and government officials locally, across states, and internationally.

This listing of issues is in no way comprehensive, but does reflect some of the major tasks ahead to advance mental health in schools. In addition to these issues, which reflect *processes* in need of enhancement, there are a number of specific content areas that represent important needs. These include broadening and improving efforts to address and prevent diverse forms of youth violence involvement and exposure (Acosta et al., 2001), and expanding programs to address substance-related problems (Center for School Mental Health Assistance, 2002). Moreover, schools are dealing with a host of issues post September 11, 2001. For example, they are now more pressed to develop well-functioning crisis prevention and response teams that are trained to handle a range of crises and traumatic events. The national crisis has also underscored the need for broad training in mental health (e.g., on stress, protective factors, emotional and behavioral problems, coping strategies) for all who work in schools, *before* any potential subsequent crises (Weist et al., in press). The magnitude of effort, knowledge, and resources required for schools to be prepared to handle significant traumatic events is staggering. Collaborative efforts led by practice and research communities in education, mental health, and the trauma fields can help move the agenda forward and reduce the burden on any one group.

Chapters in this handbook expand on all of the previously described issues and themes. The book contains five sections. The first section, *Background, Policy and Advocacy,* includes five chapters that review history and issues related to advancing policy, advocacy, research, and financing agendas. The second section, *Enhancing Collaborative Approaches,* includes five chapters reflecting connections being made in school mental health—at the federal level, between various professional disciplines, between schools and communities, and with families and other stakeholders. The third section, *School Mental Health in Context,* includes five chapters presenting the experiences of programs operating in distinctive settings and developing programs for students with distinctive needs. The fourth section, *Moving toward Best Practice,* includes five chapters focusing on principles for best practice, developing training programs, initiating quality assessment and improvement, focusing on student strengths, and implementing evidence-based programs. The fifth and final section of the book, *Cross-Cutting Issues,* includes four chapters discussing unique opportunities and challenges in the field—in preventing and responding to crises, programming for generalization, focusing on cultural competence, and negotiating unique legal and ethical issues.

At this moment in time, in the beginning of the 21st century, a constellation of factors has come together to increase not only our focus on but also our ability to improve systems of education and mental health for children, adolescents, and families. School-based mental health programs are at the nexus of this system transformation and improvement. Our hope is that this book captures the field's key issues and themes, past and present, while helping to spur its development to new levels of outreach and effectiveness.

REFERENCES

Acosta, O. M., Albus, K., Reynolds, M., & Weist, M. D. (2001). Assessing the status of research on violence-related problems among youth. *Journal of Clinical Child Psychology, 30,* 152–160.

Adelman, H. S., & Taylor, L. (1999). Mental health in schools and systems restructuring. *Clinical Psychology Review, 19,* 137–164.

Adelman, H. S., Taylor, L., Weist, M. D., Adelsheim, S., Freeman, B., Kapp, L., Lahti, M., & Mawn, D. (1999). Mental health in schools: A federal initiative. *Children's Services: Social Policy, Research, and Practice, 2,* 95–115.

Armbruster, P., & Lichtman, J. (1999). Are school-based mental health services effective? Evidence from 36 inner city schools. *Community Mental Health Journal, 35,* 493–504.

Brener, N. D., Martindale, J., & Weist, M. D. (2001). Mental health and social services: Results from the School Health Policies and Programs Study 2000. *Journal of School Health, 71,* 305–312.

Burns, B. J., Costello, E. J., Angold, A., Tweed, D., Stangle, D., Farmer, E. N. Z., & Erkanli, A. (1995). Data watch: Children's mental health service use across service sectors. *Health Affairs, 13,* 147–159.

Burns, B. J., Hoagwood, K., & Mrazek, P. J. (1999). Effective treatment for mental disorders in children and adolescents. *Clinical Child and Family Psychology Review, 2,* 199–254.

Catalano, R. F., Berglund, M. L., Ryan, J. A., Lonczak, H. S., & Hawkins, J. D. (1999). *Positive youth development in the United States: Research findings on evaluations of positive youth development programs.* Seattle, WA: Social Development Research Group, University of Washington School of Social Work.

Center for School Mental Health Assistance (2001, November). *Coping and moving forward.* Baltimore, MD: Author.

Center for School Mental Health Assistance (2002, February). *The interface between expanded school mental health and substance-related services for youth.* Baltimore, MD: Author.

Day, C., & Roberts, M. C. (1991). Activities of the Children and Adolescent Service System Program for improving mental health services for children and families. *Journal of Clinical Child Psychology, 20,* 340–350.

Douglas, L. (1998). *The new IDEA and opportunities for school mental health.* Baltimore, MD: Center for School Mental Health Assistance.

Dryfoos, J. G. (1998a). *Safe passage: Making it through adolescence in a risky society.* New York: Oxford University Press.

Dryfoos, J. G. (1998b). School-based health centers in the context of education reform. *Journal of School Health, 68,* 404–408.

Durlak, J. A., & Wells, A. M. (1997). Primary prevention mental health programs for children and adolescents. *American Journal of Community Psychology, 25,* 115–152.

Durlak, J. A., & Wells, A. M. (1998). Evaluation of indicated preventive interventions (secondary prevention) mental health programs for children and adolescents. *American Journal of Community Psychology, 26,* 775–802.

Evans, S. W. (1999). Mental health services in schools: Utilization, effectiveness, and consent. *Clinical Psychology Review, 19,* 165–178.

Flaherty, L. T., Weist, M. D., & Warner, B. S. (1996). School-based mental health services in the United States: History, current models and needs. *Community Mental Health Journal, 32,* 341–352.

Garrison, E. G., Roy, I. S., & Azar, V. (1999). Responding to the mental health needs of Latino children and families through school-based services. *Clinical Psychology Review, 19,* 199–219.

Greenberg, M. T., Domitrovich, C., & Bumbarger, B. (1999). *Preventing mental disorders in school-age children: A review of the effectiveness of prevention programs.* University Park, PA: Pennsylvania State University, Prevention Research Center.

Hibbs, E. D., & Jensen, P. (1996). *Psychosocial treatments for child and adolescent disorders: Empirically based strategies for clinical practice.* Washington, DC: American Psychological Association.

Hodges, S., Nesman, T., & Hernandez, M. (1998). *Systems of care: Promising practices in building collaboration.* Washington, DC: Center for Effective Collaboration and Practice, American Institutes for Research.

Illback, R. J., Kalafat, J., & Sanders, D. (1997). Evaluating integrated service programs. In R. J. Illback, C. T. Cobb, & H. M. Joseph (Eds.), *Integrated services for children and families: Opportunities for psychological practice* (pp. 323–346). Washington, DC: American Psychological Association.

Knitzer, J. (1982). *Unclaimed children: The failure of public responsibility for children and adolescents in need of mental health services.* Washington, DC: Children's Defense Fund.

Leaf, P. J., Alegria, M., Cohen, P., Goodman, S. H., Horowitz, S. M., Houen, C. W., Narrow, W. E., Vaden-Kiernan, M., & Regeier, D. A. (1996). Mental health service use in the community and schools: Results from the 4 community MECA study. *Journal of American Academy of Child and Adolescent Psychiatry, 35,* 889–897.

Nabors, L. A., & Reynolds, M. W. (2000). Program evaluation activities: Outcomes related to treatment for adolescents receiving school-based mental health services. *Children's Services: Social Policy, Research, and Practice, 3,* 175–189.

National Research Council and Institute of Medicine (2002). *Community programs to promote youth development.* Committee on Community-Level Programs for Youth. Board on Children, Youth, and Families. Division of Behavioral and Social Sciences and Education. Washington, DC: National Academy Press.

Nutbeam, D. (2001). Evidence-based public policy for health: Matching research to policy need. *Promotion and Education (supplement),* 15–19.

Rajala, M. (2001). European developments in health promotion. *Promotion and Education (supplement),* 5–6.

Rowling, L. (2002). Mental health promotion. In L. Rowling, G. Martin, & L. Walker (Eds.), *Mental health promotion and young people* (pp. 10–23). New York: McGraw–Hill.

Sarason, S. B. (1996). *Barometers of change: Individual, educational, and social transformation.* San Francisco: Jossey–Bass.

Sedlak, M. W. (1997). The uneasy alliance of mental health services and schools: An historical perspective. *American Journal of Orthopsychiatry, 67,* 349–362.

Simpson, J. S., Koroloff, N., Friesen, B. J., & Gac, J. (1998). *Systems of care: Promising practices in family-provider collaboration.* Washington, DC: Center for Effective Collaboration and Practice, American Institutes for Research.

Tashman, N. A., Weist, M. D., Acosta, O. M., Bickham, N. L., Grady, M., Nabors, L. A., & Waxman, R. (2000). Toward the integration of prevention research and expanded school mental health programs. *Children's Services: Social Policy, Research, and Practice, 2,* 95–115.

Tirozzi, G. N., & Uro, G. (1997). Education reform in the United States: National policy in support of local efforts for school improvement. *American Psychologist, 52,* 241–249.

U.S. Department of Health and Human Services (1999). *Mental health: A report of the Surgeon General.* Rockville, MD: U.S. Department of Health and Human Services, Substance Abuse and Mental Health Services Administration, Center for Mental Health Services, National Institutes of Health, National Institute of Mental Health.

U.S. Public Health Service (2000). *Report on the Surgeon General's Conference on Children's Mental Health: A national action agenda.* Washington, DC: U.S. Government Printing Office.

Walker, L., & Rowling, L. (2002). Debates and confusion, collaboration and emerging practice. In L. Rowling, G. Martin, & L. Walker (Eds.), *Mental health promotion and young people* (pp. 1–9). New York: McGraw-Hill.

Waxman, R. P., Weist, M. D., & Benson, D. M. (1999). Toward collaboration in the growing education–mental health interface. *Clinical Psychology Review, 19,* 239–253.

Weist, M. D. (1997). Expanded school mental health services: A national movement in progress. In T. H. Ollendick & R. J. Prinz (Eds.), *Advances in clinical child psychology* (Vol. 19, pp. 319–352). New York: Plenum Press.

Weist, M. D. (2001). Toward a public mental health promotion and intervention system for youth. *Journal of School Health, 71,* 101–104.

Weist, M. D., Paskewitz, D. A., Warner, B. S., & Flaherty, L. T. (1996). Treatment outcome of school-based mental health services for urban teenagers. *Community Mental Health Journal, 32,* 149–157.

Weist, M. D., Proescher, E., Prodente, C., Ambrose, M. G., & Waxman, R. (2001). Mental health, health, and education staff working together in schools. *Child and Adolescent Psychiatric Clinics of North America, 10,* 33–43.

Weist, M. D., Sander, M. A., Lever, N. A., Rosner, L. E., Pruitt, D. B., Lowie, J. A., Hill, S., Lombardo, S., & Christodulu, K. V. (in press). School mental health's response to terrorism and disaster. *Journal of School Violence.*

World Health Organization (1995). *The health promoting school—A framework for action in the WHO Western Pacific Region.* Regional Office for the Western Pacific: Author.

I

Background, Policy, and Advocacy

2

History of School-Based Mental Health Services in the United States

LOIS T. FLAHERTY and DAVID OSHER

INTRODUCTION

The evolution of school mental health services has occurred over a long time span and reflects social developments outside of education, changes in dominant philosophies and approaches to public education, and developments in those professional fields that relate to school mental health.

SOCIAL DEVELOPMENTS THAT SHAPED SCHOOL MENTAL HEALTH

School-based mental health services, as we know them, developed during the Progressive Era, an era of local, state, and national reform that began in the 1890s and continued until about 1930. Schools changed dramatically during this period. The average number of days in a school year increased from 135 to 173; the average days attended increased from 86 to 143; secondary school enrollment increased from 203,000 to 4.4 million; and public school enrollment increased from 12.7 to 25.7 million (Fagan, 2000). There was no longer one type of student, and as reformers looked at the implications of urbanization and industrial change, they called upon schools to address matters that had previously been viewed as the purview of the home—health, industrial education, recreation, and ultimately mental hygiene (Hunter, 1904; Levine & Levine, 1992).

Progressive Era school-based mental health reflected the confluence of four sets of factors: (1) compulsory education and laws restricting child labor services

LOIS T. FLAHERTY • University of Maryland School of Medicine, Baltimore, Maryland 21201.
DAVID OSHER • American Institutes for Research, Washington, DC 20007.

(Fagan, 1992; Richardson & Parker, 1993); (2) immigration and concerns about social order (Rothman, 1980); (3) urbanization and concerns about public health; and (4) professional and scientific developments in psychology, social work, and education. The services that developed during the Progressive Era did not reach all students, were never accepted as part of the core of schools by many educators, and changed over time. Still, they altered the landscape of schools from places where teachers were the only professionals in settings where teachers constituted a little more than half of the school staff (Kandel, 1924; U.S. Department of Education, 2000).

EDUCATIONAL DEVELOPMENTS THAT SHAPED SCHOOL MENTAL HEALTH

While Progressive Era education reforms embodied competing ideological approaches (Hendrick & MacMillan, 1989; Lazerson, 1971), they responded to a set of commonly agreed-upon problems. Progressives addressed four basic educational challenges: more students were attending schools (or supposed to attend schools) and they were not ready to learn; the presence of these students increased discipline problems for teachers; there was an increasing cultural disconnect between schools and school staff on the one hand and the students who they were supposed to teach on the other; and the failure to educate these students posed a public health and social control problem.

Fixing Schools

One set of reformers wanted to "fix" schools. This group included educators such as Julia Richman and John Dewey and social workers and reformers such as Jane Addams and her Hull House colleagues. These reformers wanted to transform education pedagogically and to create community schools that addressed barriers to learning. John Edward Wallace Wallin expressed the perspective of this group when he asked, if the child was to be compelled to attend schools, was "it not his right, under parity of reasoning, to demand that the state put him in such condition that he can assimilate those contents demanded of him by a compulsory education law?" (Wallin, 1914, pp. 17–18). The goal of fixing schools was extended by the mental hygiene movement and progressive educators such as William Heard Kilpatrick who embraced mental hygiene values and called for classroom settings that promoted mental health (Zilversmit, 1993).

Fixing Students

A second set of reformers (including some mental hygienists) viewed mental health services as a mechanism for addressing academic and behavioral problems among students. Increasingly, after 1930, failures of adaptation were explained on the basis of psychopathology and students were referred to clinics outside of the school to be treated before they could return to school (Levine & Graziano, 1972; Wallin & Ferguson, 1967).

The tension between adapting the school and fixing the child was reflected in special education where developments for children with mental health needs included the creation of nongraded and special classes. These developments had roots in concerns with unruly students (Franklin, 1994), which increased in cities during the late 19th century. "An Experiment in Discipline," by a San Francisco school principal, involved a "deportment class" created for students "of such a type that the necessity of their segregation was admitted" (U.S. Commissioner of Education, 1886, p. CVI). Similar classes for "truants, disciplinary cases, and backward children" were formed in other cities (Reigart, 1924, p. 314). While reformers such as William Henry Maxwell, New York City's Superintendent of Schools, wanted special classes for children with mental retardation in order to "develop each child, fit or unfit, to his highest education" (1910, quoted in Hendrick & MacMillan, 1989, p. 399), it was the increase in school enrollment and disciplinary concerns that drove practice so that students with behavioral problems filled special education classes (Hendrick & MacMillan, 1989).

CHANGING VIEWS OF THE CHILD

Just as progressive reforms changed how people viewed schools, so a new conceptualization of child development asked schools to adjust their approaches to improve educational and social outcomes (Sarason, 2001). Here, too, there were divergent ideological perspectives. While Granville Stanley Hall and John Dewey attempted to shape the organization of schools and learning to better fit the needs of children, other psychologists articulated a conceptualization of intelligence that had more conservative implications. Lewis Terman conceptualized human intelligence as a fixed and measurable commodity and in doing so provided educators with a mechanism to sort and segregate students who could not succeed in the school as currently organized (Chapman, 1988). These conceptualizations resulted in the development of new organizational forms. Hall created Child Study Teams in the 1880s, which promoted a child-centered as opposed to teacher-centered approach to learning. Lightner Witmer founded the first psychological clinic in the United States at the University of Pennsylvania in 1896 (Witmer, 1940), and the Chicago Juvenile Court (established in 1899) created the Juvenile Psychopathic Institute in 1909. The child guidance clinic, which evolved from these three developments, coupled individual treatment with collaboration with schools, agencies, and churches to change the child's ecology (Fagan, 2000).

THE IMPACT OF PROGRESSIVE REFORM

While the Progressive Era reformers disagreed ideologically about whether to focus interventions on schools or students, they agreed that schools should teach more than the three R's. Their agreement—an expanded agenda for public education—included "visiting teachers" (the counterparts of present-day school social workers), vocational counseling, special education classes, and school clinics. Their innovations outlived the Progressive Era, framing education between the First and Second World Wars (1914–1917 and 1940–1945) (Cremin, 1964). Despite the importance of the progressive paradigm for educational policy, four factors limited its influence on schools. First, racial segregation, which increased during the Progressive Era, limited the services that were provided to African American students (Dittmer, 1977). Second, the economic depression of the 1930s depleted schools' financial resources, so that only more affluent schools could afford any ancillary services (Tyack, 1992). Third, many educators and citizens still believed in an education model that did not include student support services as part of the mission of schools (Sarason, 2001; Tyack & Cuban, 1995). Fourth, teachers rarely changed the way they taught (Zilversmit, 1993).

The dominance of progressive ideology started to fade in the 1930s and 1940s. By then, however, the organization of schools and their relationship to community agencies had changed. Schools were no longer only for one type of student, high school was no longer for the few, and motivation and readiness to learn were considered essential (Kandel, 1924). Now, clinics helped address children's mental health problems by directly treating them, rather than consulting with schools, as the original child guidance clinics had done (Levine & Levine, 1992).

DEVELOPMENT OF CORE DISCIPLINES

Nursing

The first school nurses were placed in New York City public schools in the early 20th century. School nursing has evolved through many vicissitudes since then. While not a mental health program *per se*, school nursing from its beginnings had as its goal the improvement of children's overall health and well-being, and the recognition that social problems were at the core of many children's health problems. In 1996, about 40,000 registered nurses were working in the 82,000 public schools in the United States (Lear, 1996).

Psychology

School psychologists have provided a significant part of school mental health services. Arnold Gesell was appointed to the first officially titled "school psychologist" position in 1915—a statewide position in Connecticut. In 1939 New York State only had 67 qualified school psychologists. The National Association of School Psychologists (NASP) was founded in 1969 during a period of rapid growth in school psychology. NASP membership grew from 455 in 1969 to 5141 in 1979 to 21,488 in June 1999 (Fagan & Bose, 2000).

School psychologists started to take on intervention roles by the 1920 and have extended this role during the past decade. However, job demands and role expectations, which emphasize assessment, and the large number of students who most school psychologists serve, limit their roles.

Psychiatry

Child psychiatry as a discipline essentially began in the 20th century, with physicians from pediatrics and neurology who became centrally involved in the juvenile justice and child guidance movements (Noshpitz, 1997). Knowledge of development, skill in interviewing children and performing other assessments, organizing and leading teams, and diagnostic formulation became the core functions of this emerging discipline. As training and certification became formalized for child psychiatrists, consultation to both schools and other agencies was defined as an essential part of their role.

School Counseling

School counseling originated as part of the vocational guidance movement that began in the early 1900s (Keys, 1998). During this period of time, school counselors primarily performed vocational assessments. The term "counselor" was rarely used, and the position was generally referred to as "school guidance." Initially guidance counselors were teachers with a little extra training

The role of guidance extended in the 1920s and 1930s as course options increased and as schools attempted to individualize opportunities for students. However, the amount of time available to each student was small. For example, Muncie, Indiana, provided students in grade 7 and above with 10 minutes of counseling per term with a quarter of these students being seen again each term (e.g., Lynd & Lynd, 1937).

During the 1950s school counselors broadened their focus from the purely vocational domain to an approach that integrated issues of personality and human growth and development (Keys, 1998; Schmidt, 1996) and became known as "guidance counselors." The federal government authorized funds for school counselors in the National Defense Education Act of 1958 (Schmidt, 1996). As a result, the number of school counselors employed by schools increased dramatically in a very short period of time.

Social Work

Developments in social work came out of the feminist- and reform-driven professionalism of settlement house workers in cities like Chicago and New York. While these agencies were run by women of privilege, they were community based and had much closer ties to families than did schools and their teachers. Visiting teachers were the forerunners of today's social workers. Concerned with the disconnect that existed between poor and immigrant families and schools, settlement house workers in New York worked with the Public Education Society to create a link between families and schools that the city's Board of Education would ultimately adopt.

Visiting teachers became school employees in the 1920s and 1930s, shifting their reporting responsibility and orientation to the school (Tyack, 1992). Nonetheless, the linkage role has continued and is the core of the profession of school social work (Allen-Meares, Washington, & Welsh, 1996).

Special Education

While early special education staff received generic training or training regarding retardation, behavior disorders became a major field of training and research in the late 1950s and 1960s. The field of behavior disorders moved away from psychodynamic approaches that focused on intrapsychic conflict. Training and services, instead, built upon development of psychoeducational (Redl & Wineman, 1957) and behavioral approaches (Hewett, 1968; Skinner, 1961) that incorporated ecological strategies (Brendtro & Van Bockern, 1998).

Interactions among Disciplines

While the disciplines of psychology, psychiatry, special education, and social work were separate, they interacted. Students of Lightner Witmer and Granville Stanley Hall collaborated to expand the focus of the child study team (which had focused on both "normal development" and regular education) to include abnormal development and include special education (Fagan, 1992). Psychometric tests were employed in New York City to select children for special education (Hendrick & MacMillan, 1989). Settlement house workers produced research that framed and linked school reform and public policy (Breckenridge, 1917). Similarly, the influences of Jane Addams and John Dewey went far beyond their respective disciplines of social work and education. Addams and Dewey played roles in the creation of the Juvenile Court, and William Healy, in turn, employed Dewey's pedagogy in his design of the Juvenile Psychopathic Institute.

The Child Guidance Team included a psychologist to test and assess the child, a psychiatric social worker to visit the family, and a psychiatrist to do a clinical interview with the child. These three mental health professionals would meet as a team with the child's teachers, guidance counselor, nurse, and an administrator. The American Orthopsychiatric Association was formed in 1924 as an interdisciplinary organization of psychologists, psychiatrists, and social workers who worked in the Child Guidance Clinics (Levine & Levine, 1992).

EVOLUTION OF MENTAL HEALTH PROGRAMS

The Community Mental Health Movement and School Consultation

Public concern over the deficiencies of current systems of care for the mentally ill grew in the 1950s and culminated in the landmark Community Mental Health Centers Act of 1963, which emphasized services in the community. Prevention of mental illness through consultation and education was one of the ultimate goals, and schools were seen as ideal settings in which to implement these aims (Caplan, 1970).

The growth of the community mental health movement coincided with the social activism and idealism of the 1960s. The movement was consistent with war on poverty legislation that supported early intervention such as Head Start, improving the quality of schools that served economically disadvantaged communities, and the effective use of paraprofessionals (Riessman & Popper, 1968). It addressed matters that progressive mental health and social workers had raised a half-century before.

In the community mental health paradigm, mental health professionals were envisioned as consultants who would teach and train others to carry out therapeutic interventions, thereby extending their effectiveness. The goal of mental health consultation to schools shifted from that of assessment and treatment of individual students, along with helping teachers understand and deal with individual students on a case-by-case basis (Caplan's definition of case-oriented consultation; see Caplan (1970)) to a more far-reaching goal of not only changing the functioning of teachers but altering the system as a whole.

The efforts of community mental health centers (CMHCs) to reach out to their communities, while not always successful, helped pave the way for later school-based and school-linked mental health centers (Flaherty, Weist, & Warner, 1996). Furthermore, their concern about having therapists from the community who could speak the language of their clients as well as the use of paraprofessionals foreshadowed today's notions of cultural competence.

Systems of Care and Collaboration with Schools

Concerns that disproportionate numbers of children with serious emotional disturbance were being removed from their communities led to the development of systems of care in the 1980s. In 1992, Congress passed the Comprehensive Mental Health Services for Children and Their Families Program which supported the development of these systems of care. A system of care is in or near the home and community. In fully developed systems of care, local public and private organizations work in teams with families and children to both plan and implement individualized services for each child's physical, emotional, social, educational, and family needs. Teams include family advocates and representatives from mental health, health, education, child welfare, juvenile justice, vocational rehabilitation, recreation, substance abuse, and other services. Systems of care have supported the use of mental health clinicians in schools, school- and community-based wraparound planning and services, and student support services (Woodruff et al., 1999).

Approaches to Providing School Mental Health Services

School-Based Health Centers (SBHCs)

Historically, SBHCs played an important role in setting the stage for placement of mental health services in schools. SBHCs grew out of the traditions of school nursing and public health clinics, and began in the 1980s to meet the need for primary health care for adolescents, the most underserved age group. With over 20% of visits related to mental health concerns (Lear et al., 1991), staff in SBHCs quickly perceived the need for mental health services and expanded their scope to include mental health counseling.

SBHCs increased from a total of 200 in 1990 to 1380 in 2000. Typically these centers are staffed by a full- or part-time nurse practitioner or a physician's assistant, sometimes accompanied by an aide/receptionist, and a master's-level mental health clinician, such as a social worker. Originally most SBHCs were in urban high schools, but there has been a recent trend toward placing new centers in suburban areas and in elementary schools (Center for Health and Health Care in Schools, 2001).

Expanded School Mental Health Programs

Expanded school mental health (ESMH) programs provide a range of mental health services to youth in both regular and special education (Weist, 1997). These services include those that have historically been provided in community mental health centers, hospital outpatient clinics, and private offices, such as diagnostic assessment, individual, group, and family psychotherapy, crisis intervention, and case management. In addition, some programs implement preventive services, including classroom consultation and mental health education. ESMH programs supplement and expand upon mental health services traditionally offered in schools, which tend to focus on crisis management and the needs of students receiving special education services. Like the SBHC movement, ESMH programs also received their impetus in the 1980s, as knowledge of the high prevalence of psychosocial problems among youth, especially in poor communities, and the long-term implications of these problems in terms of morbidity and mortality increased.

Full-Service Schools

Full-service schools bring together resources from multiple sources to make an array of services available to a community, using the school as the organizing principle (Dryfoos, 1994). Services provided typically include primary health care and social services, sometimes but not always on site in the school, with the goal of replacing fragmented and overlapping services with "one-stop shopping." The emphasis is on linking the school and the community. Services included in full-service schools are extremely varied; they might include English as a second-language tutoring for adults, community policing, and childcare, in addition to more traditional health, mental health, and social services.

Comprehensive School and Systemwide Approaches

Some have argued that schoolwide interventions to address mental and social problems, which are the major reasons for school failure, be included as an essential aspect of school reform and school restructuring (Adelman & Taylor, 2000). Comer's School Development Program, which includes a mental health team that coordinates schoolwide activities to address the mental health needs of all students, is an example (Comer, 1988), as is the three-level comprehensive approach to school safety that links school safety, school reform, and addressing the mental health needs of all students (Dwyer & Osher, 2000). Services range in level of intensity in accordance with need and include preventive services.

POLICY AND FUNDING INITIATIVES

Although the federal government only supplies about 15% of the total funding for education, numerous federal mandates have shaped the course of education. A few key programs are described briefly in the following section.

Federal Education Legislation

The exclusion of over a million children with behavioral problems from public schools led to the passage of the Individuals with Disabilities Education Act (IDEA) of 1975. For the first time, a "free and appropriate public education" was to be made available to disabled children, including those with emotional and mental handicaps, in the least restrictive environment appropriate. The law also allocated resources to support preservice and in-service efforts to increase the capacity of teachers and related service providers. Subsequent amendments have continued to attempt to further define, and limit, this entitlement, and encourage help to be provided to children with special needs to remain in regular education. Despite all its problems, IDEA remains an attempt to actualize the ideal of educating all children.

While the IDEA transformed services for many students, it had less impact on children with emotional disturbances (Knitzer, Steinberg, & Fleisch, 1990), in part because they and their families were more likely to be stigmatized and because improving outcomes for them was contingent upon services from multiple service providers (Osher & Osher, 1996). The National Agenda for Improving Results for Children and Youth with Serious Emotional Disturbance (U. S. Department of Education, 1994) promoted prevention, early intervention, and collaboration, and was the base for much training and research in the 1990s. The Agenda's seven targets are (1) to expand positive learning opportunities and results, (2) to strengthen school and community capacity, (3) to value and address diversity, (4) to collaborate with families, (5) to promote appropriate assessment, (6) to provide ongoing skill development and support, and (7) to create comprehensive and collaborative systems.

The 1997 amendments to the IDEA promote collaboration. For example, Section 300.235a(2) gives local education agencies permission to use a portion of their federal special education funds to become involved in building a system of care including incorporating IEPs into other individualized service plans and in developing interagency financing strategies. Section 300.370a(7) authorizes the use of a proportion of state educational agency IDEA funds to support collaboration with other agencies.

Other Federal Initiatives

The Office of Juvenile Justice and Delinquency Prevention (OJJDP) of the U.S. Department of Justice has funded efforts to address school dropouts and truancy. The Safe and Drug Free School Program of the U.S. Department of Education, the Center for Mental Health Services of the U.S. Department of Health and Human Services, and OJJDP have jointly funded Safe Schools/Healthy Students Grants, which involve collaborations among schools, mental health, and the police. The Centers for Disease Control and Prevention (CDC) has identified youth violence and suicide as a public health issue. Accordingly, the CDC has sponsored initiatives to study interventions aimed at reducing the prevalence of high-risk behavior among children and adolescents. (For further information, see Chapter 9.)

State and Local Efforts

State support for school mental health may occur through administrative organization, support of systems of care, and through the provision of direct financial resources for schools and mental health services. Two possible models of administration are (1) Education and Mental Health are linked in a Children's

Cabinet or similar initiative (e.g., Michigan), and (2) State Departments of Education have full-time consultants in school psychology, social work, and/or emotional and behavioral disorders. Local communities' financial resources (e.g., tax base and grants) vary; consequently some schools have many mental health personnel, while others either lack these resources or have fragmented services (Woodruff et al., 1999).

SUMMARY AND CONCLUSION

The history of school mental health in the United States has been influenced by changes in society and in schools, in the development of professions, and in the expansion of the knowledge base within education and mental health. The ideals of justice and equal opportunity were embodied in notions of a common school where all learned together. These ideals evolved into a mission to help all children reach their full potential with the goals of producing citizens who were fully able to participate in a democratic society. Translating this egalitarian ideal into practice, however, meant doing something about the fact that many children did not succeed in school. While goals of academic excellence led to tracking of students and exclusion of those who did poorly, increasing awareness of the barriers posed to optimal development and learning by poverty, racism, gender discrimination, disability, and unsupportive schools has led to a renewed emphasis on helping all children to succeed. The movement from an exclusive focus on special education, with its focus on segregating children who are falling behind their peers, to expanded school mental health programs, designed to help all children, is one outcome of a broadening vision of educational opportunity. School mental health services have the potential to be part of the effort to optimize child development and to help all children succeed.

REFERENCES

Adelman, H. S., & Taylor, L. (2000). Shaping the future of mental health in schools. *Psychology in the Schools, 37,* 49–60.

Allen-Meares, P., Washington, R. O., & Welsh, B. L. (1996). *Social work services in schools.* Boston: Allyn & Bacon.

Breckenridge, S. (1917). *Truancy and non-attendance in the Chicago public schools.* Chicago: University of Chicago Press.

Brendtro, L. K., & Van Bockern, S. (1998). Courage for the discouraged: A psychoeducational approach to troubled and troubling children. In R. J. Whelan (Ed.). *Emotional and behavioral disorders: A 25 year focus* (pp. 229–252). Denver: Love Publishing.

Caplan, G. (1970). *The theory and practice of mental health consultation.* New York: Basic Books.

Center for Health and Health Care in Schools (2001). *School-based health centers: Results from a 50-state survey* school year 1999–2000. Washington, DC: The Center for Health and Health Care in Schools. http://www.healthinschools.org/sbhcs/sbhcs_table.htm.

Chapman, P. D. (1988). *Schools as sorters: Lewis M. Terman, applied psychology and the intelligence testing movement, 1890–1930.* New York: New York University Press.

Comer, J. (1988). Educating poor and minority children. *Scientific American, 259,* 42–48.

Cremin, L. A. (1964). *The transformation of the school: Progressivism in American education, 1876–1957.* New York: Vintage.

Dittmer, J. (1977). *Black Georgia in the Progressive Era, 1900–1920.* Urbana: University of Illinois Press.

Dryfoos, J. G. (1994). *Full-service schools.* San Francisco: Jossey–Bass.

Dwyer, K., & Osher, D. (2000). *Safeguarding our children: An action guide.* Washington, DC: U.S. Departments of Education and Justice, American Institutes for Research.

Fagan, T. K. (1992). Compulsory schooling, child study, clinical psychology, and special education: Origins of school psychology. *American Psychologist, 47,* 236–243.

Fagan, T. K. (2000). Practicing school psychology: A turn-of-the-century perspective. *American Psychologist, 55,* 754–757.

Fagan, T. K., & Bose, J. (2000). NASP: A profile of the 1990s. *NASP Communiqué, 29,* 10–11.

Ferinden, W. E., Jr., & Van Handel, D. C. (1974). *The handbook of school social work.* Linden, NJ: Remediation Associates.

Flaherty, L. T., Garrison, E., Waxman, R., Uris, P., Keyes, S., Siegel, M. G., & Weist, M. D. (1998). Optimizing the roles of school mental health professionals. *Journal of School Health, 68,* 420–424.

Flaherty, L. T., Weist, M. D., & Warner, B. S. (1996). School-based mental health services in the United States: History, current models and needs. *Community Mental Health Journal, 32,* 341–352.

Franklin B. M. (1994). *From 'backwardness' to 'at-risk': Childhood learning difficulties and the contradictions of school reform.* Albany, NY: State University of New York Press.

Hendrick, I. G., & MacMillan, D. L. (1989). Selecting children for special education in New York City: William Maxwell, Elizabeth Farrell, and the development of ungraded classes, 1900–1920. *Journal of Special Education, 22,* 395–417.

Hewett, F. (1968). *The emotionally disturbed child in the classroom: A developmental strategy for educating children with maladaptive behavior.* Boston: Allyn & Bacon.

Hunter, R. (1904). *Poverty.* New York: Macmillan.

Kandel, I. L. (Ed.). (1924). *Twenty-five years of American education: Collected essays.* New York: Macmillan.

Keys, S. G. (1998). *School counseling.* Unpublished work.

Knitzer, J., Steinberg, Z., & Fleisch, B. (1990). *At the schoolhouse door: An examination of programs and policies for children with behavioral and emotional problems.* New York: Bank Street College of Education.

Lazerson, M. (1971). *Origins of the urban school: Public education in Massachusetts, 1870–1915.* Cambridge, MA: Harvard University Press.

Lear, J. G., Gleicher, H. B., St. Germaine, A., & Porter, P. J. (1991). Reorganizing health care for adolescents: The experience of the school-based adolescent health care program. *Journal of Adolescent Health, 12,* 450–458.

Lear, J. G. (1996). School-based services and adolescent health: Past, present, and future. *Adolescent Medicine: State of the Art Reviews, 7,* 163–180.

Levine, M., & Graziano, A. M. (1972). Intervention programs in elementary schools. In S. E. Golann & C. Eisdorier, (Eds.) *Handbook of Community Mental Health* (pp. 541–574). New York, NY: Appleton-Century-Crofts.

Levine, M., & Levine, A. (1992). *Helping children: A social history.* New York: Oxford University Press.

Lynd, R. S., & Lynd, H. M. (1937). *Middletown in transition: A study in cultural conflicts.* New York: Harcourt, Brace.

Nastasi, B. K., Varjas, K., & Bernstein, R. (1997). *Exemplary mental health programs: School psychologists as mental health service providers.* Bethesda, MD: National Association of School Psychologists.

Noshpitz, J. D. (1997). A brief history of child mental health in the United States. In J. D. Noshpitz, P. L. Adams, & E. Bleiberg (Eds.), *Handbook of child and adolescent psychiatry* (Vol. 7, pp. 3–48). New York: Wiley.

Osher, D., & Hanley, T. V. (2001). Implementing the SED national agenda: Promising programs and policies for children and youth with emotional and behavioral problems. *Education and Treatment of Children, 24,* 374–403.

Osher, D., & Osher, T. (1996). The National agenda for children and youth with serious emotional disturbances. In M. Nelson, R. Rutherford, and B. Wolford (Eds.), *Comprehensive Collaborative Systems that Work for Troubled Youth: A National Agenda* (pp. 149–164). Richmond, KY: National Coalition for Juvenile Justice Services.

Redl, F., & Wineman, D. (1957). *The aggressive child.* New York: Free Press.

Reigart, J. F. (1924). Education of exceptional children. In I. L. Kandel (Ed.), *Twenty-five years of American education: Collected essays* (pp. 309–331). New York: Macmillan.

Richardson, J. G., & Parker, T. L. (1993). The institutional genesis of special education: The American case. *American Journal of Education, 101,* 359–392.

Riessman, F., & Popper, H. I. (1968). *Up from poverty: New career ladders for nonprofessionals.* New York: Harper & Row.

Rothman, D. J. (1980). *Conscience and convenience: The asylum and its alternatives in progressive America.* Boston, MA: Little, Brown.

Sarason, S. B. (2001). *American psychology & schools: A critique.* New York: Teachers College Press.

Schmidt, J. (1996). *Counseling in schools.* Needham Heights, MA: Allyn & Bacon.

Skinner, B. F. (1961). *Cumulative record.* New York: Appleton–Century–Crofts.

Tyack, D. (1992). Health and social services in public schools: Historical perspectives. *The Future of Children,* Spring, 19–31.

Tyack, D., & Cuban, L. (1995). *Tinkering toward Utopia: A century of public school reform.* Cambridge, MA: Harvard University Press.

U. S. Commissioner of Education (1886). *Report of the commissioner of education for the year 1884–85.* Washington, DC: U.S. Government Printing Office.

U. S. Department of Education (1994). *National agenda for improving results for children and youth with serious emotional disturbance.* Washington, DC: Author.

U. S. Department of Education (2000). *Digest of educational statistics.* Washington, DC: Author.

Wallin, J. E. W. (1914). *The mental health of the school child, the psycho-educational clinic in relation to child welfare.* New Haven, CT: Yale University Press.

Wallin, J. E. W., & Ferguson, D. G. (1967). The development of school psychological services. In J. F. Magary (Ed.), *School psychological services in theory and practice: A handbook* (pp. 1–30). Englewood Cliffs, NJ: Prentice-Hall.

Weist, M. D. (1997). Expanded school mental health services: A national movement in progress. In T. H. Ollendick & R. J. Prinz (Eds.), *Advances in clinical child psychology* (pp. 319–352). New York: Plenum Press.

Witmer, H. L. (1940). *Psychiatric clinics for children.* New York: The Commonwealth Fund.

Woodruff, D. W., Osher, D., Hoffman, C. C., Gruner, A., King, M., Snow, S., & McIntire, J. C. (1999). *The role of education in a system of care: Effectively serving children with emotional or behavioral disorders.* Washington, DC: Center for Effective Collaboration and Practice, American Institutes for Research.

Yesseldyke, J., Dawson, P., Lehr, C., Reschly, D., Reynolds, M., & Telzrow, C. (1997). *School psychology: A blueprint for training and practice II.* Bethesda, MD: National Association of School Psychologists.

Zilversmit, A. (1993). *Changing schools: Progressive education theory and practice, 1930–1960.* Chicago, IL: University of Chicago Press.

3

Toward a Comprehensive Policy Vision for Mental Health in Schools

HOWARD S. ADELMAN and LINDA TAYLOR

The process of developing formal policy is political and related to the enactment of laws, regulations, and guidelines. By way of contrast, informal "policies" emerge because of the way people in institutions pursue daily actions. These take the form of routines, customs, rules, and other regularities that determine what is and is not done in a setting, and those that endure over a lengthy period of time can be characterized as the institution's culture (Adelman et al., 1999).

Those who want to enhance mental health (MH) in schools often engage in advocating for policy change and for new policies. However, as the multitude of categorically funded programs in schools and communities demonstrates, advocacy in the absence of a comprehensive and cohesive policy vision tends to produce fragmented agendas. It is such fragmented agendas that produce piecemeal and simplistic approaches to complex, multifaceted concerns. Thus, our focus here is on a comprehensive policy vision that encompasses and reframes MH in schools. Our overarching aim is to highlight a unifying vision for policy and practice around which various policy advocates can coalesce.

Specifically, the presentation covers three matters that those who want to enhance MH in schools should consider if they want to influence school policy in a fundamental way and on a large scale. We begin by highlighting current policy initiatives that shape how MH is addressed in schools and explore basic concerns arising from these initiatives. Then, from a policy perspective, we discuss the need to reframe the argument for MH in schools. Finally, we outline needed policy changes and the importance of connecting efforts to enhance MH in schools with school reform policy.

HOWARD S. ADELMAN and LINDA TAYLOR • UCLA Center for Mental Health in Schools, Los Angeles, California 90095-1563.

CURRENT POLICY AND PRACTICE

Efforts to change policy benefit from understanding the status quo. For our purposes, it will suffice to highlight three matters: (1) how the term *mental health* usually is interpreted in making policy, (2) how school reform policy addresses students who are not succeeding, and (3) how MH in school plays out under current policy.

Mental Health or Mental Illness?

There is a widespread policy trend to use the term mental *health* and to focus only on mental *illness, disorders, or problems.* When this occurs, mental health is *de facto* defined as the absence of problems, and there is a lack of emphasis in practice on promoting positive social and emotional development. This has resulted in an MH field that is primarily focused on problems. This focus has carried over into policy for MH in schools.

A step toward redressing this limited policy perspective is seen in the *Report of the Surgeon General's Conference on Children's Mental Health* (Surgeon General, 2000). Although no formal definition of mental health is given, the vision statement provided at the outset of the report stresses that "both the promotion of mental health in children and the treatment of mental disorders should be major public health goals." This statement uses the term *mental health* in ways that are consistent with definitional efforts to use "health" as a positive concept. For example, the Institute of Medicine (1997) defines health as "a state of well-being and the capability to function in the face of changing circumstances." A similar effort to contrast positive health with problem functioning is seen in SAMHSA's Center for Mental Health Services glossary of children's mental health terms. In that source, *mental health* is defined as "how a person thinks, feels, and acts when faced with life's situations. . . . This includes handling stress, relating to other people, and making decisions." This is contrasted with *mental health problems.* The designation *mental disorders* is described as another term used for mental health problems and the term *mental illness* is reserved for severe mental health problems in adults.

Although some youngsters have serious mental health disorders (or other disabilities) that can interfere with development and learning, it is important for policymakers to recognize that few children are born with such problems. (And despite serious disorders, individuals have assets, strengths, or protective factors that help counter deficits and contribute to success.) The majority of psychosocial and MH problems that youngsters experience arise because of community, family, school, peer, and individual difference factors and are not initially rooted in internal dysfunctions (Adelman & Taylor, 1994; Catalano & Hawkins, 1995). Unfortunately, these problems often are exacerbated as youngsters internalize the frustrations of confronting barriers to development and learning and the debilitating effects of performing poorly at school, at home, and in their neighborhoods (Adelman & Taylor, 1993; Allensworth et al., 1997; Carnegie Council on Adolescent Development, 1989; Dryfoos, 1990; Sarason, 1996; Schorr, 1997). We hasten to add that a perspective that recognizes the nature and scope of external barriers to development and learning in no way denies the reality that some individuals have true disorders and disabilities. The point is that current policy overemphasizes disorders and disabilities and thus does not adequately address the entire gamut of MH and psychosocial concerns.

School Reform Policy and Students Who Are Not Succeeding

Our analysis of school reform policy indicates that the primary focus is on two major components: (1) enhancing instruction and curriculum and (2) restructuring school governance/management. Increasingly, such efforts are shaped by policy calling for (1) higher standards and expectations, (2) a focus on results, (3) strategies that enhance direct academic support, (4) movement away from a deficiency model to a strengths or resilience-oriented paradigm, and (5) devolving control to school sites.

Beyond these primary considerations, there is a *secondary* focus on students who are not doing well. Here, three types of initiatives have emerged. One line of policy stresses approaches to deal with targeted problems. These "categorical" initiatives generate auxiliary programs, some supported by school district general funds and some underwritten by federal and private sector money. Examples of activities include those related to special and compensatory education; violence reduction; prevention of substance abuse, youth pregnancy, suicide, and dropouts; immunization campaigns; early periodic screening, diagnosis, and treatment; school-based health centers; family and youth resource centers; and so forth.

A second group of overlapping policies includes an emphasis on linking a broad range of community resources to schools. Terms used in conjunction with these initiatives include school-linked services—especially health and social services, full-service schools, school–community partnerships, and community schools. In a few states where such initiatives have been under way for some time, there are discussions of strengthening the linkage between school reforms and efforts to integrate community services and strengthen neighborhoods (e.g., see recent efforts related to Missouri's Caring Communities). Paralleling these efforts is a natural interest in promoting healthy development and productive citizens and workers.

A third set of initiatives is designed to promote a narrower focus on coordination and collaboration among *governmental* departments and their service agencies to foster integrated services with an emphasis on greater local control, increased involvement of parents, and locating services at schools when feasible. The federal government has offered various forms of support to foster this policy direction (e.g., Title XI of the Improving America's Schools Act of 1994 administered by the U.S. Department of Education, which was intended to foster service coordination for students and their families; a similar provision in the 1997 reauthorization of the Individuals with Disabilities Education Act; the Centers for Disease Control and Prevention's grants to foster Coordinated School Health Programs by establishing an infrastructure between state departments of health and education). Also, to encourage organizational changes, local, state, and federal intra- and interagency committees have been established, legislative bodies are rethinking their

committee structures, and some states have gone so far as to create new executive branch structures (e.g., combining all agencies and services for children and
families under one cabinet-level department). In their most ambitious forms, these
efforts are evolving into comprehensive community initiatives with an emphasis
on community building.

All of the initiatives are relevant to addressing *some* students who are not
succeeding at school. Obviously, it is important to understand what these initiatives accomplish, but the key to improving policy is understanding what more
they could accomplish with respect to addressing MH and psychosocial concerns.

Current School Practices

Currently, there are almost 91,000 public schools in about 15,000 districts.
Over the years, most (but obviously not all) schools have instituted programs designed with a range of MH and psychosocial concerns in mind. There is a large
body of research supporting the promise of much of this activity (e.g., see Center
for Mental Health in Schools, 2000).

School-based and school-linked programs have been developed for purposes
of early intervention, crisis intervention and prevention, treatment, and promotion of positive social and emotional development. Some programs are provided
throughout a district, others are carried out at or linked to targeted schools. The interventions may be offered to all students in a school, to those in specified grades,
or to those identified as "at risk." The activities may be implemented in either
regular or special education classrooms or as "pull-out" programs and may be
designed for an entire class, groups, or individuals. With specific respect to MH,
the full range of topics arise—including matters related to promoting MH, minimizing the impact of psychosocial problems, managing psychotropic medication,
and participating in systems of care. Well-developed systems include mechanisms
for case coordination, ongoing consultation, program development, advocacy, and
quality assurance. There also may be a focus on primary prevention and enhancement of healthy development through use of health education, health services,
guidance, and so forth—though relatively few resources usually are allocated for
such activity.

School districts use a variety of *personnel* to address MH concerns. These
may include "pupil services" or "support services" specialists such as psychologists, counselors, social workers, psychiatrists, and psychiatric nurses, as well
as a variety of related therapists (e.g., art, dance, music, occupational, physical,
speech, language–hearing, and recreation therapists). Such specialists tend to focus on students seen as problems or as having problems. As outlined in Table 1,
their many *functions* can be grouped into three categories: (1) direct services and
instruction; (2) coordination, development, and leadership related to programs,
services, resources, and systems; and (3) enhancement of connections with community resources (Adelman & Taylor, 1993, 1997; Center for Mental Health in
Schools, 2001; Taylor & Adelman, 1996). In addition to responding to crises, prevailing direct intervention approaches encompass identification of the needs of
targeted individuals, prescription of one or more interventions, brief consultation,
and gatekeeping procedures (such as referral for assessment, corrective services,

Table 1. Types of Interveners and Functions

I. Interveners Who May Play Primary or Secondary Roles in Carrying Out Functions Relevant to Mental Health and Psychosocial Concerns

Instructional professionals
(e.g., regular classroom teachers, special education staff, health educators, classroom resource staff, and consultants)

Administrative staff
(e.g., principals, assistant principals, deans)

Health office professionals
(e.g., nurses, physicians, health educators, consultants)

Counseling, psychological, and social work professionals
(e.g., counselors, health educators, psychologists, psychiatrists, psychiatric nurses, social workers, consultants)

Itinerant therapists
(e.g., art, dance, music, occupational, physical, speech–language–hearing, and recreation therapists; psychodramatists)

Personnel-in-training

Others
- Aides
- Classified staff (e.g., clerical and cafeteria staff, custodians, bus drivers)
- Paraprofessionals
- Peers (e.g., peer/cross-age counselors and tutors, mutual support and self-help groups)
- Recreation personnel
- Volunteers (professional/paraprofessional/ nonprofessional—including parents)

II. Functions Related to Addressing Mental Health and Psychosocial Needs at the School and District Level

Direct services and instruction
(Based on prevailing standards of practice and informed by research)
- Crisis intervention and emergency assistance (e.g., psychological first aid and follow-up; suicide prevention; emergency services, such as food, clothing, transportation)
- Assessment (individuals, groups, classroom, school, and home environments)
- Treatment, remediation, rehabilitation (incl. secondary prevention)
- Accommodations to allow for differences and disabilities
- Transition and follow-up (e.g., orientations, social support for newcomers, follow-through)
- Primary prevention through protection, mediation, promoting and fostering opportunities, positive development, and wellness (e.g., guidance counseling; contributing to development and implementation of health and violence reduction curricula; placement assistance; advocacy; liaison between school and home; gang, delinquency, and safe-school programs; conflict resolution)
- Multidisciplinary teamwork, consultation, training, and supervision to increase the amount of direct service impact

Coordination, development, and leadership related to programs, services, resources, and systems
- Needs assessment, gatekeeping, referral, triage, and case monitoring/management (e.g., participating on student study/assistance teams; facilitating communication among all concerned parties)
- Coordinating activities (across disciplines and components; with regular, special, and compensatory education; in and out of school)
- Mapping and enhancing resources and systems
- Developing new approaches (incl. facilitating systemic changes)
- Monitoring and evaluating intervention for quality improvement, cost–benefit accountability, research
- Advocacy for programs and services and for standards of care in the schools
- Pursuing strategies for public relations and for enhancing financial resources

Enhancing connections with community resources
- Strategies to increase responsiveness to referrals from the school
- Strategies to create formal linkages among programs and services

triage, and diagnosis). In some situations, however, resources are so limited that specialists can do little more than assess for special education eligibility, offer brief consultations, and make referrals to special education and/or community resources.

Federal and state mandates play a significant role in determining how many pupil services professionals are employed. The School Health Policies and Program Study 2000 conducted by the National Center for Chronic Disease Prevention and Health Promotion sampled 51 state departments of education, 560 school districts, and 950 schools. Findings indicate that 77% of schools have a part- or full-time guidance counselor, 66% have a part- or full-time school psychologist, and 44% have a part- or full-time social worker (http://www.cdc.gov). In general, the ratio for school psychologists or school social workers averages 1 to 2500 students; for school counselors, the ratio is about 1 to 1000 (Carlson, Paavola, & Talley, 1995). Given estimates that more than half the students in many schools are encountering major barriers that interfere with their functioning, such ratios inevitably mean that more than narrow-band approaches must be used if the majority are to receive the help they need (Knitzer, Steinberg, & Fleisch, 1990). Nevertheless, the prevailing orientation remains that of focusing on discrete problems and overrelying on specialized services for individuals and small groups.

Because the need is so great, others at a school often are called upon to play a role in addressing MH and psychosocial problems of youth and their families. These include other health professionals (such as school nurses and physicians), instructional professionals (health educators, other classroom teachers, special education staff, resource staff), administrative staff (principals, assistant principals), students (including trained peer counselors), family members, and almost everyone else involved with a school (aides, clerical and cafeteria staff, custodians, bus drivers, paraprofessionals, recreation personnel, volunteers, and professionals-in-training). In addition, some schools are using specialists employed by other public and private agencies, such as health departments, hospitals, and community-based organizations, to provide MH services to students, their families, and school staff.

Because so few resources are allocated, the contexts for the activity often are limited and makeshift. That is, a relatively small proportion of this activity seems to take place in school/clinical offices earmarked specifically for such functions. Health education and skill development interventions may take place in classrooms if they are part of the regular curriculum; otherwise they tend to be assigned space on an *ad hoc* basis. Home visits remain a rarity. Support service personnel such as school psychologists and social workers must rotate among schools as "itinerant" staff. These conditions contribute to the tendency for such personnel to operate in relative isolation of each other and other stakeholders. These conditions clearly are not conducive to effective practice.

As outlined in Table 2, all this activity is provided through five major *delivery mechanisms and formats.* (For more on this, see Policy Leadership Cadre for Mental Health in Schools, 2001.) Despite the range of activity, it is common knowledge that few schools come close to having enough resources to deal with a large number of students with MH and psychosocial problems. Moreover, as is the case with most professionals who come to schools directly from preservice programs, those hired for their mental health expertise still need considerably more training once they

Table 2. Delivery Mechanisms and Formats: Five Mechanisms and Related Formats

I. School-financed student support services—Most school districts employ support service or "pupil services professionals," such as school psychologists, counselors, and social workers. These personnel perform services connected with mental health and psychosocial problems (including related services designated for special-education students). The format for this delivery mechanism usually is a combination of centrally based and school-based services.

II. School-district MH unit—A few districts operate specific mental health units that encompass clinic facilities, as well as providing services and consultation to schools. Some others have started financing their own school-based health centers with mental health services as a major element. The format for this mechanism tends to be centralized clinics with the capability for outreach to schools.

III. Formal connections with community MH services—Increasingly, schools have developed connections with community agencies, often as the result of the school-based health center movement, school-linked services initiatives (e.g., full-service schools, family resource centers), and efforts to develop systems of care (e.g., "wraparound" services for those in special education). Four formats have emerged:

- co-location of community agency personnel and services at schools—sometimes in the context of school-based health centers partly financed by community health organizations
- formal linkages with agencies to enhance access and service coordination for students and families at the agency, at a nearby satellite clinic, or in a school-based or -linked family resource center
- formal partnerships between a school district and community agencies to establish or expand school-based or -linked facilities that include provision of MH services
- contracting with community providers to provide needed student services

IV. Classroom-based curriculum and special "pull-out" interventions—Most schools include in some facet of their curriculum a focus on enhancing social and emotional functioning. Specific instructional activities may be designed to promote healthy social and emotional development and/or prevent psychosocial problems such as behavior and emotional problems, school violence, and drug abuse. And, of course, special education classrooms always are supposed to have a constant focus on mental health concerns. Three formats have emerged:

- integrated instruction as part of the regular classroom content and processes
- specific curriculum or special intervention implemented by personnel specially trained to carry out the processes
- curriculum approach is part of a multifaceted set of interventions designed to enhance positive development and prevent problems

V. Comprehensive, multifaceted, and integrated approaches—A few school districts have begun the process of reconceptualizing their piecemeal and fragmented approaches to addressing barriers that interfere with students having an equal opportunity to succeed at school. They are starting to restructure their student support services and weave them together with community resources and integrate all this with instructional efforts that effect healthy development. The intent is to develop a full continuum of programs and services encompassing efforts to promote positive development, prevent problems, respond as early after onset as is feasible, and offer treatment regimens. Mental health and psychosocial concerns are a major focus of the continuum of interventions. Efforts to move toward comprehensive, multifaceted approaches are likely to be enhanced by initiatives to integrate schools more fully into systems of care and the growing movement to create community schools. Three formats are emerging:

- mechanisms to coordinate and integrate school and community services
- initiatives to restructure support programs and services and integrate them into school reform agendas
- community schools

arrive at a school site. Those school personnel who are called upon to address MH and psychosocial concerns without training related to such matters clearly have even greater needs for capacity building and supervision. Unfortunately, there is little systematic in-service development to follow-up preservice education.

KEY CONCERNS ABOUT POLICY TRENDS

As McDonnell and Elmore (1987) state:

> A major challenge for the next generation of policy research will be to apply the lessons of past implementation studies in building a more powerful conceptual framework and in producing more useful information for policymakers.... Past research provides only limited guidance, because it has tended to focus on relatively narrow categorical programs, rather than programs targeted at all students, and has not addressed the core of schooling. (p. 3)

Viewed from the perspective of what schools do and what they could do related to students who are not succeeding, several concerns are evident. For one, there is no *cohesive* policy vision for addressing factors that interfere with learning and teaching. Relatedly, existing pupil services and school health programs do not have *high* status in the educational hierarchy and in current health and education policy initiatives (Adelman et al., 1999; Adelman & Taylor, 2000; Adler & Gardner, 1994; Center for Mental Health in Schools, 1996, 1997; Dryfoos, 1998; Kirst & McLaughlin, 1990; Knitzer et al., 1990; Kolbe, 1993; Lawson & Briar-Lawson, 1997; Palaich, Whitney, & Paolino, 1991; Tyack, 1992). The continuing trend is for schools and districts to treat such activity, in policy and practice, as desirable but not essential. Since the activity is not seen as essential, the programs and staff are marginalized. Planning of programs, services, and delivery systems tends to be done on an *ad hoc* basis; interventions are referred to as "auxiliary" or "support" services. Specialist personnel almost never are a prominent part of a school's organizational structure. Even worse, pupil services personnel usually are among those deemed dispensable as budgets tighten.

Policy aimed at students experiencing difficulty with reading and writing mostly calls for improving direct instruction and instituting higher standards and greater accountability. If necessary, students also may be referred for special services. With this in mind, there usually is provision in a school's budget for a few specialized supports. However, because such supports are costly, schools in poor neighborhoods are being encouraged to increase their linkages with community agencies in an effort to expand services and programs. The reality in poor neighborhoods, of course, is that there simply are not enough community agency resources for all services to link with all schools. Thus, the situation becomes either a matter of limiting linkages to the first schools that express an interest or of spreading limited resources (until they are exhausted) as more schools reach out.

Where school-linked services are feasible, some agencies have moved to co-locate staff on a few school campuses. In doing so, they provide a small number of clients better access to health and social services. Given that access is a prerequisite to, if not a guarantee of, effective intervention, this can be beneficial to those who are served. However, too few are likely to be served, and co-location is not a good model for fostering intervention cohesiveness. In linking with schools, community agencies often operate in parallel to the intervention efforts of school personnel (such as nurses, school psychologists, counselors, and social workers) who perform similar or complementary functions. Furthermore, by approaching school-linked services with a co-location model, outside agencies are creating a fear of job loss among personnel who staff school-owned support services. This sense of threat is growing as school policymakers in various locales explore the possibility of contracting out services. The atmosphere created by such approaches certainly is not conducive to collaboration and interferes with cohesiveness.

Given the relatively low policy priority for education support programs and services, it is not surprising that so little has been done at any administrative level to create the type of vision, leadership, and organizational structure necessary for integrating pupil services into schools in a comprehensive way. At present, specialist personnel rarely are included on governance and planning bodies. Ultimately, realignment of how pupil service personnel are governed and involved in school governance and collective bargaining and efforts to improve cost-effectiveness will play major roles in determining how many personnel address barriers to learning at a school (Hill & Bonan, 1991; Streeter & Franklin, 1993).

Clearly, policy initiatives for specific elements of school health or for coordinated school health programs are negatively affected by the piecemeal and categorical ways in which school-related intervention policies are enacted. Indeed, this is the case for all school-owned and -linked support programs and services. The roots of the problem lie in the marginalized status of such efforts vis-à-vis school reform. The symptoms of this problem are seen in the ensuing fragmentation that usually results in costly redundancy, dysfunctional competition, and limited intervention effectiveness.

To deal with the lack of policy cohesion, there has been a trend toward offering flexibility in using categorical funds, granting temporary waivers from regulatory restrictions, and offering support to encourage development of interagency infrastructure. These moves have helped in specific instances but have not provided the type of impetus for change that is needed if fundamental reforms are to play out at school sites. Direct attention to restructuring and reforming existing policy with a view toward fostering cohesive intervention is long overdue.

The most fundamental concern, however, is that prevailing intervention approaches are inadequate to the task of effectively addressing barriers to learning, and this lamentable state of affairs will not change as long as such activity is marginalized in policy and practice. This marginalization is seen clearly in how little attention is paid to dealing with the ineffective and inefficient ways resources are used in efforts to address barriers and promote healthy development. In the long run, substantially increasing intervention effectiveness requires changes that transform the nature and scope of how community- and school-owned resources are used; increasing availability and access to essential programs requires a true integration of these resources. None of this is likely to be accomplished as long as the activities involved are treated as tangential to the mission of schools.

In short, the situation is one in which, despite awareness of the many barriers to learning, education reformers continue to concentrate mainly on improving instruction (efforts to directly facilitate learning) and the management and governance of schools. Then, in the naive belief that a few health and social services will suffice in addressing barriers to learning, education reformers talk of "integrated health and social services." And in doing so, more attention has been given to linking sparse community services to school sites than to restructuring school programs and services designed to support and enable learning.

The previous discussion reflects only a few examples of fundamental policy concerns, but it underscores the point that policymakers and reform leaders have yet come to grips with the realities of students who are not succeeding. For many reasons, policymakers assign a low priority to underwriting efforts to address the needs of such students. The efforts that are made seldom are conceived in comprehensive ways, and little thought or time is given to mechanisms for program development and collaboration. Organizationally and functionally, policymakers mandate, and planners and developers focus on, specific programs. Practitioners and researchers tend to spend most of their time working directly with specific interventions and samples. Throughout the country and at all levels of political activity, policy, research, and practice initiatives remain marginalized, fragmented, and riddled with serious gaps. As a result, only a small proportion of the many students who are not succeeding are provided with the type of assistance they need, and prevailing intervention approaches tend to be narrowly focused and short term. For too many youngsters, limited intervention efficacy seems inevitable as long as a full continuum of necessary programs is unavailable, and limited cost-effectiveness seems inevitable as long as related interventions are carried out in isolation from one another.

In school districts, fragmentation and marginalization of effort are maintained by the specialized focus and relative autonomy of a district's organizational divisions. That is, the various divisions focusing on curriculum and instruction; student health and other support services; and activity related to integration and compensatory education, special education, language acquisition, parent involvement, intergroup relations, and adult and career education often operate as relatively independent entities. Thus, although these divisions usually must deal with the same common barriers to learning (e.g., poor instruction, lack of parental involvement, violence, unsafe schools, health problems, inadequate support for student transitions), they tend to do so with little in the way of a big picture framework, little or no coordination, and sparse attention to moving toward integrated efforts. Furthermore, in every facet of a school district's operations, unproductive separation is often manifested among the instructional and management components and the multiple activities that constitute efforts to address barriers to learning. This is compounded by the separation among those focusing on students experiencing problems. At the school level, this translates into situations in which teachers simply do not have access to essential supports when they identify students who are having difficulties. Prevailing school reform processes and capacity building (including pre- and in-service staff development) have not dealt effectively with such concerns.

Concentrating on matters such as curriculum and pedagogical reform, standard setting, decentralization, professionalization of teaching, shared decision making, and parent partnerships is necessary but certainly not sufficient, given the nature and scope of the barriers that interfere with school learning and performance among a large segment of students (Council of Chief State School Officers, 1992). That is, although higher standards and accountability are necessary ingredients in the final recipe for school reform, they are insufficient for turning around most schools that are in trouble. At such schools, overreliance on raising the bar and demands for rapid test score increases may even be counterproductive, because they force attention away from addressing the multitude of overlapping factors that interfere with effective learning and teaching. (And, they may be creating and exacerbating MH problems among students, their families, and school staff.) As long as the primary emphasis of those leading the movement to restructure education is limited to reforming the instructional and management components, too many students in too many schools will not benefit from the reforms. Thus, the demand for significant improvements in achievement scores will remain unfulfilled.

Given all this, it is not surprising that many schools are not making much of a dent in improving achievement test score averages. This state of affairs is undermining the move toward higher standards and efforts to minimize grade retention as social promotion is eliminated. For such initiatives to work, every school needs a comprehensive and multifaceted set of interventions not only to prevent and respond to problems early after onset but also to assist students with chronic problems. For this to be the case, however, advocates for children and families cannot pursue narrow and competing policy agendas, interventions cannot be conceived and organized in rigid categorical ways, and professionals cannot narrowly conceive their roles and functions.

Our analyses of current school policies and practices lead us to the view that the argument for MH in schools must be reframed. The new argument must be embedded in a comprehensive policy vision that encompasses an umbrella concept under which various advocates can coalesce.

REFRAMING THE ARGUMENT FOR MENTAL HEALTH IN SCHOOLS

Advocates for MH in schools include (1) those concerned about youngsters who have diagnosable mental disorders, subdiagnostic emotional and behavioral problems, and/or psychosocial problems; (2) those who want to prevent such problems; and (3) those interested in promoting healthy social and emotional development. Some of these advocates work for school districts, and their desire is for school policymakers to expand current commitments related to addressing a variety of barriers to student learning, including preventing problems by promoting healthy development. Some MH advocates who are not employed by the schools focus mainly on ways to expand school involvement in treating MH problems; others call for a greater emphasis on fostering social–emotional learning.

The various advocacy agendas have developed in relative isolation of each other. These have resulted in piecemeal policies and practices and counterproductive competition for sparse resources. Most of the agendas have narrowly framed the argument for MH in schools and have reflected an inadequate understanding of what schools are currently doing and what they can do.

The Usual Arguments for MH in Schools

With specific respect to MH in schools, the tendency of many advocates is to begin by citing the figures related to MH problems. They note, for example, that the Surgeon General's 1999 report on *Mental Health* states that "one in five children and adolescents experiences the signs and symptoms of a DSM-IV disorder during the course of a year"—with about 5% of all children experiencing "extreme functional impairment." And they stress that the picture is even bleaker when one expands the focus beyond the limited perspective on diagnosable mental disorders to the number of young people experiencing psychosocial problems and who are "at risk of not maturing into responsible adults" (Dryfoos, 1990).

The various data on need are then paired with the data on the society's response. For instance, epidemiological studies indicate that, in some communities, two-thirds of children with psychiatric disorders and significant impairment do not receive specialist care (Leaf et al., 1996). And, the Surgeon General's 1999 report on *Mental Health* estimates 6 to 9 million youngsters with serious emotional disturbances are not receiving the help they need—especially those from low-income families. Moreover, the report stresses the inadequacies of the current MH system and warns that the situation will worsen because of swelling demographics that are resulting in more children and adolescents with MH-related concerns.

Given these data, some advocates then suggest that it is self-evident that schools should expand what they do related to mental health. This position echoes the call of many others who have recognized that schools provide an important venue for enhancing the health status of children and adolescents. Such a view is well articulated, for instance, in an Institute of Medicine report (Allensworth et al., 1997) and in initiatives funded by the federal government designed to foster coordinated school health programs and MH in schools (Adelman et al., 1999; Marx, Wooley, & Northrop, 1998; Weist, 1999).

For the most part, however, school policymakers have not been swayed by the argument that schools are a good venue for addressing physical or mental health. Thus, proponents have expanded their position to make the case that a greater focus on health in schools will contribute to healthier students, and healthier students will learn and perform better. On the surface, this seems a stronger argument. However, it too has not had a great influence on school policy.

The problem with the previous arguments arises from one simple fact: *schools are not in the health business.* Education is the mission of schools, and policymakers are quick to point that out whenever schools are asked to do more about physical and mental health. Moreover, the accountability pressures on schools increasingly have focused attention on improving instruction at the expense of all matters not seen as *directly* related to raising achievement test scores. Related to this is the mandate schools have to make certain that *all* students (not just some students) experience an equal opportunity to benefit from the instruction provided.

In addition, it is important to remember that among some segments of the populace schools are not seen as an appropriate venue for MH interventions. The reasons include not only the concern that such activity will take time away from the educational mission but also the fear that such interventions are another attempt of society to infringe on family rights and values. There also is the long-standing discomfort so many in the general populace feel about the subject of mental health because it so often is viewed only in terms of mental illness. And, there is a historical legacy of conflict among various stakeholders stemming from insufficiently funded legislative mandates that have produced administrative, financial, and legal problems for schools and problems of access to entitled services for some students.

Even among those advocating for MH in schools, some argue that the involvement of schools should be restricted to those few students who have diagnosed mental disorders and qualify for special education services. Others want schools to offer a range of counseling and psychotherapeutic services to any student who is manifesting "mental health" symptoms. Still others want classrooms and schools to include a major focus on promoting healthy social and emotional development for all students.

A Rationale that Connects with the Mission of Schools

Given the previously described state of affairs, the case for MH in schools probably is best made by not presenting so many separate agendas. Our approach to framing a policy rationale for MH in schools begins with the conclusion arrived at by the Carnegie Council Task Force on Education of Young Adolescents (1989). In their report, they stress: "School systems are not responsible for meeting every need of their students. But when the need directly affects learning, the school must meet the challenge." It is evident that a variety of psychological and physical health problems affect learning in profound ways. Moreover, the problems are exacerbated as youngsters internalize the frustrations of confronting barriers (external and internal) to learning, experience the debilitating effects of performing poorly at school, and are punished for the misbehavior that often accompanies school failure.

While suburban areas are not exempt, the litany of barriers to development and learning is especially familiar to anyone who lives or works in urban or rural settings where families struggle with low income. In such locales, insufficient school and community resources often deprive youngsters of basic opportunities (not to mention enrichment activities) found in higher-income communities. Furthermore, the resources are inadequate for dealing with threats to well-being and learning such as drugs, gangs, and violence. As recent widely reported incidents underscore, violence is a specter hanging over all schools. Although the guns and killings that capture media attention fortunately are not pandemic, other forms of violence affect and debilitate youngsters at every school. Those who study the many faces of violence report that large numbers of students are caught up in cycles where they are the recipient or perpetrator (and sometimes both) of physical and sexual harassment ranging from excessive teasing and bullying to mayhem and major criminal acts. Moreover, any student may suffer the effects of severe anxiety or depression, and the rate of suicide among the young remains a constant concern. In many school settings, additional barriers to student learning and family involvement in schooling are created by inadequate attention to health problems, difficult and culturally diverse family circumstances, lack of English-language skills, and high rates of student mobility (Dryfoos, 1990; Knitzer et al., 1990; Schorr, 1997). Such conditions are breeding grounds for frustration, apathy, alienation, and hopelessness—all of which interfere with learning. In many large urban schools, the proportion of students experiencing behavior, learning, and emotional problems has climbed to over 50%, and few public schools experience less than 20%.

A strong rationale for MH in schools must be built first and foremost on the widespread need to enable more students to succeed at school. We stress that the strategy is to *build on* what school policymakers already are doing to achieve their mission. That is, those interested in enhancing the focus on MH and psychosocial concerns must recognize that such matters already are a facet of the agenda schools have for addressing barriers to learning (i.e., a variety of existing school policies and practices combine to establish a *de facto* commitment to MH). Most evident is the multifaceted enterprise that has developed to serve those students whose emotional, behavioral, and learning problems interfere with school performance and thus qualify them for special education. Also prominent are a range of counseling, psychological, and social service programs provided by schools for targeted problems related to violence, drugs, pregnancy, dropout, and so forth. Many of these programs take the form of enhancing students' assets and resiliency and reducing risk factors through an emphasis on social–emotional learning and protective factors. Clearly, school policymakers have demonstrated that they understand they must do something to assist teachers in dealing with problems that interfere with school learning.

From this perspective, we suggest that efforts to enhance and expand the *de facto* commitment to MH and psychosocial concerns are best pursued under the umbrella concept of *addressing barriers to student learning*. When this broad concept is used as a lens through which to view current policy and practices, it is quite clear that schools need to do much more and that their current efforts require considerable rethinking. Moreover, it becomes evident how low a policy priority presently is placed on the whole enterprise of addressing the factors that interfere with youngsters succeeding at school. Such awareness is a prerequisite to addressing the problems of marginalization, fragmentation, and unproductive competition.

CONNECTING WITH AND EXPANDING SCHOOL REFORM POLICY

By embedding our focus on enhancing MH in schools into the concept of addressing barriers to learning, development, and teaching, we have come to appreciate the need for shifts in policy. There is a major policy void, for example, surrounding the topic of *restructuring school-operated interventions* that are relevant to addressing barriers to learning and teaching. This is incompatible with efforts to develop truly comprehensive and multifaceted approaches to ameliorating problems and improving educational results.

Developing a Comprehensive, Multifaceted, and Cohesive Approach

Ultimately, the problems of students who are not succeeding must be approached from a societal perspective and with fundamental systemic reforms. As we have stressed elsewhere, the reforms must lead to development of a comprehensive continuum of programs (e.g., Adelman & Taylor, 1997, 1998, 2000). Such a continuum must be multifaceted and woven into three overlapping and integrated school–community systems: systems to promote healthy development and prevent problems, early intervention to address problems as soon after onset as feasible, and care for those with chronic and severe problems (see Fig. 1).

The three systems highlighted in Fig. 1 must encompass an array of effective programmatic activities that (1) enhance regular classroom strategies to improve instruction for students with mild-to-moderate behavior and learning problems,

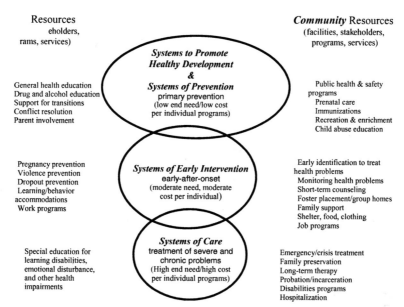

Resources
eholders,
rams, services)

Community Resources
(facilities, stakeholders,
programs, services)

Systems to Promote
Healthy Development
&
Systems of Prevention
primary prevention
(low end need/low cost
per individual programs)

General health education
Drug and alcohol education
Support for transitions
Conflict resolution
Parent involvement

Public health & safety
programs
Prenatal care
Immunizations
Recreation & enrichment
Child abuse education

Systems of Early Intervention
early-after-onset
(moderate need, moderate
cost per individual)

Pregnancy prevention
Violence prevention
Dropout prevention
Learning/behavior
accommodations
Work programs

Early identification to treat
health problems
Monitoring health problems
Short-term counseling
Foster placement/group homes
Family support
Shelter, food, clothing
Job programs

Systems of Care
treatment of severe and
chronic problems
(High end need/high cost
per individual programs)

Special education for
learning disabilities,
emotional disturbance,
and other health
impairments

Emergency/crisis treatment
Family preservation
Long-term therapy
Probation/incarceration
Disabilities programs
Hospitalization

Figure 1. Interconnected systems for meeting the needs of all students. Systemic collaboration is essential to establish interprogram connections on a daily basis and over time to ensure seamless intervention within each system and among *systems* of *prevention, systems* of *early intervention,* and *systems of care.* Such collaboration involves horizontal and vertical restructuring of programs and services (1) within jurisdictions, school districts, and community agencies (e.g., among departments, divisions, units, schools, clusters of schools) and (2) between jurisdictions, school and community agencies, public and private sectors; among schools; among community agencies. Adapted from various public domain documents authored by H. S. Adelman & L. Taylor and circulated through the Center for Mental Health in Schools at UCLA.

(2) assist students and families as they negotiate the many school-related transitions, (3) increase home and community involvement with schools, (4) respond to and prevent crises, and (5) facilitate student and family access to specialized services when necessary. Although schools cannot do everything needed, they must play a much greater role in developing the programs and systems that are essential if all students are to benefit from higher standards and improved instruction. They can, for example, do much more to welcome and provide social supports for new students and their families. They can work closely with those in the community to develop programs for recruiting, training, and deploying volunteers in ways that improve and augment ongoing social and academic supports and recreational and enrichment opportunities as well as other facets of school operation. They can work with those responsible for adult education to bring classes to school sites and facilitate enrollment of family members who want to improve their literacy, learn English, and develop job skills. And, they can play a role in ensuring that students with MH problems receive the services they need.

Establishment of comprehensive, multifaceted approaches to address barriers and promote healthy development requires cohesive policy that facilitates the blending of resources. In schools, this includes restructuring to combine parallel efforts supported by general funds, compensatory and special education entitlements, safe and drug-free school grants, and specially funded projects. With proper policy support, a comprehensive approach can be woven into the fabric of every school, and neighboring schools can be linked to share limited resources and achieve economies of scale. This scope of activity underscores the need to develop formal mechanisms for essential and long-lasting interprogram connections (collaboration in the form of information sharing, cooperation, coordination, and integration) on a daily basis and over time.

Efforts to braid and blend resources are fundamental to developing potent school–community partnerships. And, such partnerships are fundamental if we are to strengthen students and their schools, homes, and neighborhoods by creating caring and supportive environments that maximize learning and well-being.

To accomplish these goals, cohesive policy and practice seem essential. That is, policies must be realigned so that the diverse practices aimed at addressing barriers are unified. This requires moving from fragmented to cohesive policy and implies moving from narrowly focused, problem-specific, and specialist-oriented services to comprehensive general programmatic approaches. As used here, general approaches include a focus on enhancing healthy development as a key facet of prevention and encompass procedures for adding specialized services as necessary. It is time for reform advocates to expand their emphasis on improving instruction and school management to include a comprehensive component for addressing barriers to learning. To this end, we have introduced the concept of an enabling component to generate a three-component model as a framework to guide restructuring of policy and practice (see Adelman, 1996; Adelman & Taylor, 1994, 1997, 1998). And, we argue that in moving beyond the current tendency to concentrate mainly on instruction and management, school policy must elevate this third component to the same level of priority given the other two. That is, such an enabling (or learner support) component for addressing barriers to learning must be a primary and essential facet of school reform. School reformers like to say their aim is to ensure that all children succeed. We think that this third component is the key to making *all* more than the rhetoric of reform.

The Policy Leadership Cadre for Mental Health in Schools (2001) has developed a set of guidelines that are consistent with the previously described conceptual framework and reflect a comprehensive policy vision for MH in schools. The basic outline for these guidelines is presented in Table 3.

GOOD POLICY REQUIRES ADEQUATE UNDERWRITING OF SYSTEMIC CHANGE AND ESSENTIAL CAPACITY BUILDING

As discussed previously, our analyses suggest that current policy trends designed to ensure that *all* students have an equal opportunity to succeed at school generally add only a bit more of what already is being done. Moreover, in reaction to the narrow focus on categorical approaches and the related widespread fragmentation of activity, reformers are prematurely fixated on service coordination and integration. This has been especially the case with school health policy. As a result, policy is not contributing much to development of the type of comprehensive, multifaceted, and cohesive approaches that are needed to address the full range of students who are not succeeding. The type of expanded policy vision we have outlined is clearly needed.

Table 3. Guidelines for Mental Health in Schools

I. General Domains for Intervention in Addressing Students' Mental Health

1. Ensuring academic success and also promoting healthy cognitive, social, and emotional development and resilience (including promoting opportunities to enhance school performance and protective factors; fostering development of assets and general wellness; enhancing responsibility and integrity, self-efficacy, social and working relationships, self-evaluation and self-direction, personal safety and safe behavior, health maintenance, effective physical functioning, careers and life roles, creativity)
2. Addressing barriers to student learning and performance (including educational and psychosocial problems, external stressors, psychological disorders)
3. Providing social/emotional support for students, families, and staff

II. Major Areas of Concern Related to Barriers to Student Learning

1. Addressing common educational and psychosocial problems (e.g., learning problems; language difficulties; attention problems; school adjustment and other life-transition problems; attendance problems and dropouts; social, interpersonal, and familial problems; conduct and behavior problems; delinquency and gang-related problems; anxiety problems; affect and mood problems; sexual and/or physical abuse; neglect; substance abuse; psychological reactions to physical status and sexual activity)
2. Countering external stressors (e.g., reactions to objective or perceived stress/demands/crises/deficits at home, school, and in the neighborhood; inadequate basic resources such as food, clothing, and a sense of security; inadequate support systems; hostile and violent conditions)
3. Teaching, serving, and accommodating disorders/disabilities (e.g., learning disabilities; attention deficit hyperactivity disorder; school phobia; conduct disorder; depression; suicidal or homicidal ideation and behavior; posttraumatic stress disorder; anorexia and bulimia; special education designated disorders such as emotional disturbance and developmental disabilities)

III. Type of Functions Provided Related to Individuals, Groups, and Families

1. Assessment for initial (first level) screening of problems, as well as for diagnosis and intervention planning (including a focus on needs and assets)
2. Referral, triage, and monitoring/management of care
3. Direct services and instruction (e.g., primary prevention programs, including enhancement of wellness through instruction, skills development, guidance counseling, advocacy, schoolwide programs to foster safe and caring climates, and liaison connections between school and home; crisis intervention and assistance, including psychological first aid; preferral interventions; accommodations to allow for differences and disabilities; transition and follow-up programs; short- and longer-term treatment, remediation, and rehabilitation)
4. Coordination, development, and leadership related to school-owned programs, services, resources, and systems—toward evolving a comprehensive, multifaceted, and integrated continuum of programs and services
5. Consultation, supervision, and in-service instruction with a transdisciplinary focus
6. Enhancing connections with and involvement of home and community resources (including but not limited to community agencies)

IV. Timing and Nature of Problem-Oriented Interventions

1. Primary prevention
2. Intervening early after the onset of problems
3. Interventions for severe, pervasive, and/or chronic problems

V. Assuring Quality of Intervention

1. Systems and interventions are monitored and improved as necessary
2. Programs and services constitute a comprehensive, multifaceted continuum
3. Interveners have appropriate knowledge and skills for their roles and functions and provide guidance for continuing professional development
4. School-owned programs and services are coordinated and integrated
5. School-owned programs and services are connected to home and community resources
6. Programs and services are integrated with instructional and governance/management components at schools

(*Continued*)

Table 3. (*Continued*)

V. Assuring Quality of Intervention

    7. Programs/services are available, accessible, and attractive

    8. Empirically supported interventions are used when applicable

    9. Differences among students/families are appropriately accounted for (e.g., diversity, disability, developmental levels, motivational levels, strengths, weaknesses)

    10. Legal considerations are appropriately accounted for (e.g., mandated services, mandated reporting and its consequences)

    11. Ethical issues are appropriately accounted for (e.g., privacy and confidentiality, coercion)

    12. Contexts for intervention are appropriate (e.g., office, clinic, classroom, home)

VI. Outcome Evaluation and Accountability

    1. Short-term outcome data

    2. Long-term outcome data

    3. Reporting to key stakeholders and using outcome data to enhance intervention quality

At the same time, we hasten to stress that while a new policy and practice framework is necessary, it will only lay the foundation. For significant systemic change to occur, policy commitments must be demonstrated through allocation and redeployment of resources (e.g., finances, personnel, time, space, and equipment) that can adequately operationalize policy and promising practices. In particular, there must be sufficient resources to develop an effective structural foundation for systemic changes. Existing infrastructure mechanisms must be modified in ways that guarantee that new policy directions are translated into appropriate daily practices. Well-designed infrastructure mechanisms ensure there is local ownership, a critical mass of committed stakeholders, effective capacity building, processes that can overcome barriers to stakeholders' working together effectively, and strategies that can mobilize and maintain proactive effort so that changes are implemented and renewed over time.

Institutionalizing comprehensive approaches requires redesigning mechanisms for governance, capacity building, planning and implementation, coordination, daily leadership, communication, information management, and so forth. In reforming mechanisms, new collaborative arrangements must be established, and authority and power must be redistributed. All of this obviously requires that those who operate the mechanisms are adequately supported and provided with essential resources, such as time, space, materials, and equipment—not just initially but over time. And, there must be appropriate incentives and safeguards for those undertaking the risks involved in making major changes.

CONCLUDING COMMENTS

Leaders for MH in schools suggest that the well-being of young people can be substantially enhanced by addressing key policy concerns in this arena. In this respect, they recognize that policy must be developed around well-conceived models and the best available information. Policy must be realigned to create a cohesive framework and must connect in major ways with the mission of schools (Policy Leadership Cadre for Mental Health in Schools, 2001). From our perspective, we think this can be accomplished through a basic policy shift that reorganizes efforts to reform education and restructure community resources around three fundamental and essential overlapping components:

- a component encompassing all efforts to directly facilitate development and learning,
- a component encompassing all efforts to address barriers to development and learning,
- a component encompassing all efforts to manage and govern school resources and practices and school–community partnerships.

Reorganizing around three major components promises to reduce fragmentation and redundancy; enhance existing programs; increase the range of programs and services; and facilitate development of comprehensive, multifaceted, and integrated approaches. With specific respect to school health policy, the three-component model can help end the marginalized status of health initiatives in schools. To accomplish this, the focus for the immediate future must be on fully embedding school health initiatives into a component for addressing barriers to learning and advocating for inclusion of such a component as a primary facet of school reform policy.

Then, attention must be directed at restructuring the education support programs and services that schools own and operate and weave school-owned resources and community-owned resources together to provide the resources necessary for transforming the nature and scope of intervention efforts so that comprehensive, multifaceted, and integrated approaches are developed to address problems and enhance healthy development. Policymakers also must deal with the problems of creating necessary infrastructure and providing for effective capacity building to ensure appropriate implementation of comprehensive approaches and allocating the resources necessary for implementing widespread "scale-up" (e.g., underwriting model development and capacity building for systemwide replication of promising models and institutionalization of systemic changes). And, in doing all this, more must be done to involve families and to connect the resources of schools, neighborhoods, and institutions of higher education. Inadequate policy support related to any of these matters decreases the likelihood of enhancing intervention effectiveness on a large scale.

ACKNOWLEDGMENTS. This chapter was prepared in conjunction with work done by the Center for Mental Health in Schools at the University of California, Los Angeles, which is partially supported by funds from the U.S. Department of Health and Human Services, specifically from (1) the Office of Adolescent Health in the Maternal and Child Health Bureau of the Health Resources and Services Administration and (2) from the Center for Mental Health Services, Substance Abuse and Mental Health Services Administration.

REFERENCES

Adelman, H. S. (1996). Restructuring education support services and integrating community resources: Beyond the full service school model. *School Psychology Review, 25*, 431–445.

Adelman, H. S., Reyna, C., Collins, R., Onghai, J., & Taylor, L. (1999). Fundamental concerns about policy for addressing barriers to student learning. *Reading and Writing Quarterly, 15*, 327–350.

Adelman, H. S., & Taylor, L. (1993). *Learning problems and learning disabilities: Moving forward.* Pacific Grove, CA: Brooks/Cole.

Adelman, H. S., & Taylor, L. (1994). *On understanding intervention in psychology and education.* Westport, CT: Praeger.

Adelman, H. S., & Taylor, L. (1997). Addressing barriers to learning: Beyond school-linked services and full service schools. *American Journal of Orthopsychiatry, 67,* 408–421.

Adelman, H. S., & Taylor, L. (1998). Reframing mental health in schools and expanding school reform. *Educational Psychologist, 33,* 135–152.

Adelman, H. S., & Taylor, L. (2000). Shaping the future of mental health in schools. *Psychology in the Schools, 37,* 49–60.

Adelman, H. S., Taylor, L., Weist, M., Adelsheim, S., Freeman, B., Kapp, L., Lahti, M., & Mawn, D. (1999). Mental health in schools: A federal initiative. *Children's Services: Social Policy, Research, and Practice, 2,* 99–119.

Adler, L., & Gardner, S. (Eds.). (1994). *The politics of linking schools and social services.* Washington, DC: Falmer Press.

Allensworth, D., Wyche, J., Lawson, E., & Nicholson, L. (Eds.). (1997). *Schools and health: Our nation's investment.* Washington, DC: National Academy Press.

Carlson, C., Paavola, J., & Talley, R. (1995). Historical, current, and future models of schools as health care delivery settings. *School Psychology Quarterly, 10,* 184–202.

Carnegie Council on Adolescent Development's Task Force on Education of Young Adolescents (1989). *Turning points: Preparing American youth for the 21st century.* Washington, DC: Author.

Catalano, R. F., & Hawkins, J. D. (1995). *Risk-focused prevention: Using the social developmental strategy.* Seattle, WA: Developmental Research and Programs.

Center for Mental Health in Schools (1996). *Policies and practices for addressing barriers to student learning: Current status and new directions.* Los Angeles: Author.

Center for Mental Health in Schools (1997). *Addressing barriers to student learning: Closing gaps in school-community policy and practice.* Los Angeles: Author.

Center for Mental Health in Schools (2000). *A sampling of outcome findings from interventions relevant to addressing barriers to learning.* Los Angeles: Author at UCLA.

Center for Mental Health in Schools (2001). *Framing new directions for school counselors, psychologists, & social workers.* Los Angeles: Author at UCLA.

Council of Chief State School Officers (1992). *Student success through collaboration: A policy statement.* Washington, DC: Author.

Dryfoos, J. G. (1990). *Adolescents at risk: Prevalence and prevention.* London: Oxford University Press.

Dryfoos, J. G. (1998). *Safe passage: Making it through adolescence in a risky society.* New York: Oxford University Press.

Hill, P., & Bonan, J. (1991). *Decentralization and accountability in public education.* Santa Monica, CA: Rand.

Institute of Medicine (1997). *Schools and health: Our nation's investment.* Washington, DC: National Academy Press.

Kirst, M. W., & McLaughlin, M. (1990). Rethinking children's policy: Implications for educational administration. In B. Mitchell & L. L. Cunningham (Eds.), *Educational leadership and changing context of families, communities, and schools: 89th yearbook of the National Society for the Study of Education* (Part 2, pp. 69–90). Chicago: University of Chicago Press.

Knitzer, J., Steinberg, Z., & Fleisch, B. (1990). *At the schoolhouse door: An examination of programs and policies for children with behavioral and emotional problems.* New York: Bank Street College of Education.

Kolbe, L. J. (1993). An essential strategy to improve the health and education of Americans. *Preventive Medicine, 22,* 544–560.

Lawson, H., & Briar-Lawson, K. (1997). *Connecting the dots: Progress toward the integration of school reform, school-linked services, parent involvement and community schools.* Oxford, OH: The Danforth Foundation and the Institute for Educational Renewal at Miami University.

Leaf, P. J., Alegria, M., Cohen, P., Goodman, S. H., Horwitz, S. M., Hoven, C. W., Narrow, W. E., Vadem-Kierman, M., & Reiger, D. A. (1996). Mental health service use in the community and schools: Results from the four-community MECA Study. (Methods for the Epidemiology of Child and Adolescent Mental Disorders Study.) *Journal of the American Academy of Child and Adolescent Psychiatry, 35,* 889–897.

Marx, E., Wooley, S. F., & Northrop, D. (Eds.). (1998). *Health is academic: A guide to coordinated school health programs.* New York: Teachers College Press.

McDonnell, L. M., & Elmore, R. F. (1987). *Alternative policy instruments*. Santa Monica, CA: Center for Policy Research in Education.

Palaich, R. M., Whitney, T. N., & Paolino, A. R. (1991). *Changing delivery systems: Addressing the fragmentation in children and youth services*. Denver: Education Commission of the States.

Policy Leadership Cadre for Mental Health in Schools (2001). *Mental health in schools: Guidelines, models, resources & policy considerations*. Los Angeles: Center for Mental Health in Schools at UCLA.

Sarason, S. B. (1996). *Revisiting "The culture of school and the problem of change."* New York: Teachers College Press.

Schorr, L. B. (1997). *Common purpose: Strengthening families and neighborhoods to rebuild America*. New York: Anchor.

Streeter, C. L., & Franklin, C. (1993). Site-based management in public education: Opportunities and challenges for school social workers. *Social Work in Education, 15*, 71–81.

Surgeon General (1999). *Mental health: A report of the Surgeon General*. Washington, DC: U.S. Public Health Service.

Surgeon General (2000). *Report of the Surgeon General's conference on children's mental health: A national action agenda*. Washington, DC: U.S. Public Health Service.

Taylor, L., & Adelman, H. S. (1996). Mental health in the schools: Promising directions for practice. *Adolescent Medicine: State of the Art Reviews, 7*, 303–317.

Tyack, D. B. (1992). Health and social services in public schools: Historical perspectives. *The Future of Children, 2*, 19–31.

Weist, M. D. (1999). Challenges and opportunities in expanded school mental health. *Clinical Psychology Review, 19*, 131–135.

4

Effective Advocacy for School-Based Mental Health Programs

KATHY HOGANBRUEN, CAROLINE CLAUSS-EHLERS,
DAVID NELSON, and MICHAEL M. FAENZA

Reflecting the theme of this book, school-based mental health programs present an essential avenue for minimizing the barriers and increasing health care access for youth by offering services in a familiar setting where youth spend the majority of their day. Schools in collaboration with communities can play a vital role in identifying and treating children with emerging mental health needs, in addition to offering more intensive, ongoing services for those with chronic disorders. Further, the role of school-based mental health services extends beyond youth with SED to include prevention for youth who do not exhibit signs of mental illness. For instance, high rates of youth substance abuse, violence, suicide, and other preventable behaviors speak to a need for school-based programs that enhance youth resiliency by decreasing those factors that put youth at risk for mental health problems (e.g., poor anger management, academic difficulty) and increasing the factors that "protect" youth (e.g., effective communication skills, having adult mentors).

THE ROLE OF STIGMA

Stigma—negative labels, thoughts, and attitudes toward individuals with mental illness—results in barriers to appropriate and adequate mental health services (Clauss-Ehlers & Weist, 2002). An environment characterized by stigma might make parents loathe to seek services for fear they will be blamed for their child's

KATHY HOGANBRUEN, DAVID NELSON, and MICHAEL M. FAENZA • National Mental Health Association, Alexandria, Virginia 22311.   CAROLINE CLAUSS-EHLERS • Rutgers University, Graduate School of Education, New Brunswick, New Jersey 08901.

difficulties. In addition, stigma might make youth feel embarrassed about the prospect of treatment and may lead them to avoid seeking services. A common view toward children who are experiencing some type of problem is the idea that the current difficulty is somehow a developmental event that the child will "grow out of."

To truly understand the role of advocacy on behalf of youth, the climate of stigma that surrounds children's mental health must be understood. Often practitioners believe that youth are immune from difficulties like depression because their ego and cognitive capacities are not yet fully developed (Carlson & Garber, 1986; Wenar, 1994). Additionally, parents and other adults often minimize problems experienced by children and adolescents (Clauss-Ehlers & Weist, 2002). A study conducted at Ball State University and Columbia University (Chua-Eoan, 1999) found that 57% of adolescents who attempted suicide suffered from major depression. Of those adolescents, only 13% of their parents thought their child was depressed. Parents may be reluctant to acknowledge and address emotional/behavioral problems in their children related to the perception that this may worsen their own problems (e.g., being labeled a "poor parent"). This attitude may only exacerbate stigma regarding appropriate mental health treatment for youth.

ADVOCACY'S FUTURE: RESPONDING TO GAPS IN SERVICE

In addition to the public's very limited knowledge about mental health issues among youth (and adults), many other problems make the child and adolescent mental health system a "nonsystem" (see Burns & Friedman, 1990; Weisz & Weiss, 1993). These problems include (1) a lack of easily accessible community-based services, (2) a lack of capacity to respond to the mental health needs of youth (e.g., too few board-certified child psychiatrists), including an overreliance on professional staff and too little use of paraprofessionals, (3) an excessive focus on mental illness in assessment and intervention approaches rather than on mental health, (4) a failure to focus on youth strengths and competencies, (5) a failure to appropriately consider environmental factors and context, (6) extremely limited evaluation of clinical programs and the perpetuation of subjective methods of care, (7) poor collaboration of mental health professionals with others within and outside of the mental health field (e.g., primary care, education), and (8) the failure to develop integrated systems of care (Clauss, 1998; Weist & Christodulu, 2000) across child-serving systems.

However, there is a major effort to reform systems of mental health care and education for youth in the United States. Integrating mental health and education through the provision of school-based mental health services is an example of how we can work toward an improved system of care for children. This specific mental health–education reform is seeking to move beyond limiting constructs and approaches to develop a full array of effective programs for youth in natural community settings that remove barriers to their learning and improve their psychosocial adjustment. Three major developments in this reform effort are (1) the advancement of programs developed by systems of education to enable student learning, led by the work of Howard Adelman and Linda Taylor (1993, 1999); (2) the national movement toward expanded school mental health programs, which provide prevention, assessment, treatment, and case management services to youth in general, and special education, and involve strong collaboration between schools and community agencies (Flaherty & Weist, 1999; Weist, 1997a, 1999); and (3) the progress of prevention research, which is documenting that many broad-based prevention programs in schools lead to long-term positive impacts for youth (Durlak, 1995; Weissberg & Greenberg, 1998; Weist, 1997b).

In multiple ways mental illness prevention, mental health promotion, and intervention efforts in schools are moving children's mental health beyond many of the previously mentioned limitations. School-based mental health services are proactive and provided in the most universal natural setting for youth (i.e., schools). Capacity is being built to respond to the mental health needs of youth in interdisciplinary efforts that involve professional staff working with paraprofessional and nonprofessional staff (see Cowen et al., 1996; Waxman, Weist, & Benson, 1999). In most programs, youth do not need diagnoses to be seen, and there is a growing emphasis on building youth strengths and resilience factors, and placing major attention on the role of environmental variables (see Tashman et al., 1998). Quality improvement and evaluation activities are being prioritized as perhaps the most important set of activities for programs to document that they are in fact helping youth (see chapter by Ambrose et al., in press; Nabors et al., 1999). Finally, there is significant progress toward developing a system that emphasizes prevention and mental health promotion, while ensuring adequate services for youth showing early signs of problems and for those with more serious and established problems (Weist & Christodulu, 2000).

Importantly, there is very limited public awareness of limitations in child and adolescent mental health care, or of reforms that are moving us beyond these limitations. To build support for increasing capacity in children's mental health care, enhancing the focus on prevention, and moving care to natural settings such as schools, the public needs to be involved in the dialogue. There is a pressing need for the mental health advocacy community, particularly involving parents, youth, and consumers, to set the agenda for this dialogue, educate school leaders and policymakers on these issues, and move forward the call for action in the need for school-based mental health services.

Typically, the most effective advocacy efforts for mental health services in schools at the policy level (state or local governments) focus on accessing new funds for schools or increasing flexibility in the Medicaid or the Title I programs to cover school-based services. An emerging body of research exists that demonstrates both the need for and the effectiveness of school-based mental health services, presenting a solid base of evidence to inform the work of advocates. Two examples of the success of school-based mental health services/programs include the following:

- Project Achieve: Targeting at-risk students, this schoolwide prevention and early intervention program has decreased disciplinary referrals by 67% and referrals for special education by 75%, while also increasing achievement test scores and overall academic performance (Knoff & Batsche, 1995).
- School-Based Health Centers and Violence Prevention: Three community health centers in West Virginia, Maryland, and California implemented violence prevention and mental health services in school-based health centers.

All sites reported fewer suicide attempts, fewer fights in school, and improved attendance among students with discipline or attendance problems following the implementation of services (Bureau of Primary Health Care, 1996).

However, more than evidence of need and demonstrated effectiveness of services/programs is necessary to successfully advocate for broadening and improving mental health programs in schools. Despite obvious need, advocating for school-based mental health programs is a challenging task. These programs do not fit neatly into managed care systems and have evoked concerns among individuals who fear that such services could undermine parental control and turn schools into social service agencies rather than into institutions of learning (Baker, 2000; Dykeman, 1995; Schmidt, 1999). To address these anxieties, advocates must go beyond communicating statements of unmet need and/or evidence of effectiveness. Advocates must demonstrate that school-based mental health programs achieve specific goals that policymakers and society value. At the school or local level, school-based programs must be presented as an integral part of the school and the community, fully compatible with the educational mission.

In addition to established need, effectiveness of approach, and widely shared goals, successful advocacy for mental health programs in schools requires collaboration between the mental health and the education fields. Mental health advocates must expand their efforts beyond traditional mental health coalitions to include a broad-based constituency in order to secure "buy-in" outside of the mental health field. Unfortunately, too many advocacy efforts have been driven by the mental health community in an effort to force services on reluctant school systems. Such efforts are almost certain to fail since policymakers will automatically look to education advocates to determine priorities for school funding and new programs. The best advocacy efforts, as the following case studies demonstrate, are the product of communitywide coalitions and careful collaboration between multiple constituencies.

Having discussed relevant literature in the area of school-based mental health advocacy, the following case studies examine advocacy efforts at the local and state level for school-based mental health and prevention programs. Although these efforts focused on programs begun with a commitment of new federal dollars, they required advocacy to achieve support from various school and community stakeholders as well as long-term sustainability beyond the life of the federal grant. Both cases highlight important components of effective advocacy for school-based mental health service and provide a preliminary model for school mental health advocacy practice. The key components of the model are (1) groundwork, (2) obtaining initial buy-in, (3) developing a community collaboration, (4) enhancing collaboration among school service providers, and (5) increasing program resources.

ADVOCACY CASE STUDY 1: WASHINGTON, DC PUBLIC CHARTER SCHOOLS

Dr. Olga Acosta, a Chief Clinical Administrator in the Department of Mental Health in the District of Columbia, was charged with the task of developing school-based mental health programs for 17 public charter schools under a federal Safe

Schools/Healthy Students grant (funded by a consortium of federal agencies including the Department of Health and Human Services, Department of Education, and Department of Justice). Acosta's (2001) efforts highlight the five-point model for school mental health advocacy practice.

Advocacy Component 1: Groundwork

Initial groundwork for effective advocacy involves assessing which services and systems a school already has in place, with particular attention paid to whether or not a mental health infrastructure exists. While there are advantages to building on an existing infrastructure, "laying the groundwork" involves learning to work within a system the advocate may not agree with rather than having the freedom to design a potentially more logical, efficient, and responsive system of services. In contrast, in the scenario where no mental health infrastructure exists, advocates may face the difficulty of having to convince people of the need for services despite having functioned without them for years. In this capacity, mental health providers play a consultative role, working within the educational system toward the goal of helping students, teachers, and the overall system (Dougherty, 1992).

When Acosta (2001) and her team approached charter school principals to implement a system of mental health services, they met with a generally positive response and had solid systemic support. However, in individual schools where minimal levels of mental health services existed, advocates experienced difficulty in effectively explaining various aspects of mental health services. These included concerns about confidentiality, the difference between mental health and special education services, and the importance of creating a central mental health referral system. Throughout this process, relationship building and education about the need for expanded mental health services were critical to overcome resistance.

Acosta (2001) cites "readiness" as a crucial factor to assess before undertaking advocacy. She draws a parallel between advocating for mental health services in a school and beginning therapy with a client. In both cases, the "client" needs to be ready to accept the "intervention." Without such readiness, the intervention risks failure. This signifies a need to approach each school as an "individual," using clinical acumen as a guide in how to interact and advocate effectively with the school. In approaching a school, it is critical to exhibit respect for educational goals and acknowledge that the mental health team is a "school guest" with something valuable to offer. This differs subtly, but importantly, from the tone some advocates adopt, namely, "This is what you should do. This is what is best for your school."

While mental health advocates may be experts in designing service delivery systems for youth, it is important to pay attention to school signals and assess their level of interest and/or reticence. For instance, "turf" issues can be paramount. A school may feel that advocates from the outside—and perhaps even advocates on the inside—are trying to encroach upon their work, and, as a result, people in the school may be defensive and/or unwelcoming (see Waxman et al., 1999). Acosta (2001) suggests that approaching a school with a "clinical eye" toward such issues can break down barriers and help move toward a mutually beneficial, trusting relationship. Trusting relationships can ease the way for possible later challenges, such as needing to demand improved services.

Advocacy Component 2: Obtaining Initial Buy-in

By working together rather than in isolation, mental health advocates can develop mutually beneficial relationships with school personnel, students, and their families (Schmidt, 1999). To do so requires advocates to obtain "buy-in" from these individuals early on in the process of advocating for mental health services in the schools. As an example, because some school principals might feel overwhelmed by the addition of a new program (i.e., mental health services), early buy-in from a principal is necessary. According to Acosta (2001), "It is crucial to get buy-in from the principal from the beginning, because without it you will likely fail in creating or sustaining a program that will positively impact the student population."

When Acosta (2001) began the planning process for expanding school-based mental health services in the DC schools, she went to each of the 17 charter schools and met with each school leader to introduce the program and to find out more about the school's mental health needs. An advocate again needs to play the role of "consultant," assessing a school principal's goals by asking questions such as: What do you want to see changed in the school (e.g., reduced absenteeism, higher graduation rates, improved test scores)? And, what is your philosophy or mission, and how might these services support that mission? Connecting the need for mental health services to the principal's goals and interests will help obtain buy-in. For instance, if the principal's concern is a growing dropout rate, it is important to let the principal know that expanding and improving mental health services for students can help to address their emotional issues (e.g., depression) which in turn can affect motivation to stay in school. Framing a mental health intervention as a means to either reducing or removing a barrier to learning in order to enhance academic success will help secure buy-in for expansion of mental health services in schools (see Adelman & Taylor, 1999).

Related to obtaining initial buy-in is the process of conducting a preliminary needs assessment. If a school appears to be "ready" and open to the idea of expanding mental health services, a possible next step is to conduct a thorough needs assessment. A needs assessment refers to activities designed to acquire information about consumer (i.e., the schools') needs (Baker, 2000). According to Cook (1989), the needs assessment process includes identifying who will be assessed, determining the most appropriate means of assessment, devising a measuring plan, and interpreting and sharing results with decision makers in the organization.

No matter how obvious a need may appear to an advocate, it will undoubtedly take a concerted effort to convince others of the need. The needs assessment can be used for this purpose. Presenting concrete data and findings to key stakeholders in the school and community can help secure support for mental health services. Because a needs assessment catalogs existing services, it can also help prevent the creation of duplicative services. In fact, it may call attention to underutilized services and/or existing programs that can be leveraged.

The bulk of the needs assessment can be completed by talking with key stakeholders in the schools such as mental health providers, teachers, students, families, and school administrators. Acosta (2001) emphasizes the importance of connecting with any existing mental health personnel in a school (e.g., school psychologists, social workers, counselors, nurses) during the needs assessment to form allies and to secure their early support. Acosta suggests collecting data in these critical areas:

- the overall state of mental health in a school;
- the mental health needs of the student population, including what services currently exist, who currently provides services, how effective current services are, and which services can be coordinated with additional, new services;
- information on social problems in the school, such as substance abuse, violence, truancy, staff attrition, and family issues;
- school policies and procedures that directly or indirectly affect the implementation of a mental health program, such as discipline procedures and referral mechanisms.

The needs assessment should be concrete and practical. For instance, rather than reporting "violence is a problem," Acosta (2001) found collecting details such as how many fights have occurred on school grounds and how many students have been expelled for bringing a weapon to school to be far more useful. Data from the current school year were more compelling than outdated information, and data comparing current trends to previous time periods were more useful than data from just one time period.

The actual needs assessment process can propel advocacy efforts. Because conducting a needs assessment requires face-to-face interviews and discussions, it helps facilitate relationship building and the establishment of trust among advocates and school personnel and administrators. A critical part of this process is "giving people an ear." For instance, in interviewing teachers, Acosta (2001) found it helpful to ask them, "What concerns do you have about students that you would want mental health services to address?" Later these concerns can translate into services that help establish more permanent buy-in from school personnel. For instance, a concern that students frequently report psychosomatic complaints (e.g., headaches and stomachaches) as a result of stress could be addressed by advocates through the creation of stress reduction workshops.

Advocacy Component 3: Developing a Community Collaboration

Once completed, the needs assessment should be presented to the school principal to share findings and secure commitment to expand and improve mental health services. The question to key stakeholders then becomes "How would you like me to move forward with program implementation at your school?" rather than presenting one's own agenda. Such an approach facilitates the principal and others to take ownership in the movement to expand and improve mental health services.

Caplan (1970) defines consultation as "a process of interactions between two professional persons—the consultant, who is a specialist, and the consultee, who invokes a consultant's help in regard to a current work problem." Similarly, Bergan (1977) says consulting is a problem-solving process. School-based mental health consultation includes offering ideas on how best to share the findings of the needs assessment with others in the school and the community, how to design actual mental health services, how to incorporate these services with other schoolwide efforts, and assessing the need to develop policies or procedures to support mental health programs. Without such consultation, the principal may become wary or defensive of the changes suggested by the needs assessment. For instance, Acosta (2001) reported that for one charter high school, the needs assessment helped determine that substance abuse screening and treatment needed immediate attention. Relevant individuals in the school then began to plan what substance abuse services would be offered, how referrals for those services would be made, and the necessary follow-up to ensure appropriate care was in place.

In addition to the needs assessment, active collaboration with community agencies is a cornerstone to effective advocacy. Says Schmidt (1999), "Schools themselves are a major agency in the community, but schools alone cannot offer all the human services necessary to help a town, city, or county educate its citizens, provide health care, and offer basic services to improve the human condition" (p. 185). Turning to community resources is an option when schools are unable to address the myriad concerns of students and their families. Effective collaboration is a two-way process. On the one hand, it is critical that the school convey its focus to the surrounding community. On the other, it is important for the school to reach out to community agencies and learn about their services to create effective partnerships.

Acosta (2001) recommends advocates approach outpatient community centers, public and private mental health organizations, hospitals, and other service providers to build collaborative relationships with them. Community collaboration serves four main purposes: (1) to create a united voice across institutions that call for improved mental health services for youth in that region, (2) to allow interested agencies to share resources (i.e., workshops, training opportunities) and jointly conduct prevention or treatment interventions to benefit a larger number of students, (3) to capitalize on the community outreach components in hospitals or community mental health agencies that require mental health and public education services for free or at a reduced cost, and (4) to build relationships with outside mental health service providers that can receive referrals. Having an updated and thorough referral list is central to providing effective school-based mental health services. Atkinson and Juntunen (1994) call this a school–home–community liaison, whereby the school mental health program makes referrals, accepts referrals, and coordinates the referral process.

Advocacy Component 4: Establishing Collaboration among School Service Providers

In working with schools where some mental health services are already in place, it becomes critical for advocates for the expansion of mental health services to facilitate a meeting between providers to clarify roles, delineate how mental health interventions would be implemented, and establish joint goals and a timeline for services. Neglecting such collaborative planning with school-based providers can contribute to tensions between advocates and providers and undermine the possibility of a cohesive and coordinated set of mental health services (Acosta, 2001; Schmidt, 1999). Establishing collaboration early on in the planning of mental health services can help strengthen advocacy efforts by identifying allies and enlisting their support.

After forming community and internal collaborations, it is important for advocates to identify a lead organization. A lead organization (in Acosta's case, the Department of Mental Health) can help maintain and broker the process of establishing mental health services in the school to avoid fragmented services. One of the main roles of the lead organization in DC, for instance, was to establish a steering committee in each school. A steering committee should consist of representatives from all partnering organizations including school administration (e.g., the principal), school staff across disciplines (e.g., teachers, school nurse, guidance counselors, and school security), students and families, and community leaders (e.g., business leaders, representatives from the faith community) (Keys & Bernak, 1997). An interdisciplinary group maximizes the potential to do more in a school—to move mental health beyond traditional service delivery into a broader effort of comprehensive health care for children and adolescents.

For instance, Acosta (2001) shared how, due to the work of the steering committee, a mental health team in a school routinely addressed student discipline problems with a school administrator. Out of such meetings, a discussion evolved naturally regarding how the school could work to prevent, rather than treat, such problems. Without the cross-discipline steering committee, the need for preventive services would not likely have registered with the administrator.

Additionally, a steering committee can be a vehicle from which decisions about the expansion and improvement of mental health services in a school can be made. For instance, every charter school receiving services through the DC initiative has a steering committee that decides what additional targeted services should be implemented, who should be involved, and how to advocate for needed resources to support systemic change. Finally, a steering committee at the school level also serves the important function of evaluating the effectiveness and outcomes of services developed for children and families. This information can then be used to revise or adjust services to ensure that the program is individualized to meet the needs of diverse students and schools.

Advocacy Component 5: Increasing Program Resources

While this chapter assumes a school has access to funding for mental health issues, this is not the reality for many schools. Unfortunately, the scope of this chapter is too small to adequately address fundraising concerns (see Evans et al. this work). Acosta (2001) found that once program success could be demonstrated through evaluation data and utilization reports, she could approach the Department of Mental Health about building continued program funding into the agency's budget.

Community advocates, who supported the sustainability of the school mental health program, were instrumental in promoting the institutionalization of these services. Additionally, in Acosta's case, the development of a fee-for-service model through Medicaid also provided reimbursement for clinical services, and grant funding continued to be used whenever possible to augment prevention activities. Advocates can be instrumental in organizing people to help fundraise and write grant proposals as well as in advocating for systems change to incorporate permanent funding at the district or state level. The next case example will provide more detailed information about how advocates can work effectively to accomplish systems-level change.

ADVOCACY CASE STUDY 2: STATE OF CONNECTICUT

May Lum, a consultant-broker for the Safe Schools/Healthy Students (SS/HS) Action Center, provides technical assistance and capacity building for the SS/HS grantee sites located in the northeast region of the United States. The following case documents Lum's (2001) work in two Connecticut grantee communities (New Haven and Waterbury Public Schools) and further exemplifies the model for school-based mental health advocacy.

Advocacy Component 1: Groundwork

The SS/HS proactive technical assistance model which Lum (2001) and the other consultant-brokers utilize helps grantee sites anticipate problems and concerns before they arise, rather than a traditional, more reactive approach in which isolated problems are responded to as they occur. In keeping with this proactive approach, Lum's (2001) groundwork included arranging meetings with sites to help grantees determine the most effective ways to leverage federal SS/HS funding in the local community. Given the often short-lived nature of many grants, it was imperative to consider and address sustainability issues as a central component of advocacy for school-based mental health services right from the beginning. In other words, assessing from the outset how a funding source can be used to create additional revenues that supplement and eventually replace "soft money," is crucial to institute lasting mental health services in schools.

In her initial meeting with the Waterbury site, Lum (2001) learned more about the Motivate Everyone To Adopt Non-Violence Project (MEAN), a violence prevention initiative that was a precursor to the SS/HS grant and provided the foundation for the SS/HS proposal. Lum's (2001) inquiries about the history behind the project indicated a local coalition of key community stakeholders committed to youth violence prevention that formed as part of the MEAN project (McBrien, 1983; Sheeley & Herlihy, 1989).

Lum (2001) orchestrated a meeting with key coalition members, administrators, and physician leaders in the pediatrics department of Waterbury Hospital, and the project coordinator of the new SS/HS grant. Together they set an agenda focused on three key questions: (1) How can we sustain and expand violence prevention and mental health promotion efforts established from the MEAN grant? (2) Who do we know at the state level who knows of and/or supports the work being done through the SS/HS grant? (3) What are state funding sources for this type of work?

Advocacy Component 2: Obtaining Initial Buy-In

This strategic meeting led to identifying a new ally in the state legislative branch who supported the promotion of children's mental health: the policy director of the Connecticut Commission on Children (CCC). This individual was committed to children's issues and was influential in the legislative process and the development of state prevention policy. Because of the nature of the policy director's position, arranging a meeting with her required Lum's persistence and flexibility—qualities she points out as central to effective advocacy. A key aspect to obtaining buy-in is to emphasize the importance of thinking beyond traditional supporters, persisting in arranging key meetings, and asking strategic questions throughout the process of mobilizing allies and identifying supporters (Colbert, 1996).

New allies often reveal existing opportunities for advocacy and ways to develop a support base among policymakers. In Connecticut, the meeting with the policy director of the CCC facilitated a connection to a state prevention effort through the National Crime Prevention Council (NCPC). The NCPC had chosen Connecticut as one of six states nationwide to receive a planning grant to embed prevention into policy and practice across the state. With their NCPC award, Connecticut was pursuing legislation to create a line-item in the state budget to mandate that the state budget office require every state agency to identify a prevention initiative and appropriate funds for it. Through this connection, Connecticut SS/HS grantees were able to share their success stories with state legislators and highlight the need for prevention efforts.

Advocacy Component 3: Developing a Community Collaboration

Having obtained initial buy-in, Lum worked to integrate the SS/HS agenda into the CCC's prevention agenda. These actions fit with the need to develop community collaboration to effect long-term change. Keys and Bernak (1997) state that the "school-only focus is too narrow to provide the multidimensional services needed to effect long term change...help for an individual must occur within a larger network of school–community interventions targeted at families and students" (p. 259). Lum emphasized that her role as a consultant-broker to the SS/HS sites was time limited, and therefore her work aimed to create lasting structures that would sustain beyond her tenure. The result of these actions was that the CCC invited SS/HS sites to a hearing on the state's prevention legislation under the NCPC grant.

Lawmakers heard SS/HS program success stories for the two Connecticut sites and the need for continued mental health efforts in the schools (Meeks, 1968). After compelling testimony from the SS/HS grantees, the CCC was moved to utilize its ties with the local public television station to film an SS/HS prevention intervention at the New Haven site. The piece aired on public television and was then later used by the New Haven schools and the SS/HS team as a marketing tool in their efforts to sustain their prevention and mental health promotion programs. Media outreach is a key strategy to advance reforms and build child-focused systems of care. Having media outlets convey the project's story moves the issue of children's mental health to a larger, macrolevel of communication (Clauss-Ehlers & Weist, 2002).

Advocacy Component 4: Establishing Collaboration among School Service Providers

It is imperative for advocates for school-based mental health services to identify and assess mental health initiatives occurring in the community or school that have similar core values and goals. In this way, partnerships can be formed that take advantage of valuable synergies (Kameen, Robinson, & Rotter, 1985). Such efforts can facilitate a comprehensive process rather than parallel initiatives that operate in isolation.

For instance, given the similar goals for both initiatives, it was important for schools receiving ss/hs funds to talk to schools receiving Safe and Drug-Free Schools funds. Such coordination and integration greatly increase the likelihood of obtaining more permanent state- or county-level funding for advancing mental health in the schools. To achieve such integration, Lum (2001) suggests creating a "resource development team" that takes responsibility for assessing how services funded by varying initiatives/grants fit together and identifies the ongoing needs of the school district (e.g., violence prevention or mental health).

Advocacy Component 5: Increasing Program Resources

To build on the momentum created and to garner additional resources, Lum (2001) arranged a third meeting between the ss/hs grantees, the ccc, the Communications Campaign for the overall ss/hs initiative, and Connecticut public television (pbs), to discuss local and state communications on prevention. Because each ss/hs grantee site is required to have such a plan, the meeting was an opportunity to build on each other's efforts, ideas, and knowledge. Part of Lum's (2001) "sell" to the ccc involved having the two Connecticut ss/hs sites give presentations on their community impact. The compelling evidence moved the ccc to make a stronger commitment to help sustain ss/hs efforts, including offering the ss/hs sites information on funding opportunities. Ultimately, the state prevention legislation spearheaded by the ncpc initiative and supported by ss/hs was passed. This legislation will ensure longstanding state funding for prevention efforts, including violence prevention and mental health promotion.

CONCLUSION

A critical belief of effective schools is that "all children can learn" (Edmonds, 1979). And yet, over 7 million children in the United States have mental disorders or social problems (Gladding, 1996). Thus, schools focusing on instruction only potentially miss reaching an entire population of children whose academic capability is affected by emotional duress. Advocates, schools, and their surrounding communities must confront and contend with the complexity of problems and vulnerabilities faced by today's youth.

Advocates can help constituencies move beyond outdated modes of service delivery to meet the needs of future generations of students. The Washington, DC, and Connecticut case studies provide useful examples of effective advocacy for mental health services in public schools. While these communities have grant funding from the federal Safe Schools/Healthy Students program to support their work, their success at attaining the support and buy-in from school personnel, service providers, community leaders, politicians, and others offers significant lessons to all who advocate for mental health services in schools. Both cases highlight central themes in the model for school mental health advocacy practice such as building advocacy efforts around needs assessment information and collaboration between advocates, educators, and key stakeholders. The model's focus on the significance of fostering relationships is supported by Acosta's (2001) and Lum's (2001) work to develop allies and champions throughout the process. The following table summarizes the key elements of this model and those of Acosta's and Lum's successful advocacy efforts.

Key Points for School Mental Health Advocacy

- Begin thinking about program sustainability at the start of a funding source, including ways to leverage current funding.
- Capitalize on existing coalitions; be aware of initiatives with similar goals, take advantage of possible synergies, and avoid duplicating efforts.
- Form strong partnerships with prospective schools, especially with the principal and school-hired mental health staff.
- Identify key leaders and organizations in the community that are (or may be) supportive of mental health services in the schools; identify influential people who can be champions for your cause and who can be a vehicle to getting to know other influential champions.
- Look for opportunities for collaboration outside of the mental health field.
- Set up meetings with those people and organizations identified as leaders to determine what has already been done in this area, who else might be supportive, and what are the possible funding sources; follow through and be persistent and flexible to make the meetings happen.
- Once relationships are established, view them as ongoing and focus attention on developing them.

Advocates, families, school officials, mental health providers, and policymakers must work together not only to enact needed reforms but also to develop programs to be sustained over time by mental health and school systems. Both effective communication through multiple channels and being persistent with advocacy messages garnered advocates' success at instituting long-term changes in the provision of mental health services in Washington, DC, and Connecticut schools.

REFERENCES

Acosta, O. (2001). In conversation with the authors.

Adelman, H., & Taylor, L. (1993). School-based mental health: Toward a comprehensive approach. *Journal of Mental Health Administration, 20*, 32–45.

Adelman, H., & Taylor, L. (1999). Mental health in schools and systems restructuring. *Clinical Psychology Review, 19*, 137–163.

Ambrose, M. G., Weist, M. D., Schaeffer, C., Nabors, L. A., & Hill, S. (in press). In M. Weist, H. Ghuman, & R. Sarles (Eds.), Improving the quality and measuring the impact of a school mental health program. In *Providing mental health services to youth where they are: School and other community-based approaches.* New York: Taylor & Francis.

Atkinson, D. R., & Juntunen, C. L. (1994). School counselors and school psychologists as school-home-community liaisons in ethnically diverse schools. In P. Pedersen & J. C. Carey (Eds.), *Multicultural counseling in schools* (pp. 103–120). Boston: Allyn & Bacon.

Baker, S. B. (2000). *School counseling for the twenty-first century* (3rd ed.). New Jersey: Merrill, Prentice–Hall.

Bergan, J. R. (1977). *Behavioral consultation.* Columbus, OH: Merrill.

Bureau of Primary Health Care, U.S. Department of Health and Human Services (1996). *Healing fractured lives: How three school-based projects approach violence prevention and mental health care.* Washington, DC: U.S. Government Printing Office.

Burns, B. J., & Friedman, R. M. (1990). Examining the research base for child mental health services and policy. *Journal of Mental Health Administration, 17,* 87–97.

Caplan, G. (1970). *The theory and practice of mental health consultation.* New York: Basic Books.

Carlson, G. A., & Garber, J. (1986). Developmental issues in the classification of depression in children. In M. Rutter, C. E. Izard, & P. B. Read (Eds.), *Depression in young people: Developmental and clinical perspectives* (pp. 339–434). New York: Guilford.

Chua-Eoan, H. (1999, May 31). Escaping from the darkness. *Time,* 44–49.

Clauss, C. S. (1998). Cultural intersections and systems levels in counseling. *Cultural Diversity and Mental Health, 4*(2), 127–134.

Clauss-Ehlers, C. S., & Lopez Levi, L. (in press). Violence and community, terms in conflict: An ecological approach to resilience. *Journal of Social Distress and the Homeless.*

Clauss-Ehlers, C. S., & Weist, M. (2002). Children are news worthy: Working effectively with the media to improve systems of child and adolescent mental health. In H. Ghuman, M. Weist, & R. Sarles (Eds.), *Providing mental health services to youth where they are: School and community-based approaches.*

Colbert, R. D. (1996). The counselor's role in advancing school and family partnerships. *The School Counselor, 44*(2), 100–104.

Cook, D. W. (1989). Systematic needs assessment: A primer. *Journal of Counseling and Development, 67,* 462–464.

Cowen, E. L., Hightower, A. D., Pedro-Carroll, J. L., Work, W. C., Wyman, P. A., & Haffey, W. G. (1996). *School-based prevention for children at risk.* Washington, DC: American Psychological Association.

Dougherty, A. M. (1992). School consultation in the 1990s. *Elementary School Guidance and Counseling, 26,* 163–164.

Durlak, J. A. (1995). *School-based prevention programs for children and adolescents.* Thousand Oaks, CA: Sage.

Dykeman, C. (1995). The privatization of the school counselor. *School Counselor, 43,* 29–34.

Edmonds, R. R. (1979). Effective schools for the urban poor. *Educational Leadership, 37,* 15–24.

Flaherty, L. T., & Weist, M. D. (1999). School-based mental health services: The Baltimore models. *Psychology in the Schools, 36,* 379–389.

Gladding, S. T. (1996). *Counseling: A comprehensive profession* (3rd ed.). Englewood Cliffs, NJ: Merrill/Prentice–Hall.

Kameen, M. C., Robinson, E. H., & Rotter, J. C. (1985). Coordination activities: A study of perceptions of elementary and middle school counselors. *Elementary School Guidance and Counseling, 20,* 97–104.

Keys, S. G., & Bernak, F. (1997). School-family-community linked services: A school counseling role for changing times. *The School Counselor, 44*(4), 255–263.

Knoff, H. M., & Batsche, G. M. (1995). Project ACHIEVE: Analyzing a school reform process for at-risk and underachieving students. *School Psychology Review, 24,* 579–603.

Kurpius, D. J., & Fuqua, D. R. (Eds.). (1993). Special issue: Consultation: A paradigm for helping, II. *Personnel and Guidance Journal, 56,* 320–323.

Lum, M. (2001). In conversation with the authors.

McBrien, R. J. (1983). Are you thinking of killing yourself?: Confronting students' suicidal thoughts. *The School Counselor, 31,* 75–82.

Meeks, A. R. (1968). *Guidance in elementary education.* New York: Ronald Press Co.

Nabors, L. A., Weist, M. D., Tashman, N. A., & Myers, C. P. (1999). Quality assurance and school-based mental health services. *Psychology in the Schools, 36,* 485–493.

Schmidt, J. J. (1999). *Counseling in schools: Essential services and comprehensive programs* (3rd ed.). Boston: Allyn and Bacon.

Sheeley, V. L., & Herlihy, B. (1989). Counseling suicidal teens: A duty to warn and protect. *The School Counselor, 37,* 79–87.

Tashman, N. A., Waxman, R. P., Nabors, L. A., & Weist, M. D. (1998). The PREPARE approach to training clinicians in school mental health. *Journal of School Health, 68,* 162–164.

Waxman, R. P., Weist, M. D., & Benson, D. (1999). Toward collaboration in the growing education–mental health interface. *Clinical Psychology Review, 19,* 239–253.

Weissberg, R. P., & Greenberg, M. T. (1998). Social and community competence-enhancement and prevention programs. In W. Damon, I. E. Sigel, & K. A. Renninger (Eds.), *Handbook of child psychology, Volume 5: Child psychology in practice* (pp. 877–954). New York: Wiley.

Weist, M. D. (1997a). Expanded school mental health services: A national movement in progress. In T. H. Ollendick, & R. J. Prinz (Eds.), *Advances in clinical child psychology, Volume 19* (pp. 319–352). New York: Plenum Press.

Weist, M. D. (1997b). Protective factors in childhood and adolescence. In J. Noshpitz (Ed.), *Handbook of child and adolescent psychiatry, Volume 3* (pp. 27–34). New York: Wiley.

Weist, M. D. (1999). Challenges and opportunities in expanded school mental health. *Clinical Psychology Review, 19,* 131–135.

Weist, M. D., & Christodulu, K. V. (2000). Expanded school mental health programs: Advancing reform and closing the gap between research and practice. *Journal of School Health, 70*(5), 195–200.

Weisz, J. R., & Weiss, B. (1993). *Effects of psychotherapy with children and adolescents.* Newbury Park, CA: Sage.

Wenar, C. (1994). *Developmental psychopathology: From infancy through adolescence* (3rd ed.). New York: McGraw–Hill.

5

Mobilizing Research to Inform a School Mental Health Initiative

Baltimore's School Mental Health Outcomes Group

ERIC J. BRUNS, CHRISTINE WALRATH, MARCIA GLASS-SIEGEL, and MARK D. WEIST

INTRODUCTION

The Need for a Local Research Consortium on School Mental Health

Baltimore is in the fortunate position of having a national center on school mental health programs, several major universities, and a history of cooperation between the city health department, mental health core service agency, and the public school system. Along with the other 23 jurisdictions in the state, Baltimore also has a local management board (LMB), whose mission is to facilitate coordination between public and nonprofit entities toward improving the health and well-being of children and families (see Cole & Poe, 1993). One of the innovative mechanisms that has emerged from the city's increasingly coherent collaborative on behalf of young people is a network of expanded school mental health (ESMH) programs.

Baltimore's ESMH network is spearheaded by 12 different mental health provider agencies, which have agreements to provide comprehensive mental health services in 86 of the city's 183 public schools. In this partnership model, mental health clinicians, each employed by one of the mental health provider agencies,

ERIC J. BRUNS and MARK D. WEIST • University of Maryland School of Medicine, Baltimore, Maryland 21201. CHRISTINE WALRATH • Johns Hopkins Bloomberg School of Public Health, Baltimore, Maryland 21205. MARCIA GLASS-SIEGEL • Baltimore Mental Health Systems, and Baltimore Public School System, Baltimore, Maryland 21202.

work on-site in the schools, most on a full-time basis. As full partners in the school, the mental health clinicians provide a continuum of mental health services including prevention, mental health assessment, early intervention, and a range of treatment services, including individual, family, and group therapy (see Flaherty & Weist, 1999; Weist, 1997). These services are available to any student in need and primarily serve students in regular education, providing a resource for early identification and intervention before more serious problems develop. Through these interventions, as well as teacher consultation and support, ESMH services provide a method for addressing students' emotional and behavioral concerns without intervention via the special education system. Clinicians also serve on a variety of school teams and committees intended to increase coordination of services and resources available to students in a particular school (Paavola, Carey, & Cobb, 1996).

Stimulated by multiple funding streams and the promise of improving school outcomes through the reduction of emotional and behavioral barriers to learning, Baltimore's ESMH programs multiplied rapidly during the 1990s. However, despite the framework's increased visibility and expected outcomes, there was little empirical support for the approach locally or nationally, a problematic situation given the increase in local governmental and nonprofit funding. In addition, the increasingly diffuse school-based mental health service network, administered by over 10 provider agencies, was becoming difficult to effectively oversee.

As a result, in 1997, the director of the national technical assistance center in the city (Center for School Mental Health Assistance (CSMHA), University of Maryland) invited researchers from the Johns Hopkins Bloomberg School of Public Health and the city's Local Management Board and the program coordinator for CSMHA (who later became the Baltimore City Coordinator of School-Based Mental Health Services) to discuss a shared interest in developing a research base for ESMH programs in Baltimore. There was unanimous agreement on the need for an external evaluation and research consortium that could develop creative ways to document the implementation and impact of ESMH services in Baltimore, and the School Mental Health Outcomes Group (SMHOG) was born.

SMHOG's Participating Members and Intended Audiences

The core membership of SMHOG has been fluid in order to accommodate graduate students, local researchers, and advocates with specific interests. However, one aspect has been consistent: differing backgrounds, perspectives, and professional roles of participants in SMHOG have contributed to a dynamic process (see Flaherty et al., 1998; Waxman, Weist, & Benson, 1999). The Director of CSMHA, in his role with a national research and resource center, provided input on topics and questions of interest around the country, mechanisms for dissemination, and the development of research agendas and questions. The evaluators have contributed knowledge of research design and methodology, and the affiliation with the LMB has provided a necessary link to local decision makers and existing datasets. The Coordinator of School-Based Mental Health Services continually reminds the group of the need for ongoing advocacy to support and sustain the services, the need for information to improve service implementation, and potential burdens of data collection protocols. In a challenging balancing act, the diversity of the group demands that methodological rigidity does not preclude the possibility of "action research" that can inform decision making as needed, sometimes at the last minute before a school board meeting.

Initially, the school system itself (as the primary funder of ESMH programs) was the primary user of information generated from SMHOG-directed research projects. However, no formal mechanisms for dissemination were established to ensure an audience of multiple Baltimore City Public School System (BCPSS) stakeholders (e.g., clinicians, teachers, principals, and central administration). Prior to SMHOG, ESMH clinicians were required to document attendance, grades, suspensions, and special education utilization for participating students. However, they were not provided with resources or systematic guidelines for gathering data, and information from the main office was inconsistently available and often inaccurate. Further, few resources existed to analyze the data that were collected through this process. Finally, the emphasis on outcome data for individual students did not allow for system-level research that could evaluate policy developments, the climate in which programs operated, or broader-level impacts of the ESMH framework. SMHOG was initiated to oversee the student-level data collection effort to ensure it was more streamlined, purposeful, and unduplicated, while also initiating new research projects to fill gaps in knowledge around ESMH programs in Baltimore's schools.

Over time, as SMHOG's projects have yielded information about services delivered and outcomes expected and observed, the constituency of SMHOG has expanded and the research agenda has broadened. Increasingly, external stakeholders require data to support decision making. Specifically, decision makers require information on the potential of school mental health programs to achieve a wide range of school and community outcomes, such as increased school attendance, increased prosocial activities, or reduction in the impact of exposure to violence (Weist et al., 2000). In addition, provider agencies now utilize SMHOG-compiled datasets to answer questions about staff development, program implementation, and approaches to expansion. SMHOG intends to shape its research agenda by gleaning—formally and informally—the data and information needs of this expanded audience while simultaneously responding to the national policy climate and issues faced by the national research community.

Most generally, there are a number of clear foundational research questions SMHOG attempts to address. For example:

- How are ESMH services delivered across differing school sites and differing mental health provider agencies? What are the essential components in the service delivery framework?
- What are the expected outcomes of ESMH programs from the perspectives of diverse stakeholders who have a vested interested in them (e.g., youth, teachers, school system leaders, child mental health leaders, government officials)?
- What are the impacts of ESMH services on specific proposed school outcomes, such as school attendance, grades, and special education referrals? What are impacts on alternative outcomes such as school climate or teachers' perception of support?

SMHOG has developed a number of methods to address these fundamental questions, as well as more specific questions generated by stakeholders. The next section describes some of the specific methods enacted, databases compiled, analyses undertaken, and results gleaned as a result of SMHOG's work.

SMHOG ACTIVITIES AND PROJECTS

The ability of SMHOG to address the previous questions depends on the involvement of analysts with experience in measure construction, training in multivariate statistics, and, most importantly, an understanding of the research base on children's mental health systems and service delivery in schools. The team works with three major categories of information: (1) primary data collection via specific SMHOG research projects; (2) secondary school system administrative data, such as student records on grades and attendance, special education data, and mental health encounter data; and (3) secondary community-level data compiled by an affiliated initiative with a warehouse of administrative data specific to children and families. From these data sources, the following projects have been completed or are in progress.

Describing the Nature of School Mental Health in Baltimore

SMHOG was initially inspired by the need to assist the ESMH initiative in its effort to systematically and purposefully collect and analyze student-level data to document the impact of ESMH services. However, it was quickly learned via discussion with school system officials and mental health providers that the models to which clinicians adhered and the nature of clinical activities were not well described or understood. Such unexamined variation would pose a barrier to interpretation of any outcome data that were collected (see Nabors, Weist, & Reynolds, 2000). It was also discovered that there were a wide variety of proposed benefits of the ESMH framework—some supported by the existing national literature base (Armbruster & Lichtman, 1999; Weist et al., 2000), some not—which would also make design of appropriate outcome studies difficult. Thus, SMHOG's first project was to learn more about the nature of school mental health in Baltimore via a provider survey. This served to both gather process information and lay the foundation for future outcome research.

The survey provided a wealth of contextual information about ESMH programs in Baltimore, including the types of schools in which ESMH programs operated, the nature of students served, and the nature of services delivered (Walrath et al., in press). It was found that, despite the absence of an explicit approach to program siting, ESMH programs were in fact operating in schools with challenges that exceeded, on average, the school system as a whole. For example, ESMH

Table 1. Mean Number of Service Referrals and Contacts Reported by Expanded School Mental Health (ESMH) Clinicians in Baltimore City

	All ESMH schools M (SD)	Elementary M (SD)	Middle M (SD)	High M (SD)
Number of referrals	83 (105)	43 (23)	140 (163)	95 (64)
Number of contacts	705 (496)	559 (488)	910 (519)	668 (334)

NOTE: Numbers reported were for 1 school year.

Table 2. Types of Expanded School Mental Health (ESMH) Contact by Type of School (%)

	All ESMH schools (%)	Elementary (%)	Middle (%)	High (%)
Individual therapy	54	58	54	41
Group therapy	20	18	14	32
Family therapy	14	14	17	17
Assessment	13	15	12	11

schools featured higher enrollments and rates of poverty. In addition, as shown in Tables 1 and 2, school-based clinicians reported an impressive service capacity and a broad range of services delivered. Though respondent biases may have been present, results suggested that ESMH clinicians provide certain services at more intensive levels than school-employed professionals, most notably diagnostic evaluation, intake assessment, crisis evaluation, individual therapy, and group therapy. School-employed professionals were more likely to provide legally mandated services such as psychological evaluation, as well as services such as mentoring, career counseling, and drug and alcohol counseling.

Finally, the survey found that responding clinicians' most frequently voiced benefits of ESMH programs were increased mental health awareness and improved school climate (see Sutton & Fall, 1995). This was surprising given that improved school outcomes such as grades, suspensions, and attendance is an oft-stated focus of the ESMH initiative. This finding pointed to the need to assess ESMH programs' impact on additional indicators beyond traditional student-level outcomes and to the need for a greater emphasis on school-level and system-level outcomes in general (Walrath et al., in press).

Assessing System-Level Outcomes: Impact of ESMH on School Climate and Special Education Utilization

As a result of the provider survey, a second study, conducted the following school year, investigated the association between ESMH services and the two clinician-proposed but untested benefits of ESMH: improved school climate and patterns of referrals to special education (Bruns et al., in press). After adapting a pool of items from existing measures, SMHOG researchers designed and piloted a climate survey that was distributed to all faculty and staff at eight elementary schools with ESMH clinicians and seven matched schools* without ESMH components. Results found that teachers and staff in the ESMH schools gave higher ratings on the survey's mental health climate subscale than the matched comparison group. However, no differences were found for the general climate subscale of the survey. In addition, teachers in ESMH schools referred fewer students to the special education eligibility process because of emotional and behavioral issues. This result was reinforced by secondary administrative data analysis that indicated a lower rate of special education eligibility for emotional or behavioral disability in the ESMH schools (see Table 3).

The results of this study were quite intriguing and useful to BCPSS officials and mental health advocates interested in learning about potential benefits of ESMH beyond traditional student-level outcomes such as grades or school attendance.

---

*One comparison school declined to participate.

Table 3. Mean Rates of Special Education Referrals and Eligibility for Baltimore Schools with Expanded School Mental Health (ESMH) Clinicians and Comparison Schools

	ESMH schools (N = 8)		Comparison schools (N = 7)		
	Mean	SD	Mean	SD	t
Rate of all special education referrals	0.139	0.042	0.143	0.033	0.72
Rate of all students found eligible for special education	0.089	0.025	0.088	0.023	0.21
Rate of students found eligible for special education for EBD	0.010	0.008	0.018	0.005	2.02[a]

NOTE: Rates are per 100 enrolled students.
EBD, emotional/behavioral disorder.
[a] $p < 0.1$.

The results supported the notion—expressed by clinicians in previous studies and anecdotally—that helping teachers through consultation, behavior modification assistance, and interventions with students may reduce the need to rely on the special education system for students with emotional or behavioral problems.

Just as important, staff (especially teachers) in ESMH schools were found to be taking advantage of the enhanced in-school mental health resources. School personnel in ESMH schools were significantly more likely to have referred students with suspected emotional and behavioral problems to a mental health professional in the past year than were respondents in non-ESMH schools (52 to 28%). This alone was viewed as an important justification for the existence and continued expansion of ESMH components in Baltimore's schools.

Assessing Student-Level Outcomes of ESMH Participants

Despite the encouraging system- and school-level findings from the climate study described in the previous section, documenting student-level outcomes of school-based mental health services is still of critical importance. Such information remains in high demand by policymakers and school system personnel who require evidence of the ESMH framework's effectiveness in reducing individual students' barriers to learning. Such information is invaluable when determining the cost-effectiveness of ESMH services and tailoring the services delivered to those students for whom they are most effective. SMHOG is assisting in this effort in several ways. First, clinicians in the 86 schools served by ESMH programs continue to compile information on services delivered and students served. This information includes dates of initiation of mental health services for all students seen at least four times and these students' pupil identification numbers. SMHOG researchers are currently working with the BCPSS Department of Research to allow for matching of these service records to school system administrative databases that include students' enrollment, attendance, and achievement information. This approach will allow for a general assessment of the longitudinal trajectories of students who receive ESMH services.

However, despite the large amount of data that will become available for analysis, it will not provide a particularly rigorous test of program impact due to resulting gaps in information such as mental health, behavioral, and functioning status and no viable comparison group. School administrative records also are likely to be difficult to apply with precision to the research question, and data compiled on services may be of variable quality. Therefore, to augment this approach, SMHOG intends to initiative a more intensive impact study with a small subset of participating schools. Such a study will be possible through the allocation of a small evaluation budget to SMHOG via funds from the state of Maryland to support expansion of ESMH services from part time to full time in six schools in Baltimore. This targeted impact study will allow for more rigorous data collection methods, wherein functioning, behavioral, and family information, as well as school outcome data are collected at initiation of services as well as at several longitudinal points thereafter. In particular, related to experiences of other programs documenting positive changes in office referrals for discipline problems (see Jennings, Pearson, & Harris, 2000), at present SMHOG is working with the six schools to improve and standardize the way these referrals are recorded. This highlights an important lesson learned by the collaborative; that is, while exploring methods to describe and analyze school mental health programs, it is also important to improve data systems for future analyses whenever the opportunity to do so presents itself.

Compilation of a Comprehensive Data Archive

In addition to the descriptive study, climate studies, and attempts to focus and standardize the collection of student-level data, SMHOG's first 3 years were also spent building a foundation for future impact studies via the compilation of essential datasets to support ongoing evaluation activities. The following is a brief synopsis of some of the more crucial datasets.

First, a school-level dataset comprising 10 years of core descriptive data for each of Baltimore's 183 schools has been compiled. Variables include demographic data on enrolled students such as race and gender, rates of students receiving lunch subsidies, truancy and attendance rates, rates of students scoring satisfactory or better on standardized tests, dropout rates, and special education eligibility rates. This database also includes information on each school's involvement with the ESMH program, such as date(s) of entry into the initiative and the intensity of ESMH involvement, expressed in full-time equivalents. The database provides crucial contextual information to partners conducting research in the schools, supports analyses of the relationship between school-level outcomes and the presence of ESMH clinicians, and assists in grant writing. These data were recently used in regression analyses to identify schools with higher and lower than expected attendance rates, as part of a study of predictors of absenteeism. Data from the qualitative portion of this study will be used to support BCPSS's initiatives to combat truancy, which may include a targeted mental health component.

Second, a student-level dataset from the BCPSS Office of Special Education Research has been processed to describe all referrals to the special education process for the most recent 3 academic years. Variables include student demographics, referral source, presenting issues, eligibility determination information, and specific services to be included in the student's individualized educational plan (IEP). Given the expectation (and provisional finding from the study referenced previously) that ESMH programming can aid in reducing inappropriate referrals for eligibility determinations and services within the special education system, this dataset will be a major focus of future study.

Third, a number of overlapping datasets has been compiled describing the nature of mental health service encounters with school-based clinicians. One such data source is the school system's Office of Third-Party Billing, which provided a dataset of over 38,000 individual encounters submitted for reimbursement processing through avenues such as Medicaid. Though inconsistent due to differential submission patterns on the part of clinicians, this dataset includes variables such as the type of service provided and the student's DSM-IV diagnoses. Such variables required extensive data cleaning and collapsing into consistent, interpretable categories. Despite the challenge in working with these data, they are hoped to be a major supplement to existing data sources that describe the nature of school mental health in Baltimore.

Analysis of Community-Level Indicator Data to Inform ESMH

Finally, SMHOG benefits from an additional data resource that allows for the incorporation of geomappable risk and resources data for children and families into analytic activities. The Baltimore City Data Collaborative is housed at Baltimore City's Local Management Board for children and families and is directed by one of SMHOG's participating researchers. The Data Collaborative compiles individual-level information from all major child- and family-serving agencies in the city, including the Health and Police Departments, Department of Social Services, Baltimore Substance Abuse Services, Head Start, and others. The data that result—birth data such as rates of low birth weight, juvenile arrest rates by type, and child abuse and neglect rates—are continually updated and geocoded to areas such as census tracts, communities, and school catchment areas. Such information is essential to siting resources based on community need. For example, in siting ESMH or other school-based programs, school-level data are often not adequate for a full understanding of the level of risks faced by young people in the community served by a school. In siting a school-based prevention program to reduce the effects of exposure to violence, data on homicides, shootings, and juvenile arrests for the community served by the school may be necessary to appropriately target schools. In addition, the data allow evaluation studies of specific school-based initiatives— such as ESMH programs—to account for neighborhood effects.

LESSONS LEARNED

The previous section described the evolution of SMHOG, its major activities and projects, and methods through which it disseminates information to its stakeholders. The successes and challenges of each area are highlighted in the following.

The Evolution of SMHOG

The School Mental Health Outcomes Group was inspired by a need for systematic documentation of the ESMH programs in Baltimore and investigation into their impact in an effort to improve practice and expand programs. The specific foci for the group included (1) documentation of implementation efforts for existing ESMH programs, (2) provision of expanded school mental health-related

information to school- and city-level officials, individual schools, researchers, and
other stakeholders, and (3) development and implementation of ESMH outcome assessment protocols. SMHOG originated in 1997 and is an independent consortium
composed of representatives from local universities, a national technical assistance
center, and local nonprofit organizations, with each member providing a unique
and valued perspective. The group's approach to generating needed information
was to foster collaboration and draw upon existing structures and opportunities,
rather than to initiate a new "center" or academic entity. Though this approach
increased cooperation and reduced the need to obtain a large designated funding
pool for the effort, it also has created challenges, such as maintaining relationships with end users of the information and mobilizing adequate resources to
complete projects. Successes and related challenges experienced in the development of SMHOG are reviewed in the following.

Successes	Related challenges
• Diversity and commitment of SMHOG members	1. Maintaining continued school system involvement 2. Expanding group membership to include appropriate interested parties
• Cooperative designation of learning needs tailored to end users of information	1. Time and labor intensity associated with each point of focus 2. Continual generation of additional topics for inquiry
• Review and refinement of existing data collection procedures	1. Finding the balance between increased data collection burden and information required for impact assessment 2. Folding new data protocols into existing ones in a seamless and least burdensome manner

SMHOG-Related Activities and Projects

SMHOG is responsible for a variety of research projects in Baltimore City. External funding was sought and awarded for support of several of these projects,
while others were accomplished with existing resources. The projects were diverse in nature and touched upon multiple aspects of expanded school mental
health programs and their outcomes. For example, some of these projects have involved primary data collection and others the use of secondary data. Some focused
on the description of existing programs and others on the assessment of program
impact. In addition, the group has assisted university partners and local policymakers in assessing the presence of risk factors and resources at the school and
community level to inform program development and grant writing. Collectively
these projects have resulted in a data archive of ESMH programs in Baltimore City
that will be crucial to accomplishing SMHOG's mission in the future. Arguably, the
information gleaned from these efforts is only the preface to refining Baltimore's
system for delivering school mental health services. Nonetheless, it is a necessary
first step in local efforts to grapple with deeper questions around effectiveness
and impact (see Kutash & Rivera, 1996). Successes and challenges in this realm
are reviewed next.

Successes	Related challenges
• Variety of projects initiated and completed	1. Time and labor intensity associated with each project
• Use of existing databases	1. Lack of consistent coding of information; incomplete records; data gathered in a way that is not conducive to research and evaluation
	2. Linkage to the school system's internal research and evaluation division
• Collection of new data	1. Increased burden of school and clinical staff
	2. School system approval of study protocols
	3. Resource limitations precluded collecting data from multiple perspectives (e.g., teacher, clinical staff, student)
• Compilation of a data archive of ESMH services in Baltimore City	1. Due to different targets and sources of information, complete information does not exist for every ESMH school

Dissemination of the Information Generated by SMHOG

The information gathered via SMHOG efforts has been used in a variety of ways. There is clear indication that it has been used to further understand, expand, and refine school mental health services in Baltimore City. Furthermore, great strides have been made toward a heightened awareness of the need for systematic and consistent documentation of impact. Local providers and advocates have gained a more thorough understanding of the types of services provided within programs across the city. Funds have been leveraged for continued work by SMHOG, and information generated has been used to advocate for expansion of the school mental health initiative. Nonetheless, while information was made available to the school system, cultivating formal avenues of communication and dissemination to multiple and diverse audiences within the school system (e.g., clinicians, teachers, administrators) has remained a challenge. Successes and challenges related to information dissemination are presented in the following.

Successes	Related challenges
• Information and findings were provided to the ESMH program staff	1. Formal mechanisms were not established to ensure widespread dissemination across school system audiences
• Funds were leveraged for continued SMHOG efforts	1. Limited resources restrict the complexity of possible study designs
• Funding was justified for expansion of ESMH	1. Multiple factors are considered when selecting schools for expansion
	2. Leverage of funds for ESMH
• Information was made available to the school system	1. Establishing clear lines of communication and dissemination with the local school system

CONCLUSIONS AND RECOMMENDATIONS

The mission of SMHOG has remained consistent over the past 4 years, but the nature of its work continues to evolve. For example, while there is no doubt that current members will remain active, a commitment to expanding the membership to other relevant parties and developing better linkages to the local school system's research and evaluation department are essential. In addition, qualitative and case studies will be necessary to augment our understanding of the impact of ESMH programs, and additional outcome indicators, including child-level clinical and academic indicators, will be proposed in an effort to demonstrate impact. Finally, there is a continued need for SMHOG to aid in the collection of systematic outcome information. Reaching this goal will require SMHOG to specify the specific research questions to be addressed, convene clinical providers and the BCPSS Research Division, and specify data collection methods that minimize participant burden. These activities to build research infrastructure will serve to facilitate the conduct of more formal, experimental research on the impact of expanded school mental health services.

The evolution of SHMOG and implementation of its related projects has resulted not only in useful information for local ESMH stakeholders, but also in a wealth of experience about developing an independent research consortium. In reflecting back and looking forward we have identified the following recommendations for others who may wish to implement such a consortium:

1. The consortium should be independent of any one organization or agency.
2. Consortium membership must include multiple stakeholders: a group of individuals who collectively can describe the state of the field, design robust studies, analyze collected information, disseminate information, influence local decision making, keep advocacy issues on the table, and communicate the findings to a variety of audiences.
3. Consortium membership must evolve to include new stakeholders as they present themselves in the community.
4. Links to the local school board and their preexisting research teams is essential.
5. Clearly define the mission, goals, and core research questions of the consortium.
6. Develop a mechanism for interested parties to bring questions and topics to the consortium.
7. Utilize existing databases in an effort to decrease data collection burdens and be creative in the use of existing sources of information.
8. Explore local funding sources for projects generated via your consortium.
9. Make your presence known—put yourself on the map.
10. Identify all of your potential audiences and disseminate as frequently and widely as possible.

At the time of this writing the School Mental Health Outcomes Group in Baltimore is a vibrant, interdisciplinary group that is well respected by leaders in child education, mental health, and health in Baltimore. Meetings are being convened to expand and formalize the consortium. For example, activities that are being discussed include: increasing and diversifying the membership, electing a chair and cochair, formalizing mechanisms for input to the group from diverse stakeholders, forming subcommittees, developing strategies for outreach, developing and prioritizing research agendas, and pursuing more significant external funding. For the members of SMHOG the benefits of our activities over the past 4 years are clear, even compelling. The challenges have also been clear, even daunting. We hope that this chapter captures essential benefits and challenges to spur the development of similar consortia in other communities.

ACKNOWLEDGMENTS. Mark Weist's work on this article was supported by cooperative agreement U93 MC 00174 from the Office of Adolescent Health, Maternal and Child Health Bureau (Title V, Social Security Act), Health Resources and Services Administration, with cofunding by the Center for Mental Health Services, Substance Abuse, and Mental Health Services Administration.

REFERENCES

Armbruster, P., & Lichtman, J. (1999). Are school-based mental health services effective? Evidence from 36 inner city schools. *Community Mental Health Journal, 35*(6), 493–504.

Bruns, E. J., Walrath, C., Siegel, G. M., & Weist, M. D. (in press). School-based mental health services in Baltimore: Association with school climate and special education referrals. *Behavior Modification.*

Cole, R., & Poe, S. (1993). Partnerships for care: Systems of care for children with serious emotional disturbances and their families. *Interim report of the mental health services program for youth.* Washington. DC: Washington Business Group on Health.

Flaherty, L. T., Garrison, E., Waxman, R., Uris, P., Keyes, S., Siegel, M. G., & Weist, M. D. (1998). Optimizing the roles of school mental health professionals. *Journal of School Health, 68*(10), 420–424.

Flaherty, L. T., & Weist, M. D. (1999). School-based mental health services: The Baltimore models. *Psychology in the Schools, 36*(5), 379–389.

Jennings, J., Pearson, G., & Harris, M. (2000). Implementing and maintaining school-based mental health services in a large urban school district. *Journal of School Health, 70*(5), 201–296.

Kutash, K., & Rivera, V. R. (1996). *What works in children's mental health services? Uncovering answers to critical questions.* Baltimore, MD: Paul H. Brookes.

Nabors, L., Weist, M. D., & Reynolds, M. W. (2000). Overcoming challenges in outcome evaluations of school mental health programs. *Journal of School Health, 70*(5), 206–209.

Paavola, J. C., Carey, K., & Cobb, C. (1996). Interdisciplinary school practice: Implications of the service integration movement for psychologists. *Professional Psychology: Research and Practice, 27,* 34–40.

Sutton, J. M., & Fall, M. (1995). The relationship of school climate factors to counselor self-efficacy. *Journal of Counseling and Development, 73*(3), 331–336.

Walrath, C., Bruns, E. J., Anderson, K., Glass-Siegel, M., & Weist, M. (in press). The nature of expanded school mental health services in Baltimore. *Behavior Modification.*

Waxman, R. P., Weist, M. D., & Benson, D. M. (1999). Toward collaboration in the growing education–mental health interface. *Clinical Psychology Review, 19,* 239–253.

Weist, M. D. (1997). Expanded school mental health services: A national movement in progress. In T. H. Ollendick & R. J. Prinz (Eds.), *Advances in clinical child psychology* (Vol. 19, pp. 319–352). New York: Wiley.

Weist, M. D., Nabors, L. A., Myers, C. P., & Armbruster, P. (2000). Evaluation of expanded school mental health programs. *Community Mental Health Journal, 36,* 395–412.

6

Overcoming the Challenges of Funding School Mental Health Programs

STEVEN W. EVANS, MARCIA GLASS-SIEGEL,
ALICIA FRANK, RON VAN TREUREN,
NANCY A. LEVER, and MARK D. WEIST

One of the largest obstacles to the delivery of expanded school mental health (ESMH) services is developing and sustaining funding sources. The school mental health approach to care integrates mental health, education, and in some cases other systems such as health, social services, and juvenile justice. With the involvement of multiple systems and disciplines, the problematic question becomes which agency or organization is responsible for payment. No one payer can realistically take on all of the responsibility, leaving many ESMH programs to creatively meet fiscal challenges and repeatedly come up with solutions to the next fiscal crisis.

The fiscal solutions that have been developed to support ESMH programs are extremely diverse and constantly evolving. Knowing that funding opportunities change quickly over time, it is a challenge to provide useful and current information. Furthermore, fiscal opportunities vary greatly between communities and states, complicating an attempt to provide a useful snapshot of the financial issues that impact expanded school mental health. This chapter consolidates some of the financial aspects behind school mental health programs and provides an overview of the complexity of the issue. The chapter concludes with the stories of three ESMH programs that have successfully maintained funding over the years and describes their funding successes and failures.

STEVEN W. EVANS and ALICIA FRANK • James Madison University, Harrisonburg, Virginia 22807. MARCIA GLASS-SIEGEL • Baltimore Mental Health Systems, and Baltimore City Public School System, Baltimore, Maryland 21202. RON VAN TREUREN • Seven Counties Services, Inc., Louisville, Kentucky 40220. MARK D. WEIST and NANCY A. LEVER • University of Maryland School of Medicine, Baltimore, Maryland 21201.

There are two important caveats to this chapter. First, while there are many school mental health programs funded by schools and systems of education, these are not within the purview of the chapter. Instead, this chapter addresses programs that receive grant, contractual, fee-for-service, or other forms of revenue to sustain operations. Second, most of the literature on funding is specific to school-based health centers (SBHCs) and these may or may not include mental health services. In fact, only about 60% of SBHCs have mental health professionals on staff (Center for Health and Health Care in Schools (CHHCS), 2001a). Furthermore, there are many ESMH services that are not connected to SBHCs. Therefore, our literature review depends heavily on articles on mental health programs developed within SBHCs, and we acknowledge that this does not capture the full range of issues related to school mental health funding.

OVERVIEW OF FUNDING OPPORTUNITIES

Federal and State Funding

Federal grants provide some states with a substantial portion of funding that potentially can be used to support expanded school mental health. A portion of these funds may be allocated for SBHCs. The Healthy Schools, Healthy Communities program administered by the Bureau of Primary Health Care is a primary source of support for SBHCs, allocating over $14 million in 2000 (CHHCS, 2001a). In 1999, through landmark collaboration at the federal agency level, the Departments of Education, Justice, and Health and Human Services jointly created the Safe Schools/Healthy Students Initiative, which provided $98.7 million in funding to 54 sites. Other types of federal grants that have been successfully used to provide support are the Title XX Social Services block grant and the Preventive Health and Health Services block grant (CHHCS, 1998, 2001a). On the state and local level, many SBHCs obtain funding from Maternal and Child Health block grants that contributed approximately $10 million to 19 schools in 2000 (CHHCS, 2001b).

In addition to federal funding, some states have included school-based health and mental health services in their budgets. State general funds contributed almost $32 million to SBHCs in 18 different states during 1999–2000 (CHHCS, 2001a). Some states rely heavily on state funding; for example, in Louisiana approximately 60–65% of the centers' budgets are financed through state appropriations (CHHCS, 1998). States also can budget funding from specific sources to supplement monies reserved in the general fund. An example of this type of funding is exemplified by the Title XI program, which provides education dollars from the federal government to support SBHCs. Some states have targeted programs such as the U.S. Department of Education "Safe and Drug Free Schools" program to supplement their budgets (Making the Grade National Program Office (MTG), 1995). Specific health initiatives also provide opportunities for funding SBHCs. For example, North Carolina increased funding in its adolescent health initiative to assist in the support of SBHCs (CHHCS, 1998).

State taxes also provide substantial support for SBHCs. In particular, tobacco tax dollars in Arizona and Massachusetts provided almost $8 million to SBHCs (CHHCS, 2001a). Moreover, an additional $5.5 million was given to SBHCs from tobacco settlements in Florida, Louisiana, and Massachusetts (CHHCS, 2001a). Other states have used a supplemental sales tax to help support SBHCS (MTG, 1995).

Third-Party Payments/Fee-for-Service Reimbursements

Third-party payers including the various State Children's Health Insurance Programs (SCHIP) programs, commercial insurance, and Medicaid provide support for school mental health through fee-for-service reimbursements. In many localities, fee-for-service reimbursement is possible based on a medical home model. In this framework, centers are viewed as providers of primary care and preventive services, as well as offering a mechanism for expanding the child health care delivery system. When the SBHC is viewed as a provider of nonduplicative care, much of the SBHC's budget can come through patient care reimbursement (MTG, 1995).

A primary disadvantage of the fee-for-service model is that many services offered in a school-based setting are not reimbursable (National Assembly on School-Based Health Care (NASBHC), 2000). For example, consultation with teachers and parents, classroom observations, case management, and parent education are examples of common mental health services that typically are not covered by Medicaid or commercial insurance (NASBHC, 2000), yet these services are central to the tenets of school-based health care. Additionally, some Medicaid programs define specific provider types for mental health services and, accordingly, many SBHCS are ineligible for mental health reimbursement (NASBHC, 2000). Exceptions to this trend exist in North Carolina and New Mexico where Medicaid reimbursement codes specific to SBHC mental health services have been developed that include enhancement and preventive services (NASBHC, 2001). In addition, some Medicaid managed care organizations (e.g., Community Care Behavioral Health, Pittsburgh, PA) have agreed to provide payment for some school-based mental health services such as teacher consultation. In addition, Community Care Behavioral Health has actively worked with providers and schools in the community to facilitate additional school-based services for students. While Medicaid managed care companies are not often seen in the role of facilitating ESMH services, they can be very effective in this role and have been in some areas.

To encourage managed care programs to increase their support of school-based programs, it may be necessary to emphasize the fiscal advantages. Although there are few studies comparing the cost effectiveness of school mental health compared to care delivered in other settings, one study concluded that school-based services cost about a half to a quarter of what similar services would cost in the private sector (Nabors, Leff, & Metrick, 2001). An additional concern about fee-for-service models is that they require considerable administrative and bureaucratic activities to recover funds as well as the necessity of diagnosing students for fee reimbursement. Negotiating the bureaucratic requirements of fee-for-service takes time away from preventive and clinical activities. However, given the tentative funding picture for most programs, capitalizing on every funding stream, including fee-for-service billing, is usually necessary.

Despite disadvantages, links to fee-for-service revenue (particularly funds available through Medicaid) are seen as an integral part of the long-term financial success of SBHCS. This is partially due to the increasing scarcity of public and private grant dollars and to the questions related to Medicaid managed care (NASBHC, 2001). Currently over half of SBHCs operate in areas with Medicaid managed care providers, and 80% of the centers report billing Medicaid and Medicaid health plans (NASBHC, 2000). The difficulty of billing and collecting reimbursement from Medicaid has prevented SBHCs from relying on Medicaid as a primary source of support. Only a small percentage (3–10%) of the SBHCs' budgets in most states comes from Medicaid reimbursements (CHHCS, 1998). In fact, some SBHCs lose money when trying to collect from Medicaid, since the revenue recovered from it frequently does not cover the cost of billing (CHHCS, 1998). Notably, based on information gathered from round table discussions sponsored by the National Assembly on School-Based Health Care regarding Medicaid reimbursement in SBHCs, the "overwhelming sentiment of the participants was that billing is not regarded as advantageous or profitable" (NASBHC, 2001, p. 6).

Some centers have obtained support successfully from Medicaid through carve-out dollars under "related health services" for special education as defined by the Individuals with Disabilities Education Act (IDEA) (CHHCS, 1998). In Vermont, for example, the schools provide administrative functions on behalf of Medicaid to ensure comprehensive and preventive health services to enrolled students. One problem with this arrangement has been some difficulty obtaining funds for program expansion (CHHCS, 1998).

In other states, schools are listed as "essential care providers" which has led to requirements on managed care providers to contract with them (CHHCS, 1998). Despite such regulation, SBHCs still have found it difficult to obtain reimbursement. For example, some primary care physicians do not want to permit children to receive services at an SBHC. Even in states with legislation related to paying for SBHC services (e.g., Rhode Island), reimbursement from insurance programs usually is not sufficient to cover the operating budget for an SBHC (CHHCS, 1998). In Oregon, managed care providers are not required to contract with the schools, and there has been extreme difficulty in negotiating contracts between the SBHCs and managed care (CHHCS, 1998). This was also the case in one state where it took 2 1/2 years to negotiate contracts between the SBHCs and most managed care plans (CHHCS, 1998). Some states have attempted to simplify the billing and reimbursement process. In Illinois and North Carolina, centers that meet standards set by the Health Department, School Health Office, and Office of Medical Assistance do not have to receive prior approval to bill Medicaid for services (NASBHC, 2001).

SCHIP has the potential to be a principal source of support for many SBHCs. Like Medicaid, it is a publicly funded insurance program that is supported through state funds with matching federal dollars. SCHIP was designed to insure children whose family income excluded them from qualifying for Medicaid, but were unable to afford private insurance (Center for School Mental Health Assistance (CSMHA), 2000). States were allowed to choose how to develop and implement this plan with the majority of states choosing to implement their SCHIP program through managed care delivery systems (CHHCS, 1998). Therefore, the extent to which an SCHIP program will reimburse SBHCs for general or mental health services depends on the state.

Outpatient Mental Health Center Funding

Alternative strategies for funding school-based programs are to partner with already existing outpatient mental health centers (OMHCs) or to form an independent center. In many states, a program must be or be affiliated with an outpatient mental health center to bill private and public insurance programs for services. By joining forces, two or more agencies can generate additional services to more children and can provide new revenue that neither agency could access on its own (Bundy & Wegener, 2000). That is, while ESMH programs have the staff, capability, and connections to serve children in schools, the outpatient program has the structure, mechanisms, and recognition needed to bill for services. In our experience, it is more expeditious for a school program to join forces with a licensed OMHC than to create their own center. This is because developing an OMHC usually involves an intensive level of activity including negotiating multiple bureaucracies, having buildings inspected and certified, credentialing staff, developing paperwork, and other tasks that can take many months to accomplish.

Solicited Funds

Many expanded school mental health programs obtain at least some of their financial support from private donors, private foundations, and federal agencies. One private foundation that has been a significant supporter in establishing and developing SBHCs is the Robert Wood Johnson Foundation (RWJF). In 1993, the RWJF created a national program called "Making the Grade" with the purpose of "support(ing) states in developing financial and other strategies to foster replication of SBHCs" (CHHCS, 1998). For most states involved in the Making the Grade program, approximately 10% of their budget is provided through contributions from private donors and foundations (CHHCS, 1998). In North Carolina, the Duke Endowment has financed planning and start-up costs for SBHCs. Private foundations and businesses can also help support other school-based mental health initiatives by providing funds and added resources to programs. For example, a program operated by the University of Maryland School of Medicine has benefited from contributions ($10,000–$15,000 a year) from businesses and local foundations to initiate special activities such as qualitative assessment with community stakeholders, and initiating peer mentoring programs.

Pooled, Blended, or Braided Funds

Many SBHCs combat the tenuous nature of funding sources by relying on pooled, blended, or "braided" (conveying that programs still retain control of funds and staff) sources. Using this approach, SBHCs rely on many different funding streams rather than just one or two in order to ensure that the majority of the budget will be covered even if one of the funding sources should end. This also has the advantage of allowing the SBHC to offer comprehensive services, since funding sources differ on which services, providers, and clientele are covered (Committee for the Advancement of Professional Practice, 1995). This strategy of relying on mixed funding sources is also common among school mental health programs that are not connected to SBHCs.

The following section contains descriptions of the fiscal decision making and advocacy efforts that resulted in growth and stability for three strong ESMH programs. These programs developed independently in Pittsburgh, Pennsylvania; Louisville, Kentucky; and Baltimore, Maryland. As demonstrated by these descriptions, each took very different routes dependent on unique opportunities and obstacles within each community.

MODELS OF INNOVATIVELY FUNDED EXPANDED SCHOOL MENTAL HEALTH PROGRAMS

Bridges for Education Program

The Bridges for Education Program began as a pilot project by faculty and staff at the Western Psychiatric Institute and Clinic (WPIC—part of the University of Pittsburgh Medical Center). The pilot school included self-contained special education programs including a program for severely emotionally disturbed (SED) high school students. Many of these students had previous psychiatric hospitalizations, were taking psychiatric medications, and exhibiting severe impairment in home and school functioning. Using an outpatient model of care, a clinician joined the school to enhance the array of services. As Medicaid covered most of the students, the clinician set up services to be billed through the hospital to Medicaid. The clinician billed an average of slightly over 30 hours per week at the school. In addition to providing services directly to the students, she met with teachers and parents on a regular basis. A child psychiatrist also came regularly and took over the medication management for many of the students. Initial data on this model of service were encouraging and resulted in the hospital supporting the expansion of the program.

Many schools were eager to receive these services; however, since Medicaid was the primary revenue source, the program targeted expansion into schools in economically depressed areas. This was a good public relations move for the hospital and brought care to many students who otherwise would not have received it. Schools in other areas also wanted the program, which led the director of the Bridges Program to begin a lobbying effort with the commercial insurance companies to pay for services provided at schools. Contracts between the hospital and the major insurance companies restricted payment to services provided only to licensed sites. Since licensing all of the schools was viewed as impractical, efforts were begun to modify the language in the agreements to allow payment for services provided at nonlicensed sites.

The program rapidly expanded and clinicians were meeting productivity levels above the outpatient clinic, but not at the level achieved in the pilot project. The financial promise of the program was short-lived, because after expanding the program, Medicaid managed care began in the area. In Pennsylvania, behavioral health services are carved out and managed by one managed care organization (MCO) within each county; however, during the first 2 years of Medicaid managed care, this was not the case. Four MCOs began providing coverage and competing for customers. Initially, WPIC was not a provider for any of these MCOs. As these companies continued to expand their customer base, the number of students who were covered by unmanaged Medicaid began to diminish rapidly. In addition, the program discovered that it frequently did not receive payments for services because families had signed up with a particular Medicaid MCO without informing the program. Usually these families reported that the representative from the MCO assured them that they could continue to receive services from the Bridges Program after becoming a customer of their MCO. As a result, the bills from the Bridges Program went unpaid by Medicaid, and the families and clinicians struggled with problems resulting from being in the middle of treatment without any means of paying for care. The options were limited since those providers who participated in these MCO plans did not have school-based mental health services available for these families. With a shrinking population of clients and financial chaos related to the transition to Medicaid managed care, the Bridges for Education Program was collapsing financially.

While the program was struggling financially, the reputation of the program in the community was strong. Schools and families valued the services and felt that children were benefiting from them. As a result, some schools offered to pay for a defined set of services that could be provided in their school without having to use insurance reimbursement. This led to the Bridges for Education program reinventing itself. In its new form, staff were trained to provide a diverse set of services including traditional school-based care, peer mediation, schoolwide interventions, teacher training and consultation, substance abuse prevention, and other services desired by the schools. These services were marketed to the schools, and largely based on the initial clinical reputation of the program, contracts with several schools were established.

Schools paid for the services using a variety of funding sources, including general funds, federal and state grants, and contracts. The director of the Bridges Program worked with school administrators to help them prepare and submit state and federal grants that led to contracts. One of the contracts involved working with special education administrators to set up magnet programs for youth classified as SED and then jointly staffing the programs. Other contracts involved working with teachers to revise the school's discipline policy and other consultation and training services; however, most of the contracts involved working directly with children, teachers, and families.

As the Bridges Program completed its transition to contractual services, many of the initial barriers to third-party payment were resolved. Medicaid managed care switched to a behavioral health carve-out which meant that all children in the county who were covered by Medicaid could now receive services from the Bridges Program and the program would be paid. Furthermore, the stature and importance of school mental health services in the community had grown, and the managed Medicaid company in the county supported this effort and began reimbursing for teacher consultation. In addition, lobbying efforts to commercial insurance companies achieved success, and the largest commercial insurance company in the region agreed to cover mental health services provided in schools.

The Bridges for Education Program continues to grow and work with community partners to pursue funding opportunities. The program has expanded to include an arm called Bridges for Medicine that involves contracting with physician practices to provide mental health services. While primarily remaining a contracted service, the program has begun to move toward mixing contractual work with third-party billing. This return to relying on Medicaid and commercial insurance has been done cautiously and in small steps with the hope that the current stability provided by contracts can buffer challenges of third-party billing. The advantages of the ESMH approach to care have kept the enthusiasm and motivation for this program high, resulting in many children receiving much-needed services in spite of the financial challenges.

Seven Counties Services, Inc.

Seven Counties Services (SCS), located in Louisville, Kentucky, serves a diverse region with urban, suburban, and rural communities. Seven Counties has a longstanding relationship with the various school districts in the region. Nine years ago, the SCS developed a school-based division with the mission of partnering with educators to help each child maximize his/her potential. The program goals are framed in educational terms and include improving academic proficiency, increasing attendance, and making schools safe environments for children to learn. Seven Counties' school-based program provides individual, family, and group psychotherapy, and psychoeducational groups in over 110 schools.

Since 1990, several factors in Kentucky have supported the development of expanded school mental health programs. For example, the 1990 Kentucky Education Reform Act (KERA) presented significant opportunities for partnerships with schools. KERA established a network of Family Resource and Youth Service Centers (FRYSCs). The centers are located within qualifying schools, and are mandated to provide a variety of services to families including easily accessible health and mental health resources. The FRYSCs receive state funding, and schools qualify for services based on the percentage of students who receive free and reduced lunches. There are currently 89 FRYSCs serving Jefferson County, the largest district served by SCS.

In most cases, the FRYSC coordinators become the program's main school contact and referral source. They identify children and families in need, and coordinate referrals from teachers, principals, and parents. Some FRYSCs include funds in their budget to contract with SCS for psychoeducational groups. These prevention groups are topical and time limited, covering areas such as conflict resolution, anger management, social skills, and grief/loss. With a school-based program budget of nearly $2,000,000, Medicaid continues to be the program's main source of revenue. In 1997, the program's budget was funded nearly 90% by Medicaid reimbursement, while in 2001 it was 75%. This decline reflects an increase in contract, grant, and insurance revenue.

Throughout the past decade, Medicaid has undergone major changes affecting eligibility in Kentucky. The Personal Responsibility and Work Opportunity Reconciliation Act of 1996, better known as "Welfare Reform," redefined how assistance to low-income families can be provided. Most notably, the Act reduced the number of Medicaid-eligible families and showed a commensurate reduction in the number of children eligible for the school lunch program. This directly affected the FRYSC budgets, which are tied to the number of students eligible for free and reduced lunches in their school. It had the effect of lowering their overall discretionary dollars to pay for mental health services. However, in the fall of 1997, Title XXI of the Social Security Act passed, which enabled states to develop guidelines for expanding health insurance to children. Currently, the Kentucky Children's Health Insurance Program (KCHIP) covers children whose family income is up to 200% of the poverty index. This greatly increased the number of children eligible for mental health services and helped increase available funding.

Seven Counties' funding from the Kentucky Department of Mental Health is capped and has not increased in recent years. The program's Board of Directors designates this money to provide services for individuals who are eligible for sliding scale fees. Eligibility is available to members of the community who belong to priority populations (e.g., adults with severe and persistent mental illness, children with severe emotional disturbance) who do not have any coverage for mental health services. While this money primarily covers clinical services, there is some flexibility in its use. Under the state contract, "consultation and education" services are encouraged in the community. This allows all Seven Counties' clinical staff to connect with teachers, either by direct consultation about behavioral issues or through classroom observations. The connection with teachers and other educators is an essential part of the program's model, and something that most insurance plans will not reimburse. The funds also may be used for in-service trainings, parent education groups, and participation in school meetings.

The SCS program has recognized the value of advocacy and positioning at the state level. Since 1995, an interagency work group has met monthly to promote the advancement of school mental health in the state. Much of this group's work has focused on a legislative initiative, House Bill 843 (HB 843), which established local planning boards for community mental health centers. The interagency work group has been working with the boards to coordinate community needs assessments, to enhance working relationships and develop contracts with school boards, and to provide local training on effective practice in the schools.

Expanded School Mental Health Programs in Baltimore

Through a longstanding partnership between the health department, the public mental health authority, and the school system, ESMH programs provide a continuum of services (prevention through treatment) to students in nearly 50% of the Baltimore City Public School System (BCPSS). While the significant contribution from the city school system has historically been the most visible source of funding and has helped establish the standard of services for *any* student in need regardless of reimbursement potential, over the years, the mental health system has increased its contribution. The current funding mix closely reflects the continuum of mental health prevention and treatment services available through coordinated, integrated ESMH services.

Expanded school mental health services were introduced into a few schools in 1987 with the initial funding coming from two sources: the mental health system, which at that time was part of the Baltimore City Health Department, and the BCPSS. Mental health system funding was identified for a pilot project at one large urban middle school, creating the first formal ESMH partnership agreement between the local health department/public mental health system and the public school system in Baltimore City. Around the same time, through a creative partnership between the Baltimore City Health Department and the BCPSS, one other school began to receive ESMH services on a half-time basis (with a total funding contract of $20,000/year). The following year, four additional schools received half-time ESMH services with a total of $100,000 in funding from the school system. ESMH services also began to be provided as a component of several SBHCs, and full-time mental health services became a standard part of the service array of the SBHCs in Baltimore

City. By the 1993–1994 school year, 32 public schools had ESMH services provided through partnership agreements with 8 major public mental health programs. Most recently, in the 2001–2002 school year, the number of schools participating in these partnerships has increased to 86, representing nearly 50% of the 183 schools in the city.

In 1993, Baltimore Mental Health Systems (BMHS), the local mental health authority, was established as a separate entity, rather than continuing as part of the city health department. Each year, some state mental health dollars have been included in the BMHS pool of contract dollars with almost $500,000 allocated annually in support of the prevention and early intervention components of the ESMH programs.

Over the years, the number of different funding sources has expanded to include funding not only from the school system's third-party billing revenues, state mental health funding, and contracts with the city health department, but also federal funding, reimbursements through the public mental health fee-for-service system, and funding from some of the principals. Additionally, the state of Maryland has a system of reimbursement for preapproved community prevention and mental health education activities, which has increasingly been used to support some of the prevention services offered by ESMH programs. This diverse array of funding supports a continuum of services and enables ESMH programs to identify students in need and to provide timely interventions.

In 1997, a new managed mental health care system was initiated throughout the state of Maryland. Under this new system, only providers who were individually licensed or who were affiliated with a state-licensed outpatient mental health center could become paneled with the public mental health system managed care organization. Prior to this carve-out, through an agreement with the city health department, the BCPSS Office of Third-Party Billing was able to access reimbursement for some portion of the mental health services provided by ESMH clinicians. During this challenging 2-year period, BCPSS managed to become recognized by the state Medicaid office as a billing-only Medicaid entity. With the support of BMHS, BCPSS was able to create a new practice group consisting of participating licensed outpatient mental health centers and all participating individually licensed ESMH clinicians. The BCPSS Office of Third-Party Billing then became the central entity for seeking reimbursement for services rendered to students in general education who met the criteria for a mental health diagnosis.

This new system was extremely demanding for those clinicians who had not previously been involved in the process of accessing reimbursement. With the new system, clinicians were responsible for the following: (1) registering each student for whom reimbursement would later be sought with the managed care organization, (2) developing and submitting treatment plans for students needing more than 12 sessions, and (3) submitting data on each service delivered to the BCPSS Office of Third-Party Billing. For BCPSS, the new system required an entirely new method of tracking services and submitting claims, which was qualitatively different from the well-developed system for submitting claims on behalf of students receiving evaluations and services within the special education system. Large numbers of claims were rejected due to lack of timely registration of students, problems with coding of diagnoses, problems with navigating the computerized system for mental health claims, and problems submitting claims electronically. Although having a school system manage the billing had been a major achievement, after 2 years of trying to work within this system, it was determined that the billing staff's time and effort continued to be excessive in relation to the total reimbursements received. As a result, beginning in July 2000, the participating agencies that received funding from BCPSS were given permission to seek reimbursement and to make use of any fees collected to support their existing ESMH programs or to enable expansion to additional schools.

An opportunity for funding for prevention services developed in conjunction with the 1997 mental health "carve-out" and was called the Community Prevention and Support (CPS) process. Prior to the shift to statewide mental health managed care, licensed OMHCs had received state operating grants that included funding for "consultation and education." Funding for these services was maintained through the CPS process which allowed clinicians affiliated with licensed OMHCs to submit proposals for prevention/mental health education activities to the mental health core service agency in each jurisdiction, and if the proposals were preapproved, reimbursement was possible through the public mental health system, using state-only dollars.

Two major federally funded projects have provided partial support to the network of ESMH providers in Baltimore City. In 1994, thanks to a federal grant awarded by the Center for Mental Health Services, the East Baltimore Mental Health Partnership was born, enabling the Johns Hopkins Hospital to expand their ESMH services from 7 schools to all 19 schools located in their geographic area. The Safe Schools/Healthy Students (SS/HS) Initiative that began in the fall of 1999 was the second federal grant that benefited ESMH services in Baltimore. That project, which was funded for a total of 3 years, provided additional financial support to several existing programs and enabled ESMH services to expand to 6 new schools that had not previously had them. Baltimore's success in securing SS/HS Initiative funding was related to the years of alliance building between the school system, the public mental health system, the health department, the local management board, and Johns Hopkins University.

One of the most exciting new funding developments was the success of a statewide school-based mental health budget initiative in 2001. The process had begun several years earlier with the Maryland chapter of the National Assembly on School-Based Health Care partnering with the Mental Health Association of Maryland to formally advocate for additional funding for those aspects of ESMH services that were not reimbursable through the fee-for-service system. The funding was intended to support a model of integrated services including direct treatment services (services provided to students who meet the criteria for a formal mental health diagnoses), indicated prevention (services to students who have been identified as having a behavioral or emotional need, typically related to an environmental stressor, but who are not diagnosable), selective prevention (services to students who are at risk), and universal prevention (mental health education; social skills development) in the proportions noted in Fig. 1. Through a series of meetings with the Maryland Department of Mental Hygiene and the active advocacy efforts of the Maryland Assembly on School-Based Health Care in partnership with the Mental Health Association of Maryland, $2 million in new funding was included in the state Mental Hygiene Administration's 2002 budget to support this model.

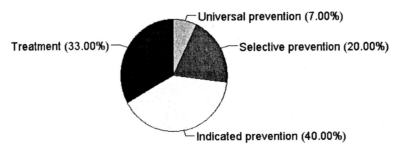

Figure 1. Model of distribution of ESMH services

While it appears that at this moment in time (2002), the Baltimore ESMH programs have achieved a funding continuum that supports the model in Fig. 1, the reality is a bit different. As discussed earlier, funding for ESMH services does not tend to be stable from year to year and this is true in Baltimore City. While most of the funding is expected to remain stable in 2003, the most notable exception is the federal SS/HS Initiative grant that will end in September 2002. Without replacement grant funds, the congruence between the model and the actual funding distribution will no longer exist. Additionally, the composite funding for all the services in the city is not the same as the funding mix for any *one* ESMH provider agency. Regrettably, no one program offering these services has the exact proportion of contract to fee-for-service funding that is illustrated in the citywide composite. On the other hand, the University of Maryland's School Mental Health Program and the East Baltimore Mental Health Partnership, which are the two largest providers of ESMH services in Baltimore, do in fact receive some funding from *each* of the sources reflected in the funding chart. This fact in conjunction with the funding distribution for these services on a citywide composite basis is a positive indicator of the current strength of ESMH programs in Baltimore. These diverse funding sources help to provide stability and support the broad continuum of services from prevention through early intervention and treatment.

CONCLUDING COMMENTS

In spite of the increasing prominence of ESMH as a means to improve child and adolescent mental health and reduce barriers to learning, funding the programs remains a major challenge. To meet this challenge means addressing a number of critical needs. First, there is a need for enhancing communication mechanisms to enable the sharing of lessons learned and funding strategies (as reviewed in this chapter) among and between programs, communities, and states. National technical assistance centers for mental health in schools (see Adelman et al., 1999) are currently engaged in sharing information about school mental health funding, as are other groups (e.g., the Centers for Disease Control and Prevention, the Center for Health and Health Care in Schools). A major step forward would be to further enhance resources of each of these groups to create one evolving guide that reviews the full panoply of school mental health funding opportunities and strategies, with this information broadly shared with diverse constituents (e.g., through list-serves, websites, and conferences). This advance would help to assist in addressing the second need—to build advocacy for mental health in schools (see Chapters 3–5). It is becoming increasingly clear that if the American public is not fully engaged in the major dialogues about school mental health (e.g., the advantages, impacts, and challenges), then support for the programs will continue to be marginal at best.

However, meaningful advocacy is related to many factors. Funding for expanded school mental health programs, like most goods and services in this country, is driven by consumer demand and supply. Unfortunately, there is not an economically meaningful demand for ESMH. Large corporations are not insisting that commercial insurance companies include coverage for ESMH in their policies. Similarly, employees are not making insurance choices based on coverage for ESMH. Most communities are not demanding or even expecting schools to provide this care, and advocacy groups have not barraged their legislators with demands for this coverage.

In fact, there are reasons that may contribute to avoidance of expanded school mental health. Arguments about improved access to care were recently interpreted as expensive "child-find" efforts by an insurance company representative. Schools may fear that ESMH services may end up on individual educational plans and thereby fall on the school district to fund. School-employed mental health professionals have expressed concerns that partnerships with outside agencies could reduce their roles. These economic and professional issues may serve to keep ESMH marginally funded and positioned unless there are some important changes.

These issues notwithstanding, there is a tremendous opportunity for ESMH to become a distinct model of care that is demanded by consumers and stakeholders in schools and communities. The advantages of ESMH are described in many of the chapters in this book. The cumulative effect of these advantages should result in greater access, greater consumer satisfaction, and better outcomes than clinic-based models of care that are currently available. These advantages need to be demonstrated through local program evaluations and through larger scale research. While current advocacy efforts resound with passion, testimonials, and some data and experience, they are lacking the real ammunition that will secure widespread stable funding. Outcome, satisfaction, and economic data demonstrating the value to children and families are needed to achieve this goal. Once obtained, large companies will expect insurance companies to fund ESMH, employees will consider ESMH when selecting coverage, and communities will insist that ESMH services are a part of the schools. At that point, future editions of this book will not need to include this chapter.

REFERENCES

Adelman, H. S., Taylor, L., Weist, M. D., Adelsheim, S., Freeman, B., Kapp, L., Lahti, M., & Mawn, D. (1999). Mental health in schools: A federal initiative. *Children's Services Social Policy, Research, and Practice, 2*(2), 95–115.

Bundy, A., & Wegener, V. (2000). Maximizing Medicaid funding to support health and mental health services for school-age children and youth: Strategy brief. *Tools for out-of-school time and community school initiatives, 1*(5). Washington, DC: The Finance Project.

Center for Health and Health Care in Schools (1998). Nine state strategies to support school-based health centers—Executive summary. http://www.healthinschools.org/school based health centers/papers/ninestrategies.asp.

Center for Health and Health Care in Schools (2001a). 1999–2000 school-based health center initiatives: Number of centers and state financing. http://www.healthinschools.org/school based health centers/school based health centers_table.htm.

Center for Health and Health Care in Schools (2001b). School-based health centers: Results from a 50-state survey: School year 1999–2000. http://www.healthinschools.org/school based health centers/survey2000.htm.

Center for School Mental Health Assistance (2000). Issue brief: Involvement of expanded school mental health programs in the State Children's Health Insurance program (CHIP). Baltimore, MD: University of Maryland School of Medicine.

Committee for the Advancement of Professional Practice (1995). Executive summary, schools as health service delivery sites: Historical, current, and future roles for psychology. Report of the schools as health service delivery sites work group. Washington, DC: American Psychological Association.

Making the Grade National Program Office (1995). Issues in financing school-based health centers: A guide for state officials. Center for health and health care in schools. The George Washington University, Washington, DC. http://www.healthinschools.org/school based health centers/papers/issues-financing.asp.

Nabors, L. A., Leff, S. S., & Mettrick, J. E. (2001). Assessing the costs of school-based mental health services. *Journal of School Health, 71*(5), 199–200.

National Assembly on School-Based Health Care (2000). *Medicaid reimbursement in school-based health centers: State association and provider perspectives.* Washington, DC: Author.

National Assembly on School-Based Health Care (2001). *Medicaid reimbursement in school based health centers gets regional attention.* Washington, DC: Author.

II

Enhancing Collaborative Approaches

7

Mental Health in Schools†

Programs of the Federal Government

TRINA MENDEN ANGLIN

The United States federal government has a vested interest in the mental health of children and adolescents. It considers the current state of mental health care for children a public crisis (U.S. Public Health Service, 2000). Approximately 21% of children and adolescents between the ages of 9 and 17 have a diagnosable mental or addictive disorder that causes at least minimal functional impairment; almost half of these youth, or 11% of all youth, have significantly impaired functioning, and about one-quarter of youth with mental disorders, or 5% of all youth, experience extreme functional impairment (Shaffer et al., 1996; U.S. Department of Health and Human Services, 1999a). Although only limited population and community-based data are currently available, decade-old findings indicate that only one of five school-aged children and adolescents with a mental disorder actually receives specialty mental health services, and only two of five receive mental health services from any source, including the mental health, general health, education, human services, and juvenile justice sectors (Burns et al., 1995). It has been concluded that the unmet need for mental health services for young people did not change in the 10 years between 1980 and 1990 (Burns et al., 1995). Because education is an entitlement for all children, schools represent the single location through which virtually every child and the large majority of adolescents can be reached. Schools have the potential to contribute to the solution of this problem.

The federal government supports an array of programs that promote the mental health of children and adolescents in school settings. This chapter describes

TRINA MENDEN ANGLIN • Health Resources and Services Administration, Rockville, Maryland 20857.

†The author acknowledges and deeply appreciates the thoughtful review of, and very helpful suggestions made to, the manuscript for this chapter by Nancy Davis, Ph. D., Cento for Mental Health Services, Substance Abuse and Mental Health Services Administration, U.S. Department of Health and Human Services.

consensus report recommendations issued by the U.S. Department of Health and Human Services. This chapter focuses on school-based programs for school-aged children and adolescents that have a comprehensive purview of mental health issues and also describes surveillance efforts that monitor school-based mental health educational and service programs.

BACKGROUND OF FEDERAL INVOLVEMENT IN SCHOOL MENTAL HEALTH

Although many schools and communities have a century-long history of programming that addresses the mental health and social well-being of students (Hoagwood & Erwin, 1997; Sedlak, 1997), the federal government has only recently formally addressed mental health issues of children and adolescents in school settings. Six forces have contributed to the federal government's heightened attention to student mental health problems and to schools as a prime service delivery site. First, Public Law 94-142 (Education for All Handicapped Children Act of 1975, more recently amended in 1990 and in 1997 as the Individuals with Disabilities Education Act (IDEA)) requires that children between the ages of 3 and 21 with serious emotional disturbances, which are considered a disability, receive a free and appropriate education in the least restrictive environment as well as mental health services necessary for promoting their ability to learn (U.S. Department of Education, 2001a). This law has been the major force leading to the expansion of school-based mental health services for children with serious emotional disturbances. For a single geographic region of the country, it was found that at least three-quarters of children receiving professional care for a mental health problem obtained services through a school-based program, and that schools were the *only* source of services for about two-thirds of school-aged children with a mental health diagnosis and for about 45% of children with a serious emotional disturbance (Burns et al., 1995). Given these findings, it has been suggested that schools function as the *de facto* mental health system for children and adolescents (Burns et al., 1995; Rones & Hoagwood, 2000).

A second influence on federal attention to school-based mental health services has come from the systems of care reform movement, which has aimed to strengthen services and improve outcomes for children and adolescents with serious emotional disturbances. This model of service transcends the requirements of IDEA. Described as a "comprehensive spectrum of mental health and other supportive services that are organized into a coordinated network for children with severe emotional disturbances," the system of care model requires collaboration across agencies and sectors and wraps needed services around individual children and their families. Although a key focus of the model is the partnership between parents and service providers, the model contains eight domains of service, including mental health, social, educational, health, substance abuse, vocational, recreational, and operational (e.g., case management, transportation, family support, legal) services (Stroul, 1996).

A third influence has been the school-based health care movement, which alerted the federal government that mental health issues are a major problem for children and adolescents seeking health care. Through attention to school-based health centers, the federal government recognized that schools represent the single best site for addressing students' mental health needs.

Fourth, concern about adolescent drug and alcohol use has led to categorical prevention programming through the U.S. Department of Education's Safe and Drug Free Schools Program and through the Substance Abuse and Mental Health Services Administration's Center for Substance Abuse Prevention, located in the U.S. Department of Health and Human Services. The close associations between mental health status and substance abuse cannot be overemphasized; co-morbid or co-occurring disorders are common among adolescents and adults (Kessler et al., 1994, 1996; Lewinsohn et al., 1993; Merikangas et al., 1998; Regier et al., 1993; U.S. Department of Health and Human Services, 1999b; Weinberg et al., 1998). However, it is not known whether categorical programming directed at specific behavioral problems, such as abuse of alcohol and illicit drugs, is also able to ameliorate other mental disorders.

Fifth, concern about student-perpetrated violence has led to specific programming around school safety through the efforts of the Safe and Drug Free Schools Program and the U.S. Department of Justice's Office of Juvenile Justice and Delinquency Prevention and Office of Community Oriented Policing Services. Categorical funding for substance abuse programs and violence and delinquency prevention programs has laid a firm foundation for interest in more comprehensive mental health programs.

A sixth force driving interest in school-based mental health has been the well-publicized spates of lethal student violence in which multiple students and faculty have been killed and injured on school campuses. Analysis of these incidents has sparked recognition that certain mental disorders and a nonsupportive school social climate can be major risk factors for student-perpetrated violence.

As recently as 1993, virtually no federal programs focusing primarily on mental health in school settings were listed in a directory of federal activities related to health promotion through schools, despite ongoing multidepartment federal interest in school health since at least 1980. However, the directory listed many programs that were closely allied with mental health, such as family advocacy, drug-free schools, child abuse and neglect, sexual abuse prevention, alcohol and drug abuse prevention, high-risk youth, and community and migrant health centers (U.S. Department of Health and Human Services, 1993). The three listed programs with a primary mental health focus included schools as part of a larger context. These programs, which are described in the next section of the chapter, were (1) two rehabilitation research and training centers on children's mental health and services for children with serious emotional disturbances supported by the Department of Education's Office on Special Education and Rehabilitation Services, which are discussed below, and (2) the Child and Adolescent Service System Program (CASSP), a former initiative that had been supported by the National Institute of Mental Health/Alcohol, Drug Abuse, and Mental Health Administration (ADAMHA) of the U.S. Department of Health and Human Services. (ADAMHA was reorganized in 1992.)

The following problems have been identified in considering the roles that schools play in serving children and adolescents with emotional and behavioral problems: (1) The number of students recognized as having problems is disproportionately low compared to national prevalence rates. Schools only identify about 1% of students, but up to 5% of children and adolescents have severe emotional and behavioral problems and up to 21% of students have diagnosable mental disorders. (2) The educational programs offered to students with emotional and behavioral problems do not focus sufficiently on academic learning and social skills development; they overemphasize behavioral controls and tend to place affected students in segregated settings. (3) Families are construed as adversaries rather than as partners. (4) Students with emotional and behavioral problems have poor outcomes in terms of decreased chances of graduation and employment and heightened risk for involvement in the juvenile justice system (Knitzer, 1996). The reader is asked to remember these points and to consider how currently funded programs, new legislation, and consensus recommendations might be able to address these serious concerns.

FEDERAL PROGRAMS THAT INCLUDE SCHOOL-BASED MENTAL HEALTH EFFORTS

This section of the chapter describes five current federal programs that include a school-based mental health focus. Two programs have a primary focus on the mental health of children and adolescents and include school-based activities as part of a larger context. Two programs focus on schools and include mental health activities as part of broader efforts. One program combines these two concepts for an exclusive focus on mental health in schools.

Federal Programs with a Primary Mental Health Focus that Include School-Based Activities

Rehabilitation Research and Training Centers

Sponsoring Agency. Historically, the Department of Education, Office of Special Education and Rehabilitative Services (OSERS) has funded rehabilitation research and training centers for children with emotional disabilities through its National Institute on Disability and Rehabilitation Research (NIDRR). OSERS provides leadership for achieving full integration into and participation in society of people with disabilities by ensuring access to equal opportunities and excellence in education, employment, and community living (U.S. Department of Education, 2001b). In practice, OSERS supports programs that educate children and adolescents with disabilities, provides for the rehabilitation of youth and adults with disabilities, and supports research to improve the lives of people with disabilities. The mission of NIDRR, one of OSERS' three components, is to generate, disseminate, and promote new knowledge for improving the options available to people with disabilities so that they can perform fully in the community and receive appropriate supports from society (U.S. Department of Education, 2001c).

Description of the Program. Rehabilitation research and training centers (RRTCS) are a key program category supported by NIDRR. The RRTCS, which were first legislatively mandated in 1973, are expected to conduct synergistic research, training, and service activities. Of the 40 RRTCs currently funded, 3 include activities that are school-directed, but none is primarily focused on school-based mental health services for children. The three centers include the Rehabilitation Research and Training Center to Improve Services for Children with Serious Emotional and Behavioral Disabilities and Their Families, the Rehabilitation Research and Training Center for Children's Mental Health, and the Rehabilitation Research and Training Center on Positive Behavioral Support (National Rehabilitation Information Center for Independence, 2001).

Comprehensive Community Mental Health Services for Children and Their Families Program

Sponsoring Agency. The Children's and Communities Mental Health Services Improvement Act of 1992 authorized the Comprehensive Community Mental Health Services for Children and Their Families Program (CCMHP), which is administered by the Center for Mental Health Services/Substance Abuse and Mental Health Services Administration (SAMHSA). SAMHSA is mandated to improve the quality and availability of prevention, treatment, and rehabilitative services for mental illness and substance abuse in order to reduce illness, death, disability, and other societal cost caused by these problems (Substance Abuse and Mental Health Services Administration, 2002). The Center for Mental Health Services (CMHS), placed within SAMHSA, aims to improve the availability and accessibility of high-quality care for people affected by or at risk for mental disorders and works toward the development of an effective community-based mental health infrastructure for the nation (Substance Abuse and Mental Health Services Administration, 2002).

Description of the Program. CCMHP is built on the principles of the earlier Child and Adolescent Service System Program (CASSP), which had been congressionally authorized as the mental health component of Title II, Treatment and Prevention Programs, of the Anti-Drug Abuse Act of 1988. CASSP was designed to improve systems of service delivery for children and adolescents with severe emotional disturbances; its main goal was to improve and integrate the way diverse services are delivered to this population by states and communities. This program had been active in every state and had also helped to support the two rehabilitation research and training centers mentioned previously (U.S. Department of Health and Human Services, 1993). Both CASSP and CCMHP are based on the systems of care model.

CCMHP is the current federal program providing coordinated, community-based, family-centered, culturally competent, accessible, and least restrictive services for children and adolescents with serious emotional, behavioral, or mental disorders accompanied by functional impairment. Development of these systems of care is based on the premise that the mental health needs of children, adolescents, and their families can be met in their home, school, and community environments (Substance Abuse and Mental Health Services Administration, 1999). A variety of community agencies are involved, including mental health, child welfare, education, and juvenile justice. Funded service systems are tailored to the needs of individual children and adolescents and include evaluation and diagnosis, emergency, intensive home-based and day treatment services, transitional and case management, and respite care.

School-based practices endorsed by CCMHP project sites include use of clinicians and other student support providers from the larger community in the school, use of school-based "wraparound" services to support learning and transition, use of school-based case management, provision of schoolwide prevention and early intervention programs for learning social skills and behaviors, creation of centers of support within the school, and the use of family liaisons or advocates to help empower family members in strengthening their roles in their children's education and care (Woodruff et al., 1999). Evaluation of sites funded in 1993 demonstrated positive educational performance; after 6 months in the program, the percentage of children rated as at least average in their school performance increased by 12 percentage points, and after 1 year in the program, the rating increased by 19 percentage points. Evaluation measures also demonstrated improvements in children's overall functional status and in contacts with law enforcement agencies (Substance Abuse and Mental Health Services Administration, 1999).

Federal Programs with a Primary School-Based Focus that Include Mental Health Activities

Providing Mental Health Services through School-Based Primary Care

Comprehensive health service delivery in schools started during the 1980s with the advent of the school-based health center (SBHC) movement. SBHCs provide primary health care services to students; they are most likely to be located in schools where student access to other health care services is limited and students' home neighborhoods increase their vulnerability for engaging in health risk behaviors (Lear et al., 1991). At this time, more than one-third of this country's approximately 1500 school-based health centers receive federal support, either directly from the Healthy Schools, Healthy Communities Program of the Health Resources and Services Administration's Bureau of Primary Health Care (which began in 1994 and is based on a comprehensive model of health services, including mental health services) or indirectly through support by federally funded community health centers (which administer 19% of school-based health centers) and/or by Title V (Social Security Act) Maternal and Child Health State Block Grant funding. At least 45 states contain SBHCs. Specialty mental health providers are integral staff in 57% of SBHCs and provide a mean of 33 hours of service each week (Schlitt et al., 2000). Mental health concerns represent the modal reason for visits to SBHCs with comprehensive mental health services; at least a quarter of all visits carry mental health diagnoses.

Safe Schools, Healthy Students Interdepartmental Initiative

Sponsoring Agencies. The Safe Schools, Healthy Students Initiative (SS/HS) is a collaborative effort sponsored by the U.S. Departments of Education, Health and Human Services, and Justice. Partners within these departments include the Safe and Drug-Free Schools Program, Substance Abuse and Mental Health Services Administration/Center for Mental Health Services, Office of Juvenile Justice and Delinquency Prevention, and Office of Community Oriented Policing Services (COPS).

Activities of the Safe and Drug-Free Schools (SDFS) Program are authorized under Part A, the Safe and Drug-Free Schools and Communities Act, contained within Title IV, 21st-Century Schools, of the No Child Left Behind Act of 2001, which represents reauthorization of the Elementary and Secondary Education Act. This program aims to prevent violence in and around schools and to strengthen efforts that prevent the illegal use of alcohol, tobacco, and other drugs. The SDFS States Grant Program provides formula-based grants to state and local education agencies, and the national program's activities support a variety of discretionary initiatives that can respond to the emerging needs of school districts and their communities (U.S. Department of Education, 2001d). It is further described in the section, No Child Left Behind Act of 2001.

The mission of the Office of Juvenile Justice and Delinquency Prevention (OJJDP), which is placed within the U.S. Department of Justice, is to prevent and respond to juvenile delinquency and victimization. OJJDP is guided by the Juvenile Justice and Delinquency Prevention Act of 1974 and subsequent amendments; it works with both states and communities (U.S. Department of Justice, 2002a). COPS is responsible for advancing community policing, including the placement of police officers in schools as part of the COPS in Schools (CIS) Program. These positions enforce laws and educate students about crime prevention, help students to solve social problems, and serve as liaison to the larger community (U.S. Department of Justice, 2002b).

Description of the Program. Started in Federal Year 1999 through a congressional appropriation, the purpose of the SS/HS Initiative is to develop practical knowledge about effective policies and programs that reduce school violence. It is the most comprehensive, largest single initiative to date that addresses the multiple issues, including promotion of mental health, that foster both the healthy development of children and a safe school environment.

The SS/HS Initiative is a grant program that has awarded a total of 97 three-year grants of $1 to $3 million to local education agencies (LEAs). Eligible LEAs must have established formal partnerships with local mental health and law enforcement agencies. They must develop comprehensive plans for promoting the healthy development of children and youth, fostering resilience, and preventing violence. There are six required program components: a safe school environment and safe school policies; educational reform; violence prevention, alcohol, and other drug prevention and early intervention; school and community mental health prevention and treatment intervention services; and early childhood social and emotional development services. Together, these components are expected to accomplish four goals: to improve/increase services to "at-risk" children and their families, to link child-serving agencies in a consistent and complementary way, to decrease violence and drug abuse and to make school disciplinary activity less necessary, and to enhance the healthy development of all children (National Criminal Justice Reference Service, 2001; Substance Abuse and Mental Health Services Administration, 2001).

Key mental health objectives of the SS/HS initiative emphasize early childhood development, capitalize on developing resilience, establish a formal connection between schools and the public mental health system, and for students with more serious problems, provide for screening and assessment, treatment by mental health specialists, and follow-up. Major education objectives include the development of comprehensive strategies for addressing community needs, such as increased school security; firm, caring discipline policies, schoolwide education on safety and violence prevention and counseling/social services; integration of school reform with safe environments; emphasis on research-based programs; and promotion of successful school/family/community linkages. Key justice and law enforcement objectives ensure safety, control delinquent behavior in and around schools, prevent dropping out and school failure, establish closer working relationships with mental health and education sectors, and create positive opportunities for students to be successful (Substance Abuse and Mental Health Services Administration, 2001).

Funded sites are encouraged to use programs already scientifically shown to be effective and are expected both to participate in a national evaluation of the initiative and to develop a local evaluation. The national evaluation, which is being conducted in two waves, is expected to provide information on such areas as the optimal combination of community characteristics needed to achieve an integrated, strategic approach to violence prevention; the major challenges faced by communities as they develop comprehensive and integrated strategies for violence prevention; and the economic costs and benefits for communities in developing a strategic approach to violence prevention. In addition to collecting core information from all sites, the evaluation is collecting supplemental data for 18 randomly selected sentinel sites. Initial evaluation results should be available in 2002.

Program with an Exclusive Focus on Mental Health in Schools

Mental Health in Schools Program

Sponsoring Agency. This initiative is sponsored by the Health Resources and Services Administration's (HRSA) Maternal and Child Health Bureau (MCHB). HRSA's mission is to improve and expand access to quality health care for all Americans. It works to assure the availability of quality health care for low-income, uninsured, isolated, vulnerable, and special needs populations (HRSA, 2002). As part of HRSA, the MCHB aims to improve the health, safety, and well-being of the maternal and child population, which includes school-aged children and adolescents. The Maternal and Child Health Services Program was authorized by Congress in 1935 as Title V of the Social Security Act (Maternal and Child Health Bureau, 2002).

Description of the Program. The Mental Health in Schools Program was developed in 1995 in response to the awareness that the school-aged population needed enhanced access to mental health services. It is perhaps the first recent federal program with an exclusive focus on children's mental health in a school-based context. MCHB was concerned that 20% of students have a significant mental health problem that compromises their ability to learn and ultimately to succeed at school. The intent of the initiative was to assist schools, educators, community-based organizations, and health/mental health providers to build the infrastructure necessary for enhancing primary mental health resources and services for children

and adolescents in school settings. The initiative sought to facilitate early attention to mental health problems and to promote preventive activities designed to
reduce the prevalence of psychosocial problems among school-aged children and
adolescents.

The program was initially operationalized in two ways: (1) State-level partnership grants were awarded to five state departments of health for building partnerships among health, mental health, and education agencies in order to assist
communities' efforts to develop mental health services for school-aged children
and adolescents. (2) Two training and technical assistance centers were established
to develop resources and instructional materials for strengthening the ability of
school personnel, primary care health providers, and mental health specialists to
provide mental health services within school settings (Adelman et al., 1999). The
initiative was partially renewed on a competitive basis in 2000 with co-support
by SAMHSA's Center for Mental Health Services; two awards were made for training
and technical assistance centers for mental health in schools. The specific intent of
the current initiative is to strengthen the personnel and administrative abilities of
schools and their communities to address psychosocial issues and mental health
problems, including substance abuse, for school-aged children, adolescents, and
their families.

FEDERALLY SPONSORED SURVEILLANCE AND STUDIES OF SCHOOL MENTAL HEALTH EFFORTS

School Health Policies and Programs Study

Sponsoring Agency. The School Health Policies and Programs Study (SHPPS)
is supported by the Centers for Disease Control and Prevention's (CDC) Division
of Adolescent and School Health (DASH). CDC's mission is to promote health and
quality of life by prevention and controlling disease, injury, and disability (Centers for Disease Control and Prevention, 2002a). Within CDC, the mission of DASH
is to prevent the most serious health risk behaviors among children, adolescents,
and young adults. It employs the following four strategies: identifying and monitoring critical health problems and school health policies and programs to reduce
these problems; synthesizing and applying research to increase the effectiveness
of school health policies and programs; enabling constituents to implement effective policies and programs; and conducting evaluations to assess and improve
the effectiveness of implemented school health policies and programs (Centers for
Disease Control and Prevention, 2002b).

DASH has organized many of its activities around an eight-component model
of a coordinated school health program. Mental health issues are integral to several of its components, which include: comprehensive school health education;
physical education; school health services; school nutrition services, school counseling, psychological and social services; healthy school environment, school-site
health promotion for staff; and family and community involvement in school
health (Marx, Wooley, & Northrop, 1998). Sixteen state education agencies receive
funding for building the mechanism, or infrastructure, for developing coordinated
school health programs within their school districts.

Description of Study. First conducted in 1994, SHPPS is a national survey that monitors and assesses school health policies and programs at the state, school district, individual school, and classroom levels. It provides a "big picture" perspective, but is not designed to elicit details of specific activities at the school level. The original study addressed mental health issues and programs in a limited way. SHPPS 2000 has broader content and scope and addresses mental health issues in greater detail than its predecessor. It specifically assesses the eight school health program components, including mental health and social services, as well as school policies and environments. Despite these differences, it is possible to compare some findings across the two surveys to determine whether student services have changed across the 6 years between the two studies (Brener, Martindale, & Weist, 2001; Small et al., 1995).

Study Findings. Only five categories of service relevant to mental health are directly comparable between the two studies. In 1994, these domains were assessed only for middle/junior and senior high schools, but the 2000 survey also included elementary schools. Each category of service was provided by a greater percentage of schools in 2000 compared to 1994: Individual counseling services were provided by 86% of middle/junior and senior high schools overall in 1994 and by 90% of all surveyed schools in 2000. All other categories of services started from lower baselines and demonstrated greater increases across time: Group counseling services were provided by 60% of schools in 1994 and by 76% in 2000; provision of family counseling services increased from 46 to 61%; suicide prevention services (provided individually or in small groups) increased from 47 to 77%; and alcohol and other drug use treatment services increased from 43 to 58% between 1994 and 2000 (Brener et al., 2001; Small et al., 1995). As discussed later in this chapter, the Department of Education is mandated to sponsor national programs for elementary school counseling and for preventing substance abuse. It is likely that the high percentages of schools with counseling services can be attributed to these programs.

School Health Education Profiles

Study Findings. CDC/DASH has also conducted surveillance on the characteristics of health education among secondary schools (encompassing grades 6 through 12), most recently in 1998 (Grunbaum et al., 2000). Across states, the median percentage of schools requiring health education for secondary schools was 93%. The following findings of the school health education profiles are relevant to mental health. Median percentages of schools that mandated the following content areas to be included in required health education classes were: prevention of alcohol and other drug use—99%; violence prevention—85%; and suicide prevention—74%. In addition, the large majority of schools attempted to improve students' skills. For example, the median percentage of schools mandating instruction in skills for nonviolent conflict resolution was 83%; resisting social pressures was 95%; and stress management was 86% (Grunbaum et al., 2000). However, neither the quality nor effectiveness of these health education topics was assessed. Interestingly, less than half of health education teachers overall had received inservice training on topics relevant to student mental health over the previous 2 years:

prevention of alcohol and other drug use—50%; violence prevention—43%; and suicide prevention—26% (Grunbaum et al., 2000).

Characteristics and Funding of School Mental Health Services Study

Sponsoring Agency. Substance Abuse and Mental Health Services Administration/Center for Mental Health Services.

Description of Study. Very little formal information is known about the extent of mental health services provided in schools (Rones & Hoagwood, 2000). This national survey of a representative sample of schools, which will be fielded during the 2002–2003 school year, seeks to provide an information baseline. The survey has four aims: (1) to identify and describe models and arrangements for the delivery of mental health services within public elementary, middle/junior, and senior high schools and to document which are most prevalent; (2) to identify and describe the numbers and types of professional mental health staff available in public school settings, the amounts of time they are available, and their qualifications; (3) to document the types of mental health problems most frequently encountered in the school setting and the nature and amount of mental health services delivered; and (4) to identify and categorize the ways in which school mental health services are currently funded and explore the ways in which various funding mechanisms may affect the delivery of services.

LOOKING TO THE FUTURE

This chapter concludes with descriptions of two federal consensus reports critical to children's school-based mental health and the newly reauthorized Elementary and Secondary Education Act, the No Child Left Behind Act of 2001. Each contains sections pivotal to the advancement of school-based mental health for children and adolescents. Given the recency of release of the reports and passage of the legislation, however, their potential is largely untapped.

Federally sponsored consensus reports serve two major functions: to call national attention to serious and emerging problems and to offer recommendations on how to address them. Such recommendations provide an important impetus for developing future federal programs. In addition, states, communities, and private sector organizations look to these reports for guidance in developing their own activities. The Surgeon General's Office has recently issued two reports that have the potential to influence both public and private sector investments in school-based mental health. They are the *Report of the Surgeon General's Conference on Children's Mental Health: A National Action Agenda* (U.S. Public Health Service, 2000) and the *National Strategy for Suicide Prevention: Goals and Objectives for Action* (U.S. Public Health Service, 2001).

The *Report of the Surgeon General's Conference on Children's Mental Health: A National Action Agenda* (September 2000) provides a blueprint for addressing the mental health needs of our nation's children and adolescents. The conference report reaffirms the critical roles that schools can play in addressing children's mental health problems. The report specifically includes schools in action steps for five of the eight national goals. Action steps relevant to schools are summarized in the following and are placed in the context of education.

The third goal of the conference report on children's mental health seeks to improve the recognition and assessment of mental health needs in children. Schools are considered a key player for meeting this goal as the report lists several recommended action steps that focus on the education community: (1) encourage early identification of mental health needs in existing education systems; (2) create tangible tools for educators to help them assess children's social and emotional needs, discuss mental health issues with both parents and children, and make appropriate referrals; (3) train all education personnel in ways to enhance child mental health and recognize early indicators of mental health problems; and (4) promote proactive systems of behavior support at the school level, including both universal prevention methods and selective, individual student supports for children with more intense and long-term needs.

The fourth goal of the conference report on children's mental health calls for the elimination of racial/ethnic and socioeconomic disparities in access to mental health care services. Schools are perceived as an important part of the strategy for enhancing access to mental health services for children. The conference report recommends that mental health services be colocated with other key systems, such as education, to improve access, especially in remote or rural communities. It also advises that if schools' resource capacities are strengthened, they can serve as a key link to a comprehensive system of school- and community-based identification, assessment, and treatment services for meeting the needs of youth and their families.

The sixth goal of the conference report on children's mental health aims to increase access to and coordination of quality mental health care services. Several of the activities recommended for implementing this goal are school based. For example, it is recommended that a common language be developed to describe children's mental health in order to facilitate delivery of services across systems. Similarly, definitions and evaluation procedures used by education systems to identify and serve children and youth with mental health needs should be modified in order to facilitate access to essential services. Access to mental health services can be increased by providing them where youth and families congregate, such as in schools. The report also recognized that schools can be complicated systems for families to negotiate, and recommended the use of family advocates to assist families in interacting effectively with them.

The seventh goal of the conference report on children's mental health aims to increase the capacity of frontline providers, such as educators, to recognize and manage mental health care issues. Specific action recommendations relevant to education include: (1) engaging professional organizations in educating new teachers about child development, enhancing their skills for addressing children's mental health, and training them to recognize early symptoms for proactive intervention; and (2) facilitating training of new providers by building knowledge of child development into the existing curricula of professional schools and encouraging training opportunities across disciplines that can facilitate the development of effective partnerships.

In summary, the *Report of the Surgeon General's Conference on Children's Mental Health: A National Action Agenda* recognizes that mental health needs of children and adolescents could be better met if our nation (1) enhanced schools' and educators' abilities to identify and respond proactively constructively to children with mental health needs; (2) promoted children's and adolescents' access to mental health services by colocating them in schools and coordinating effort with community-based agencies; (3) developed a common language describing children's mental health and behavioral issues that could be used across sectors; and (4) helped parents and school systems to work effectively together. The conference report emphasized training of school personnel as part of several action recommendations. In addition to helping address the national problem of unmet mental health needs, the action recommendations of the conference report also respond to the problems identified by Knitzer (1996) regarding schools' current roles in child and adolescent mental health.

The *National Strategy for Suicide Prevention: Goals and Objectives for Action* (U.S. Public Health Service, 2001) was developed by a broad array of stakeholders and seeks to integrate suicide prevention into existing health, mental health, education, human service, and justice settings. Suicide is a serious public health problem. It is the third leading cause of death among adolescents. Suicide rates continue to increase from early adolescence (ages 10–14 years) until young adulthood (20–24 years); among males, rates are almost double for young adults compared to adolescents aged 15–19 years. Suicide attempts increase the burden of disability and suffering; it is estimated that for every completed suicide, 50 to 100 attempts are made. In addition, adolescents who attempt suicide are at heightened risk for suicide in the future (U.S. Public Health Service, 2001).

The *National Strategy* includes schools as part of several objectives. As part of calling for the development and implementation of community-based suicide prevention programs, the *National Strategy* includes an objective (4.2) to increase by 2005 the proportion of school districts and private school associations with evidence-based programs designed to address serious childhood and adolescent distress and prevent suicide. The sixth goal calls for the implementation of training for recognition of at-risk behavior and delivery of effective treatment. Key gatekeepers, which include teachers and school staff (e.g., bus drivers, custodians, office secretaries) as well as school health personnel, interact with children and adolescents in "natural" settings and have opportunities to intervene with troubled students. Formal objective 6.5 aims by 2005 to increase the proportion of educational faculty and staff who have received training on identifying and responding to children and adolescents at risk for suicide. Goal 8 seeks to improve access to and community linkages with mental health and substance abuse services. Within the context of this goal, objective 8.5 aims to increase by 2005 the proportion of school districts in which school-based health centers incorporate mental and substance abuse assessment and management into the scope of their activities.

The recommendations of the *National Strategy for Suicide Prevention* were developed independently from the recommendations of the conference report on children's mental health, yet the two sets of recommendations are highly consistent with each other. The recommendations for strategies to decrease suicide rates represent concrete examples of how the more general recommendations of the conference report on children's mental health can be operationalized. Training of school personnel, use of evidence-based programs, and enhancing access to mental health services are emphasized as key school-based strategies for preventing suicide.

The No Child Left Behind Act of 2001

The No Child Left Behind Act of 2001 (H.R. 1), which was signed into Public Law No. 107-110 in January 2002, is the reauthorization of the Elementary and Secondary Education Act of 1965, which had been previously reauthorized in 1994. In particular, Titles IV and V contain sections with high relevance to school mental health (No Child Left Behind Act, 2001).

Title IV is now named 21st Century Schools; Part A is the Safe and Drug-Free Schools (SDFS) and Communities Act. Its primary purpose is to support programs that prevent violence in and around schools and that prevent the illegal use of alcohol, tobacco, and other drugs; it fosters a safe and drug-free learning environment supportive of student academic achievement. This act also mandates that parents and the communities that surround schools be involved in relevant activities. Local education agencies (LEAs) that receive grants from the SDFS State Grants Program (Subpart 1, Section 4115) are authorized to develop a wide range of activities for the prevention of violence and drug use. Of the 22 authorized activities listed, 5 are directly relevant to mental health. The first 2 include expanded and improved school-based mental health services related to illegal drug use and violence as well as counseling, mentoring, referral services, and other student assistance programs. Services can include early identification of violence and illegal drug use, assessment, and direct or group counseling services provided to students, parents, families, and school personnel by qualified school-based mental health service providers. Teachers can be trained by school-based mental health service providers in appropriate identification and intervention techniques for students at risk for violent behavior and illegal use of drugs. A third possible activity that LEAs could undertake is the establishment of emergency intervention services following traumatic crisis events that have disrupted the learning environment. A fourth activity is the development of programs for training school personnel on the prevention of youth suicide. The final activity directly related to mental health that is included as part of the SDFS State Grants Program for LEAs is the development of programming that responds to the needs of students faced with domestic violence or child abuse.

The SDFS and Communities Program also has National Program (Subpart 2) activities that are administered at the federal level. One key example of an authorized national program activity with direct mental health implications calls is the development, demonstration, evaluation, and dissemination of child abuse education and prevention programs for elementary and secondary students (Section 4121). A second authorized program with direct relevance to mental health will provide assistance to LEAs and community-based organizations for the prevention of hate crimes (Section 4123). A newly authorized third activity calls for the establishment of a National Center for School and Youth Safety by the Secretary of Education and the Attorney General (Section 4128). This center would offer emergency assistance to local communities as they respond to school safety crises. Part of the assistance effort would include counseling for victims and the community. The center would also maintain a toll-free anonymous student hotline for reporting possible warning signs of violent behavior and would function as a clearinghouse for best practices in school violence prevention, intervention, and crisis management.

A fourth activity, new to the 2001 legislation, is the creation of a national grants program for LEAs for the reduction of alcohol abuse among secondary school students (Section 4129). This activity would be carried out jointly with the Substance Abuse and Mental Health Services Administration. The final national program activity promoting mental health mandates the establishment of mentoring programs at LEAs and community-based organizations for children at risk for educational failure, dropping out of school, or involved in criminal or delinquent activities (Section 4130). (This program is similar to the Juvenile Mentoring Program (JUMP), which is sponsored by the U.S. Department of Justice's Office of Juvenile Justice and Delinquency Prevention.)

Title V, Promoting Informed Parental Choice and Innovative Programs, is the other title of the No Child Left Behind Act of 2001 that specifically addresses mental health issues. The overall purposes of Title V are to (1) support education reform efforts and school improvement programs that are based on scientific research; (2) meet the education needs of all students, including at-risk youth; and (3) develop and implement education programs that improve school, student, and teacher performance. Subpart 3, Local Innovative Education Programs, of Part A, Innovative Programs, provides for State allocations to LEAs for innovative assistance programs. Included in the list of 27 authorized assistance programs is the expansion and improvement of school-based mental health services, including early identification of drug use and violence; assessment; and direct individual or group counseling services provided to students, parents, and school personnel by qualified school-based mental health services personnel (Section 5131).

The remaining three programs that address mental health issues within Title V are each contained in Part D, Fund for the Improvement of Education (FIE). Through national activities, as well as funding of state education agencies (SEAs), LEAs, institutions of higher learning, and other types of organizations, this section supports nationally significant programs to improve the quality of elementary and secondary education at the state and local levels and helps children meet state academic content and student academic achievement standards. The Elementary and Secondary School Counseling Program, Subpart 2 of FIE (Section 5421), reauthorizes competitive grants to LEAs for establishing and expanding comprehensive counseling services for students in elementary schools and extends eligibility to secondary schools. This program also expands the set of mental health professionals who can provide counseling services. Child and adolescent psychiatrists and "other" qualified psychologists have been added to the traditional school-based mental health professionals, which include school counselors, school psychologists, and school social workers. This provision is key for schools being able to call upon community-based mental health professionals as service providers. In addition, counseling services can be provided in "settings that meet the range of student needs," so that it is possible that services could be provided off campus.

There are two categories of Grants to Improve the Mental Health of Children contained in Subpart 14 of Part D of Title V of the Leave No Child Behind Act of 2001. These programs were not previously authorized. The first category, Grants for the Integration of Schools and Mental Health Systems (Section 5541), authorizes a program of competitive awards to SEAs, LEAs, and Indian tribes for the purpose of enhancing student access to high-quality mental health care by developing innovative programs that link local school systems with community mental health systems. These collaborative efforts provide and improve prevention, diagnosis, referral, and treatment services for students; increase the availability of crisis intervention services; provide training for both school personnel and mental health professionals; and provide technical assistance and consultation to school systems, mental health agencies, and families.

The second category, Promotion of School Readiness Through Early Childhood Emotional and Social Development (Section 5542), authorizes a program of Foundation for Learning Grants to LEAs and community-based organizations to help young children become ready for school by fostering their emotional, behavioral, and social development. Eligible children must be younger than 7 years and be at risk for poor scholastic outcomes because of such characteristics as exposure to violence, homelessness, parental mental disorder or substance abuse, extreme poverty, low birth weight, early behavioral problems, and cognitive deficit or developmental disability.

The program also supports the coordination and facilitation of access to a wide range of services available through community resources. This program could facilitate community partnerships that build toward a community system of care composed of child-serving agencies and organizations that provide individualized supports for eligible children and their families.

The final program in Part D of Title V with direct mental health implications is Subpart 17, Combating Domestic Violence (Section 5571). This new program of competitive grants to LEAs strengthens effective prevention and intervention strategies for children exposed to domestic violence through training for school personnel and development of support services, relevant educational programming for students, and development and implementation of school system policies on behalf of students exposed to domestic violence.

In summary, the No Child Left Behind Act of 2001 addresses student mental health needs from multiple perspectives. In addition to continuing programs directed at reducing substance abuse and violence, the act addresses important social issues that have serious implications for children's mental health, such as child abuse, domestic violence, and hate crimes. In addition to expanding comprehensive counseling services within schools, the No Child Left Behind Act supports linkages between schools and community-based mental health systems and permits clinical mental health specialists to provide services to students on and off campus. Training of teachers is also included. The developmental needs of young children are considered. Full implementation of the multiple components of this legislation can help schools to identify larger numbers of students with mental health needs, build the service capacity for meeting these needs, and encourage schools to work collaboratively with their communities. Programs developed by the education sector under the auspices of the No Child Left Behind Act have the potential to implement the school-based action steps recommended by the *Report of the Surgeon General's Conference on Children's Mental Health*. Most importantly, they have the potential to increase children's and adolescents' access to mental health services and to reduce the unmet need for them.

REFERENCES

Adelman, H. S., Taylor, L., Weist, M. D., Adelsheim, S., Freeman, B., Kapp, L., Lahti, M., & Mawn, D. (1999). Mental health in schools: A federal initiative. *Children's Services: Social Policy, Research, and Practice, 2,* 95–115.

Brener, N. D., Martindale, J., & Weist, M. D. (2001). Mental health and social services: Results from the School Health Policies and Programs Study 2000. *Journal of School Health, 71,* 305–312.

Burns, B. J., Costello, E. J., Angold, A., Tweed, D., Stangl, D., Farmer, E. M. Z., & Erklani, A. (1995). Children's mental health service use across service sectors. *Health Affairs, 14,* 147–159.

Centers for Disease Control and Prevention (2002a). About CDC. http://www.cdc.gov/aboutcdc.htm.

Centers for Disease Control and Prevention (2002b). About the adolescent and school health program. http://www.cdc.gov/nccdphp/dash/what.htm.

Flaherty, L. T., Weist, M. D., & Warner, B. S. (1996). School-based mental health services in the United States: History, current models and needs. *Community Mental Health Journal, 32,* 341–352.

Grunbaum, J. A., Kann, L., Williams, B. I., Kinchen, S. A., Collins, J. L., Baumler, E. R., & Kolbe, L. J. (2000). Surveillance for characteristics of health education among secondary schools—School health education profiles, 1998. In CDC surveillance summaries. *Morbidity and Mortality Weekly Report, 49*(SS-8), 1–41.

Health Resources and Services Administration (2002). About HRSA. http://www.hrsa.gov/about.htm.

Hoagwood, K., & Erwin, H. D. (1997). Effectiveness of school-based mental health services for children: A 10-year research review. *Journal of Child and Family Studies, 6,* 435–451.

Kessler, R. C., McGonagle, K. A., Zhao, S., Nelson, C. B., Hughes, M., Eshleman, S., Wittchen, H. U., & Kindler, K. S. (1994). Lifetime and 12-month prevalence of DSM-III-R psychiatric disorders in the United States. Results from the National Comorbidity Survey. *Archives of General Psychiatry, 51,* 8–19.

Kessler, R. C., Nelson, C. B., McKonagle, K. A., Edlund, M. J., Frank, R. G., & Leaf, P. J. (1996). The epidemiology of co-occurring addictive and mental disorders: Implications for prevention and service utilization. *American Journal of Orthopsychiatry, 66,* 17–31.

Knitzer, J. (1996). The role of education in systems of care. In B. A. Stroul & R. M. Friedman (Eds.), *Children's mental health: Creating systems of care in a changing society* (pp. 197–213). Baltimore: Paul H. Brookes.

Lear, J. G., Gleicher, H. B., St. Germaine, A., & Porter, P. J. (1991). Reorganizing health care for adolescents: The experience of the school-based adolescent health care program. *Journal of Adolescent Health, 12,* 450–458.

Lewinsohn, P. M., Hops, H., Roberts, R. E., Seeley, J. R., & Andrews, J. A. (1993). Adolescent psychopathology: I. Prevalence and incidence of depression and other DSM-III-R disorders in high school students. *Journal of Abnormal Psychology, 102,* 133–144.

Marx, E., Wooley, S. F., & Northrop, D. (Eds.). (1998). *Health is academic: A guide to coordinated school health programs.* New York: Teachers College Press.

Maternal and Child Health Bureau (2002). About MCHB. http://www.mchb.hrsa.gov.

Merikangas, K. R., Mehta, R. L., Molnar, B. E., Walters, E. E., Swendsen, J. D., Aguilar-Gaziola, S., Bigl, R., Borges, G., Caraveo–Anduaga, J. J., Dawit, D. J., Kolody, B., Voga, W. A., Wittchen, H. U., & Kessler, R. C. (1998). Comorbidity of substance use disorders with mood and anxiety disorders: Results of the International Consortium on Psychiatric Epidemiology. *Addictive Behaviors, 23,* 893–907.

National Criminal Justice Reference Service (2001). OJJDP Annual Report 2000, Chapter 2, Preventing and intervening in delinquency. http://www.ncjrs.org/html/ojjdp/annualreport2000/chap2.html.

National Rehabilitation Information Center for Independence (NARIC) (2001). Rehabilitation research and training centers program descriptions. http://www.naric.com/search/pd.

No Child Left Behind Act of 2001. http://thomas.loc.gov/cgi-bin/query or http://www/ed/gov/legislation/ESEA02.

Regier, D. A., Narrow, W. E., Rae, D. S., Manderscheid, R. W., Locke, B. Z., & Goodwin, F. K. (1993). The de facto U.S. mental and addictive disorders service system. Epidemiologic catchment area prospective 1-year prevalence rates of disorders and services. *Archives of General Psychiatry, 50,* 85–94.

Rones, M., & Hoagwood, K. (2000). School-based mental health services: A research review. *Clinical Child and Family Psychology Review, 3,* 223–240.

Schlitt, J., Santelli, J., Juszczak, L., Brindis, C., Nystrom, R., Klein, J., Kaplan, D., & Seiboum, D. (2000). *Creating access to care: School-based health center census 1998–99.* Washington, DC: National Assembly on School-Based Health Care.

Sedlak, M. W. (1997). The uneasy alliance of mental health services and the schools: An historical perspective. *American Journal of Orthopsychiatry, 67,* 349–362.

Shaffer, D., Fisher, P., Dulcan, M. K., Davies, M., Piacentini, J., Schwab-Stone, M. E., Lahey, B. B., Bourdon, K., Jensen, P. S., Bird, H. R., Canino, G. B., & Regier, D. A. (1996). The NIMH Diagnostic Interview Schedule for Children Version 2.3 (DISC-2.3): Description. Acceptability, prevalence rates, and performance in the MECA study. Methods for the epidemiology of child and adolescent mental disorders study. *Journal of the American Academy of Child and Adolescent Psychiatry, 35,* 865–877.

Small, M. L., Majer, L. S., Allensworth, D. D., Farquhar, B. K., Kann, L., & Pateman, B. C. (1995). School health services. *Journal of School Health, 65,* 319–326.

Stroul, B. A. (1996). The system of care concept and philosophy. In B. A. Stroul & R. M. Friedman (Eds.), *Children's mental health: Creating systems of care in a changing society* (pp. 3–21). Baltimore: Paul H. Brookes.

Substance Abuse and Mental Health Services Administration (1999). CMHS programs, comprehensive community mental health services for children and their families. http://mentalhealth.samhsa.gov/cmhs/childrenscampaign/ccmhs.asp.

Substance Abuse and Mental Health Services Administration (2001). SAMHSA programs in brief: Safe schools and healthy communities. http://www.samhsa.gov/programs/content/brief2001/kda/01kda_cmhs-18.htm.

Substance Abuse and Mental Health Services Administration (2002). SAMHSA—Who we are. http://www.samhsa.gov/about/content.

U.S. Department of Education (2001a). IDEA. Lesson 1: History and impact. http://www.ed.gov/offices/OSERS/Policy/IDEA25th/Lesson1_History.html.

U.S. Department of Education (2001b). OSERS (Office of Special Education and Rehabilitative Services) mission statement. http://www.ed.gov/offices/OSERS/About/mission.html.

U.S. Department of Education (2001c). NIDRR (National Institute on Disability and Rehabilitation Research). About NIDRR. http://www.ed.gov/offices/OSERS/NIDRR/About/.

U.S. Department of Education (2001d). About safe & drug-free schools program. http://www.ed.gov/offices/OESE/SDFS/aboutsdf.html.

U.S. Department of Health and Human Services, Office of Disease Prevention and Health Promotion, Public Health Service (1993). *Healthy schools. A directory of federal programs and activities related to health promotion through the schools.* Washington, DC: Author.

U.S. Department of Health and Human Services (1999a). *Mental health: A report of the Surgeon General.* Rockville, MD: U.S. Department of Health and Human Services, Substance Abuse and Mental Health Services Administration, Center for Mental Health Services, National Institutes of Health, & National Institute of Mental Health.

U.S. Department of Health and Human Services, Substance Abuse and Mental Health Services Administration (1999b). *The relationship between mental health and substance abuse among adolescents.* Rockville, MD: SAMHSA, DHHS Publication No. (SMA) 99-3286.

U.S. Department of Justice (2002a). OJJDP home page. http://ojjdp.ncjrs.org/.

U.S. Department of Justice (2002b). COPS grants, programs and activities. http://www.usdoj.gov/cops.

U.S. Public Health Service (2000). *Report of the Surgeon General's conference on children's mental health: A national action agenda.* Washington, DC: U.S. Department of Health and Human Services.

U.S. Public Health Service (2001). *National strategy for suicide prevention: Goals and objectives for action.* Rockville, MD: U.S. Department of Health and Human Services.

Weinberg, N. Z., Rahdert, E., Colliver, J. D., & Glantz, M. D. (1998). Adolescent substance abuse: A review of the past 10 years. *Journal of the American Academy of Child and Adolescent Psychiatry, 37,* 252–261.

Woodruff, D. W., Osher, D., Hoffman C. C., Gruner, A., King, M. A., Snow, S. T., & McIntire, J. C. (1999). *The role of education in a system of care: Effectively serving children with emotional or behavioral disorders. Systems of care: Promising practices in children's mental health, 1998 Series, Vol. III.* Washington, DC: Center for Effective Collaboration and Practice, American Institutes for Research.

8

Enhancing Collaboration within and across Disciplines to Advance Mental Health Programs in Schools

NANCY RAPPAPORT, DAVID OSHER,
ELLEN GREENBERG GARRISON,
CORINNE ANDERSON-KETCHMARK,
and KEVIN DWYER

Schools across the country are increasingly utilizing the expertise of multiple disciplines to enhance the mental health of their students and address barriers to learning through the provision of a range of services in schools. School mental health providers, including nurses, counselors, school psychologists, school social workers, special educators, and their clinical partners—psychologists, psychiatrists, and psychiatric nurses—have a unique opportunity to address the mental health needs of students. The continuum of mental health services offered support, primary prevention (e.g., universal interventions targeting bullying, abuse, and violence), early intervention (e.g., counseling for students whose behavior indicates that they are at risk), and intensive treatment for students with severe and/or chronic problems (e.g., proven therapies, crisis intervention, and wraparound supports). Collaboration is critical to avoid competition for scarce resources, fragmentation of services, needless duplication of effort, and the potential isolation of

NANCY RAPPAPORT • Teen Health Center, Cambridge, Rindge and Latin School, Cambridge, Massachusetts 02139.   DAVID OSHER and KEVIN DWYER • American Institutes for Research, Washington, DC 20007.   ELLEN GREENBERG GARRISON • American Psychological Association, Washington, DC 20002.   CORINNE ANDERSON-KETCHMARK • School Social Workers Association of America, Northlake, Illinois 60164.

service providers. To ensure more comprehensive, cost-effective, and accessible services, collaboration must involve concerted efforts by all stakeholders.

Collaboration to enhance overall student adjustment and academic performance arises between and among mental health professionals in several contexts. First, it occurs between and among various school-hired mental health personnel working in the school setting. Second, if systems are to coordinate family-friendly services, collaboration can take place between and among school-hired personnel and mental health professionals offering services in the community. And third, collaboration can increasingly be found in school settings among school-hired and community-based mental health professionals working with other educators, families, and clinicians in school health clinics, or as adjunct school staff members in intensive special programs. For those community mental health professionals working within the school, the overall degree of collaboration with school-hired personnel and with students and their families may vary as a function of how well integrated they are into the school's culture and daily operations and how well they align their services to the school's existing services.

This chapter presents collaboration as a vital tool for effective mental health service delivery in school settings. It describes the critical components of collaboration, including the involvement of school administrators, educators, and school- and community-based mental health personnel, and most importantly, of the students and their families. Attention is also directed to the need to recognize and overcome potential obstacles to collaboration and to address such critical issues as school policy, educational leadership, and school culture.

CRITICAL COMPONENTS OF EFFECTIVE COLLABORATION

Although collaboration is generally accepted as a useful and laudable goal, realizing effective collaboration is not easy. Collaboration, when successfully implemented in schools, comprises more than its building blocks of cooperation and coordination. It involves altering the means by which mental health practitioners and schools traditionally do business. To ensure the implementation of effective collaborative relationships in school settings, those involved need to engage in the following four tasks: (1) Define mutually agreed upon goals that provide incentive for the investment of effort in the collaborative process. (2) Decide on an overall strategy that integrates services and accept shared responsibilities for designated activities. (3) Create a working environment that fosters accountability for actions and outcomes. (4) Where possible, shift from separate funding sources to viable integrated mechanisms for the allocation of financial resources to support collaborative strategies.

A critical component of successful interdisciplinary collaboration is a capacity to appreciate and build on the competencies of the individual disciplines involved. Professionals from different disciplines bring unique frames of reference, as well as different backgrounds, priorities, expectations, and clinical responsibilities. They may have different ways of conceptualizing students' strengths and difficulties, which, taken together, provide a comprehensive view to guide interventions. Ideally, early on in the collaborative process, school teams can devote time to understand the function of each participant, clarify roles, and understand professional paradigms. They also need to understand one another's technical language to enhance communication. Otherwise, professionals run the risk of engaging in discipline turf wars and rigidly adhering to a certain body of knowledge without exploring alternative perspectives. Avoiding this narrow approach involves practicing the disciplinary equivalent of cultural competency.

Providers need to value interdisciplinary diversity and recognize how multidisciplinary resources enhance their ability to respond to the complex needs of students. Mental health professionals benefit from opportunities within the collaborative process to conduct self-assessment. The process of self-assessment allows providers to reflect upon their own discipline and how their training and practice knowledge may lead them to interpret and respond to situations in a certain predictable way.

> John, a ninth grader, was displaying progressively more disruptive behavior in school and was suspended for the fifth time in two months for fighting with another student. His school confidential record noted that he was under the supervision of a probation officer for a prior assault charge. The probation officer and assistant principal were frustrated with John's recurring discipline problems and threatened his expulsion and return to juvenile court for probation violation. Likewise, one of his teachers was becoming increasingly irritated with his outbursts in class and low frustration tolerance. The school psychologist was discouraged that John refrained from participating in the psychoeducational group provided by the counselor. John was receiving anger management training from the school psychologist as a related service to his special education program. Due to the parents' initial desire for confidentiality, school personnel were not informed that John was receiving psychiatric medication and individual therapy from a community clinic psychiatrist. None of the providers or agencies were communicating with each other as a problem-solving team. Out of concern for John's welfare, the parents requested a meeting of school, clinic, and court personnel. Once all the professionals understood the complexity of the problems and the nature of services being provided, they began to collaborate in providing a network of supportive school, home, and community wraparound services, which enabled John to remain in the school setting and improve academically and socially.

Another prerequisite to successful collaboration is preventing status differentials between professions (e.g., physicians working with counselors), including differential authority and access to resources, from impeding interdisciplinary collaboration. Sometimes, interdisciplinary efforts generate questions concerning the respective competencies of individual professions. Through open and honest communication such potentially problematic issues can be raised and addressed, early and effectively.

As this vignette suggests, collaboration is increasingly challenging when there are multiple providers from many arenas, and there is no clear forum established for communication. Potential conflicts may arise when professionals interpret the involvement of other disciplines as an imposition and/or challenge to their competency or diagnostic capabilities. Professionals may also feel threatened by the involvement of family members who may question their professional competence to understand the specific problems at issue. However, with the mutual investment of time and resources, along with a clear understanding of one another's professional contributions, the student and family can feel even more supported. The process of detailing responsibilities and opportunities for each team member to enhance student competencies will contribute to the achievement of this goal.

CONTRIBUTIONS OF SEVERAL KEY MENTAL HEALTH DISCIPLINES TO SCHOOL COLLABORATION

Each of the core mental health disciplines of psychology, social work, and psychiatry offers unique and significant contributions (alone and in conjunction with one another) in the school context. The following sections provide a brief overview of their respective functions and the ways in which they collaborate with other school- and community-based mental health professionals. For a more detailed description of the roles, as well as education and training, of each of the school mental health disciplines (including counseling and nursing), see the article on this topic by Flaherty et al. (1998).

PSYCHOLOGY

School psychologists contribute to collaboration by applying learning and other psychological theory to improve instruction and behavior of children. They utilize consultation and teaming skills to support behavioral interventions and strategies, and they provide individual and group counseling to students and families. They are responsible for conducting psychological and educational assessments to identify students' needs for additional regular education support or special education services. School psychologists provide individual and group counseling, consultation, and also evaluate educational and treatment plans to address the needs of students with special learning, behavioral, and/or emotional problems (Marx & Wooley, 1998). School psychologists draw upon psychological research, theory, and practice to develop learning and behavioral interventions for individual students or groups of students, classrooms, or on a schoolwide basis (e.g., prevention and crisis intervention programs). School psychologists are adept at helping connect and monitor clinical mental health interventions in the classroom helping support both learning and behavior.

Health service psychologists in the community (e.g., clinical and counseling psychologists) can increasingly be found in schools working closely with teachers and other school-based personnel in providing counseling services to referred students and their families and in providing support and consultation to staff. In this regard, they may conduct professional training for teachers to enable them to identify students in need of mental health counseling, particularly students who may be overlooked, since they may be anxious or withdrawn (rather than disruptive). These psychologists also work closely with school psychologists in providing related psychological services to special education students, and also partner in assessing and treating students whose mental health disturbance is intensely affecting their lives. These professionals engage families in treatment and frequently have more flexibility than school-hired personnel in conducting in-home intensive services and meeting with families during evening or weekend hours. In some cases, agency personnel are more familiar with the network of community providers and can help connect families with a range of needed services.

SOCIAL WORK

School social workers provide individual and group counseling on a limited basis and conduct social skills or other specialty groups as determined necessary by the schools they serve. They also offer in-service training to school staff on a variety of topics, ranging from how to teach social skills, conduct functional behavioral assessments, and access resources in the community. School social workers also work together as members of the pupil services team, which supports students in their learning environment. They are often part of the assessment team to determine eligibility for special education. They are also responsible for making the appropriate referrals for interventions that are needed to improve student progress, prior to a special education assessment.

School social workers often provide the primary link between the home, school, and community. They can provide case management to assist student learning and adjustment. Their role extends from the coordination of school and community services to accessing systems and resources to better address the learning and related needs of students. School social workers are trained to understand how to bring together different and oftentimes competing systems for the benefit of the student and family. When *clinical social workers* provide services in the schools, school social workers benefit from the opportunity to refer students to them and to engage in case consultation for the betterment of students and their families. Clinical social workers also provide intensive therapeutic counseling to students and families.

PSYCHIATRY

Child and adolescent psychiatrists may consult in school settings and with other mental health professionals and school staff. They also participate in diagnostic evaluations and make treatment recommendations. Because psychiatrists are relatively few in number, compared to the other mental health professionals, their role as consultant allows for maximal use of their expertise. In keeping with their general training emphasis on the more severe psychiatric disorders, child and adolescent psychiatrists tend to be more involved with students in mental health and special education facilities as well as with public school students eligible for special education services.

Importance of Family Involvement in Collaboration

Meaningful involvement of family members can provide critical information in the mental health assessment process and further the adoption and implementation of treatment plans. When families are involved with decision making, treatments are likely to be more culturally competent and better designed to build on child and family strengths. Parents can help by providing critical direction about approaches and incentives that may work, while also encouraging the child and reinforcing adherence to the treatment plan. Parents are also in a unique position to monitor daily the impact of the therapeutic interventions.

Under federal education law, active participation is mandated for those children eligible for special education and related services to ensure that they and their parents feel supported by the school system. While an exceedingly valuable mandate, there are often barriers to family involvement created by administrative structures and service delivery mechanisms within schools. To address these difficulties, the National Agenda for Achieving Better Results for Children and Youth with Serious Emotional Disturbance (2000) suggests the following approaches that schools can employ:

> Any collaborative relationship should be marked by a demonstration of respect and compassion for family members; an understanding and an accommodation of different styles of social interaction; the use of straightforward language; creative outreach efforts; respect for families' cultures and experiences; providing families with crucial information and viable options; and the scheduling of individual education plan meetings at convenient times and places for families, caregivers, and surrogates.

Meeting processes can be refined to facilitate family participation. Schools in Westerly, Rhode Island, for example, have premeetings with families to discuss the individual education plan (IEP) process, solicit family input into the agenda, and provide families with necessary background on concerns that may arise at the meeting.

Educators as Key Collaborators

Collaboration with educators is also vital, since classroom teachers spend the most time with students and are often the most knowledgeable about them. Consequently, they can provide critical insights about student motivation and behavior. They also tend to be the most committed, both personally and professionally, to the success of individual students in the classroom and beyond. Difficulty may arise, however, when teachers and administrators feel increased pressure to focus on short-term academic goals and standardized test scores, often at the expense of student and family adjustment. They may also find themselves overattending to the time and energy demands of a disruptive student who may undermine the progress of other students. Understandably, teachers may need to be convinced by mental health providers that their efforts to monitor and encourage a student are likely to yield positive change in academic outcomes. There is better "buy in" from teachers if there are mechanisms to allow for them to support strategic planning. For example, school-based wraparound initiatives in Illinois and Nebraska provide substitute teachers in the classroom to enable the regular teachers to engage in planning activities and participate in the IEP meetings.

> Sonia, a sixth-grader in middle school, was suspended for swearing and other disrespectful behavior toward her teachers and classmates. Previous offers of counseling support had been rejected by

her parents. The school administrator recently discovered that both of Sonia's parents were alcoholic and that her father was terminally ill. Prior to Sonia's return to school, the school administrator, recognizing the seriousness of the problem, called a student support team meeting with the school psychologist, social worker, and teachers and the school mental health clinic representative to share their observations and shape their interventions to be most responsive to Sonia's pressing needs. As a result, the student and her family agreed for the first time to meet with a substance abuse counselor. The parents also consented for Sonia to join a group run by the school psychologist to address the stress related to her father's terminal illness and her vulnerability to peer risk behaviors. Parents also agreed to have Sonia meet with a child and adolescent psychiatrist to be evaluated for possible attention deficit/hyperactivity disorder. The school administrator made adjustments in Sonia's schedule to allow for these services and additional academic support. However, even though Sonia began to take many positive steps, some teachers were still exhausted by her challenging behavior and wanted her out of their classrooms. Classroom observation was then initiated by the school social worker to identify and remove precipitants of Sonia's disruptive behavior. Encouragement by the school social worker, concrete steps by the administrator, more focused mental health and educational services, and the sharing of realistic expectations with the teachers allowed the school to successfully maintain this fragile girl in the regular classroom.

Mental health providers and teachers engaged in collaborative relationships may have different expectations about how quickly students should and can turn around their performance. Accordingly, all those involved need to adopt realistic expectations for students. There also needs to be flexibility in prioritizing areas in which students need to improve and developing concrete ways of achieving progress. The previous vignette illustrates the commitment by educators, administrators, and mental health clinicians to carefully craft opportunities for student progress. Mental health providers may also be involved in offering whole classroom interventions to promote social competency skills, either directly or through training teachers to offer various modules. They also can provide teachers with suggestions about ways to encourage positive student behavior in the classroom and improve school climate.

EXPANDED SCHOOL MENTAL HEALTH SERVICES

As a means to extend school-based mental health services, schools are increasingly turning to community mental health professionals to provide group or individual therapy for students in the school setting or in the community. This collaborative process works well when the following four conditions are met. First, community mental health providers are oriented to the school culture and daily routines and have the opportunity to observe students in structured and unstructured settings (e.g., recess and lunch) and gain insights from the teachers and school personnel. Second, school professionals are included in the planning and implementation process of adding community mental health providers to the school environment. Third, the roles and responsibilities for school-based and community-based professionals are clearly delineated. And fourth, there is a mechanism or structure in place to facilitate productive, meaningful, and ongoing communication between school- and community-based providers.

Special Issues to Address

Confidentiality

All school mental health providers and counselors are required to adhere to a code of ethics respecting confidentiality. In the school setting, mental health providers including those from different disciplines and professional affiliations (e.g., hospitals and community health centers), negotiate the delicate balance of protecting the confidentiality of students against the desire of the school and parents to obtain important information. School administrators and parents may need to be informed of these necessary confidentiality requirements for any therapeutic relationship to be sustained. Clinicians tactfully can avoid this situation by being explicit about their policies surrounding confidentiality and working to encourage students to give permission for information sharing with educators when it may allow the school to make certain critical modifications beneficial to the student. Sharing information with parents should follow the same principles.

Complementary Roles

Another challenge involves how community-based mental health clinicians can complement the delivery of services by school personnel. Sometimes, school personnel may turn to community-based mental health providers to assist students in need of more acutely intensive services provided through a continuum of care in the community (e.g., family stabilization teams, emergency room coverage, and psychiatric hospitalization). In these instances, collaboration between school and community mental health personnel is essential to engage the student and family in treatment to ensure necessary consultation and follow-up.

> An illustrative example concerns Leroy, a high school junior, who was tearful in a guidance counselor's office, and irritable and withdrawn in class. During a more detailed interview with a clinical psychologist, Leroy revealed that his mother, who had schizophrenia, had temporarily moved back home with him and his father. This recent change in his family situation had led to his increased sense of being overwhelmed. With the family's permission, the clinical psychologist initiated an emergency evaluation of the mother and then continued to monitor the student and family's progress. Leroy chose an autobiographical literature course with the psychologist's encouragement and was able to examine his protective feelings toward his mother, while also negotiating some needed psychological distance from her. The collaboration with the school enabled Leroy to be more engaged in academics and feel more supported in his family situation.

Protocol for Initiating Mental Health Services

It is also critical that all involved school- and community-based providers appreciate the protocol for initiating mental health evaluation or treatment with a student. Oftentimes, the decision to access specific providers is shaped by whether students have an IEP, certain types of health insurance (if the student does not have an IEP), or certain types of identifiable problems (e.g., substance abuse, oppositional behavior). It can also be challenging to offer mental health support in ways that can enhance the student's sense of competency. School administrators and teachers need to present mental health services in a positive light as an opportunity rather than as a form of punishment or the last resort in a declining trajectory. This is facilitated in a school climate that does not stigmatize mental health needs.

Emergency Care

Emergency situations, where students are hospitalized psychiatrically or evaluated for violent intentions or acts, can strain the collaboration among mental health and school personnel. Oftentimes, when an emergency hospitalization occurs, there is no immediate communication with the school staff. School clinicians might not be contacted until the hospitalization is well under way or after the student is discharged. Other times, the adequacy or appropriateness of the student's educational placement may be questioned by hospital staff during or following the admission period. Yet communication is vital in these instances. School staff not only are likely to possess critical information about the student to enhance the hospital treatment, but they also need guidance from hospital staff to facilitate the student's transition back to school. Procedures need to be developed regarding communication about and monitoring of the student, and how to delineate meeting the needs of the student in a nonthreatening way.

External Supervision

External supervisors and consultants can provide significant assistance to school mental health personnel, especially when the supervision (or consultation) is provided by clinicians who are familiar with the challenges of a school environment. Supervisors can help provide access to a broad continuum of services and therapeutic approaches. They can help recognize when a student needs more extensive testing or offer unique perspectives on complicated diagnostic questions. The external supervisor's clinical experience can give school personnel added confidence and impetus to manage a complex situation. Also, external supervision can optimally provide protected time when school personnel can have the opportunity to be more reflective. Sometimes, school personnel may be on the frontlines and in crisis mode for extended periods of time. Supervision allows time to look at recurrent patterns and to determine necessary systemic changes. External supervisors can also reinvigorate staff by validating their efforts and encouraging them to be vigilant about potential burnout and gain needed support within the school. Similarly, experienced school-hired mental health professionals can provide effective strategies and supervision for clinicians providing services in the schools.

POLICY AND LEADERSHIP

School and districtwide leadership can facilitate or undermine interdisciplinary collaboration. Collaboration can more readily be developed and sustained when it is supported at a policy level, embraced by senior-level school managers (e.g., superintendents and principals) and middle managers (e.g., district coordinators), and implemented by providers on a student-by-student level (Hodges, Nesman, & Hernandez, 1999). The effective implementation of collaboration often depends upon policymakers and administrators ensuring adequate staffing allocations for teaming, training across disciplines, and sufficient time for collaboration. Leaders within the school system, such as principals and special education administrators, often are pressured to follow certain priorities that do not involve mental health. Mental health may also be viewed as beyond the primary academic mission of the school system. Typically, there is no regular funding base for mental health services. These services may only be regarded as necessary to respond to crises involving individual students or within the broader school environment.

Negotiating with leaders and policymakers is a long-term proposition, particularly when advocating for increased resource allocation to expand mental health services for students. Mental health clinicians need to understand how schools order their priorities and maintain an ongoing dialogue with school administrators about how mental health fits into the larger priorities that schools are expected to meet. For example, school-based mental health professionals are often assigned to multiple sites at different times, which naturally hinders their accountability and capacity to collaborate. In such a case administrators should be apprised of how they can enhance mental health services in the school setting, through aligning the schedules of mental health professionals and prioritizing needs.

Working with Schools

Schools have distinct cultures (Sarason, 2001), which are different from those of mental health agencies. To be responsive to the needs of the school community, mental health providers should understand the context of their work (i.e., the culture of the school and its history with school improvement efforts), try to become part of the school culture, and attend to the concerns of the educators. Carefully outlined protocols can establish a process for decision making that can avoid conflicts.

Mental health personnel can successfully integrate their work into schools through a variety of ways. One approach is to find a good navigator, someone who is seasoned and well respected within the school community. This individual can help avoid and resolve stalemates and describe effective strategies employed in the past to overcome and promote change in the school. Another approach is to establish a positive working relationship with the school-hired mental health professionals, plan with them, and complement their services. Some have developed a forum for clinical case reviews. While this tactic has the potential to be somewhat more confrontational in nature, it can be carried out in a respectful, nonthreatening way. It allows for the resolution of potentially problematic situations in a direct, objective manner. This type of debriefing is particularly useful after a crisis (e.g., the evaluation of a violent threat or act of a student), where staff are encouraged to comment on management decisions and offer suggestions for future actions in such situations.

A fourth approach involves systemic change through the creation of a school-wide team to integrate mental health, safety procedures, and school reform, and link to a student support team that works with individual students. The school-wide team plans, aligns, and oversees all schoolwide activities, while the student support team assesses, consults about, and develops mental health interventions for individual students. Both teams include three key personnel: the principal to harness the authority of senior leadership; a teacher to link to educators; and a mental health professional to focus on the mental health needs of the students and school. This model has been cited in two major documents, *Safeguarding Our Children: An Action Guide* (Dwyer & Osher, 2000), which was released by the U.S. Departments of Education and Justice, and *Every Student Learning: Safe and Supportive Schools* (Learning First Alliance, 2001), which was produced by 12 leading educational organizations.

CONCLUSION

As described in this chapter, collaboration is well worth the commitment and investment of time and energy for all those involved in the school setting—the school administrators, teachers, and school- and community-based mental health professionals, as well as for the students and their families. Collaboration almost inevitably has the "ebb and flow" of relationships. It is a precious commodity that needs to be safeguarded by structures that provide for sufficient resources, adequate time for teachers and mental health staff to work effectively, and professional training to help staff build new skills. Commitment to collaboration entails the capacity to recognize conflicts and barriers, and to address them systematically and creatively. Building upon professional and familial relationships, interdisciplinary collaboration has the potential to transform a loosely knit patchwork of school- and community-based services into a quilted fabric of comprehensive, coordinated, and integrated services to the benefit of individual students, their families, and the larger school community.

REFERENCES

Dwyer, K., & Osher, D. (2000). *Safeguarding our children: An action guide.* Washington, DC: U.S. Departments of Education and Justice, American Institutes for Research.

Flaherty, L. T., Garrison, E. G., Waxman, R., Uris, P. F., Keys, S. G., Glass-Siegel, M., & Weist, M. D. (1998). Optimizing the roles of school mental health professionals. *Journal of School Health, 68*(10), 420–424.

Hodges, S., Nesman, T., & Hernandez, M. (1999). *Promising practices: Building collaboration in systems of care. Systems of care: Promising practices in children's mental health, 1998 Series, Volume VI.* Washington, DC: Center for Effective Collaboration and Practice, American Institutes for Research.

Learning First Alliance (2001). *Every student learning: Safe and supportive schools.* Baltimore, MD: Author.

Marx, E., & Wooley, S. F. (Eds.). (1998). *Health is academic: A guide to coordinated school health programs.* New York: Teachers College Press.

National Agenda for Achieving Better Results for Children and Youth with Serious Emotional Disturbance (2000). Washington, DC: U.S. Department of Education: Author.

Sarason, S. B. (2001). *American psychology & schools: A critique.* New York: Teachers College Press.

9

The Community Schools Approach

Improving Student Learning, Strengthening Families and Communities

MARTIN J. BLANK, JANE QUINN, and HAYIN KIM

INTRODUCTION

Most conversations about what we want for our young people in communities across America begin with an emphasis on the kinds of people we want them to be, thereby holding implications for our society as a whole. The most common phrases suggest larger societal values—caring adults, engaged family members, productive workers and contributors to American society. Although academic achievement is seen as part of the equation, it is not the first issue raised. There is a recognition that young people must develop socially, ethically, civically, and personally, as well as academically.

The Carnegie Council on Adolescent Development framed this well in *Turning Points* (Carnegie Council on Adolescent Development, 1989) when it recommended five goals for successful adolescent development. Every adolescent should be "an intellectually reflective person, a person en route to a lifetime of meaningful work, a good citizen, a caring and ethical individual, and a healthy person" (p. 15).

Educators today, pressed by the demands to improve academic achievement, realize that their efforts to raise grades necessitate nurturing young people in all of these other ways as well. Teachers cannot effectively teach *and* serve as social workers, police officers, and enrichment tutors. Above all, regardless of socioeconomic status or location, schools cannot attain their goals without the support of families and communities.

MARTIN J. BLANK • Institute for Educational Leadership, Washington, DC 20036. JANE QUINN and HAYIN KIM • Children's Aid Society, New York, New York 10010.

This sentiment is articulated by John Gardner, former head of Common Cause and Secretary of the Department of Health, Education and Welfare, who asserts that collaborative effort is *the* basis for success; "in a tumultuous swiftly changing environment, in a world of multiple colliding systems the hierarchical position of leaders within their own system is of limited value because some of the most critically important tasks require lateral leadership—cross boundary leadership—involving groups over whom they have no control.... Leaders unwilling to seek mutually workable arrangements with systems external to their own are not serving the long-term institutional interests of their constituents" (Gardner, 1990, pp. 98–99).

Educators who understand Gardner's message are working in close collaboration with an array of community partners—parents and residents, youth development organizations, health, mental health, and social services agencies, community organizing and community development groups, institutions of higher education, faith-based institutions, business and civic groups—to ensure that young people have the kinds of learning experiences, supports, and opportunities that they need to succeed. They are creating community schools—places and partnerships that support student learning and strengthen families and communities. These educators and their partners believe that the school, as the single institution in our society that serves all children, has a unique role to play and a vital interest in bringing this array of supports and opportunities together.

This chapter characterizes community schools as a strategy for creating the conditions for successful student learning by also attending to critical social and developmental goals. It is intended to help mental health professionals see how mental health programs fit into a broader community school context. The chapter begins with a discussion of what young people need to succeed, reviews initiatives to connect school and community resources, defines a new vision of community schools, and provides evidence of the promise of the community school approach. Examples of innovative community schools with strong mental health programs are included. The chapter reviews the challenges in making community schools a permanent part of the education and community landscape and recommends steps for addressing those challenges. It closes with suggestions on how mental health leaders working in schools can contribute to the community schools movement.

WHAT YOUNG PEOPLE NEED TO SUCCEED

Research evidence strongly demonstrates (Benard, 1991; Clark, 1988; Eccles, 1999; Epstein, 1995; Henderson & Berla, 1995; Ianni, 1990; Marx, Wooley, & Northrop, 1998; McLaughlin, 2000; Vandell & Shumow, 1999) that in order for young people to succeed academically and developmentally, they need access to several kinds of ongoing supports and opportunities including:

- A strong core instructional program—taught by qualified teachers in small classes—designed to engage children in learning, enabling all of them to succeed academically

- Student and family support services (medical, dental, mental health, and social services) designed to strengthen families and reduce barriers to learning
- Enrichment opportunities designed to expand student learning, develop their personal and social competencies, and build their engagement and motivation
- Parent, family, and community involvement to create a natural network of support to encourage and enable young people

Based on this research-supported foundation, different sectors are beginning to develop very similar lists of supports and opportunities that young people need to succeed. For example, in *Every Child Learning* (Learning First Alliance, 2001), the Learning First Alliance—which includes the nation's largest education associations—suggests the following core elements of a safe and supportive learning environment: a facility that provides safety and community; schoolwide approaches to improve school climate, safety, and discipline; orderly and focused classrooms; a challenging and engaging curriculum; frequent opportunities for student participation, collaboration, service, and self-direction; respectful supportive relationships among and between students, school staff, and parents; and the involvement of family, students, school staff, and the surrounding community. The Forum for Youth Investment (Yohalem & Pittman, 2001) suggests that young people need stable places, high expectations and standards, high-quality instruction and training, challenging experiences, opportunities to participate and contribute, basic care and services, and healthy relationships with peers and adults, role models, resources, and networks.*

The commonality in these frameworks is a heartening sign that people and organizations in different sectors are finding common ground and exploring ways to work together to help young people succeed. Specifically, each holds a primary focus on the school as a central institution around which to organize many supports for young people and their families. They also made clear that schools cannot do all of this work by themselves. They need to build deep and intentional partnerships with organizations who share their goals.

BACKGROUND: COMMUNITY–SCHOOL INITIATIVES IMPROVING RESULTS FOR CHILDREN AND YOUTH IN THE PAST DECADE

The past decade has been a period of exponential growth in efforts to link schools and community partners. These efforts build on a rich history of related work dating back to John Dewey's vision of the school as center of community (Dewey, 1902) and Jane Addams's work on the school as settlement house at the beginning of the 20th century (Addams, 1904). It also reflects the ongoing work of the community education movement that began in the 1930s

---

*Similar frameworks have been articulated by Jobs for the Future (Almeida & Steinberg, 2001), the Community Action for Youth Project (http://www.irre.org/7critical.htm,), the Center for Youth Development (http://www.nydic.org/devdef.html#need), and the Public Education Network (McLaughlin, 2000).

(see http://www.ncea.com) and the work of Communities in Schools starting in the 1970s (see http://www.cisnet.org).

Beginning in the late 1980s, a new wave of school and community partnerships emerged. Schools, youth development organizations, human services agencies, community-building organizations, community organizers, parent leadership and education networks, family support groups, and others renewed efforts to create strong relationships and help young people and their families succeed. Local and state governments, United Ways, institutions of higher education, neighborhood organizations, business, civic, religious, and social organizations also were involved. In many cases these organizations initiated and led new partnerships with schools aspiring to achieve a variety of different goals.

An analysis of the new wave of these "school–community initiatives" was provided in the publication *Learning Together* (Melaville, 1998).[†] The intent of *Learning Together* was to "map" the range of activity occurring between school and community so that policymakers, administrators, and practitioners could have a clear understanding of the nature of this burgeoning work. The analysis revealed that school–community initiatives employed four major approaches (p. 14):

- *Services Reform:* The services reform approach seeks to remove the nonacademic barriers to school performance by providing access to improved health and human services to young people and families. These efforts are manifested in the establishment of mental health services, family support centers, health clinics, crisis intervention programs, and other supports for students, families, and sometimes the greater community.
- *Youth Development:* Youth development strategies serve to help students develop their talents and abilities to participate fully in adolescence and in adult life by increasing young people's opportunities to be involved in learning, decision making, service opportunities, and supportive relationships with others. This includes such activities as mentoring, community service/service-learning, after-school programs, recreation, leadership development, and career development programs.
- *Community Development:* Community development approaches focus on enhancing the social, economic, and physical capital of the community through economic development and job creation. They also emphasize community organizing, advocacy, and leadership development among community members, parents, and students.
- *Education Reform:* Education reform strategies seek to improve educational quality and academic performance by focusing on improving the management, curriculum, instruction, and general culture within schools and classrooms. This includes engaging parents, families, and teachers more directly

---

[†]The 20 initiatives included Alliance Schools; Beacon Schools; Bridges to Success; Caring Communities; Children's Aid Society Schools; Communities in Schools Community Education programs in Birmingham, AL, St. Louis, MO, and St. Louis Park, MN; COZI; Family Resources and Youth Services Centers (KY); Family Resource Schools (Denver); Full Service Schools (Jacksonville, FL); New Beginnings (San Diego); New Jersey School-Based Youth Services Program; New Visions for Public Schools (NY); Pacoima Urban Village (Pacoima, CA); Readiness to Learning Initiative (WA); WEPIC (Philadelphia).

in school-based decision making, engaging the private sector, and a range of additional activities referenced under the previous approaches.

Not surprisingly, collaboration across sectors and organizations was also a priority for nearly all of the initiatives.

Most of these school–community partnerships used services reform and youth development approaches, with others focusing on community development and education reform. Perhaps the most significant finding in *Learning Together,* however, was that "while each initiative is more closely aligned with one major approach than another, most are influenced by all of them. Thus the school–community terrain is not so much characterized by disconnected or conflicting approaches, as by blended and complementary approaches that constitute an emerging field of practice" (Melaville, 1998, p. 18). On this ground, a new vision of schooling was emerging "bringing the unique and valuable perspectives of multiple fields to bear on teaching and learning, school and education" (Melaville, 1998, p. 18).

From the perspective of education reform, how have these school–community initiatives influenced teaching and learning? They follow an evolutionary path: "Beginning with parent participation, they move to affecting the school environment and eventually influence school policies and classroom instruction" (Melaville, 1998, p. 93). Most initiatives have only recently evolved to the point where they are in a position to influence school policies and classroom instruction. They are beginning to make more explicit connections with the school day to become true community partners in the educational process.

The growth in school–community initiatives, increasingly referred to as "community schools," continues, and the work is deepening. According to the August 2001 issue of *The School Administrator* published by the American Association of School Administrators, "the number of school–community partnerships nationally is soaring as school leaders capitalize on the potential benefits that can be gleaned from bringing schools, parents, and community agencies together to help students learn" (Pardini, 2001, p. 7).

COMMUNITY SCHOOLS: AN EMERGING VISION

In light of the school–community initiatives of the past decade, a coherent vision of the relationship between schools and community is now emerging. It is the vision of a community school. A community school provides a framework within which all of the relationships between schools and many different community partners[‡] come together to improve learning and development for children, while strengthening families and communities. The work of community partners is integrated with the teaching and learning work of the school, and there is an intentional focus on how their joint efforts can reach the shared goals that they desire for students, their families, and the community. The partnerships with the

---

[‡]The term community partner includes any organization or agency regardless of particulars that works toward common results with educators.

community are not just nice "add-ons;" they are integral to the mission and life of the school. The community helps to re-create schools as new kinds of educational and social institutions.

The Coalition for Community Schools has crafted a vision for community schools that provides a context for the design of such schools across the country (adapted from *Community Partnerships for Excellence;* Coalition for Community Schools, 2000):

A community school, operating in a public school building, is open to students, families, and the community before, during, and after school, 6 days a week, all year long. It very often operates through a partnership between the school system and an anchor institution (e.g., a community-based organization, child and family service agency, community development group, institution of higher education). Families, youth, principals, teachers, neighborhood residents, and community partners help design and implement activities that promote high educational achievement and use the community as a resource for learning.

The school curriculum is based on high standards and expectations. The curriculum deliberately uses the history, assets, and problems of the community as a primary resource in the teaching and learning process. Professional development supports for teachers and other school personnel are in place, and there is a strong sense of accountability to the community.

Ideally, a full-time community school coordinator manages a range of supports provided by local agency partners and participates on the management team for the school. A before- and after-school learning component is rich and diverse in content, giving students the opportunity to expand their horizons, build on their classroom experiences, contribute to their communities, and have fun. A family resource center develops parent leaders, helps families with parenting education, adult education, employment, housing and other services, and empowers parents to become better advocates for their children's education. Medical, dental, and mental health services are available on site for the students and sometimes for their families.

Volunteers from business, religious and civic organizations, youth development workers, health and social service professions, college faculty and students, and especially family members come into the school to share their energy, knowledge, and skills.

Citizens, neighbors, and family members come to support, promote, and bolster what schools are working hard to accomplish—ensuring young people's academic, vocational, and interpersonal success. Community schools crackle with the excitement of doing, experiencing, and discovering unknown talents and strengths. Community schools open up new channels for learning and self-expression. Students come early and stay late—because they want to.

A community school is also different because multiple partners bring different but complementary strengths, styles, and leadership to the school. Schools, youth organizations, health and human service agencies, community organizations, community development groups, government, and philanthropy bring their unique competencies and work together toward common results. Furthermore, their work is not "business as usual." They are changing their funding patterns, transforming the practices of their personnel, working creatively and respectfully with youth, families, and community residents in order to create a different kind of institution—a school that takes a comprehensive approach to strengthening children, youth, families, and communities.

WHAT WE KNOW ABOUT THE EFFECTIVENESS OF THE COMMUNITY SCHOOLS APPROACH

In a summary of what we know about the effectiveness of community schools, Joy Dryfoos, a recognized authority in this field (see *Full Service Schools,* 1994), suggests "the weight of the evidence is substantial that community schools are beginning to be able to demonstrate their positive effects on students, families, and communities" (Dryfoos, 2000). Dryfoos reviewed some 48 reports on different community school initiatives that focus on one or more outcome measures, such as academic achievement, changes in student behavior, or increases in parental involvement. The community school initiatives offered varying arrays of supports and opportunities to young people and their families depending on the model they used and on the needs in the community.

In 46 of the reports positive outcomes were reported. The quality of the reports varied enormously, from evaluations that relied on very small nonrepresentative samples to those that were based on carefully designed management information systems and control groups. The variation in numbers reporting positive for particular outcomes reflects the specific data which each initiative chose to collect and present. Overall, in a world where most improvements are incremental, the results are promising not only in terms of academic achievement but also with regard to conditions that are critical for student learning, e.g., attendance, parent involvement, and the reduction of high-risk behaviors.

- *Achievement:* Academic gains were reported by 36 of the 48 programs with any form of documentation. These were generally improvements in reading and math test scores, looked at over a 2- or 3-year period.
- *Attendance:* Nineteen programs reported improvement in school attendance. Several reported lower dropout rates including one that specifically targeted pregnant and parenting teens.
- *Suspensions:* Ten programs reported reduction in suspensions suggesting improvements in school climate.
- *High-Risk Behaviors:* Reductions in substance abuse, teen pregnancy, disruptive behavior in the classroom, or general improvement in behavior were shown in 10 of the reports.
- *Access to Services:* Better access to health care, lower hospitalization rates, higher immunization rates, or access to dental care were reported at least once. Many of the after-school programs cited improved access to childcare as a significant outcome.
- *Parent Involvement:* Eleven of the programs specifically showed increases in parent involvement and in other programs; parents said that they "felt better." Providers reported lower rates of child abuse and neglect among participants, less out-of-home placement, better child development practices, less aggression, and generally improved social relationships. Students reported a heightened sense of adult support from both parents and teachers.

• *Neighborhood:* Several programs (five) noted lower violence rates and safer streets in their communities. A unique finding was the reduction in student mobility reported by a program, suggesting that adding services to the school encouraged families to stay in the neighborhood.

Community Schools in Action

The stories of three community schools bring to life the vision and strategy we have been discussing. In each case a strong mental health component is integrated into the community school.

Quitman Street Community School Partnership, Newark, NJ

George Worsley *knows* the Quitman School in Newark, NJ, not only as a staff social worker and community member but also as a child who attended the school while growing up in the surrounding impoverished community. Far more in-depth than any needs assessment could reveal, Worsley is cognizant of the deeply ingrained problems facing both the community and the school. Now, as a social worker at the Quitman School, he brings with him a lifelong urge to face and remedy the social problems in the community—most importantly, those affecting the children.

The Quitman Street Community School is a full-service community school collaboration between the Community Agencies Corporation of New Jersey (CACNJ), the Prudential Foundation, and the Newark Board of Education. They provide after-school educational and recreational programs, health care services, counseling services, and adult education. The Children's Hospital of Newark Beth Israel Medical Center-Health Place provides on-site medical, dental, and counseling services free to the students. A school site director, hired by the lead agency, CACNJ, manages all of the supports of this extensive and highly integrated partnership. The school governance body, established by the local Board of Education, is comprised of the principal, the site director, head social worker, and the pediatric nurse practitioner, among other school faculty and staff.

The wide array of services, supports, and opportunities, though impressive and responsive to the needs of the surrounding community, rests on a larger deep-seated commitment to provide students with the assurance that they can succeed. On the most basic level, this means making sure that all of their students know that their lives—education, families, challenges, accomplishments, and opinions—matter. Worsley relates that students who come from the community where drug and alcohol abuse is commonplace, often feel neglected and mistreated by the system. "Many of our kids suffer from low and no self-esteem," he says. "It is very difficult to counteract these feelings of worthlessness." These emotions are manifested in larger social and mental health issues—learning disabilities, illiteracy, attention deficit hyperactivity disorder, conduct and personality disorders, and several other social and personal illnesses.

Accordingly, the staff and faculty at the Quitman Community School have worked proactively to promote a healthy school environment. One highly successful vehicle, the Child Well-Being Committee, brings together all of the adults in the school who come into contact with the children during the course of each day—teachers, guidance counselors, cafeteria workers, janitors, school crossing guards, and mental health staff—to discuss how they can promote a child-friendly environment where children are uplifted and made to feel like they count. As one administrator says, "The foremost value of the clinic has been its advocacy for the well-being of the child, not only physical but emotional. The clinic staff has created a hope-filled place. That is their legacy, that they've done a great deal to make this a child-centered friendly school." One illustration of this committee's work was in managing cafeteria unrest as staff found it difficult to deal with the needs/behaviors of students who finished their lunches early, or finished late, wanted to go outside, or wanted to stay indoors. Involving them in the problem-solving and planning process, the Child Well-Being Committee polled the students to come up with solutions—showing movies, having quiet games, even deciding on the cafeteria menus. Students felt that their opinions mattered, and they were included in a healthy decision-making process.

Quitman's therapeutic services are based on the continuous relationships in and outside of the school. Teachers are in regular communication with social workers, learning about the possible warning signs of serious mental health disorders as well as about other problems that could affect the child's ability to learn, such as speech impediments or developmental delays. Together, the teacher and the social worker work to assess the child's situation and then bring in the parents and other family members as part of the treatment team. After a thorough diagnostic assessment, therapeutic services are provided, usually on site.

By relying on the entire school community to keep their ears and eyes open for all of the students, the Quitman Community School seeks to address the problems that might otherwise go undiagnosed and untreated from birth to adulthood.

INTERMEDIATE SCHOOL 218 (IS 218), SALOMÉ UREÑA MIDDLE ACADEMIES, THE CHILDREN'S AID SOCIETY, NEW YORK, NY

Within an urban school filled to overcapacity, located in the heart of a large immigrant community, structure is essential. Mental health staff at the Salomé Ureña Middle Academies (SUMA), IS 218 in the largely Dominican community of Washington Heights knows that, without working collaboratively and comprehensively with all members of the school community, their students are at great risk of falling through the cracks.

The full-service approach of the Children's Aid Society's (CAS) community schools addresses the multiple needs of children by recognizing that learning is influenced by ongoing experiences within families, schools, and communities. The mission at IS 218 is to prepare students to meet the highest standards and challenges of life through an academically challenging curriculum and to bring them to their full potential through the cooperative efforts of family and faculty. In line with this mission, collaborating partners at IS 218 offer an extended-day program that includes educational, social, and vocational enrichment activities, physical and health programs, and cultural arts activities before and after school, on the weekends, and during school holidays and summer vacations. IS 218 also offers full-service medical and dental services for students as well as a myriad of enrichment and continuing education programs for parents and community members. Families and community members also take advantage of the on-site social services, whether it be registering their children for health insurance or meeting with the Parent Coordinator to discuss other needs.

The highly integrated range of supports and services requires strong management and ongoing attention to interpersonal relationships with the school. A full-time community school director oversees and continually cultivates the partnership, ensuring that the work of all partners reflects the changing needs of the middle school and its 1700 students.

CAS social workers work side by side with school administrators, special education specialists, psychologists, and counselors on the Enhanced Pupil Personnel Committee to review weekly those students who are dealing with mental health and special education issues. Oftentimes, student referrals are made by teachers who maintain regular contact with social workers. Together, they build strategies to work with children in the classroom and to be aware of behaviors that may be symptomatic of more severe disorders.

The primary asset of CAS mental health staff is assuring that their presence influences all parts of the school—during the school day and in the extended day. At IS 218, the work of the social worker is primarily out of the office and instead is in the hallways, classrooms, and lounges—even on the school's front steps. Weekly "town meetings" are held during the school day to give students an opportunity to voice their opinions and discuss key issues such as domestic violence, sex education, relationships, and drug and alcohol abuse. Oftentimes, town meetings allow social workers to identify students who may be in need of additional counseling or group work. In addition, mental health staff are available throughout the extended-day program, sometimes in the school until 9 PM. Teen programs that are held at IS 218 meet 3 days a week from 6 to 9 PM where staff and social workers work with teens, providing recreational activities as well as various workshops on topics such as the college application process, sex and life classes, résumé writing, and working in the community. Mental health referrals are often tied to health issues so the mental health staff works closely with the health care staff to better assess the full needs of the child. Additionally, mental health staff are often the primary liaisons to parents and the wider community. Integrating families in the assessment and treatment process is often the entry point necessary for serving the needs of the entire family. Accordingly, mental health staff work with the school's parent coordinator to serve families more effectively.

A unique feature of the mental health program at IS 218 is the use of a computerized assessment tool, called the Diagnostic Interview Schedule for Children (DISC). Initially employed to screen all students at the school for serious mental health problems, DISC is now used more selectively, once a student is referred to the mental health program. Throughout the mental health program at IS 218, but especially in this initial assessment component, CAS benefits greatly from a long-term collaborative relationship with Columbia University's Division of Child and Adolescent Psychiatry (Quinn, 1999).

PARKWAY HEIGHTS MIDDLE SCHOOL, FAMILIES ON TRACK, SOUTH SAN FRANCISCO, CA

The Parkway Heights Middle School is committed to keeping its students and families "on track" and provides an innovative level of wraparound student services. Each component works in conjunction with the other to build a community in South San Francisco with students and families of promise.

Families on Track is a project funded by the Bothin Foundation, in partnership with the South San Francisco Unified School District and more than 15 other community partners. The "school within a school" at Parkway Heights Middle School offers educational support services and an extended-day program. In order to fully support the educational curriculum of the school, Families on Track also provides parent activities, continuing education opportunities, and comprehensive mental health and social services. Their extended-day program includes individual tutoring, homework centers, and other academic enrichment activities, as well as recreational and youth development activities through the Boys and Girls Club and through other collaborating partners. All of these services are woven together as a support network for all of their students and families.

Site governance is reflective of the intensive collaborative. A dual line of supervision is shared between the executive director of the lead agency and a social services coordinator employed by a collaborating agency. These on-site directors work hand in hand with school administrators to manage both the operational affairs and the clinical and programmatic areas of the school. Evaluators of the collaborative are also highly involved in the planning and continuous development of the project as they regularly meet with staff and parents, conducting various focus groups and measuring the progress of the initiative quantitatively and qualitatively. Accordingly, Families on Track is very attentive to the recommendations of the evaluators in their efforts to respond to the needs of students and families.

Families on Track realizes that support services are not as effective individually as when they are woven together. In light of that fact, mental health staff are integrated at every level of the school from governance, planning, school-day curriculum, staff development, and the extended-day programs for youth and parents. For example, case managers—both youth and family advocates—are required to sit in the classroom for 7 to 10 hours a week, observing and providing on-the-spot interventions. These social workers serve as antennae to gauge whether students are in need of early intervention; referrals for individual, group, and family therapy; or appropriate social services. They also set the tone for a supportive classroom and overall school environment.

Additionally, mental health is seen as a shared responsibility with all parties—teachers, advocates, therapists, and families—playing an important role. The social services team—the site coordinator, advocates, and therapists—meet once a week to discuss individual cases and to coordinate treatment plans. Advocates also meet every other week with teachers to call attention to particular students without revealing specifics about the case, in order to monitor behavioral disorders and include the teachers in their holistic approach to treatment. The social service team also provides professional development in-services to train teachers on specific mental health issues such as suicide training and abuse reporting.

During the after-school program, advocates coordinate Socialization and Well-Being groups. Those students who need help with general social skills, conflict resolution, or anger management are referred to Socialization groups. Well-Being groups support those students who have experienced some sort of direct trauma. Both groups are led by therapists and co-led by advocates. Similar to their work with school-day staff, advocates meet regularly with extended-day staff to determine how they can best work with certain students.

Parents are brought in alongside teachers and social services staff to get a better and deeper understanding of the issue at hand. Every other week "team meetings" are held on a case-by-case basis to serve those students who are most at risk. This example of proactive engagement with parents has brought many into the school for the first time. Despite the circumstances under which they are introduced to the services of the school, the parental response has been extremely favorable. Parkway Heights also offers bilingual parent support groups that meet in the evenings and are led by therapists and advocates. Oftentimes, these support groups are held concurrently with the Well-Being and Socialization groups, thereby meeting the childcare needs of these parents. Advocates also conduct many home visits that further strengthen the relationship between students, schools, home, and social services.

CHALLENGES TO CREATING AND SUSTAINING PROGRAMS

The data and stories we have presented begin to make the case for community schools as an important strategy for improving student learning and development and strengthening families and communities. Still, in an era of standards-based reform and high-stakes testing, many challenges remain if this strategy is to become deeply embedded in the way educators, parents, community agencies, and organizations of all kinds think about their work.

First, we must continue to break down the boundaries between disciplines. Irrespective of the divides between educators, health, mental health, human services providers, youth development organizations, community development and community-building groups, and others, we must keep in mind that each one brings something of importance to the lives of children and their families. The experience of community schools demonstrates that people from these disciplines can learn to work together without giving up their unique languages, philosophies, values, or professional practices. In fact, it is in the intersection of these differences that the most effective ways to support families and build on family strengths will happen. The past decade has seen important advancements in crossing these boundaries. More professional and interprofessional preparation programs, in-service professional development experiences, and day-to-day interactions are necessary in order to deepen these shifts and make them permanent.

Second, agencies and organizations working in the same school must work together. There are many schools with "partners." There are too few schools where these partners are working together in strategic ways to achieve a common set of results. If a mental health agency, a youth development organization, a family support center, a business-led tutoring program, a mentoring program, or any other type of service is present in a school, it is incumbent on the staff of those programs and school personnel to think and plan together for the well-being of the children in the school, their families, and the surrounding neighborhood. In the absence of such planning, school personnel see these important services as fragmented and disconnected from the primary teaching and learning mission of the school.

Third, partners must focus on results. Different sectors have articulated results for their own work in the past decade. Whether it is education, mental health, youth development, family support, community organizing, or any other field, each has seen the value of starting with a clear definition of outcomes that can be used as a tool for planning and accountability. In a community school setting, a clear definition of desired results enables partners to define an intentional strategy that takes advantage of the capacity each offers and allows partners to see where they can bring added value to each others' work.

Fourth, there must be mechanisms for ensuring that the voices of parents and students are heard within the community school. Most importantly, there must be a place where they can work with school staff and community partners to plan, organize, and evaluate the community school, and find ways to sustain it. Organizing and maintaining parent and youth participation takes relentless commitment and requires an understanding that community participation in decision making is essential in building a constituency and sustaining a community school. Additionally, this helps to create "social capital" enabling parents, youth, and families to create networks of support to help solve problems without professional intervention.

Fifth, it is important to find a way to manage the relationships among partners and the school. This is particularly important in a school environment where there are so many pressures on school personnel with regard to academic achievement. The community schools we described and most school–community initiatives reviewed in *Learning Together* (Melaville, 1998) chose to have full-time coordinators. The community school coordinator becomes part of the fabric of the school by understanding the school culture, learning the needs and assets of the school, its students, families, and staff, and becoming a resource to the school principal and the teachers.

Ideally, from our perspective, the community school coordinator is a member of the staff of a community-based organization or agency (e.g., a mental health center, a child and family services agency, a youth development organization) that has chosen to make a long-term commitment to work at the school. Long-term commitment means that the agency sees the school as a permanent locus for the delivery of its services; the agency is not just at the school for the life of a grant. This is a challenging scenario, but establishing an institutional anchor is key to creating and sustaining a community school. The Children's Aid Society, YMCAs, Boys and Girls Clubs, institutions of higher education, family service agencies, and youth and community development organizations are among the entities making this kind of commitment. These lead partners are then in a position to mobilize the assets of other service providers as well as neighborhood-based organizations and associations.

Finally, if a community school strategy is to reach scale, there must be community partnerships in place that bring together the array of individuals and organizations committed to better results for children and families. The community school approach argues that communities, not just educators, are responsible for the education of our children. If community responsibility is to become a reality, then there must be a forum where leaders from among parents, neighborhood leaders, and youth come together with different sectors (e.g., K-12 education, higher education, youth development, family support, health, mental health and social services, community development, neighborhood, government, business, religious, and philanthropy) to build and sustain a community school strategy. These partnerships must be "significant, sustained and systemic" (Harkavy, 2000). At the community level, they should assume responsibility for articulating a vision of community schools, defining desired results, promoting accountability, mobilizing financing and resources, educating the public, building constituency for community schools, setting broad policy, facilitating professional development, and overseeing the long-range effectiveness and financial stability of the initiative (Melaville, 1998, p. 26). Such partnerships, challenging as they are, are a crucial mechanism for redirecting existing community resources and mobilizing public opinion to invest the necessary resources to meet the needs of all children and families.

IMPLICATIONS FOR THE MENTAL HEALTH COMMUNITY

The mental health community has a major role to play in the community schools movement. The work that has already been done to build constituency for mental health services in schools is a strong foundation on which to build. In order to be consistent with the goals of community schools, mental health services should abide by the following principles.

Most importantly, mental health services should not be isolated from other parts of the school or community; rather they should be an integral part of the fabric of the community school. Mental health programs should be developed from a common philosophical, professional, and procedural framework shared by all collaborating partners. Context also is crucial, with needs assessment and evaluation data driving the planning process. This includes mapping all available resources to deal with documented needs.

Mental health should not be viewed strictly as a direct service; rather interventions should seek to influence school climate and address schoolwide challenges. For instance, providing school staff with assistance on child and adolescent development issues, conflict resolution strategies, classroom behavior management, and promotion of self-discipline should be on the agenda.

Mental health staff should work closely with a Site Coordinator or Community School Director, if available, to ensure integration at the service delivery level. Mental health staff should also be represented on local planning and oversight teams. Where these coordination and planning resources are not in place, mental health staff can play pivotal roles in helping to create them.

Finally, mental health staff should use existing school structures such as school cabinets, school leadership teams, and pupil personnel committees for planning, recommendations, and discussion of documented student needs. Furthermore, mental health staff should use these structures to help clarify the goals for all collaborating partners in the school as well as to articulate their own expectations for the mental health program.

CONCLUSION

The efforts to promote mental health services in schools and the movement for community schools have much in common. By sharing their assets, expertise, and commitment, leaders in these closely related arenas can help make schools places that support and nurture all young people and help them reach their highest potential.

REFERENCES

Addams, J. (1904). *On education.* New Brunswick, NJ: Transaction Publications.

Almeida, C., & Steinberg, A. (Eds.). (2001). *Connected learning communities: A toolkit for reinventing high school.* Boston, MA: Jobs for the Future.

Benard, B. (1991). *Fostering resiliency in kids: Protective factors in the family, school and community.* Portland, OR: Northwest Regional Educational Laboratories, Western Regional Center for Drug-Free Schools and Communities.

Carnegie Council on Adolescent Development (1989). *Turning points: Preparing American youth for the 21st century.* New York: Carnegie Corporation of New York.

Center for Youth Development (2001). *Definitions of youth development.* Available on-line: http://www.nydic.org/devdef.html#needs.

Clark, R. M. (1988). *Critical factors in why disadvantaged children succeed or fail in school.* New York: Academy for Educational Development.

Coalition for Community Schools (2000). *Community partnerships for excellence.* Washington, DC: Institute for Educational Leadership.

Dewey, J. (1902). The school as social center. In J. Boydston (Ed.), *John Dewey: The middle works, 1902–1903* (Vol. 2, pp. 80–93). Carbondale, IL: Southern Illinois University Press.

Dryfoos, J. (1994). *Full service schools.* San Francisco, CA: Jossey–Bass.

Dryfoos, J. (2000, September). *Community schools: Evaluation of findings to date.* Paper presented to the Coalition for Community Schools, Washington, DC. Available on-line: http://www.communityschools.org/evaluation/evalcontents.html.

Eccles, J. (1999). The development of children ages 6 to 14. In R. E. Behrman (Ed.), *The future of children: Vol. 9, No. 2, Fall 1999, When school is out* (pp. 30–44). Los Altos, CA: The David and Lucile Packard Foundation.

Epstein, J. L. (1995). School, family, community partnerships: Caring for the children we share. *Phi Delta Kappan, 77*(9), 701–712.

Gardner, J. (1990). *On leadership.* New York, NY: Free Press.

Harkavy, I. (2000, June). *Governance and the community-higher education-school connection.* Paper presented at The Learning Connection: New Partnerships between Schools and Colleges, Kansas City, MO.

Henderson, A. T., & Berla, N. (1995). *A new generation of evidence: The family is critical to student achievement.* Washington, DC: Center for Law and Education.

Ianni, F. A. J. (1990). *The search for structure.* New York: Free Press.

Learning First Alliance (2001). *Every child learning: Safe and supportive schools.* Washington, DC: Author.

Marx, E., Wooley, S. F., & Northrop, D. (Eds.). (1998). *Health is academic.* New York: Teachers College Press.

McLaughlin, M. W. (2000). *Community counts: How youth organizations matter for youth development.* Washington, DC: Public Education Network.

Melaville, A. (1998). *Learning together: The developing field of school–community initiatives.* Flint, MI: Charles Stewart Mott Foundation.

Pardini, P. (2001). School–community partnering. *The school administrator, August 2001,* 6–11.

Quinn, T. (1999). *Helping troubled youth: The Columbia teen screen suicide prevention program.* New York, NY: Columbia University and the New York State Psychiatric Institute.

Vandell, D. L., & Shumow, L. (1999). After-school child care programs. In R. E. Behrman (Ed.), *The future of children: Vol. 9, No. 2, Fall 1999, When school is out* (pp. 64–80). Los Altos, CA: The David and Lucile Packard Foundation.

Yohalem, N., & Pittman, K. (2001). *Powerful pathways: Framing options and opportunities for vulnerable youth.* Flint, MI: The Charles Steward Mott Foundation.

10

Partnering with Families in Expanded School Mental Health Programs

JENNIFER AXELROD LOWIE, NANCY A. LEVER,
MELISSA G. AMBROSE, SUSAN B. TAGER,
and SUSAN HILL

Systems of education and child and adolescent mental health recognize that close partnerships with families are essential for the success of almost any endeavor. Service providers in the emerging expanded school mental health (ESMH) field echo this realization. While working with families is a priority within the ESMH field and has been identified as a key best practice (Weist et al., 2001), little has been written about how to systematically incorporate families into the ESMH framework and involve them as full partners in their child's care. Drawing on experiences and research in the education field, expanded school mental health programs can expand their efforts to integrate effective strategies into daily practice by utilizing existing knowledge bases.

FAMILY INVOLVEMENT FROM THE EDUCATION PERSPECTIVE

On a broad level, family involvement in education has been well documented in the literature to support the improvement of children's academic success, overall school quality, and the health and well-being of students and families (Brener, Dittus, & Hayes, 2001; Hampton & Mumford, 1998). In addition, Epstein (1992) offered a clearly articulated model of family involvement in education. This model outlines a comprehensive long-term system for involving families in schools. Research supports that family involvement in education has positive impact across

JENNIFER AXELROD LOWIE, NANCY A. LEVER, MELISSA G. AMBROSE, SUSAN B. TAGER, and SUSAN HILL • University of Maryland School of Medicine, Baltimore, Maryland 21201.

the developmental age span (Eccles & Harold, 1993; Marcon, 1999). Thus, it is important to involve families throughout their children's education. Recognizing that families tend to become less engaged in schools as their children enter secondary school raises the need to develop innovative outreach to families (Cristenson, 1995; Eccles & Harold, 1993). Furthermore, research has demonstrated differences in family involvement depending on stress and resources (Tolan & McKay, 1996). These differences have implications for the manner and type of service provision necessary to ensure that services are provided appropriately and respectfully. Involving families in care has been associated with substantive change and improvement in children's functioning. In fact, in a study by the Search Institute, it was found that as parental involvement in schools increased, problem behaviors decreased (e.g., alcohol use, violence, and antisocial behaviors) (Roehlkepartain & Benson, 1994).

INVOLVING FAMILIES IN MENTAL HEALTH SERVICES

While the value of family involvement in youth education is widely accepted, recognition of the importance of family involvement in the mental health treatment of youth is a more recent development. "In the past, families were seen primarily as contributing to the mental health problems of their children, and their only role in treatment was to alter their structure and/or functioning" (Osher, van Kammen, & Zaro, 2001, p. 63). Currently, family collaboration in mental health service provision has emerged as a crucial factor in the success of interventions with youth. As the Surgeon General's report on mental health states, "families have become essential partners in the delivery of mental health services for children and adolescents" (U.S. Department of Health and Human Services, 1999). Rather than blaming parents and caregivers for children's mental health issues, families are being brought into the process as change agents and seen as key collaborators in treatment.

According to the Federation of Families for Children's Mental Health, services provided to families should "utilize the strengths of families by: ensuring that they are equal partners in the planning, implementation, and evaluation of services; viewing the child as a whole person and the family as a whole unit, rather than emphasizing the disability; empowering families and children to make decisions about their own lives" (Federation of Families, 2001). Stakeholders recognize that family involvement is necessary; however, the difficulty remains in translating those beliefs into successful practice. This shift in practice needs to occur in traditional models of service provision as well as in the expanded school mental health movement. School-based mental health programs are uniquely positioned to partner with schools and families to better integrate children's mental health care.

This chapter seeks to characterize and define best practices of family involvement in expanded school mental health programs. Barriers to care and strategies for the development of a framework for integrating families into their children's care will be presented. The chapter addresses unique aspects of family involvement within a school-based mental health program, presents "model" examples of family involvement, and describes training issues for clinicians and for successful partnerships. Finally, we explore future directions for the field and make recommendations for next steps.

DEFINING A MODEL OF FAMILY COLLABORATION

For the purpose of this chapter, it is important to have a clear definition of family collaboration. Jivanjee and Friesen (as cited in Simpson et al., 1999) define family–provider collaboration as a partnership "in which parents and professionals develop mutually agreed goals, share responsibilities in planning and decision making, are seen as mutually respected equals, and engage in open and honest two-way sharing of information" (p. 8). The model of therapist as expert is replaced by a shared-learner framework in which both parties contribute knowledge and insight. Underlying the framework are three aspects of family–provider collaboration: "shared vision and goals, shared power in decision-making in all levels, and long-term commitment to the process of developing collaboration" (Simpson et al., 1999). In this model of care, families and providers must be willing to form a team, overcome resistance and reluctance to partner as equals, and engage in a process of open dialogue and communication.

A collaborative family–provider framework offers potential for empowering families and enhancing clinician satisfaction. When families are involved in clinical services, they are more likely to feel that their children's needs are being met and that there are improved outcomes (Farmer et al., 1997). Family involvement in mental health care has been linked to improved service coordination (Koren et al., 1997) and to the reduction of stress on the family system (Farmer et al., 1997). While the literature related to successful models of family–provider collaboration is increasing, overall, the research related to the topic is limited, leaving many basic questions unanswered (e.g., How should families best be engaged and involved in treatment? How does family collaboration with the therapist impact overall outcomes at the individual, child, and systems level?) (Cheney & Osher, 1997; Simpson et al., 1999).

One national study of family involvement efforts elaborated the gap between theory and practice with regard to schools involving families. The School Health Policies and Programs Study collected data from states, districts, schools, and classrooms to evaluate components of school health programs (Brener et al., 2001). Family involvement in these programs was assessed through questionnaires. Responses indicated that 32.8% of schools invited family members to tour school mental health and social services facilities, 41.6% met with parents' organizations to discuss available mental health services, and 78.4% provided information to families on school mental health and social services programs. While over three-quarters of the studied schools were providing information about mental health services, less than one-third had outreach efforts to demystify the mental health services through tours. The findings from this study suggest the need to develop more effective outreach and communication strategies with families to better inform them about available mental health resources.

BARRIERS TO FAMILY INVOLVEMENT IN EXPANDED SCHOOL MENTAL HEALTH PROGRAMS

Within the field of school-based mental health, several barriers exist that inhibit successful family–provider collaboration in mental health services. Many of these barriers occur across treatment settings (e.g., community mental health centers, university-based treatment programs, private practitioners); however, recognizing how they specifically impact service provision in ESMH programs will allow for the development of more family-sensitive care. The availability of appointment times and accessibility of services is one barrier to care (Bickham et al., 1998; McKay, McCadam, & Gonzales, 1996). For working families and families needing to negotiate childcare, daytime appointments can be difficult, if not impossible, for them to attend. In some cases, schools may not be in walking distance or on easily accessed transportation routes, making it difficult for families to access care. Additional transportation barriers, including financial costs, unreliable modes of transportation, and lengthy travel times, may prevent families from being able to follow through with appointments (Weist, 1997).

Bickham and colleagues (1998) also identify other challenges to involving families in school-based mental health, including stigma of mental health care, fear by families that they will be blamed for problems, students' desire not to involve families in treatment, and families feeling unwelcome or uncomfortable with the school system. Stigma can be an especially difficult challenge to overcome in involving families in therapy efforts (McKay et al., 1996). Depending on the method used to present the clinical services, families may feel as if their children are being labeled, and feel the need to defend themselves and their children. Limited information and misinformation concerning mental health services may leave families very hesitant to pursue treatment. Also, lack of knowledge about available services may prevent families from seeking care (McKay et al., 1996; Weist, 1997). Many times, there is a significant communication disconnect resulting in families underutilizing community and school resources. In addition, family members may have had negative prior experiences either in the school setting or in their own mental health care that may inhibit their willingness to seek support services for their children.

Another major barrier for family–provider collaboration is a perceived lack of mutuality. Some families have indicated that there is an imbalance of power in the mental health care of their child, resulting in their input not being valued or incorporated into treatment (Simpson et al., 1999). Rather than feeling like an expert on their child's needs, families have described feeling like they have only a token role in service planning. Families also have reported concerns about confidentiality (Simpson et al., 1999), resulting in a reluctance to share information and to engage in the therapeutic process. This lack of full participation and disclosure may inhibit the provision of quality care.

A final barrier to family–provider collaboration relates to the role of the clinician in shaping family participation in school-based mental health (Bickham et al., 1998; McKay et al., 1996). Some clinicians have not been trained to work with families and may not feel comfortable collaborating and participating in the shared-learner model. Clinicians also may not feel supported by the larger systems in which they work, and may not feel they have the necessary time or resources to appropriately involve families.

A PILOT STUDY OF CLINICIAN PERSPECTIVES ON FAMILY INVOLVEMENT

In an effort to explore clinicians' perspectives of family involvement in expanded school mental health programs, clinicians from the University of Maryland

School Mental Health Program (SMHP) completed the Family Involvement Survey for Clinicians (FISC), a pilot questionnaire assessing views and practices related to family involvement. Twenty-three clinicians completed a survey of the activities they utilize to engage families and maintain involvement throughout the course of the intervention. Clinicians rated their perceptions on a scale of 1 (not important) to 5 (very important) of the importance of family involvement, their success in engaging families, and their success of ongoing family involvement. Clinicians reported that they considered family involvement to be critical to the outcomes of intervention (mean = 4.19, SD = 0.15). However, clinicians reported that they were only somewhat successful at engaging families (mean = 3.05, SD = 0.13) and in maintaining family involvement (mean = 3.05, SD = 0.11). Further analysis of the data indicates that clinicians' perceptions of the importance of family involvement are significantly higher than their self-rated competence in engaging families (t = 6.19, p < 0.05) and continuing that engagement (t = 6.60, p < 0.05). The differences between these two scores highlight the need for additional clinical training and support related to effective strategies and practices for family involvement (Jivanjee & Friesen, 1997).

To further elaborate on the quantitative ratings, the FISC included open-ended questions to explore the strategies that clinicians have used to engage families in the treatment process. Over half of the clinicians reported that they made phone calls to families, sent letters home, and tried to have flexible hours to accommodate family work schedules. Of the clinicians surveyed, approximately one-fourth indicated that they tried to have a visible presence in the school: attending Parent Teacher Association meetings, presenting at schoolwide functions, and coordinating with family liaisons in the school. Clinicians reported that they hoped that their visibility would increase families' awareness of services and increase family engagement in the initial stages of therapy. Underlying many of the responses was the belief that services had to be pragmatic, offer immediate assistance, and help to remediate family stressors. In general, the strategies used by clinicians for engaging families were similar to those used in maintaining family involvement in therapy. It is notable that there were differences in the degree of family involvement that were dependent on the grade level of the students. Clinicians in high schools reported that they had greater difficulty engaging families, as youth were often reluctant to bring families into the therapeutic relationship.

Clinicians also reported on family-related schoolwide activities in which they participated. One of the aspects of expanded school mental health that makes it a unique form of intervention is the ability to collaborate with the school to promote increased awareness of mental health issues within the school environment. The results of the survey were concerning in that 10 of the clinicians reported that they were involved in no other family-related activities at the school. In part this may be due to the fact that many of the clinicians are only in their schools 2 or 3 days a week. In addition, the demands on their time to deliver a full range of mental health services including focused prevention activities, outreach and consultation, and therapy (which may include significant administrative demands related to pursuing fees) have impinged upon their abilities to engage in broader family outreach. Of those clinicians who did report involvement in other activities, 5 were involved in the Student Support Team, and 4 were involved with the Parent Teacher Association. Other involvement strategies included presentations, back-to-school nights, working intensively with family advocates and liaisons, and hosting family support groups.

What is clear from this survey is that while school-based clinicians are appreciative of the need to involve families, their actual work with families is far from the ideal described in the literature. This relative lack of family involvement in school-based mental health has been reported in other programs. In reviewing the school mental health literature, Atkins et al. (1998) reported that while the programs have been successful at outreaching to children, they have not done as well in involving families in treatment or in providing program guidance.

One possible explanation for the lack of family involvement is limited clinical preparedness to offer those services. Of the clinicians surveyed, few reported that they had received significant clinical training and coursework related to family involvement. Three clinicians reported that they had received no coursework on the topic, while the majority reported that the topic had been included as part of family therapy classes or had been integrated into other classwork. A number of clinicians reported that they had sought additional training in family involvement through continuing education classes, in supervision, and in didactic seminars included in the School Mental Health Program training. This clearly illustrates the need for school mental health clinicians to have additional training and education on diverse ways to work closely with and involve families, both in treatment efforts and in program development and guidance. In addition, it appears that broadening the scope of the training to include supervisors and program managers will be critical in improving services to families as a way of influencing clinical practice and policy.

AN EXAMPLE OF FAMILY INVOLVEMENT IN AN EXPANDED SCHOOL MENTAL HEALTH PROGRAM

As part of a collaborative partnership between the School Mental Health Program, one of its elementary schools, and the Safe Schools/Healthy Students Initiative, a creative outreach program to families in one school community was started. In this initiative, the school mental health clinician partnered with a family advocate and a parent liaison to outreach to caregivers in the school. The project was designed to systematically reach out to families in the school, destigmatizing mental health services by becoming partners in the school community, and creating effective linkages for families to ensure that they felt supported by the mental health team.

The project began with the help of the school in the identification of a parent liaison and a family advocate. The parent liaison identified was from the local community and her children had attended the school in previous years. She already was familiar with the school, as she had been employed as a paraprofessional aide. The parent liaison had well-established relationships with caregivers in the school community. It was felt to be crucial to the success of the project that the parent liaison was from the community and had well-developed relationships with families in the school neighborhoods. The family-to-family worker had significant experience with facilitating family support groups as well as personal experience with her son who had significant mental health needs.

In order for this project to be successful, it involved the development of collaborative and trusting relationships between all of the participants. From the inception of the project, the school administration was very supportive of this work. The principal identified areas at the school that would provide a comfortable environment for families to gather and agreed to grant the team access to those areas during school hours. For example, the cafeteria was identified as a neutral place in the school that parents frequented and was removed from the stigma of many of the other gathering places, i.e., the front office, conference meeting rooms, and the counseling suite. The outreach team members interacted with families in this informal setting. This allowed the team to introduce themselves, engage in informal conversations, to share information, and to discuss family issues in a nonthreatening manner. As a result, family members were more willing to discuss their feelings about their concerns regarding their children's school experience and any mental health concerns. These conversations played a key role in linking families with the school-based mental health services when more intensive child or family mental health services were required.

Together, the outreach team developed and coordinated ongoing family meetings. These groups provided basic parenting support to families as well as encouraging an open dialogue between families. The partnership also resulted in three family events at the school: a bingo night and annual mother–daughter and father–son luncheons. These activities enabled the outreach team to become more visible, brought in other members of the school community, and gave clinicians an opportunity to informally discuss mental health concerns.

The partnership within the school demonstrated the value of involving families and family advocates in mental health care. The clinician reported that developing informal relationships with families led to increased service utilization as well as to increased comfort with clinicians and the therapeutic process. In addition, the outreach efforts led to more effective service implementation, as families were more involved in their children's treatment. In addition, the clinician was able to respond to the broad family needs in the school community by partnering with the family advocate and parent liaison to provide education on topics of interest to families and to develop opportunities for networking and support. The school mental health clinician and the principal of the school recognized the importance of including paraprofessionals in outreach and quality care. They hope to continue this model of collaboration and outreach to families to promote involvement.

STRATEGIES FOR EFFECTIVE FAMILY–PROVIDER COLLABORATION

Bickham et al. (1998) provided a discussion of strategies that can be effective in fostering family involvement in ESMH programs. The strategies they identified included developing a philosophy of family involvement, being flexible and creative, assessing and respecting the needs of the families served, linking families with resources, allocating and obtaining resources necessary to promote family involvement, and establishing quality improvement procedures to inform and improve the process of involving families. The following section presents examples of programs that exemplify these strategies within their clinical practice.

Developing a Philosophy of Family Involvement

Two school-based programs that incorporate a philosophy of family involvement are the Comer School Development Program (SDP) and Linkages to Learning. The Comer School Development Program is a model that schools across the country have adopted in an effort to restructure and mobilize adults to support student learning and development. In this model, traditional school organization and management is replaced with an innovative operating system coupled with a commitment to family involvement. The goal of this program is to support the child's development and to create a strong and inclusive community that involves families (Zigler, Fin-Stevenson, & Stern, 1997). Comer's SDP is comprised of three equally important components: a School Planning and Management Team, a Mental Health Team, and a Parent Program. This model posits that, for a family involvement initiative to succeed, the school's ecology must foster positive and supportive relationships among all stakeholders (Comer & Haynes, 1991). The Parent Program provides a range of involvement at differing levels of time commitment and responsibility, enabling families to participate at a level that is comfortable for them. SDP conceptualizes parent involvement at three levels. The first level is the provision of general support and participation in a variety of school activities, such as attending parent/teacher conferences, monitoring children's homework, and supporting fundraising activities. The second level involves parents as volunteers in daily school activities where parent volunteers are given meaningful tasks and each parent is paired with a compatible staff member. The third level allows for parents to participate in school decision making by serving on the School Planning and Management Team and related committees (Comer School Development Program, 2001). The Comer model demonstrates the range and variability of opportunities for the involvement of families in broader educational contexts and can be applied to school mental health practice through the development of multiple avenues for families to participate in their children's care.

Linkages to Learning (LTL) is another program that consistently demonstrates a strong philosophy about the importance and value of family involvement. LTL is a school-based/school-linked service delivery system representing a collaborative effort between the public school system, the Maryland Department of Health and Human Services, and multiple community service organizations. The partnership was established to reduce the social and family problems that serve as barriers to learning. From the beginning, LTL adopted a user-friendly atmosphere that served to facilitate family involvement. For example, in an effort to outreach to all families, the program hires bilingual staff in order to enhance communications and interactions with families. Parents participating in LTL are viewed by program staff as partners in developing asset-based, culturally appropriate solutions to the challenges confronting their children, schools, and communities (Linkages to Learning, 1999). School-based services offered to families by LTL include mental health, social services, educational support, and health care.

Be Flexible and Creative in Facilitating Family Involvement

Professionals working in schools often learn that successful facilitation of family involvement requires an increased level of flexibility and creativity. One example is the Youth and Family Centers (YFC) in Dallas, Texas. The YFC provides mental health and other support services to students and families at 10 strategically placed school-based centers (each center serving approximately 20 schools) with a focus on involving families (Jennings, Pearson, & Harris, 2000). They illustrate the importance of family involvement in their model of school mental health service provision, stating as one of their main objectives that "every child must have a family member who loves him/her and a teacher who cares (and the family and teacher must be involved in the children's health/mental care)" (Jennings et al., 2000, p. 201). The YFC has incorporated the use of a family greeter to welcome families on their initial visits and to assist them in completing forms (Jennings et al., 2000). By using a family greeter, they are working to increase the comfort level of the family from the onset of care. The YFC also has developed a number of programs to support family involvement in school-based mental health services and the school community, including Adult Basic Education (ABE), Power of Parenting (POP), and Family Youth Interactions (FYI). Additionally, the YFC has made a concerted effort to be flexible in service delivery, reflected in the availability of evening appointments (centers are required to provide evening appointments at least 2 evenings a week).

Another example of creative outreach to families is exemplified by the Primary Mental Health Project (PMHP), one the oldest school-based prevention programs for children in the country. In an effort to better address the needs of families, they developed the Parent Associate Program (Cowen et al., 1996). Parent Associates are paraprofessionals trained by the PMHP to focus their work primarily on the linkages between schools and families. They help the PMHP team to gather information from families (family history, significant family events, developmental history) and to provide families with information about the PMHP. Furthermore, parent advocates assist in crisis management and the development of effective home–school communication strategies (Cowen et al., 1996).

Assess and Respect the Needs of the Families Served by the Program

Best practices in establishing ESMH programs include conducting needs assessment to determine the specific needs of the community and how services will be developed (Acosta et al., 2002; Weist et al., 2000). Families and other key stakeholders should be included in the needs assessment (Acosta et al., in press). This can be accomplished by conducting focus groups with families, and recruiting family members for active participation in steering committees and advisory boards. The University of Maryland School Mental Health Program, which operates in 23 Baltimore City Schools, has incorporated both of these activities into their program. For example, a needs assessment to explore desired aspects of program services was conducted with key stakeholder groups, including families. In response to this survey, specific family recommendations included educating families about mental health issues, increasing education about teen parenting, and reducing stigma related to mental health through media campaigns. Families also suggested that services be offered after school and in the summer. Family participants expressed their strong commitment to and interest in being involved in their children's treatment (Nabors et al., 1999). It is clear that families want to be involved in the development, implementation, and evaluation of services. The SMHP strives to meet this goal by having family and youth members on their advisory board to guide program development. The program also employs a family advocate who attends program meetings and helps to shape the training agenda to increase clinicians' sensitivity to families' needs.

Linking Families with Resources

Many schools and mental health providers have learned that locating family-oriented resources in schools leads to increased levels of family involvement in schools and related programs such as ESMH. This is one reason why full-service community schools have been effective in increasing access to and utilization of services (Warger, 2001). A full-service community school is one that integrates education with health, social, and mental health services into a specific community (Dryfoos, 1998). An example of a full-service program is the School of the 21st Century (also known as Family Resource Centers). The School of the 21st Century is a school-based childcare and family support program, providing children and families with access to a variety of support services including childcare, mental health, and health and nutrition. Examples of initiatives include year-round all-day daycare; before-school, after-school, and vacation care for students; home visits, developmental screenings, and support groups for parents with children aged 0 to 3; and daycare provider training (Comer/Zigler Initiative, no date). There are more than 300 participating schools located in 13 states across the country (Zigler et al., 1997). While full-service schools are a model of integrated service provision and resources, it also is possible to provide meaningful resources to parents on a smaller scale. Many clinicians link families to resources by hosting parenting workshops and support groups or publishing newsletters, while others disseminate handouts and fliers on mental health topics, healthy development, and resources in the community (Lowie et al., 2001).

Allocate or Obtain Resources Necessary to Promote Family Involvement

Moving beyond a philosophy of family involvement, promoting and maintaining such involvement may require additional resources. Such resources may be obtained by enlisting the help of schools and community agencies, and through local, state, and national grants that can assist in funding such efforts (Bickham et al., 1998). (For further information about funding, please review the related chapter in this book.)

Establish Quality Improvement Procedures to Inform and Improve the Process of Involving Families

There has been increasing recognition among both researchers and practitioners that children and family members can significantly contribute to evaluating children's mental health programs (Anderson, Rivera, & Kutash, 1998). The literature includes several studies that have looked at adolescent and parent satisfaction with mental health services (Brannan, Sonnichsen, & Heflinger, 1996; Garland &

Besinger, 1996; Kopec-Schrader et al., 1994; Lambert, Salzer, & Bickman, 1998; Stuntzner-Gibson, Koren, & DeChillo, 1995) as well as studies that have specifically examined satisfaction with school-based mental health services (Jennings et al., 2000; Nabors et al., 1999). Youth and Family Centers in Dallas, Texas, have used family satisfaction measures, which have provided overwhelmingly positive responses (Final Report Youth and Family Centers Program, 1999–2000). Satisfaction questionnaires completed by students and family members who received services through YFCs indicated that more than 90% were happy with services and would return if needed (Jennings et al., 2000). To continue to ensure quality services, families need to be involved in the evaluation process. Their input regarding program strengths and weaknesses should be incorporated into program improvement plans.

RECOMMENDATIONS FOR ENHANCED FAMILY INVOLVEMENT IN ESMH

Based on existing research and clinical practice, the points in Table 1 summarize recommendations to promote family involvement in expanded school mental health programs.

Table 1. Summary Recommendations for Clinicians in Expanded School Mental Health Programs to Promote Family Involvement

1. Clinicians should be involved in a full array of activities at the school to increase their visibility and acceptance as a member of the school team. These interactions also may help to reduce the stigma of mental health services as individuals become more aware of the types of services offered and comfortable with the clinician offering those services.
2. Families' confidentiality should be respected and their input should be valued and actively included in treatment planning.
3. Services should be accommodating to the schedules of families (e.g., early morning and evening appointments).
4. Programs and clinicians should strive to partner with and gain the support of the school administration to promote family involvement in mental health and the broader school community.
5. Clinicians need to be familiar with school and community resources and should provide families with appropriate referrals.
6. Programs should offer families workshop trainings, conferences, and other opportunities to develop skills and share knowledge and expertise (e.g., discussion dinners, family-to-family linkages).
7. Programs should consider hiring paraprofessionals, including parent associates and family-to-family support advocates, to help facilitate connections between caregivers and service providers.
8. Programs should provide intensive training opportunities to clinicians and supervisors in enhancing family outreach and involvement with an emphasis on cultural sensitivity and recognition of differences in family needs.
9. Programs should actively seek to become full partners in the healthy development of the school community. Clinicians should strive to improve academic outcomes for youth.
10. Programs should involve families as equal members on advisory boards/program committees and should include families in all aspects of program development, implementation, and evaluation.

NEXT STEPS AND FUTURE DIRECTIONS TO INVOLVE FAMILIES IN ESMH PROGRAMS

Despite the widely recognized importance of family involvement in expanded school-based mental health programs, there remains a gap between best practice and what is actually practiced. The effort to further involve families in all aspects of the ESMH movement begins with enhancing access to care and perceptions of mental health services (e.g., having early morning, evening, and weekend appointments available, calling families to remind them of appointments, and reducing the stigma of mental health services by being an active participant in the school community). In order to provide progressive family-friendly care, ESMH programs need to address such fundamental issues as program philosophy, mission, training of providers, and allocation of resources. By developing and enhancing clinicians' roles in the schools, empowering clinicians with useful tools/resources, and allocating resources to ensure that clinicians are better able to meet family needs, it is likely that all parties (e.g., youth, families, and clinicians) will benefit. Appropriate training and resources are needed to help clinicians feel competent to work with families. Programs also should allocate resources (e.g., training, workshops, funding to hire family advocates/greeters) to increase families' comfort level with and knowledge about mental health. Clinicians need to be willing to adopt less traditional roles and be responsive to feedback from the school community regarding their service provision model. This may necessitate that clinicians act in ways outside of their scope of service (e.g., case managers) to help families meet their mental health, health, and basic living needs.

Allocating resources may be the most challenging of these efforts since expanded school mental health programs are often in a state of constant challenge to maintain and secure ongoing funding. Nonetheless, if these programs are to have the far-reaching impacts that they have the potential for, efforts for family involvement need to be prioritized, and it is clear that designated funding for them is one way to ensure that they are prioritized.

Finally, the expanded school mental health field is very young (see Weist & Christodulu, 2000). A review of the literature reveals limited information about the process of or outcomes related to family–provider collaboration in ESMH programs. Developing a systematic research and training agenda to advance family involvement in school mental health programs will hopefully lead to improved access to care, reduced barriers to learning, and improved emotional and behavioral functioning of youth.

REFERENCES

Acosta, O. M., Tashman, N. A., Prodente, C., & Proescher, E. (2002). Establishing successful school mental health programs: Guidelines and recommendations. In H. S. Ghuman, M. D. Weist, & R. Sarles (Eds.), *Providing mental health services to youth where they are: School and community based approaches.* New York: Routledge.

Anderson, J. A., Rivera, V. R., & Kutash, K. (1998). Measuring consumer satisfaction with children's mental health services. In M. H. Epstein, K. Kutash, & A. Duchnowski (Eds.), *Outcomes for children and youth with emotional and behavioral disorders and their families: Program and evaluation best practices.* Austin, TX: Pro-ED.

Atkins, M., McKay, M., Arvanitis, P., London, L., Madison, S., Costigan, C., Haney, P., Zevenbergen, A., Hess, L., Bennett, D., & Webster, D. (1998). An ecological model for school-based mental health services for urban low-income aggressive children. *Journal of Behavioral Health Services & Research, 25*(1), 64–75.

Bickham, N. L., Pizarro, J., Warner, B. S., Rosenthal, B., & Weist, M. D. (1998). Family involvement in expanded school mental health. *Journal of School Health, 68*(10), 425–428.

Brannan, A. M., Sonnichsen, S. E., & Heflinger, C. A. (1996). Measuring satisfaction with children's mental health services: Validity and reliability of the satisfaction scales. *Evaluation and Program Planning, 19*(2), 131–141.

Brener, N. D., Dittus, P. J., & Hayes, G. (2001). Family and community involvement in schools: Results from the school health policies and programs study 2000. *Journal of School Health, 71*(7), 340–344.

Cheney, D., & Osher, T. (1997). Collaborate with families. *Journal of Emotional and Behavioral Disorders, 5*(1), 36–44.

Comer, J. P., & Haynes, N. M. (1991). Parent involvement in schools: An ecological approach. *The Elementary School Journal, 91*, 272–277.

Comer School Development Program (2001). Comer School Development Program: Program Overview. Retrieved October 24, 2001, from http://www.med.yale.edu\comer\index.html.

Comer/Zigler Initiative (no date). *What is the Comer/Zigler Initiative (CoZi)?* Retrieved June 15, 2001, from http://www.med.yale.edu/comer/about/alliances.htm.

Cowen, E., Hightower, A., Pedro-Carroll, J., Work, W., Wyman, P., & Haffey, W. (1996). *School based prevention for children at risk: The primary mental health project.* Washington, DC: American Psychological Association.

Cristenson, S. (1995). Best practices in supporting home–school collaboration. In A. Thomas & J. Grimes (Eds.), *Best practices in school psychology—III* (pp. 253–267). Washington, DC: National Association of School Psychologists.

Dryfoos, J. G. (1998). *A look at community schools in 1998.* Occasional paper #2. New York: National Center for Schools and Communities.

Eccles, J., & Harold, R. (1993). Parent–school involvement during the early adolescent years. *Teachers College Record, 94*(3), 568–588.

Epstein, J. (1992). School and family partnerships: Leadership roles for school psychologists. In S. L. Cristenson & J. C. Conoley (Eds.), *Home–school collaborations: Enhancing children's academic and social competence* (pp. 499–515). Silver Spring, MD: National Association of School Psychologists.

Farmer, E. M. Z., Burns, B. J., Angold, A., & Costello, E. J. (1997). Impact of children's mental health problems on families: Relationships with service use. *Journal of Emotional & Behavioral Disorders, 5*(4), 230–238.

Federation of Families for Childrens Mental Health (n.d.). Retrieved December 1, 2001, from http://www.ffcmh.org/Eng_one.htm.

Garland, A. F., & Besinger, B. A. (1996). Adolescents' perceptions of outpatient mental health services. *Journal of Child and Family Studies, 5*(3), 355–375.

Greenberg, M., Domitrovich, C., & Bumbarger, B. (1999). Preventing mental disorders in school-age children: A review of the effectiveness of prevention programs. Retrieved from http://www.prevention.psu.edu/.

Hampton, F., & Mumford, D. (1998). Parent involvement in inner-city schools. *Urban Education, 98*(33), 410–428.

Jennings, J., Pearson, G., & Harris, M. (2000). Implementing and maintaining school-based mental health services in a large, urban school district. *Journal of School Health, 70*(5), 201–205.

Jivanjee, P. R., & Friesen, B. J. (1997). Shared expertise: Family participation in interprofessional training. *Journal of Emotional & Behavioral Disorders, 5*(4), 205–211.

Kopec-Schrader, E. M., Rey, J. M., Plapp, J. M., & Beumont, P. J. V. (1994). Parental evaluation of treatment in an adolescent service. *Journal of Adolescence, 17*, 239–249.

Koren, P., Paulson, R., Kinney, R., Yatchmenoff, D., Gordon, L., & DeChillo, N. (1997). Service coordination in children's mental health: An empirical study from the caregiver's perspective. *Journal of Emotional & Behavioral Disorder, 5*(3), 162–172.

Lambert, W., Salzer, M. S., & Bickman, L. (1998). Clinical outcome, consumer satisfaction, and ad hoc ratings of improvement in children's mental health. *Journal of Consulting and Clinical Psychology, 66*(2), 270–279.

Linkages to Learning (1999). *Linkages to Learning: Orientation manual to new staff.* Rockville, MD: Author.

Lowie, J., Ambrose, M., Lever, N., & Tager, S. (2001, May). Family involvement in ESMH programs. Presentation conducted at the Maryland State School Health Council and the Maryland Assembly on School-Based Health Care Annual Spring Conference 2001, Ocean City, MD.

Marcon, R. (1999). Positive relationships between parent school involvement and public school inner-city preschoolers' development and academic performance. *School Psychology Review, 28*(3), 395–413.

McKay, M. M., McCadam, K., & Gonzales, J. (1996). Addressing the barriers to mental health services for inner city children and their caretakers. *Community Mental Health Journal, 32*(4), 353–361.

Nabors, L. A., Weist, M. D., Reynolds, M., Tashman, N. A., & Jackson, C. Y. (1999). Adolescent satisfaction with school-based mental health services. *Journal of Child and Family Studies, 8*(2), 229–236.

Osher, T., van Kammen, W., & Zaro, S. (2001). Family participation in evaluating systems of care: Family, research and service system perspectives. *Journal of Emotional & Behavioral Disorders, 9*(1), 63–70.

Roehlkepartain, E., & Benson, P. (1994). Measuring the impact of involvement [Electronic Version]. *Source Newsletter.* Retrieved January 9, 2001, from http://www.search-institute.org/archives/csf.htm.

Simpson, J., Koroloff, N., Friesen, B., & Gac, J. (1999). Promising practices in family–provider collaboration. *Systems of care: Promising practices in children's mental health, 1998 series, volume II.* Washington, DC: Center for Effective Collaboration and Practice, American Institutes for Research.

Stuntzner-Gibson, D., Koren, P. E., & DeChillo, N. (1995). The Youth Satisfaction Questionnaire: What kids think of services. *Families in Society: The Journal of Contemporary Human Services,* 616–624.

Tolan, P., & McKay, M. (1996). Preventing serious antisocial behavior in inner-city youth: An empirically based family intervention program. *Family Relations, 45,* 148–155.

U.S. Department of Health and Human Services (1999). *Mental health: A report of the Surgeon General—Executive summary.* Rockville, MD: U.S. Department of Health and Human Services, Substance Abuse and Mental Health Services Administration, Center for Mental Health Services, National Institutes of Health, National Institute of Mental Health.

Warger, C. (2001). *Research on full-service schools and students with disabilities* (ERIC/OSEP Digest Number E616). Arlington, VA: The Eric Clearinghouse on Disabilities and Gifted Education.

Weist, M. D. (1997). Expanded school mental health services: A national movement in progress. *Advances in Clinical Child Psychology, 19,* 319–351.

Weist, M. D., & Christodulu, K. V. (2000). Expanded school mental health programs: Advancing reform and closing the gap between research and practice. *Journal of School Health, 70*(5), 195–200.

Weist, M. D., Nabors, L. A., Myers, C. P., & Armbruster, P. (2000). Evaluation of expanded school mental health programs. *Community Mental Health Journal, 36,* 395–412.

Weist, M. D., Sander, M. A., Link, B., & Carrillo, K. (2001, November). *Developing principles for expanded school mental health programs.* Workshop presented at the meeting of the American School Health Association, Albuquerque, NM.

Zigler, E. F., Fin-Stevenson, M., & Stern, B. M. (1997). Supporting children and families in the schools: The school of the 21st century. *American Journal of Orthopsychiatry, 67*(3), 396–407.

11

System, Agency, and Stakeholder Collaboration to Advance Mental Health Programs in Schools

NANCY A. LEVER, STEVE ADELSHEIM,
CHRISTINE A. PRODENTE, KRISTIN V. CHRISTODULU,
MELISSA G. AMBROSE, JOHN SCHLITT,
and MARK D. WEIST

The U.S. Surgeon General's report on mental health underscores that prevention and treatment are both needed to help reduce social, emotional, and behavioral problems in children and adolescents (U.S. Department of Health and Human Services, 1999). The report also emphasizes that schools are a "major" setting for identifying mental health concerns in youth. Schools are one of the most universal, natural settings and provide unparalleled access to youth (Weist, 1997). In fact, it is estimated that one-fourth of the U.S. population can be found in schools (Jamieson, Curry, & Martinez, 2001).

Considering the extensive mental health needs of today's youth, it is not surprising that any single agency or organization would have difficulty meeting the rising demand for services. There is growing acceptance that collaboration among school and community health, primary care, mental health, and education is crucial for effectively delivering services to youth and their families (Dryfoos, 1994; Flaherty et al., 1998). As reflected in other chapters in this book, expanded school mental health (ESMH) programs are built around these school–community partnerships (Weist, 1997). By blending the partners' skills and resources, students

NANCY A. LEVER, MELISSA G. AMBROSE, and MARK D. WEIST • University of Maryland School of Medicine, Baltimore, Maryland 21201.   STEVE ADELSHEIM • New Mexico Department of Health, Santa Fe, New Mexico 87502.   CHRISTINE A. PRODENTE • Partial Hospitalization Program, Medical College of Ohio, Kobacker Center, Toledo, Ohio 43614.   KRISTIN V. CHRISTODULU • State University of New York, Albany, Albany, New York 12222.   JOHN SCHLITT • National Assembly on School-Based Health Care, Washington, DC 20001.

and families are afforded a richer array of mental health services (Acosta, Tashman, Prodente, & Proescher, 2002). However, collaboration among people of different backgrounds and disciplines and between agencies and programs from throughout the community and state is by no means easy. In this chapter we provide background to and ideas and examples of effective school–community–state collaboration to advance mental health in schools.

Throughout the chapter, we use the term stakeholder to refer to individuals, agencies, and groups who have some stake or investment in the development, implementation, and evaluation of a given endeavor. For expanded school mental health, key stakeholders include the following groups: youth, parents or guardians, teachers, administrators, school and community mental health and health staff, local and state government officials, staff from other child-serving agencies, community leaders, faith leaders, businesses, civic organizations, funders, and advocates (Kretzmann & McKnight, 1993; Nabors et al., 1998; Waxman, Weist, & Benson, 1999).

There is some literature emphasizing the need to work with diverse stakeholders and multiple community and state organizations to develop or improve child and adolescent mental health programs (U.S. Department of Health and Human Services, 1999; Nabors, Weist, Holden, et al., 1999; Weist, 1997). However, examples of and explicit guidance for this work are lacking. Within this chapter, the definition of, barriers to, and components of successful collaboration at multiple levels will be explored. Specific use of these collaborative strategies in developing and improving expanded school mental health programs will then be addressed. The chapter concludes with two examples—one focusing on state-level collaboration to advance school mental health in New Mexico and a second focusing on the experiences of a program in Baltimore in its efforts to connect with diverse stakeholders to enhance resources and to improve quality.

DEFINING COLLABORATION

Collaboration is a process of participation through which people, groups, and organizations work together to achieve desired results (National Network for Collaboration, 1995). Collaboration can be viewed as a process to reach goals that cannot be achieved acting singly (or, at least not achieved as efficiently) (Bruner, 1991). For collaborations to be successful, individuals and groups must be able to see a contribution to their own mission and purpose (Golden, 1991). Research involving children's services shows that collaboration can lead to improved access, better tracking of services, and a reduction in barriers to care for families (Bruner, 1991). Collaboration can help to expand available resources through cooperative programming and the sharing of facilities, information, training, and staff (Lippitt & Van Til, 1981). By demonstrating improved outcomes, increased client satisfaction, and increased savings due to the reduction of service duplication, working collaboratively can also change the way agencies are perceived by the community (National Assembly of National Voluntary Health and Social Welfare Organizations (NASWO), 1991; Roberts, 1994).

Barriers to Successful Collaboration

Several researchers have explored why collaboration is difficult in the area of child and family services (see Gardner, 1989; Schorr, 1988; Weiss, 1981;

Weissbourd, 1990). Reasons include insufficient funding, organizational rigidities, and inadequate resources. Barriers to collaboration described in the literature might be categorized as personal, systemic, or environmental (Hodges, Nesman, & Hernandez, 1999). A primary personal barrier is the American ethos of competition and independence that works against collaborating with others, promotes turfism, and leads to fear of losing power (Lippitt & Van Til, 1981). Conflicts between "outside" professionals brought into schools and district personnel may arise over "turf," use of space, confidentiality, and liability (Waxman et al., 1999). System-level barriers may include limited resources such as time, specialized staff, technology, funding, and limited experience with collaboration (Gray, 1989; Powell, Koput, & Smith-Doerr, 1996; Skiba, Polsgrove, & Nasstrom, 1996). Environmental barriers include racial or cultural polarization, which can lead to distrust and lack of communication (NASWO, 1991). Other barriers include state-level factors such as competing mandates for each agency or insufficient resources allocated with the mandate (Macbeth, 1993; Magrab, Young, & Waddell, 1985).

Elements of Successful Collaboration

Successful collaborative relationships require groups to come together for a joint endeavor. Though each organization may have different missions to achieve, a successful partnership requires that each group be willing to work toward one overarching shared goal or vision (Friend & Cook, 1990). The partnership requires redefined and overlapping missions that may push organizations to expand their missions beyond what may be conventional for their agency. Golden (1991) describes common elements of successful collaboration based on research on welfare agencies and children's services. An important element is the ability to resolve conflicts, as these will occur in any genuine collaborative endeavor. Second, organizational leaders must express and demonstrate a commitment to collaboration and the development of relationships; without such role modeling, program staff should not be expected to collaborate. Third, those involved in the collaborative relationship must perceive that it is mutually beneficial. Finally, as organizations and their staff come together to create programs, an effort should be made to outreach to and involve stakeholders who will be impacted.

Early in the collaborative relationship, it is important for leaders to convey that the autonomy of individuals and programs will be retained, while pursuing a joint agenda (Goldman & Intriligator, 1990; Lippitt & Van Til, 1981; Melaville & Blank, 1991). This has led to the emphasis on "braided" funding and programming, where programs share resources and funding while maintaining control over staff and funding streams, versus true "blended" funding and programming, which implies the merging of two organizations into one. It is essential that equality in decision making and in voicing of opinions and perspective be maintained when working collaboratively (National Network for Collaboration, 1995). It is also important for members of the collaborative team to decide who is responsible for the completion of specific duties (Lippitt & Van Til, 1981). Established procedures for settling disagreements can help avoid friction that can be caused by turf issues commonly found when people from different types of agencies work together (Goldman & Intriligator, 1990). In addition, agencies working collaboratively must develop a shared method of communication early in the process, so that differing terminologies do not interfere with participants recognizing their common goals (Himmelman, 1993).

Collaboration in Expanded School Mental Health Programs

The Importance of Collaboration

In contrast to "multidisciplinary" collaboration, which conveys that multiple disciplines are in some way involved in a common agenda, "interdisciplinary" collaboration conveys that they are genuinely and seriously working together. Interdisciplinary collaboration can reap many benefits including increased resources, decreased fragmentation, and reduced costs (Flaherty et al., 1998). Through collaborative efforts, service providers and agencies can accomplish goals that neither could achieve alone (U.S. Department of Education, 1996). Because schools, homes, and communities share goals related to educating and socializing youth, they must collaborate in order to minimize problems and maximize results (Taylor & Adelman, 2000). For most children, but especially for children from disadvantaged environments, schools are the most readily available and easily accessible sites for the provision of a continuum of community-based mental health services (Flaherty & Weist, 1999; Tuma, 1989).

The inherently interdisciplinary nature of school-based mental health provides the opportunity for an integrated and comprehensive approach as opposed to fragmented and piecemeal approaches (Rosenblum et al., 1995). Highly effective programs tend to be guided by a shared, strategic, and systemic planning perspective rooted at the community level (Knoff, 1996). Such an approach places a high value on stakeholder involvement during three stages: planning, implementation, and evaluation. Involving key stakeholders in these stages increases the likelihood that community members will feel some responsibility for and commitment to supporting the program (Acosta, Tashman, et al., 2002). Meaningful stakeholder participation in these three stages also helps to ensure that the goals of the program are consistent with stakeholder priorities as well as the current needs of the community (Nabors et al., 1998).

Initial Collaborative Planning

One way of ensuring that community needs, perspectives, and resources are taken into consideration early on is to include representatives from the various stakeholder groups on a planning committee, which is responsible for guiding the early development of the school mental health program (Acosta, Tashman, et al., 2002). Educators, school administrators, mental health providers, coordinators of the collaborating mental health agencies, and other community leaders should be included on the planning committee (Waxman et al., 1999). Initially, it will be important to the success of the program that these collaborative partners focus on identifying and agreeing upon the overall mission and goals of the program (Bruner, 1991; Gray, 1989; Hodges et al., 1999; Magrab et al., 1985). Another goal of the planning committee is to network with the various community groups in a position to benefit from and/or contribute to a school mental health program (Acosta, Tashman, et al., 2002). Soliciting meaningful input from community stakeholder groups early on helps to ensure that the program's mission is consistent with stakeholder goals and increases the likelihood of broad-based community support for the emerging program (Nabors et al., 1998).

Stakeholder involvement through the planning committee will also be important when identifying community needs, current gaps in services, and available resources. This information is then used to assist the planning committee in making decisions about the overall structure of the program. It may be, for example, that the planning committee elects to improve coordination among existing school-linked programs as one step in developing a comprehensive, integrated school mental health program. Thus, one of the first tasks of the planning committee will be to conduct a community needs assessment. Needs assessments are critical for establishing program priorities, identifying gaps in service provision, securing start-up funds, and identifying barriers that prevent youth from accessing mental health services (Acosta, Weist, et al., 2002; Weist, Nabors, et al., 2000; Wolf, Yung, & Cotton, 1994). Soliciting input from key stakeholders is an important part of conducting a needs assessment, as the more they are involved in the process of identifying needs, the more likely they are to agree that the appropriate needs were identified and decided upon (Brandon & Wang, 1994).

Stakeholder involvement in the needs assessment process can be accomplished by such means as focus groups, informal interviews, and surveys (Nabors et al., 1999). The process of conducting a community needs assessment also facilitates networking among program developers and key stakeholders and enables developers to learn what would motivate the various stakeholder groups to want to support the program. In addition to a thorough assessment of current community needs, the planning committee can assess what resources are available within the school and community as a means of identifying important collaborative partners and gaps in services (Acosta, Tashman, et al., 2002). Finally, the planning committee can collaboratively help to negotiate expectations regarding schedules, organizational policies, funding responsibilities, professional roles and responsibilities, and legal/ethical mandates (Hodges et al., 1999; Magrab et al., 1985; NASWO, 1991).

Program Implementation

Involving stakeholders as partners in the ongoing governance of school mental health programs is critical to maintaining program support and viability (Christenson & Conoley, 1992; Henderson, Marburger, & Ooms, 1986). One effective strategy for accomplishing this is to establish an advisory board comprised of a wide array of stakeholders (Acosta, Tashman, et al., 2002; Waxman et al., 1999). Distinguished from the planning committee, which represents the core team that meets frequently to develop the framework for the program, the advisory board should broadly reflect the needs of the school and community, meeting every month to few months. Advisory boards help shape the program's vision, mission, and activities; assist in publicizing and bringing resources into the program; and assist in continuous program evaluation and improvement. It is also important for advisory boards to monitor and guide the program in legal, fiscal, and public matters to promote internal accountability and the recognition of such (Melaville & Blank, 1991; Nabors, Weist, Holden, et al., 1999).

In addition to feedback from advisory boards, ideally stakeholders will be involved in the daily operation of the school mental health program. The presence of interdisciplinary teams comprised of school- and community-hired health and mental health staff, educators, supportive personnel (e.g., resource officers, juvenile justice staff), parents, and student leaders can help achieve this goal (Haynes & Comer, 1996; Waxman et al., 1999). These teams, which have many names, such as "student support," "mental health," "learning support," or "healthy school" teams, provide a mechanism for ongoing coordination of school mental health services, while at the same time offering a means for mutual support between team members. By mobilizing and coordinating resources, such collaborative teams can help promote family and community involvement. Further, such collaborative teams can assist in developing quality assessment and improvement measures, raising community awareness of mental health issues, guiding outreach efforts, raising funds, and creating resources for stakeholders (e.g., educational literature, parent–peer mentoring groups).

There are a number of other ways for stakeholder groups to partner with school mental health programs. Faith-based organizations, for example, may offer nonprofessional volunteer services such as mentoring, assisting the school with special events, and monitoring and serving as positive role models and supports for students (Prodente et al., 2002). Community and business leaders can provide mentoring and financial support to the program. University staff can offer expertise on evaluation, the use of evidence-based programs, and implementing schoolwide preventive programs (Dwyer & Bernstein, 1998; Golden, 1991). Schools can also link with other agencies and organizations to provide additional on-site services (e.g., adult education and career development, child care, financial and social services, parenting classes, social and recreational activities, health services) to promote youth, family, and community involvement in the school (Hendrickson & Omer, 1995). In ongoing therapeutic interactions with students, school mental health clinicians can (and should) solicit their active feedback on positive *and* negative aspects of treatment. This kind of ongoing feedback can (and should) also be provided by teachers and other staff (e.g., school-hired health and mental health staff) who work closely with the program.

Collaborative Program Evaluation

Meaningful stakeholder involvement in program evaluation activities contributes to a sense of shared responsibility for outcomes and guides the future direction of the program (Dryfoos, Brindis, & Kaplan, 1996; Gray, 1989; Weist, Nabors, et al., 2000). Program evaluation findings can help to improve service delivery, provide feedback to stakeholders about the effectiveness of the services, and document fiscal, legal, and public accountability (Nabors & Reynolds, 2000; Nabors, Weist, Holden, et al., 1999).

There are several recommended approaches for involving stakeholders in the evaluation process. First, a "Quality Assessment and Improvement Team" with both community- and school-based participants can be established with the goal of developing and implementing strategies for assessing service utilization and effectiveness. Second, it will be important to involve mental health staff, school staff, parents, youth, and other stakeholders in the assessment process by asking them to complete questionnaires or participate in focus groups, peer review teams, and/or interviews. Last, stakeholders may wish to assist the program by sharing and disseminating evaluation results in an effort to build broad-based community support (Prodente, Sander, & Weist, 2002; Taylor & Adelman, 2000).

The following section presents examples of state and local efforts that involve systems and stakeholders joining together in collaborative efforts to advance mental health programs in schools. The two examples help to demonstrate how school mental health programs can outreach to key stakeholders and involve them in program development, implementation, and improvement.

System and Stakeholder Collaboration at State and Local Levels

Collaboration to Advance School Mental Health in New Mexico

New Mexico's children currently face some of the highest rates of poverty, substance abuse, suicide, and school dropout of any children in the United States. New Mexico has the largest percentage of children in poverty; the highest rate of teens not in school/working; the second highest dropout rate; the second highest teen death rate due to accident, suicide, homicide; and the sixth highest teen suicide rate in the United States (Annie E. Casey Foundation, 2001). Many of these issues have major mental health problems at their core. While 35% of New Mexico's children live in rural counties, 12% live in counties designated as "frontier," having a population density of less than six people per square mile. Access to skilled providers is difficult to come by, particularly in rural and frontier communities. These painful statistics speak to the clear need for expanded advocacy efforts statewide. The New Mexico School Mental Health Initiative, a joint effort of the University of New Mexico Department of Psychiatry and the New Mexico Department of Health, has been advocating for expansion of school-based behavioral health programs in an effort to improve the lives of New Mexico's children.

The Initiative is housed in the Department of Health's Office of School Health. The Office, with its 23 staff members, is in the Health Systems Bureau of the Public Health Division. The Office of School Health has grown dramatically in the last few years, with the expansion of the New Mexico School Mental Health Initiative (Adelman et al., 1999; Adelsheim, 2000; Adelsheim, Carrillo, & Coletta, 2001; Annie E. Casey Foundation, 2001). Funded initially by a Federal Maternal and Child Health grant, this collaboration of state agencies, schools, families, and community partners has made great strides in expanding both programs and support for addressing the mental health needs of students so they may be successful in school.

Initially, the staff of the School Mental Health Initiative consisted of the child psychiatrist director, a master's-level social worker as program director, and an administrative assistant. Due to the needs of schools for training in school mental health directed to teachers, the Behavioral Educational Consultant position was created, and a former special education teacher with a strong background in teacher training was hired.

While it was clear that New Mexico needed expanded children's behavioral health programs in schools, no program funding was initially available. Furthermore, obtaining this funding was complicated by the fact that services for children's mental health at the state level is splintered between five different divisions in four different state agencies. Bringing together these agencies to support a focus on school behavioral health became the next critical priority. Discussions with directors of each of these state programs led to the eventual formation of the Interdepartmental School Behavioral Health Partnership (ISBHP). This state-level, interdepartmental collaborative has coordinated and expanded critical school mental health programs for New Mexico's children. Members include representatives from the Divisions of Public Health and Behavioral Health in the Health Department; the School Health Unit and Special Education Division in the State Department of Education; the Prevention and Intervention Division of the Children, Youth, and Families Department; and the Medical Assistance Division of the Human Services Department. In a true state-level partnership, these agencies collaborated over the past 5 years to now provide over $1.4 million yearly in staff and program support for school mental health programs.

One innovative staff role created by this collaboration was that of five School Mental Health Advocate positions. Each regional School Mental Health Advocate, a master's-level trained therapist with school mental health experience, was assigned to a state Public Health district office to work closely with local schools, parents, health professionals, and mental health providers. These critical community partners have provided essential technical assistance, training, and support to schools, families, and communities to expand regional understanding and local capacity to provide collaborative prevention, early intervention, and treatment for students.

One of the first steps in implementing the Initiative at the community level was to establish statewide workgroups. An *Advocacy Workgroup* was created to promote legislation and expand policy support for school mental health, leading in 1998 to the passage by the legislature of a special "Memorial" in support of expanded school mental health. The Mental Health in the Schools Memorial called for increasing intra- and interagency collaboration and training to enhance school mental health programs. State agencies involved were the Departments of Health; Education; Children, Youth, and Families: Human Services; Corrections; the Administrative Office of the Courts; the Children's Subcommittee of the Governor's Mental Health Planning Council; the Developmental Disabilities Planning Council; and the Individuals with Disabilities Education Act (IDEA) Council. In addition, the text called for inclusion of consumers, advocates, and providers working in the mental health field and schools. The Memorial recommendations were made following four regional meetings on school mental health around the state. Over 240 New Mexicans spent a half-day discussing these issues in small groups and making recommendations. Some of the final recommendations became policy that impacted critical state program development and funding.

Examples of the programs coming from these recommendations include the expansion of behavioral health services in school-based health centers. The Office of School Health, with additional financial support from the ISBHP, currently provides funding for 17 school-based health centers statewide, which serve over 40 schools. The New Mexico School Mental Health Awareness Project, also created through the ISBHP, made its first advocacy effort *Childhood Revealed New Mexico* in 2001. This art exhibit, coordinated by staff from the New York University Child Study Center and highlighting artwork of children with mental illness from across the United States, was used as a vehicle to increase awareness of and advocacy for the mental health needs of our state's children. This exhibit spent 4 months in New Mexico, in both urban and rural communities, and included newspaper articles, lecture series, a film series, performances, and citywide proclamations. The exhibit brought together schools, community members, and community leaders from throughout the state to discuss the impact of childhood mental illness, while also addressing the stigma issues that complicate communication around this issue. Our School Behavioral Health Training Institute, a train-the-trainers model for school teachers and school health personnel focused on children's mental health, has also had an advocacy component in helping school personnel become more sensitized to the social and emotional needs of students. Thus far in the 2001–2002 school year, over 160 school staff have been trained. This staff will in turn train over 1200 teachers in their home schools.

Efforts have also been made to bring mental health assessments to schools. A legislative memorial was approved in 1999, followed by funding in the 2000 and 2001 legislative sessions for mental health assessments for students (kindergarten through sixth grade). The goals include early identification of high-risk youth, supportive intervention for the child and family, and a plan to help children get on track and succeed in the classroom. This legislation is accompanied by funds for teacher training in school mental health and funds for assessment tools, as well as service dollars.

Further indications of the impact of various collaborative efforts to increase attention to children's behavioral health have been the state Summits on Children's Mental Health. The School Mental Health Initiative took the lead, with the support of the Governor's Mental Health Planning Council, in developing the first of two New Mexico Summits on Children's Mental Health. Attended by over 200 people each year, these annual Summits brought together statewide advocates for youth, parents, and providers to share information about children's mental health. In addition, the yearly Head to Toe state conference on school health, attended by 400–500 people per year, provides information on many aspects of school behavioral health programs.

Collaboration with parents and parent advocates has been one of the critical priorities of the School Mental Health Initiative. With parent organizations, the initial thrust has been one of joint advocacy for increased support to address children's mental health concerns such as expanding awareness of mental health symptoms and improving access to services. The School Mental Health Initiative provides for reimbursement for parent transportation and time to attend meetings and asks for parents to co-present to legislative committees. Acknowledgment of parents as the true experts in understanding the needs of their children and the community has been one of the cornerstones of the School Mental Health Initiative's collaborative model.

With awareness of the expanding numbers to be served and the growing emphasis on wraparound services, New Mexico's legislature and state government is increasingly coming to understand that effective collaboration in school behavioral health is essential to improving the social and academic success of New

Mexico's youth. In keeping with this understanding, the state is now working to make school- and community-level collaboration a priority and is beginning to build an infrastructure that can effectively turn policy into practice.

The University of Maryland School Mental Health Program

The University of Maryland School Mental Health Program (SMHP) began providing expanded school mental health services in four Baltimore City schools in 1989. In 2002, the program is operating in 23 schools, at the elementary, middle, and high school levels. Coinciding with the growth of this program has been increasing levels of stakeholder involvement and collaboration. The increasing involvement of diverse stakeholders in the program has helped to ensure that services provided are reflective of the needs of the schools and their communities. Mechanisms for this increased stakeholder involvement are presented in the following.

Advisory Board

In 1999, the program's advisory board was created and included representatives from the following stakeholder groups: children's health, children's mental health, teachers and school administrators, school-hired mental health providers, juvenile justice, families, students, faith community, legal community, other school mental health programs, local and national media, and the business community. Over the past 3 years, there have been three major streams of activity that the advisory board has recommended and guided: (1) increasing local awareness about the program and its advantages and impacts, (2) enhancing connections with communities of faith, and (3) developing a peer leadership program. These activities are briefly reviewed in the following.

Related to the board's inclusion of key leaders in education, health, and mental health systems in Baltimore, program staff has had the opportunity to present in front of highly influential groups (e.g., the school board, state legislators, staff from the mayor's office). This has assisted the program in maintaining a high local profile. Board members and state leaders have expressed that this has been important in increasing grant and contract revenues in spite of the fact that these are declining statewide. These presentations and meetings have also helped to forge collaborative relationships between program staff and city and state leaders. These relationships have been important for program leaders to stay current on critical developments and to have a voice in the city and state on the way school-based mental health programs should move forward.

With active guidance from faith leaders on the advisory board, the program is now developing a mentoring program involving people from local churches (and eventually other religious institutions) volunteering time in schools to mentor "at-risk" youth. At present, this program is established in a middle school, with people from two local churches participating. In the current school year, it is also beginning to take shape in one of the high schools. This initiative is enhancing the connection between youth in need and responsible community adults and also increasing opportunities for program staff to interact with leaders and parishioners from local communities of faith. It is also affording the opportunity to work through issues that have not been worked through before (e.g., the mutual reticence of the faith and mental health communities to work together) (Prodente et al., 2002).

With active guidance from both a social worker and a teacher on the board, a peer leadership program in one of the high schools is being developed. The peer leadership program is based on a national model, Peer Group Connection (Powell, 2000), and for the past 7 years has been implemented at the St. Paul's Academy, a local and highly prestigious private school in Baltimore. One of the board members is a teacher from St. Paul's who coordinates their peer leadership program. Based on the board's involvement on this project, a fundraising dinner was held and raised $6000 in funds to support the implementation of the program in one of the high schools. Since then, the SMHP has identified an additional $8000 in funds, completed all preliminary planning in the high school, and submitted a foundation grant to support the program in the school for 3 years. The board and program leaders are optimistic about the funding potential for this project and planning is fully under way to formally begin implementing the program (recruiting senior mentors) in the spring of 2002. Based on national data (Powell, 2000), it is expected that there will be improved outcomes for participating ninth graders (120 a year for 3 years) and seniors (20 a year for 3 years). The program will also establish a unique collaboration between a highly resourced private school and a high school serving students from more disadvantaged communities.

Quality Assessment and Improvement Activities (QI)

For the past 4 years, with support from two small grants from the Agency for Healthcare Research and Quality, the SMHP has been exploring multiple dimensions for assessing and improving the quality of school mental health care. These activities have included (1) holding separate focus groups with teachers, students, school health staff, and parents to gauge their impressions of program services and to gather their recommendations for program improvement; (2) implementing a peer review process, whereby clinicians received intensive feedback on randomly identified cases from a team of peers; (3) assessing and improving core indicators of school mental health quality, including the percentage of referred students actually seen, latency between referral and initial contact, daily productivity, effective participation on school teams, and leadership in implementing special projects in the school; (4) evaluating the impact of therapeutic services on student grades, attendance, and discipline encounters; (5) developing and implementing measures of student, teacher, and parent satisfaction with services; and (6) conducting a formal treatment outcome evaluation of the impact of therapeutic services on clinician-, parent-, teacher-, and student-rated behavioral functioning. These activities have been critically important in generating information to improve services, provide accountability data for funders, and discover what quality assessment and improvement activities are realistic for program staff given other demands. Findings from this work are also helping to develop important research avenues.

CONCLUDING COMMENTS AND FUTURE DIRECTIONS

Child and adolescent mental health is increasingly recognized as a priority within our nation. Given that no one agency, organization, or stakeholder could possibly address all youth mental health concerns, and given that each seeks to improve child psychosocial functioning and success in school, it is logical to pool resources and expertise. Collaboration at the system, agency, and stake-holder levels is necessary for effective school-based mental health program development, implementation, and evaluation. While the process of engaging and maintaining collaborative initiatives can be arduous and time consuming, the benefits, including greater support and commitment, improved accountability, opportunities for enhanced advocacy, improved service delivery, greater consumer satisfaction, and increased resources, easily outweigh the required effort. While school-based mental health care has grown in the last 20 years, research related to best practices in collaboration within the field lags far behind. Programs that are able to create effective collaborative initiatives should consider creating dissemination plans that will allow them to share effective collaborative practices with one another. Such sharing of information could help programs develop guidelines related to partnering to advance expanded school mental health, for example, helping to answer questions such as "What form of collaboration is needed?," "When should the collaboration occur?," "How should it occur?," "Which stake-holders and agencies should be included?," "What strategies work best in different communities?" This knowledge base will help enhance partnerships and create more efficient and effective models of mental health service delivery in schools.

REFERENCES

Acosta, O. M., Tashman, N. A., Prodente, C., & Proescher, E. (2002). Implementing successful school mental health programs: Guideline and recommendations. In H. Ghuman, M. Weist, & R. Sarles (Eds.), *Providing mental health services to youth where they are: School and other community-based approaches* (pp. 57–74). New York: Taylor Francis.

Acosta, O. M., Weist, M. D., Lopez, F. A., Shafer, M. E., & Pizarro, L. J. (in press). Assessing the mental health and academic needs of Latino youth. *Behavior Modification.*

Adelman, H. S., Taylor, L., Weist, M. D., Adelsheim, S., Freeman, B., Kapp, L., Lahti, M., & Mawn, D. (1999). Mental health in schools: A federal initiative. *Children Services: Social Policy, Research, and Practice, 2,* 99–119.

Adelsheim, S. (2000). Addressing barriers to development and learning: School, family, community, and agency partnerships in New Mexico. *Counseling and Human Development, 32,* 1–12.

Adelsheim, S., Carrillo, C., & Coletta, E. (2001). Developing school health in a rural state: The New Mexico school mental health initiative. *Child and Adolescent Psychiatric Clinics of North America, 10*(1), 151–159.

Annie E. Casey Foundation (2001). *Kids count data book.* Baltimore, MD: Author.

Brandon, P. R., & Wang, Z. (1994). Teacher involvement in school-conducted needs assessments. *Evaluation Review, 18*(4), 458–471.

Bruner, C. (1991). *Thinking collaboratively: Ten questions and answers to help policy makers improve children's services.* Washington, DC: Education and Human Services Consortium.

Christenson, S. L., & Conoley, J. C. (1992). *Home-school collaboration: Enhancing children's academic and social competence.* Silver Spring, MD: National Association of School Psychologists.

Dryfoos, J. G. (1994). *Full service schools.* San Francisco: Jossey–Bass.

Dryfoos, J. G., Brindis, C., & Kaplan, D. W. (1996). Research and evaluation in school-based health care. *Adolescent Medicine: State of the Art Reviews, 7*(2), 207–220.

Dwyer, K. P., & Bernstein, R. (1998). Mental health in the schools: 'Linking islands of hope in a sea of despair.' *School Psychology Review, 27*(2), 277–287.

Flaherty, L., Garrison, E., Waxman, R., Uris, P., Keys, S., Glass-Siegel, M., & Weist, M. (1998). Optimizing the roles of school mental health professionals. *Journal of School Health, 68*(10), 420–424.

Flaherty, L., & Weist, M. D. (1999). School-based mental health services: The Baltimore models. *Psychology in the Schools, 36,* 379–389.

Friend, M., & Cook, L. (1990). Collaboration as a predictor for success in school reform. *Journal of Educational and Psychological Consultation, 1*(1), 69–86.

Gardner, S. (1989). Failure by fragmentation. *California Tomorrow, Fall,* 20–21.

Golden, O. (1991). Collaboration as a means, not an end: Serving disadvantaged families and children. In L. B. Schorr, D. Both, et al. (Eds.), *Effective services for young children: Report of a workshop* (pp. 84–101). Washington, DC: National Academy Press.

Goldman, H., & Intriligator, B. A. (1990). *Factors that enhance collaboration among education, health, and social service agencies.* Paper presented at the 1990 Annual Meeting of the American Educational Research Association.

Gray, B. (1989). *Collaborating: Finding common ground for multiparity problems.* San Francisco: Jossey–Bass.

Haynes, N. M., & Comer, J. P. (1996). Integrating schools, families, and communities through successful school reform: The school development program. *School Psychology Review, 25*(4), 501–506.

Henderson, A. T., Marburger, C. L., & Ooms, T. (1986). *Beyond the bake sale: An educator's guide to working with parents.* Columbia, MD: The National Committee for Citizens in Education.

Hendrickson, J. M., & Omer, D. (1995). School-based comprehensive services: An example of interagency collaboration. In P. Adams & K. Nelson (Eds.), *Reinventing human services: Community- and family-centered practice* (pp. 145–162). Hawthorne, NY: Aldine de Gruyter.

Himmelman, A. T. (1993, July). *Helping each other help others: Principles and practices of collaboration. ARCH Factsheet Number 25.* Washington, DC: ARCH.

Hodges, S., Nesman, T., & Hernandez, M. (1999). Promising practices: Building collaboration in systems of care. *Systems of care: Promising practices in children's mental health, 1998 series, Volume VI.* Washington, DC: Center for Effective Collaboration and Practice, American Institutes for Research.

Jamieson, A., Curry, A., & Martinez, G. (2001). School enrollment in the United States—Social and economic characteristics of students. *Current population reports.* Washington DC: U.S. Census Bureau.

Knoff, H. M. (1996). The interface of school, community, and health care reform: Organizational directions toward effective services for children and youth. *School Psychology Review, 25*(4), 446–464.

Kretzmann, J., & McKnight, J. (1993). *Building communities from the inside out: A path toward finding and mobilizing a community's assets.* Chicago: ACTA Publications.

Lippitt, R., & Van Til, J. (1981). Can we achieve a collaborative community? Issues, imperatives, potentials. *Journal of Voluntary Action Research, 10*(3–4), 7–17.

Macbeth, G. (1993). Collaboration can be elusive: Virginia's experience in developing an interagency system of care. *Administration and Policy in Mental Health, 20,* 259–282.

Magrab, P. R., Young, T., & Waddell, A. (1985). *Developing collaborative services for seriously emotionally disturbed children.* Washington, DC: Georgetown University Child Development Center.

Melaville, A. I., & Blank, M. J. (1991). *What it takes: Structuring interagency partnerships to connect children and families with comprehensive services.* Washington, DC: Education and Human Services Consortium.

Nabors, L. A., & Reynolds, M. W. (2000). Program evaluation activities: Outcomes related to treatment for adolescents receiving school-based mental health services. *Children's Services: Social Policy, Research, and Practice, 3*(3), 175–189.

Nabors, L. A., Weist, M. D., Holden, E. W., & Tashman, N. A. (1999). Quality service provision in children's mental health care. *Children's Services: Social Policy, Research and Practice, 2*(2), 57–79.

Nabors, L. A., Weist, M. D., & Tashman, N. A. (1999). Focus groups: A valuable tool for assessing male and female adolescent perceptions of school-based mental health services. *Journal of Gender, Culture, and Health, 4*(1), 39–48.

Nabors, L. A., Weist, M. D., Tashman, N. A., & Myers, C. P. (1998). Quality assurance and school-based mental health services. *Psychology in the Schools, 36*(6), 485–493.

National Assembly of National Voluntary Health and Social Welfare Organizations (1991). *The community collaboration manual.* Washington, DC: Author.

National Network for Collaboration (1995). *Collaboration framework—Addressing community capacity.* Cooperative State Research, Education, and Extension Service, USDA. Retrieved November 30, 2001, from http://www.cyfernet.org/nnco/framework.html.

Powell, S. R. (2000). *The power of positive peer influence: Leadership training for today's teens.* Retrieved March 3, 2002, from http://www.princetonleadership.org/peerinfluence.html.

Powell, W. W., Koput, K. W., & Smith-Doerr, L. (1996). Interorganizational collaboration and the locus of innovation: Networks of learning and biotechnology. *Administrative Science Quarterly, 41,* 116–145.

Prodente, C., Sander, M., Hathaway, A., Sloane, T., & Weist, M. (2002). Children's mental health: Partnering with the faith community. In H. S. Ghuman, M. D. Weist, & R. M. Sarles (Eds.), *Providing mental health services to youth where they are: School-and other community-based approaches* pp. 209–224. New York: Taylor-Francis.

Prodente, C., Sander, M., & Weist, M. (in press). Furthering Support for Expanded School-Based Mental Health Programs. *Children's Services; Social Policy, Research, and Practice.*

Roberts, M. C. (1994). Models for service delivery in children's mental health: Common characteristics. *Journal of Clinical Child Psychology, 23,* 212–219.

Rosenblum, L., DiCecco, M. B., Taylor, L., & Adelman, H. S. (1995). Upgrading school support programs through collaboration: Resource coordinating teams. *Social Work Education, 17,* 117–124.

Schorr, L. (1988). *Within our reach: Breaking the cycle of disadvantage.* New York: Doubleday/Anchor Press.

Skiba, R., Polsgrove, L., & Nasstrom, K. (1996). *Developing a system of care: Collaboration for students with emotional/behavioral disorders.* Reston, VA: The Council for Children with Behavioral Disorders.

Taylor, L., & Adelman, H. S. (2000). Connecting schools, families, and communities. *Professional School Counseling, 3*(5), 298–307.

Tuma, J. M. (1989). Mental health services for children: The state of threat. *American Psychologist, 44,* 188–198.

U.S. Department of Education (1996). Putting the pieces together: Comprehensive school-linked strategies for children and families. Washington, DC: author.

U.S. Department of Health and Human Services (1999). *Mental health: A report of the Surgeon General.* Rockville, MD: U.S. Department of Health and Human Services, Substance Abuse and Mental Health Services Administration, Center for Mental Health Services, National Institutes of Health, National Institute of Mental Health.

Wagner, M., Golan, S., Shaver, D., Newman, L., Weschsler, M., & Kelley, F. (1994). *A healthy start for California's children and families: Early findings from a statewide evaluation of school-linked services.* Menlo Park, CA: SRI International.

Waxman, R., Weist, M., & Benson, D. (1999). Toward collaboration in the growing education-mental health interface. *Clinical Psychology Review, 19*(2), 239–253.

Weiss, J. A. (1981). Substance vs. symbol in administrative reform: The case of human services coordination. *Policy Analysis* (Winter), 20–45.

Weissbourd, R. (1990). Making the system work for poor children. Unpublished paper prepared for the Executive Session on Making the System Work for Poor Children.

Weist, M. D. (1997). Expanded school mental health services: A national movement in progress. In T. H. Ollendick & R. J. Prinz (Eds.), *Advances in clinical child psychology* (pp. 319–352). New York: Plenum.

Weist, M. D., Myers, C. P., Danforth, J., McNeil, D. W., Ollendick, T. H., & Hawkins, R. (2000). Expanded school mental health services: Assessing needs relate to school level and geography. *Community Mental Health Journal, 36,* 259–274.

Weist, M. D., Nabors, L. A., Myers, C. P., & Armbruster, P. (2000). Evaluation of expanded school mental health programs: *Community Mental Health Journal, 36*(4), 395–412.

Wolf, E. M., Yung, B. R., & Cotton, K. L. (1994). Collaborative needs assessment for child mental health program development. *Journal of Mental Health Administration, 21*(2), 161–169.

III

School Mental Health in Context

12

School-Based Mental Health Services in Urban Communities

MARC S. ATKINS, STACY L. FRAZIER, JALEEL ABDUL ADIL, and ELIZABETH TALBOTT

The large gap between efficacy and effectiveness research has resulted in a new consensus regarding the need for research that will inform practice (National Institute of Mental Health, 1999; Weisz, 2000). Epidemiological studies indicate that fewer than 20% of children who need mental health care actually receive any services (Goodman et al., 1997). Earlier studies indicated that of those children who did receive services, fewer than 50% received the appropriate service relative to their need (Kazdin, 1996). These realities have led to two important movements in child mental health services: efforts to increase the effectiveness of services principally by advocating evidence-based treatments (Hibbs & Jensen, 1997; Weisz, 2000) and calls for alternative models for mental health services (Burns, 1999; National Institute of Mental Health, 1999).

Nowhere are these efforts more needed than in urban, low-income communities where the unprecedented rise in community violence, poverty, and substance abuse places children at high risk of becoming perpetrators and/or victims of aggressive conduct (Attar, Guerra, & Tolan, 1995; Hess & Atkins, 1999). In fact, children in low-income, urban settings are exposed to violent crime rates that exceed the national average by 4 to 10 times (Gorman-Smith, Tolan, & Henry, 1999). For example, a recent survey in Baltimore indicated that 90% of students knew at least one victim of violence, 77% witnessed violence, and 47% reported victimization by violence (Weist, Acosta, & Youngstrom, 2001). The effects of increasing community violence, gang activity, drug use, and poverty place urban, minority children at substantial risk for mental health difficulties (Gorman-Smith et al., 1999).

MARC S. ATKINS, STACY L. FRAZIER, and JALEEL ABDUL ADIL • University of Illinois at Chicago, Chicago, Illinois 60680.   ELIZABETH TALBOTT • Institute for Juvenile Research, Chicago, Illinois 60612.

The effects of community violence on parents may also mediate the impact of community violence on children. Violence and poverty affect parents' ability to monitor and discipline their children consistently and to provide needed support and nurturance (Gorman-Smith et al., 2000). Inner-city children's exposure to violence predicted increases in aggression and depression at a 1-year follow-up, even after controlling for prior levels of these problems (Gorman-Smith & Tolan, 1998). However, family support moderated the effect of community violence, such that in families with high levels of parent–child conflict, high-witnessed violence had no additional influence on antisocial outcome (Miller et al., 1999).

With the advent of welfare reform, urban families have been facing these extraordinary pressures with the added strain of diminishing mental health services and community-based resources (Knitzer et al., 2001). A decade ago, a nationwide survey of parents found that those living in urban, low-income communities reported less than half the access to after-school programs as compared either to parents (either poor or nonpoor) living in nonurban communities or to nonpoor families living in urban communities (National Commission on Children, 1991). More recently, Halpern (1999) surveyed after-school programs in low-income communities and found that there were only enough programs to provide for fewer than one-third of families in need of services. The lack of community resources exacerbates the already pernicious effect of poverty by increasing parental burdens to provide for their children's safety (Jarrett, 1995). Not surprisingly, prevalence rates for children's disruptive behavior in low-income communities are almost three times the national estimates (Tolan et al., 1997), placing it among the most significant mental health problems in these communities (Bell, 1997).

The urgent and unique needs of low-income, urban families demand a response from the mental health community in the form of accessible, effective, culturally sensitive, and ecologically meaningful services. In this chapter we will present the case for how school-based services can overcome obstacles to services for urban communities and the rationale for a school-based services model focused on keeping children, parents, teachers, and community members invested in services that promote healthy outcomes. As we will describe, given the enormous mental health needs of children and families living in these communities, it is important that school-based services are integrated with more traditional social and clinical services to form a coordinated mental health services system.

LIMITATIONS OF MAINSTREAM MENTAL HEALTH SERVICES FOR INNER-CITY FAMILIES

Despite the large need for effective mental health services, children and families in urban communities remain a largely underserved population. Longitudinal studies in urban clinics indicate no-show rates of 50% or greater, with low-income, African American children experiencing particular problems in gaining access to programs (Kazdin, 1993). Furthermore, there is evidence that clinic-based mental health services are perceived by urban parents as insensitive to the needs of their children, suggesting that this dissatisfaction may account for high rates of attrition after the initial appointment (Pottick, Lerman, & Micchelli, 1992).

Fostering positive attitudes about mental health service providers and reducing stigma associated with mental health services have been identified as critical to the engagement of minority families in these services (e.g., Leaf et al., 1987). Underutilization has also been explained by concrete obstacles, such as inaccessible locations, lack of information about available services, and lack of social support (McKay, 2000). Thus, the overall consensus is that alternative models for mental health services that take into consideration the attitudes and obstacles experienced by urban families are necessary to successfully engage and retain inner-city families in services.

ECOLOGICAL MODELS FOR MENTAL HEALTH SERVICES

Research based on ecological models has found strong support for the cumulative effects of poverty, scarce community resources, and increased parental burdens on children's development and adaptation (Tolan & Guerra, 1998). Recent studies have established the central role of ecological factors on childhood conduct problems such as neighborhood context, school involvement, and family functioning (e.g., Gorman-Smith et al., 2000). The implication of these studies is to guide mental health services toward community-based, collaborative models (Tolan & Guerra, 1998). However, despite more than 30 years of research documenting the effectiveness of prevention and intervention programs to reduce disruptive school behavior (e.g., Cowen, 1997), school-based mental health programs in urban, low-income communities have failed to show enhanced effectiveness. This may be in large part because the prevailing treatment modality in school-based mental health programs is individual therapy or counseling (Weist, 1997), an ineffective strategy due to a shortage of mental health providers and the lack of evidence for counseling as an effective intervention for children's mental health difficulties (Adelman & Taylor, 1999; Atkins et al., 1998).

In response to the inadequacy of counseling-focused, school-based, mental health programs for urban low-income families, school-based models need to expand their focus to adapt services to the needs and competencies of teachers, parents, and children in order to capitalize on schools' unique opportunities to provide mental health-promoting activities for children in these communities (Atkins et al., 1998). We propose four key foci for school-based mental health programs in urban communities: (1) focus on children's academic performance, (2) teacher collaboration and support, (3) parental involvement, and (4) reliance on indigenous resources. The rationale for each goal will follow.

FOCUS ON ACADEMIC PERFORMANCE

There is considerable evidence that children's schooling plays a critical role in their adjustment. For example, children evidencing disruptive behavior disorders are at high risk for poor school adjustment (Willcutt & Pennington, 2000), and low participation in academic tasks is predictive of oppositional behavior (Finn & Cox, 1992). Intensive educational interventions have been shown to reduce aggression as a function of increased achievement (Kellam et al., 1998). In addition, in a study of urban, African American families, academic self-esteem and academic achievement were protective factors for negative life events and for youth perceptions of family conflicts (Spencer et al., 1993). Thus, success in school is clearly associated with positive mental health and well-being for students, and this association may be particularly salient for urban students (Gorman-Smith et al., 1999). In a recent study of African American adolescents from low-income Chicago neighborhoods, youth *without* mental health problems reported substantial academic support from teachers, parents, and school staff, suggesting the importance of these positive links for all children (Talbott & Fleming, 2001).

These associations suggest that providing students with access to high-quality instruction is an important mental health goal. Mental health staff can help to support students' academic goals by keeping abreast of their academic progress through sensitive measures of student performance, such as curriculum-based assessment (Shapiro, 1996), and by providing support for the use of effective instructional methods by teachers (Fuchs & Fuchs, 1998). These supportive activities may require additional training for mental health staff, but they could also help to foster better opportunities for collaboration between mental health staff and teachers. Because enhancing academic performance is the primary task of teachers, the association between academic learning and disruptive classroom behavior establishes a logical rationale for teachers to collaborate with mental health staff.

An example of an academic intervention that can benefit from collaboration from mental health staff is peer tutoring (Fuchs & Fuchs, 1997). Student pairs are matched according to ability level and engaged in exercises designed to improve oral reading and comprehension, with the combined goal to both improve reading and build supportive peer relationships (Mastropieri et al., 2000). This requires that mental health staff learn curriculum-based assessment procedures to help teachers identify appropriate tutoring goals and to track the progress of the intervention (Shapiro, 1996).

There are several advantages to this approach. Peer tutoring provides students with access to one-to-one instruction, as well as valuable opportunities to ask questions, receive corrective feedback, maintain academic engagement, and sustain on-task behavior (Mastropieri et al., 2000). Results of peer tutoring research reveal that both tutors and tutees not only improve their academic performance but also improve in social functioning and social responsibility and enjoy tutoring each other (Heller & Fantuzzo, 1993; Utley, Mortweet, & Greenwood, 1997). Therefore, peer tutoring is in many ways a hallmark mental health program that capitalizes on indigenous resources in schools to support students.

Teacher Collaboration and Support

In a meta-analysis of influences on student learning in inner-city schools, Wang, Haertel, and Walberg (1997) found 22 factors associated with learning. Classroom management exerted the largest influence on learning, followed by home environment and parental support, student–teacher social interactions, and peer group support; each of these had a greater influence on learning than did quality of instruction and school culture. The mental health literature has also found that teachers' behavior management practices, such as reinforcement for positive behavior and appropriate negative consequences for inappropriate behavior, are important predictors of student on-task behavior and academic performance (Hawkins, 1997) and that positive student–teacher relationships are associated with students' attachment to school and achievement (Baker, 1999). Therefore, the most successful interventions for students with behavioral difficulties at school rely on teachers to implement classroom-based contingency management programs (Cohen & Fish, 1993).

However, many teachers hold largely negative attitudes toward the use of behavior management programs. For example, in a recent survey of 900 Chicago public school educators, 200 of whom were classroom teachers, only 25% of teachers reported that classroom-based interventions were usually or always effective for students with ADHD (Graczyk et al., 2002).The generally negative view that many teachers hold regarding classroom-based behavior management programs probably reflects the failure of these programs to account for the realities of teaching such as the many competing demands in classrooms and the limited resources (Fantuzzo & Atkins, 1992). This view may also reflect a lack of training and support for general education teachers who work with students with behavioral difficulties (Scruggs & Mastropieri, 1996). Realities associated with teaching and lack of training are only exacerbated in urban, low-income schools, where teachers and students struggle to manage the enormous stressors associated with inner-city living (Boyd & Shouse, 1997).

Social Diffusion Theory

A new model for consultation to teachers is suggested by social diffusion theory which proposes that key opinion leaders influence the dissemination of novel information through a social network (Valente, 1996). We are examining the applicability of this model in Chicago inner-city public schools through a study in which peer-nominated teacher opinion leaders are paired with community-based mental health providers on behalf of students diagnosed with ADHD. Teacher key opinion leaders (KOL) and community-based mental health providers will obtain knowledge of evidence-based practices for students with ADHD via a Web-based course. Upon completion of the course, KOL teachers and mental health providers will work collaboratively to recommend classroom-based interventions for students with ADHD in grades 1–4. A comparison group in matched schools will provide evidence-based training to mental health providers via the Web-based course but these providers will *not* be teamed with teacher opinion leaders. We hypothesize that teachers in KOL schools will show more positive attitudes toward educational and mental health services, will make greater use of recommended classroom accommodations for ADHD students, and will evidence greater parental involvement and improved academic and social behavior for students. Results from this study could suggest new strategies for mental health consultation to urban schools.

Models of School Reform

To address the difficulty of implementing school-based mental health services, large-scale, schoolwide programs have been suggested which attempt to address school-level barriers to mental health service use (e.g., Adelman & Taylor, 1999). These comprehensive models provide an important guide for future development but are problematic in regard to the substantial resources needed for implementation and to the extent to which mental health needs of children are addressed. As Weisz, Han, and Valeri (1997) noted in regard to the Fort Bragg study investigating a coordinated care model of mental health service delivery (Bickman, 1996), a focus on comprehensive models often neglects attention to the quality of services offered.

Furthermore, whereas school reform movements have inspired renewed hope for urban schools, there is less evidence that these reforms are sufficient to impact children with mental health difficulties, especially for children living in urban communities. Historically, school reforms have been difficult to implement and often conflict on key goals. For example, there is no clear consensus on how to define school climate, in part because of the failure of any climate measure to predict school performance reliably, and many of these characteristics are not easily amenable to intervention, especially by mental health staff who lack the authority and resources to effect such changes (Boyd & Shouse, 1997).

The lack of agreement on the optimal features of school climate that promote children's social adaptation to school and the variety of factors associated with school climate suggest that successful mental health services in urban schools must be responsive to the range of conditions that may inhibit mental health service utilization. Collaboration with teachers is important to overcome inconsistent implementation of school-based mental health programs and to enhance the integration of services into ongoing school routines (Adelman, 1996; Hoagwood, 2000). Designing services that are "teacher-centered and classroom-based" (Fantuzzo & Atkins, 1992) may enable teachers to collaborate effectively with mental health service providers in response to the urgent and large need for mental health services in urban schools. In addition, teacher-directed services are the norm in urban schools, in part because mental health specialists are unavailable to teachers due to their preoccupation with the provision of direct services to relatively few students (Adelman & Taylor, 1998). Therefore, community-based mental health staff support to teacher-directed programs can provide an important resource that is often unavailable in urban schools.

PARENTAL INVOLVEMENT

Parental involvement in support of children's academic functioning and behavioral performance in both school and home settings are often-mentioned academic and mental health goals (e.g., Gorman-Smith et al., 1999). In fact, empirical support for increasing parental involvement in children's schooling is based on over two decades of research that links parental involvement to positive academic performance (Henderson & Berla, 1994) and improved mental health (Gorman-Smith et al., 1999). However, inner-city, African American parents remain a largely untapped resource for addressing the academic and mental health needs of urban children. Low participation rates by urban, minority parents at formally sanctioned school activities represent an ongoing concern for educators and school-based mental health providers and may relate to parents' frustration regarding limited input into their children's education (Connors & Epstein, 1995; Harry, Allen, & McLaughlin, 1995).

There is also evidence that low-income parents of color might experience unique obstacles to involvement at school. These include concerns regarding the lack of confidentiality in school-based services, prior negative experiences with school staff, perceived negative attitudes by school staff, concerns regarding their abilities to provide educational assistance to their children, and perceptions of racism or clashes regarding cultural values (e.g., Connell, Spencer, & Aber, 1994). Conversely, there is increasing evidence that inner-city parents will join parental involvement activities that are perceived as responsive to their concerns and abilities. Positive attitudes toward education and schools and confidence in their child's academic abilities are associated with parental involvement in children's schooling (Connors & Epstein, 1995). Low-income, minority parents are often eager to be involved in their children's education but may lack the knowledge of ways to be involved at home or at school (Chavkin & Williams, 1993).

Other researchers have criticized traditional definitions of parental involvement, including attendance at school events, workshops, PTA meetings, and academic conferences, as not adequately representing the involvement of parents of color in their children's lives. For example, in a study involving parents of low-income, African American sixth and eighth graders, 61% of parents did not attend school events, although 86% of students reported that their parents helped them with their homework (Chavkin & Williams, 1993). In a recent reexamination of the National Education Longitudinal Study (NELS) data, Stone and McKay (in press) identified four types of parental involvement with a sample of 4276 parents of students attending urban public elementary schools: (1) home–school communication, (2) volunteering, (3) setting school-related rules at home, and (4) discussing school-related concerns. Similarly, others have noted the importance of parents' reading to children, ensuring that children have proper school supplies, monitoring the amount of sleep that children get, and supporting the child in arriving at school on time (e.g., Epstein & Lee, 1995). Activities included in these expanded definitions of parental involvement may play a crucial role in the academic, social, and emotional success of children and are therefore important targets for school-based mental health services.

Little research has focused on the specific influence of cultural values and perceptions of racism in relation to the involvement activities or parenting strategies of low-income parents of color (Jarrett, 1995). Yet, emerging research suggests that African American parents adjust their parenting practices to buffer youth from the impact of racism (Stevenson et al., 1995), suggesting the need to modify mainstream parental involvement programs to be more responsive to these distinct values and practices. McKay et al. (in press) examined how racial socialization (i.e., Afrocentrism, religiosity) may mediate the relationship between at-home and at-school parental involvement. Results indicated that parental perceptions of racism predicted *higher* reports of at-home parental involvement and *lower* reports of at-school involvement. The authors recommended increased efforts to bridge a cultural gap between parents and teachers in inner-city communities.

Evidence from our initial study of a model for school-based mental health services provided support for a broadly defined parental involvement program (Atkins, Adil, Jackson, Talbott, et al., 2001). Extensive efforts to recruit and engage families in services resulted in initial recruitment rates above 90%, and of those 60 families, 86% remained involved in services at 9-month follow-up (Atkins et al., 2001). Because only about half of the families attended one or more parent groups, and fewer than a third attended sessions regularly, all families received home-based services in addition to consultation with the child's teacher and other school-based interventions, such as academic tutoring. In contrast, of the 36 families randomly assigned to a control group "services as usual" condition, only 2 of 24 families who agreed to enter services received any services at all. In each case, the child received one session for medication evaluation with no follow-up. These results suggest that a flexible model for service delivery, along with intensive outreach to parents, are effective strategies for overcoming barriers to services for families living in urban low-income communities.

RELIANCE ON INDIGENOUS RESOURCES

Community Collaborators

During the past few decades there has been expanding interest in the incorporation of community members as mental health service providers in low-income communities as a means to enhance the availability of services, reduce stigmatization, increase accessibility, and reduce cost. In addition to these benefits, change that takes place without the help of an "expert" may create a sense of personal empowerment to help maintain the change (Christensen & Jacobson, 1994). Community members who share certain demographic characteristics with the target population may be more likely to influence behavior change due to their shared experiences, opportunities for natural empathy, and reduced social distance (Hiatt, Sampson, & Baird, 1997). Similarly, paraprofessionals or "indigenous therapists" who have either conquered similar problems or triumphed in equally challenging circumstances may be perceived as realistic role models by clients (Nielsen, 1995). Given these advantages, paraprofessionals may be more likely to overcome the multiple barriers to mental health service use that often keep inner-city families from accessing mental health services.

Two models have emerged for the incorporation of community members into service provider roles. The "paraprofessional model" uses community volunteers with little formal education who are trained extensively and supervised closely to perform clinical duties in high-risk communities. A successful example is the Parent–Child Assistance Program in Seattle, Washington, a paraprofessional home visitation model targeting high-risk, poly-substance-abusing mothers for 3 years beginning with the birth of their first child (Grant, Ernst, & Streissguth, 1999). The program has experienced positive outcomes for clients with regard to drug treatment and recovery, family planning, child well-being, and linkage to social services. They attribute much of their success to particular characteristics of the advocates themselves, including shared history with clients and subsequent personal achievements, empathy, persistence, problem-solving skills, a direct but nonjudgmental approach, and the shared conviction that each client has value and promise regardless of her past history.

The second model is the "collaborative model" in which community members work with clinical researchers to design and implement educational and mental health services that are ecologically meaningful and acceptable to consumers. Compared to the paraprofessional model in which community members are trained to follow an existing protocol, the collaborative model invites community partners to provide information that would not otherwise be available to mental health staff, including knowledge of neighborhood strengths and needs, familiarity with local resources, and advice regarding which program elements would be acceptable to and utilized by their communities (McCormick et al., 2000). In one innovative HIV prevention program in Chicago, a collaborative board was established consisting of community parents, school staff, and university-based researchers to oversee the design, implementation, and evaluation of the program (Madison et al., 2000). Based on this literature, we have been studying the role of community members in the development and implementation of our school mental health program since its inception (Frazier et al., 2002). Our goal is to study the influence of community consultants on the development of effective and culturally sensitive mental health services for families living in inner-city communities.

Links to School District Initiatives

Coincident with diminishing community resources and escalating child and family problems, schools serving urban, low-income communities are under unprecedented scrutiny and surveillance to be accountable for the academic performance of their students. In most urban school districts, school reform policies have been enacted that place schools on probation if achievement scores are persistently low, which triggers a series of interventions directed to improving teaching and school management. For example, in Chicago, "zero-tolerance" policies in place since 1997 have resulted in a more than 800% increase in expulsions from 1997 to 1999, to nearly 700 per year (Chicago Public Schools, 1999). Bans on "social promotion" have resulted in dramatic increases in grade retention. Social promotion is a much-maligned educational procedure with poor empirical support including evidence that it is overused with low-income, African American male students (Owings & Magliaro, 1998). Children with learning or behavioral difficulties are least likely to benefit from these programs. For these children, either expulsion or grade retention offers no advantages and may exacerbate their difficulties (Atkins et al., 2001). Furthermore, these policies are often perceived by teachers as blaming them for the students' difficulties which further escalates already chronic problems of negativity and stress (Boyd & Shouse, 1997).

Therefore, an additional goal for school-based mental health services is the need to link mental health services with school district initiatives to enhance mental health promotion. Most urban school districts have many initiatives that link with mental health, such as programs regarding special education referrals and placement, violence prevention, inclusion, parental involvement, and teacher support. Schools are required to develop plans for each of these needs. For example, in Chicago, a school-based problem-solving program has been implemented districtwide to provide teachers with practical strategies for classroom management issues and students with remedial education to address academic deficits that are not related to a learning disability. However, whereas districts provide considerable support to schools in the selection of programs, support for implementation is less available, and therefore programs are implemented with varying fidelity. Often mental health providers are not aware of such initiatives in the schools and at times recommend programs that compete with existing schoolwide initiatives. Developing a model for effective linkages between mental health programs and school district initiatives requires considerable expertise in education and program development that is often beyond the expertise of mental health providers. Therefore, collaboration between mental health programs and educators in schools or universities is often necessary to build and sustain effective linkages with school district initiatives.

Recently, in collaboration with the Chicago Public Schools, the Illinois State Board of Education, and the Illinois State Department of Mental Health, we have begun to study the implementation of a comprehensive program focused on the academic and mental health needs of students and their families living in urban, low-income communities. The program combines a model for school reform, Positive Behavior Intervention and Support (Horner et al., 2001), Chicago Public Schools' School-Based Problem-Solving Program, and our model for mental health consultation in urban schools (Atkins et al., 2001). Key questions of the study are the effectiveness of the program on the development of classroom-based supports for students' academic and behavioral goals and of parental involvement. A key hypothesis is that the involvement of community-based mental health providers will enable schools to accommodate students with moderate and high mental health needs, an often-neglected population for school reform programs (Adelman & Taylor, 1999; Atkins et al., 1998).

Collaboration with Community-Based Programs

Children's involvement in after-school programs and family involvement in socially supportive activities in the community are also strongly associated with positive outcomes (Morrison et al., 2000). For families with children evidencing disruptive behavior problems, social isolation is common and associated with poor long-term prognosis (Atkins & McKay, 2000). In addition, these children often present with behavior problems that risk their attendance in or limit the advantages offered by after-school programs. Thus, an important goal for mental health providers is to educate program staff regarding children's psychosocial needs as well as to provide consultation on behavior management issues.

By supporting community-based after-school programs or other neighborhood resources available to children and families, mental health programs can provide direct relief to families and also help to lessen the burden on schools to provide for the social service needs of children and families. Inner-city communities are undergoing vast changes associated with gentrification and abandonment of public housing. As families are relocated throughout the city, few resources are allocated for their support. This leaves the burden on schools to provide for the enormous social and emotional needs of the families and children. However, although schools can and do provide many socially supportive opportunities for children and families, they are often plagued by some of the same barriers that interfere with families' use of mental health services, such as poor communication between staff and parents, and parents' perceptions of stigma associated with discussions of their child's school difficulties (Adelman & Taylor, 1999; Boyd & Shouse, 1997). Thus, it would be unwise to rely on schools to provide for all the social service needs of children and families, and therefore mental health support for community-based social service programs can be an important element in supporting schools.

CONCLUSION

The development and implementation of accessible and effective school-based mental health services respond to several policy mandates and urban school reform initiatives for children's services, including the need for least restrictive services, greater coordination among service systems, greater linkages to existing community resources, parental involvement, and flexible and individualized support. Based on our work to date, we have recognized the need to specify more clearly linkages with community-based programs and also the need for guidelines for intensive home-based services (e.g., Burns et al., 2000; Evans & Armstrong, 2002). These modifications acknowledge the strain on schools, families, and after-school programs to provide for the needs of children and families and the need for mental health services to support caretakers and educators in these normative settings. In addition, each of these settings will be strained by the needs of children exhibiting disruptive behavior which requires additional expertise from mental health providers.

Extensive examination of the cultural context and perceptions of low-income, urban families is a particularly important task for those serving low-income, urban, African Americans, who historically display mistrust of mainstream institutions. While often neglected by traditional mental health agencies and professionals, racial identity and sociopolitical awareness among urban African Americans have historically been mobilizing forces in individual and community development and can be resources to cultivate ecologically sensitive services for children and families. In light of the nationally recognized need for reorganization of child mental health services (http://www.surgeongeneral.gov/library/mentalhealth), there is an opportunity for school-based services to develop a new standard of care for the delivery of effective services for children and families living in urban, low-income communities.

REFERENCES

Adelman, H. (1996). Restructuring education support and integrating community resources: Beyond the full service school model. *School Psychology Review, 25,* 431–445.

Adelman, H., & Taylor, L. (1998). Reframing mental health in schools and expanding school reform. *Educational Psychologist, 33,* 135–152.

Adelman, H., & Taylor, L. (1999). Mental health in schools and system restructuring. *Clinical Psychology Review, 19,* 137–163.

Atkins, M., Adil, J., Jackson, M., McKay, M., & Bell, C. (2001). An ecological model for school-based mental health services. *13th annual conference proceedings: A system of care for children's mental health: Expanding the research base.* Tampa: University of South Florida.

Atkins, M., Adil, J. A., Jackson, M., Talbott, E., & Bell, C. C. (2001). PALS: An ecological approach to school-based mental health services in urban schools. *Report on Emotional & Behavioral Disorders in Youth, 1,* 75–77, 91–92.

Atkins, M., & McKay, M. (2000). Conduct disorder. In M. Hersen & V. Van Hasselt (Eds.), *Advanced abnormal psychology* (2nd ed., pp. 209–222). New York: Plenum.

Atkins, M., McKay, M., Arvanitis, P., London, L., Madison, S., Costigan, C., Haney P., Zevenbergen, A., Hess, L., Bennett, D., & Webster, D. (1998). An ecological model for school-based mental health services for urban low income aggressive children. *The Journal of Behavioral Health Services & Research, 5,* 64–75.

Atkins, M., McKay, M., Frazier, S. L., Jakobsons, L., Arvanitis, P., Cunningham, T., Brown, C., & Lambrecht, L. (2002). Suspensions and detentions in an urban, low-income school: Punishment or reward? *Journal of Abnormal Child Psychology, 30*, 361–371.

Attar, B., Guerra, N., & Tolan, P. (1995). Neighborhood disadvantage, stressful life events, and adjustment in urban elementary-school children. *Journal of Clinical Child Psychology, 23*, 391–400.

Baker, J. A. (1999). Teacher–student interaction in urban at-risk classrooms: Differential behavior, relationship quality, and student satisfaction with school. *Elementary School Journal, 100*, 57–70.

Bell, C. C. (1997). Community violence: Causes, prevention, and intervention. *Journal of the National Medical Association, 89*, 657–662.

Bickman, L. (1996). A continuum of care: More is not always better. *American Psychologist, 51*, 689–701.

Boyd, W., & Shouse, R. (1997). The problems and promise of urban schools. In H. Walberg, O. Reyes, & R. Weissberg (Eds.), *Children and youth: Interdisciplinary perspectives* (pp. 141–165). Thousand Oaks, CA: Sage.

Burns, B. J. (1999). A call for a mental health services research agenda for youth with serious emotional disturbance. *Mental Health Services Research, 1*, 5–20.

Burns, B., Schoenwald, S., Burchard, J., Faw, L., & Santos, A. (2000). Comprehensive community-based interventions for youth with severe emotional disorders: Multisystemic therapy and the wraparound process. *Journal of Child and Family Studies, 9*, 283–314.

Chavkin, N. F., & Williams, D. L. (1993). Minority parents and the elementary school: Attitudes and practice. In N. Chavkin (Ed.), *Families and schools in a pluralistic society* (pp. 73–84). Albany: State University of New York Press.

Chicago Public Schools (1999). *Annual report from the Office of Specialized Services.* Chicago: Author.

Christensen, A., & Jacobson, N. S. (1994). Who (or what) can do psychotherapy: The status and challenge of nonprofessional therapies. *Psychological Science, 5*, 8–13.

Cohen, J., & Fish, M. (1993). *Handbook of school-based interventions: Resolving student problems and promoting healthy educational environments.* San Francisco: Jossey–Bass.

Connell, J. P., Spencer, M. B., & Aber, J. L. (1994). Educational risk and resilience in African-American youth: Context, self, action, and outcomes in school. *Child Development, 65*, 493–506.

Connors, L. J., & Epstein, J. L. (1995). Parents and school partnerships. In M. H. Bornstein (Ed.), *Handbook of parenting, Vol. 4: Applied and practical parenting* (pp. 437–458). Mahwah, NJ: Erlbaum.

Cowen, E. L. (1997). Schools and the enhancement of children's wellness: Some opportunities and some limiting factors. In R. Weissberg & T. Gullotta (Eds.), *Healthy children 2010: Establishing preventive services* (Vol. 9, pp. 97–123). Thousand Oaks, CA: Sage.

Epstein, J., & Lee, S. (1995). National patterns of school and family connections in the middle grades. In B. Ryan, G. Adams, T. Gullotta, R. Weissberg, & R. Hampton (Eds.), *The family-school connection: Theory, research, and practice* (pp. 108–154). Thousand Oaks, CA: Sage.

Evans & Armstrong (2002). What is case management? In B. Burns & K. Hoagwood (Eds.), *Community treatment for youth. Evidence-based interventions for severe emotional and behavioral disorders* (pp. 39–68). New York, Oxford University Press.

Fantuzzo, J., & Atkins, M. S. (1992). Applied behavior analysis for education: Teacher centered and classroom based. *Journal of Applied Behavior Analysis, 25*, 35–42.

Finn, J. D., & Cox, D. (1992). Participation and withdrawal among fourth-grade pupils. *American Educational Research Journal, 29*, 141–162.

Frazier, S., Adil, J., Atkins, M., Gathright, T., & Jackson, M. (2002). *Community collaboration on PALS: Reflections, discoveries, and lessons learned.* Manuscript submitted for publication.

Fuchs, D., & Fuchs, L. S. (1997). Peer-assisted learning strategies: Making classrooms more responsive to diversity. *American Educational Research Journal, 34*, 174–206.

Fuchs, D., & Fuchs, L. S. (1998). Respecting the importance of science and practice: A pragmatic view. *Learning Disability Quarterly, 21*, 281–287.

Goodman, S., Lahey, B. B., Fielding, B., Dulcan, M., Narrow, W., & Regier, D. (1997). Representativeness of clinical samples of youths with mental disorders: A preliminary population-based study. *Journal of Abnormal Psychology, 106*, 3–14.

Gorman-Smith, D., & Tolan, P. H. (1998). The role of exposure to community violence and developmental problems among inner-city youth. *Development & Psychopathology, 10*, 101–116.

Gorman-Smith, D., Tolan, P. H., & Henry, D. B. (1999). The relations of community and family to risk among urban-poor adolescents. In P. Cohen & C. Slomkowski (Eds.), *Historical and geographical influences on psychopathology* (pp. 349–367). Mahway, NJ: Erlbaum.

Gorman-Smith, D., Tolan, P. H., Henry, D. B., & Florsheim, P. (2000). Patterns of family functioning and adolescent outcomes among urban African American and Mexican American families. *Journal of Family Psychology, 14,* 436–457.

Graczyk, P., Atkins, M., Jackson, M., Baumann, B., Kim, J., Letendre, J., McCoy, J., Harley, R., & Sykes, K. (2002). *Urban educators' attitudes about mental health services for students with ADHD.* Manuscript submitted for publication.

Grant, T. M., Ernst, C. C., & Streissguth, A. P. (1999). Intervention with high-risk alcohol and drug-abusing mothers: I. Administrative strategies of the Seattle model of paraprofessional advocacy. *Journal of Community Psychology, 27,* 1–18.

Halpern, R. (1999). After-school programs for low-income children: Promise and challenges. *The Future of Children, 9,* 81–95.

Harry, B., Allen, N., & McLaughlin, M. (1995). Communication versus compliance: African-American parents' involvement in special education. *Exceptional Children, 6,* 364–377.

Hawkins, J. D. (1997). Academic performance and school success: Sources and consequences. In R. Weissberg, T. Gullofta, R. Hampton, B. Ryan, & G. Adams (Eds.), *Enhancing children's wellness* (pp. 278–305). Thousand Oaks, CA: Sage.

Heller, L., & Fantuzzo, J. (1993). Reciprocal peer tutoring and parent partnership: Does parent involvement make a difference? *School Psychology Review, 22,* 517–534.

Henderson, A., & Berla, N. (1994). *A new generation of evidence: The family is critical to student achievement.* Washington, DC: National Committee for Citizens in Education.

Hess, L., & Atkins, M. (1998). Victims and aggressors at school: Teacher, self, and peer perceptions of psychosocial functioning. *Applied Developmental Science, 2,* 75–89.

Hiatt, S. W., Sampson, D., & Baird, D. (1997). Paraprofessional home visitation: Conceptual and pragmatic considerations. *Journal of Community Psychology, 25,* 77–93.

Hibbs, E. D., & Jensen, P. S. (1997). *Psychosocial treatments for child and adolescent disorders: Empirically based strategies for clinical practice.* Washington, DC: American Psychological Association.

Hoagwood, K. (2000). State of the evidence on school-based mental health services—NIMH perspectives. *Report on Emotional & Behavioral Disorders in Youth, 1,* 13–17.

Horner, R. H., Sugai, G., Lewis-Palmer, T., & Todd, A. W. (2001). Teaching school-wide behavioral expectations. *Report on Emotional & Behavioral Disorders in Youth, 1,* 77–79, 93–96.

Jarrett, R. (1995). Growing up poor: The family experience of socially mobile youth in low-income African American neighborhoods. *Journal of Adolescent Research, 10,* 111–135.

Kazdin, A. (1993). Premature termination from treatment among children referred for antisocial behavior. *Journal of Child Psychology & Psychiatry, 31,* 415–425.

Kazdin, A. (1996). Dropping out of child psychotherapy: Issues for research and implications for practice. *Clinical Child Psychology & Psychiatry, 1,* 133–156.

Kellam, S., Mayer, L., Rebok, G., & Hawkins, W. (1998). Effects of improving achievement on aggressive behavior and of improving aggressive behavior on achievement through two preventive interventions: An investigation of causal paths. In B. P. Dohrenwend (Ed.), *Adversity, stress, and psychopathology* (pp. 486–505). New York: Oxford University Press.

Knitzer, J., Yoshikawa, H., Cauthen, N., & Aber, L. (2001). Welfare reform, family support, and child development: Prespectives from policy analysis and developmental psychopathology. *Development & Psychopathology, 12,* 619–632.

Leaf, P., Bruce, M., Tischler, G., & Holzer, C. (1987). The relationship between demographic factors and attitudes toward mental health services. *Journal of Community Psychology, 15,* 275–284.

Madison, S., McKay, M., Paikoff, R., & Bell, C. (2000). Basic research and community collaboration: Necessary ingredients for the development of a family-based HIV prevention program. *AIDS Education and Prevention, 12*(4), 281–298.

Mastropieri, M., Spencer, V., Scruggs, T., & Talbott, E. (2000). Students with disabilities as tutors: An updated research synthesis. In T. Scruggs & M. Mastropieri (Eds.), *Advances in learning and behavioral disabilities* (Vol. 14, pp. 247–279). Greenwich, CT: JAI.

McCormick, A., McKay, M., Wilson, M., McKinney, L., Paikoff, R., Bell, C., Baptiste, D., Coleman, D., Gillming, G., Madison, S., & Scott, R. (2000). Involving families in an urban HIV preventive intervention: How community collaboration addresses barriers to participation. *AIDS Education and Prevention, 12,* 299–307.

McKay, M. M. (2000). What can we do to increase involvement of urban children and families in mental health services and prevention programs. *Report on Emotional & Behavioral Disorders in Youth, 1,* 11–20.

McKay, M., & Stone, S. (2000). Predictors of urban parent involvement. School Social Work Journal, 15, 12–28.

Miller, L. S., Wasserman, G. A., Neugebauer, R., Gorman-Smith, D., & Kamboukas, D. (1999). Witnessed community violence and antisocial behavior in high-risk, urban boys. Journal of Clinical Child Psychology, 28, 2–11.

Morrison, G., Storino, M., Robertson, L., Weissglass, T., & Dondero, A. (2000). The protective function of after-school programming and parent education and support for students at risk for substance abuse. Evaluation and Program Planning, 23, 365–371.

National Commission on Children (1991). Speaking of kids: A national survey of children and parents. Washington, DC: Author.

National Institute of Mental Health (1999). Bridging science and service: A report by the National Advisory Mental Health Council's Clinical Treatment and Services Research Workgroup. Washington, DC: Author.

Nielsen, B. A. (1995). Paraprofessionals: They can be competent, and there is more good news. Journal of Psychological Practice, 1, 133–140.

Owings, W. A., & Magliaro, S. (1998). Grade retention: A history of failure. Educational Leadership, 56, 86–88.

Pottick, K. J., Lerman, P., & Micchelli, M. (1992). Of problems and perspectives: Predicting the use of mental health services by parents of urban youth. Children & Youth Services Review, 14, 363–378.

Scruggs, T. M., & Mastropieri, M. A. (1996). Teacher perceptions of mainstreaming/inclusion, 1958–1995: A research synthesis. Exceptional Children, 63, 59–74.

Shapiro, E. S. (1996). Academic skills problems: Direct assessment and intervention. New York: Guilford Press.

Spencer, M. B., Cole, S. P., DuPree, D., Glymph, A., & Pierre, P. (1993). Self-efficacy among urban African American early adolescents: Exploring issues of risk, vulnerability, and resilience. Development and Psychopathology, 5, 719–739.

Stevenson, H., Davis, G., Weber, E., Wieman, D., & Abdul-Kabir, S. (1995). HIV prevention beliefs among urban African American youth. Journal of Adolescent Health, 16, 316–323.

Stone, S., & McKay, M. (in press). Predictors of urban parent involvement. School Social Work Journal.

Talbott, E., & Fleming, J. E. (2001). The role of social contexts and special education in the mental health problems of urban adolescents. Manuscript in preparation.

Tolan, P. H., Gorman-Smith, D., Huesmann, L. R., & Zelli, A. (1997). Assessing family process to explain risk for antisocial behavior and depression among urban youth. Psychological Assessment, 9, 212–223.

Tolan, P. H., & Guerra, N. (1998). Societal causes of violence against children. In P. K. Trickett & C. J. Schellenbach (Eds.), Violence against children in the family and the community (pp. 195–209). Washington, DC: American Psychological Association.

Utley, C., Mortweet, S. L., & Greenwood, C. R. (1997). Peer mediated instruction and interventions. Focus on Exceptional Children, 29, 1–23.

Valente, T. W. (1996). Social network thresholds in the diffusion of innovations. Social Networks, 18, 69–89.

Wang, M., Haertel, G., & Walberg, H. (1997). Fostering educational resliience in inner-city schools. In H. Walberg, O. Reyes, & R. Weissberg (Eds.), Children and youth: Interdisciplinary perspectives (pp. 119–140). Thousand Oaks, CA: Sage.

Weist, M. D. (1997). Expanded school mental health services: A national movement in progress. Advances in Clinical Child Psychology, 19, 319–352.

Weist, M. D., Acosta, O., & Youngstrom, E. (2001). Predictors of violence exposure among inner-city youth. Journal of Clinical Child Psychology, 30, 187–198.

Weisz, J. (2000). Agenda for child and adolescent psychotherapy research: On the need to put science into practice. Archives of General Psychiatry, 57, 837–838.

Weisz, J. R., Han, S. S., & Valeri, S. M. (1997). More of what? Issues raised by the Fort Bragg study. American Psychologist, 52, 541–545.

Willcutt, E., & Pennington, B. (2000). Psychiatric comorbidity in children and adolescents with reading disability. Journal of Child Psychology and Psychiatry, 41, 1039–1048.

13

The Mental Health for Immigrants Program

Program Design and Participatory Research in the Real World

BRADLEY D. STEIN, SHERYL KATAOKA,
LISA JAYCOX, ERIKA M. STEIGER, MARLEEN WONG,
ARLENE FINK, PIA ESCUDERO,
and CATALINA ZARAGOZA

TAKING THE INITIATIVE

Schools are increasingly becoming the primary source of a variety of services for children, especially disadvantaged and minority children. This is particularly true in the realm of mental health. The Surgeon General (U.S. Public Health Service, 2000) and others (Weist, 1997) have called for an increase in schools' capacity to meet children's mental health needs and for greater development of evidence-based treatments that can be disseminated and sustained in the community (U.S. Public Health Service, 2000; Weisz, 2000). The Los Angeles Unified School District (LAUSD) Mental Health Services Unit has taken a proactive stance in developing programs to address these issues.

One problem of substantial importance in the multicultural LAUSD is meeting the needs of new immigrants. There are estimated to be over 2.2 million

BRADLEY D. STEIN • University of Southern California, Los Angeles, California 90089. SHERYL KATAOKA • University of California, Los Angeles, Los Angeles, California 90095. LISA JAYCOX • RAND, Santa Monica, California 90407. ERIKA M. STEIGER, PIA ESCUDERO, and CATALINA ZARAGOZA • Los Angeles Unified School District Mental Health Services Unit, Van Nuys, CA 91406. MARLEEN WONG • National Center for Traumatic Stress, Los Angeles, California 90095. ARLENE FINK • University of California, Los Angeles, Los Angeles, California 90095.

school-aged newly immigrant children in the United States (Schmidley & Gibson, 1999), many of whom live under poor and overcrowded conditions (Hernandez & Darke, 1999). Immigrant parents seeking mental health care for their children face many barriers (Arroyo, 1998; Gong Guy, Cravens, & Patterson, 1991; Guarnaccia & Lopez, 1998; Kim, 1997), with the result that many do not receive necessary services (Munroe-Blum et al., 1989; Vega et al., 1999). These barriers include a lack of understanding of the U.S. mental health system, inadequate health insurance, and a shortage of culturally sensitive, bilingual mental health clinicians. Parents may also either misinterpret their children's psychological distress or fear the stigma of receiving mental health care (Arroyo, 1998; Gong Guy et al., 1991; Guarnaccia & Lopez, 1998; Kim, 1997).

To help these children, the LAUSD sought to develop and evaluate a mental health treatment appropriate for the school setting that would address a problem that all stakeholders, including teachers and immigrant parents, would recognize as being important. While other mental health issues are also relevant, the LAUSD Mental Health Services Unit, in consultation with school principals and administrators, chose to address the impact of violence on the mental health of immigrant children. The clinicians knew from experience that the stressful living situations of many poor immigrant families are associated with an increased risk of violence exposure (Coulton et al., 1995; Garbarino, 1995; Straussner & Straussner, 1997). Immigrants have often experienced political instability, social upheaval, and high rates of poverty and crime in their countries of origin (Partida, 1996), and the migration process itself may also be traumatic (Arroyo, 1998). Although immigrant children who have experienced traumatic events might need help in addressing their psychological distress, they often do not know where to turn (Guarnaccia & Lopez, 1998). Newly immigrant children enrolled in the LAUSD commonly receive a variety of services through the Emergency Immigrant Education Program (EIEP), such as orientation classes, medical and dental screening, language classes, and tutoring, but mental health services have not traditionally been offered.

The LAUSD Mental Health Services Unit wanted to develop and rigorously evaluate a mental health program that could be disseminated across the district if effective. Wanting this intervention to be evidence-based and thoroughly evaluated, yet responsive to the district's needs and limitations, school district officials sought to develop a partnership with clinician/researchers from RAND, the University of California, Los Angeles (UCLA), and the University of Southern California (USC). To guide this collaborative relationship, the Mental Health Services Unit and clinician/researchers chose to work together in the context of a participatory research partnership (Mittelmark, 1990), a model in which the knowledge and expertise of all collaborators is considered complementary. The focus is on the production of local knowledge to improve interventions and practice, and parties work together to educate each other (Macaulay et al., 1999). At its most effective, participatory research brings academic and community stakeholders together to benefit a community while producing generalizable knowledge (Macaulay et al., 1999). Participatory research has been offered as a framework for program development, evaluation, and dissemination that is well suited to schools (Stoiber & Kratochwill, 2000).

This partnership created the Mental Health for Immigrants Program (MHIP), with the school district serving as the senior partner, identifying both the problem (psychological sequelae of violence exposure) and the desired intervention setting (school-based mental health services). The academic partners assisted in the development of the clinical intervention and in the evaluation of the program's effectiveness.

DEVELOPING AN INNOVATIVE PROGRAM

The first task for the partnership was to determine what kind of treatment program would be most appropriate. The school district desired an intervention that (1) was empirically supported, (2) could serve as many children as possible with limited school resources, (3) would be consistent across schools, and (4) would be easy to disseminate if found to be effective. After examining several potential interventions with the academic partners, the school district chose to base the MHIP clinical intervention on the Cognitive–Behavioral Intervention for Trauma in Schools (CBITS) (Jaycox, 2000). The CBITS is an evidence-based clinical intervention designed to decrease depression and anxiety symptoms, particularly symptoms of posttraumatic stress disorder (PTSD). It is a group intervention that utilizes a detailed manual to train children in the following cognitive–behavioral skills and techniques: education about common reactions to trauma, relaxation training, cognitive restructuring for maladaptive thoughts, approach rather than avoidance of trauma-related cues, exposure to trauma memories through imagination and drawing, and social problem solving. Cognitive–behavioral therapy (CBT) was chosen for the student component of the program because of its effectiveness in reducing symptoms of both depression and PTSD (Cohen & Mannarino, 1996; Deblinger & Heflin, 1996; March et al., 1998; Pelcovitz & Kaplan, 1996), its effectiveness in group formats and educational settings, and its emphasis on a skills-building approach rather than on treatment per se. The eight-group CBT student sessions were complemented by several parent and teacher psychoeducational sessions. The detailed CBITS manual also allowed multiple school district personnel to be trained in this treatment while maintaining some degree of consistency across group leaders, facilitating future dissemination if appropriate.

The next task was to determine which schools and which students would participate. Due to funding restrictions, only recent immigrants, defined as having been in the United States less than 3 years, were eligible to receive services through the MHIP. Schools were targeted on the basis of having a large immigrant population, which resulted in students being drawn from relatively disadvantaged neighborhoods. First, a school district assistant superintendent introduced the MHIP to school administrators at a district meeting. Then the MHIP Clinical Director followed up with principals at elementary and middle schools selected by LAUSD Mental Health and Immigrant Education personnel. If school administrators expressed an interest in having their school participate, a presentation about the program and the effects of violence on children was made to school faculty as part of a staff development program. Of the 13 schools approached, 11 agreed to participate. Those that declined expressed concern about space limitations and about involving students in this nonacademic activity during school hours.

It was necessary to restrict the program to third to eighth graders given the cognitive level required to participate in the child component of the intervention, and the program was offered only to children and families whose native language was Spanish, Korean, Armenian, or Russian because of limited staffing resources.

The children were screened with the use of a questionnaire about recent and life-time violence exposure, symptoms of posttraumatic stress, and symptoms of depression. Parents of children who reported both significant violence exposure and symptoms in the clinical range for either PTSD or depression were then contacted to provide them with information about the MHIP intervention groups. At this time, written informed consent was obtained from parents, and assent was obtained from the children, for participation in the program.

This first contact was complicated by the circumstances of many of these families. As LAUSD staff anticipated, many of the parents of the recent immigrant children targeted for this program were poorly educated, and a number were functionally illiterate. The MHIP sought to address this by providing information to parents verbally as well as in writing. Bilingual and multicultural psychiatric social workers from the LAUSD Mental Health Services Unit were also responsible for reviewing all program materials to ensure that the content, language, and concepts were culturally appropriate and accurately translated into the relevant languages.

Another initial obstacle was that, although immigrant parents are concerned about the effects of violence exposure, they often do not recognize subsequent problems as being the psychological sequelae of these events (Garrison, Roy, & Azar, 1999), and this unrecognized need may present an important barrier to treatment. To address this often low perception of need, MHIP psychiatric social workers provided general information to all parents enrolled in the program about the effects of violence on children and encouraged parents to attend more in-depth parent education sessions.

By providing services directly on local school campuses, the MHIP sought to reduce the difficulties parents have in taking their children to treatment, such as lack of transportation. Home visits were also conducted by the social workers if necessary to meet with the parents. Because these parents were often unfamiliar with programs available to assist them, MHIP staff provided information about community mental health programs and social service agencies covering a wide array of services. Ongoing clinician contacts with the families and parent sessions were used to reinforce and support this attempt to overcome barriers faced by participants.

The intervention itself also needed to be adapted to the specific needs of these students. The CBITS intervention was modified for work with recent immigrant children in schools via feedback from the bilingual, multicultural psychiatric social workers. The school psychiatric social workers participated in a 2-day training and continued to receive ongoing supervision throughout the course of the clinical intervention. The modification process occurred over several months, both during training and as the first few groups were run in schools. The partnership worked to ensure that the clinical intervention could be easily delivered in schools, was appropriate for the treatment of traumatized immigrant children, yet continued to adhere to the core treatment elements. Modifications included reducing the time of each session to allow it to be delivered during a single school period, developing examples that were culturally appropriate and relevant for recent immigrants and developing a consensus on how to handle certain cultural issues. For instance, several children in the program complained of seeing spirits or ghosts of deceased relatives, and the psychiatric social workers reached consensus on how they would handle these disclosures in the groups.

Modifications also occurred during implementation, as the school and academic partners worked together to overcome the logistical challenges faced in the delivery of a child mental health program in disadvantaged urban schools. An example is the changes made to the MHIP's original plan to offer the CBT groups after school. Many principals favored this, as classroom space was more available after school in overcrowded schools, and students would not miss class to participate in the MHIP. However, there was a significant decline in participation when the program was offered after school. While decreased participation would be expected in any school as the result of opportunities to participate in other after-school programs, this effect was very pronounced in these schools. The MHIP social workers reported that some children were unable to participate because they had to care for younger siblings after school, while others would leave school immediately to go to a bathroom off the school grounds, as they did not feel safe using school bathrooms. Other students would leave immediately after school to get food, since in some schools the lunch break occurred as early as 10 AM. Finally, staying after school would have required some children to pass through dangerous areas going to and from school alone rather than with their classmates. Based on this experience, the MHIP staff, school principals, and academic partners worked to modify the MHIP so that it could be conducted at times when children were in school and when the school was able to provide space.

EVALUATING THE INTERVENTION

A need for reliable assessment was one of the central reasons for creating the program, and LAUSD staff worked closely with the academic partners from as early as the program design stage to develop an evaluation plan that could be used to determine the MHIP's effectiveness. A participatory evaluation methodology was used (Fink, 1993) in which the school district stakeholders provided advice and guidance about the selection of evaluation questions and hypotheses, performance standards, and data collection measures, and the academic partners were responsible for identifying potential measures, organizing and conducting data analysis and reporting the results (see Table 1).

This meant that while the academic partners conducted the literature review to identify the variables for research questions and the relevant measures, it was the school district staff that prioritized and ultimately selected the most important questions and hypotheses and the measures to be used. The school district was also interested in outcomes in multiple domains and chose to focus on school performance, overall functioning, and psychological symptoms after reviewing information provided by the academic partners on the range of potential outcomes suggested by Hoagwood et al. (1996). Some measures to assess these outcomes, such as the Achenbach Child Behavior Checklist (CBCL) (Achenbach, 1991), the Child Depression Inventory (CDI) (Kovacs, 1992), and the Life Events Scale (Singer et al., 1995, 1998), were then selected because the Mental Health Services Unit was familiar with them from prior use in clinical settings. The availability of the CBCL and the CDI in Spanish was an added advantage. Others, such as the Child PTSD Symptom Scale measure (Foa et al., 2001), were selected after school personnel had pilot-tested several similar instruments suggested by the academic partners.

Table 1. Participatory Program Evaluation

MHIP evaluation tasks	Program evaluators' tasks	Mental health services unit and EIEP tasks
Identify research questions/ hypotheses	Conduct literature review to identify variables for research questions and to set directions for hypotheses	Advise on selection of most important questions and hypotheses; inform evaluators if priorities change
Formulate study design	Set up incentives to ensure "encouragement" to adhere to robust research design	Advise on best methods for assuring fidelity to design
Choose sample	Determine sample size and method of selection	Provide guidance on methods for assuring "representation"
Select measures	Recommend measures	Choose measures based on suitability and cultural appropriateness
Implement data collection	Train staff; monitor quality	Collect data
Analyze data	Choose methods appropriate to quality of data	Provide feedback on interpretation of analysis
Report results	Write report	Advise on formats that will promote usability of results
Disseminate findings	Adhere to integrity of data in reports to other researchers and persons responsible for program planning and policy	Support program dissemination throughout school district and share clinical experience with educators, administrators, school board, and other school clinicians
Develop Evaluation Users' Guide	Develop methods for providing continued technical assistance after completion of the evaluation	Provide examples based on experiences in delivering intervention

The academic partners also recommended random assignment of eligible students to either the MHIP intervention or a comparison group. The LAUSD Mental Health Services Unit and EIEP staff felt that all eligible children should be offered the school-based MHIP and decided that the comparison group would consist of children who were placed on a waiting list for the MHIP intervention. Whenever possible, children were randomly assigned. However, it was sometimes necessary either to randomize groups of children rather than individuals or to assign children only to immediate treatment so that all eligible children could get the MHIP intervention prior to the end of the school year.

Families and children participating in the MHIP completed symptom measures at three points: (1) screening and program enrollment, (2) when the children assigned to the MHIP intervention completed the intervention, immediately prior to the comparison group beginning the intervention; and (3) when the children in the comparison group completed the intervention. The main evaluation will be of the MHIP's effectiveness in reducing symptoms of PTSD and depression and will compare changes in symptoms between the intervention and comparison group.

RESPONSE FROM PARTICIPANTS

The feedback from participants in the MHIP was overwhelmingly positive. Many parents, even some who were initially reluctant to allow their children into the program, became enthusiastic supporters. One parent said, "My son is not afraid to come to school anymore. He comes home and talks to me. Before he would just cry and not say anything. Now he'll come home and tell us what's bothering him. I realize how important it is to spend time with our kids and listen to them." Some parents wanted services for other members of their family, including adults not living in the family home.

Teachers and administrators were also very happy with the program. The MHIP Clinical Director sought their opinions using a semistructured interview as part of a feedback/exit interview at the end of the academic year. These discussions were conducted with both the school principal and the school official who acted as the liaison with the MHIP at all schools that participated in the program. There were several common themes in their responses.

The involvement of parents and teachers in addition to students was viewed as a program strength. One elementary school principal remarked that "the school benefited in that teachers were able to learn about how trauma impacts kids," while another commented on "the comprehensiveness of the intervention model in which parents, teachers, and students were served." A number of school administrators remarked on the importance of school mental health programs such as the MHIP involving teachers while "requiring little from the school."

When asked what would be the most important changes to make to the MHIP, the majority of respondents wanted to extend the program, either in the number of sessions or in the population served. Despite the concern on the part of many that the MHIP was limited to only immigrants and not meeting the needs of all of their students, every principal and administrator wanted the MHIP to return to their school the following year.

The MHIP program was strongly supported by a variety of stakeholders, including parents, teachers, principals, school district administrators, and mental health staff. In the case of the MHIP, this support likely resulted in large part from the collaborative efforts to address each group's concerns throughout the development and implementation of the program. Given the many challenges that often face the successful dissemination and adoption of mental health programs in schools, it is encouraging that the MHIP was able to develop broad support across many stakeholders through its use of a collaborative approach.

CHALLENGES FACED BY THE PARTNERSHIP

While participatory research is a promising model for community-based research, developing and implementing such a partnership can be challenging (Macaulay et al., 1999). For others seeking to develop similar partnerships, the MHIP may offer one example of how these challenges may be addressed.

The successful development of the MHIP was greatly facilitated by the preexisting relationship between the school staff and the clinician/researchers. Several members of the academic team had been working clinically with the LAUSD Mental Health Services Unit, in one case for a period of several years. This commitment reassured the school district partners that the academic partners were interested in improving local school mental health services as well as in research. As important, the conversations that had occurred over the years had convinced the LAUSD Mental Health Services Unit leadership and some of the school clinicians of the benefits and importance of evaluating the effectiveness of school mental health programs. These conversations occurred at a time when there was tremendous discussion both nationally and locally about accountability in schools. The resulting commitment by the LAUSD Mental Health Services Unit to improving program evaluation led to the MHIP being staffed with school mental health clinicians who understood the importance of the evaluation activities, which helped to overcome some of the resistance to research among some of the Unit's other clinicians.

The participatory research partnership was maintained and strengthened by constant communication between the partners as the program evolved. Weekly phone meetings and frequent face-to-face meetings allowed problems to be identified and addressed early and also helped create an understanding between the school and academic partners of the priorities and challenges being faced by both groups. This facilitated the compromises necessary to successfully operating the program in the schools on a daily basis, while maintaining the critical components of the evaluation design and data collection necessary for the generation of scientific publications. In fact, several school district personnel have become formally involved in the authorship of peer-reviewed articles, while others have influenced the research questions and analysis by sharing their perceptions of what are the key MHIP components and what factors most affected participants' improvement.

While the effectiveness of the MHIP intervention will not be known until the analysis of the program data is completed, the success of the participatory research model can be judged by recent developments in the MHIP program and in other school mental health activities. The MHIP has continued to receive funding from the EIEP program, with efforts now focusing on improving the program based on experiences from the first year. Many school mental health clinicians involved in these efforts have continued their work with the MHIP from the first year. There are also several efforts being made to use the same model to pilot the MHIP clinical intervention in a general student (nonimmigrant) population and evaluate its effectiveness. Finally, the participatory research model is being considered for use in examining a number of mental health programs offered by LAUSD, and efforts are currently under way to use this model for an examination of LAUSD's mental health counseling program for emotionally disturbed children and for its Suicide Prevention Program.

Still, while participatory research may serve as a useful model for establishing collaborative research with schools, other challenging issues remain. The funding of school mental health programs is one such challenge, as few schools have sufficient resources to meet the needs of students with mental health and psychosocial problems (Adelman et al., 1999). This was less a problem for the MHIP, as the EIEP was committed to developing mental health services to complement other immigrant student services. However, the collaborative nature of the intervention and evaluation, the increasing emphasis in schools on outcomes and accountability, and school officials' desire to get more "bang for the mental health buck" increased the willingness of school officials to commit substantial resources to developing a high-quality clinical intervention and to evaluating the program. While this type of funding for mental health interventions for special populations may be available to a few other school districts, it is likely to remain a relatively unusual funding source, and further evidence of the effectiveness of school mental health interventions is necessary in order to obtain the funding necessary to expand this type of program to the general school population. A collaborative approach, increasing schools' sense of program ownership by engaging school personnel in all aspects of intervention design and evaluation, may increase the likelihood that schools would be willing to commit the resources necessary for the development and evaluation of such programs.

The MHIP also presented many logistical challenges likely to be faced by others developing child mental health programs in disadvantaged urban schools. As a response to tremendous overcrowding, many schools now divide the students into tracks and teach all year; there are now over 2 million students in year-round schools in 44 states (Growth of Public Year-Round Education in the United States over a 15-Year Period, San Diego, CA: National Association for Year-Round Education, 2002. Accessed February 22, 2002, at http://nayre.org/statistics.html). Since record enrollments are expected for the next several years (Digest of Education Statistics, 2000, Washington, DC: National Center for Education Statistics, 2000. Accessed February 22, 2002, at http://nces.ed.gov/pubs2001/digest/introduction.html), this trend is likely to continue.

Year-round calendars can result in unusual school schedules with 1- to 3-month "vacation periods" scattered throughout the year, far different from the traditional September-to-June school calendar, and can disrupt the continuity of many interventions. Another challenge that results from the overcrowding is the lack of a room for mental health professionals to meet with children, a problem exacerbated by new laws mandating class size reductions. This is most likely to occur in the poorest and most disadvantaged urban schools, precisely in those schools where mental health services may be most needed.

These and other difficulties can be daunting, but the success of the Mental Health for Immigrants Program demonstrates that a true community–research collaboration can overcome many of the challenges of designing, delivering, and evaluating an evidence-based child mental health intervention that is intended to be disseminated throughout a school system.

A NEW MODEL FOR SCHOOL MENTAL HEALTH PROGRAM EVALUATIONS

Schools are increasingly being seen as a promising way to improve the delivery of mental health services to poor and minority children (Dryfoos, 1994; Garrison et al., 1999; Weist, 1997) in order to address current inequities and their underutilization of traditional mental health services (U.S. Department of Health and Human Services, 1999). Prior attempts to deliver mental health services in schools and evaluate effectiveness of such services have been hampered by the different school and mental health cultures (Knoff & Batsche, 1990; Weist, 1997) as well as by challenges faced by researchers in conducting research on school-based mental health systems (Forness & Hoagwood, 1993).

The participatory research partnership used in the MHIP development and evaluation is not a panacea, but it does provide a framework that is useful in overcoming many of the challenges faced in conducting school-based mental health research. This framework guided the overall program development, while the clinical intervention and evaluation components drew upon more specific models of community–researcher collaborations in the areas of treatment development and evaluation. The framework also allowed the LAUSD Mental Health Services Unit and EIEP staff to set the MHIP's priorities, while assigning important roles to academicians and school district stakeholders such as principals in the modification of the clinical intervention and the program's evaluation.

Flexibility from all partners is crucial to the success of such a collaboration. The work of the partnership at each phase of the program's development added a critical piece to the resulting MHIP, yet the roles and responsibilities of the partners varied during different stages of the program design. The academic and school partners worked together to choose an evidence-based clinical intervention, well suited to the school environment, that addressed the problem of violence exposure. This ensured that the resulting program would incorporate the values and needs of a variety of stakeholders, and increased participation and acceptance of the program, ingredients Jensen and colleagues have noted are associated with successful outcomes (Jensen, Hoagwood, & Trickett, 1999). The modifications made to the CBITS intervention to increase its appropriateness for the school setting greatly increase the likelihood that the intervention, if found to be effective, will be able to be replicated and disseminated without having to undergo further substantial revisions. Finally, the collaborative efforts regarding the MHIP evaluation led to the school district's support of the use of standardized mental health assessments and random assignment, two factors that have limited prior school-based mental health research (Forness & Hoagwood, 1993; Hoagwood & Erwin, 1997).

At the same time, it is important to acknowledge limitations in the MHIP and, more generally, in collaborative community partnerships. Despite efforts to involve all stakeholders in the MHIP, the time frame in which the program was developed and implemented limited the involvement of immigrant parents and community representatives. Their influence was primarily indirect, via school principals, teachers, EIEP Program staff, and others with whom they had frequent contact. Parents also communicated with MHIP staff through phone calls, letters, and in-person discussions. In the future, however, more direct involvement of recent immigrant parents would be desirable. Developing and maintaining a collaborative community partnership also requires a substantial amount of time and energy on the part of all involved and the willingness among all participants not only to become educated about the priorities of other stakeholders but also to work to achieve compromises that will allow all participants to gain from participation in the project. It is therefore not a suitable approach for all projects, investigators, or communities.

As the gap between what can be achieved under optimal versus real-world conditions is increasingly acknowledged, more collaborative partnerships between university researchers and community groups will be needed in both the development and the evaluation of mental health interventions (Jensen et al., 1999). Schools already provide the majority of mental health services to children (Burns et al., 1995) and are obvious partners with whom researchers interested in child mental health services can collaborate. While others have described the key elements of this type of collaboration (Hoagwood et al., 1995; Jensen et al., 1999), there is little in the literature regarding how these elements come together to develop a school-based mental health program.

The MHIP provides a detailed example of how such a community research partnership may function during all phases of the design of a school-based mental health intervention, from conceptualization through clinical intervention to evaluation, to meet the specific needs of underserved, vulnerable populations such as immigrants. Additional examples of school–researcher partnerships are needed if schools and researchers are to overcome the challenges inherent in such a partnership in order to design, implement, and evaluate school-based mental health programs.

REFERENCES

Achenbach, T. M. (1991). *Manual for the Child Behavior Checklist/4–18 and 1991 Profile.* Burlington, VT: Department of Psychiatry, University of Vermont.

Adelman, H. S., Taylor, L., Weist, M. D., Adelsheim, S., Freemna, B., Kapp, L., Lahti, M., & Mawn, D. (1999). Mental health in schools: A federal initiative. *Children's Services: Social Policy, Research, and Practice, 2*(2), 95–115.

Arroyo, W. (1998). Immigrant children and families. In M. R. Isaacs (Ed.), *Promoting cultural competence in children's mental health services. Systems of care for children's mental health* (pp. 251–268). Baltimore, MD: Paul H. Brookes.

Burns, B. J., Costello, E. J., Angold, A., Tweed, D., Stangl, D., Farmer, E. M., & Erkanli, A. (1995). Children's mental health service use across service sectors. *Health Affairs, 14*(3), 147–159.

Cohen, J. A., & Mannarino, A. P. (1996). A treatment outcome study for sexually abused preschool children. *Journal of the American Academy of Child and Adolescent Psychiatry, 35,* 42–50.

Coulton, C. J., Korbin, J. E., Su, M., & Chow, J. (1995). Community level factors and child maltreatment rates. *Child Development, 66*(5), 1262–1276.

Deblinger, E., & Heflin, A. H. (1996). *Treating sexually abused children and their nonoffending parents: A cognitive behavioral approach.* Thousand Oaks, CA: Sage.

Dryfoos, J. (1994). *Full-service schools: A revolution in health and social services for children, youth, and families.* San Francisco: Jossey–Bass.

Fink, A. (1993). *Evaluation fundamentals: Guiding programs, research, and policy.* Newbury Park, CA: Sage.

Foa, E. B., Johnson, K., Feeny, N. C., & Treadwell, K. (2001). The child PTSD symptom scale (CPSS): A preliminary examination of its psychometric properties. *Journal of Clinical Child Psychology, 30*(3), 376–384.

Forness, S. R., & Hoagwood, K. (1993). Where angels fear to tread: Issues in sampling, design, and implementation of school-based mental health services research. *School Psychology Quarterly, 8*(4), 291–300.

Garbarino, J. (1995). The American war zone: What children can tell us about living with violence. *Journal of Developmental & Behavioral Pediatrics, 16*(6), 431–435.

Garrison, E. G., Roy, I. S., & Azar, V. (1999). Responding to the mental health needs of Latino children and families through school-based services. *Clinical Psychology Review, 19*(2), 199–219.

Gong Guy, E., Cravens, R. B., & Patterson, T. E. (1991). Clinical issues in mental health service delivery to refugees. *American Psychologist, 46*(6), 642–648.

Guarnaccia, P. J., & Lopez, S. (1998). The mental health and adjustment of immigrant and refugee children. *Child and Adolescent Psychiatric Clinics of North America, 7*(3), 537–553.

Hernandez, D. J., & Darke, K. (1999). Socioeconomic and demographic risk factors and resources among children in immigrant and native-born families: 1910, 1960, and 1990. In D. J. Hernandez (Ed.), *Children of immigrants: Health, adjustment, and public assistance* (pp. 19–125). Washington, DC: National Academy Press.

Hoagwood, K., & Erwin, H. D. (1997). Effectiveness of school-based mental health services for children: A 10-year research review. *Journal of Child & Family Studies, 6*(4), 435–451.

Hoagwood, K., Hibbs, E., Brent, D., & Jensen, P. (1995). Introduction to the special section: Efficacy and effectiveness in studies of child and adolescent psychotherapy. *Journal of Consulting & Clinical Psychology, 63*(5), 683–687.

Hoagwood, K., Jensen, P. S., Petti, T., & Burns, B. J. (1996). Outcomes of mental health care for children and adolescents: I. A comprehensive conceptual model. *Journal of the American Academy of Child & Adolescent Psychiatry, 35*(8), 1055–1063.

Jaycox, L. H. (2000). Cognitive-Behavioral Intervention for Trauma in Schools, (unpublished manual).

Jensen, P. S., Hoagwood, K., & Trickett, E. J. (1999). Ivory towers or earthen trenches? Community collaborations to foster real-world research. *Applied Developmental Science, 3*(4), 206–212.

Kim, W. (1997). Korean immigrant children. In J. Noshpitz (Ed.), *Handbook of child and adolescent psychiatry* (Vol. 4, pp. 600–610). New York: Wiley.

Knoff, H. M., & Batsche, G. M. (1990). The place of the school in community mental health services for children: A necessary interdependence. *Journal of Mental Health Administration, 17*(1), 122–130.

Kovacs, M. (1992). *The children's depression inventory manual.* North Tonawanda, NY: Multi-Health Systems, Inc.

Macaulay, A. C., Commanda, L. E., Freeman, W. L., Gibson, N., McCabe, M. L., Robbins, C. M., & Twohig, P. L. (1999). Participatory research maximises community and lay involvement. North American Primary Care Research Group. *BMJ, 319*(7212), 774–778.

March, J. S., Amaya-Jackson, L., Murray, M. C., & Schulte, A. (1998). Cognitive–behavioral psychotherapy for children and adolescents with posttraumatic stress disorder after a single-incident stressor. *Journal of the American Academy of Child & Adolescent Psychiatry, 37*(6), 585–593.

Mittelmark, M. (1990). Balancing the requirements of research and the needs of communities. In N. Bracht (Ed.), *Health promotion at the community level* (pp. 125–139). Newbury Park, CA: Sage.

Munroe-Blum, H., Boyle, M. H., Offord, D. R., & Kates, N. (1989). Immigrant children: Psychiatric disorder, school performance, and service utilization. *American Journal of Orthopsychiatry, 59*(4), 510–519.

Partida, J. (1996). The effects of immigration on children in the Mexican-American community. *Child & Adolescent Social Work Journal, 13*(3), 241–254.

Pelcovitz, D., & Kaplan, S. (1996). Post-traumatic stress disorder in children and adolescents. *Child & Adolescent Psychiatric Clinics of North America, 5*(2), 449–469.

Schmidley, D. A., & Gibson, C. (1999). *Profile of the foreign-born population in the United States, 1997* (Currne Population Reports Series P23-195). Washington, DC: U.S. Census Bureau.

Singer, M. I., Anglin, T. M., Song, L. y., & Lunghofer, L. (1995). Adolescents' exposure to violence and associated symptoms of psychological trauma. *Journal of the American Medical Association, 273*(6), 477–482.

Singer, M. I., Miller, D. B., Guo, S., Slovak, K., & Frierson, T. (1998). *The mental health consequences of children exposed to violence: Final report.* Cleveland: Case Western Reserve University.

Stoiber, K. C., & Kratochwill, T. R. (2000). Empirically supported interventions and school psychology: Rationale and methodological issues—Part I. *School Psychology Quarterly, 15*(1), 75–105.

Straussner, J. H., & Straussner, S. L. (1997). Impact of community school violence on children. In S. L. A. Straussner (Ed.), *Children in the urban environment: Linking social policy and clinical practice* (pp. 61–77). Springfield, IL: Charles C. Thomas.

U.S. Department of Health and Human Services (1999). *Mental health: A report of the Surgeon General—Executive summary.* Rockville, MD: U.S. Department of Health and Human Services, Substance Abuse and Mental Health Services Administration, Center for Mental Health Services, National Institutes of Health, National Institute of Mental Health.

U.S. Public Health Service (2000). *Report of the Surgeon General's conference on children's mental health: A national action agenda.* Washington, DC: Department of Health and Human Services.

Vega, W. A., Kolody, B., Aguilar-Gaxiola, S., & Catalano, R. (1999). Gaps in service utilization by Mexican Americans with mental health problems. *American Journal of Psychiatry, 156*(6), 928–934.

Weist, M. D. (1997). Expanded school mental health services: A national movement in progress. *Advances in Clinical Child Psychology, 19*, 319–352.

Weisz, J. R. (2000). Agenda for child and adolescent psychotherapy research: On the need to put science into practice. *Archives of General Psychiatry, 57*(9), 837–838.

14

School-Based Mental Health on a United States Army Installation

MICHAEL E. FARAN, MARK D. WEIST,
ALBERT Y. SAITO, LINDA YOSHIKAMI,
JEFFREY W. WEISER, and BJARNE KAER

In 2000, the report of the Surgeon General's Conference on Children's Mental Health dramatically summarized the state of our nation's mental health system for children and adolescents as follows: "Children and families are suffering because of missed opportunities for prevention and early identification, fragmented treatment services, and low priority for resources." The Surgeon General, Dr. David Satcher, made the analogy that "there is no mental health equivalent to the federal government's commitment to childhood immunization," implying that such an approach is necessary to address the mental health crisis for youth in our nation (U.S. Public Health Service, 2000).

School-based mental health programs are a centerpiece of the Surgeon General's report and are improving access to effective prevention, early intervention, and treatment for students and families around the nation (Adelman et al., 1999; Weist, 2001). As reviewed in other chapters in this book, these programs are showing progressive growth related to the increasing recognition that they reduce barriers to the receipt of mental health services by children, adolescents, and families (Catron, Harris, & Weiss, 1998), while at the same time reducing barriers to student learning (Adelman & Taylor, 1999). Further, *preliminary* evaluation findings support the impact of the programs in improving student emotional and behavioral functioning (Armbruster, Gerstein, & Fallon, 1997; Nabors & Reynolds, 2000; Weist et al., 1996), school behavior (Hall, 2000; Jennings, Pearson, & Harris,

MICHAEL E. FARAN, ALBERT Y. SAITO, and JEFFREY W. WEISER • Child and Adolescent Psychiatry Service, Tripler Army Medical Center, Honolulu, Hawaii 96859.   MARK D. WEIST • University of Maryland School of Medicine, Baltimore, Maryland 21201.   LINDA YOSHIKAMI and BJARNE KAER • Solomon Elementary School, Department of Education, Nahiawa, Hawaii 96786.

2000), and student attendance (Britto & Klostermann, 2000; Jennings et al., 2000).

However, research on school-based mental health programs remains limited (Rones & Hoagwood, 2000), and issues related to the effective implementation of these programs in diverse contexts remain to be explored (see Weist & Albus, in press). One context that has received almost no attention in the published literature on school mental health is military schools. In this chapter, we describe the development of a school-based mental health program in an elementary school serving military children in Hawaii.

Military families are unique in many ways as compared to their civilian counterparts (see Isay, 1968; LaGrone, 1978). On average, a military family will move every 3 years, often to locations overseas. Children are therefore required to change schools and make new friends on a frequent basis. In many families both parents are in the military, potentially compounding disruptions at home. There are also many single-parent military families. Often children go exclusively to schools dominated by military children and recognize that their lives are different from those of "civilian" children. Military parents are required to have a plan that specifies who is to take care of their children if they are deployed, and deployment itself places enormous strain on the military family.

These stresses clearly operate in the lives of military families in Hawaii, where the 25th Infantry Division of the U.S. Army operates. Deployment for soldiers from this division occurs on a fairly frequent basis. Often the children are cared for by the other parent, a relative, or, at times, by a good family friend. Many times the nonmilitary spouse and children move back to the mainland to be with relatives, an event that is difficult for the children's social and academic adjustment. Whenever there is a national crisis, many children begin to worry if their parents are going to leave and, more importantly, if they will return.

An additional stress for military families in Hawaii is being isolated from extended family members and friends on the mainland. In Hawaii, children are several thousand miles from their relatives, and sometimes this separation is from one of the biological parents (as with children of divorce). In addition, Hawaii has a high cost of living that strains family budgets, resulting in many spouses being required to take jobs outside the house, leaving less time for their families. Junior-enlisted families frequently fall below the poverty level. Moreover, Hawaii's culture and multiethnic composition is very different from that of the mainland, which presents an adjustment challenge for many families. Related to these unique stresses, many military children in Hawaii view themselves differently from other children (e.g., as "Army Brats").

In this chapter, we describe the Solomon Wellness for Education Program, a school mental health program being developed on a military base in Hawaii. We describe a range of services being developed in the school along with plans for assessing and improving program quality and for evaluating program outcomes. We then discuss unique issues the program is confronting related to the events of September 11, 2001. The chapter concludes with a discussion of challenges and opportunities that lie ahead in the advancement of school-based mental health-based mental health programs in U.S. schools with largely military populations, and Department of Defense schools abroad.

THE SOLOMON WELLNESS FOR EDUCATION PROGRAM

The goal of the Solomon Wellness for Education Program (SWEP) is to develop a comprehensive school mental health program at Solomon Elementary School located on the U.S. Army's Schofield Barracks, Hawaii. This is a collaborative project between the Child and Adolescent Psychiatry Service of Tripler Army Medical Center (TAMC) and the Solomon Elementary School, Department of Education, Hawaii. Schofield Barracks is the home of the Army's 25th Infantry Division. There are 15,356 active duty soldiers and 27,892 family members, of which 5600 family members are under the age of 18. On post there are two elementary schools: Hale Kula and Solomon. The middle schools and high school are off-post in the surrounding town of Wahiawa. At present, there are plans to establish a model program at Solomon Elementary School and then to progressively extend the program to other schools in the central district of Oahu, a district containing the majority of military families in Hawaii.

Solomon Elementary School

Solomon Elementary School has an enrollment of 830 students in grades pre-kindergarten through 5, with 58 teachers. It is funded and administered by the state of Hawaii. There are four classes of preschool special education (about 40 students) and 90 other special education students with problems that range from severe autistic disorder in self-contained classes to mild learning-disabled students who may spend as little as 1 hour per day in a special education setting. The school provides a breakfast and lunch program as well as an after-school program until 5:30 PM on school days. Seventy percent of the students are eligible for free or reduced meals. The school is considered a federal Title I school with greater than 51% of students coming from low-income households.

The great majority of the children in the school (97%) come from military families, mostly from the junior-enlisted ranks. Many students come from single-parent families, and a large number of students are from blended families. At Schofield Barracks, consistent with other Army installations, assignments for soldiers change every 3 years. This means that every third year, there is virtually a 100% turnover of students, making continuity of the education for these students very difficult and presenting a unique challenge in school mental health programming (e.g., to establish special programs to assist students and families with the transitions of coming and leaving). Also, students often move during the year, complicating an already inconsistent education and creating higher levels of psychosocial stress.

The school has two school counselors, a Student Services Coordinator, a Parent–Community Networking Coordinator (PCNC), and a Primary School Adjustment Project. The PCNC is a parent who is paid by the school to coordinate all parent activities. There is a classroom that has been set aside as a gathering place for parents where they can have meetings, socialize, and participate in various projects. There are computers with on-line capabilities so parents can e-mail their spouses when they are deployed. The Primary School Adjustment Project provides assistance to children who are having problems adjusting to school and includes two staff members under the supervision of the school counselors. Often these are children who have recently moved to Hawaii who may present temporary difficulties adjusting, developing friends, and so on. All services for children are coordinated by the student services coordinator and by the two school counselors. Child and adolescent psychiatry fellows from TAMC have been providing limited consultation to Solomon for about 15 years. Prior to SWEP, this consisted primarily of classroom observations and of evaluation and triage of students referred by the school counselors. Before the 2000–2001 school year, if more intensive services were required these were provided at TAMC, referred out to a school-contracted counselor, or seen by a civilian TRICARE provider (the Department of Defense's Military Health Care Program). All students at Solomon are eligible for services through the Hawaii Department of Education and Department of Health as mandated by Public Law 105-17, the Individuals with Disabilities Education Act Amendments of 1997.

The Solomon Wellness for Education Program in Year 1

The vision of SWEP is to provide comprehensive mental health services as an integral part of Solomon Elementary School. Teachers are viewed as the "experts" in the school, leading the critical task of educating the students. Beginning in the 2000–2001 school year, services were expanded to include child psychiatry fellows in the school for 2 days per week (up from 1/2 day per week the year before), with the chief of the Child and Adolescent Psychiatry Service meeting weekly with the fellows, the school principal, and school staff with behavioral responsibilities to provide consultation and direction in addressing child mental health issues. In this year, child psychiatry fellows began offering intensive evaluation and treatment (including psychotropic medication when indicated) to identified students and families. They also began to expand program services by starting a parent outreach program and initiating preventive activities in classrooms.

Midway through the 2000–2001 school year, a meeting was held with staff and leaders from TAMC, Solomon's elementary school, Hawaii's Departments of Health and Education, and the Center for School Mental Health Assistance, a technical assistance center for school-based mental health at the University of Maryland. The focus of the meeting was to discuss mental health and educational needs of military children and options for school-based mental health. The state of Hawaii was interested in SWEP, as the state system for providing mental health service was in flux. Responsibility for all mental health services, except for the most serious cases, was being shifted from the Department of Health to the Department of Education. The outcome of this meeting was to unanimously support going forward with SWEP.

Subsequently, numerous organizational meetings were held with Department of Education and TAMC staff to further refine plans for the development of school-based mental health programs at Solomon. From the onset, it was emphasized that all involved in the process would share in SWEP's development and be equal partners and co-workers in the process. The first task was to form an Advisory Council composed of all the significant stakeholders who could provide support, guidance, and recommendations to SWEP from the early onset of its conception (see Nabors et al., 1999). The Advisory Council was initially made up of the school principal, the Chief of the Child and Adolescent Psychiatry Service, the PCNC, the two school counselors, teachers, the two individuals from the Primary School Adjustment Project, the student services coordinator, and a representative from the Army Oahu Base Support Command. Later a chaplain and a psychologist were added to the group. The Advisory Council came up with the name Solomon Wellness for Education Program to convey the goal for program services to enhance wellness, which in turn will enhance educational success for students at Solomon. Two "temporary" bungalows were chosen as sites for establishing SWEP. Each bungalow is being converted into two separate evaluation and treatment rooms so there will be a total of four rooms for SWEP. Several unique system issues such as having a "clinic" as part of a school are still being addressed with the support of the Department of Health and TAMC.

In the spring of 2001, the SWEP Plan was presented to the parents and teachers of Solomon. A significant concern for teachers, who already were overworked, was how much more of their time was this project going to demand. Teachers were assured that the goal was for SWEP to provide them with support and, ideally, decrease the amount of time that they needed to spend to address behavioral issues in students. Parents were most concerned about confidentiality and about the stigma around seeing someone for a mental health problem. Both of these issues are potentially of greater concern for military communities. These will be ongoing concerns that will require reassurance that confidentiality will be maintained according to federal and state statutes.

The Solomon Wellness for Education Program in Year 2

In the beginning of the 2001–2002 school year, it was decided to increase child psychiatry fellow involvement at Solomon from 2 to 3 days per week. In addition, the school hired a social worker to expand clinical services. At present, two child psychiatry fellows work at the school on Tuesdays, and one works at the school on Wednesdays. On Tuesdays, the fellows are joined by the Chief of the Child and Adolescent Psychiatry Service at TAMC and a staff psychiatrist who supervise the fellows and work with the principal and other Department of Education staff to further develop and integrate SWEP into the school milieu. Monthly Advisory Council meetings are held to provide recommendations and guidance. SWEP is highly dynamic in that its goal is to be flexible in meeting student and community needs. Requests for services are coming from several different sources, not only from within the Solomon school community but also from the district superintendent, parents with children in home-schooling, private schools outside of Solomon, and the 25th Infantry Division Command. The organizational structure of SWEP is presented in Fig. 1.

In addition to more intensive evaluation and intervention services, the child psychiatry fellows have begun to be involved in prevention activities. One set of activities relates to the prevention of bullying, based on the recommendation of the Advisory Council that this has become a pressing problem in the school. In the beginning of the school year, the fellows developed a "show" on handling interpersonal conflict. They role-played conflictual and then positive behaviors in a variety of interpersonal situations associated with student conflict. After the fellows modeled a positive response to conflict, student volunteers did the same.

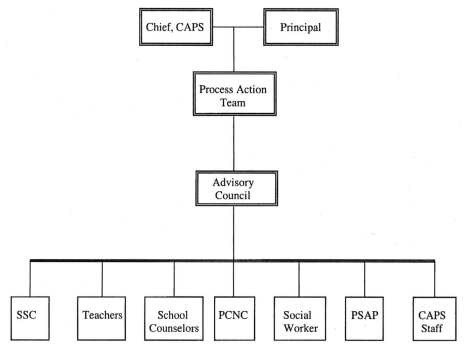

Figure 1. Organizational structure of the Solomon Wellness for Education Program. CAPS, Child and Adolescent Psychiatry Service, Tripler Army Medical Center; SSC, student services coordinator; PCNC, Parent–Community Networking Coordinator; PSAP, Primary School Adjustment Project.

These conflict resolution presentations were made in each of the nine classrooms of the fourth- and fifth-grade classrooms of the school.

Responding to the Terrorist Attacks

The September 11, 2001 terrorist attacks in New York City and Washington, DC greatly impacted the military community. Children are being separated for extended periods from their parents not knowing if their parents will return home. For the first time since World War II, people in Hawaii are expressing concerns about being attacked. The military was placed on high alert, increasing anxiety almost universally. The District Superintendent generated a list of schools in the Central Oahu District that have military children and adolescents. This list was used by SWEP staff in developing and implementing a number of presentations to school staff on "Helping Children with Disaster Related Anxiety." In these presentations, TAMC child and adolescent psychiatry fellows and staff discussed strategies for talking to children about disaster, presented signs and symptoms of traumatization and anxiety, presented tips for helping students and families, and reviewed a strategy for triaging students presenting more intensive problems. The briefing was derived from essentially two Internet websites—"Helping Children Handle Disaster-Related Anxiety" (www.nmha.org/reassurance/children.cfm) and "Helping Children Cope with Loss" (www.nmha.org/reassurance/childcoping.cfm).

Based on the success of the initial presentations, staff from the Hawaii Department of Education requested that they be made at other schools. Eventually, presentations were given at a total of 15 schools in the central district of Oahu.

Strategic Planning Meeting in Year 2

Midway through the 2001–2002 school year, a strategic planning meeting was held including TAMC leadership and fellows; the principal at Solomon, teachers, and all staff involved with student behavior, representatives from the Hawaii Departments of Health and Education, and a consultant from the University of Maryland, Center for School Mental Health Assistance. The focus of this meeting was to analyze progress made by the SWEP program, to collaboratively develop recommendations to overcome challenges, and to expand and improve the program. A major conclusion of the program analysis was that while a good collaboration had been established between the school and TAMC staff in starting the program, efforts needed to be made to make it a *full and equal* partnership. It was decided that the chief of the Child and Adolescent Psychiatry Service and the school principal should formally assume the roles of program co-directors. In addition, it was decided to establish the SWEP Process Action Team, which would be jointly led by a TAMC staff psychiatrist and a social worker/program coordinator from Solomon.

After addressing these structural issues for the program, the vision and goals for the program were redefined. The group decided on the following vision statement and program goals:

> Vision: To develop and implement a comprehensive array of school-based programs and services to support students, family, and community. Goals: (1) To provide a full continuum of mental health promotion and intervention programs and services to include early identification and intervention, prevention, evaluation, and treatment. (2) To remove barriers to learning and improve the academic success of students. (3) To enhance strengths and protective factors in students, families, and the school community. (4) To promote the quality of life and wellness in military families. (5) To provide training, staff development, and research opportunities to improve children's mental health and education.

After developing the program vision and goals, the group discussed activities toward the accomplishment of the strategic plan. These included:

1. Addressing logistical issues and improving the functioning of services provided by child psychiatry fellows in the school. Plans were established to assist fellows in the transport of students to and from appointments, to involve volunteers so that fellows would not be in the portable buildings alone with students, and to enhance phone and computer access in the buildings.
2. Increasing resources for the program and expanding the staff. The group decided to extend an invitation to be on the Advisory Council to local legislators and business leaders, with the view that these connections could assist in developing financial resources. In addition, plans were developed to recruit trainees in psychology and in social work from local graduate programs to solidify intervention services and to assist in the expansion and improvement of prevention activities.
3. Conducting a program needs assessment. It was decided to hold two meetings, with parents and teachers, in which details of the program would

be presented, an open dialogue would be held on needs of students and families, and strategies would be recommended to address them.

4. Improving outreach and services to families. It was decided to present the idea of a "parent empowerment" group to parents during the parent needs assessment meeting. The group also discussed ways to increase parental involvement in the school and to increase interactive time between them and the child psychiatry fellows (e.g., through a coffee hour one morning a week).

5. Developing an algorithm and making the referral process for services more systematic. Prior to the strategic planning meeting, decisions about which students should see the child and adolescent psychiatry fellows were being made by experienced school counselors, without a written description on how they were making these decisions. It was decided to develop a written description of referral processes to improve the objectivity of decision-making processes and to assist in both documenting and assisting cases identified as below the threshold for referral to one of the psychiatrists.

6. Increasing prevention activities in the school. In addition to recruiting psychology and social work trainees, the group decided to more purposefully use evidence-based prevention programs. With assistance from the Center for School Mental Health Assistance, a number of evidence-based programs will be obtained and reviewed by both the program's Advisory Council and the Process Action Team (PAT), with the goal to implement two evidence-based approaches by the start of the 2002–2003 school year.

The group then focused on establishing plans for program quality assessment and improvement (QAI) and for outcome evaluation. A formal QAI program was established involving monitoring of all referrals in terms of number, number seen, and latency between referral and first contact. In addition, plans were established to evaluate grades, attendance, tardiness, and disciplinary encounters before and after intervention for all students seen four or more times by the child psychiatry fellows (see Weist et al., 2000). Also, staff from the Center for School Mental Health Assistance presented 10 principles for best practice in expanded school mental health, and the group agreed that these principles should be in the forefront of planning and evaluation of the program. (For example, programs are implemented to address school and community needs and assets. Staff are respectful of and competently address developmental, cultural, and personal differences among students, families, and staff.)

Since being established, PAT has been meeting weekly to implement recommendations of the strategic plan and to ensure joint accountability (between the school and the TAMC staff) to ensure that progress is being made on all fronts.

Future Plans for the Solomon Wellness for Education Program

While some level of mental health consultative services have been available at Solomon Elementary School for 15 years, the increase and improvement of services in the past 2 years have generated considerable enthusiasm and growth of the program. Already, the program at Solomon has been called a "model" for other schools that serve high numbers of students from military families. The SWEP program is receiving significant support from the Child and Adolescent Psychiatry

Service of Tripler Army Medical Center and has been fully embraced and supported by the principal and staff at Solomon, and leaders in the state's Departments of Education and Health. In addition, the program has benefited from consultation from a national technical assistance center for mental health in schools and is generating the interest of leaders from local universities, most notably from those of the University of Hawaii.

At present, the collaborative team involved in SWEP is focused on moving the program's recently formulated vision and goals from plans to reality. The Advisory Council will be expanded and will meet monthly. PAT will meet weekly, and team leaders and members are committed to moving each area of the strategic plan forward quickly and with joint accountability between leaders from TAMC and Solomon.

Plans are under way to build a coalition to support the effort at Solomon and, in the near future, to extend services to other military schools in the central Oahu district. As mentioned, through PAT, a program coordinator has been hired by the school, and activities are being co-led with a staff psychiatrist from Tripler. The SWEP co-directors, the school principal, and chief of the Child and Adolescent Psychiatry Service are participating in most meetings of PAT and are ensuring that the Advisory Council is both kept abreast of its activities and providing guidance to them. As this chapter is being written in February 2002, plans are in place to (1) add psychology and social work trainees in this academic year, (2) to increase staff, (3) to move the program toward more of an interdisciplinary focus, and (4) to enhance program services toward a full continuum of promotion, prevention, and intervention services. A federal grant to support all of this work is being pursued, with a late-spring submission hopefully leading to enhanced support for local planning and to improvement and expansion of the program into at least one additional school for the 2002–2003 school year.

In addition, consistent with our fifth goal to advance training, staff development, and research in child and adolescent mental health in schools, our experiences are being shared with leaders within the U.S. Department of Defense. Our goal is to both enhance resources for the program here and provide training to extend the program to other schools with military family members. Further, plans are being formulated to develop a number of collaborative research programs involving staff and trainees from Solomon, TAMC, Hawaii Departments of Education and Health, and interested local universities.

Consistent with the increased national focus on preventing child and adolescent suicide (National Strategy for Suicide Prevention, 2001), we are beginning to develop plans for systematic screening of students in higher elementary grades, using the Child and Adolescent Suicide Prevention Index (CASPI; Pfeffer, Jiang, & Kakuma, 2000). Plans are also under way to expand the school training, *Helping Children with Disaster-Related Anxiety,* to develop this into a training manual, and to evaluate its impacts on preparedness and comfort level of school staff in assisting students with disaster-related trauma. We are also developing systematic strategies to assist students and families with the transitions of coming and leaving, related to the 100% turnover of the student body every 3 years at Solomon and at other military schools.

We are also developing a program to assist students and families to prepare and handle the myriad stresses associated with military deployment. At Schofield Barracks, a large contingent of soldiers are going to be deployed to Bosnia in the spring of 2002. Our goal is to conduct a qualitative study of the impacts of this deployment on students, families, and school staff this spring, which we hope will lead to more systematic program development and research concerning an area of critical importance within the military community.

CONCLUDING COMMENTS

As in any new project we wait to see how successful the Solomon Wellness for Education Program will be in improving students' and their families' lives—"the proof is in the pudding." To date, there has been an overall enthusiastic acceptance by students, parents, and school staff. Because of the demand for services, it has been a challenge switching from the old model of school consultation to an approach that integrates a more comprehensive array of services into the fabric of the school. As SWEP takes shape, services expand, and we increase our focus on quality, an important outcome has been the recognition that the need and demand for services are much greater than what was previously believed. In the 2000–2001 school year in which the SWEP program was born, approximately 50 students were evaluated and treated by child and adolescent psychiatry fellows from Tripler, representing about 6% of the school population. At the middle point of our second year of operation (in February 2002), already more than 50 students have been served. Based on our projections, by the end of the current school year the SWEP program will have served over 80 students and families, representing an increase of 60% over last year.

As the reality of our rapid growth is being processed by program staff and the Advisory Council, an increasing theme in planning discussions is how to meet this growing need in a cost-efficient and cost-effective manner. An emerging conclusion of these discussions is that at least for the short term, the implementation of more comprehensive mental health services in the school will cost substantially more, in dollars and in personnel, than prevailing models of care. This is consistent with national discussions on the theme that any effort involving enhanced screening and assessment of problems will likely identify issues that exceed the ability of the current system to effectively address (see U.S. Public Health Service, 2000; Weist, 2001). However, we remain undeterred, cognizant of the fact that, in the long term, these costs will likely be compensated for by savings from reduced costs for high-end services and programs (e.g., psychiatric hospitalizations, juvenile justice involvement) as well as by the increased productivity of our youth when they become adults.

The World Health Organization (WHO) documented that mental and neurological disorders accounted for 12% of the total disability-adjusted life years (DALYs) lost due to all diseases and injury. One DALY is equivalent to 1 lost year of healthy life. Thus, investing in addressing problems like depression early should result in improved functioning of citizens and decreased costs to health systems downstream (WHO, 2001). Consistent with WHO findings, prior to the events of September 11, 2001, within the military, there was growing recognition of the benefits of promoting the psychosocial health of soldiers, their spouses, and their families toward improving their effectiveness in military service. The national tragedy has served to underscore and provide a sense of urgency to this work.

In addition to the impact of September 11, a number of other factors are contributing to an increased awareness within the military of attending to mental health issues among soldiers and their families. For example, women now comprise 15% of the population of the U.S. Army as compared to 1.3% in 1970. This is a dramatic increase from what initially was a predominantly male institution. Mothers (and frequently single mothers) are being deployed to defend our country and are being placed in harm's way. There are considerable financial stresses on families, particularly among those in lower enlisted ranks. Also, there is isolation from extended families and often separation from spouses for extended periods, leading to "periodic" single-parent families. As mentioned previously, there are considerable stresses associated with students and families transitioning from one environment to another every 3 years, as well as the very significant stresses caused by military deployment. All of these issues can be addressed in school-based mental health, as demonstrated by our experiences within SWEP over the past 2 years.

In preparing this chapter we were struck by how limited the literature is on the psychosocial needs of military families. In particular, we found no other articles on school-based mental health programs in military schools. Thus, while our efforts at Solomon elementary school are beginning; we are excited about the project's potential to both improve the lives of students and families in the school and serve as an example to spur the improvement and expansion of school mental health in military schools.

REFERENCES

Adelman, H. S., & Taylor, L. (1999). Mental health in schools and systems restructuring. *Clinical Psychology Review, 19*, 137–164.

Adelman, H. S., Taylor, L., Weist, M. D., Adelsheim, S., Freeman, B., Kapp, L., Lahti, M., & Mawn, D. (1999). Mental health in schools: A federal initiative. *Children's Services: Social Policy, Research, and Practice, 2*, 95–115.

Armbruster, P., Gerstein, S. H., & Fallon, T. (1997). Bridging the gap between service need and service utilization: A school-based mental health program. *Community Mental Health Journal, 32*, 341–352.

Britto, M. B., & Klostermann, B. (2000). *Children first plan: Final evaluation report for years 1–3.* Cincinnati, OH: Children's Hospital Medical Center and the Institute for Health Policy and Services Research, University of Cincinnati.

Catron, T., Harris, V. S., & Weiss, B. (1998). Posttreatment results after 2 years of services in the Vanderbilt School-Based Counseling project. In M. H. Epstein, K. Kutash et al. (Eds.), *Outcomes for children and youth with emotional and behavioral disorders and their families: Programs and evaluation best practices* (pp. 653–656). Austin, TX: PRO-ED, Inc.

Hall, S. (2000). *Final report youth and family centers program: 1999–2000.* Division of Evaluation, Accountability, and Information Systems. Dallas, TX: Dallas Public Schools.

Isay, R. A. (1968). The submariners' wives syndrome. *Psychiatric Quarterly, 42*, 260–265.

Jennings, J., Pearson, G., & Harris, M. (2000). Implementing and maintaining school-based mental health services in a large urban school district. *Journal of School Health, 70*, 201–296.

LaGrone, D. M. (1978). The military family syndrome. *American Journal of Psychiatry, 135*, 1040–1043.

Nabors, L. A., & Reynolds, M. W. (2000). Program evaluation activities: Outcomes related to treatment for adolescents receiving school-based mental health services. *Children's Services: Social Policy, Research, and Practice, 3*, 175–189.

Nabors, L. A., Weist, M. D., Tashman, N. A., & Meyers, C. P. (1999). Quality assurance and school-based mental services. *Psychology in the Schools, 36*, 485–493.

National Strategy for Suicide Prevention (2001). *Goals and objectives for action.* SMA01-3517, www.mentalhealth.org/suicideprevention.

Pfeffer, C., Jiang, H., & Kakuma, T. (2000). Child-adolescent suicidal potential index (CASPI): A screen for risk for early onset suicidal behavior. *Psychological Assessment, 12,* 304–318.

Rones, M., & Hoagwood, K. (2000). School-based mental health services: A research review. *Clinical Child and Family Psychology Review, 3,* 223–241.

U.S. Public Health Service (2000). *Report on the Surgeon General's Conference on Children's Mental Health: A national action agenda.* Washington, DC: U.S. Government Printing Office.

Weist, M. D. (2001). Toward a public mental health promotion and intervention system for youth. *Journal of School Health, 71,* 101–104.

Weist, M. D., & Albus, K. E. (in press). Expanded school mental health: Exploring program details and developing the research base. *Behavior Modification.*

Weist, M. D., Nabors, L. A., Myers, C. P., & Armbruster, P. (2000). Evaluation of expanded school mental health programs. *Community Mental Health Journal, 36,* 395–411.

Weist, M. D., Paskewitz, D. A., Warner, B. S., & Flaherty, L. T. (1996). Treatment outcome of school-based mental health services for urban teenagers. *Community Mental Health Journal, 32,* 149–157.

World Health Organization (2001). *The World Health Report 2001: Mental health: New understanding, new hope.* www.who.int/whr/2001/main/en/contents.htm.

15

Serving the Most Severe of Serious Emotionally Disturbed Students in School Settings

JOSEPH E. NYRE, ERIC M. VERNBERG, and MICHAEL C. ROBERTS

An increasing number of children and youth enrolled in public schools have severe psychiatric disturbances, yet few school systems are adequately prepared to meet the needs of this population (Rones & Hoagwood, 2000). This unfortunate scenario arises in part from a relative dearth of school-based models that are effective and affordable for working with youngsters with serious emotional disturbances. Developing and garnering financial support to implement evidence-based models for helping youth with serious emotional disturbances succeed in school and other domains represents a significant and immediate challenge facing school systems, but also social services, mental health agencies, and, increasingly, the juvenile justice system (Osher, Osher, & Smith, 1994).

This chapter focuses on children with extreme forms of psychopathology and very poor adaptive functioning. Many school and community mental health settings label this group of children as having serious emotional disturbance (SED) for purposes of funding and access to services, but there is variability in local or state criteria for SED. Common elements of SED definitions generally include the federal definition of the Individual with Disabilities Education Act (IDEA, 1997). As defined by Federal Law (CFR Parts 300 and 303):

> "(i) The term [emotional disturbance] means a condition exhibiting one or more of the following characteristics over a long period of time and to a marked degree that adversely affects a child's educational performance:

JOSEPH E. NYRE • Harvard Medical School, Boston, Massachusetts 02115. **ERIC M. VERNBERG and MICHAEL C. ROBERTS** • University of Kansas, Lawrence, Kansas 66045.

     (a) An inability to learn that cannot be explained by intellectual, sensory, or health factors.
     (b) An inability to build or maintain satisfactory interpersonal relationships with peers and teachers.
     (c) Inappropriate types of behavior or feelings under normal circumstances.
     (d) A general pervasive mood of unhappiness or depression.
     (e) A tendency to develop physical symptoms or fears associated with personal or school problems.
   (ii) The term includes schizophrenia. The term does not apply to children who are socially maladjusted, unless it is determined that they have an emotional disturbance" (*Federal Register,* Vol. 64, No. 48, March 12, 1999/Rules and Regulations p. 12422).

Additional criteria for SED often include a stipulation of *critical need*. Criteria for critical need often include imminent risk of hospitalization or other institutional care, suspension/expulsion, or out-of-home placement due to extreme disturbances in behavior or emotional regulation (Nyre, 1997).

Specification of SED criteria is important in allocating resources and services equitably and fairly. However, the term SED may contribute to a disconnection between systems of care that rely on other criteria and terminology for defining children with severe mental health problems. Child psychiatrists, clinical child psychologists, and other mental health practitioners, for example, generally utilize DSM-IV diagnoses in communications of many types (e.g., case formulation, communication with other providers, reimbursement for services), but the more general label of SED does not fit in this nosology. Child protection services use event- (physically or sexually abused) or circumstance-oriented terms (child in need of care) to justify services, and the juvenile justice and family court systems employ yet another set of terms and criteria to allocate services or sanctions. These variations in terminology reflect different mandates and conceptual traditions among schools, social services, mental health providers, and legal systems when confronted with severely disturbed children and adolescents.

In addition to contributing to communication barriers, variability in criteria and mandates for providing services to seriously disturbed children often contributes to a constantly changing set of service providers, each with a different agenda and plan. For example, child protection or family preservation services may be withdrawn after a standard period of time whether or not family functioning has improved. Similarly, community mental health services may hinge on a family's ability to pay or willingness to participate in services that are offered. Many families of seriously disturbed children struggle with finances, transportation, and parental adjustment, posing serious barriers to participation in the clinic-based mental health services that continue to be the predominant model of service delivery. Overlapping services are offered. For example, protective service agencies may fund psychotherapy focusing closely on sexual or physical abuse at the same time a community mental health agency is offering individual or family counseling for behavior management or other psychological issues. In court-involved families, parenting classes or visits with parole or truancy officers may be ordered, leaving the family with a patchwork of conflicting advice or directives. At the same time, important services such as respite care or after-school care often do not fit the mandate of any of the systems involved with disturbed children and their families.

The available epidemiological evidence reveals that approximately 20% of children and adolescents currently meet, or within the last 6 months have met criteria for a psychological disorder (Roberts, Attkinsson, & Rosenblatt, 1998), with 5–9% meeting criteria for serious emotional disturbance (Friedman et al., 1996). Moreover, research on mental health economics indicates mental health expenditures increased threefold from $3.5 billion to $11.75 billion during the period of 1986 to 1998 (National Advisory Mental Health Council, 2001). While positive correlations between rates of psychopathology and mental health expenditures may be noted, few would argue that agencies, specifically schools, continue to struggle to meet the needs of children and youth encountering significant psychiatric disturbance.

In recognition of the significant, present, and immediate mental health needs of this nation's children, much attention in recent years has been directed toward valuing school settings as an appropriate environment to provide access to a continuum of high-quality mental health services (Vernberg, Roberts, & Nyre, in press). By augmenting traditional school-based services through the development of expanded school mental health (ESMH) programs (Weist, Ginsburg, & Shaffer, 1999), researchers, practitioners, administrators, and policymakers have worked to develop effective programs and disseminate their key ingredients to better serve this population.

Federal and state laws require educational, social service, and mental health agencies to implement either individual or collaborative programs to meet the educational and mental health needs of children encountering severely debilitating psychiatric disturbance, yet these agencies have collectively struggled to develop effective programs (Quinn & McDougal, 1998). As a result, children and youth exhibiting SED often receive the least effective interventions, consume the greatest amount of resources, and show the poorest outcomes (Vernberg et al., in press).

Embedded in this movement is the notion of a "true continuum of interventions." A true continuum of interventions is generally defined as a full range of mental health services that includes assessment, individual, group, and family therapies, and consultation at the primary, secondary, and tertiary prevention levels (Weist et al., 1999). Presumably, this continuum of interventions effectively encompasses children and families exhibiting various levels of psychiatric need, but it is unclear how often these services are actually provided, especially to those at the most severe ends of the problem index. Thus, although this population also often requires the most intensive and coordinated services (Rones & Hoagwood, 2000), children and youth encountering severely debilitating psychiatric disturbance predominately receive ineffective, disjointed, and difficult-to-access piecemeal mental health services. Therefore, it is not surprising that researchers and practitioners have called for a more comprehensive provision of empirically validated programs for children exhibiting serious emotional disturbances.

In this chapter we briefly review the approaches schools have taken to serve children with SED. Next, we discuss general tenets of successful school-based mental health programs. Last, with a foundation in best practices, increased accessibility, and ecological validity, we present a school-based program for children encountering severely debilitating SED that is developing empirical validation.

PROGRAM OPTIONS AND OUTCOMES

In the collective struggle to educate and treat children with SED, schools and affiliated mental health service providers often utilize one or more program options. These have included inpatient hospitalization, partial-hospital (day treatment) programs, outsourced services of community mental health agencies, and traditional special education behavioral programs. These options are discussed in the following, with specific emphasis on traditional school-based approaches.

Inpatient Hospitalization

Referral and placement in an inpatient psychiatric facility or unit typically occurs via one of two methods. School-initiated placements may occur upon the consensus of the multidisciplinary individual educational plan (IEP) team that the student's educational needs are unable to be met in any other manner. This team would include but not be limited to the student's parents, teachers, administrator, and the school psychologist, counselor, and/or social worker. Upon this placement, the medical team and the multidisciplinary IEP team will make decisions regarding future educational placements. The second avenue for placement in an inpatient psychiatric unit or facility requires a referral outside the school district. Although the problems often arise in school settings, decision making about hospitalization is not under the control of the schools. Concerns, background information, and initiation of referral may be made by either psychologists or social workers in the school districts, but typically others make the final decision to place. Once in such a unit, decisions about discharge and aftercare are similarly out of the hands of the schools—despite the fact that schools ultimately take responsibility for educational services to a child manifesting SED.

Inpatient hospitalization represents an effective tool in crisis stabilization but has been shown to not produce good long-term outcomes (Friesen & Koroloff, 1990; Henggeler, 1994; Kiesler, 1993; Lyman & Wilson, 2001; Weisz et al., 1995). While there may be many underlying factors effecting these outcomes, the inability of hospitalization to improve environmental variables precipitating hospitalization (Friesen & Koroloff, 1990) diminishes its value to school districts as a program option. Further complicating this option are recent changes in health care funding resulting in a reduction in two major areas: the allowable number of days per inpatient psychiatric admission and the quantity of psychiatric services per year. Consequently, these issues combined with an average cost of over $500.00 per day, developing school district-controlled hospitalization does not represent a viable option for school districts attempting to maximize benefits with existing funds.

Day Treatment

Various mental health units for intensive therapeutic interventions for children with serious emotional disturbances have been created over the years under various labels such as day treatment, therapeutic day care centers, therapeutic classrooms, partial hospitalization, and psychoeducational treatment. Combinations of labels are sometimes used as well, such as partial day treatment. In these units, the child patient lives at home or with a caregiver (e.g., foster parents) within their own community while receiving services on a daily basis at the day treatment center. When "partial" is attached to the day treatment, the child or adolescent may spend at least part of the day in other activities that may include attendance at a regular school or special education service unit, or in a job-training program. Typically, day treatment involves psychiatric staff and settings where the focus is on the psychotherapeutic modality with a strong psychiatric orientation. If any educational components are included, the teaching staff is employed by the psychiatric center. Although models may differ, these settings are separate from the regular schools attended by the child patient. Services provided in day treatment closely resemble those associated with inpatient or hospitalization, such as medication, individual psychodynamic therapy, group psychotherapy, family therapy, parent groups, milieu therapy, behavior modification, and educational/special education programs and other treatment and supportive counseling (Farley, 1991). Thus, day treatment is a less restrictive environment and perhaps carries less stigma often associated with inpatient hospitalization (Zimet & Farley, 1991). Because evening and overnight expenses are not involved, day treatment costs are less than inpatient treatment, but the therapeutic elements may be just as intense and expensive.

Community Mental Health Services

Outsourcing services to community mental health agencies represents a common practice employed by school districts. Outsourced services often include consultation, group psychotherapy, or self-contained psychoeducational treatment programs. While less expensive than inpatient and partial hospitalization, community mental health services also have questionable effectiveness and poor ecological validity (Friesen & Poertner, 1995; Knitzer, 1993; Koyanagi & Gaines, 1993; Weisz, Weiss, & Donenberg, 1992). That is, they often lack comprehensive services, are plagued with accessibility problems, and are often uncoordinated in organizing care (Friesen & Poertner, 1995; Knitzer, 1993; Koyanagi & Gaines, 1993). While such services represent an available, often necessary option for school districts that are frequently used, problems in location, ecological validity, accessibility, comprehensiveness, and co-administrative responsibilities underscore the need for integrated school-based models.

Traditional Educational Programs

Within the context of schools, programs for children with SED are most often limited to traditional special education environments. These services include education for part or all of the day in resource rooms, self-contained classes, or special centers, which often vary within and across schools, districts, regions, and states. Notwithstanding, small adult-to-student ratios in special settings are a common component of special education environments. While these service programs often include a strong behavioral modification component and are effective for some students requiring special education, such programs seldom offer psychotherapy or other mental health services (Conoley & Conoley, 1991; Knitzer, 1993; Marder, 1992) and may not be sufficient for addressing the comprehensive needs of children with SED. Consequently, the overt behaviors may be addressed, but issues underlying problem behaviors may either go unaddressed or be addressed in an uncoordinated fashion. As a result, children and youth with SED receiving services in these programs often do not transition to less restrictive settings and have shown significantly lower academic performance, graduation rates, and attendance at postgraduate institutions (Duchnowski, 1994). Moreover, this population is at high risk for inpatient psychiatric hospitalization, incarceration, and school failure or expulsion (Patterson, Reid, & Dishion, 1992). These traditional school-based programs are often limited by problems of a narrow focus on in-school behavior (Conoley & Conoley, 1991), limited knowledge, skills, and confidence of service providers, piecemeal noncomprehensive practices (Adelman, 1993; Adelman & Taylor, 1998), and general lack of services (Knitzer, 1993; Marder, 1992).

School-Based Mental Health Programs

In response to acknowledged difficulties in these various ways of treating and educating children with SED, school-based mental health programs have proliferated. However, few studies have specifically focused on programs for children with SED. The evidence that is available suggests such programs often continue to be planned and implemented in a narrow piecemeal fashion resulting in little coordination, integration, and continuity among staff- and community-based programs (Adelman & Taylor, 1998). The absence of these critical collaborative components may result in fragmented and disjointed services leading to (1) a lack of monitoring of the overall plan, (2) the child's needs not being addressed, and (3) duplications or omissions of services (Quinn, Epstein, & Cumblad, 1995; Stroul & Friedman, 1996). The tendency for schools and communities to rely on narrowly focused, short-term, cost-intensive crisis interventions for a small number at the extreme end of the continuum of the many students requiring some assistance (Adelman & Taylor, 1998) further complicates the matter. In our view, this situation intensifies the need for research focusing on tenets of successful school-based programs for children with SED.

In summary, school systems, administrators, and staff are seeking empirically validated school-based mental health programs for children with SED. In response, a growing movement has taken form to create comprehensive school-based centers, which include staff and services usually accessed in community mental health and private practice arenas. Presented in the following sections are general program descriptors and guidelines for school-based mental health programs and a detailed description of a promising school-based Intensive Mental Health Program (IMHP) for children with debilitating SED.

GENERAL COMPONENTS OF INTENSIVE MENTAL HEALTH PROGRAMS

In a review of research on school-based mental health services, Rones and Hoagwood (2000) examined common features of successful ESMH programs and noted the absence of research focusing specifically on the SED population. While not identified specifically for the SED special education population, common features of successful programs are relevant, in that they serve as a general platform from which programs for children with SED may be constructed. These common features include: "(a) consistent program implementation; (b) inclusion of parents, teachers, or peers; (c) use of multiple modalities; (d) integration of program content into general classroom curriculum; and (d) developmentally appropriate program components" (Rones & Hoagwood, 2000, p. 223). While these features are often described as "best practice" approaches to program implementation, school and mental health agencies do not uniformly adopt these basic principles. Additionally, given the lack of research on implementation of these features in outcome evaluation, the effectiveness is not known. Expanding on these common features and responding to the increased need for effective school-based programs for children with SED, in the subsequent sections we describe key ingredients and features of an effective school-based mental health program.

Intensive Mental Health Program

The IMHP model, now in its fifth year of operation, was developed through a public school–university collaboration to treat elementary school children (5–12 years old) with the most severe SED who (1) have extreme disturbances with emotional regulation; (2) have severe deficiencies in behavioral control resulting in an inability to function in general or special education settings; and (3) typically consume multiple social service, medical, therapeutic, and legal resources in the community (Vernberg, Nyre, & Roberts, 2000).

Focusing on interprofessional collaboration, the program develops and implements a coherent, consistent service plan for each child, using collaboration and consensus building among key stakeholders (teaching staff, mental health providers, social service agencies, parents, and the children themselves). Initially, children diagnosed with SED attend the IMHP classroom for one-half of each school day (either morning or afternoon), where they receive intensive mental health services from a highly trained interdisciplinary staff. (See Table 1 for a description of these personnel.) Unique to the IMHP, children continue to attend their regular

Table 1. Staffing and Functions of the Intensive Mental Health Program[a]

Title	Functions	Hours per week
Special education teacher	Lead teacher for classroom	20
Paraprofessional teacher	Behavior management and classroom instruction	20
Master's-level therapists	Individual and group therapists, coordination of service plan, and contacts with home and neighborhood school	20 each for two therapists
Doctoral-level psychologist	Supervision of mental health services	3
School social work intern	Consultation with neighborhood school and home, assist with service plan	10
School social worker	Supervision of social work intern, facilitate service coordination	3
School psychologist	Consultation on service plan	2
Child psychiatrist	Consultation on service plan and management of medication	As needed

[a]Classes last 3 hours with a maximum of six children per classroom.

school (the "neighborhood school") during the remaining half-day throughout the treatment process, thus allowing effective functioning at home and across school settings to remain a primary objective.

Program evaluation is especially critical in demonstrating the efficacy and cost-effectiveness of emerging school-based programs, which often require state and federal moneys for continued operation. A review of research published to date on the IMHP model of service delivery reveals program effectiveness in the domains of child-specific outcomes, family functioning, and systemic benefits (Nyre & McVey, 2000; Randall et al., 1998; Vernberg et al., 2000, in press). In a series of reports, it was noted that 95% of the children admitted to the IMHP maintained a part-time educational placement in their neighborhood schools, with 74–80% successfully returning to less restrictive educational environments in their respective neighborhood schools (Nyre & McVey, 2000; Randall et al., 1998; Vernberg et al., in press). Moreover, children receiving services through the IMHP have shown significant decreases in rates of suspensions, removal from the home, and hospitalization (Vernberg et al., 2000, in press). More specific to level of functioning, analysis of preadmission and discharge scores for these children on the Child and Adolescent Functional Assessment Scale (Hodges, 1990, 1994) revealed significant improvement in functioning across the domains of school, home, community, moods, self-harm, and thinking (Vernberg et al., 2002). Within the context of family involvement, a significant majority of the parents were rated as having "good involvement" in treatment and experienced improved family functioning during and after services were provided through the IMHP (Vernberg et al., in press).

Evidence of the systemic benefit of the IMHP may be found in the combination of cost-effectiveness and treatment success. Cost-effectiveness may be defined in several manners dependent upon the intended outcome of the system. Benefits of the IMHP include (1) training opportunities for future practitioners who concurrently assist the system and the children within the system; (2) diminished future expenditures allocated to the target population resulting from effective early or initial intensive intervention; and (3) by reductions in inpatient psychiatric hospitalizations, diversion from the juvenile justice system, and reductions in the duplication of community-based services (likely drawing funds from similar sources). Of the 74–80% of students successfully returning to less restrictive educational environments in their respective neighborhood schools, no student has returned to the IMHP (Nyre & McVey, 2000; Vernberg et al., in press). Consequently, the costs to the system (transportation, staff allocation, paraeducator support, supplies, etc.) are significantly smaller over time when compared to the aforementioned alternatives.

The summarized available research indicates that the IMHP model is a feasible alternative to inpatient hospitalization and private day treatment programs that are more expensive than the IMHP. This model holds promise in terms of cost-effectiveness and beneficence by reducing the redundancy or omission of services and by actively countering "piecemeal" treatment approaches, which are typified by the lack of coordination, integration, and continuity among service providers working with a child and his/her family system (Adelman & Taylor, 1998). By targeting the elementary level, the IMHP also serves a preventive function (secondary and tertiary), arresting the persistence of symptoms over time, and diminishing the exacerbation of existing problems (Randall et al., 1998). This model merges the formats of traditional specialized classrooms (e.g., Behavior Disorders (BD) or SED Classrooms), which emphasize behavior modification and educational assistance, with those of psychiatric inpatient or day-treatment programs, which emphasize group and individual therapy (Nyre & McVey, 2000; Randall et al., 1998; Vernberg et al., 2000, in press).

Common Features of Other School-Based Programs and IMHP Innovative Contributions

IMHP provides a unique and intensive model of intervention for children and youth with SED. By definition, these children encounter severe impairments in functioning at school and at home. Components of effective school-based mental health programs identified by Rones and Hoagwood (2000) are embedded in the foundation of the IMHP structure. However, these components alone do not sufficiently describe the IMHP. For the purposes of elucidation, IMHP innovations and components are discussed within the context of those presented by Rones and Hoagwood (2000). Following this section, IMHP service and treatment features are presented.

1. Consistent Program Implementation. The IMHP model provides a highly structured and consistent system to manage children's behavior. Data are gathered for the clinical assessment of children and for program evaluation. Data are collected from referral sources, consultation partners, and community providers to formulate a comprehensive conceptualization of factors influencing each child's functioning. These data are reviewed at weekly staff meetings, in weekly supervision, and by the IMHP oversight committee to ensure program continuity and consistency across each program site.
2. Inclusion of Parents, Teachers, or Peers. As children continue to attend their neighborhood schools for one-half of the day and receive IMHP services for the remaining half-day, a natural avenue exists for the inclusion of parents, teachers, and peers. IMHP staff communicates continuously with each student's neighborhood schoolteachers and special education staff regarding progress in the IMHP classroom, including consultation on effective behavior management strategies. This communication and information sharing facilitates the eventual transition to full-time attendance to a less restrictive environment within the neighborhood school. IMHP therapists continuously consult with parents and childcare providers concerning management issues, educational concerns, and therapeutic issues. In addition to working continuously with families and school personnel, IMHP staff collaborate and coordinate with community agencies often including case managers, therapists, and psychiatrists at the community mental health center, private psychotherapists, foster care providers and support staff, protective service providers from the state social service agency, health specialists, and family court. This interprofessional and multidisciplinary collaboration among various treatment providers and community-based professionals is intended to facilitate generalization of treatment effects and decrease fragmentation of services between agencies. Last, because children attend their neighborhood schools for a portion of each academic day, access to same-age and socially appropriate peers may be accomplished and monitored.
3. Use of Multiple Modalities. Treatment planning and implementation by IMHP staff focuses on individual-, group-, family-, and system-based

interventions. The IMHP also creates a treatment setting for children offering an individually tailored array of empirically supported psychosocial and biomedical interventions including group and individual therapy, social skills training, relaxation training, targeted behavior management, and carefully evaluated medication trials (see Fig. 1 for an example of the typical service plan for a child in the IMHP). For example, behavior management programs, token economies, and positive reinforcement contingent upon displaying appropriate behavior are similar to those found in more traditional BD classrooms. In the IMHP behavior management systems are extended to the neighborhood school and the child's home.

4. Integration of Program Content into General Classroom Curriculum. As mentioned earlier, the IMHP benefits from the unique approach of having children remain in their neighborhood school program during a portion of the day. As a result, integration of IMHP group and child-specific interventions are accomplished through *in vivo* consultation and implemented daily in the child's neighborhood school. Effectiveness of this daily integration is then monitored. Further, IMHP staff continuously consults with neighborhood school staff in the development and daily monitoring of child-specific interventions. Last, the program structure includes a certified teacher and the ability to approximate classroom settings within the IMHP environment. This provides a measure of viability for program content integration.

5. Developmentally Appropriate Program Components. Upon meeting admission criteria, children are admitted to one of four classrooms based on the child's developmental level. This practice allows for program components to be developed and implemented based on a more narrow range of development (i.e., 2 years). In addition to program components, individual treatment plans are based on empirically valid data gathered from referral sources, consultation partners, and community providers to formulate a comprehensive conceptualization of factors influencing each child's functioning ultimately resulting in a developmentally appropriate treatment plan.

The IMHP model is intensive and comprehensive in providing therapeutic services for students who have significant emotional and psychological needs not effectively served in the aforementioned traditional special education programs or in traditional mental health settings. As its primary goal, the IMHP model focuses on (1) returning children with SED to a less restrictive educational environment; (2) increasing the accessibility of mental health services; (3) coordinating separate services into a coherent, consistent whole; (4) utilizing empirically supported treatments or "best practices" where evidence is not fully developed; and (5) increasing the probability of positive outcomes. The integrative combination of these intervention modalities and orientations makes IMHP a promising model for mental health services for children with SED.

IMHP Principles: Service and Treatment Features

Expanding on the five common features of effective ESMH programs (Rones & Hoagwood, 2000), IMHP is predicated on nine principles encompassing service and

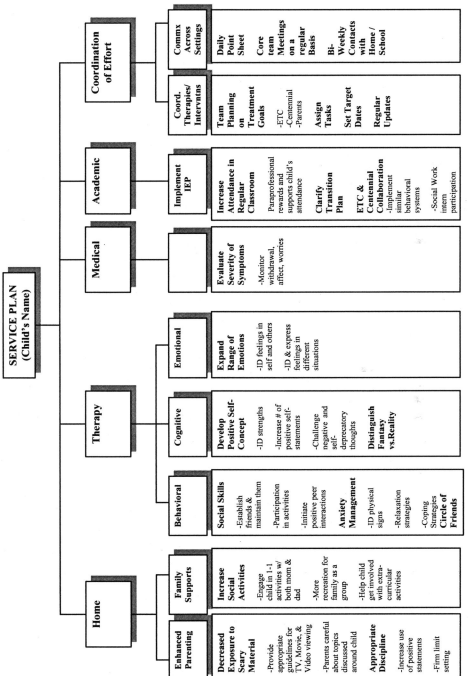

Figure 1. Example of service plan for child in the intensive mental health program.

treatment features. It is important to differentiate the service delivery features (i.e., how treatment is delivered) and treatment features (i.e., what is delivered) of IMHP. Service delivery features are the same for each child, whereas treatment features are tailored to individual needs and psychopathology. Both the service delivery features and the treatment features are designed to be consistent with the following nine basic principles guiding IMHP.

1. Maintain Placement in the Child's Home and Neighborhood School. This allows children to maintain relationships with family members, teachers, and peers. This has important bidirectional components, in that relationships are not severed and the responsibility to care for and educate the child is not diminished.
2. Emphasize an Empirical Approach to Guide Interventions. Treatment components are selected consistent with current research on empirically supported (evidenced-based) psychosocial and pharmacological interventions (e.g., American Academy of Child and Adolescent Psychiatry, 1998; Lonigan, Elbert, & Johnson, 1998).
3. Focus on Cognitive and Behavioral Skill Development. Specific attention in treatment planning is given to teaching and promoting appropriate behaviors and social–cognitive skills. Cognitive–behavioral and behavioral techniques for specific child problems have thus far achieved the strongest empirical support among psychosocial interventions (Lonigan et al., 1998) and can be directly applied to improve functioning in the home and in neighborhood school settings.
4. Attend to Cross-Setting Linkages and Events. Point sheets are completed each day in the neighborhood school, IMHP, and the child's home. All respondents view ratings to facilitate communication. These data are aggregated by the IMHP staff and child to assist in understanding the interrelationship between settings and events and to make data-driven treatment decisions. Service plans are developed to directly assess and intervene in multiple settings. By utilizing this data set, individual problem behaviors can be targeted in multiple settings by various providers, thereby maximizing effort and impact.
5. Emphasize Generalization and Maintenance of Treatment Outcomes. An analog classroom schedule is used in the IMHP to focus on skills needed in the neighborhood school and family for successful functioning. Additionally, frequent communication occurs with the school, home, and community providers, resulting in an enhanced active involvement in the child's treatment by every important adult in the child's life. Moreover, collaborating agencies often use the interagency collaboration model established by IMHP when providing follow-up care after the child has been discharged from IMHP.
6. Collaborate with Everyone Involved with Child. Based on the foundations established by the Child and Adolescent Service System Program (CASSP) principles (Day & Roberts, 1991), team and individual meetings are used to establish consensus on goals and treatment. Collaborative services are therefore child centered, family focused, community based, culturally competent, and least restrictive/least intrusive.

7. View Assessment and Diagnosis as Ongoing Process. Children have significant daily therapeutic contact with master's-level clinicians, who receive close supervision by doctoral-level, licensed clinical child or school psychologists. Comprehensive case conceptualizations are formulated based on the child's history, ongoing observations, and clinical/psychosocial assessments. Detailed records of school reports and hospitalization summaries are maintained and integrated into the overall treatment and planning process for each child.

8. Maintain a Developmental Focus. The nature of the intervention varies based on the developmental level of each child and his or her family. The child's maturity and ability to reason are considered throughout treatment planning. A developmental perspective consistent with literature on best practice is integrated with behavioral and cognitive–behavioral approaches.

9. Cultivate an Authoritative Parenting Style for Adults Involved with the Child. An interaction approach consistent with an authoritative style is taught to each significant adult involved with each IMHP student. Warmth and emotional closeness are cultivated, effective discipline techniques are taught, and age-appropriate expectations, demands, and challenges are nurtured with families, teachers, and other caregivers.

IMHP KEY INGREDIENTS

In the following section, key ingredients leading to successful service delivery are discussed. These key ingredients include, among other things, a unique staffing formula, treatment features, and characteristics of the family, home, school, and community. A common theme throughout this discussion focuses specifically on effective collaboration and consistency.

Staffing Requirements

Each IMHP classroom requires multiple personnel working collaboratively toward implementation of service plans (see Table 1). The atypical allocation of time for the master's-level therapists is worth special mention. Specifically, each therapist is allocated 20 hours per week for each IMHP classroom (sessions are 3 hours per day, morning or afternoon). Two therapists are assigned to each classroom, and each therapist is on site in the classroom every other day, resulting in a constant therapeutic presence. Through this arrangement, each therapist spends an average of 7.5 hours weekly with the six children assigned to each classroom, with primary therapeutic responsibilities for three of the six children. This allocation results in 2.5 hours per week for clinical supervision and 10 hours per week for home visits, consultations with the neighborhood school and/or with community service providers, and other collateral contacts.

Direct classroom instruction remains the primary responsibility of the special education classroom teacher, who is vital to successful implementation of group and individual interventions. Consequently, the classroom teacher also fulfills the following functions: (1) assists in group therapy as needed; (2) maintains active individual education plans; (3) helps implement the discipline and behavior management plans; (4) attends weekly IMHP staff meetings; (5) conducts group check-in; (6) consults with the home school teacher regarding instructional behavioral components; and (7) attends parent–teacher conferences, provides grades, and assists in transition planning.

The therapists and social workers are assigned to a child's family to conduct case management and interagency coordination. Therapists and social workers often coordinate access to other community-based services available for the family outside IMHP. Similarly, therapists, social workers, and classroom teachers coordinate Core Team Meetings with the student's parents, neighborhood school, community agencies, and IMHP staff. IMHP therapists, social workers, teacher, and paraprofessionals provide consultation to the neighborhood school. While only therapists and social workers consult at the administrative level, the teacher, therapist, or social worker may consult at the direct-service level by modeling appropriate classroom use of point sheets, a modified token economy (using a "Gotcha Ticket" system adapted from Jenson, Rhode, & Reavis, 1996), and other child-specific interventions. By design, the point sheets utilize a response cost system where points are lost for failing or refusing to exhibit specific target behaviors. For example, losing more than 20% of total available weekly points costs the child an opportunity to participate in a weekly special fun activity. The Gotcha Ticket system operates entirely on positive reinforcement. Gotcha Tickets are disbursed liberally for appropriate or desired behavior and are exchanged for a variety of rewards in the "Gotcha Ticket Store." The awarding of a Gotcha Ticket for appropriate behavior is always paired with a positive verbal statement identifying the behavior. Gotcha Tickets serve as reinforcements for the children and measure the frequency of adults' positive comments to the child. Finally, therapists and social workers also conduct biweekly home visits to provide support to parents and to implement various home-based interventions.

Service Delivery

Key elements of the IMHP service delivery model are summarized in Table 2. These include *IMHP classroom features* (e.g., individual and group therapy, behavior management system), *IMHP supervision features* (e.g., weekly 2-hour supervisory sessions with doctoral-level psychologist), *IMHP collaboration features* (e.g., consultation with neighborhood school, families, other service providers), and *IMHP transition features* (e.g., written plan for transition and regular monitoring of postdischarge implementation of plan). For each child in IMHP, the provision of each feature is recorded continuously, providing documentation of treatment fidelity (Vernberg et al., in press).

Treatment Features

The IMHP treatment planning process utilizes empirically validated interventions employed for each child through the service delivery model described previously. Service plans differ depending on each child's symptomatology, psychopathology, and life circumstances, and are developed following comprehensive review of the potential factors causing and maintaining the child's symptoms (see Fig. 1 for the organization of the interventions). Service plans are developed and

Table 2. Key Elements of Service Delivery Model for the Intensive Mental Health Program[a]

Elements of service delivery model

IMHP classroom features
Child attends classroom daily, 3 hours/day
Individual therapy 2 days/week, 30 minutes each
Group check-in, 15 minutes/day
Group therapy, 4 days/week, 40 minutes each
Target behaviors recorded on point sheet, daily
Psychiatric and behavioral symptoms rated by therapist, daily
"Gotcha Ticket" coupons awarded, daily
"Gotcha Ticket" shopping offered, daily

IMHP supervision features
Therapists discuss child with doctoral-level psychologist during clinical supervision, $\geq$1/week
Classroom staff meets weekly, $\geq$40 minutes
Staff complete comprehensive evaluation form, giving baseline history and assessment of current functioning within 1 month of program entry, with updates $\geq$1/month thereafter

IMHP collaboration features
Consult with home school staff regarding behavior, $\geq$1/week
Meet individually with parents/guardians, $\geq$1/2 weeks
Attend core team meeting with home school staff and community service providers, $\geq$1/month
Provide summary of target behaviors and psychiatric/behavioral symptoms to medication prescriber (if applicable), $\geq$1/month
Distribute "Collaborative Contacts" form, which lists all service providers involved with child to all these providers within 1 month of program entry, into program, with updates $\geq$1/month
Distribute Service Plan schematic to service providers within 1 month of program entry, update $\geq$1/month thereafter (see Fig. 1 for example)
Observe home school use of behavior management system, $\geq$1/month

Home school service features
Child attends home school classes daily, 3 hours/day
Target behaviors recorded on point sheet daily
Teaching staff uses "Gotcha Tickets" to reward desired behavior daily
"Gotcha Ticket" shopping offered daily

Home service features
Child lives with parents or guardians daily (whenever possible)
Target behaviors recorded on point sheet daily
Parents use "Gotcha Ticket" coupons to reward desired behavior daily
Parents/guardians allow home visits by IMHP staff, $\geq$2/month

Transition features (upon completion of IMHP)
Sign written agreement with home school, family, and other service providers for services to be offered following transition
Review transition plan implementation with above team 2 and 4 weeks after transition
Follow-up contact with family and home school 3 and 6 months posttransition

[a]From Vernberg, E. M., Roberts, M. C., & Nyre, J. E. (in press). School-based intensive mental health treatment. In D. T. Marsh & M. A. Fristad (Eds.), *Handbook of serious emotional disturbance in children and adolescents.* New York: Wiley.

refined in consultation with the family and other service providers. Service plans are then distributed to providers and parents to establish treatment congruency, determine roles, and assign responsibilities.

Ongoing assessment of behavioral, cognitive, and emotional status is conducted to guide decision making. Daily point sheets are utilized to track three or four (dependent upon developmental level) specific target behaviors developed by the treatment team. The students earn points across all settings (i.e., home, neighborhood school, and IMHP classroom). Thus, the point sheet serves as an indicator of cooperation and involvement in the therapeutic mission of the program. Sometimes the daily sheets include written critical comments, are mismarked with inappropriately removed or added points, or not returned at all. In these situations, the treatment team redoubles efforts to engage the neighborhood school and the parents who misunderstand, misuse, or sabotage the point sheets. When cooperation from neighborhood school staff and families is sufficient, point sheets provide a detailed record of the child's behavior. The point sheets also serve as a tool to identify patterns in children's behavior related to medication changes, treatment gains, and environmental factors. Daily ratings of symptoms observed in the IMHP classroom serve as another valuable source of continuous, high-quality clinical data.

The treatment features listed in Table 3 are tracked continuously to assess fidelity to the principles guiding the IMHP, monitor overall therapeutic progress, and guide treatment decisions. Categories of treatment features include (1) case conceptualization (e.g., review of data from multiple sources and conceptual paradigms), (2) treatment selection (e.g., utilize empirically supported treatments for each identified target of change), and (3) treatment implementation (e.g., continuous program monitoring).

Child Characteristics

Severity and chronicity of disturbance at the time of admission often influence treatment outcomes (Nyre & McVey, 2000; Vernberg et al., 2000, in press). Detailed descriptions of severity and chronicity are gained from the comprehensive, in-depth review of history and careful attention to conflicting information typically found in case materials and histories for seriously disturbed children. Specific variables include the age of onset of severely disruptive or abnormal behavior; the degree to which impairment has been continuous versus episodic; and the intensity of disturbance in mood, thought qualities, and activity or arousal (Vernberg et al., in press).

Characteristics of Family and Home Environment

Parental psychopathology is a frequent barrier to a child's treatment progress, especially when manifested as erratic, antisocial, or dysregulated behavior. The extensive contact with parents and caregivers represents an excellent opportunity to examine these indicators as prognostic signs. Parents who exhibit psychological problems are referred to practitioners in the community, especially to local mental health practitioners. Many of the parents have already had previous contact with the mental health system for their own problems and may simply need to reaccess treatment.

Table 3. Treatment Features of the Intensive Mental Health Program

Case conceptualization

Case history and assessment of current functioning conforms to practice parameters for primary presenting problems (American Association of Child and Adolescent Psychiatry).

Empirically supported, psychometrically sound, age-normed measures of child functioning are included in evaluation.

Information from multiple sources considered including:

    Home school personnel

    Other service providers

    Parents or guardian

    Direct observation using validated observational system

    Child self-report

Case formulation includes consideration of presenting problems from multiple conceptual paradigms, including:

    Biological

    Behavioral

    Cognitive and cognitive–behavioral

    Family systems

    Attachment relationships

    Cultural and socioeconomic

Treatment selection

Explicitly identify measurable targets for change in each of the following areas:

    Biological regulation (e.g., arousal, mood, activity level, basic cognitive processes)

    Overt behavior

    Social cognition (e.g., social information processing, knowledge structures)

    Family relations

    Peer relations

    Teaching staff–child relations

    Other environmental factors contributing to dysfunction

Utilize empirically supported interventions to address each identified target for change (i.e., defined as efficacious or probably efficacious using criteria specified by Lonigan et al. (1998)).

Treatment implementation

Review in clinical supervision ≥1/month

    Progress on implementing selected strategies for each child

    Objective indicators of child functioning (i.e., graphs of point sheets from home, home school, IMHP settings, data from daily ratings of symptoms in IMHP)

    Level of cooperation from home school and family in carrying out service

    Progress in individual therapy for each child

    Progress in group treatment for each child

Clinical supervision provided as needed for:

    Therapists addressing difficulties in individual therapy

    Therapists addressing difficulties in cooperation from families/home school staff

    Therapists addressing difficulties in group therapy

    References to relevant research-based justification for treatment decisions

Characteristics of Schools and Community

Children served by the IMHP often receive a notably higher standard of education and mental health service than do others (Vernberg et al., in press). For example, the willingness, level of understanding, and ability of neighborhood school staff to implement basic behavior management strategies and IMHP interventions vary. As a result, children appear to make much less progress if they attend neighborhood school settings wherein staff is unwilling or unable to implement basic IMHP interventions. Daily ratings of child behavior and weekly visits to the neighborhood school provide robust data pertaining to the quality of service offered to IMHP children.

Similarly, community service providers vary in either their willingness or their ability to collaborate in both developing and implementing a consistent, coherent service plan. Once again, data gathered underscore the importance and impact of teamwork in the pursuit of a well-developed, empirically based effective service plan. Ongoing ratings of cooperation and follow-through by other providers are gathered routinely, enabling empirical testing of the intuitively posited influence on treatment outcomes.

DISCUSSION

The professional literature regarding school reform, social reform, and mental health reform has collectively identified schools as having the potential to provide effective mental health services. As a result, a growing body of research is being conducted on ESMH programs. However, few studies to date have identified components, features, and active ingredients of effective school-based mental health programs for children with SED.

As school, social service, and mental health agencies continue to develop programs for children and youth encountering SED, the IMHP as described here represents a fiscally sound, effective school-based approach. Strong leadership, a collaborative environment, and adherence to program components, features, and ingredients outlined in this chapter combine to offer a viable solution to the significant difficulties encountered by systems attempting to meet the critical needs of children encountering debilitating SED. While this model is not free from barriers, it can be successfully replicated and may serve as a foundation for future development of school-based programs for children with SED.

REFERENCES

Adelman, H. S. (1993). School-linked mental health interventions: Toward mechanisms for service coordination and integration. *Journal of Community Psychology, 21,* 309–319.

Adelman, H. S., & Taylor, L. (1998). Reframing and mental health in schools and expanding school reform. *Educational Psychologist, 33,* 135–152.

American Academy of Child and Adolescent Psychiatry (1998). Practice parameter of the assessment and treatment of children and adolescents with posttraumatic stress disorder. *Journal of the American Academy of Child and Adolescent Psychiatry, 37*(4S–26S).

Burns, B. J., & Friedman, R. M. (1990). Examining the research base for child mental health services and policy. *The Journal of Mental Health Administration, 17,* 87–97.

Conoley, J. C., & Conoley, C. W. (1991). Collaboration for child adjustment: Issues for school- and clinic-based child psychologists. *Journal of Consulting and Clinical Psychology, 59,* 821–829.

Day, C., & Roberts, M. C. (1991). Activities of the child and adolescent service system program for improving mental health services for children and families. *Journal of Clinical Child Psychology, 20,* 340–350.

Duchnowski, A. J. (1994). Innovative service models: Education. *Journal of Clinical Child Psychology, 23*(Suppl.), 13–18.

Friedman, R. M., Katz-Leavy, J. W., Mandersheid, R. W., & Sonderheimer, D. L. (1996). Prevalence of serious emotional disturbance in children and adolescents. In R. W. Mandersheid & M.A. Sonnenschein (Eds.), *Mental health, United States, 1996* (p. 83) (DHHS Publication No. SMA 96-3098). Washington, DC: U.S. Government Printing Office.

Friesen, B. J., & Koroloff, N. M. (1990). Family-centered services: Implications for mental health administration and research. *Journal of Mental Health Administration, 17,* 13–25.

Friesen, B. J., & Poertner, J. (1995). *From case management to service coordination for children with emotional, behavioral, or mental disorders: Building on family strengths.* Baltimore, MD: Brookes.

Henggeler, S. W. (1994). A consensus: Conclusion of the APA Task Force report on innovative models of mental health services for children, adolescents, and their families. *Journal of Clinical Child Psychology, 23*(Suppl.), 3–6.

Hoagwood, K., Jensen, P. S., Petti, T., & Burns, B. J. (1996). Outcomes of mental health care for children and adolescents: I. A comprehensive conceptual model. *Journal of the American Academy of Child and Adolescent Psychiatry, 35,* 1055–1063.

Hodges, K. (1990, 1994 revision). *Child and Adolescent Functional Assessment Scale.* Ypsilanti, MI: Eastern Michigan University, Department of Psychology.

Individuals with Disabilities Act, 20, U.S.C., & Sect 1400 et. seq. (I.D.E.A. 1997).

Jenson, W. R., Rhode, G., & Reavis, H. K. (1996). *The tough kid toolbox.* Longmont, CO: Sopris West.

Kazdin, A. E., & Kendall, P. C. (1998). Current progress and future plans for developing effective treatments: Comments and perspectives. *Journal of Clinical Child Psychology, 27,* 217–226.

Kiesler, C. A. (1993). Mental health policy and mental hospitalization. *Current Directions in Psychological Science, 2,* 93–95.

Knitzer, J. (1993). Children's mental health policy: Challenging the future. *Journal of Emotional and Behavioral Disorders, 1,* 8–16.

Koyanagi, C., & Gaines, S. (1993). *All systems failure: An examination of the results of neglecting the needs of children with serious emotional disturbance.* Alexandria, VA: National Mental Health Association.

Lonigan, C. J., Elbert, J. C., & Johnson, S. B. (1998). Empirically supported psychosocial interventions for children: An overview. *Journal of Clinical Child Psychology, 27,* 138–145.

Lyman, R. D., & Wilson, D. R. (2001). Residential and inpatient treatment of emotionally disturbed children and adolescents. In C. E. Walker & M. C. Roberts (Eds.), *Handbook of clinical child psychology* (3rd ed., pp. 881–894). New York: Wiley.

Marder, C. (1992). *Secondary school students classified as serious emotionally disturbed: How are they being served?* Menlo Park, CA: SRI International.

National Advisory Mental Health Council Workgroup on Child and Adolescent Mental Health Intervention Development and Deployment (2001). *Blueprint for change: Research on child and adolescent mental health.* Washington, DC: Author (website: http://www.nimh.nih.gov/childhp/councildesc.cfm accessed: February 4, 2002).

Nyre, J. E. (1997, November). Serving mental health needs of children and families in school settings: An integrated model of service delivery. *KASP Examiner,* 16–17.

Nyre, J. E., & McVey, D. (2000, March). *Integrating mental health services in schools.* Paper presentation at convention of the National Association of School Psychologists, New Orleans, LA.

Osher, D., Osher, T., & Smith, C. (1994). Toward a national perspective in emotional and behavioral disorders. *Beyond Behavior, 6,* 6–17.

Patterson, G. R., Reid, J. B., & Dishion, T. J. (1992). *Antisocial boys.* Eugene, OR: Castalia.

Quinn, K. P., Epstein, M. H., & Cumblad, C. (1995). Developing comprehensive individualized community-based services for children and youth with emotional and behavior disorders: Direct service providers' perspective. *Journal of Child and Family Studies, 4,* 19–42.

Quinn, K. P., & McDougal, J. L. (1998). A mile wide and a mile deep: Comprehensive interventions for children and youth with emotional and behavioral disorders and their families. *School Psychology Review, 27,* 191–203.

Randall, C. J., Vernberg, E. M., Nyre, J., & McVey, D. (1998, August). *Effecting individualized treatment within uniform procedures in a therapeutic classroom.* Poster presented at the convention of the American Psychological Association, San Francisco, CA.

Roberts, R. E., Attkinsson, C. C., & Rosenblatt, A. (1998). Prevalence of psychopathology among children and adolescents. *American Journal of Psychiatry, 155,* 715–725.

Rones, M., & Hoagwood, K. (2000). School-based mental health services: A research review. *Clinical Child and Family Psychology Review, 3,* 223–241.

Stroul, B. A., & Friedman, R. M. (1996). The system of care philosophy. In B. A. Stroul (Ed.), *Children's mental health: Creating systems of care in a changing society* (pp. 2–22). Baltimore, MD: Brookes.

Vernberg, E. M., Nyre, J. E., Puddy, R. W., Jacobs, A. K., & Roberts, M. C. (2002, March). CAFAS outcomes for a school-based Intensive Mental Health Program. Paper presented in K. Hodges (chair), Evaluation of Intensive Interventions for youth with SED using the CAFAS. Symposium presented at the annual research conference A System of Care for Children's Mental Health: Expanding the Research Base, Tampa, FL.

Vernberg, E. M., Nyre, J. E., & Roberts, M. C. (2000, August). Helping SED children succeed in school: Keeping the door open. Paper presented in V. J. Look-Morales (chair), Opening the doors—School and SED. Symposium presented at the annual convention of the American Psychological Association, Washington, DC.

Vernberg, E. M., Roberts, M. C., & Nyre, J. E. (2002). School-based intensive mental health treatment. In D. T. Marsh & M. A. Fristad (Eds.), *Handbook of serious emotional disturbance in children and adolescents* (pp. 412–427). New York: Wiley.

Weist, M. D., Ginsburg G., & Shafer, M. (1999). Progress in adolescent mental health. *Adolescent Medicine: State of the Art Reviews, 10,* 165–174.

Weisz, J. R., Donenberg, G. R., Han, S. S., & Weiss, B. (1995). Bridging the gap between lab and clinic in child and adolescent psychotherapy. *Journal of Consulting and Clinical Psychology, 63,* 688–701.

Weisz, J. R., Weiss, B., & Donenberg, G. R. (1992). The lab versus the clinic: Effects of child and adolescent psychotherapy. *American Psychologist, 47,* 1578–1585.

16

Children with Special Health Care Needs in School

Responding to the Challenge through Comprehensive School-Based Health Care

CINDY M. SCHAEFFER, MARK D. WEIST, and JANE W. McGRATH

It is estimated that between 15 and 20% of children in the United States have a significant ongoing need for health care (Newacheck et al., 1998). In order to clearly define the group of children and youth discussed in this paper, the term "children with special health care needs" as defined by the Federal Bureau of Maternal and Child Health will be used. "Children with special health care needs are those who have or are at increased risk for a chronic physical, developmental, behavioral, or emotional condition, and who also require health and related services of a type or amount beyond that required by children generally" (American Academy of Pediatrics (AAP), 1993). This definition includes children with chronic illness that is defined as a condition that lasts at least 3 months and requires extensive hospitalization or in-home health services (AAP, 1993).

Paradoxically, this high prevalence of children with special health care needs is related to advances in medical science, which have greatly increased survival rates for a number of health conditions. For example, the median survival age for children with cystic fibrosis has more than doubled in the last 3 decades, up from 11 years in 1966 to 29 years in 1993 (Cystic Fibrosis Foundation, 1994). Similarly, acute lymphoblastic leukemia (ALL), a disease that was once almost uniformly fatal, now has an average childhood survival rate of 5 years or more (Mulhern &

CINDY M. SCHAEFFER • Johns Hopkins University Bloomberg School of Public Health, Baltimore, Maryland 21205. **MARK D. WEIST** • University of Maryland School of Medicine, Baltimore, Maryland 21201. **JANE W. McGRATH** • University of New Mexico School of Medicine, Albuquerque, New Mexico 87131.

Friedman, 1990). Moreover, while accidents remain the most common cause of childhood death, more children are surviving them—but often with permanent disabilities and complex medical needs (U.S. Department of Health and Human Services, 1994). Schools around the country are feeling the impact of these trends, as they are faced with more children with special health care needs than ever before.

In addition to inherent illness-related stressors (e.g., complying with complicated regimens, coping with physical limitations and discomfort), children with special health care needs face considerable stress in negotiating the multifaceted aspects of attending school. These include preparing for and getting to school, adjusting to being around peers (and often coping with questions, teasing, or rejection) and teachers, moving around the building, and facing academic demands while continuing to monitor and manage their illness. Related to these compounding stressors, children with special health care needs are at high risk for low educational attainment, poor adjustment to school, and a range of emotional and behavioral problems (Boekaerts & Roeder, 1999). In turn, these emotional and behavioral problems may exacerbate physical problems, in a negative snowballing effect leading to school avoidance and dropout.

Physical, emotional, and behavioral functioning is closely intertwined in youth with special health care needs. This complexity requires that programs address children's physical, emotional, and behavioral needs in an integrated fashion. One of the best ways to deliver such integrated care is through school-based health centers (SBHCs). The ideal SBHC provides a full range of care, including treatment of illnesses and accidents, management of chronic conditions, physical and laboratory assessment, and a continuum of mental health services (Juszcak et al., 1995). Due to their intuitive appeal (i.e., bringing needed services to youth "where they are") and to their demonstrated impacts on health and mental health outcomes, SBHCs are growing throughout the United States so that they now number over 1200 (Dryfoos, 1999). Importantly, SBHCs can be a critical resource for youth with special health care needs, enabling ongoing assessment, intervention, and support to address their physical, emotional, and behavioral issues.

In this chapter, we review the physical and mental health issues common to children with special health care needs and discuss how SBHCs and related school-based mental health programs can be instrumental in addressing these needs. Although specific medical conditions in children can be associated with unique stressors and issues, many common features also exist. In this paper, we provide a more general review based on the presumption that the psychosocial needs of children with various medical conditions are more similar than they are different (Rinehart, 1998).

CHILDREN WITH SPECIAL HEALTH CARE NEEDS

In addition to ongoing physical challenges, children with special health care needs also have significantly more school problems and psychosocial difficulties than do their healthy peers (Gortmaker et al., 1990; Lavigne & Faier-Routman, 1992; Pless, Power, & Peckham, 1993). Youth with chronic illness often present with low self-esteem, social withdrawal, problems in peer and adult relationships, and negative feelings about their conditions (Bowden, Dickey, & Greenberg, 1998). In all children, behavior, emotion, thought, and physical functioning are closely related. Problems in one domain are likely to be associated with problems in another domain. Anxiety and depression, for example, may cause or aggravate colitis in a child, and many conditions, such as lupus and asthma, are negatively affected by stress.

In some cases, social and educational difficulties are directly related to the medical condition itself, as when children have compromised cognitive functioning or are significantly disfigured by their condition. In other cases, difficulties in functioning stem from factors secondary to the medical condition, such as limited involvement in activities, inadequate social support, or poor coping skills. Often, these "secondary" problems are not recognized by teachers, school administrators, or even by school health and mental health staff. When problems are recognized, the teacher or staff member may not know how to address them.

Limitations in Activities

As many as one in eight youth report a limitation in their usual activities because of a special health care need (Newacheck & Taylor, 1992). School attendance is one prominent example. One study found that youth with special health care needs were three times more likely to spend days in bed and had three times as many days absent from school than other youth (Newacheck et al., 1998). Absence from school obviously interferes with academic performance; it also significantly interferes with peer and adult relationships and social development. Indeed, several studies have shown a significant positive relationship between school attendance and positive adjustment in children with special health care needs (Colgrove & Huntzinger, 1994; Stein & Jessup, 1984; Weitzman, Walker, & Gortmaker, 1986).

Even when children with special health care needs are able to attend school, they often are excluded from many activities such as special clubs, student government, and athletics. For some, frank physical limitations adversely affect communication, mobility, and activity level, making sports and extracurricular involvement difficult or impossible. However, some children with special health care needs are excluded from activities by parents, coaches, teachers, and schools only as a matter of routine, despite a lack of research to support such exclusion.

Inadequate Social Support

Social isolation and stigmatization by peers are commonly experienced by children with special health care needs in schools (LaGreca, 1990). On a website for children with special health care needs, stigma is a pervasive theme in the children's writings (Fleitas, 1999). For example, an 8-year-old wrote: "I have cystic fibrosis and sometimes I cough a lot. Here's what happens when I get in line at school. The kids in front of me walk real fast, and the kids behind me walk real slow. So it's sort of like I'm all alone." Sadly, teachers and other school staff often miss opportunities to reach out to these youth when they experience such isolation.

Maladaptive Coping Styles

Children with special health care needs, in a variety of ways, cope with the stress of managing their condition in school. For many children, school is a respite from a world of hospitals and medical procedures. For these children, especially for those with life-threatening illnesses, expectations of school attendance impart a clear and reassuring message that there is a future. In reaction to their strong desire to be in school, some children may disregard serious limitations in an attempt to be like everyone else and fit in. These children may be less compliant with medical regimens and more resistant to missing school for necessary medical care.

Other children have difficulty shedding the sick role they played while in the hospital to assume the role of student in school. Because they have been necessarily dependent on parents and health care providers, they may be less well equipped to meet the challenges of autonomy, achievement, and peer acceptance valued by their classmates. As a result, some children may replace developmentally appropriate goals of independence and achievement with more regressive attempts to maintain caretaking behavior by teachers and peers. Some may feign inability to perform a task to avoid having to do it.

This brief discussion underscores the many challenges youth with chronic illness experience when they attend school. School staff also face significant challenges in their attempts to educate, promote healthy development, and care for these youth.

INADEQUATE TRAINING OF SCHOOL PERSONNEL

In an era when children are discharged from hospitals in hours and days instead of weeks and months, children often return to school with medical needs that cause understandable tension for many classroom teachers. Teachers may not be fully informed about a student's health problem and may not know how to respond should a health crisis occur in the classroom. In addition, school staff may inappropriately prohibit students from taking needed medication for conditions such as asthma and diabetes. Teachers also may have concerns about medical devices that students need for daily living such as gastric catheters and glucometers. Schools are faced with the need for significant teacher and staff training in order to ensure that the school environment is safe for students with special health care needs.

In addition to anxiety and poor training in dealing with youth with special health care needs, teachers are often handicapped in their efforts to educate these students. In many cases when children are discharged from hospitals, limited information is given to the school. Without information on past academic and behavioral functioning, and without specific educational plans and administrative support, teachers may quickly feel frustrated or defeated in their efforts to work with these students.

Another problem can be an imbalanced focus on illnesses. For example, a child's diabetes may be relatively ignored (increasing physical risks) or it may receive excessive attention (increasing frustration). One child rebuked her teacher, using the anonymity of a web page to share this concern: "I hate it when you keep asking if I can eat this or do that. I know what my limitations are and I can look after myself. It also embarrasses me in front of my friends" (Fleitas, 1999).

Confidentiality of student health records and information is a major concern for schools. There are several federal statutes that are relevant including: Family Educational Rights and Privacy Act of 1974 (FERPA), Individuals with Disabilities Education Act (IDEA), as well as state laws concerning a minor's right to medical treatment. It is beyond the scope of this chapter to present a detailed discussion on confidentiality. However, the confidentiality of health records and a student's desire for privacy may limit the information on a student's health condition that can be shared with teachers. All schools should have policies and procedures regarding student confidentiality. These policies should distinguish health records from academic records and have clear guidelines for how confidential health information is shared within the school (American School Health Association (ASHA), 2000).

RESPONDING TO THE NEEDS OF CHILDREN WITH SERIOUS MEDICAL CONDITIONS

Given the challenges of successfully integrating students with special health care needs into schools, a critical mass of supportive health and educational staff is necessary. Moreover, past and recent laws require that the health and educational needs of youth with these conditions must be met. But schools may have difficulty in complying with the magnitude of demands imposed by these laws.

Public Law 94-142, IDEA, and Special Education Services

In the most recent reauthorization of Public Law 94-142, the Individuals with Disabilities Education Act (IDEA), schools are mandated to provide children with chronic illness and other disabling conditions individualized educational and supportive services in the least restrictive educational setting. To qualify for special services under IDEA, a child must have a disability that is "adversely affecting (his/her) educational performance." The disability category that usually applies to children with special health care needs is "other health impaired." This classification is defined as "having limited strength, vitality or alertness, due to chronic or acute health problems such as a heart condition, tuberculosis, rheumatic fever, nephritis, asthma, sickle cell anemia, hemophilia, epilepsy, lead poisoning, leukemia, or diabetes, which adversely affects a child's educational performance."

Although designed to benefit youth with a wide range of academic difficulties, there are several limitations to placing a child with special health care needs in the special education system. A widespread problem is the lack of resources in schools to adequately address student needs. Schools are often deficient in human and programmatic resources for both educational and health concerns.

Another significant issue with special education placement is the risk of further stigmatizing youth who already feel stigmatized. Most parents of children with special health care needs do not want them to be singled out or treated differently as a result of their conditions. In some cases, parents may be reluctant to accept services for their children that are genuinely needed.

Finally, special education services can fail to address problems in the broader school environment. In general, special education services are focused on individual students and neglect the needs of their teachers and their classmates. Although teachers are sometimes provided with aides to assist special education students in their classrooms, little attention is paid to educating and supporting teachers in modifying their teaching to meet the child's needs. Similarly, special education does not intervene with other students who encounter children with special health care needs, thus failing to help students learn important lessons about diversity and respect (which hurts both well and ill children). Because the difficulties faced by children with special health care needs in schools are due in part to the way others respond to them, interventions that focus only on the child will likely be inadequate.

ROLES AND CONTRIBUTIONS OF SCHOOL-BASED HEALTH CENTERS AND SCHOOL MENTAL HEALTH PROGRAMS

Although special education services are certainly warranted and valuable for many children with special health care needs, school-based health centers (SBHCs) offer another mechanism to address the needs of these students. As mentioned, SBHCs now number over 1200 in the United States and have expanded to include a range of preventive, primary care, and mental health services. A common staffing pattern for an SBHC would include a medical assistant, nurse coordinator (often an RN), nurse practitioner or physician assistant, a mental health professional (usually master's-level or doctoral trainee), and a consulting physician. Some centers have additional staff, including health educators, outreach workers, and dentists (Juszcak et al., 1995).

School-based health centers are uniquely positioned to provide services to students who are most in need. Most SBHCs are established in low-income communities with inadequate health care resources and many unmet health care needs. This is reflected in a 1998–1999 survey of SBHCs nationally; two-thirds of the population served by the centers were members of a minority group (National Assembly on School-Based Health Care, 2000). Studies of children with special health care needs reveal that those who face the most serious problems in accessing health care are children who live at or below the federal poverty line, live in single-parent families, are uninsured, are older children and teens, or members of a racial or ethnic minority group. SBHCs are designed to provide easily accessible health care services to this population.

An important impact of SBHCs has been increased awareness about the mental health needs of youth. As SBHCs become established, mental health issues quickly become the number one or two source of referrals, and staff may feel overwhelmed in their attempt to respond to this significant need (Dryfoos, 1999; Flaherty, Weist, & Warner, 1996). This awareness has led to advocacy by leaders in health and education sectors for the advancement of expanded school mental health programs (Weist, 1997, 1999), as reviewed in other chapters in this book.

In many ways the ideal arrangement is when an expanded school mental health program operates out of a school-based health center. This partnership promotes a coordinated approach to student health and mental health issues, helps to "market" both the health and the mental health services, and can reduce the stigma associated with seeking mental health care (see Juszcak et al., 1995; Weist, 1997). In addition, although findings related to youth are limited, there is now notable evidence for adults that integrating mental health and medical care decreases overall costs (i.e., the "medical cost offset"; Chiles, Lambert, & Hatch, 1999; Cummings, 1990; Groth-Marnat & Edkins, 1996). Similarly, there is evidence to suggest that health outcomes are improved when mental health and medical services are integrated (Kibby, Tye, & Mulhern, 1998; Levinson, 1992).

School-based health centers are successful at connecting students in need with mental health services. For example, Kaplan et al. (1998) found that adolescents with access to an SBHC were *10* times more likely to make a mental health or substance abuse visit than students who had commercial health insurance but did not have access to an SBHC.

An ideal scenario for a school would be an ongoing effort to better and more efficiently respond to the full range of student needs. For example, a school could have an SBHC that is well established and is providing a full array of primary care, and has an affiliated ESMH program that provides assessment, case management, and therapy services for youth, as well as assisting the school in launching prevention programs. Center-related services would be provided by community agency staff who collaborate with school-hired professionals such as school nurses, counselors, social workers, and psychologists (Flaherty et al., 1998; Waxman, Weist, & Benson, 1999). Center staff work closely with school staff and leadership to develop a full range of services such as classroom-focused strategies, community outreach, and crisis prevention and response (Adelman & Taylor, 1999; Weist & Christodulu, 2000). It is within this context that the multifaceted needs of students with special health care needs can be best addressed.

In the following, we present ideas for school-based programs to better address the health and mental health needs of children and adolescents with special health care needs. Recommendations are built upon studies and articles on SBHCs and expanded school mental health as reviewed earlier. We also draw on studies and articles that have generally discussed interdisciplinary collaboration in pediatric settings (e.g., Drotar, 1995; Roberts, 1995; Schroeder, 1996).

Student-Level Interventions

Medical services provided by nurses, nurse practitioners, and physicians' assistants within SBHCs can meet many of the daily medical needs of students. Usually, when SBHC staff are working with these students, an important initial step is to develop strong channels of communication with their primary care providers (PCPs). In cases where a student does not have a PCP the SBHC can either refer the student to a PCP in the community or if appropriate, one of the SBHC providers can become the student's PCP. Through increased communication and coordination with the student's PCP, SBHC staff can gain a better understanding of the child's capabilities, limitations, and needed environmental accommodations. With this knowledge, medical staff in SBHCs can serve as translators of the child's physical needs (e.g., dietary restrictions, medication schedules) to other school personnel, who can then plan modifications accordingly. SBHC staff are also in a position to observe day-to-day changes in a child's condition and can communicate this information back to outside service providers. This ability to frequently touch base with the student without disrupting the flow of the student's day at school can be a powerful way to monitor the student's health condition.

School-based mental health clinicians can effectively address the emotional and behavioral needs of students with special health care needs by adapting interventions from pediatric psychology to the school setting. For example, cognitive–behavioral strategies such as relaxation training, distraction, and imagery have been found to be highly effective in helping children with special health care needs manage and cope with pain (Holden, Deichmann, & Levy, 1999; Janicke & Finney, 1999; Larsson & Carlsson, 1996; Powers, 1999; Walco et al., 1999). School-based clinicians can help children rehearse and use the techniques learned in pediatric care settings, or can train children in the techniques directly, since manuals for many pediatric approaches now exist (Walco et al., 1999). Similarly, school-based clinicians can partner with other health care staff involved with the student to promote compliance with the illness regimen (Anderson & Collier, 1999; Murphy, Thompson, & Morris, 1997). Since schools are natural settings, training and reinforcing students for regimen compliance within them should promote the generalization of this compliance to other settings (e.g., home, neighborhood) and its maintenance over time (see Chapter 18).

Students with special health care needs often respond to their conditions by withdrawing from classmates and teachers, both of whom represent potential sources of support (Bowden et al., 1998; Logan et al., 1998). Accordingly, interventions which seek to enhance support of youth with special health care needs by peers and teachers are extremely valuable. In addition to working directly with peers and teachers to help them better understand and hence better respond to the student's medical condition, social skills training for youth with illnesses is an important factor in improving their interpersonal relationships. Students with medical conditions may need to learn a number of social skills to compensate for their conditions, such as entering peer groups, reading social cues, responding to provocation, interpreting feedback from peers, and communicating with teachers (Dodge, McClaskey, & Feldman, 1985).

Children and youth with special health care needs may have difficulty navigating the physical and emotional changes that occur normally with pubertal development. The literature shows conflicting results about the impact of chronic illness on adolescents. However, some things are relatively clear. Adolescents with chronic illness may be more dependent on family members than matched controls and, depending on the severity of their condition, may have difficulty transitioning to an independent life. In addition, parents and physicians often forget that chronically ill adolescents have the same concerns about their sexuality as normal peers (Anderson, 1991). School-based health centers with ESMH can help ease these transitions by providing family and individual therapy as well as health education and case management services.

School-based health centers with ESMH can assume an important role in integrating children and youth with special health care needs into the community system of health care. This role is most important for youth who are uninsured. Uninsured children are four times more likely than insured children to have an unmet health need such as a need for medical care, mental health care, and prescriptions (Newacheck & Taylor, 1992). Case managers and clinicians in schools can help families sign up for public health insurance programs as well as help ensure that students with special health care needs are reconnected to a PCP as well as specialty pediatric services in the community.

Family-Level Interventions

One of the most important roles for a school-based health professional is to serve as a liaison between the school and parents. Parents need to be involved in co-managing the care of their seriously ill children while they are in the school. Parents are more likely to be involved in their children's education if they perceive the classroom environment to be welcoming and if their input about the needs of their children is respected. School health and mental health personnel, by virtue of their training and accessibility (they are usually much more accessible by phone than other school staff), are well suited to respond to parent inquiries about a child during the school day or to communicate observations about a child's condition to parents.

SBHC professionals are also an important source of information for parents regarding community resources for the management of medical conditions. For example, providers can direct parents to disease-specific websites that advise parents about how to best communicate with schools and advocate for services for their child (Fleitas, 1999). Also, SBHC providers can assist parents in obtaining financial support and in making connections to community support groups and educational programs. If supportive and educational programs do not exist in the community, SBHCs may consider offering such services to parents directly.

In addition to supportive and educational services, parents may also need direct interventions to help them manage the demands of a child's medical condition. A growing body of research suggests that individual pediatric interventions are more effective when families are included in treatment (Rodrigue, 1994; Sanders et al., 1994). For example, parents may inadvertently reinforce a child's maladaptive coping skills. Parent training can help to identify and modify these negative interactions (Thompson et al., 1992). For some parents, issues of grief and loss are important targets of intervention. Family-level interventions may also be warranted for siblings, who may struggle to understand their brother or sister's condition, or may feel guilty (related to their physical health) or jealous (related to special treatment received by the ill sibling).

Classroom- and School-Level Interventions

An important task for school health and mental health programs is to provide support to teachers who must manage students with special health care needs in their classrooms. SBHC staff can educate teachers about the specific needs of a particular child, help the teacher develop ways to encourage interactions with healthy peers, and can respond to medical or emotional crises that may occur within the classroom. SBHC staff can also help teachers balance the amount of attention given to a student's medical condition to ensure that it is adequate but not at a level that reinforces negative coping behaviors. With the support of school health and mental health professionals, teachers are free to focus on teaching and may be more open to having students with special health care needs in their classrooms.

Interventions that target a student's entire classroom can also contribute greatly to the adjustment of children with special health care needs. For example, SBHC staff can educate students about a child's illness to reduce the stigma and fear that classmates often convey. Carefully implemented classroom education and support programs have been found to enhance the reintegration of children back into the school after hospitalization (Katz et al., 1992). In addition, simulation exercises that allow classmates to experience an aspect of the child's condition (e.g., ride in a wheelchair, try on a heavy cast) can increase classmate sensitivity toward and admiration for the impaired child.

One website testimonial illustrates the benefits of this type of classroom intervention: "When I went back to school, two of the nurses from the clinic came with me to explain my illness. They brought some dolls with them so that everyone could understand, and they even showed the kids the needles that I got. They said that leukemia was not contagious, so that the kids would understand they couldn't catch it. The students asked lots of questions, like 'how did you get leukemia, why are your cheeks so fat and what happened to all of your hair'" (Fleitas, 1999). Clearly, providing students with a forum for discussing their own fears and others' misconceptions about a student's illness minimizes stigma and can facilitate social interaction. Of course, children with special health care needs and their parents need to be included in any planning of educational efforts to inform other students of the nature of their medical condition in order to ensure that privacy is respected (Bowden et al., 1998).

School-based health center staff also can be instrumental in keeping children connected to their teachers and classmates during hospitalizations. For example, overburdened teachers may value the help of SBHC staff in initiating letter-writing campaigns to a hospitalized child. Technology now exists for teleconferencing from hospital sites to schools, presenting new opportunities for youth with special health care needs to remain connected to peers and teachers. Such strategies have benefits for students in the classroom as well, providing them with opportunities to learn about hospitals and medical procedures in a positive way.

CONCLUDING COMMENTS

The trend of increasing numbers of youth with special health care needs in schools fortunately coincides with a trend toward better and more comprehensive health and mental health care in schools. Nationally there is an increase in the number of SBHCs with related mental health programs. Unfortunately, most schools remain very poorly equipped to respond to the physical, emotional, and behavioral needs of students. As such, much work needs to be done in enhancing physical and mental health realms, and in forging truly interdisciplinary efforts between staff, educators, and youth and families. This interdisciplinary effort should be based on existing knowledge regarding integrated approaches to health and mental health care, and on pediatric psychology. A focus on measuring outcomes and the cost benefits of integrated approaches will be one of our most critical tasks. There are many challenges ahead in the development of integrated approaches to the biopsychosocial needs of youth with special health care needs. But it is evident that SBHCs with expanded school mental health services are an important new approach with the potential to significantly improve student health and academic outcomes.

ACKNOWLEDGMENTS. We express our appreciation to Joan Fleitas and Laura Nabors for contributing ideas to this paper. This chapter was supported by Project MCJ24SH02-01-0 from the Office of Adolescent Health, Maternal and Child Health Bureau (Title V, Social Security Act), Health Resources and Services Administration, Department of Health and Human Services; by Project R03 HS09542 from the Agency for Health Care Policy Research; and by Project T32 MH18834 from the National Institute of Mental Health.

REFERENCES

Adelman, H. S., & Taylor, L. (1999). Mental health in schools and system restructuring. *Clinical Psychology Review, 19,* 137–163.

American Academy of Pediatrics, Committee on Children with Disabilities (1993). Psychosocial risks of chronic health conditions in childhood and adolescence. *Pediatrics, 92*(6), 876–878.

American School Health Association, National Task Force on Confidential Student Health Information (2000). *Guidelines for protecting confidential student health information.* ASHA 7263 State Route 43/ P.O. Box 708, Kent, OH 44240.

Anderson, C. A., & Collier, J. A. (1999). Managing very poor adherence to medication in children and adolescents: An inpatient intervention. *Clinical Child Psychology and Psychiatry, 4,* 393–402.

Anderson, M. M. (1991). Principles of care for the ill adolescent. *Adolescent Medicine State of the Art Reviews: Acute and Chronic Medical Disorders,* October.

Boekaerts, M., & Roeder, I. (1999). Stress, coping, and adjustment in children with a chronic disease: A review of the literature. *Disability and Rehabilitation: An International Multidisciplinary Journal, 21,* 311–337.

Bowden, V. R., Dickey, S. B., & Greenberg, C. S. (1998). Chronic conditions as a challenge to health maintenance. In V. R. Bowden, S. B. Dickey, C. Smith Greenberg, & K. Law (Eds.), *Children and their families: The continuum of care* (pp. 577–594). Philadelphia, PA: Saunders.

Chiles, J. A., Lambert, M. J., & Hatch, A. L. (1999). The impact of psychological interventions on medical cost offset: A meta-analytic review. *Clinical Psychology: Science and Practice, 6,* 204–220.

Colgrove, R. W., & Huntzinger, R. M. (1994). Academic, behavioral, and social adaptation of boys with hemophilia/HIV disease. *Journal of Pediatric Psychology, 19,* 457–473.

Cummings, N. A. (1990). Brief intermittent psychotherapy throughout the life cycle. In J. K. Zeig & S. G. Gilligan (Eds.), *Brief therapy: Myths, methods, and metaphors* (pp. 169–184). New York: Brunner/Mazel.

Cystic Fibrosis Foundation (1994). *Patient registry 1993: Annual data report.* Bethesda, MD: Author.

Dodge, K. A., McClaskey, C. L., & Feldman, E. (1985). A situational approach to the assessment of social competence in children. *Journal of Consulting and Clinical Psychology, 53,* 344–353.

Drotar, D. (1995). *Consulting with pediatricians: Psychological perspectives.* New York: Plenum.

Dryfoos, J. G. (1999). *Full-service schools.* San Francisco: Jossey–Bass.

Flaherty, L. T., Garrison, E., Waxman, R., Uris, P., Keys, S., Siegel, M. G., & Weist, M. D. (1998). Optimizing the roles of school mental health professionals. *Journal of School Health, 68,* 420–424.

Flaherty, L. T., Weist, M. D., & Warner, B. S. (1996). School-based mental health services in the United States: History, current models and needs. *Community Mental Health Journal, 32,* 341–352.

Fleitas, J. (1999). *In Bandaids and blackboards: When a chronic illness—or some other medical problem—goes to school* [On-line]. Available: http://www.funrsc.fairfield.edu/.

Gortmaker, S. L., Walker, D., Weitzman, M., & Sobol, A. M. (1990). Chronic conditions, socioeconomic risks, and behavioral problems in children and adolescents. *Pediatrics, 85,* 267–276.

Groth-Marnat, G., & Edkins, G. (1996). Professional psychologists in general health care settings: A review of the financial efficacy of direct treatment interventions. *Professional Psychology: Research and Practice, 27,* 161–174.

Holden, E. W., Deichmann, M. M., & Levy, J. D. (1999). Empirically-supported treatments in pediatric psychology: Recurrent pediatric headache. *Journal of Pediatric Psychology, 24,* 91–109.

Janicke, D. M., & Finney, J. W. (1999). Empirically-supported treatments in pediatric psychology: Recurrent abdominal pain. *Journal of Pediatric Psychology, 24,* 115–127.

Juszcak, L., Fisher, M., Lear, J. G., & Friedman, S. B. (1995). Back to school: Training opportunities in school-based health centers. *Journal of Developmental & Behavioral Pediatrics, 16,* 101–104.

Kaplan, D. W., Calonge, B. N., Guernsey, B. P., & Hanrahan, M. B. (1998). Managed care and school-based health centers: Use of health services. *Archives of Pediatric and Adolescent Medicine, 152,* 25–33.

Katz, E. R., Varni, J., Rubenstein, C. L., Blew, A., & Hubert, N. (1992). Teacher, parent, and child evaluative ratings of school reintegration intervention for children with newly diagnosed cancer. *Children's Health Care, 21,* 69–75.

Kibby, M. Y., Tye, V. L., & Mulhern, R. K. (1998). Effectiveness of psychological intervention for children and adolescents with chronic medical illness: A meta-analysis. *Clinical Psychology Review, 18,* 103–117.

LaGreca, A. M. (1990). Social consequences of pediatric conditions: Fertile area for future investigation and intervention? *Journal of Pediatric Psychology, 15,* 285–307.

Larsson, B., & Carlsson, J. (1996). A school-based, nurse-administered relaxation training for children with chronic tension-type headache. *Journal of Pediatric Psychology, 21,* 603–614.

Lavigne, J. V., & Faier-Routman, J. (1992). Psychological adjustment to pediatric physical disorders: A meta-analytic review. *Journal of Pediatrics, 17,* 133–158.

Levinson, J. L. (1992). Psychosocial interventions in chronic medical illness: An overview of outcome research. *General Hospital Psychiatry, 14*(Suppl.), 43–49.

Logan, K. R., Jacobs, H. A., Gast, D. L., Murray, A. S., Daino, K., & Skala, C. (1998). The impact of typical peers on the perceived happiness of students with profound multiple disabilities. *Journal of the Association for Persons with Severe Handicaps, 23,* 309–318.

Mulhern, R. K., & Friedman, A. G. (1990). Psychological issues associated with treatment of childhood acute lymphocytic leukemia. In S. B. Morgan & T. M. Okwumabua (Eds.), *Child and adolescent disorders: Developmental and health psychology perspectives* (pp. 267–300). Hillsdale, NJ: Erlbaum.

Murphy, L. M., Thompson, R. J., & Morris, M. A. (1997). Adherence behavior among adolescents with Type I insulin-dependent diabetes mellitus: The role of cognitive appraisal processes. *Journal of Pediatric Psychology, 22,* 811–825.

National Assembly on School-Based Health Care (2000, June). *Creating access to care for children and youth; School-based health center census 1998–1999.*

Newacheck, P. W., Strickland, B., Shonkoff, J. P., Perrin, J. M., McPherson, M., McManus, M., Lauver, C., Fox, H., & Arango, P. (1998). An epidemiologic profile of children with special health care needs. *Pediatrics, 102,* 117–123.

Newacheck, P. W., & Taylor, W. R. (1992). Childhood chronic illness: Prevalence, severity and impact. *American Journal of Public Health, 82,* 364–371.

Pless, I. B., Power, C., & Peckham, C. S. (1993). Long-term psychosocial sequelae of chronic physical disorders in childhood. *Pediatrics, 91,* 1131–1136.

Powers, S. W. (1999). Empirically supported treatments in pediatric psychology: Procedure-related pain. *Journal of Pediatric Psychology, 24,* 131–145.

Rinehart, P. M. (1998). In *The first five years* [On-line]. Available: http://www.cyfc.umn.edu/Documents/I/H/IH1002.htm.

Roberts, M. C. (Ed.). (1995). *Handbook of pediatric psychology* (2nd ed.). New York: Guilford.

Rodrigue, J. R. (1994). Beyond the individual child: Innovative systems approaches to service delivery in pediatric psychology. *Journal of Clinical Child Psychology, 23*(Suppl.), 32–39.

Sanders, M. R., Shepherd, R. W., Cleghorn, G., & Woolford, H. (1994). The treatment of recurrent abdominal pain in children: A controlled comparison of cognitive–behavioral family intervention and standard pediatric care. *Journal of Consulting and Clinical Psychology, 62,* 306–314.

Schroeder, C. S. (1996). Psychologists and pediatricians in collaborative practice. In R. J. Resnick & R. H. Rozensky (Eds.), *Health psychology through the lifespan: Practice and research opportunities* (pp. 109–131). Washington, DC: American Psychological Association.

Stein, R. E. K., & Jessup, D. J. (1984). Relationship between health status and psychological adjustment among children with chronic conditions. *Pediatrics, 73,* 169–174.

Thompson, R. J., Gustafson, K. E., Hamlett, K. W., & Spock, A. (1992). Psychological adjustment of children with cystic fibrosis: The role of child cognitive processes and maternal adjustment. *Journal of Pedatric Psychology, 17*, 573–585.

U.S. Department of Health and Human Services (1994). *Healthy people (2000): National health promotion and disease prevention objectives.* Washington, DC: U.S. Government Printing Office.

Walco, G. A., Sterling, C. M., Conte, P. M., & Engel, R. G. (1999). Empirically supported treatments in pediatric psychology: Disease-related pain. *Journal of Pediatric Psychology, 24*, 155–167.

Waxman, R. P., Weist, M. D., & Benson, D. (1999). Toward collaboration in the growing education–mental health interface. *Clinical Psychology Review, 19*, 239–253.

Weist, M. D. (1997). Expanded school mental health services: A national movement in progress. In T. H. Ollendick & R. Prinz (Eds.), *Advances in clinical child psychology* (Vol. 19, pp. 319–352). New York: Plenum.

Weist, M. D. (1999). Challenges and opportunities in expanded school mental health. *Clinical Psychology Review, 19*, 131–135.

Weist, M. D., & Christodulu, K. (2000). Expanded school mental health programs: Advancing reform and closing the gap between research and practice. *Journal of School Health, 70*, 195–200.

Weitzman, M., Walker, D. K., & Gortmaker, S. (1986). Chronic illness, psychosocial problems, and school absences. *Clinical Pediatrics, 25*, 137–141.

IV

Moving toward Best Practice

17

School Mental Health in Systems of Care

PHILIP J. LEAF, DAVID SCHULTZ, LAUREL J. KISER, and DAVID B. PRUITT

The Center for Mental Health Services (1997) estimates that from 9 to 13% of all children aged 9–17 have a serious emotional disturbance that either impairs or substantially interferes with their ability to function effectively at home, school, or within the community. More than 20 years ago, Knitzer (1982) found that two-thirds of children in need did not receive mental health services. Since the publication of that landmark report, concerns about the small number of youth with mental disorders who receive mental health services have not lessened (Leaf, Bogrov, & Webb, 1997; U.S. Department of Health and Human Services, 1999). Although recent research suggests that a greater proportion of children in need of mental services now receive them (Costello et al., 1993; Leaf et al., 1996), few communities can claim that all or even most youth identified as having mental or emotional problems receive effective services.

In most communities, mental health services have been provided primarily in outpatient clinics and inpatient units (Kiser, King, & Lefkovitz, 1999). Concern over the poor outcomes experienced by many youth with mental disorders, however, has led to a call for (1) the increased use of research-based treatments (Hoagwood et al., 2001; Kazdin & Weisz, 1998; Kutash & Rivera, 1996) and (2) a more effective "system of care" (Kiser, Lefkovitz, & Kennedy, 2001). The promise and controversy surrounding expanded use of research-based treatments has been widely discussed (Hoagwood et al., 2001; Kazdin & Kendall, 1998; Persons, 1995). Considerable evidence exists that, when implemented well, evidence-based services can result in significant improvements in children's outcomes. As discussed in other chapters in this volume, however, we are still learning how to implement and sustain these preventive and treatment interventions in school settings.

PHILIP J. LEAF and DAVID SCHULTZ • Johns Hopkins University Bloomberg School of Public Health, Baltimore, Maryland 21205.   LAUREL J. KISER and DAVID B. PRUITT • University of Maryland School of Medicine, Baltimore, Maryland 21201.

A system of care is "a comprehensive spectrum of mental health and other necessary services which are organized into a coordinated network to meet the multiple and changing needs of severely emotionally disturbed children and adolescents" (Stroul & Friedman, 1996, p. 3). In response to the numerous reports describing deficiencies in the mental health services available to our nation's youth, the federal government, family advocacy groups, and academic training centers have devoted considerable time and effort to disseminating the concepts and philosophy of the Child and Adolescent Service System Program (CASSP). This program develops infrastructures necessary for publicly funded community-based services for children and adolescents with serious emotional disturbances (Davis et al., 1995; Stroul & Friedman, 1986, 1996).

Communities will probably require both more effective systems of care and greater utilization of evidence-based practices to produce the outcomes they desire for emotionally disturbed children. To date, improvements in a community's system of care have been shown to improve access to and coordination between services for children but not, by themselves, to improve children's behaviors or school functioning significantly (Bickman, Noser, & Summerfelt, 1999). A community's system of care may coordinate services well between providers and between agencies such that more children with needs are identified and come into contact with service providers. The ultimate effectiveness of the system, however, remains dependent upon the individual, direct services provided to children and their families. If those delivering services to children continue to use practices not proven to affect children significantly, greater access to and coordination between services will not impact youth greatly.

Most discussions concerning systems of care have focused on individual service needs of the youth and their families or home-based services (e.g., Multisystemic Therapy; Schoenwald, Borduin, & Henggeler, 1998). Increasingly, however, mental health professionals and policymakers have focused on schools as a critical component of the system of care approach (Elias et al., 1997; Gottfredson, 2001; Leaf et al., 1997). Clinicians working in schools can access youth more easily than can those working in more traditional clinical settings (e.g., outpatient or inpatient clinics). In addition, these clinicians have a greater opportunity to establish procedures that will help *prevent* mental disorders, substance abuse, and violence; that will facilitate the early detection and referral of youth with behavioral or emotional problems; that can provide an array of services delivered to children directly in the schools; and that can reintegrate youth with serious emotional or behavioral problems back into schools.

This chapter suggests ways to think about school-based services from a system of care perspective. We first present six principles associated with the system of care approach and suggest ways in which mental health professionals working with and in schools might apply these principles to their work. We then provide an overview of the different types of services mental health clinicians might help provide within the school setting. As an example of a system of care approach, we then present a description of the school-based services provided within the Safe Schools, Healthy Students (SS-HS) project in Baltimore City. We conclude this chapter by suggesting ways in which to fund the system of care approach.

PRINCIPLES OF A SYSTEM OF CARE

Fifteen years ago, Stroul and Friedman (1986) outlined many principles that now constitute the most frequently cited description of the characteristics of a "system of care." These principles are organized around optimizing outcomes for emotionally disturbed children by increasing access to and coordination between mental health services. Too often, well-implemented interventions fail to impact children significantly because either the other domains of children's functioning remain unchanged (e.g., a child learns anger management techniques well but remains unmonitored after school and associates with delinquent peers) or the interventions do not receive consistent or sustained reinforcement (e.g., a child learns a set of anger management techniques during placement at a day school but does not receive encouragement to utilize these techniques when returning to a regular education classroom). In this section, we present six principles relevant to school-based mental health care and suggest how clinicians might apply these principles to their work.

Children Need Access to a Comprehensive Array of Services

"Access" reflects the extent to which children in need of mental health and substance abuse care receive services that match both the severity and the complexity of their needs (Institute of Medicine, 1993; Kiser, 2001). Addressing access issues from a system of care philosophy mandates an assessment of population needs, an evaluation of resources and management structures for meeting those needs, and delivery of the array (quantity, variety, and intensity) of services that match the level of need determined. The delivery of mental health services within schools provides multiple opportunities for improving access to care.

First, improving access to care for children requires assessing population need. School mental health programs can help produce an accurate picture of the prevalence of risk and resilience factors and also disorders present in the school-age population. Mental health clinicians can help conduct school-based needs assessments by randomly sampling the children in their schools and conducting screening surveys regarding lifestyles, risk behaviors, general health and behavioral health concerns.

Second, once needs are identified, school mental health programs can work to improve access to care by decreasing need, managing demand, and improving population health. Typically, we determine need by assigning a diagnostic classification to those individuals who meet specific illness-related criteria. Within traditional mental health systems, diagnosis, the presumptive criterion for medical necessity, is the key to access to services. In contrast, school mental health services can extend access to mental health care to children before they are diagnosed with an illness. By targeting those at high risk or with premorbid conditions, the numbers of children actually diagnosed should decrease.

School mental health programs also can improve access to services through a focus on improving the mental health of all children within the school. To reach this desired outcome, clinicians within schools can provide specific tools to children, parents, and teachers to assist them in achieving wellness, including health-risk assessments, selected screening programs, outreach to high-risk groups, and behavioral health education and promotion programs.

Finally, school mental health programs improve access because involvement with them is typically less stigmatizing than involvement with community mental health clinics. Through mental health clinicians' activities with preventive interventions and other roles, many children and families interact with the mental health care system for the first time, and these initial interactions are often comfortable ones not related to individualized treatment services. School-based services therefore act as an excellent "portal of entry" into the system of behavioral health care (Booney & Pumariega, 2001).

Children Need to Receive Services in Accordance with Their Individual Needs

Once needs have been assessed and demand is being managed, programs working within a systems of care philosophy develop and implement a comprehensive array of services that can meet the individual needs of the children they serve. Although the primary mission of schools remains to educate our nation's youth, in many schools and school systems the content of primary and secondary education has expanded beyond simple academic learning. In order to maximize the academic potential of their students, many schools have accepted the task of reducing individual children's barriers to learning (Adelman & Taylor, 2000). These barriers include learning difficulties (e.g., attention deficit hyperactivity disorder (ADHD)), emotional and behavioral challenges (e.g., anxiety, conduct disorder), and contextual risk factors (e.g., familial or neighborhood violence). As a result, elementary, middle, and high schools increasingly provide a good home for clinicians interested in the prevention, early detection, and effective treatment of emotional and behavioral problems. The types and intensity of services required to address different children's barriers to learning vary. While some children will require individualized interventions across multiple domains (e.g., academic, behavioral, and familial), less intense and less individualized interventions will sufficiently address other children's barriers to learning. Later in this chapter we will present in detail different categories of interventions that are required to meet children's varying needs.

Early Identification and Intervention of Children Should Be Promoted

Many youth experience serious episodes of disruption, in part because of the limited ability of many teachers to manage the behaviors of students and/or because the school environment supports and possibly even fosters bullying. With negative school climates existing in many of our schools, clinicians are forced to attend to many children whose emotional or behavioral problems could have been prevented or, at least, the disruption accompanying these problems greatly reduced. In a later section of this chapter we describe universal and indicated preventive interventions that can help address these needs and concerns. A community-based system of care approach can provide support for preventive interventions by providing school-based clinicians and clinical agencies with access to a variety of funding streams. For many emotional or behavioral challenges, early prevention and intervention not only prevent or alleviate later difficulties but also prove fiscally advantageous for the community (Reynolds & Temple, 1998; Seitz, Rosenbaum, & Apfel, 1985; Zigler & Styfco, 1994).

Services Should Be Provided within the Least Restricted Most Normative Settings

CASSP proposed that services be delivered as close to the child's home and community as possible and thus avoid separating children from natural family and community supports. Rather than referring a child to an alternative educational or residential setting, the formulation of treatment and preventive interventions within a regular school setting provides important opportunities for keeping youth engaged with positive peers and for maintaining linkages with natural support systems in the home and in the community. There is growing evidence that grouping youth with other children with similar behavioral difficulties (e.g., group therapy, inpatient hospitalizations) can increase rather than decrease disruption and delinquent activity (Dishion & Andrews, 1995). The effects of the group norm and modeling of behavior by other disruptive children often prove a stronger influence on children than do the interventions mental health providers deliver. Mental health services delivered within school settings offer clinical service providers unique opportunities to craft interventions that aid in either maintaining or developing positive peer relationships.

Families Should Participate in the Planning and Delivery of Services

Although delivering treatment within and from the context of the school holds many advantages over a traditional outpatient clinic, the uncertain role of caregivers in treatment remains a challenge. In a traditional outpatient clinic, caregivers have to transport children to treatment and then participate in, or at least wait for the conclusion of, therapeutic sessions. For their children to receive individualized treatment from school mental health professionals, however, caregivers typically only have to sign a consent form sent home by a teacher. But the most effective treatments for ADHD and disruptive behaviors include parental involvement (Kazdin, 2000). School mental health professionals often encounter situations in which they have access to children with mental health needs but do not have access to the caregivers whose participation could make treatment successful. The professional may face the unenviable decision of whether to treat the child with an approach less likely to prove effective (e.g., individual or group therapy by itself) or not to provide services for the child at all.

Most school-based clinical programs have yet to organize around facilitating access to family members. One advantage school-based services have over traditional outpatient clinics in terms of engaging caregivers is the academic setting within which they operate. In many communities, a stigma associated with the use of mental health services still exists. Parents may be more motivated to involve themselves in preventive and remedial interventions that use school performance—and not just "mental health"—as an indicator of outcome. Although a child's frequent failure to follow teacher directions may concern the provider and teacher, the family may be most motivated to address the child's lack of academic achievement. In a later section, we discuss how school-based health clinicians in Baltimore have coordinated with "parent liaisons" to promote access to caregivers. School-based clinicians should pursue collaborations such as these.

Services from One Agency Should Be Linked and Integrated with Services from Other Agencies

CASSP advocated for interagency coordination among child- and family-serving agencies in the provision of services for children and adolescents with SED. Many children are involved with various mental health providers, receive mentoring, attend after-school or summer school programs, receive alternative educational or residential placements, are involved with the juvenile justice system, etc. If youth are to achieve the most positive outcomes possible, especially children with more serious problems, clinicians—school-based or not—will need to collaborate actively with family members and other service providers.

When communities pay attention to the need to integrate and link services, opportunities are provided for clinicians to utilize more extensive intervention strategies. These strategies should not just link service providers together but also interventions across providers. For example, if a school-based mental health clinician works to teach a child how to respond to teasing, then other service providers for that child should know the techniques taught in order that other providers might reinforce these techniques when the opportunity presents itself. If a youth is in an out-of-home placement, staff there should utilize the same techniques. If the youth is at home, training and support should be provided to caregivers at home to use these techniques. Within an effective system of care, the adults present recurrent and consistent messages to youth.

We challenge school-based clinicians and clinical agencies to examine their activities in light of the preceding six principles. Does your school offer a "comprehensive" array of services? How often are families engaged in the planning and delivery of treatment? These six principles can be used to improve and expand the practice within school-based mental health services.

In the next section we elaborate more fully on what a "comprehensive array" of services should include within a school-based setting in order that children receive services of appropriate intensity to meet their needs.

THE CONTINUUM OF CARE WITHIN A SCHOOL BUILDING

Mental health services have been categorized within the following four domains: (1) universal, (2) selected, and (3) indicated preventive interventions, and (4) treatment of clinical disorders (Tolan & Guerra, 1994). These categories differ in terms of the nature of the services, the problems targeted by the services, and the intensity and duration of the interventions provided. Most schools and communities need this entire array of services in order to match the mental health needs of their children with the most appropriate level of service. In this section, we describe these four domains, provide examples of interventions, suggest roles for school-based mental health clinicians within the domains, and discuss limitations to the implementation of the interventions.

Universal Interventions

Preventive interventions delivered to all children within a school, a grade, or a classroom—regardless of children's levels of symptomatology—are considered "universal" in nature. Within schools, these interventions attempt to provide information or skills useful for all students. For example, schools are mandated to provide instruction about positive health practices, such as related to substance use, HIV, and the prevention of pregnancy. In some school systems, this mandate extends to include the teaching of social skills to all elementary-aged children in order to reduce the risk of aggression or violence. Universal interventions therefore frequently take the form of a prescribed curriculum of lessons on a topic (e.g., sex education) that either a general teacher or a specialist delivers.

One example of a universal intervention that might be familiar to clinicians is the *Good Behavior Game,* which attempts to reduce aggression in elementary-aged children (Barrish, Saunders, & Wolf, 1969). Teachers divide their classrooms into teams, ensuring that each team has a roughly equivalent number of impulsive and aggressive children. Teachers then identify behaviors upon which the game will focus (e.g., only talking when it's one's turn, keeping one's hands to oneself) and choose times of the day to play the game. When teachers initiate the game, teams receive marks if a team member breaks a rule. At the end of the game, all team members on any team that stays below a predetermined number of marks receive a prize. The game promotes both a group expectation of and a group reinforcement for appropriate behavior. Results of a randomized trial show the Good Behavior Game to reduce levels of aggression in lower-income, urban, elementary school children (Kellam et al., 1998).

School-based clinicians can play an important role in the implementation of universal programs. First and foremost, clinicians can make themselves familiar with universal programs and then initiate conversations with school administrators and teachers regarding the usefulness of initiating these programs. For example, many excellent universal programs exist that focus on the prevention of aggression and violence among elementary-aged children (e.g., the Good Behavior Game; PATHS (Greenberg & Kusche, 1998)). As the perceived expert in violence reduction, consequences of teen pregnancy, etc., the clinicians' expressions of support for a program can be critical during the early phases of program planning or implementation. Once a school adopts a program, clinicians can also train staff, monitor the fidelity of program implementation, determine whether treatment referrals come disproportionately from teachers who implement the program poorly, and/or provide support to teachers who have difficulty implementing the program.

Clinicians also can provide an important function by providing training and supervision for new teachers in a school. Even when schools are able to organize a program for effectively training and supervising teachers in the program's initial year, the infrastructure typically does not exist to deal with teacher turnover. The impact of teacher turnover on the long-term effectiveness of school-based programs should not be underestimated. For example, last year the Baltimore City Public School System lost or transferred nearly one-fifth of the teachers employed. In school districts with high staff turnover, each new school year brings a need for substantial time and energy to train and support teachers. School-based clinicians can play an important role if they learn universal programs well and play a leadership role in initiating trainings for new staff.

Consistent implementation of classroom universal programs depends on principals actively supporting programs, such as by securing time during the day for teachers to deliver components of the programs and providing incentives for teachers to do so (e.g., including program implementation in teacher evaluations). In many schools, principals may not feel at liberty to attempt to deal with any issues other than the academic performance of the children in their schools. Increasingly, school officials, legislatures, and the media judge principals and entire school systems by their students' average scores on standardized achievement tests. Schools with consistently low scores may become candidates for state takeover, negative publicity, or both. The overwhelming importance placed on academic achievement leaves many principals and teachers with little interest in classroom time not specifically spent on academic learning. School-based clinicians need to present universal programs to school administrators not only as mental health programs but also as reducing barriers to learning.

Selected Interventions

Many children are placed at risk for emotional or behavioral difficulties because of familial or other environmental circumstances, such as exposure to violence or death, alcoholism, or divorce in the family, etc. Many intervention programs focus on children or adolescents with one or more identified risk factors in an attempt to prevent the appearance of specific emotional or behavioral difficulties and are considered "selected" in nature. Mental health professionals typically deliver selected interventions.

An example of an empirically supported "selective" intervention that could be implemented in a school context is the Children of Divorce Intervention Program (CODIP; Pedro-Carroll & Cowen, 1985). CODIP focuses on helping children of divorce experience less anxiety and exhibit less behavioral disturbance. CODIP includes 10 to 14 group sessions, facilitated by a mental health professional, that typically occur during the school day. Through games and exercises, children learn to express feelings about their caregivers' divorce, learn why caregivers typically divorce, and learn how to cope with typical feelings and situations they will encounter. Results of clinical trials show the CODIP to improve adjustment in urban children in early and middle childhood (Pedro-Carroll & Alpert-Gillis, 1997; Pedro-Carroll, Alpert-Gillis, & Cowen, 1992).

School-based mental health clinicians are often needed to overcome the typical barriers to the implementation of selected preventive interventions. Again, before selected interventions are implemented, schools must first identify their needs. Although individual teachers often know a considerable amount of information about their children's home lives, rarely does an administrator, teacher, or other staff person gather that type of information within an entire school building. School-based mental health clinicians can play a critical role by initiating mental health needs assessments within schools.

In addition, education about, identification of, and implementation of selected preventive interventions usually require the initiative of the mental health clinician. School personnel often are not familiar or comfortable with organized, preventive interventions for children with common risk factors. School-based mental health clinicians can play an important role by explaining this need and educating other staff, especially administrators, about the need for and implementation of selected preventive interventions.

Indicated Interventions

Many children have a particular set of emotional or behavioral difficulties (e.g., anxiety, aggression, poor social skills) but fall below levels of "clinically significant" impairment. These behaviors may constitute disruptions to classrooms or the school setting, but the youth may not meet criteria for a clinical disorder. Services that focus on particular emotional or behavioral difficulties in order to prevent clinically significant manifestations of these or other symptoms are considered "indicated" in nature. Because "indicated" interventions often require a developed understanding of emotional or behavioral symptomatology, mental health professionals typically deliver them. The delivery of indicated preventive interventions in schools presents an exciting opportunity for mental health professionals because we can easily monitor changes in students' classroom and social behaviors and modify interventions accordingly.

One indicated preventive intervention is the Coping Power Program (Lochman et al., 1996). The Coping Power Program focuses on the reduction of aggressive and disruptive behaviors among children in late childhood and the prevention of substance use. The program includes both a child component and a parent component. Program developers based the child component on an existing program they developed entitled the Anger Coping Program (Lochman & Lenhart, 1993). The child component includes 33 one-hour group sessions, facilitated by a mental health professional, that typically occur during the school day. Sessions include exercises that focus on examining the intentions behind others' behaviors, recognizing physiological signs of anger arousal, solving social problems systematically, and expanding children's repertoires of behavioral responses to negative social events. The parent component includes 16 one-hour group sessions that focus on identifying and promoting positive behaviors in children, disciplining effectively, stress management, and building family cohesion. Multiple randomized clinical trials have shown the Coping Power Program both to decrease levels of aggression and to prevent the use of substances in middle school (Lochman et al., 1996).

Mental health professionals typically deliver indicated preventive interventions, often in conjunction with another school staff. To expand the reach and sustainability of indicated preventive interventions, however, school-based mental health clinicians can play an important role by training other school staff in these interventions. In high-risk neighborhoods the number of children who need interventions to address disruptive and aggressive classroom behaviors typically extends beyond a single clinician's capacity to deliver services. In these situations multiple school staff, with facilitation by a mental health professional, need to learn to deliver indicated preventive interventions.

Although the Coping Power Program and other indicated preventive interventions have proven successful, mental health professionals should consider options carefully before utilizing group interventions for aggressive and disruptive children. As stated previously, when disruptive children come together, *positive* reinforcement for inappropriate behaviors often occurs. Group treatment of delinquent early adolescents, for example, has led to *increases* in substance abuse and delinquent and violent behaviors (Dishion, McCord, & Poulin, 1999). The Coping Power Program minimizes disruptive behaviors within groups and enhances desired outcomes by providing stimulating, scripted exercises that focus specifically on the affective–cognitive and behavioral patterns common in aggressive children. It also includes a behavioral reward system during and following each session. Mental health professionals should *only* implement group interventions with disruptive children if (1) group facilitators can minimize disruptive and delinquent behaviors within the group, such as by developing a behavioral reward system for behaviors within group sessions; and (2) previous research shows that the intervention can work.

Treatment

Children who exhibit clinically significant levels of impairment, as diagnosed by a mental health professional, require "treatment" services. Treatment services offered within a school mental health program can incorporate a variety of service delivery options at multiple levels of care.

Several recent documents provide excellent reviews of empirically supported treatments for childhood depression, anxiety, ADHD, and disruptive behavior (Kazdin, 2000; U.S. Department of Health and Human Services, 1999). One treatment for depression, self-control therapy (Stark, Reynolds, & Kaslow, 1987; Stark, Rouse, & Livingston, 1991), reduces symptoms of depression and anxiety. Self-control therapy utilizes a cognitive–behavioral approach to group treatment and includes twenty-four 45-minute sessions. Sessions focus on restructuring maladaptive cognitions (e.g., I'll never win at anything) and training in social skills, assertiveness, and relaxation.

As mentioned previously, clinicians who operate solely or primarily from within the local school increasingly serve emotionally disturbed youth. Some of these services have been established in conjunction with efforts aimed at reducing the number of youth who need to leave their local school or their homes in order to receive treatment for their problems. School-based clinicians have an opportunity to produce more beneficial functional outcomes for children because they can easily observe outcomes, modify treatment regimes, and collaborate with the child's other providers.

As problems become more severe, the intensity of services needed increases. In addition to clinician visits, it is possible to offer ambulatory programs, such as after-school services or day-treatment programs within an integrated mental health and school setting. These programs can infuse a student's academic program with daily mental health services (individual therapy, family therapy, case management, psychiatric evaluation, and nursing services) delivered within the classroom setting.

Finally, school mental health clinicians can be involved with children if they need to leave school to receive acute or long-term mental health services, such as hospitalization, residential care, or homebound instruction. School mental health clinicians can provide these treatment settings with essential information regarding the child's functioning and also the changes necessary before coming back to school. Most essential is the school mental health clinician's role as an advocate for the child upon reentry.

Researchers are only beginning to investigate how well these four different types of services, if available simultaneously within a school building, meet the needs of different children. We believe the most effective system of care will include all four categories and that school-based clinicians are critical for the development of the full continuum. Universal interventions will likely protect children with some, but relatively low, levels of risk for future emotional and behavioral disturbance but not protect those with the highest levels of risk. Lower-income, urban first-grade children who initially exhibited *moderate* levels of aggressiveness, for example, exhibited the greatest improvement in response to the previously described Good Behavior Game (Ialongo et al., 1999); children with the *highest* initial levels of aggression exhibited relatively less improvement. Similarly, selected and indicated programs might prove intense and individualized enough to meet the needs of another proportion of children (i.e., a group of children slightly more "at risk"). The needs of a small percentage of children might not be met by either universal, selected, or indicated services, however, and require even more intense, individualized treatment services.

Although universal programs might not provide the level of individualized care required to change emotionally disturbed children's behaviors, these programs still may play a critical role in their mental health care. In some cases a school's climate may need to change in order for more individualized services to prove effective. For example, a colleague of ours once talked to a 10-year-old boy within a lower-income community characterized by violence about nonviolent techniques he could use to respond to bullying (e.g., not shoving back, expressing how he felt). After listening attentively for a while, the boy interrupted, "But Ms. Johnson, if I do that, I'll get beat up!" Universal interventions may prove beneficial not only because they teach skills that directly help some children but also because they promote a school climate (e.g., a less violent one) within which children and families can respond positively to other, more individualized interventions.

In the Safe Schools, Healthy Students (ss-hs) project in Baltimore City, we have implemented interventions in schools that include services within each of the preceding four categories. As an example of how clinicians and clinical agencies might establish a continuum of mental health care within a school building, in the next section we describe some of the services provided within the ss-hs project.

THE SAFE SCHOOLS, HEALTHY STUDENTS PROJECT

The federal and state governments have presented a number of opportunities to integrate school-based mental health systems into a communitywide system of care, even if these programs and funding sources were not developed specifically for that purpose. For example, the ss-hs programs funded by a consortia of federal agencies attempt to increase the coordination of care for many of America's children. Four federal departments—Education, Health and Human Services, Labor, and Justice—collaborate to fund projects entitled Safe Schools, Healthy Students (ss-hs) projects in over 80 communities across the country. In the ss-hs project in Baltimore, the Baltimore City Public School System (bcpss) collaborates with the Baltimore Mental Health Systems, Baltimore City Police Department, Mayor's

Office, Department of Juvenile Justice, Department of Social Services, Family League of Baltimore (a Baltimore City initiative that coordinates services for children and families), Safe and Sound Campaign (a Baltimore City initiative that focuses on health and safety for children), Archdiocese of Baltimore, and Johns Hopkins Bloomberg School of Public Health.

In the SS-HS project in Baltimore, we have attempted both to provide a continuum of care within each elementary school building based on the preceding four categories of care and to promote a citywide system of care by connecting schools and school personnel with other city agencies. The following sections highlight some of these services and provide one example of a potential continuum of care within a school building.

Universal

A central component to the system of mental health care in BCPSS SS-HS schools is a curriculum of lessons delivered to all children by their classroom teachers entitled promoting alternative thinking strategies (PATHS; Greenberg & Kusche, 1998). This comprehensive, developmentally based curriculum promotes the development of essential social and emotional skills. Lessons cover the following three conceptual domains: (1) emotional understanding, (2) self-control, and (3) problem solving. Teachers deliver two or three lessons a week for 20 minutes at a time and incorporate skills learned into activities throughout the school day.

Selected

Almost 1 in every 10 adult residents of Baltimore abuse substances heavily. The Baltimore City Department of Health supplies staff for health clinics in BCPSS schools and has begun a program aimed at children of substance-abusing parents. This program involves students identified by school staff as having disruptions at home because of substance-abusing parents and provides group sessions to strengthen social skills and provide resiliency. Efforts are also made to facilitate treatment for the substance-abusing parent.

The BCPSS SS-HS project also recruited and paid a parent from each school community to function as a parent liaison to the neighborhood. These liaisons perform multiple functions that fall within different categorizations of care. Within the selected level, parent liaisons identify informational needs that certain caregivers have and coordinate appropriate responses to these. Activities may include hosting an informational session on lead poisoning or a group question-and-answer session with an attorney.

Evaluation activities of the SS-HS project in Baltimore have also helped schools and, in particular, student support teams (SST) identify their students' needs. In order to help facilitate decision-making surrounding services for children, the BCPSS recently required SSTs to exist within each school. The BCPSS hopes that the SSTs will coordinate all referrals for special services (except special education services, which existing child study teams handle) within a school. The SST consists of administrators, mental health professionals, teachers, and other school staff. School staffs refer all children for whom they have academic, emotional, or behavioral concerns to the SST. The SST reviews the child's functioning and develops a plan of services for the child. Regular reviews provide opportunities to evaluate and modify services the child receives.

Although SSTs predominantly respond to individual children's needs, in collaboration with the SS-HS project some SSTs have taken on the responsibility to address issues that require preventive efforts and school climate issues. For example, some mental health professionals have asked all teachers to complete a needs assessment form that identifies students in their classrooms and issues of concern for that student (e.g., family member death, drug exposure or use). Mental health professionals have worked collaboratively with their SSTs to determine how to provide services to respond to these identified needs. Twice a year teachers in all SS-HS schools also complete behavioral checklists on all children in their classrooms. SS-HS project staff provide reports based on these checklists to administrators and SSTs to help them discuss needs not only of individual students but also entire classrooms and the whole school climate.

Indicated

Even after training in the PATHS curriculum, some children will continue to display inappropriate and maladaptive social behaviors. Teachers may refer these children to an intervention entitled Skillstreaming (McGinnis & Goldstein, 1997). Skillstreaming typically occurs either within the context of the whole classroom or within smaller groups of children. In the BCPSS SS-HS project we utilize small group formats of four to eight children and two adult facilitators, with mental health professionals in the school most commonly functioning as group facilitators. Groups focus on a particular social skill (e.g., alternatives to aggression, expressing feelings) for several sessions. Through role-plays during group meetings and assignments completed outside group meetings, facilitators help children develop the identified skill. To monitor and encourage transfer of training outside the group setting facilitators communicate weekly with children's teachers to discuss whether or not children exhibited the skill throughout school days.

Parent liaisons also function at the indicated level of care by helping communicate with caregivers of children exhibiting moderate academic, behavioral, or emotional concerns. Often teachers cannot reach caregivers during the day or, because of the lack of a working phone, at all. In these cases, teachers contact the parent liaison, who makes home visits or evening phone calls to communicate with caregivers. Because parent liaisons reside in the communities, caregivers often respond more favorably to their presence and encouragement than to teachers or other school staff.

In order to respond to significant incidents of classroom or school disruption, we have also established alternative classrooms in each school. The school office may refer children to the alternative classroom from several hours to several days following inappropriate behaviors by children. Placement of children into the classroom represents an alternative to suspension away from school. While in the classroom the alternative classroom aide and appropriate school personnel (e.g., mental health professionals) work with the child to examine the child's behaviors and their antecedents, continue academic assignments, and make an action plan for the child's successful return to the classroom.

Treatment

Through funds provided by the BCPSS SS-HS grant, mental health agencies in Baltimore place mental health clinicians in participating SS-HS schools. These clinicians work alongside BCPSS school psychologists and social workers to provide mental health services to children. SSTs or teachers refer children with more serious or persistent behavioral or emotional problems to these mental health clinicians. Clinicians use a variety of modalities—family therapy, teacher consultation, group therapy, and individual therapy—to best meet the needs of the children. These clinicians have received training in PATHS and Skillstreaming so that they may incorporate the language and concepts of these programs into their therapeutic work with children and families. These clinicians also have received ongoing clinical training alongside other community service providers. The SS-HS "specialty services" committee, with participation from various community stakeholders, has identified common concerns and priorities and organized "cross-training" sessions in which clinicians from schools, mental health clinics, social service agencies, group homes, and juvenile justice programs receive training together. Cross-training not only helps pool resources for training and ongoing support of clinical programs but also increases the likelihood that youth served will experience the same intervention regardless of the setting (i.e., school, group home, or family). School-based clinicians, such as those in the SS-HS project, have become involved in a variety of preventive interventions and treatment programs and play a multifaceted role in many community treatment programs.

The preceding opportunities are not yet available within many other school-based programs. Clinicians who attempt to broaden their skills or to employ both preventive and remedial intervention strategies frequently encounter attitudinal, organizational, and fiscal problems. Collaborations with other agencies within most communities provide opportunities for clinicians and clinical agencies to avert some of these barriers, through both coordination of intervention efforts and financial resources. The concluding section presents some ways in which collaborations with other agencies in Baltimore led to communitywide efforts to deal with emotional and behavioral problems. These efforts have helped fund school-based clinicians, support staff, and other mental health activities.

FUNDING SCHOOL MENTAL HEALTH SERVICES WITHIN A SYSTEM OF CARE

In many communities, the quantity and range of services they can provide is limited because of the way in which services are funded. Many communities provide school-based mental health services only to students requiring these services as part of their special education program. In other communities, clinicians work solely on a fee-for-service basis. Paired with large caseloads, fee-for-service reimbursement leaves little room to conduct evaluations with students who may not meet criteria for a psychiatric diagnosis (i.e., students who can be compensated), to provide consultation to school personnel and parents, to participate in the prevention or early intervention of mental health or substance abuse problems, or to connect and collaborate with other community agencies and service providers (e.g., juvenile justice, mentors). The fee-for-service system not only limits which children a clinician can see but also frequently limits the range of services that a clinician can provide.

Developing a system of care within a community frequently provides clinicians more flexibility in their clinical activities. This occurs because agencies blend or braid various funding sources and tie these sources not to the delivery of services but to the documentation of reduced behavioral problems within classrooms and schools and reduced hospitalizations or out-of-school placements. Communities that create systems of care frequently establish multiagency oversight boards that include representation from local health, mental health, substance abuse, child welfare, and juvenile justice agencies. Some of these oversight boards additionally include representation for housing agencies, mayoral or county executives, local foundations, parent groups, advocacy organizations, and local academic institutions. The diversity of the membership not only tends to expand the definitions of need employed in discussions of school-based services, but also brings to the table alternative funding strategies.

Within Baltimore a variety of agencies provide funds and support for school-based mental health. As described previously, some school-based clinicians have access to home-based services and parent and neighborhood liaisons. These services and liaisons work with students and their families to implement clinical programs. The state has provided money from the child welfare system to fund both preventive and remedial services provided by school-based clinicians. An agency in Baltimore charged with the oversight of the public mental health system, Baltimore Mental Health Systems, Inc., has provided money to several clinical service agencies to provide preventive services in preschool and school settings. The Baltimore City Public School System subcontracts with these same clinical service agencies to provide mental health clinicians in schools charged with preventive, remedial, and treatment responsibilities. The Mayor's Office provides funding for staff to work with students after school and to provide mentors to those youth who require additional adult support. The Department of Juvenile Justice has located some of their staff in schools to aid in sustaining delinquent youth in their schools and to provide additional support for in-school mental health efforts. Finally, at the time of our writing meetings are occurring between the State of Maryland and local communities in an attempt to consolidate funding sources and develop an integrated approach to the prevention of mental illness, substance abuse, and delinquency. These funds will, in part, fund more mental health clinicians to work in schools.

A final, important note is necessary concerning the funding of school-based mental health services. It took time to develop the relationships necessary between agencies to establish the aforementioned funding streams in support of school-based mental health services, and they only became possible because of the vision and active involvement of mental health clinicians and others interested in school-based services in planning and oversight activities. Local clinical directors may need to call meetings with other community agencies to place school-based mental health on their radar screens. Adelman and Taylor (2000) have written extensively about the need for greater attention to be paid to the development of resources for the reduction of mental health and behavioral problems in schools. In communities in which school-based clinicians and their agencies do not actively participate in the development of program priorities and intervention strategies; however, it is unlikely that funds will be available to support a multifaceted preventive and intervention strategy.

REFERENCES

Adelman, H. S., & Taylor, L. (2000). Looking at school health and school reform policy through the lens of addressing barriers to learning. *Children's Services: Social Policy, Research, and Practice, 3*, 117–132.

Barrish, H. H., Saunders, M., & Wolf, M. M. (1969). Good behavior game: Effects of individual contingencies for group consequences on disruptive behavior in a classroom. *Journal of Applied Behavior Analysis, 2*, 119–124.

Bickman, L., Noser, K., & Summerfelt, W. T. (1999). Long-term effects of a system of care on children and adolescents. *Journal of Behavioral Health Services, 26*, 185–202.

Booney, V. H., & Pumariega, A. (Eds.). (2001). *Clinical assessment of child and adolescent behavior.* New York: Wiley.

Center for Mental Health Services (1997). *Comprehensive community mental health services for children program.* Substance Abuse and Mental Health Services Administration: Technical Report.

Costello, J. E., Burns, B. J., Angold, A., & Leaf, P. J. (1993). How can epidemiology improve mental health services for children and adolescents? *Journal of the American Academy of Child and Adolescent Psychiatry, 32*, 1106–1114.

Davis, M., Yelton, S., & Katz-Leavy, J. (1995). "Unclaimed Children" revisited: The status of state mental health services. *Journal of Mental Health Administration, 22*, 147–176.

Dishion, T. J., & Andrews, D. W. (1995). Preventing escalation in problem behaviors with high-risk young adolescents: Immediate and 1-year outcomes. *Journal of Consulting and Clinical Psychology, 63*, 538–548.

Dishion, T. J., McCord, J., & Poulin, F. (1999). When interventions harm: Peer groups and problem behavior. *American Psychologist, 54*, 755–764.

Durlak, J. A., & Wells, E. (1997). Primary prevention mental health programs for children and adolescents: A meta-analytic review. *American Journal of Psychology, 24*, 115–152.

Elias, M. J., Zins, J. E., Weissberg, R. P., Frey, K. S., Greenberg, M. T., Haynes, N. M., Kessler, R., Schwab-Stone, M. E., & Shriver, T. P. (1997). *Promoting social and emotional learning.* Alexandria, VA: Association for Supervision and Curriculum Development.

Gottfredson, D. C. (2001). *Schools and delinquency.* New York: Cambridge University Press.

Greenberg, M. T., & Kusche, C. (1998). *Promoting Alternative Thinking Strategies (PATHS).* Boulder, CO: Center for the Study and Prevention of Violence.

Hoagwood, K., Burns, B. J., Kiser, L., Ringeisen, H., & Schoenwald, S. K. (2001). Evidence-based practice in child and adolescent mental health services. *Psychiatric Services, 52*, 1179–1189.

Ialongo, N. S., Werthamer, L., Kellam, S. G., Brown, C. H., Wang, S., & Lin, Y. (1999). Proximal impact of two first-grade preventive interventions on the early risk behaviors for later substance abuse, depression, and antisocial behavior. *American Journal of Community Psychology, 27*, 599–641.

Institute of Medicine (1993). *Access to health care in America.* Washington, DC: National Academy Press.

Kazdin, A. (2000). *Psychotherapy for children and adolescents: Directions for research and practice.* New York: Oxford University Press.

Kazdin, A. E., & Kendall, P. J. (1998). Current progress and future plans for developing effective treatments: Comments and perspectives. *Journal of Clinical Child Psychology, 27*, 217–226.

Kazdin, A. E., & Weisz, J. R. (1997). Identifying and developing empirically supported child and adolescent treatments. *Journal of Abnormal Child Psychology, 5*, 367–387.

Kellam, S. G., Mayer, L. S., Rebok, G. W., & Hawkins, W. E. (1998). Effects of improving achievement on aggressive behavior and of improving aggressive behavior on achievement through two preventive interventions: An investigation of causal paths. In B. P. Dohrenwend (Ed.), *Adversity, stress, and psychopathology* (pp. 486–505). New York: Oxford University Press.

Kiser, L. J., King, R., & Lefkovitz, P. M. (1999). A comparison of practice patterns and a model continuum of ambulatory behavioral health services. *Psychiatric Services, 50,* 605–606, 618.

Knitzer, J. (1982). Mental health services to children and adolescents: A national view of public policies. *American Psychologist, 39,* 905–911.

Kutash, K., & Rivera, V. R. (1996). *What works in children's mental health services? Uncovering answers to critical questions.* Baltimore: Paul H. Brookes.

Leaf, P. J., Alegria, M., Cohen, P., Goodman, S. H., Horwitz, Hoven, Narrow, Vaden-Keirnan, & Regier (1996). Mental health service use in the community and schools: Results from the four-community MECA study. *Journal of the American Academy of Child and Adolescent Psychiatry, 35,* 889–897.

Leaf, P. J., Bogrov, M., & Webb, M. B. (1997). The East Baltimore Mental Health Partnership. In S. W. Henggeler & A. B. Santos (Eds.), *Innovative approaches for difficult-to-treat populations.* Washington, DC: American Psychiatric Press.

Lochman, J. E., & Lenhart, L. A. (1993). Anger coping intervention for aggressive children: Conceptual models and outcome effects. *Clinical Psychology Review, 13,* 785–805.

Lochman, J. E., & Wells, K. C. (1996). A social-cognitive intervention with aggressive children: Prevention effects and contextual implementation issues. In R. D. Peters & R. S. McMahon (Eds.), *Preventing childhood disorders, substance abuse, and delinquency.* Thousand Oaks, CA: Sage.

Lochman, J. E., Wells, K. C., Lenhart, L., & Colder, C. (1996, May). *Cognitive-behavioral and behavioral parent training preventive intervention for boys at risk for substance use: Initial analyses of the Coping Power Program.* Poster presented at the National Prevention Research Conference, Washington, DC.

Lourie, I. S., Stroul, B. A., & Friedman, R. M. (1998). Community-based systems of care: From advocacy to outcomes. In M. H. Epstein & K. Kutash (Eds.), *Outcomes for children and youth with emotional and behavioral disorders and their families: Programs and evaluation best practices* (pp. 3–19). Austin, TX: PRO-ED, Inc.

McGinnis, E., & Goldstein, A. P. (1997). *Skillstreaming the elementary school child.* Champaign, IL: Research Press.

Pedro-Carroll, J. L., & Alpert-Gillis, L. J. (1997). Preventive interventions for children of divorce: A developmental model for 5 and 6 year old children. *Journal of Primary Prevention, 18,* 5–23.

Pedro-Carroll, J. L., Alpert-Gillis, L. J., & Cowen, E. L. (1992). An evaluation of the efficacy of a preventive intervention for 4th–6th grade urban children of divorce. *Journal of Primary Prevention, 13,* 115–130.

Pedro-Carroll, J. L., & Cowen, E. L. (1985). The Children of Divorce Intervention Program: An investigation of the efficacy of a school-based prevention program. *Journal of Consulting and Clinical Psychology, 53,* 603–611.

Persons, J. B. (1995). Why practicing psychologists are slow to adopt empirically-validated treatments. In S. C. Hayes, V. M. Follette, R. M. Dawes, & K. E. Grady (Eds.), *Scientific standards of psychological practice: Issues and recommendations.* Reno, NV: Context Press.

Reynolds, A. J., & Temple, J. A. (1998). Extended early childhood intervention and school achievement: Age thirteen findings from the Chicago Longitudinal Study. *Child Development, 69,* 231–246.

Schoenwald, S. K., Borduin, C. M., & Henggeler, S. W. (1998). Multisystemic therapy: Changing the natural and service ecologies of adolescents and families. In M. H. Epstein & K. Kutash (Eds.), *Outcomes for children and youth with emotional and behavioral disorders and their families: Programs and evaluation best practices* (pp. 485–511). Austin, TX: PRO-ED, Inc.

Seitz, V., Rosenbaum, L. K., & Apfel, N. H. (1985). Effects of family support intervention: A ten-year follow-up. *Child Development, 56,* 376–391.

Stark, K. D., Reynolds, W. M., & Kaslow, N. J. (1987). A comparison of the relative efficacy of self-control therapy and a behavioral problem-solving therapy for depression in children. *Journal of Abnormal Child Psychology, 15,* 91–113.

Stark, K. D., Rouse, L., & Livingston, R. (1991). Treatment of depression during childhood and adolescence: Cognitive-behavioral procedures for the individual and family. In P. Kendall (Ed.), *Child and adolescent therapy* (pp. 165–206). New York: Guilford.

Stroul, B. A. (1993). *Systems of care for children and adolescents with severe emotional disturbances: What are the results?* Washington, DC: CASSP Technical Assistance Center, Georgetown University Child Development Center.

Stroul, B. A., & Friedman, R. M. (1986). *A system of care for seriously emotionally disturbed children and youth.* Washington, DC: CASSP Technical Assistance Center, Georgetown University Child Development Center.

Stroul, B. A., & Friedman, R. M. (1996). The system of care philosophy. In B. A. Stroul (Ed.), *Children's mental health: Creating systems of care in a changing society* (pp. 3–22). Baltimore, MD: Brookes.

Tolan, P. H., & Guerra, N. G. (1994). Prevention of delinquency: Current status and issues. *Applied and Preventive Psychology, 3,* 251–273.

U. S. Department of Health and Human Services (1999). *Mental health: A report of the Surgeon General.* Rockville, MD: U.S. Department of Health and Human Services, Substance Abuse and Mental Health Services Administration, Center for Mental Health Services, National Institutes of Health, National Institute of Mental Health.

Zigler, E., & Styfco, S. J. (1994). Head Start: Criticisms in a constructive context. *American Psychologist, 49,* 127–132.

18

Training for Effective Practice in the Schools

THOMAS J. POWER, PATRICIA H. MANZ, and STEPHEN S. LEFF

Reforms in health care and education have highlighted the value of schools as a setting for the delivery of intervention and prevention services for children with or at risk for mental health problems (Kolbe, Collins, & Cortese, 1997). These reforms have focused attention on the resources of the school for coordinating mental health services to reduce the fragmentation that exists among systems in the community. Further, the key role that schools can serve in preventing mental health disorders and promoting health for all children has been emphasized in the literature (Dryfoos, 1994).

Although training programs have been developed to prepare mental health professionals for some of the challenges that arise in schools, very few programs have been designed to take full advantage of the opportunities for exciting intervention and prevention work available through schools (Power & Blom-Hoffman, in press). Part of the problem is that guidelines for the preparation of school mental health providers are lacking.

The intent of this chapter is to offer broad guidelines and to outline core domains of training that need to be addressed to prepare mental health professionals to become scientist-practitioners in schools. Guidelines for training are derived from the eight priorities for the future outlined in the Surgeon General's recent report on mental health (U.S. Department of Health and Human Services, 1999). These guidelines are then used to specify core domains of training and specific competencies that should be addressed in a comprehensive training program. A model program based in a doctoral-level school psychology training program is described to illustrate how a set of didactic and practicum training experiences can be integrated to address these guidelines.

THOMAS J. POWER and STEPHEN S. LEFF • Children's Hospital of Philadelphia, University of Pennsylvania School of Medicine, Philadelphia, Pennsylvania 19104.   PATRICIA H. MANZ • Lehigh University College of Education, Bethlehem, PA 18015.

GUIDELINES FOR TRAINING: IMPLICATIONS OF THE SURGEON GENERAL REPORT

Ensure the Delivery of State-of-the-Art Programs

Although countless programs have been developed to address the mental health needs of children, these initiatives vary greatly in their effectiveness and in the extent to which they have been adequately evaluated (Leff et al., 2001). Often programs chosen for implementation in the schools have not been subjected to systematic outcome evaluation. As a result, there may be a substantial gap between best practice and the services that are actually implemented in the community (U.S. Department of Health and Human Services, 1999).

Several professional groups, including the Agency for Health Care Policy and Research, the American Psychiatric Association, and the American Psychological Association, have developed guidelines for identifying empirically supported approaches to intervention (see Nathan, 1998). In psychology, criteria have been established for differentiating programs into those that are efficacious (i.e., established) and possibly efficacious (i.e., very promising; see Chambless & Hollon, 1998). The criteria used for determining if programs are efficacious or possibly efficacious include the following: (1) an experimental group design utilizing random assignment or carefully controlled single-case experiments, (2) a well-documented set of intervention procedures, (3) uniform therapist training and monitoring, (4) reliable and valid outcome assessment measures, (5) assessment of effects at follow-up, and (6) independent replication. Programs that meet all criteria are termed "efficacious," and those that meet all criteria except for independent replication are termed "possibly efficacious."

The school mental health professional can serve a valuable role in evaluating the existing research literature to identify empirically supported programs that may be effective in school and community settings. Training in research design, quantitative and qualitative methods of data analysis, and procedures for critically evaluating the research literature is essential for school mental health providers to serve as a resource in this capacity.

Tailor Programs to Developmental Level, Gender, Race, and Culture

A significant pitfall in providing child mental health services is to assume that "one size fits all." In other words, it is erroneous to claim that an empirically supported approach to intervention for a particular set of problems is effective for all children regardless of developmental level, gender, or cultural and racial background (Hughes, 2000). Research has affirmed repeatedly the importance of children's developmental level, race, culture, and gender in the delivery of appropriate and effective mental health services (Gibbs & Huang, 1998; Wilson, Rodrique, & Taylor, 1997). Nonetheless, developmental, cultural, and gender appropriateness are often not adequately considered when devising assessment and intervention strategies (Leff et al., 2001; Manz, Fantuzzo, & McDermott, 1999).

A guiding principle for examining the developmental, racial, cultural, and gender appropriateness of psychological interventions was offered by Paul (1967). Referred to as the "ultimate question," mental health professionals must constantly ask: "*What* treatment, provided by *whom,* is most effective for *this* individual, under *what* set of circumstances?" Mental health professionals will often find only partially complete answers to this question based upon their training and experience as well as available empirical literature. Establishing a partnership between the mental health team and stakeholders within the school and community, including school professionals, community leaders, parents, and children, is crucial to ensuring that programs are responsive to developmental, racial, cultural, and gender factors (Fantuzzo & Mohr, 2000; Manz et al., 2002). School mental health professionals need training to establish partnership relationships with school professionals and community residents that can lead to effective, appropriate, and culturally responsive services.

Overcome Stigma

When operating within a traditional clinical framework, emotional and behavioral problems are perceived as inherent dysfunctions in children that typically yield socially undesirable consequences (Wakefield, 1997). Employing a deficit-oriented approach perpetuates negative attributions of children and their families, which in turn reinforces the stigma associated with mental health programs (Fantuzzo, Coolahan, & Weiss, 1997). Alternative, strength-based approaches for providing mental health services are emerging based upon a proliferation of research related to resiliency and positive psychology that has highlighted the importance of affirming children's competencies and building the resources of the school, family, and community (Masten, 2001; Seligman & Csikszentmihalyi, 2000).

Several distinctive aspects of a resiliency model counteract the negative stigma often associated with mental health services (Doll & Lyon, 1998; Fantuzzo & Mohr, 2000). This model highlights the strengths within individuals, families, and communities who historically have been described narrowly by diagnostic nomenclature and risk factors. In addition, the model promotes the active engagement of children, families, schools, and communities in the development, implementation, and evaluation of intervention and prevention programs. Instead of feeling victimized by disorders and high levels of environmental risks, individuals are empowered by the invitation to work as equal partners with mental health professionals to build on existing competencies and address mutual concerns (Benson, 1997).

Knowledge of research and practice related to resiliency, and the integration of this perspective with a developmental psychopathology framework, is necessary to achieve a balanced approach to service delivery that capitalizes on protective factors while addressing risk factors (Masten, 2001). In addition, training in methodologies for conducting participatory action research can be invaluable in developing programs that are embraced and sustained by the community (Nastasi et al., 2000).

Ensure the Supply of Mental Health Services and Providers

Establishing mental health programs in schools is a justifiable approach to increase the supply and availability of services to children and families of various socioeconomic and cultural backgrounds (Weist et al., 2000). However, the extent to which school-based mental health programs can comprehensively address a wide range of student needs and provide a broad array of services is contingent upon the degree to which these programs are integrated into the schools. Often school administrators, motivated by a commitment to address the enormous needs of many students, look for problem-specific programs that have been developed in clinics, hospitals, or university settings. Addressing mental health needs in this manner produces disconnected programs and a fragmented approach to service delivery (Dryfoos, 1994).

Alternatively, expanding the school's capacity to provide integrated mental health services involves cultivating and supplementing natural resources within the school and restructuring service delivery systems (McLaughlin et al., 1997). Using school and community resources as a foundation for building mental health programs is both an efficient way of increasing the supply of services and a potentially effective method of service delivery (Adelman & Taylor, 1998). For example, enlisting and training community residents to serve as paraprofessionals can expand program capacity for providing effective mental health services to students and families (Blalock, 1991; Cowen et al., 1996). Moreover, given that these paraprofessionals share racial, cultural, and socioeconomic backgrounds with the students and families, the cultural responsiveness of the program can be significantly enhanced (Dowrick et al., 2001; Manz et al., 2002). In addition, developing strategies to promote family involvement in schooling (Christenson & Sheridan, 2001) and using peer-mediated learning and social skills strategies (Fantuzzo, King, & Heller, 1992) are effective ways of using the natural resources of the community to address important student needs.

School mental health professionals need to understand the culture of the school and the communities in which they work in order to identify and build upon natural resources in the community. In addition, these professionals should learn strategies for linking community systems to promote family–school and community–school partnerships to address the educational and mental health needs of children (Christenson & Sheridan, 2001; Comer et al., 1996).

Facilitate Entry into Programs

Many factors can facilitate entry and consistent involvement in intervention and prevention programs. A key factor is the social validity of the program, referring to the extent to which the program's goals, methods, and intended outcomes are viewed by children, families, and other major stakeholders as reasonable, developmentally appropriate, and culturally responsive (Nastasi et al., 2000; Schwartz & Baer, 1991). Feasibility issues, such as transportation, financial costs, day care considerations, and scheduling, also are important in facilitating program entry and maintenance (Bennett et al., 1996). Families of lower socioeconomic and/or ethnic minority status are particularly likely to encounter barriers in seeking mental health services and often seek help from other sources. For example, McMiller and Weisz (1996) found that over 65% of African American and Latino families expressed reluctance to seek assistance from mental health professionals to address concerns or difficulties with their children. Alternatively, these families generally reported a preference to seek help from their extended families or from residents or leaders in the community.

Several cultural factors may account for the discrepancy in help-seeking behaviors between Caucasian and ethnic minority families (Weisz et al., 1997).

Cultural groups may vary with regard to perceptions about whether a behavior problem is a disciplinary issue or a mental health concern. In addition, families may differ in the degree to which they feel it is appropriate to seek professional help for private family matters. Many African American and Latino families are inclined to value the privacy of family matters and feel it is undesirable to disclose these issues to persons outside of the family or community. Similarly, families vary in their comfort level in approaching mental health professionals. Ethnic minority families commonly mistrust mental health professionals and agencies (McMiller & Weisz, 1997). Further, communication difficulties may prevent participation in mental health services among ethnic minority families for whom English is not their primary language (Toppelberg, 1997).

Differences in help-seeking behaviors among families of varying ethnic backgrounds underscore how important it is for school mental health professionals to understand the cultural values of the children and families they serve. These providers need training in methods of overcoming barriers and facilitating access to intervention and prevention programs for families of diverse socioeconomic and cultural backgrounds.

Reducing Financial Barriers

Financial issues are major barriers to entry into mental health programs. Financial barriers include (1) a lack of insurance coverage for children and their families, (2) differential rates of third-party reimbursement for mental health versus physical health problems, and (3) a family's restricted access to preferred providers. Not surprisingly, families from low-income households are much more vulnerable to these financial barriers than higher-income groups. It is estimated that 11 million children under the age of 18 years are not insured (Children's Defense Fund, 2001). A very high percentage of these children live in families with income levels well below the federal poverty threshold (Children's Defense Fund, 2001).

The health reform movement has resulted in a dramatic shift in service delivery for children and families coping with mental health problems. Increasingly, the emphasis is being placed on building the capacity of community-based institutions, such as schools, primary care pediatric settings, and faith-based centers, to address the social and emotional needs of children (McMahon et al., 2000). Less emphasis has been placed on expending private and public resources to support mental health programs situated in hospital and clinic settings.

School mental health professionals need to understand the paradigm shift in mental health service delivery and the impact that this has had on children and families from diverse backgrounds. They need training to take advantage of new opportunities that have been created in the community in primary care, school, and faith-based centers, and they need to understand and be prepared to address the barriers that continue to exist, particularly for children from low-income and ethnic minority groups.

Continue to Build the Scientific Database

Although advances in mental health research are occurring at a rapid rate, the need to develop and validate approaches to intervention and prevention for children with or at risk for mental health problems is enormous (U.S. Department of Health and Human Services, 1999). Empirically supported approaches to intervention and prevention have been developed to address many mental health concerns, but research generally has failed to address the unique needs and perspectives of children from varying ethnic and cultural groups (Hughes, 2000). Developing and validating approaches to service delivery for each cultural group are not feasible. An alternative approach is to use research methods that balance the use of empirically supported procedures with perspectives of the stakeholders of intervention and prevention services (Greenwood, Whyte, & Harkavy, 1993). Participatory action research is a model that has been developed to ensure that programs of service are both efficacious and socially valid. Participatory action research involves stakeholders from the school, community, and family along with the clinical–research team in every step of program development and evaluation including: identifying target problems, conducting a needs assessment, developing the program, selecting outcome measures, implementing procedures, monitoring procedural integrity, collecting outcome data, interpreting the data, and developing recommendations for further research and practice (Schensul & LeCompte, 1999).

School mental health providers need to be trained to critically evaluate the research literature to determine which approaches to intervention are empirically supported and for which populations of children. In addition, these professionals need to understand the important role that they can serve in developing and validating community responsive programs within their schools and in contributing to an accumulating database regarding empirically supported intervention and prevention approaches for diverse populations.

Improving Public Awareness of Effective Strategies

School mental health professionals can play a leading role in disseminating information about evidence-based practice to educators, families, and community leaders. In doing so, emphasis should be placed on strategies to promote mental health and to intervene early when risk factors emerge. School mental health providers may provide workshops for professionals and paraprofessionals through school districts, and they may contribute to articles published in local, regional, and national periodicals. In addition, school mental health providers can offer workshops to parent and community groups within schools or community organizations.

School mental health professionals can also use the mass media to disseminate information related to effective prevention and intervention programs. Over the past decade, a number of researchers have studied how a carefully planned and implemented mass media approach can positively influence children or adolescent behaviors, including cigarette smoking (e.g., Worden et al., 1996), disclosure of child abuse (Hoefnagels & Baartman, 1997), and violent behaviors (American Psychological Association, 1999). However, the school mental health professional must be vigilant in these activities to ensure that the media accurately portrays their main points.

School mental health professionals would benefit from learning strategies to disseminate information about important mental health issues by delivering presentations to national, state, and local associations, contributing to periodicals and journals, and collaborating with the media. Having opportunities to observe mentors, engage in role playing with guided practice, and participate in dissemination activities under supervision are extremely helpful in training professionals about methods of raising public awareness about mental health topics.

CORE DOMAINS OF TRAINING

Since the early 1990s, several task forces have been established to develop guidelines to prepare child-oriented psychologists to respond to reforms in health care and mental health. In particular, the National Institute of Mental Health Task Group convened in 1992 (see Roberts et al., 1998) and the American Psychological Association (APA) Practice Directorate Task Force convened in 1996 (APA, 1998) outlined several core components of training critical in the preparation of child-oriented psychologists. Many areas of training outlined by these task forces are highly pertinent to the preparation of school mental health professionals. The conclusions of these task forces have been adapted to delineate five core domains for the training of school mental health professionals. Table 1 provides a description of these core domains and examples of the types of graduate level courses that could be offered to address each domain. The following is a brief description of each domain.

Core Domain I: Child Development

School mental health professionals must have a thorough understanding of the principles of child development, including factors that promote and impede normal development. Bronfenbrenner's (1979) social–ecological model of development is particularly important for school mental health providers to understand. According to this model, development is promoted when systems in the

Table 1. Core Domains of Training for School Mental Health Providers and Examples of Coursework for Each Domain

Core domains	Examples of courses
Domain I: Child development	Developmental psychology Developmental psychopathology
Domain II: Multimodal assessment and intervention design	Categorical and dimensional assessment Strength-based and ecological assessment Functional assessment of behavior
Domain III: Empirically supported and culturally responsive interventions	Empirically supported interventions Empirically supported prevention programs Designing culturally competent interventions
Domain IV: Program development and evaluation	Action research and research design Quantitative methods of data analysis Qualitative methods of data analysis
Core Domain V: Systems change and professional issues	School ecology and climate Coordinating systems of care Ethical and legal issues Dissemination strategies

community (e.g., family, school, neighborhood peer group, health system, community agencies) are connected effectively with each other and when each system operates to maximize the functioning of the other systems (Power & Bartholomew, 1987).

School mental health professionals also need a strong foundation in developmental psychopathology. Although it is important for professionals to become familiar with the diagnostic schemata outlined in the DSM-IV, primary emphasis should be placed on understanding developmental pathways that lead to externalizing and internalizing disorders (Donovan & Spence, 2000; Patterson, Reid, & Dishion, 1992). In exploring these pathways, the focus should be on understanding risk factors that need to be targeted for intervention as well as on enhancing protective factors to promote resilience (Masten, 2001).

Core Domain II: Multimodal Assessment and Intervention Development

Several assessment paradigms are highly useful in understanding children's functioning and designing potentially effective, socially valid, and feasible interventions. Categorical assessment, which generally involves the use of structured interview procedures, is useful in determining whether children meet criteria for psychiatric disorders as defined by diagnostic criteria such as the DSM-IV. Dimensional assessment, which usually involves the use of rating scales, are useful in acquiring norm-referenced information about children from a variety of sources (e.g., parent, teacher, child) (Achenbach & McConaughy, 1996).

Categorical and dimensional methods are limited because of their reliance upon a deficit model, their sole focus on the functioning of an individual child, and their lack of utility for designing interventions (Power & Eiraldi, 2000). Alternative methods of assessment have been developed to address these limitations. Strength-based assessment approaches are designed to identify assets of the individual and resources in the environment that can be enhanced to promote resilience and adaptive functioning (Epstein & Sharma, 1998). Ecological assessment methods provide information about the systems in which individuals function and the manner in which systems interact to either foster or impede healthy development (Garcia Coll et al., 1996). Functional assessment is highly useful in designing instructional and behavioral interventions (McComas & Mace, 2000). Functional assessment is designed to identify variables in the child and environment that trigger and maintain behavior for the purpose of determining hypothesized functions of behavior. School mental health professionals need to understand the strengths and limitations as well as the complementarity of these assessment paradigms. They need to be exposed to categorical methods of assessment, and they need focused training in dimensional, strength-based, ecological, and functional methods.

Core Domain III: Empirically Supported and Culturally Responsive Interventions

For intervention strategies to be effective, they should be based upon empirical research demonstrating their efficacy and they should have strong social validity.

More specifically, the goals, methods, and outcomes of intervention should be viewed by participants as reasonable and appropriate (Schwartz & Baer, 1991). School mental health professionals need to be trained to examine and critically evaluate the research literature pertaining to intervention, including both psychosocial and pharmacological approaches (Phelps, Brown, & Power, 2001). School mental health providers need to learn how to determine which programs are efficacious or possibly efficacious in addressing mental health problems, and they should be trained to be skeptical about generalizing findings derived from a specific sample to samples of varying gender, developmental level, and cultural background.

The research literature is limited in informing practitioners about efficacious, socially valid, and culturally responsive approaches to programming for children from diverse backgrounds (Hughes, 2000). To address this gap between science and practice, school mental health professionals need to learn methods of partnering with stakeholders in the school and community to develop and evaluate programs of intervention and prevention (Nastasi et al., 2000).

Core Domain IV: Program Development and Evaluation

Schools are a venue that provides numerous opportunities for the development and implementation of programs that have the potential to address the needs of large groups of children and their families. These initiatives may include intervention programs to address the needs of children with identified problems as well as prevention programs for at-risk and healthy children. Efforts to develop programs typically have been initiated and directed by school mental health professionals, and the focus of these initiatives often has been to orchestrate school personnel and resources to address mental health needs. However, such efforts may fail to address important community needs and to build upon existing resources in the community to develop and sustain mental health programs (Nastasi, 2000; Power, 2000).

School mental health professionals need to understand that effective program development builds upon existing resources of the school and community and needs to be conducted in partnership with school professionals as well as with community leaders and residents. Training in participatory action research is particularly useful for program development and evaluation. With participatory action research, members of the research team (e.g., school mental health professionals and university-based consultants) collaborate with project stakeholders (e.g., educators, community leaders, parents, youth) in all stages of program development and evaluation, including (1) problem identification, (2) needs assessment, (3) program development, (4) program implementation, (5) outcome assessment, (6) data interpretation, and (7) program redesign (Nastasi & Berg, 1999). Enlisting and empowering natural helpers from the community, including family members, community residents, and peers, can be an effective approach to increase the resources for program implementation and to provide services in a culturally sensitive manner (Dowrick et al., 2001). In addition, partnerships between researchers and community stakeholders are essential in planning effective replication and dissemination projects.

Programs need to be developed in a way that facilitates their systematic evaluation. For this reason, school mental health providers need training in experimental, quasiexperimental, correlational, and descriptive methods of research design. In addition, training in quantitative as well as in qualitative methods of analysis is needed to organize and interpret process and outcome data that are generated during the course of action research (Nastasi & Berg, 1999).

Core Domain V: Systems Change and Professional Issues

School mental health providers need to understand the mission, culture, and legal policies pertaining to the major systems that have an effect on children, including the family, the school, the health care system, the mental health system, and the child welfare system. In addition, they need to understand factors that promote and serve as barriers to the coordination of systems of care.

Many children have problems gaining access to potentially beneficial intervention and prevention programs. Lower socioeconomic status, ethnic minority status, and single parenting are some of the factors that prevent families from becoming involved and staying involved in services. School mental health providers need to understand the many barriers to program access and maintenance, and they need to develop strategies to reduce these obstacles and promote ongoing involvement (Adelman & Taylor, 1998).

School mental health providers encounter numerous ethical and legal issues in their research and practice. These issues include maintaining the confidentiality of mental health information in the public world of the school, addressing cases of suspected child abuse, and obtaining informed consent for the participation in research projects. School mental health providers need to know federal, state, and local policies that govern the delivery of mental health services, and they need to be well informed about ethical principles and their implication for practice in the schools. In addition, training in strategies to raise public awareness about effective intervention and prevention strategies is needed.

Integrated Learning Experiences

The preparation of school mental health providers requires an integrated set of coursework and practicum experiences (Power et al., 1995). Ideally, courses are conducted by a multidisciplinary faculty with experience in service delivery as well as in program development and evaluation in school and community settings. Courses are linked with practicum experiences that provide trainees the opportunity to apply models of assessment, intervention, and prevention in actual situations under supervision. Practicum experiences are offered in school settings as well as in mental health centers and primary care pediatric settings and afford students opportunities to coordinate systems of care for children and their families. Practicum experiences provide students with opportunities to engage in a broad range of clinical, programmatic, and research activities addressing each of the core domains of training. Further, university faculty engage in an ongoing collaboration with practicum supervisors to ensure the complementarity of didactic and applied learning activities.

A MODEL TRAINING PROGRAM

Many pathways are available for the preparation of school mental health professionals (Power, Shapiro, & DuPaul, in press). The following is a description of a model program that is nested within a doctoral-level school psychology training program. A unique feature of this program is that it has been designed to prepare professionals to effectively link the educational, health, and mental health systems to provide coordinated care for children and their families (Shapiro, DuPaul, & Power, 1997). Although this model has been developed specifically for the preparation of school psychologists, many of its components have relevance for professionals in other psychology specialties and other disciplines.

Through the collaborative efforts of Lehigh University and The Children's Hospital of Philadelphia (CHOP), a program linking pediatric, clinical child, and school psychology, referred to as the pediatric school psychology program, was established in 1997 with funding from the U.S. Department of Education, Office of Special Education Programs. In 2001, a subsequent grant was awarded to continue the project with an expanded focus.

Goals of the Lehigh/CHOP Program

The program is designed for students in the school psychology doctoral training program at Lehigh University. Students in the third and fourth year of training have the option of applying to this specialized program. The goal of the Lehigh/CHOP training initiative is to develop school professionals as leaders in linking the educational, health, mental health, and family systems to address the needs of children with or at risk for mental health disorders and chronic health conditions. The program is designed to prepare professionals to provide intervention services to children with or at risk for health conditions and mental disorders, as well as to develop and evaluate programs of prevention and health promotion. The program focuses primarily on providing services and conducting research on behalf of children from low-income neighborhoods of diverse ethnic backgrounds, given that these individuals are at greatest risk for becoming functionally impaired as a result of developing a chronic health condition (Talley & Short, 1995).

Required Coursework

The doctoral training program at Lehigh University is strongly grounded in principles of developmental and behavioral psychology. In their first 2 years of doctoral training, students receive intensive training in child development, behavioral assessment including functional assessment of behavior, data-based decision-making and intervention design, research design and statistical analysis, school ecology, and educational psychology. In the next 2 years, students in the pediatric school psychology program complete the components of training for each of the core domains presented in Table 1. The courses offered to students in the third and fourth years are indicated in Table 2. In the third year the focus of coursework is on strategies of intervention for children with or at risk for mental health disorders and chronic health conditions, including psychosocial and medical interventions, as well as on principles and strategies of organizational change. In the fourth

**Table 2. Course Requirements during the Third and Fourth Year
of Doctoral Study in the Lehigh/CHOP Program**

Third year—fall semester
  Health/pediatric psychology
  Theory and practice of organizational management
  Advanced seminar in family and child interventions
Third year—spring semester
  Applications in pediatric school psychology—intervention
  Advanced seminar in child psychopathology
Third year—summer
  Neuropharmacology
Fourth year—fall semester
  Comprehensive school health programs
  Advanced seminar in multicultural counseling
Fourth year—spring semester
  Applications in pediatric school psychology—health promotion
  Advanced seminar in child development

year the focus of coursework is on strategies of prevention and health promotion, action research methods, multicultural assessment and intervention strategies, and advanced concepts and applications in child development.

Courses offered through this specialized program are taken at Lehigh University and at CHOP. Courses at Lehigh are offered by a multidisciplinary faculty including professors in Biology, School and Counseling Psychology, Special Education, and Educational Leadership. Courses at CHOP are offered by faculty in Psychology and Developmental and Behavioral Pediatrics from CHOP and the University of Pennsylvania School of Medicine.

Practicum Experiences

Because the goal of training is to prepare professionals to effectively link systems of care in the community, practicum experiences are divided equally between school and health care settings. School practica are offered in Philadelphia and in the Lehigh Valley of Pennsylvania. During the school practica, students provide assessment and intervention services in an interdisciplinary context for children with or at risk for health and mental health disorders. In addition, the students learn to develop and evaluate prevention programs for children at risk for developing health problems. Students learn to apply action research methodologies with a focus on building partnerships with school professionals and community residents to develop and evaluate intervention and prevention programs. In the health care practica, students focus on addressing the needs of children with chronic health conditions and mental health problems who are having difficulties with adaptation into the school and community. For example, students complete practica in a variety of programs including: the Center for Management of Attention-Deficit/Hyperactivity Disorder (ADHD), the Behavioral Pediatrics Clinic, the Feeding and Dysphagia Center, the Oncology Center, and the Neonatal Follow-up Program. In these rotations, they are given opportunities to contribute to the development of intervention programs that address the needs of children with chronic health conditions in the school and community.

RETRAINING AND CONTINUING EDUCATION

Many professionals have not had the comprehensive training required to take advantage of the numerous opportunities available in schools to engage in exciting intervention and prevention activities. For example, many school mental health professionals are very effective in providing intervention services to children and families, but they may have limited knowledge about strategies of prevention, community partnership, and action research. As a result, they may lack skills in developing and evaluating innovative health promotion projects. Similarly, many clinic-based providers are interested in expanding their practice to include school mental health activities, but they may be lacking in knowledge of school ecology, organizational change in the community, and prevention programming in school settings.

Professionals seeking to become retrained to broaden their range of skills related to school mental health practice and research can often receive this training through graduate programs at local universities. A limited number of university departments actually have formal retraining programs, but many departments are willing to provide mentoring to assist professionals in designing an individualized retraining program. In some cases, it may be possible to enroll in a series of courses and practicum experiences to achieve the individualized learning objectives. Another option is to identify mental health agencies and school districts (e.g., see Fischetti & Mortati, 1998; Wooten, 1997) that provide systematic and integrated training. Typically, these programs are designed for preservice training at the graduate level, but often program directors are willing to accommodate professionals who seek retraining.

Critical to the success of any retraining program is for professionals to become aligned with mentors who have a broad vision of school mental health, who have a wide range of intervention and prevention skills related to school mental health practice, and who are highly invested in the career development of the professional. Because retraining programs are typically highly individualized experiences, it is essential that the professional works closely with mentors to design, implement, and evaluate an individualized training program (Power, Shapiro, et al., in press).

Ongoing continuing education is essential for all school mental health providers, regardless of their level of preservice training. Numerous resources are available to assist with the professional development needs of school mental health providers, but two excellent resources are the Center for School Mental Health Assistance at the University of Maryland—Baltimore and the Center for Mental Health in Schools at the University of California—Los Angeles.

CONCLUSIONS

Schools are a setting that provides exciting opportunities for school mental health professionals to offer intervention and prevention services. Professionals from multiple disciplines are making important contributions in schools as mental health providers, but guidelines for the preparation of school mental health providers are lacking. In this chapter we used the eight priorities outlined in the Surgeon General's report on mental health to derive five essential domains of training for school mental health providers. These core domains of training include (1) child development, (2) multimodal assessment and intervention design, (3) empirically supported and culturally responsive intervention strategies, (4) program development and evaluation, and (5) systems change and professional issues. Important components of training within each domain were outlined. The chapter described a model training program based in a doctoral-level school psychology program, which has been developed through a collaboration between Lehigh University and The Children's Hospital of Philadelphia. This program provides an integrated set of courses and practicum experiences that focus on the preparation of professionals for practice and research related to intervention as well as prevention.

Given the rapid growth of school mental health programs since 1990, standards for the preparation of school mental health professionals across multiple disciplines are needed. Also, research regarding the implementation of training standards and outcomes derived from programs that utilize these standards should be conducted to direct training efforts in the future.

ACKNOWLEDGMENT. Preparation of this chapter was supported in part by funding from the U.S. Department of Education, Office of Special Education Programs (H325D010002).

REFERENCES

Achenbach, T. M., & McConaughy, S. H. (1996). Relations between DSM-IV and empirically-based assessment. *School Psychology Review, 25,* 329–341.

Adelman, H. S., & Taylor, L. (1998). Mental health in schools: Moving forward. *School Psychology Review, 27,* 175–190.

American Psychological Association (1998). *Report of the Task Force on Child and Adolescent Professional Psychology to the Board of Professional Affairs.* Washington, DC: Author.

American Psychological Association (1999). *Warning signs.* Washington, DC: American Psychological Association.

Bennett, D. S., Power, T. J., Rostain, A. L., & Carr, D. E. (1996). Parent acceptability and feasibility of ADHD interventions: Assessment, correlates, and predictive validity. *Journal of Pediatric Psychology, 21,* 643–657.

Benson, P. L. (1997). *All kids are our kids: What communities must do to raise caring and responsible children and adolescents.* San Francisco: Jossey–Bass.

Blalock, G. (1991). Paraprofessionals: Critical team members in our special education programs. *Intervention in School and Clinic, 36,* 200–214.

Bronfenbrenner, U. (1979). *The ecology of human development.* Cambridge, MA: Harvard University Press.

Chambless, D. L., & Hollon, S. D. (1998). Defining empirically supported therapies. *Journal of Consulting and Clinical Psychology, 66,* 7–18.

Children's Defense Fund (2001). *Accessing health services: Moving beyond enrollment.* Washington, DC: Author.

Christenson, S. L., & Sheridan, S. M. (2001). *Schools and families: Creating essential connections for learning.* New York: Guilford Press.

Comer, J. P., Haynes, N. M., Joyner, E. T., & Ben-Avie, M. (1996). *Rallying the whole village: The Comer process for reforming education.* New York: Teachers College Press.

Cowen, E. L., Hightower, A. D., Pedro-Carroll, J. L., Work, W. C., Wyman, P. A., & Haffey, W. G. (1996). *School-based prevention for children at risk: The primary mental health project.* Washington, DC: American Psychological Association.

Doll, B., & Lyon, M. A. (1998). Risk and resilience: Implications for the delivery of mental health services in the schools. *School Psychology Review, 27,* 348–363.

Donovan, C. L., & Spence, S. H. (2000). Prevention of childhood anxiety disorders. *Clinical Psychology Review, 20,* 509–531.

Dowrick, P. W., Power, T. J., Manz, P. H., Ginsburg-Block, M., Leff, S. S., & Kim-Rupnow, S. (2001). Community responsiveness: Examples from under-resourced urban schools. *Journal of Prevention and Intervention in the Community, 21,* 71–90.

Dryfoos, J. G. (1994). *Full-service schools: A revolution in health and social services for children, youth, and families.* San Francisco: Jossey–Bass.

Epstein, M. H., & Sharma, J. (1998). *Behavioral and Emotional Rating Scale: A strength-based approach to assessment.* Austin, TX: PRO-ED.

Fantuzzo, J. W., Coolahan, K., & Weiss, A. (1997). Resiliency partnership-directed research: Enhancing the social competencies of preschool victims of physical abuse by developing peer resources and community strengths. In D. Cicchetti & S. Toth (Eds.), *Developmental perspective on trauma: Theory, research and intervention* (pp. 463–514). Rochester, NY: University of Rochester Press.

Fantuzzo, J. W., King, J. A., & Heller, L. R. (1992). Effects of reciprocal peer tutoring on mathematics and school adjustment: A component analysis. *Journal of Educational Psychology, 84,* 331–339.

Fantuzzo, J. W., & Mohr, W. (2000). Pursuit of wellness in Head Start: Making beneficial connections for children and families. In D. Cicchetti, J. Rapapport, I. Sandler, & R. Weissberg (Eds.), *The promotion of wellness in children and adolescents* (pp. 341–369). Thousand Oaks, CA: Sage.

Fischetti, B. A., & Mortati, A. L. (1998, Fall). Post-doctoral school-based clinical supervision: A training model for credentialling as a licensed psychologist. *The School Psychologist, 52,* 105, 120–121.

Garcia Coll, C., Crnic, K., Lamberty, G., Wasik, B. H., Jenkins, R., Garcia, H. V., & McAdoo, H. P. (1996). An integrative model for the study of developmental competencies in minority children. *Child Development, 67,* 1891–1914.

Gibbs, J. T., & Huang, L. N. (Eds.). (1998). *Children of color: Psychological interventions with culturally diverse youth.* San Francisco, CA: Jossey–Bass.

Greenwood, D. J., Whyte, W. F., & Harkavy, I. (1993). Participatory action research as a process and as a goal. *Human Relations, 46,* 175–192.

Hoefnagles, C., & Baartman, H. (1997). On the threshold of disclosure. The effects of a mass media field experiment. *Child Abuse & Neglect, 21,* 557–573.

Hughes, J. N. (2000). The essential role of theory in the science of teaching children: Beyond empirically supported treatments. *Journal of School Psychology, 38,* 301–330.

Kolbe, L. J., Collins, J., & Cortese, P. (1997). Building the capacity of schools to improve the health of the nation: A call for assistance from psychologists. *American Psychologist, 52,* 256–265.

Leff, S. S., Power, T. J., Manz, P. H., Costigan, T. E., & Nabors, L. A. (2001). School-based aggression prevention programs for young children: Current status and implications for violence prevention. *School Psychology Review, 30,* 344–362.

Manz, P. H., Fantuzzo, J. W., & McDermott, P. A. (1999). The parent version of the preschool social skills rating scale: An analysis of its use with low-income, ethnic minority children. *School Psychology Review, 28,* 493–504.

Manz, P. H., Power, T. J., Ginsburg-Block, M., & Dowrick, P. W. (2002). Community paraeducators: Improving the effectiveness of urban schools through the engagement and empowerment of low-income, ethnically diverse community residents. Manuscript submitted for publication.

Masten, A. S. (2001). Ordinary magic: Resilience processes in development. *American Psychologist, 56,* 227–238.

McComas, J. J., & Mace, F. C. (2000). Theory and practice in conducting functional analysis. In E. S. Shapiro & T. R. Kratochwill (Eds.), *Behavioral assessment in schools: Theory, research, and clinical foundations.* New York: Guilford Press.

McLaughlin, J. M., Leone, P. E., Meisel, S., & Henderson, K. (1997). Strengthen school and community capacity. *Journal of Emotional and Behavioral Disorders, 5,* 15–23.

McMahon, T. J., Ward, N. L., Pruett, M. K., Davidson, L., & Griffith, E. (2000). Building full-service schools: Lessons learned in the development of interagency collaboratives. *Journal of Educational & Psychological Consultation, 11,* 65–92.

McMiller, W. P., & Weisz, J. R. (1997). Help-seeking preceding mental health clinic intake among African-American, Latino, and Caucasian youths. *Journal of the American Academy of Child and Adolescent Psychiatry, 35,* 1086–1094.

Nastasi, B. K. (2000). School psychologists as health-care providers in the 21st century: Conceptual framework, professional identity, and professional practice. *School Psychology Review, 29,* 540–554.

Nastasi, B. K., & Berg, M. (1999). Using ethnography to strengthen and evaluate intervention programs. In J. J. Schensul & M. D. LeCompte (Eds.), *The ethnographer's toolkit: Using ethnographic data: Interventions, public programming, and public policy* (Vol. 9, pp. 1–56). Walnut Creek, CA: AltaMira Press.

Nastasi, B. K., Varjas, K., Schensul, S. L., Silva, K. T., Schensul, J. J., & Ratnayake, P. (2000). The participatory intervention model: A framework for conceptualizing and promoting intervention acceptability. *School Psychology Quarterly, 15,* 207–232.

Nathan, P. E. (1998). Practice guidelines: Not yet ideal. *American Psychologist, 53,* 290–299.

Patterson, G., Reid, J., & Dishion, T. (1992). *Antisocial boys.* Eugene, OR: Castalia Publishing.

Paul, G. L. (1967). Outcome research in psychotherapy. *Journal of Consulting Psychology, 31,* 109–118.

Phelps, L., Brown, R. T., & Power, T. J. (2001). *Pediatric psychopharmacology: Facilitating collaborative practices.* Washington, DC: American Psychological Association.

Power, T. J. (2000). Commentary: The school psychologist as community-focused, public health professional: Emerging challenges and implications for training. *School Psychology Review, 29,* 557–559.

Power, T. J., & Bartholomew, K. L. (1987). Family-school relationship patterns: An ecological assessment. *School Psychology Review, 14,* 222–229.

Power, T. J., & Blom-Hoffman, J. (in press). The school as venue for managing and preventing health problems: Opportunities and challenges. In R. Brown (Ed.), *Handbook of pediatric psychology in school settings.* Mahwah, NJ: Erlbaum.

Power, T. J., DuPaul, G. J., Shapiro, E. S., & Parrish, J. M. (1995). Pediatric school psychology: The emergence of a subspecialty. *School Psychology Review, 24,* 244–257.

Power, T. J., & Eiraldi, R. B. (2000). Educational and psychiatric classification systems. In E. S. Shapiro & T. R. Kratochwill (Eds.), *Behavioral assessment in schools: Theory, research, and clinical foundations.* New York: Guilford Press.

Power, T. J., Shapiro, E. S., & DuPaul, G. J. (in press). Preparing psychologists to link the educational and health systems in managing and preventing children's health problems. *Journal of Pediatric Psychology.*

Roberts, M., Carlson, C., Erickson, M., Friedman, R., LaGreca, A., Lemanek, K., Russ, S., Schroeder, C., Vargas, L., & Wohlford, P. (1998). A model for training psychologists to provide services for children and adolescents. *Professional Psychology: Research and Practice, 29,* 293–299.

Schensul, J. J., & LeCompte, M. D. (Eds.). (1999). *Ethnographer's toolkit* (Vols. 1–7). Walnut Creek, CA: AltaMira Press.

Schwartz, I. S., & Baer, D. M. (1991). Social validity assessments: Is current practice state of the art? *Journal of Applied Behavior Analysis, 24,* 189–204.

Seligman, M. E., & Csikszentmihalyi, M. (2000). Positive psychology. *American Psychologist, 55,* 5–14.

Shapiro, E. S., DuPaul, G. J., & Power, T. J. (1997, August). Pediatric school psychology: A new specialty in school health reform. *The Pennsylvania Psychologist Quarterly,* 20–21.

Talley, R. C., & Short, R. J. (1995). *School health: Psychology's role. A report to the nation.* Washington, DC: American Psychological Association.

Toppelberg, C. O. (1997). Minority help seeking. *Journal of the American Academy of Child and Adolescent Psychiatry, 36,* 443–444.

U.S. Department of Health and Human Services (1999). *Mental health: A report of the Surgeon General.* Rockville, MD: U.S. Department of Health and Human Services, Substance Abuse and Mental Health Administration, Center for Mental Health Services, National Institutes of Health, National Institute of Mental Health.

Wakefield, J. C. (1997). When is development disordered? Developmental psychopathology and the harmful dysfunction analysis of mental disorder. *Development and Psychopathology, 9,* 269–290.

Weist, M. D., Nabors, L. A., Myers, P. C., & Ambruster, P. (2000). Evaluation of expanded school mental health programs. *Community Mental Health Journal, 36,* 395–411.

Weisz, J. R., McCarty, C. A., Eastman, K. L., & Chaiyasit, W. (1997). Developmental psychopathology and culture: Ten lessons from Thailand. In S. S. Luthar & J. A. Burak (Eds.), *Developmental psychopathology: Perspectives on adjustment, risk and disorder* (pp. 568–592). New York, NY: Cambridge University Press.

Wilson, D. K., Rodrique, J. R., & Taylor, W. C. (Eds.). (1997). *Health-promoting and health-compromising behaviors among minority youth.* Washington, DC: American Psychological Association.

Wooten, S. A. (1997, Fall). School psychology into the twenty-first century: The internship in the Dallas public schools. *The School Psychologist, 51,* 114–117.

Worden, J. K., Flynn, B. S., Solomon, L. J., & Secker-Walker, R. H. (1996). Using mass media to prevent cigarette smoking among adolescent girls. *Health Education Quarterly, 23,* 453–468.

19

Continuous Quality Improvement and Evaluation of Expanded School Mental Health Programs

LAURA A. NABORS, HEATHER D. LEHMKUHL, and MARK D. WEIST

In the emerging expanded school mental health (ESMH) field, quality is one of the most, if not the most important, issues to focus on. Program quality is fundamental to effectiveness, and in this era of increased accountability, documenting effectiveness is paramount to the advancement of the field. Although some preliminary evaluation studies have been conducted (e.g., Armbruster, Gerstein, & Fallon, 1997; Nabors & Reynolds, 2000), more information about quality of care and outcomes for youth receiving school mental health services is needed. In this chapter we review ideas for implementing continuous quality improvement (CQI) activities and evaluating the outcomes of expanded school mental health programs. We also discuss challenges to CQI and evaluation and present ideas for future work and research in the field.

CONTINUOUS QUALITY IMPROVEMENT

Quality improvement, broadly defined, is "a systematic framework for investigating the reasons for service outcomes, thus setting the stage for further improvement" (Chowanec, 1994, p. 792). Many different types of program evaluation and research methods, incorporating both qualitative and quantitative techniques, may be subsumed under the rubric of quality improvement (Hibbs, 1995). Including the

LAURA A. NABORS and HEATHER D. LEHMKUHL • Department of Psychology, University of Cincinnati, Cincinnati, Ohio 45221.   MARK D. WEIST • University of Maryland School of Medicine, Baltimore, Maryland 21201.

term "continuous" implies that activities are ongoing, in essence representing a feedback loop that never ends, as the program progressively improves based on quality assessment findings. As Bickman and Noser (1999) stated:

> CQI requires that we understand the link between process of care and outcome, that we systematically collect data on this link, and that we create an atmosphere of change at all levels of the organization that supports the implementation of changes in treatment based on that [sic] data. (p. 247)

We recommend designing CQI activities that will examine the (1) impact of treatment; (2) building blocks of effective programs, such as emphasizing training, quality assurance, wraparound service planning, and collaboration; (3) treatment process; and (4) satisfaction with treatment. In the following sections of this chapter, we present ideas for conducting CQI activities for evaluation of ESMH services and describe the benefits and challenges related to doing this.

Theoretical Framework for Conducting CQI Activities

Avedis Donabedian (1980), one of the foremost theorists on quality improvement, recommended assessing quality indicators in three areas: program structure, treatment process, and treatment outcome. Indices of quality for the program structure are variables representing the setting (e.g., attractiveness of physical space; accessibility of offices) and characteristics of the health care providers (e.g., therapeutic orientation, experience) (Eppel et al., 1991). Examination of treatment process should include recording information about the (1) referral process (e.g., time between referral and intake), (2) training that occurs during supervision, and (3) interventions used during therapy. The area that has received the most attention is measurement of treatment outcomes, which typically involves examining changes in the child's functioning over the course of treatment. Examples of outcome indicators include measurement of changes in student self-concept, academic achievement, attendance, as well as student and parent satisfaction with treatment.

A significant amount of shared variance exists between indicators in the three areas, and Donabedian (1980) proposed that quality improvement activities could overlap across areas. This is a similar notion to Bickman and Noser's (1999) definition of CQI programs as examining linkages between therapy process and outcomes. Investigating the relationship between indicators for treatment process and outcomes will provide information about the interactions between interventions and changes in functioning for youth receiving therapy.

Area 1: Evaluation of Program Structure

As mentioned, the first phase of CQI activities may center on examining program structure, or factors that are crucial to the appearance of and managing the program, such that these factors form the foundation for operating the program. Successful programs develop a mission statement and standards that serve to guide program evaluation activities, such as examining the efficiency, effectiveness, and costs of services. An expert panel for the Center for School Mental Health

Assistance (CSMHA) identified several standards of high-quality care for expanded school mental health services:

> (1) Providing comprehensive direct clinical assessment and treatment services for underserved youth, (2) emphasizing preventive programs that provide early identification and treatment for youth in need, (3) ensuring that mental health programs have a strength or competency focus, versus an exclusive focus on reducing psychopathology, and (4) seeking to maximize the impact of mental health services by improvement in collaborative efforts aimed at improving the global school environment. (CSMHA, 1996, p. 4)

Several other CQI activities can be implemented during a structural appraisal. Assessing consumer perceptions of the quality of office space, in terms of its adequacy for conducting therapy, is one recommended activity. Ensuring that the office space is inviting allows youth to feel comfortable, laying the groundwork for the development of the relationship and therapeutic intervention. Other structural indicators include the adequacy of the referral system or time from referral to first contact, percentage of referrals actually seen, percentage of students referred to other settings for treatment, and "show rate" (appointment keeping).

Conducting a needs assessment to examine stakeholder perceptions of program strengths and areas for improving services is an activity that can be conducted during a structural appraisal. Stakeholder views may be assessed using surveys, interviews, or focus groups. Nabors, Weist, and Tashman (1999) reported on a study involving the use of focus groups to provide ideas and feedback to a school mental health program operating in Baltimore. Groups were conducted with various stakeholder groups such as adolescents receiving and not receiving treatment, teachers, parents, clinicians, health center staff, and administrators. Results indicated that services were highly valued by adolescents, parents, administrators, and teachers. Increasing staff to serve more youth was a frequently mentioned goal by all stakeholder groups. Students reported that they valued opportunities to talk about their problems with "counselors" who they felt comfortable with, rather than disclosing their problems to teachers or school staff.

Area 2: Evaluation of Treatment Process

Donabedian (1980) referred to a second area, appraisal of treatment process, as crucial in quality improvement. This refers to assessing the process of therapy, supervision, relationships between clinicians and school staff, family involvement in therapy, and service coordination and case management activities. Recording prevention activities conducted in schools, and interactions between clinicians and students during these activities, is another indicator of the process of care. Also, documenting clinicians' and students' perceptions of what they consider to be "successful" interventions, or treatment techniques associated with positive outcomes, is an important first step in recording information about treatment process. Taping or recording notes on the process of supervision and the interventions discussed by supervisors and trainees will provide knowledge about how clinicians are being trained. Relating the process of supervision to what happens during therapy will enhance knowledge about how supervision is translated into clinical practice. The collaborative relationship between the clinician and school staff often is a "foundation" for implementing interventions in the classroom. Describing successful and unsuccessful collaboration efforts can be used to guide training for new clinicians.

Peer review teams are an evaluation activity for examining treatment process, and results emanating from these meetings may be used to enhance the effectiveness of existing interventions as well as to guide the development of new ones. Peer review teams are made up of clinicians who have experience working in the setting of interest. The peer review teams typically conduct record reviews and hold meetings to evaluate the success of treatment and the clinician's skills (Eppel et al., 1991; Sechrest, 1987). Reviewers conduct detailed reviews of cases randomly assigned for evaluation or of cases identified as high risk by clinicians (Lavender et al., 1994). After a case is reviewed, recommendations for improving therapy are made by reviewers (Lawthers & Wood, 1996). Reviewers can provide ideas on useful therapeutic techniques and interventions as well as provide supportive yet corrective feedback when a particular approach does not seem to be working (Lavender et al., 1994). Peer review of progress notes and treatment plans provides information about compliance with standards and promotes the development of "best practice" guidelines. Conducting peer reviews may be costly, because time is lost from clinical practice, both for the peer reviewers and for the clinician undergoing review. It is also relatively time and labor intensive. Meetings may take several hours, involving a significant amount of time and effort for both the treating clinician and the other program clinicians. It may be difficult for clinicians in busy ESMH clinics to devote this much time to an evaluation activity. Thus, other methods for assessing therapy process, such as focused interviews, may be more cost-effective in gathering information on factors influencing treatment process (Nabors, Reynolds, & Weist 2000).

Area 3: Evaluation of Outcomes

The third area for evaluation efforts is assessing the outcomes of treatment. These may be assessed in a variety of ways, such as (1) examining changes in student functioning using self-report or parent report on behavioral checklists or standardized questionnaires; (2) documenting consumer perceptions of treatment using interviews, focus groups, or satisfaction surveys; or (3) documenting the number of children referred for Special Education Services, medical evaluations, to the Juvenile Justice System, etc. (Weist et al., 2000).

Importantly, since evaluation and research efforts on ESMH programs remain relatively limited, there is a wide range of possible approaches that have yet to be explored. For example, different methods (e.g., focus groups, behavior observations, questionnaires) can be used to examine children's functioning across different domains (e.g., social, behavioral, academic) and contexts (e.g., classroom, lunchroom, playground, home, or community). Advancing and increasing the diversity of the outcome evaluation/research agenda in ESMH will be facilitated by partnerships between programs and by researchers in child and adolescent mental health (see Tashman et al., 2000). For example, in Baltimore, the School Mental Health Outcomes Group is an interdisciplinary group of practitioners, researchers, administrators, and educators that is guiding the evaluation of school

Table 1. Guidelines for CQI Activities in ESMH Programs[a]

1. Develop or reevaluate mission statement and standards for the program.
2. Select or recruit an Advisory Board (include multiple stakeholders) to guide program evaluation efforts and monitor CQI activities.
3. Hire or select staff to form an evaluation team to conduct CQI activities.
4. Assess stakeholder needs.
5. Assess mental health resources in the school and community.
6. Foster working relationships with other mental health providers and agencies.
7. Develop or improve staff orientation programs.
8. Implement an ongoing training and continuing education program for staff.
9. Evaluate supervision quality.
10. Conduct structural appraisal activities.
11. Examine therapy process indicators.
12. Evaluate multiple therapy outcome indicators for youth and families.
13. Assess the relationship between process and outcome indicators.
14. Present a report summarizing activities to the program staff and advisory board; revise report based on their feedback.
15. Provide results and feedback to funders and stakeholders.
16. Use feedback to reexamine the program; return to step 1.

[a]This table was adapted and revised based on material presented in Nabors, Weist, Tashman, and Myers (1999).

mental health programs in the city. The collaborative and diverse nature of this group enables the identification of novel evaluation strategies, the improvement of research methods, and the development of strategies to translate research findings into effective advocacy (see Chapter 5, this work).

The press to increase practice activities may make it difficult to conduct all planned CQI activities in a short period of time. It may take 1, 2, or more years to complete evaluation efforts in the three areas. In most cases, then, it may be beneficial to conceptualize CQI programs as being conducted in phases and to consider implementing either one or some of the CQI activities over a period of time. This means that the process of CQI will be long term and developed in stages based on program funding and on the availability of staff to participate in evaluation activities.

Table 1 presents key steps in developing continuous quality improvement activities in school mental health. We emphasize that implementation of a CQI program is a process that takes time, money, and effort from all who are involved in the program, including its leaders, staff, collaborating stakeholders, advisory board members, and funders.

Challenges of Conducting Outcomes Research

Evaluation of children's mental health services is a difficult area to study. It can be difficult to select outcome indicators. Therapy may influence many aspects of children's lives, making the range of possible outcome factors diverse. Also, understanding the treatment process is challenging, because many variables such as clinician characteristics (e.g., therapeutic orientation), child characteristics (e.g., diagnoses, previous therapy experiences), family dynamics, and the types of interventions used influence what happens during therapy sessions (Farmer, 2000).

Additional complications may arise when results do not provide evidence showing that clinically significant change resulted from treatment or when results indicate that youth are still functioning within the "clinical range" in terms of symptomatology (Luk et al., 2001; Nabors & Reynolds, 2000; Weisz, Weiss, & Donenberg, 1992). Clinical significance may be defined as a "meaningful change" in functioning for youth, measured by a significant improvement (e.g., one standard deviation) on survey or questionnaire data (Jacobsen & Truax, 1991). Implementing data analysis techniques that provide information about the clinical significance of results may provide more meaningful data for clinicians, parents, teachers, and other stakeholders.

Clinicians may be convinced of the value of CQI activities, if they see project results as having positive implications for the children they serve (such as increasing funding for services or improving office space). Also, when results are shared with clinicians they can use this information to improve treatment. Similarly, school administrators and funders may be more supportive of research efforts when they learn about positive outcomes for youth, such as improved grades and academic achievement and decreased absences for youth.

To complicate matters even further, unique issues are associated with conducting research in schools (see Forness & Hoagwood, 1993; Nabors, Weist, & Reynolds, 2000). Additional challenges faced by researchers evaluating ESMH programs include (1) working with multiple Institutional Review Boards, (2) reducing attrition from pre- to postassessment, (3) convincing clinicians to participate in the evaluation, (4) finding adequate space to conduct the evaluation and to store data in order to maintain confidentiality, and (5) selecting outcome measures that are brief and have a proximal relationship to the intervention (see Nabors, Weist, & Reynolds, 2000; Weist et al., 2000). Additionally, recruiting comparison groups in evaluation efforts is a significant challenge, in terms of both recruiting the groups and addressing associated barriers (e.g., obtaining institutional approval) and also in ensuring comparability with the treatment group. Several of the barriers inherent in conducting outcome evaluations of ESMH programs are reviewed in Table 2.

It will remain challenging to untangle what aspects of therapy process as well as child, family, environmental, and clinical factors are exerting key influences to shape changes—positive or negative—in a child's social–emotional functioning. Forness and Hoagwood (1993) have aptly named research in schools as an "area where angels fear to tread" (p. 291). Challenges to conducting outcome evaluations

Table 2. Barriers to Conducting Evaluation Activities in ESMH Programs

1. Different outcomes are of interest to different stakeholders.
2. Obtaining approval from schools to conduct the research.
3. Finding a comparison group or getting permission to use a wait-list control group.
4. Obtaining approval from multiple institutional review boards (e.g., school, university, local health department).
5. Obtaining informed consent.
6. Motivating clinicians, students, families, and teachers to participate.
7. Finding space for data collection and storage.
8. Collecting objective data on behavior change.
9. Determining the optimal interval between pre- and post-tests.
10. Determining the right measures to include in the evaluation.
11. Reducing attrition and evaluating reasons for dropouts.
12. Assessing the effects of unique contexts.

can be overcome when administrators are supportive of the evaluation team and make efforts to implement findings to improve the program.

The costs and longitudinal nature of outcomes research may make it difficult for school mental health program administrators, clinicians, and school staff to support evaluation efforts. Often, evaluation goals are determined by program funders or other outside agencies, without input from the program about the resources that would be needed to conduct a CQI program. In order to attain evaluation goals, adequate funding and protected staff time need to be allocated to ensure success of evaluation efforts. It is notable that most contracts to fund school mental health programs do not include funds for evaluation or research. This "unfunded mandate" stresses the program and places contingencies on obtaining extramural funding for research.

Ideally, ESMH programs should have an advisory board in place that is providing input into all areas of program functioning. Strategies for evaluating the program and for using results to improve program support are key advisory board functions (see Tashman et al., 2000, Chapter 11). It is also useful for programs to have in place quality improvement/evaluation teams representing a core group that includes expertise on evaluation/research issues (see Flaherty & Weist, 1999). Developing a research and service agenda, based on program-level and national goals, to guide the team's efforts will both ground and drive evaluation efforts (see Kratochwill & Stoiber, 2000).

Future Directions

Several processes may be used to direct the implementation of a continuous quality improvement approach for ESMH programs: (1) receiving ongoing feedback and guidance from stakeholder groups (e.g., youth, families, school staff, agency staff, community and faith leaders, government officials) who have a vested interest in the program; (2) implementing a full range of services from broad approaches that seek to improve the environment of the school and promote mental health to intensive therapeutic interventions; (3) striving for principles of best practice and providing ongoing training; and (4) evaluating the program, engaging in collaborative research, and disseminating findings and lessons learned. These interrelated processes are presented in Fig. 1.

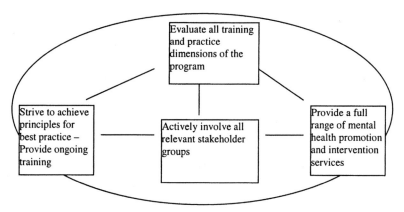

Figure 1. Ensuring high quality in ESMH programs.

Table 3. Guidelines for Improving ESMH Programs

Guidelines for enhancing preventive and clinical interventions
1. Provide clinical services to youth in need, irrespective of ability to pay.
2. Be involved in the school as a change agent to improve school environment and broadly promote mental health for students and staff.
3. Develop prevention activities; use evidence based interventions when possible.
4. Build treatment efforts on the evidence base (e.g., manualized approaches).
5. Develop and implement a Continuous Quality Improvement (CQI) Program.

Guidelines for striving for best practice and enhancing training efforts
1. Have principles for best practice guide the program.
2. Develop a broad range of experiences to enhance training efforts.
3. Emphasize interdisciplinary training for clinicians and trainees.
4. Improve cultural diversity of training.
5. Provide quality supervision of trainees.
6. Implement orientation, training, and continuing education programs.
7. Conduct CQI activities to examine the effects of training sessions and to document their impact on treatment process.

Guidelines for enhancing evaluation and research activities
1. Develop an evaluation plan with guidance from and involvement of stakeholders.
2. Implement the evaluation plan, with findings used to improve program services and increase support.
3. Work cooperatively with other community-based programs to develop joint evaluation projects.
4. Encourage researchers, clinicians, parents, teachers, and students to work on evaluation teams.
5. Develop/take advantage of forums for practitioners and researchers to exchange information.
6. Build dissemination mechanisms, attending to the "user friendliness" of evaluation findings and implications.

Guidelines for involving stakeholders
1. Develop an advisory board that includes all relevant stakeholder groups.
2. Enhance communication mechanisms between program staff and stakeholders (e.g., newsletters, e-mail distribution lists).
3. Conduct needs assessments involving quantitative (e.g., school record information, sociodemographic data) and qualitative (e.g., focus groups) approaches.
4. Build dissemination mechanisms, attending to the "user friendliness" of evaluation findings to deploy effective treatments in the field.
5. Involve families as collaborators in treatment and in improving the program.

Guidelines for improving the program in each of these four areas are presented in Table 3.

In that expanded school mental health is an emerging field, there are countless issues that represent important future directions for the field to advance. As mentioned, improving program quality is perhaps the most important overarching issue for the field. Some of the key themes that should guide the future work include:

- Determining the most effective approaches for ongoing stakeholder involvement.
- Building strategies for active communication between stakeholders and program staff.
- Moving toward a full continuum of mental health promotion and intervention in schools and effectively merging school and community resources and programs.

- Identifying the role of expanded school mental health programs in local systems of care and improving communication and collaboration between each service site.
- Developing principles for best practice, quality indicators, and quality improvement programs for each principle (see Weist et al., 2002).
- Enhancing training for effective school-based practice for mental health trainees and professionals and increasing mental health training for frontline staff, such as teachers and school nurses.
- Creating algorithms for programs to choose the best evaluation approaches and outcome indicators based on their size, goals, and activities.
- Developing formal strategies to bridge research and practice in order to promote collaborative relationships between researchers and practitioners in the widespread application and improvement of the evidence base.

These are just a few major themes that should be pursued in the work ahead. To make progress in each area will require a focus on efficiency and the embracing of technological advances. For example, developing standardized outcome evaluation systems for school mental health programs in a community or state and providing technical assistance and support for the conduct of evaluations would be of major assistance. Such systems would facilitate accountability as different ESMH programs would be able to compare findings and engage in discussions related to reasons for effectiveness or ineffectiveness (Mason, 2000). The national evaluation of the Comprehensive Community Mental Health Services for Children and Their Families Program (see Special Issue in the *Journal of Emotional and Behavioral Disorders,* 2001) documents the development and effectiveness of the system-of-care approach. In that expanded school mental health programs are key players in the system of care (Pumariega & Vance, 1999), funding a similar project focusing on them would no doubt yield significant dividends in both improving practice and shaping future evaluation and research agendas.

ACKNOWLEDGMENTS. The authors would like to thank the Agency for Healthcare Research and Quality for funding this project (Grant RO3 HSO9542). Additionally, we would like to thank the clinicians and students participating in the School Mental Health Program, in Baltimore, Maryland, as well as the University of Cincinnati, University of Maryland, the Baltimore City Health Department, and the Baltimore City Schools for supporting our research efforts.

REFERENCES

Armbruster, P., Gerstein, S. H., & Fallon, T. (1997). Bridging the gap between need and service utilization: A school-based mental health program. *Community Mental Health Journal, 33,* 199–211.

Bickman, L., & Noser, K. (1999). Meeting the challenges in the delivery of child and adolescent mental health services in the next millennium: The continuous quality improvement approach. *Applied and Preventive Psychology, 8,* 247–255.

Center for School Mental Health Assistance (1996). *Documenting the effectiveness of school mental health programs.* Baltimore, MD: Author.

Chowanec, G. D. (1994). Continuous quality improvement: Conceptual foundations and application to mental health care. *Hospital and Community Psychiatry, 45,* 789–793.

Donabedian, A. (1980). *The definitions of quality and approaches to its assessment*. Ann Arbor, MI: Health Administration Press.

Eppel, A. B., Fuyarchuk, C., Phelps, D., & Tersigni-Phelan, A. (1991). A comprehensive and practical quality assurance program for community mental health services. *Canadian Journal of Psychiatry, 36*, 102–106.

Farmer, E. M. Z. (2000). Issues confronting effective services in systems of care. *Children and Youth Services Review, 22*, 627–650.

Flaherty, L. T., & Weist, M. D. (1999). School-based mental health services: The Baltimore models. *Psychology in the Schools, 36*, 379–389.

Forness, S. R., & Hoagwood, K. (1993). Where angels fear to tread: Issues in sampling, design, and implementation of school-based mental health services research. *School Psychology Quarterly, 8*, 291–300.

Hibbs, E. D. (1995). Child and adolescent disorders: Issues for psychosocial treatment research. *Journal of Abnormal Clinical Psychology, 23*, 1–10.

Jacobsen, N. S., & Truax, P. (1991). Clinical significance: A statistical approach to defining meaningful change in psychotherapy research. *Journal of Consulting and Clinical Psychology, 59*, 12–19.

Kratochwill, T. R., & Stoiber, K. C. (2000). Uncovering critical research agendas for school psychology: Conceptual dimensions and future directions. *School Psychology Review, 29*, 591–603.

Lavender, A., Leiper, R., Pilling, S., & Clifford, P. (1994). Quality assurance in mental health: The QUARTZ system. *British Journal of Clinical Psychology, 33*, 451–467.

Lawthers, J., & Wood, P. (1996). In search of psychiatric performance measures. *Clinical Performance and Quality Health Care, 4*, 38–40.

Luk, E. S. L., Staiger, P., Mathai, J., Wong, L., Birleson, P., & Adler, R. (2001). Evaluation of outcome in child and adolescent mental health services: Children with persistent conduct problems. *Clinical Child Psychology and Psychiatry, 6*, 109–124.

Mason, M. M. (2000). Meeting the challenges of data collection in outcome systems. *Education and Treatment of Children, 23*, 75–95.

Nabors, L. A., & Reynolds, M. W. (2000). Program evaluation activities: Outcomes related to treatment for adolescents receiving school-based mental health services. *Children's Services: Social Policy, Research, and Practice, 3*, 175–189.

Nabors, L. A., Reynolds, M. W., & Weist, M. D. (2000). Qualitative evaluation of a high school mental health program. *Journal of Youth and Adolescence, 29*, 1–13.

Nabors, L. A., Weist, M. D., & Reynolds, M. W. (2000). Outcome evaluation in school mental health: Overcoming challenges and developing a research agenda. *Journal of School Health, 70*(5), 206–209.

Nabors, L. A., Weist, M. D., & Tashman, N. A. (1999). Focus groups: A valuable research tool for assessing adolescents' perceptions of school based mental health services. *Journal of Gender, Culture, and Health, 4*, 39–48.

Nabors, L., Weist, M., Tashman, N., & Myers, P. (1999). Quality assurance and school-based mental health services. *Psychology in the Schools, 36*, 485–493.

Pumariega, A. J., & Vance, H. R. (1999). School-based mental health services: The foundation of systems of care for children's mental health. *Psychology in the Schools, 36*, 371–378.

Sechrest, L. B. (1987). Research on quality assurance. *Professional Psychology: Research and Practice, 18*, 113–116.

Special Issue: The national evaluation of the Comprehensive Community Mental Health Services for Children and Their Families Program (2001). *Journal of Emotional and Behavioral Disorders, 9*.

Tashman, N., Weist, M. D., Acosta, O., Bickham, N. L., Grady, M., Nabors, L., & Waxman, R. P. (2000). Toward the integration of prevention research and expanded school mental health programs. *Children's Services: Social Policy, Research, and Practice, 3*, 97–115.

Weist, M. D., Nabors, L. A., Myers, C. P., & Armbruster, P. (2000). Evaluation of expanded school mental health programs. *Community Mental Health Journal, 36*, 395–412.

Weist, M. D., Sander, M., Lowie, J. A., & Christodulu, K. (2002). The expanded school mental health framework. *Childhood Education, 78*, 269–273.

Weisz, J. R., Weiss, B., & Donenberg, G. R. (1992). The lab versus the clinic: Effects of child and adolescent psychotherapy. *American Psychologist, 47*, 1578–1585.

20

Strength-Based Approaches to Assessment in Schools

MICHAEL H. EPSTEIN, MARK K. HARNISS,
VESTENA ROBBINS, LINDA WHEELER,
SHELLY CYRULIK, MICHAELA KRIZ,
and J. RON NELSON

Strength-based assessment has received considerable acceptance from across a wide range of stakeholders involved in youth services including child welfare (Saleeby, 1992), mental health (Lourie, Katz-Leavy, & Stroul, 1994), family services (Dunst, Trivette, & Deal, 1994), and education (Nelson & Pearson, 1991). Several education and mental health initiatives as well as established treatment models have stressed the need for strength-based assessment including the Child and Adolescent Service System Program (CASSP) (Stroul & Friedman, 1994), the U.S. Department of Education's National Agenda for Achieving Better Results for Children and Youth with Serious Emotional Disturbance (1994), multisystemic therapy (Henggeler et al., 1998), and the wraparound approach (VanDenBerg & Grealish, 1996). Strength-based assessment has been defined as "the measurement of those emotional and behavioral skills, competencies, and characteristics that create a sense of personal accomplishment; contribute to satisfying relationships with family members, peers, and adults; enhance one's ability to deal with adversity and stress; and promote one's personal, social, and academic development" (Epstein & Sharma, 1998, p. 3). In this chapter, we briefly overview strength-based assessment, discuss informal and formal assessment techniques, and end with applied examples of strength-based assessment.

MICHAEL H. EPSTEIN, MICHAELA KRIZ, and J. RON NELSON • University of Nebraska, Lincoln, Nebraska 68583.   **MARK K. HARNISS** • University of Washington, Seattle, Washington 98195.   **VESTENA ROBBINS** • REACH, Louisville, Kentucky 40208.   **LINDA WHEELER and SHELLY CYRULIK** • Alliance for Children and Families, Milwaukee, Wisconsin 53224.

OVERVIEW OF STRENGTH-BASED ASSESSMENT

Strength-based assessment is founded upon the following set of beliefs:

1. All children have strengths.
2. Focusing on children's strengths instead of weaknesses may result in enhanced motivation and improved performance.
3. Failure to demonstrate a skill should first be viewed as an opportunity to learn the skill as opposed to a problem.
4. Service plans that begin with a focus on strengths are more likely to involve families and children in treatment.

All Children Have Strengths

A primary goal of practitioners and researchers in the social sciences has been the development of assessment tools that provide reliable and valid indicators of various skills. In general, assessment instruments have been used to identify deficits or problems in an individual's or a group's performance for the purpose of screening, diagnosis, identification, or remediation. In the area of emotional and behavioral disorders, there are many formal assessments that possess strong psychometric properties and provide useful information to practitioners and researchers. These include the Revised Behavior Problem Checklist (Quay & Peterson, 1987), Behavior Rating Profile (Brown & Hammil, 1990), and the Child Behavior Checklist (Achenbach, 1991). However, the deficit-oriented focus of these measures may unnecessarily limit the range of information collected on the behaviors of children by reducing the focus of those who provide the data. Such a restricted focus may result in the failure to collect additional information about individuals that may be relevant to developing, implementing, and monitoring comprehensive service plans, such as individual education programs (IEPs). The field of assessment is certainly not limited to the identification of problems and weaknesses, however. Salvia and Ysseldyke (1998) define assessment at its most general level as a process for gathering data to inform decisions about a group or an individual. From this broader standpoint, information about strengths is equally as important as information about weaknesses. Thus, strength-based assessment fits within a holistic model in which each child is viewed as an individual, possessing unique strengths and weaknesses. Such a focus may change the current assessment approach that emphasizes "fixing" a child's deficits to an emphasis on enhancing a child's strengths. If professionals focus on the identification and development of strengths, children may develop a stronger foundation upon which to face personal challenges.

Focus on Strengths

When professionals focus on a child's deficit areas, they may inadvertently respond to the child more negatively and with less enthusiasm. A child may read this either as "giving up" or as a lack of interest, which may lead to less motivation to change or grow. As Kral (1989) noted, "If we ask people to look for deficits, they will usually find them, and their view of the situation will be colored by this. If we ask people to look for successes, they will usually find it, and their view of the situation will be colored by this" (p. 32). Recent research (Oswald et al., 2001) suggests a child's strengths already play a large part in decisions about where a child is placed. In comparing children with similar weaknesses but differing strengths, they found that children with a lower number of identified strengths were placed in more restrictive settings. They note that "individual child strengths may mitigate the impact of serious psychiatric symptoms and risk, allowing children to remain in homelike settings more successfully" (p. 196).

Opportunity to Learn

When a child fails, it may not mean the child does not have the capacity to function successfully; rather it might mean the child has not learned the skills to perform successfully. Inadequate or nonexistent instruction may explain a child's failure to demonstrate a skill. Based on this principle, school personnel, caregivers, and direct service providers need to consider how to provide sufficient instruction for the child to learn and master competencies.

Service Plans

Service plans (e.g., IEPs, transition plans) that begin with a focus on strengths rather than with a focus on incompetence and failure, are more likely to be acceptable to children, families, and service providers as they provide a foundation of competence upon which to improve. In 1997, the reauthorization of the Individuals with Disabilities Education Act (IDEA) mandated the use of strength-based assessment in the development of the IEP. Specifically, IDEA states that the IEP team shall consider "the strengths of the child and the concerns of the parents for enhancing the education of their child" (34 CFR 300.346).

This added strength-based component of IDEA has the potential to change the IEP process from a focus on a child's problems to a broader focus on the child's entering strengths in conjunction with her or his areas for improvement. The IEP team could then develop an inventory that highlights a child's current strengths and resources, identifies critical needs across all life domains, and includes parental goals and the services and supports that will be used to build upon the child's strengths and ameliorate the child's weaknesses.

Collecting a range of assessment data that represent both strengths and weaknesses may be very useful in communicating with parents and caregivers who are interested not only in what is "wrong" with their child but also in knowing what is "right" and in building upon the skills and competencies they see in their child. Moreover, such an orientation to families may lead to a positive parent–professional relationship characterized by mutual trust, supportiveness, and clarity of goals.

INFORMAL STRENGTH-BASED ASSESSMENT

Counselors and diagnosticians have frequently practiced informal strength-based assessment (VanDenBerg & Grealish, 1996, 1998). However, there is no single model of informal strength assessment that applies to all situations. Generally in an informal approach, a professional engages in a "strength chat" with the child, family, and/or informal supports (e.g., relatives, friends, pastors). In this chat, the professional asks questions about the strengths, resources, vision, and goals for the future that the child and family hold in order to identify the needs of the child and family. The format of this chat, as well as the questions and data collection, varies from professional to professional and from situation to situation. Examples of questions that would appear in an informal interview are as follows: "If you were in trouble, who would you ask for help?" "What do you see yourself doing in three years?" "What are your favorite hobbies or activities?" The chief benefit of informal approaches to strength-based assessment is in their clinical utility for service planning. The following is an abbreviated case study of how an informal strength assessment was used to identify goals and establish a treatment plan.

Applied Example

The Hill family was referred to a school-based mental health program and assigned to Ms. Alice Schademann, a family service worker. The family consisted of Sandy (mother), Jason (first grader), and Jeff (third grader). Sandy was a single parent working two jobs; Jason and Jeff were both receiving special education services. The family had very little in terms of financial resources. At home, Sandy was struggling with discipline and with finding time to spend as a family. She also was in need of some respite time. At school, Jason and Jeffrey were defiant, noncompliant, academically underachieving, and constantly sent to the office. The boys were in need of positive activities outside of school.

As part of the intake to the school program, an informal strength assessment was conducted between Sandy (the mother) and Alice (the family service worker). The purpose of the assessment was to gather important information about the family's interests. Alice asked questions about family interests, strengths, past experiences, traditions, goals, and values. Sample questions included "Life would be better six months from now if . . . " and "The things I like best about my children are . . . " The information obtained was then used in the planning process to identify and write goals with the family. A copy of the completed strength-based assessment is presented in Table 1.

The information from Sandy was very informative and helpful in designing the plan of care. Sandy stated that the family enjoyed watching movies and eating popcorn on weekends. The family loved animals, going to the zoo, and had several pets of their own. The Hills had a strong extended family to whom they could turn for support; specifically the boys' grandfather and aunt. Sandy expressed that what she loved most about her children was their sense of humor and athletic ability. Sandy also identified as a need her desire to work one job as opposed to two jobs, and that would enable her to spend more time with her boys.

A family planning team, consisting of Sandy, the boys' grandfather and aunt, the principal, a special education teacher, a community recreation worker, and Alice, was convened. Alice presented the results of the strength-based assessment and other relevant data, and Sandy identified a number of needs and goals. The family initially had three goals: employment, parenting skills, and after-school activities for the boys. First, Sandy wanted a new job that paid well. The team focused on Sandy's interests of animals, children, and nature, reviewed classified ads, and brainstormed possible employment options. Based on her strength of love

Table 1. Example of an Informal Strength-Based Assessment

1. **The things I like most about my child(ren) are:** They have a great sense of humor. They are athletic. They enjoy soccer, swimming, basketball.
2. **My life would really be better 6 months from now if:** I could work one job, instead of two, and make ends meet.
3. **My child's/children's life would be really better 6 months from now if:** If they had activities to keep them busy and out of trouble; if these activities occur after school.
4. **The most important thing I have ever done is:** Become a Mom.
5. **I am happiest when:** I am with my family.
6. **The best times we have had as a family are:** Saturday nights, watching movies, and eating popcorn. We sit around and laugh and tell stories.
7. **My best qualities as a parent are:** I keep trying, I am patient, and I want the best for my boys.
8. **Name some special rules that your family has:** We tell each other what we're thinking. We share what we have. We pray together at night.
9. **Who are persons you call when you need help and want to talk? Who have you turned to in the past for support?** The boy's grandfather and aunt.
10. **What activities does your family enjoy?** We like to spend time with our pets, go for walks, and go to the park, watch movies, have extended family over.
11. **What are your family traditions? In which cultural events does your family participate?** The boy's father was Hispanic. We still practice a lot of the Hispanic traditions.
12. **Are there any special values or beliefs that were taught to you by your parents or others who are important to you?** We were raised to always put our family first and talk problems through.
13. **Does your family belong to any part of the faith community? In what way?** We have started to attend a local church.

of animals, Sandy agreed to apply for work as an assistant to a veterinarian and was offered the position. The second goal was for Sandy to improve her parenting skills, especially how to discipline her boys. Alice mentioned that a class on effective parenting strategies was being offered at the elementary school one evening a week for 10 consecutive weeks. Sandy's father agreed to watch the boys one night a week so Sandy could attend a parenting class. Sandy incorporated her strength of extended family support (i.e., her father) to work toward her goal (i.e., effective parenting skills). The third goal was for the boys to experience planned, positive age-appropriate activities outside of school. Sandy wanted the boys to have male mentors that would engage them in athletic activities and offer variety to their schedules. At the suggestion of the principal, Sandy agreed to sign the boys up for a mentoring program at the local YMCA. The boy's grandfather and aunt also offered to take the boys on monthly outings that tapped into the athletic ability of the boys. This provided the much-needed respite Sandy required. The boys focused on their strengths of athletic ability and got involved in soccer and basketball with their mentors. The third goal (i.e., positive after-school activities) was achieved by building on the strengths of Sandy (i.e., family support) and her sons (i.e., athletic ability).

FORMAL STRENGTH-BASED ASSESSMENT

Only recently has strength-based assessment, particularly informal assessment, received the same rigorous psychometric consideration as deficit-oriented approaches. Specifically, proponents of strength-based assessment are just beginning to investigate the reliability, validity, and fidelity of implementation of their strength-oriented measures. Without such evidence, it is difficult to be certain that strength-based measures assess the variables of interest consistently. Strength-based measures have also lacked the normative data that allow researchers and practitioners to compare an individual's ratings to the ratings of other individuals from a specific population.

In response to these concerns about informal strength-based assessment, several standardized strength-based measures have been developed, field-tested, and published in recent years. In the following section, a few of these instruments and their psychometric qualities are reviewed. Specifically, we briefly review the Strengths and Difficulties Questionnaire (SDQ) (Goodman, 1997), the Children and Adolescent Strengths Assessment Scale (CASA) (Lyons, Kisiel, & West, 1997), and work by the Search Institute (Benson et al., 1998; Leffert et al., 1998). Finally, we review the Behavioral and Emotional Rating Scale (BERS) (Epstein & Sharma, 1998) and describe how formal strength-based data can be used for planning and evaluation purposes.

Strength and Difficulties Questionnaire

A widely accepted measure (available in over 30 languages), the SDQ is used in basic and applied research and as a screening tool in educational and mental health environments. The SDQ (Goodman, 1997) is a brief screening instrument with 25 positive and negative items. The strength-oriented items in the SDQ were added to make the measure more acceptable to respondents. The measure is divided into five domains: Prosocial Behavior, Peer Problems, Emotional Symptoms, Inattention Hyperactivity, and Conduct Problems. Parents, teachers, or mental health professionals complete the primary version of SDQ or youth, ages 11–16, can complete a different version as a self-report. The measure has adequate concurrent and predictive validity as well as test–retest reliability (Goodman, 1997; Goodman & Scott, 1999).

Child and Adolescent Strengths Assessment Scale

Designed to be included as part of an overall mental health evaluation, the CASA (Lyons et al., 1997) is a 30-item measure divided into five domains. These domains include morality/spirituality (4 items), peer strengths (3 items), psychological strengths (5 items), school/vocational strengths (8 items), family strengths (6 items), and extracurricular strengths (4 items). The CASA is administered by either a child's caregiver or therapist. Evaluators rate a youth on a 3-point scale for each item (1 = no evidence, 2 = interest/potential, 3 = yes, definitely). Results of the CASA indicate the presence of strength and the potential for development of that strength. The scale appears to possess adequate content and concurrent validity as well as internal reliability.

Search Institute

The Search Institute is a nonprofit social science research organization that seeks to promote positive youth development (Benson et al., 1998; Leffert et al., 1998). In particular, the Institute focuses on community-based programs that address the strengths and assets of families and individuals. Their recent work has centered on the development of two theoretical constructs: The Developmental Asset Framework (a set of benchmarks for positive development of children and adolescents) and the Asset-Building Community (a model for developing communities with more positive supports for youth).

The Developmental Asset Framework is operationalized in the Search Institute's revised Profiles of Student Life: Attitudes and Behaviors (PSL-AB), a self-report survey designed to measure developmental assets. Developmental assets are defined as "a set of 'building blocks' that when present or promoted appear to enhance significant developmental outcomes among youth" (Benson et al., 1998, p. 142). The 156-item survey measures 40 developmental assets as well as other constructs (e.g., developmental deficits, thriving indicators, high-risk behaviors). The developmental assets are grouped into categories that represent external (i.e., environmental) and internal (e.g., values) assets. In the PSL-AB, these broad categories are broken down into eight additional external or internal subcategories. External developmental assets include (1) support, (2) empowerment, (3) boundaries and expectations, and (4) constructive use of time. Internal developmental assets include (1) commitment to learning, (2) positive values, (3) social competencies, and (4) positive identity. The PSL-AB possesses reasonable internal consistency and strong content validity (Leffert et al., 1998). It has been used in a large-scale study ($N = 99,462$) to evaluate the developmental assets of communities in the United States and to investigate correlations between developmental assets and risk behavior (Benson et al., 1998).

Behavioral and Emotional Rating Scale

The Behavioral and Emotional Rating Scale (BERS; Epstein & Sharma, 1998) is composed of 52 items rated on a scale of 0 to 3 (0 = not at all like the child; 1 = not much like the child; 2 = like the child; 3 = very much like the child). Five factor analytically derived subscales of emotional and behavioral strengths and an overall strength quotient are derived from the BERS. Factor 1, Interpersonal Strengths (14 items) (e.g., "accepts criticism"), measures a child's ability to control his/her emotions or behaviors in social situations. Factor 2, Family Involvement (10 items) (e.g., "interacts positively with parents"), measures a child's participation and relationship with his/her family. The third factor, Intrapersonal Strengths (11 items) (e.g., "is self-confident"), assesses a child's outlook on his/her competence and accomplishments. Factor 4, School Functioning (9 items) (e.g., "completes school tasks on time"), focuses on a child's competence on school and classroom tasks. Factor 5, Affective Strengths (7 items) (e.g., "acknowledges painful feelings"), assesses a child's ability to accept affect from others and express feelings toward others. Summing the standard scores of the five subscales and converting that sum into a quotient derives an overall strength quotient.

The BERS development process followed rigorous content validity procedures (Epstein, 1999). In addition, the BERS has been normed using national samples of children with emotional disturbance ($N = 861$) and without emotional disturbance ($N = 2176$) (Epstein & Sharma, 1998), demonstrated convergent (Harniss et al., 1999) and discriminant validity (Reid et al., 2000), and shown short-term and long-term test–retest and interrater reliability (Epstein et al., 1998; Epstein, Hertzog, & Reid, 2001; Friedman, Leone, & Friedman, 1999). Based on these studies, the BERS appears to be a psychometrically sound, norm-referenced assessment tool. It possesses acceptable content validity, strong internal consistency, moderate to high convergent and discriminant validity, high interrater and test–retest reliability, and stability over time. Based on these sound psychometric characteristics, the BERS is recommended for the following uses: (1) documenting children's emotional and behavioral strengths, (2) identifying children with limited emotional and behavioral strengths, (3) setting goals for an individual education program, and (4) documenting progress in strength areas as a result of intervention.

APPLIED EXAMPLES OF STRENGTH-BASED ASSESSMENT

The next section provides examples of the use of strength-based assessment, in general, and the BERS, in particular. In the first example, the BERS was used to assess the outcomes of a school-based wraparound program in Kentucky over a 6-month period. In the second example, the BERS was used to monitor the outcomes of the Families and Schools Together program, a national school-based program to prevent violence, dropout, and substance abuse.

Kentucky

Program Description

In 1998 the Children and Youth Services Branch of the Kentucky Division of Mental Health received a five year federal grant. The grant, entitled Building Bridges of Support: One Community at a Time, from the Center for Mental Health Services was awarded to help them to expand its system of care in three rural Appalachian regions. Acknowledging schools as a critical partner in system of care efforts, the central focus of the project was on developing and implementing a comprehensive, multilevel, integrated school-based mental health model that focused on prevention, early intervention, and intensive intervention efforts. Within the Bridges Project, a full staff of mental health professionals (i.e., a three-member student service team and regional behavior consultant) were located on the school campus. The Student Service Team (SST) included the service coordinator, family liaison, and intervention specialist. The service coordinator worked as the child's case manager by facilitating wraparound team meetings and linking the family with natural supports and formal resources in the community. The family liaison was a parent of a child with an emotional disability who served in a professional role by providing peer-to-peer mentoring for families and building local and regional family support networks. The intervention specialist was a mental health clinician who had received additional training in developing behavioral interventions and school-based supports. The regional behavior consultant provided assistance to schools in implementing universal supports and consultation on targeted and intensive interventions and supports. In collaboration with school staff, these mental health professionals facilitated the implementation of a continuum of positive behavior supports (Sugai & Horner, 1999; Todd, Horner, Sugai, & Sprague, 1999) in 21 schools.

The positive behavior supports (PBS) model was developed initially as an alternative to aversive interventions for children with severe disabilities who engaged in self-injurious and aggressive acts (Durand & Carr, 1985). Recently, however, the approach has extended from a focus on individual children to an intervention approach for schools (Dwyer & Osher, 2000; Todd, Horner, Sugai, & Colvin, 1999; Todd, Horner, Sugai, & Sprague, 1999). The assumption underlying the model is that a continuum of effective behavior supports is required to meet the needs of all children (Sugai et al., 2000). That is, schools are comprised of three groups of students, each requiring a different level of intervention.

The majority of students (80 to 90%) will not exhibit problem behaviors. Universal interventions, which constitute a form of primary prevention, focus on improving the overall level of appropriate behavior for all students. These strategies focus on enhancing protective factors in the school and preventing the development of problems through the efforts of all school personnel. Within the Bridges Project, regional behavior consultants facilitate the development of a positive behavior support committee responsible for planning, monitoring, and maintaining the schoolwide program (Scott & Nelson, 1999; Sugai et al., 2000). However, not all students are responsive to universal interventions, with about 10 to 15% requiring targeted interventions. Targeted interventions are designed to provide support to students who are at risk of developing emotional and behavioral problems. Within the Bridges Project, SSTs work with teachers, other school staff, and parents to address the specific behavior of a student or group of students. Targeted interventions may, for example, include mentoring, tutoring or other academic support, small group counseling, or the development of a positive behavior plan. There will remain, however, 3 to 5% of the student body for which targeted interventions are not effective. Students experiencing chronic and intense problem behavior in the home, school, and community require more intensive interventions, services, and supports that usually extend beyond school resources to other community agencies. Using a wraparound approach to meet the needs of students with the most intense needs (Eber & Nelson, 1997; VanDenBerg & Grealish, 1996), SSTs facilitate the establishment of a child and family team. The team is comprised of family members, school personnel, community agency service providers, and others who have a positive relationship with the child and family (e.g., extended family, clergy, and friends).

Data Collection

While evaluation efforts have been implemented to assess all three levels of intervention, the most comprehensive efforts were focused upon the impact of intensive wraparound services. As part of the evaluation, caregivers complete the BERS (Epstein & Sharma, 1998) at intake and every 6 months thereafter.

Results

At intake, the majority of children tended to possess average behavioral and emotional strengths in comparison to a national sample of children with emotional and behavioral problems. To examine change in behavioral and emotional strengths over time, paired sample t-tests were conducted for a sample of

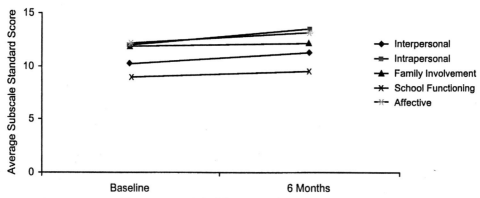

Figure 1. BERS Subscale Standard Scores ($N = 47$).

children ($N = 47$) for whom 6-month follow-up scores were available. Average strength standard scores increased from baseline to 6-month follow-up for all five BERS subscales (see Fig. 1). All increases were statistically significant with the exception of the family involvement and school functioning subscales. Strength Quotient scores increased significantly from baseline ($M = 105.3$) to 6-month follow-up ($M = 113$).

Implications

It is encouraging to note that overall emotional and behavioral strengths as well as interpersonal strengths, intrapersonal strengths, and affective strengths significantly increased from baseline to 6-month follow-up, particularly given the strength-based philosophy of the project. Additional analyses, however, will need to be conducted to determine whether these changes are sustained and, if so, the pattern of these changes over time. The use of the BERS as a tool for conducting strength-based assessments has practical and programmatic implications for the Bridges Project. Results from the BERS are used at both a clinical and a program level. When used within the context of clinical treatment and service planning, the wraparound process is placed in a more positive context. Meetings, conversations, and plans are focused on strengths rather than on deficits as team members begin to view the child as possessing strengths from which to build. Additionally, the results of the BERS are used to monitor the child's progress and facilitate the refinement of interventions and plans. At a program level, an examination of changes in aggregate BERS scores is useful in assessing the program's performance with respect to improving the emotional and behavioral strengths of the children receiving intensive school-based wraparound services.

Families and Schools Together

Program Description

The Families and Schools Together (FAST) program is a collaborative prevention and parent involvement program designed to reduce factors related to alcohol and drug abuse, violence and delinquency, and school dropout. FAST was developed in 1988 by Dr. Lynn McDonald and by Family Service, Madison, Wisconsin. In 1993, the Alliance for Children and Families (formerly Family Service America), with support from DeWitt Wallace-Reader's Digest Fund, became the national training and replication center for the program. The FAST program has since expanded from 6 to 38 states, the District of Columbia, Canada, and Australia.

FAST is a 2-year program focused on strengthening the entire family unit. The program invites families with children aged 4 to 9 who display behavior problems at school or at home, low self-esteem, short attention span, or hyperactivity to participate in 8 or 10 weekly multifamily meetings at their child's school. During the sessions, families participate in research-based activities that are not only fun but also are designed to build on the natural strength of the family unit. The FAST curriculum works toward four general goals: enhancing family functioning, promoting child success in school, preventing substance abuse by the child and the family, and reducing the stress that parents and children experience from daily life situations.

The weekly multifamily meetings are at the core of the FAST program. A collaborative team comprised of four community members facilitates FAST weekly sessions: a parent partner, a school partner, a community-based mental health partner, and a community-based substance abuse partner. Each individual team member brings unique skills and experiences to the program and serves as a resource in achieving the program goals. The four core team members also operate as a team of coaches supporting the parents in strengthening their own family units, building a social support network of their design, and modeling the power of a respectful and supportive team approach to problem solving. Furthermore, the team facilitates communication among program administrators, collaborative community partners, and parents.

Each of the weekly sessions includes six key components: (1) a meal shared as a family unit, (2) several communication games played at the family table, (3) time for adults to talk one-on-one with another adult, (4) a parent self-help group, (5) one-to-one quality play, and (6) a door prize, in which each family wins once. The six components are designed to strengthen the bonds within and between families and their community. Protective factors are built through strengthening the parent–child bond, creating an intimate support network, building a cohesive family unit, and connecting families to the community. Following the weekly sessions, the families graduate into FASTWORKS, a 2-year follow-up program that meets monthly to continue building on the bonds created during FAST.

Evaluation

FAST uses a nonexperimental, pretest–posttest evaluation design that focuses on initial outcomes and protective factors. The factors assessed by FAST are child behavior, family functioning, parent–school involvement, and families' experience of the program and its impact. Families complete a series of questionnaires before the start and at the end of the program. Teachers complete the child behavior questionnaire at both time points.

FAST uses two different measures to assess child behavior: The Revised Behavior Problem Checklist (RBPC) (Quay & Peterson, 1987) and the BERS. With respect to family functioning, families complete two scales that assess social characteristics of healthy families: the Family Adaptability and Cohesion Scale (FACES III; Olson, Portner, & Lavee, 1985) and the social isolation subscale of the Parenting Stress Inventory (Abidin, 1995). Parent school involvement is assessed by the Witte Parent Survey (Witte, 1991).

Data Collection

Families are contacted by school personnel about FAST. Those who volunteer to participate receive home visits from FAST team members. At this visit, team members explain more about the program and ask the parents to complete the evaluation instruments and bring them to the first meeting. Likewise, teachers of the children are given evaluation instruments to complete and return to the school team members before the first meeting. When the program has ended, team members make home visits to the families to distribute the evaluation forms and also to recruit for the FASTWORKS follow-up program. Teachers are also given forms to complete at this time.

Results

In an evaluation supported by the Dewitt Wallace-Readers Digest Fund FAST was found to reduce factors related to alcohol and drug abuse, violence and delinquency, and school dropout. Outcomes reported in child behavior, family functioning, and parent involvement indicate positive changes at the home, school, and community levels. With respect to the BERS, the results showed statistically significant parent and teacher posttest increases of 6 and 12%, respectively, in the overall behavioral and emotional strength score. The parents (see Table 2) reported statistically significant increases on each of the five subscales: a 10% increase in interpersonal strength, a 7% increase in family involvement, a 7% increase in intrapersonal strength, a 7% increase in school functioning, and a 5% increase in affective strength. After the program, teachers (see Table 3) reported statistically significant increases on each of the three measured subscales: a 12% increase in interpersonal strength, a 13% increase in intrapersonal strength, and an 11% increase in school functioning.

Table 2. Parent Average Scores on the Behavioral and Emotional Rating Scales ($N = 959$)[a]

	Pretests		Posttests	
	M	SD	M	SD
Total score	105.62	22.31	113.51	21.67
Subscales				
Interpersonal strength	26.91	7.96	29.67	7.66
Family involvement	21.50	4.78	23.00	4.45
Intrapersonal strength	24.34	5.33	25.95	4.98
School functioning	16.98	5.41	18.17	5.31
Affective strength	15.88	3.34	16.72	3.14

[a]All pre- and posttest comparisons statistically significant at $p \leq 0.001$.

Table 3. Teacher Average Scores on the Behavioral and
Emotional Rating Scale ($N = 901$)[a]

	Pretests		Posttests	
	M	SD	M	SD
Total score	59.18	19.91	66.25	20.15
Subscales				
Interpersonal strength	25.42	9.93	28.44	9.85
Intrapersonal strength	19.13	6.35	21.62	6.23
School functioning	14.63	6.31	16.19	6.37

[a]All pre- and posttest comparisons statistically significant at $p \leq 0.001$.

Implications

As a result of feedback from practitioners and parents and changing needs and evaluation trends, FAST made the decision to move toward strength-based evaluation. This move serves to better align the evaluation component with the program philosophy and goals. While FAST was building upon child and family strengths through program activities, the program was asking parents to assess their child's behavior by looking at the negative behaviors or deficits that their child was exhibiting. Beginning in the fall of 1999, the deficit-based measure of child behavior was replaced with an asset-based instrument, the Behavioral and Emotional Rating Scale. The BERS serves as a better match with FAST philosophy in its composition, presentation, and reception. The change to strength-based evaluation has been favorably received by all involved. Both verbal feedback and outcomes have both been positive.

CONCLUSION

In this chapter, we provided an overview of strength-based assessment, described informal and formal strength-based assessment, and offered examples of the use of strength-based assessment in the evaluation of children's services in school settings. The applied examples document the value of strength-based assessment in planning and evaluating children's services. This assessment approach affords several advantages to direct service providers. Strength-based assessment (1) engages the child and family in a positive way in receiving specialized services; (2) minimizes the frustration of parents and practitioners by emphasizing solutions as opposed to problems; (3) identifies for the child, family, and professionals what is going well in the life of the child and what skills and competencies can be developed; (4) fosters a positive parent–professional relationship characterized by open communication, mutual trust, cooperation, and supportiveness; and (5) empowers the family and, in some cases, the child to assume responsibility for decisions and actions.

Although the number of psychometrically sound instruments has increased, much work needs to be completed in this area. First, additional strength scales need to be developed that assess the strengths and assets of families, preschoolers, and young adults. Second, further research on the psychometric characteristics of these instruments, particularly with respect to their predictive validity, needs to be conducted. Third, the value of strengths and assets as an outcome measure needs to be documented in school- and community-based research projects. Finally, school personnel and other practitioners need to be trained not only to identify the strengths of children and families but also to use this information in writing and in implementing treatment plans. Professionals need to be trained and supervised so that they regularly gather and use strength-based information in making decisions about service plans and treatments. To this end, administrators and policymakers need to encourage staff to identify and emphasize what children and families do well.

REFERENCES

Abidin, R. R. (1995). *Parenting Stress Index: Professional manual* (3rd ed.). Odessa, FL: Psychological Assessment Resources.

Achenbach, T. M. (1991). *Manual for the Child Behavior Checklist/4-18 and 1991 profile*. Burlington, VT: University of Vermont, Department of Psychiatry.

Benson, P. L., Leffert, N., Scales, P. C., & Blyth, D. A. (1998). Beyond the "village" rhetoric: Creating healthy communities for children and adolescents. *Applied Developmental Science, 2*(3), 138–159.

Brown, L. L., & Hammil, D. D. (1990). *Behavior Rating Profile: An ecological approach to behavioral assessment*. Austin, TX: PRO-ED.

Dunst, C. J., Trivette, C. M., & Deal, A. G. (Eds.). (1994). *Supporting and strengthening families: Methods, strategies, and practice* (Vol. 1). Cambridge, MA: Brookline Books.

Durand, M. V., & Carr, E. G. (1985). Self-injurious behavior: Motivating conditions and guidelines for treatment. *School Psychology Review, 14*, 171–176.

Dwyer, K., & Osher, D. (2000). *Safeguarding our children: An action guide*. Washington, DC: U.S. Departments of Education and Justice, American Institutes for Research.

Eber, L., & Nelson, C. M. (1997). School-based wraparound planning: Integrating services for students with emotional and behavioral needs. *American Journal of Orthopsychiatry, 67*(3), 385–395.

Epstein, M. H. (1999). Development and validation of a scale to assess the emotional and behavioral strengths of children and adolescents. *Remedial and Special Education, 20*, 258–262.

Epstein, M. H., Harniss, M. K., Pearson, N., & Ryser, G. (1998). The Behavioral and Emotional Rating Scale: Test–retest and inter-rater reliability. *Journal of Child and Family Studies, 8*, 319–327.

Epstein, M. H., Hertzog, M. A., & Reid, R. (2001). The Behavioral and Emotional Rating Scale: Long term test–retest reliability. *Behavioral Disorders, 26*, 314–320.

Epstein, M. H., & Sharma, J. (1998). *Behavioral and Emotional Rating Scale: A strength-based approach to assessment*. Austin, TX: PRO-ED.

Friedman, K. A., Leone, P. E., & Friedman, P. (1999). Strengths-based assessment of children with SED: Consistency of reporting by teachers and parents. *Journal of Child and Family Studies, 8*(2), 169–180.

Goodman, R. (1997). The Strengths and Difficulties Questionnaire: A research note. *Journal of Child Psychology and Psychiatry, 38*, 581–586.

Goodman, R., & Scott, S. (1999). Comparing the Strengths and Difficulties Questionnaire and the Child Behavior Checklist: Is small beautiful? *Journal of Abnormal Child Psychology, 27*, 17–24.

Harniss, M. K., Epstein, M. H., Ryser, G., & Pearson, N. (1999). The Behavioral and Emotional Rating Scale: Convergent validity. *Journal of Psychoeducational Assessment, 17*(1), 4–14.

Henggeler, S. W., Schoenwald, S. K., Bourdin, C. M., Rowland, M. D., & Cunningham, P. B. (1998). *Multisystemic treatment of antisocial behavior in children and adolescents*. New York: Guilford Press.

Kral, R. (1989). *Strategies that work: Techniques for solutions in the schools*. Milwaukee, WI: Brieg Family Therapy Center.

Leffert, N., Benson, P. L., Scales, P. C., Sharma, A. R., Drake, D. R., & Blyth, D. A. (1998). Developmental assets: Measurement and prediction of risk behaviors among adolescents. *Applied Developmental Science, 2*(4), 209–230.

Lourie, I. S., Katz-Leavy, J., & Stroul, B. A. (1994). Individualized services in a system of care. In B. A. Stroul (Ed.), *Children's mental health: Creating systems of care in a changing society.* Baltimore, MD: Brookes, 429–452.

Lyons, J. S., Kisiel, C., & West, C. (1997). Child and adolescent strength assessment: A pilot study. *Family Matters,* 30–32.

Nelson, C. M., & Pearson, C. A. (1991). *Integrating services for children and youth with emotional and behavioral disorders.* Reston, VA: Council for Exceptional Children.

Olson, D. H., Portner, J., & Lavee, Y. (1985). *Family Adaptability and Cohesion Scale.* St. Paul, MN: Family Social Sciences, University of Minnesota.

Oswald, D. P., Cohen, R., Best, A. M., Jenson, C. E., & Lyons, J. (2001). Child strengths and the level of care for children with emotional and behavioral disorders. *Journal of Emotional and Behavioral Disorders, 9,* 192–199.

Quay, H. C., & Peterson, D. (1987). *Revised Behavior Problem Checklist.* Coral Gables, FL: University of Miami, Department of Psychology.

Reid, R., Epstein, M. H., Pastor, D. A., & Ryser, G. (2000). Strengths-based assessment differences across students with LD and EBD. *Remedial and Special Education, 21*(6), 346–355.

Saleeby, D. (Ed.). (1992). *The strengths perspective in social work practice.* New York: Longman.

Salvia, J., & Ysseldyke, J. (1998). *Assessment* (7th ed.). Boston: Houghton Mifflin.

Scott, T. M., & Nelson, C. M. (1999). Universal school discipline strategies: Facilitating positive learning environments. *Effective School Practices, 17*(4), 54–64.

Stroul, B. A., & Friedman, R. M. (1994). *A system of care for children and youth with severe emotional disturbances.* Washington, DC: Georgetown University, CASSP Technical Assistance Center.

Sugai, G., & Horner, R. H. (1999). Discipline and behavioral support: Practices, pitfalls, and promises. *Effective School Practices, 17*(4), 10–22.

Sugai, G., Sprague, J. R., Horner, R. H., & Walker, H. M. (2000). Preventing school violence: The use of office discipline referrals to assess and monitor school-wide discipline interventions. *Journal of Emotional and Behavioral Disorders, 8*(2), 94–101.

Todd, A. W., Horner, R. H., Sugai, G., & Colvin, G. (1999). Individualizing school-wide discipline for students with chronic problem behaviors: A team approach. *Effective School Practices, 17*(4), 72–82.

Todd, A. W., Horner, R. H., Sugai, G., & Sprague, J. R. (1999). Effective behavior support: Strengthening school-wide systems through a team-based approach. *Effective School Practices, 17*(4), 23–37.

U.S. Department of Education (1994). *National agenda for achieving better results for children and youth with serious emotional disturbance.* Washington, DC: Author.

VanDenBerg, J. E., & Grealish, E. M. (1996). Individualized services and supports through the wraparound process: Philosophy and procedures. *Journal of Child and Family Studies, 5,* 7–22.

VanDenBerg, J. E., & Grealish, E. M. (1998). *The wrap-around process: Training manual.* Pittsburgh: Community Partnership Group.

Witte, J. F. (1991). *First year report: Milwaukee parental choice program.* Madison, WI: Robert LaFollette Institute of Public Policy, University of Wisconsin–Madison.

21

Facilitating the Implementation of Evidence-Based Prevention and Mental Health Promotion Efforts in Schools

PATRICIA A. GRACZYK, CELENE E. DOMITROVICH, and JOSEPH E. ZINS

Within the field of school-based mental health, a call for greater integration between treatment and prevention efforts has been sounded (Tashman et al., 1999). This integration is appropriate and logical for several reasons. First, practitioners in both fields are attempting to provide interventions that reduce youth risk for poor outcomes and improve their functioning in social, emotional, and academic domains. Second, innovative models of school-based mental health (e.g., Adelman & Taylor, 1999; Nastasi, Varjas, Bernstein, & Pluymert, 1998; Weist, 1997) and prevention (Institute of Medicine, 1994) have been proposed that are comprehensive and call for a spectrum of services to meet the needs of *all* students. While recipients of traditional school mental health services include primarily special education students or students with diagnosed disorders, potential recipients of comprehensive school-based mental health services and prevention programs can include the entire student body. Third, a union of school-based mental health and prevention efforts can reduce duplicity of efforts. Fourth, both fields recognize schools as an important setting for intervening with children and youth. Schools have extended and intensive accessibility to the majority of children and can provide ample opportunities for students to develop, practice, and receive recognition for emotionally appropriate and socially competent behaviors that are the foundation

PATRICIA A. GRACZYK • University of Illinois at Chicago, Chicago, Illinois 60637.   CELENE E. DOMITROVICH • Pennsylvania State University, University Park, Pennsylvania 16802. JOSEPH E. ZINS • University of Cincinnati, Cincinnati, Ohio 45221.

of mental health both within and beyond the classroom setting (Consortium on the School-Based Promotion of Social Competence, 1994; Evans, 1999; Weissberg, Caplan, & Sivo, 1989; Weissberg & Greenberg, 1998).

The major topic of this chapter is the implementation of effective school-based prevention and mental health promotion practices. We begin by providing an overview of the current state of the field. We then summarize what is meant by effective or evidence-based practices by using information garnered from two major program reviews, one of which has recently been completed and another that is ongoing. Next, we provide a conceptual lens through which implementation of school-based prevention programs can be viewed. Critical factors are identified, and a framework is presented that ties these factors together in a coherent and meaningful way. The ensuing discussion illustrates how this framework can help guide efforts to assess and monitor implementation quality to result in effective program delivery. The chapter concludes with a discussion of some of the challenges existing within the field relative to the utilization and evaluation of sound implementation practices.

CURRENT STATE OF THE FIELD

This is an exciting time in the field of school-based prevention and mental health promotion. The past decade has seen a proliferation of evidence that school-based efforts to promote young people's emotional and social development work (Durlak & Wells, 1998; Institute of Medicine, 1994; Rones & Hoagwood, 2000). Major reviews have identified effective school-based programs that promote positive outcomes for children and adolescents in the areas of positive youth development (Catalano et al., 1998), violence prevention (e.g., Elliot, 1998), drug prevention (e.g., Drug Strategies, 1999; Center for Substance Abuse Prevention, 2001), health education (American School Health Association, 1998), and the prevention of mental disorders (Greenberg, Domitrovich, & Bumbarger, 1999, 2001; Rones & Hoagwood, 2000).

At the same time, recognition of the critical importance of competence-promotion and prevention efforts has also grown significantly, as was evidenced in the December 1999 report on mental health disseminated by the Surgeon General of the United States. In that report the Surgeon General recommended that mental health and mental illness be viewed as two points on a continuum. The report went on to say that, although past efforts in the mental health field had focused primarily on mental illness, it has become increasingly evident that the prevention of mental illness and promotion of mental health warrant greater attention (U.S. Department of Health and Human Services, 1999). Similarly, the Centers for Disease Control and Prevention acknowledged the connections between physical health and mental health and the need to coordinate services and efforts (Kolbe, Kann, & Brenner, 2001).

Oftentimes, "prevention" and "promotion" efforts are viewed as interchangeable. Although high-quality programs that prevent mental disorders and promote mental health are similar in many respects, they also have their differences (Weissberg & Greenberg, 1998). In 1994, the Institute of Medicine (IOM) established a framework for prevention by differentiating it from treatment and distinguishing levels of prevention interventions that differ according to the risk status of targeted participants. These levels of prevention, referred to as *universal, selective,* and *indicated,* were based in part on the work of Gordon (1983, 1987) and replace the terms primary, secondary, and tertiary that had been used in the field until that point. *Universal interventions* are the broadest form of intervention (e.g., mandatory school attendance). They target all students in a school or in a grade, and are conducted in a positive, proactive way, independent of risk. *Selective interventions,* on the other hand, are delivered to individuals or a subgroup with some risk factors that makes them significantly more likely to develop a negative outcome (e.g., children of depressed parents). Finally, *indicated interventions* target individuals or a subgroup of individuals already showing signs, symptoms, or markers related to a problem outcome or diagnosis (e.g., oppositional defiant disorder).

Mental health promotion extends beyond preventive efforts. While preventing negative outcomes such as mental illness is a critical goal in itself, "building wellness from the start, and promoting conditions that maintain and enhance it, is a promising strategy in its own right" (Cowen, 1998, p. 455). Wellness and promotion efforts come under a variety of names including positive youth development, asset building, social-competence promotion, life skills education, character building, and social and emotional learning (SEL). Accordingly, our discussion pertains to programs with these designations as well.

CHARACTERISTICS OF EFFECTIVE PROGRAMS

Although a comprehensive presentation of the characteristics of effective school-based prevention and mental health promotion efforts is beyond the scope of this chapter, summaries of two recent program reviews will be presented to represent current thinking on the topic.[†]

Review of Programs to Prevent Mental Health Disorders in School-Aged Children

Greenberg and colleagues (1999, 2001) conducted a systematic search for universal, selective, and indicated prevention programs with empirical support for their effectiveness in generating positive mental health outcomes for school-aged children. Interventions included in the review were those that had been evaluated in randomized or quasiexperimental trials with school-aged children and youth and that demonstrated significant reductions in psychological symptomatology. Of over 130 programs screened for inclusion in the review, 34 were determined to be efficacious in preventing emotional and behavioral problems.

In summarizing their findings, Greenberg et al. (1999, 2001) identified characteristics that effective programs had in common and proposed that these common elements represent "best practices" in prevention and promotion programming. First, high-quality prevention programs are theoretically based and developmentally appropriate. A preventive intervention needs to be based on a theory of change

---

[†]More thorough coverage of program characteristics can be found in a number of resources (e.g., Consortium on the School-Based Promotion of Social Competence, 1994; Elias et al., 1997; Graczyk et al., 2000; Weissberg & Greenberg, 1998).

that specifies how a program is expected to achieve particular outcomes (Chen, 1998; Harachi et al., 1999). As a result, the theory of change justifies program content and activities. Most interventions target several factors (often referred to as "mediating factors" or "proximal outcomes") that are theoretically linked to more distal problems. The interventions are either attempting to reduce risks or build competencies that research has shown are associated or causally linked to the outcome of interest. For example, the Anger Coping Program (Lochman, 1985, 1992) is an indicated intervention that targets children exhibiting aggressive behavior. The program contains lessons that are designed to improve children's perspective taking skills, affect recognition, self-control, and social problem-solving skills. These social–cognitive skills are the "proximal outcomes" for the program. Research has shown that aggressive children often have deficits in these domains and that difficulties in these areas also may contribute to the maintenance of aggressive behavior. Therefore, according to the theoretical model of the Anger Coping Program, building these skills should reduce the participant's aggressive behavior.

Most theoretical models that form the basis for high-quality preventive interventions are drawn from larger developmental models. Developmental models of disorders specify the pattern of individual and environmental risk and protective factors that interact to cause and maintain problem behaviors. A comprehensive developmental model charts the course of problem behavior over an extended period of time and includes factors on multiple levels (i.e., individual, environmental, social) that are involved in the emergence and maintenance of the problem. Developmental models are useful because they provide an overall framework for the timing of interventions and, as described previously, can also provide guidelines for the specific nature and content of interventions (Weissberg & Greenberg, 1998).

Greenberg et al. (1999, 2001) also concluded that the highest-quality programs are multiyear in duration and address a range of risk and protective factors rather than unitary problem behaviors (e.g., aggression). Furthermore, effective programs target multiple domains (e.g., school, family), with an emphasis on changing environments as well as individuals, and consequently require a package of integrated and collaborative interventions. To ensure sustainability of prevention efforts in schools, the authors recommended that programs be integrated with other systems of treatment both within the school and in the community. Arguments for greater integration also have been made by advocates of expanded models of school-based and school-linked mental health (e.g., Adelman & Taylor, 1999; Hoagwood & Koretz, 1996; Nastasi et al., 1998; Weist, 1997).

SEL Program Review

The second program review is currently being conducted by the Collaborative for Academic, Social, and Emotional Learning (CASEL; www.casel.org) and encompasses multiple categories of universal school programs including character, drug, sexuality, social skills enhancement, violence prevention, and comprehensive health education. Programs included in the review are multiyear in duration and most include a classroom instructional component. Over 80 programs have met criteria for inclusion.

Table 1. Key Competencies to Promote Social and Emotional Development[a]

Competencies	Definition
I. Knowledge of self	
Identifying emotions	Identifying and labeling one's feelings
Being responsible	Recognizing and understanding one's obligation to engage in ethical, safe, and legal behaviors
Recognizing strengths	Identifying and cultivating one's strengths and positive qualities
II. Caring for others	
Perspective taking	Identifying and understanding the thoughts and feelings of others
Appreciating diversity	Understanding that individual and group differences complement each other and make the world more interesting
Respecting others	Believing that others deserve to be treated with kindness and compassion and feeling motivated to contribute to the common good
III. Responsible decision making	
Managing emotions	Monitoring and regulating one's feelings so that they facilitate rather than impede the handling of situations
Analyzing situations	Accurately perceiving situations in which a decision is to be made and assessing factors that might influence one's response
Goal setting	Establishing and working toward the achievement of short- and long-term prosocial goals
Problem solving	Generating, implementing, and evaluating solutions to problems
IV. Social effectiveness	
Communication	Using verbal and nonverbal skills to express oneself and promote positive and effective exchanges with others
Building relationships	Establishing and maintaining healthy and rewarding connections with individuals and groups
Negotiation	Achieving mutually satisfactory resolutions to conflict by addressing the needs of all concerned
Refusal	Effectively conveying and following through with one's decision not to engage in unwanted, unsafe, unethical, or unlawful conduct
Help seeking	Identifying the need for and accessing appropriate sources of help and support

[a]From Payton et al. (2000).

Based on a thorough review of the literature and consultation with experts in the field of social and emotional learning, 22 evaluation criteria were established to identify quality SEL programs (Payton et al., 2000). These criteria include coverage of 15 SEL competencies (see Table 1) and 6 characteristics of program design: quality of lesson plans, student assessment measures, classroom-implementation monitoring tools, and strategies to promote schoolwide coordination, school–family partnerships, and school–community partnerships. Programs are rated for their coverage of each of these elements. In addition, each program is assigned a rating based on the evidence supporting its effectiveness in producing positive behavioral outcomes for students. A summary of the findings is forthcoming and will be reported in a program guide for educators.

The reviews summarized previously are representative of those published in the last several years. The majority of identified evidence-based interventions have demonstrated their efficacy under highly rigorous conditions where there was a great deal of control over the quality of delivery. These efficacy studies minimize threats to internal validity and delineate the powerful components of a treatment (Seligman, 1996), but the results are difficult to generalize to the field where treatments typically are delivered in less rigorous ways. Thus, a major issue facing educators and school-based mental health providers today is not whether evidence-based prevention and mental health-promotion programs are available to schools but rather how to select and implement appropriate interventions effectively under "real-world" conditions when many components cannot be controlled as well. As a result, implementation, the major topic of this chapter, has now come to the forefront and warrants attention in a more comprehensive and systematic fashion than it generally has received in the past.

IMPLEMENTING EFFECTIVE PROGRAMS

Implementation Quality

Implementation is the process by which interventions are put into action. Implementation quality is the degree to which an intervention is conducted as it was intended originally (Durlak, 1995; Yeaton & Sechrest, 1981), and it refers to the discrepancy between the intervention as designed and the intervention as delivered. Variation in program implementation occurs each time school-based mental health practitioners and educators attempt to replicate a program or strategy in a community setting, as there always are some changes from the original effort. These modifications can have either negative or positive effects. Negative implementation discrepancies are often due to unforeseen events, planning failures, or a lack of resources that undermine the quality of the program that is delivered. For example, a school district might train a set of teachers to conduct an intervention, but during the school year the teachers go on strike. If union teachers are replaced with substitutes who receive brief training and are organized with little notice by people other than the official trainers, it is unlikely that the program will be implemented as well as it would have been originally by the teachers.

Other types of implementation discrepancies can lead to positive benefits for students. These discrepancies are usually intentional changes to the intervention. For instance, implementers of preventive interventions need to tailor programs to match the unique needs of their students, teachers, schools, parents, and communities. While these changes are necessary and have the potential to make the program more effective in the target community than it would have been without adaptations, these adjustments can be complicated and should be done with great care. At this time there is little empirically derived information available to guide schools in their adaptation efforts. What information is available suggests that the more schools digress from a program or preventive strategy as it was designed and evaluated, the greater the risk that program effects will be compromised (e.g., Botvin et al., 1990, 1995; Connell, Turner, & Mason, 1985; Gottfredson, Gottfredson, & Hybl, 1993).

Within the field of school-based prevention and mental health promotion, factors that influence effective program implementation have been identified, and there are several excellent references available that highlight them (e.g., Durlak,

1998; Elias et al., 1997; Gottfredson et al., 1997; Zins & Erchul, 2002). Identified factors pertain to characteristics of the program itself (e.g., program complexity, provision of technical assistance and user-friendly materials) and the environment in which the program is to be implemented (i.e., community, district, school, teacher, and participant characteristics).

Lack of Attention to Implementation

In spite of the seemingly obvious connection between implementation quality and program outcomes, recent research reviews have revealed that few evaluation studies of prevention programs have looked at this relationship. For example, Durlak (1998) found that less than 5% of over 1200 published prevention studies provided data on program implementation. Of the 162 studies of primary and early secondary prevention programs reviewed by Dane and Schneider (1998), 39 studies specified how implementation was documented, and of these, only 13 actually evaluated how variations in implementation impacted program outcomes. Domitrovich and Greenberg (2000) also analyzed outcome studies for 34 school prevention programs that demonstrated effectiveness in producing positive mental health outcomes for students. They found that all 34 programs promoted integrity in some fashion and 56% used multiple strategies (i.e., manual, training, and supervision). Over 67% of the programs verified implementation integrity in some way (e.g., monitored how much of the program was actually provided to students), but less than 33% of the programs examined whether quality of implementation influenced program outcomes. Moreover, Kolbe et al. (2001), in reporting on the School Health Policies and Programs Study 2000, noted that they could not include information about the use of specific health education curricula because such information would be misleading without detailed knowledge of the related implementation fidelity.

These three reviews (Dane & Schneider, 1998; Domitrovich & Greenberg, 2000; Durlak, 1998) generated similar conclusions. First, implementation integrity varies significantly across settings and implementers. Second, implementation can be seriously compromised by program modifications. Finally, implementation quality is related to program outcomes.

MODEL TO GUIDE SCHOOL-BASED IMPLEMENTATION EFFORTS

Recently, a model of implementation was developed and described in a paper commissioned by the Center for Mental Health Services (CMHS) of the Substance Abuse and Mental Health Services Administration (SAMHSA) (Greenberg, Domitrovich, Graczyk, & Zins in press). The rationale for the model was to provide a summary of the critical factors identified in the literature as having the potential to affect implementation quality and to organize the factors in a coherent way. The model was inspired by work conducted in the field of evaluation research focused on program theory and theory-driven evaluations (e.g., Weiss, 1995), particularly Chen's work (1990, 1998). It is intended for use by a broad audience including practitioners, researchers, and other stakeholders who are invested in delivering high-quality prevention programs. A brief summary of the model follows.

Overview of Model

According to Chen (1990, 1998), there are two major components of a comprehensive program theory. The first is the *causative or causal theory,* also known as the program's theory of change, which specifies how the program produces its intended outcomes. The second is the *prescriptive theory,* which provides guidelines for delivering the interventions and describes the context that is necessary for the successful implementation of the intervention.

For a number of reasons both the causal and prescriptive theories of an intervention need to be considered. The causal theory can inform the practitioner about the process of identifying the appropriate intervention to be used when a particular outcome is targeted. As stated previously, the causal theory also should be considered when modifications are made to a program because it specifies what aspects of the intervention are the change mechanisms and, as such, are the key elements of the intervention. The prescriptive theory is equally important because it guides the daily activities of the program and identifies the environmental supports needed to ensure high-quality programming.

Ideally, practitioners will utilize the entire program model throughout the implementation process—from the planning stages when a school is considering a program, to the selection process, and then throughout the program's implementation. Because very few programs are ever delivered in the real world exactly as they are designed, the factors outlined in the model can be used to identify what to monitor during the actual implementation of the program. Measures of these factors can then be utilized to evaluate the quality of implementation and the effects of implementation quality on program outcomes.

For this chapter, we focus on the prescriptive portion of the model as it has been applied to school-based prevention and mental health-promotion programs. The model is presented in a format that facilitates its use as a guide to school-based mental health providers and educators in their efforts to provide their students with evidence-based practices.[†] The prescriptive model has three components. The first refers to characteristics of the intervention, the second to training and technical support, and the third to the environment in which the program is to be implemented. For conceptual and evaluation purposes, the three components of the prescriptive model can be viewed as mediators or moderators of program outcomes. Descriptions of each component follow, and factors within each component are listed in Table 2.

Characteristics of the Intervention

Characteristics of a program or intervention itself can impact intervention quality. The first, and perhaps most important of these, are the essential components or "active ingredients" of an intervention. The essential components of an intervention can include the specific content of the program (i.e., broad components or processes, individual sessions within a component, or specific sections of a lesson) or the specific activities that are part of the program (i.e., role plays, group problem discussions). Current estimates indicate that, on average,

---

[†]Readers are encouraged to refer to Greenberg et al. (in press) for a more complete description.

Table 2. Factors in the Three Components of the Prescriptive Theory

Components

I. Characteristics of the intervention
    Program characteristics
        Content
        Program structure
        Timing
        Dosage
        Quality of materials
    Quality of delivery
    Target audience
    Participant responsiveness

II. Training and technical support
    Training model
        Content
        Modeling
        Practice
        Coaching & feedback
    Trainer characteristics
    Implementer characteristics
    Supervision model
        Availability
        Quality of implementer–trainer relationship

III. Environmental conditions
    Classroom level
        Teacher characteristics & behavior
        Classroom climate
        Peer relationships
    School level
        Positive relationships
        Open communication & effective problem solving
        Awareness
        Administrative support
    District level
        Shared goals
        Administrative support
    Community level
        Quality of school–community collaboration
        History of collaboration

school-based prevention activities utilize approximately 54% of methods and 71% of the content considered representative of best practices (Gottfredson et al., 2000).

    Other program characteristics that have the potential to affect implementation quality if they are not delivered as originally intended are the structure, timing, and dosage. The structure of the program refers to who delivers the program and how it is delivered (e.g., classroom teachers presenting skill-building lessons). Timing is the pace at which the program should be administered (e.g., three times a week or once a week for 20 weeks), and dosage is the prescribed level of exposure to the intervention and refers to "how much" of the intervention participants should be provided. Although current estimates vary widely, the Gottfredson et al.

(2000) study also revealed that school-based prevention efforts typically involve 32 sessions and last about 25 weeks.

Successful program implementation is more likely when program materials are visually appealing, user-friendly, age-appropriate, and culturally sensitive. Thus, quality of materials is a critical factor that can affect implementation quality. Manuals are probably the single resource most widely used by mental health staff and teachers who are implementing mental health interventions (Graczyk et al., 2000). Consequently, the content and design of program manuals may have a significant impact on the quality of program delivery. Along with manuals, materials such as videotapes, handouts, overhead slides, and student workbooks have been found to facilitate program implementation and integrity because they provide additional guidance and structure to implementers beyond that which is provided during training and consultation (Gottfredson et al., 2000).

In order to achieve high-quality programming, implementers need to do more than stay faithful to the program model. High-quality delivery is also essential for achieving successful outcomes. This dimension refers to the affective quality of the presentation when the program is delivered and whether the program was delivered to the targeted participants. As described earlier, the IOM (1994) classification system for prevention efforts (i.e., universal, selective, and indicated) is based on characteristics of the designated target audience. The target audience for an intervention refers to the group for whom the program was intended. Even if a program is delivered with fidelity and in an engaging manner, if it does not reach its intended audience an implementation breakdown has occurred. For example, getting parents to join and remain involved in universal school-based programs for parents and youth can be a considerable challenge (Spoth, Redmond, & Shin, 2001).

The final dimension in this component is participant responsiveness. This aspect refers to the way targeted students react to the program. Along with treatment integrity, acceptability and adherence are central to the success of the implementation process. Acceptability refers to judgments or beliefs that a treatment is "appropriate, fair, and reasonable" (Kazdin, 1981). Adherence involves the willingness of students to engage in certain behavior changes indicated in the intervention plan (Meichenbaum & Turk, 1987). When students acknowledge the benefits of an intervention and actively engage in its activities, they are more likely to achieve positive outcomes. Integrity acceptability, and adherence are two elements that link intervention use with effectiveness.

Training and Technical Support

The amount and quality of training and technical support have been found to be important correlates of successful program implementation (Gottfredson et al., 2000). The purpose of training is to prepare implementers to deliver an intervention (i.e., to develop their readiness to facilitate program delivery). Effective training models are guided by four basic principles: (1) present the relevant information or concepts; (2) model the knowledge, skills, and attitudes to be learned; (3) provide trainees with opportunities to practice the skills; and (4) coach trainees during practice and provide feedback after practice (Salas & Cannon-Bowers, 2001). Efforts to specifically apply the intervention in the real world rounds out the training in delivery. In the case of school-based mental health interventions, implementers need to be informed about the underlying theoretical model of the program, become familiar with program content, and be prepared to conduct the major activities of the program.

Training opportunities can vary in quality, and usually the ones conducted by knowledgeable, motivated individuals are best. For some programs, trainers are recruited from those individuals who have used the intervention in the field (e.g., Life Skills Training; Botvin, 2000). Regardless of their experience, trainers should be prepared, use high-quality materials, and have an engaging presentation style.

While knowledge and skills are important outcomes for prospective program implementers, successful training should also address implementer attitudes, beliefs, and perceptions. As an example, for teachers to facilitate students' social and emotional development, they need to see the value of fostering such growth, have the necessary background knowledge of children's social and emotional development (e.g., perspective-taking ability, emotional self-regulation), and then be able to integrate these into their pedagogical practices (Adalbjarnardottir & Selman, 1997). Individuals who believe in a program and who are confident in their ability to use an intervention will be more likely to implement the program well. Conversely, if a teacher or school-based clinician does not feel confident or comfortable conducting lessons about a particular topic (e.g., sexuality, suicide), that individual may be more likely to skip those lessons even though they are a necessary part of the program (i.e., essential to achieving positive student outcomes).

A final aspect of the training and technical support that should be mentioned is the availability of ongoing support, consultation, or supervision. Situations occurring after training are as important to a program's success as those that occur during training (Salas & Cannon-Bowers, 2001), yet some prevention efforts require preimplementation training but have no contact with implementers once the program begins. This approach has the potential to undermine implementation quality, because it is inevitable that problems will be encountered once the intervention is started. Related to this issue is the quality of communication between the implementers and the technical support staff. Even when support is available, if the implementers do not feel comfortable talking with a consultant or do not view that person as particularly helpful, it is unlikely that the problem will be resolved in a way that facilitates program delivery.

Technical support during program implementation is also important because it can facilitate transfer of training. During actual program implementation, a consultant can model, coach, or provide other kinds of support to implementers to strengthen their ability to apply, generalize, and maintain the knowledge, skills, and attitudes acquired during the training session in "real-world" classroom, school, family, or community settings.

Environmental Conditions that Influence Program Implementation

School-based prevention programs do not exist in a vacuum. Instead they are nested within different ecological systems. Different factors within these systems can either support or undermine program implementation in any given setting. Contextual factors may vary in relevance to program implementation and outcomes depending on the characteristics of the particular intervention. For example, the loss of a particular teacher most likely would have a greater impact on a social skills intervention within that teacher's classroom than on an intervention involving a change in district discipline policies. "Key" ecologies for school-based efforts typically include the classroom, school, district, and community.

Factors at the Classroom Level

In addition to teacher characteristics and behaviors, other relevant classroom-level factors include those that contribute to the classroom climate, such as relationships among classmates and between teachers and students. No single factor defines a classroom's climate. Rather, classroom climate refers to the psychological and social aspects of the classroom environment, including shared goals, the level of cooperation and mutual respect that exists among classroom members, and the relationships between teacher and students and among students (Wang, Haertel, & Walberg, 1997).

Factors at the School Level

Positive relationships at the school level are needed to build a sense of professional community that is crucial in promoting positive student outcomes (King & Newmann, 2000). As such, relationships at the school level can also have a strong effect on the quality of implementation. Principals, teachers, and staff need a strong foundation of goodwill, respect, and collaboration in order to meet the challenges of implementing a new program, especially if the intervention includes multiple integrated components. They need to share common goals, communicate openly, exchange ideas, and actively problem-solve with one another. All school personnel should be aware of a new program and understand any implications it may have for their role in the school. A positive school environment allows staff to take risks, support one another, learn from mistakes, and grow professionally.

Other school-level factors that impact implementation include the school's ability to provide physical and administrative supports for interventions. For example, there must be adequate time for a new program or curriculum to fit into the day. School administrators have the power to make schedule changes or even modify the curriculum to make room for new programs. By providing support through organization, motivation, and direction, the principal can substantially affect program implementation (Gottfredson et al., 2000). Of course, if a school does not have positive principal–teacher relationships, principal support could have less influence.

Factors at the District Level

Although implementation usually occurs at the building and classroom levels, district administrators as well as school board members can have substantial influence. Prevention programming is likely to receive stronger endorsement as well as resources if it targets an aspect of the district's mission statement or addresses a district objective or school board concern. Further, the support of influential school board members can directly affect awareness and engagement at all levels, as well as assignment of resources. For example, there are numerous ways that these types of programs can be funded, including Title I, Federal Safe and Drug-Free Schools funds, and state- and local-level funds. There is little research on how decisions regarding the use of funds are made, but such decisions may have dramatic effects on program implementation.

Factors at the Community Level

Schools function within larger systems at the local, county, state, and federal levels. Schools or districts may not have the power to make decisions if their agenda is different from the political system or if they have to balance competing external demands. Certain interventions require collaborations between educational and other community organizations. Depending on the structure and provision of services by community agencies or the history of the relationship between agencies, collaborations could present an added challenge to implementation.

In addition to the contextual factors indicated previously, it is widely acknowledged that parents exert a profound influence on a child's social, emotional, and cognitive development through their parenting practices, attitudes, and behaviors (Patrikakou, Weissberg, & Rubenstein, 1999). Consequently, any efforts to promote children's mental health should involve parents and other primary caregivers.

In summary, implementation quality and the overall success of prevention initiatives are affected by the attitudes and beliefs of students, teachers, school administrators, mental health personnel, parents, and members of the broader community who make school-related decisions. For prevention efforts to be successful, these key stakeholders must believe that a need exists and view change as a necessary goal. They also must see the problem as preventable and the intervention as effective. This shared vision can provide the necessary initial impetus to ensure that the intervention will become a priority and be allotted adequate attention, time, and financial resources.

UNRESOLVED ISSUES AND FUTURE DIRECTIONS

The first goal of this chapter was to highlight the body of knowledge that has accumulated within the field of prevention over the past decade, as it has the potential to expand and strengthen the services that are currently being provided by school-based mental health clinicians. The second goal was to draw attention to the issue of implementation. A focus on implementation is critical because the conditions under which schools are attempting to provide evidence-based programs can and oftentimes do vary significantly from the settings where the interventions were originally developed and evaluated. In addition, the field of prevention as a whole is moving beyond the question of "Does the program work?" to "How were the outcomes achieved?" To provide quality services to their students, school-based mental health practitioners need a theoretical model to guide their activities. The model outlined in this chapter can serve as a guide in the selection of appropriate interventions, the planning and monitoring of services, and the integration of implementation information into decision-making and program improvement.

As alluded to earlier, a lingering conundrum for educators and school-based mental health practitioners involves the determination of a proper balance between the need to maintain fidelity to an intervention and the co-occurring need to tailor an intervention to fit a particular school or community. In the real world of schools, programs generally cannot be "taken out of the box" and implemented "as is." Instead, adaptations and modifications need to be made to meet local circumstances, needs, and expertise. Specification of essential elements or "active ingredients" of a program can help guide local adaptation efforts because such information differentiates program elements that should be provided with fidelity from the less essential ones that can be adapted without compromising program effects (Center for Substance Abuse Prevention, 2001). While helpful, such distinctions alone do not provide the complete solution to a very complex set of issues. Questions remain unanswered as to the degree to which an evidence-based intervention can be modified without violating its integrity and compromising its effectiveness. For example, how much or to what extent must essential elements be delivered as designed? Is there a critical threshold for a program's active ingredients above which program effects are ensured but below which effects are jeopardized?

In addition to program components, are there contextual factors that are critical for the success of school-based prevention efforts? In their study of prevention efforts in 1279 schools across the United States, Gottfredson et al. (2000) found that higher levels of principal support and greater integration of prevention efforts with other aspects of school activities resulted in higher levels of implementation quality. Interestingly, budgetary issues were not associated with implementation quality. Thus, more research is needed to verify the strength of putative active ingredients of preventive interventions and to clarify the role of contextual factors in supporting or impeding programmatic efforts.

Another concern involves how information about implementation quality is utilized. When implementation quality is assessed, this information often results in minimal influence on decision making and practice or ongoing program improvement (Sproull & Zubrow, 1981). Results need to be disseminated to practitioners and to decision makers effectively so that there is an increase in their utilization. Fostering collaboration among those involved in the evaluation effort (e.g., evaluators, school staff, district administrators) can build trust and interest in the results, factors that are predictive of whether the information is utilized (Beer & Walton, 1990).

CONCLUDING COMMENTS

It is clear that the importance of understanding and solving issues relative to implementation is becoming increasingly important as schools attempt to provide their students with evidence-based interventions to prevent emotional and behavioral problems and promote sound mental health. To maintain a focus on implementation, the following suggestions are offered.

- The definition of implementation quality should be expanded to include *both* the degree to which the intervention was delivered as planned *and* the degree to which the implementation support system was utilized as planned.
- Further research is needed to specify active ingredients of interventions, clarify the role of contextual factors in supporting implementation efforts, and develop psychometrically sound implementation measures.

- Program developers should identify the active ingredients of an intervention and provide clear implementation guidelines to schools to support their efforts to maintain sufficient fidelity to the intervention yet adapt a program to meet local needs and resources.
- The assessment of implementation needs to be considered in the initial planning stage of prevention programs (rather than as an afterthought) and included as part of the entire intervention package.
- Measurement of the quality of implementation should become routine practice and expectation for evaluators, consultants, trainers, implementers, and program developers.
- Efforts are needed to ensure that implementation data are used by decision makers and shared with practitioners.
- Training programs for implementers such as school-based mental health providers and educators need to include an understanding of the importance of intervention integrity into their curriculum and also incorporate the assessment of implementation as an expectation of professional practice.

We hope that by devoting greater attention to these issues in the future, the field can attain a high degree of confidence that evidence-based prevention and health-promotion practices can be implemented successfully in local schools and a thorough understanding of whether what is being done makes a difference and why.

ACKNOWLEDGMENTS. We would like to thank Mark Greenberg for his helpful feedback on earlier drafts of this chapter. Correspondence concerning this chapter should be addressed to Patricia A. Graczyk, Institute for Juvenile Research, University of Illinois at Chicago, 840 South Wood Street - Suite 130 (MC 747), Chicago, Illinois 60612-7347; e-mail: pgraczyk@psych.uic.edu.

REFERENCES

Adalbjarnardottir, S., & Selman, R. L. (1997). "I feel I have received a new vision:" An analysis of teachers' professional development as they work with students on interpersonal issues. *Teaching and Teacher Education, 13,* 409–428.

Adelman, H. S., & Taylor, L. (1999). Mental health in schools and system restructuring. *Clinical Psychology Review, 19,* 137–163.

American School Health Association (1998). *School health: Findings from evaluated programs* (2nd ed.). Rockville, MD: U.S. Department of Health and Human Services.

Beer, M., & Walton, E. (1990). Developing the competitive organization: Interventions and strategies. *American Psychologist, 45,* 154–161.

Berndt, T. J., & Keefe, K. K. (1995). Friends' influence on adolescents adjustment to school. *Child Development, 66,* 1312–1329.

Botvin, G. J. (2000). *Life skills training: Promoting health and personal development. Teacher's Manual 1.* Princeton, NJ: Princeton Health Press.

Botvin, G. J., Baker, E., Dusenbury, L., Botvin, E. M., & Diaz, T. (1995). Long-term follow-up results of a randomized drug abuse prevention trial in a white middle-class population. *Journal of the American Medical Association, 273,* 1106–1112.

Botvin, G. J., Baker, E., Dusenbury, L., Tortu, S., & Botvin, E. M. (1990). Preventing adolescent drug abuse through a multi-modal cognitive-behavioral approach: Results of a 3-year study. *Journal of Consulting and Clinical Psychology, 58,* 437–446.

Catalano, R. F., Berglund, M. L., Ryan, J. A. M., Lonczak, H. C., & Hawkins, J. D. (1998). *Positive youth development in the United States: Research findings on evaluations of positive youth development programs* (NICHD Publication). Washington, DC: U.S. Department of Health and Human Services.

Center for Substance Abuse Prevention (2001). *2001 annual report of science-based prevention programs. Rockville,* MD: Author.

Chen, H. T. (1990). *Theory-driven evaluations.* Thousand Oaks, CA: Sage.

Chen, H. (1998). Theory-driven evaluations. *Advances in Educational Productivity, 7,* 15–34.

Connell, D. B., Turner, R. R., & Mason, E. F. (1985). Summary of the findings of the School Health Education Evaluation: Health promotion effectiveness, implementation, and costs. *Journal of School Health, 55,* 316–323.

Consortium on the School-Based Promotion of Social Competence (1994). The school-based promotion of social competence: Theory, research, practice, and policy. In R. J. Haggerty, L. R. Sherrod, N. Garmezy, & M. Rutter (Eds.), *Stress, risk, and resilience in children and adolescents: Processes, mechanisms, and interventions* (pp. 268–316). New York: Cambridge University Press.

Cowen, E. L. (1998). Changing concepts of prevention in mental health. *Journal of Mental Health, 7,* 451–461.

Dane, A. V., & Schneider, B. H. (1998). Program integrity in primary and early secondary prevention: Are implementation effects out of control? *Clinical Psychology Review, 18,* 23–45.

Domitrovich, C. E., & Greenberg, M. T. (2000). The study of implementation: Current findings from effective programs that prevent mental disorders in school-aged children. *Journal of Educational and Psychological Consultation, 11,* 193–221.

Drug Strategies (1999). *Making the grade: A guide to school drug prevention programs.* Washington, DC: Author.

Durlak, J. A. (1995). *School-based prevention programs for children and adolescents.* Thousand Oaks, CA: Sage.

Durlak, J. A. (1998). Why program implementation is important. *Journal of Prevention and Intervention in the Community, 17,* 5–18.

Durlak, J. A., & Wells, A. M. (1998). Evaluation of indicated preventive intervention (secondary prevention) mental health programs for children and adolescents. *American Journal of Community Psychology, 26,* 775–802.

Elias, M. J., Zins, J. E., Weissberg, K. S., Greenberg, M. T., Haynes, N. M., Kessler, R., Schwab-Stone, M. E., & Shriver, T. P. (1997). *Promoting social and emotional learning: Guidelines for educators.* Alexandria, VA: Association for Supervision and Curriculum Development.

Elliot, D. (1998). *Blueprints for violence prevention.* Golden, CO: Venture Publishing.

Evans, S. W. (1999). Mental health services in schools: Utilization, effectiveness, and consent. *Clinical Psychology Review, 19,* 165–178.

Gordon, R. (1983). An operational classification of disease prevention. *Public Health Reports, 98,* 107–109.

Gordon, R. (1987). An operational classification of disease prevention. In J. A. Steinberg & M. M. Silverman (Eds.), *Preventing mental disorders* (pp. 20–26). Rockville, MD: Department of Health and Human Services.

Gottfredson, D. C., Fink, C. M., Skroban, S., & Gottfredson, G. D. (1997). Making prevention work. In R. P. Weissberg, T. P. Gullotta, R. L. Hampton, B. A. Ryan, & G. R. Adams (Vol. Eds.), *Healthy children 2010: Establishing preventive services* (pp. 219–252). Thousand Oaks, CA: Sage.

Gottfredson, D. C., Gottfredson, G. D., & Hybl, L. G. (1993). Managing adolescent behavior: A multiyear, multischool study. *American Educational Research Journal, 30,* 179–216.

Gottfredson, G. D., Gottfredson, D. C., Czeh, E. R., Cantor, D., Crosse, S. B., & Hantman, I. (2000). *National study of delinquency prevention in schools.* Ellicott City, MD: Gottfredson Associates, Inc.

Graczyk, P. A., Weissberg, R. P., Payton, J. W., Elias, M. J., Greenberg, M. T., & Zins, J. E. (2000). Criteria for evaluating the quality of school-based social and emotional learning programs. In R. Bar-On & J. D. A. Parker (Eds.), *The handbook of emotional intelligence* (pp. 391–410). San Francisco: Jossey–Bass.

Greenberg, M. T., Domitrovich, C., & Bumbarger, B. (1999). *Preventing mental disorder in school-aged children: A review of the effectiveness of prevention programs.* Report submitted to The Center for Mental Health Services (SAMHSA), Prevention Research Center, Pennsylvania State University (obtainable at http://www.psu.edu/dept/prevention/).

Greenberg, M. T., Domitrovich, C., & Bumbarger, B. (2001). Preventing mental disorder in school-aged children: Current state of the field. *Prevention & Treatment, 4*, 1–64.

Greenberg, M. T., Domitrovich, C., Graczyk, P. A., & Zins, J. E. (in press). *The study of implementation in school-based prevention research: Implications for theory, research, and practice.* Report submitted to The Center for Mental Health Services. Rockville, MD: Substance Abuse and Mental Health Services Administration.

Harachi, T. W., Abbott, R. D., Catalano, R. F., Haggerty, K. P., & Fleming, C. B. (1999). Opening the black box: Using process measures to assess implementation and theory building. *American Journal of Community Psychology, 27*, 711–731.

Hoagwood, K., & Koretz, D. (1996). Embedding prevention services within systems of care: Strengthening the nexus for children. *Applied & Preventive Psychology, 5*, 225–234.

Institute of Medicine (1994). *Reducing risks for mental disorders: Frontiers for preventive intervention research.* Washington, DC: National Academy Press.

Kazdin, A. E. (1981). Acceptability of child treatment techniques: The influence of treatment efficacy and adverse side effects. *Behavior Therapy, 12*, 493–506.

King, M. B., & Newmann, F. M. (2000). Will teacher learning advance school goals? *Phi Delta Kappan, 81*, 576–580.

Kolbe, L. J., Kann, L., & Brener, N. D. (2001). Overview and summary of the findings: School health policies and programs study 2000. *Journal of School Health, 71*, 253–259.

Linn, R. L. (2000). Assessments and accountability. *Educational Researcher, 29*, 4–16.

Lochman, J. E. (1985). Effects of different treatment lengths in cognitive-behavioral interventions with aggressive boys. *Child Psychiatry and Human Development, 16*, 45–56.

Lochman, J. E. (1992). Cognitive-behavioral intervention with aggressive boys: Three year follow-up and preventive efforts. *Journal of Consulting and Clinical Psychology, 60*, 426–432.

Meichenbaum, D., & Turk, D. (1987). *Facilitating treatment adherence.* New York: Plenum.

Nastasi, B. K., Varjas, K., Bernstein, R., & Pluymert, K. (1998). *Exemplary mental health programs: School psychologists as mental health service providers.* Bethesda, MD: National Association of School Psychologists.

Newcomb, A. F., Bukowski, W. M., & Pattee, L. (1993). Children's peer relations: A meta-analytic review of popular, rejected, neglected, controversial, and average sociometric status. *Psychological Bulletin, 113*, 99–128.

Parker, J. G., & Asher, S. R. (1987). Peer relations and later personal adjustment: Are low-accepted children at risk? *Psychological Bulletin, 102*, 357–389.

Patrikakou, E. N., Weissberg, R. P., & Rubenstein, M. I. (1999). School–family partnerships. In A. J. Reynolds, H. J. Walberg, & R. P. Weissberg (Eds.), *Promoting positive outcomes: Issues in children's and families' lives* (pp. 95–127). Washington, DC: CWLA Press.

Payton, J., Wardlaw, D., Graczyk, P. A., Tompsett, C., Ragozzino, K., Bloodworth, M., Fleming, J., Garza, P., Bailey, J., & Weissberg, R. P. (2000). *A review of school-based social and emotional learning (SEL) programs: Project coding manual.* Unpublished manuscript, University of Illinois at Chicago.

Rones, M., & Hoagwood, K. (2000). School-based mental health services: A research review. *Clinical Child and Family Psychology Review, 3*, 223–241.

Salas, E., & Cannon-Bowers, J. A. (2001). The science of training: A decade of progress. *Annual Review of Psychology, 52*, 471–499.

Seligman, M. E. P. (1996). Science as an ally of practice. *American Psychologist, 51*, 1072–1079.

Spoth, R. L., Redmond, C., & Shin, C. (2001). Randomized trial of brief family interventions for general populations: Adolescent substance use outcomes 4 years following baseline. *Journal of Consulting & Clinical Psychology, 69*, 627–642.

Sproull, L. S., & Zubrow, D. (1981). Performance information in school systems: Perspectives from organization theory. *Educational Administration Quarterly, 17*, 61–79.

Tashman, N. A., Weist, M. D., Acosta, O., Bickham, N. L., Grady, M., Nabora, L., & Waxman, R. (1999). Toward the integration of prevention research and expanded school mental health programs. *Children's Services: Social Policy, Research, and Practice, 3*, 97–115.

U.S. Department of Health and Human Services (1999). *Mental health: A report of the Surgeon General.* Rockville, MD: Author.

Wang, M. C., Haertel, G. D., & Walberg, H. (1997). Learning influences. In H. J. Walberg & G. D. Haertel (Eds.), *Psychology and educational practice* (pp. 199–211). Berkley, CA: McCutchan Publishing Company.

Weiss, C. H. (1995). Nothing as practical as good theory: Exploring theory-based evaluation for comprehensive community initiatives for children and families. In J. P. Connell, A. C. Kubisch, L. B. Schorr, & C. H. Weiss (Eds.), *New approaches to evaluating community initiatives: Concepts, methods, and contexts.* New York: Aspen Institute.

Weissberg, R. P., Caplan, M. Z., & Sivo, P. J. (1989). A new conceptual framework for establishing school-based social competence promotion programs. In L. A. Bond & B. E. Compas (Eds.), *Primary prevention and promotion in the schools* (pp. 255–296). Thousand Oaks, CA: Sage.

Weissberg, R. P., & Greenberg, M. T. (1998). School and community competence-enhancement and prevention programs. In W. Damon (Series Ed.) & I. E. Sigel & K. A. Renninger (Vol. Eds.), *Handbook of child psychology: Vol. 4. Child psychology in practice* (5th ed., pp. 877–954). New York: Wiley.

Weist, M. D. (1997). Expanded school mental health services: A national movement in progress. In T. Ollendick & R. J. Prinz (Eds.), *Advances in clinical child psychology* (Vol. 19, pp. 319–352). New York: Plenum.

Yeaton, W. H., & Sechrest, L. (1981). Critical dimensions in the choice and maintenance of successful treatments: Strength, integrity, and effectiveness. *Journal of Consulting & Clinical Psychology, 49,* 156–167.

Zins, J. E., & Erchul, W. P. (2002). Best practices in school consultation. In A. Thomas & J. Grimes (Eds.), *Best practices in school psychology IV* (pp. 424–436). Silver Spring, MD: National Association of School Psychologists.

V

Cross-Cutting Issues

22

Preventing and Addressing Crises and Violence-Related Problems in Schools

MARY MARGARET KERR

- An elementary school principal, estranged from her abusive husband, arrives at work early one morning. Thirty minutes later, her husband, armed, comes to school in a rage.
- A 6-year-old is abducted from the playground of her school during the first day of school. Other children witness the event helplessly.
- A 9-year-old boy playing near a stairwell falls three stories inside his elementary school. Classmates witness it. Paramedics take the child, seriously injured, to the hospital.
- A member of the high school football team collapses and dies during a practice.

These four vignettes depict the range of crises facing schools today. With each school crisis come psychological repercussions, many of which challenge even the most experienced crisis responders. This chapter offers an overview of each phase of crisis preparation, responding, and aftermath, with essential concepts to guide school and agency personnel. First, however, we offer a national perspective for those preparing crisis plans. This context is important, because schools often fall prey to the heightened attention paid by the media to acts of intentional violence. For example, a school might spend its resources preparing for a hostage situation while overlooking the more probable crisis of a teacher having a heart attack.

SCHOOL CRISES: A NATIONAL PERSPECTIVE

There is less than one in a million chance of suffering a school-associated violent death. Put another way, in 1998, twice as many people were killed by

MARY MARGARET KERR • University of Pittsburgh, Pittsburgh, Pennsylvania 15260.

lightning as were killed in schools. Despite media coverage to the contrary, only 10% of schools reported any instances of serious crime during the 1996–1997 school year, while 43% reported no crime at all (U.S. Department of Education and U.S. Department of Justice, 1999).

While these statistics offer hope, others have dismissed them as overly optimistic. "Realistically, a major organizational crisis can be expected in a moderate-sized to large school district almost every year (Pitcher & Poland, 1992)" (Poland & McCormick, 1999). Calming parents and the public is a job often assigned to the school mental health specialist. The task for school crisis responders, therefore, is to strike a balance between irrational fear on the one hand and reasonable preparation for probable crises on the other. One way to accomplish this balance is to review current reports about school safety and violence. The National Center for Educational Statistics (http://www.nces.ed.gov/index.html) publishes an annual report on U.S. schools' crime data. An excellent review of targeted school shootings is the United States Secret Service Report written by Vossekuil et al. (2000).

School mental health specialists will find that staff members are more capable of following crisis plans when they do not feel personally unsafe or vulnerable. This is another reason to share with staff the findings of government agencies regarding their workplace and its safety. In this regard, the Occupational Safety and Health Administration has produced several training series for preventing workplace violence prevention, including "Guidelines for Preventing Workplace Violence for Health Care and Social Service Workers" downloadable from www.osga.gov.

In summary, school mental health specialists can help their districts by first sharing a factual national perspective on school crime and violence as well as highlighting other crises that are likely to take place. The next section includes suggestions to help agency and school personnel establish *local* priorities for their crisis preparedness.

SCHOOL CRISES: A LOCAL PERSPECTIVE

Before embarking on a school crisis campaign, school districts should thoughtfully consider several sources of *local* information. No textbook or crisis planning kit can possibly replace the insights of those who live and work in a community. To gain this local perspective, we recommend an *interagency school safety council* (Table 1) with representatives from local, county, state, and federal law enforcement agencies; juvenile and family court; fire department; emergency medical services; mental health agencies; health department; businesses (e.g., Chamber of Commerce); faith community (e.g., religious leaders); public transportation (e.g., bus company); telecommunications (e.g., telephone company); media; local emergency management agency representatives; Parent Teacher Student Association; union leadership for school employees; school district legal counsel; school security; and school psychological services.

This advisory body should meet at least four times each year to establish priorities for their joint work, to identify anticipated crises, to develop and review protocols to follow in the event of a crisis, and to critique crisis responses. We

Table 1. Sample Interagency School Safety Council Agenda

March 18, 2002, Agenda
Perrone School District Interagency School Safety Council

1. Review of minutes from last meeting.

2. Spring prom (May 10, 2002)
   * Alcohol and drug use (See 11-19-01 police report on ecstasy)
   * Weapons—need for metal detectors/staff
   * Admissions: nonstudent guests/fake student id cards/suspended and expelled students
   * Parking and traffic control/DUI
   * Smoking in restrooms
   * Crowd control; "mosh pits"
   * Students leaving the dance without permission
   * Training for chaperones
   * Undercover security
   * After prom—supervisions and security at hotel and restaurant
   * "Dirty dancing": how to confront students

3. Basketball tournament (March 28–30)
   * Security for visiting team
   * Alcohol use among adult spectators (See security report from 2-8-02 game)
   * Safeguards for vandalism after game (See photos of graffiti after the Carlson game)

4. Review of bomb threat drill
   * Problems with phone call-back system
   * Concerns expressed by union reps for custodial union (Custodians are asked to search school grounds with police)

5. Update on flood emergency plan from local Emergency Management Agency reps.

6. Review of questions from school safety teams
   * Bruce Elementary: What should the school secretaries ask when a visitor buzzes for entry into the school?
   * Roberts Middle School: We need a plan for students who are dropped off early by working parents. We have at least 40 kids each morning before school opens.
   * Williams High School: We are seeing an increase in "self-cutting." Should we follow the suicide policy on these cases? Not all of the students seem suicidal. Problem is especially noticeable in the ninth grade.

7. Other items (Please call in your items as soon as possible.)

Next meeting is June 15, 2002, 5–8 PM, Chamber of Commerce.

---

cannot overemphasize the importance of this guidance *before* a crisis. Interagency coordination and communication are the hallmarks of successful crisis prevention. Mental health specialists working in schools, often more experienced in interagency collaboration than educators, can make a unique contribution to such a leadership body.

Table 1 illustrates a sample agenda for a school safety advisory group. Attention to detail, as seen in the discussion items, characterizes a well-coordinated school safety council that anticipates future events while learning from the past. Note that the agenda also provides for the exchange of information about topics typically unfamiliar to school leaders. Also, in keeping with one of the basic principles for the prevention of workplace violence—employee involvement—schools are invited to raise their own concerns.

Table 2. Checklist for Preparation of School Crisis Plans

1. Locate present policies and procedures:
   * Agency directives and memoranda
   * Bulletins from central office
   * Community agencies' files (police, protective services, emergency management agency, courts, mental health agencies, hospitals, and health care agencies)
   * Individual school building guidebooks

2. Review policies and procedures for:
   * Facilities problems (electrical outage, heating, plumbing)
   * "Unrest," protests, strikes
   * Natural disasters or events (weather)
   * Transportation delays, problems, and accidents
   * Individual child accidents (indoors and outside)
   * Medical problems affecting many (head lice, meningitis), individual medical crises (including alcohol and other drugs), individual mental health crises (depression, suicidality, trauma), intentional acts against persons (abuse; assault; rape; assaults with chemical, syringe, mace; bomb threats), hostage situations
   * Kidnapping or missing person
   * Intentional acts against property (theft, vandalism, graffiti)
   * Events outside school that affect school community (witnessing a crime or accident, airline crash)

3. Collaborate on policies.
   * Share your policies and procedures with others.
   * Request policies from comparable institutions.

4. Host joint sessions to review policies and procedures.

5. Check the link between policies and procedures.
   * Are they current?
   * Are they complete?
   * Have they worked?
   * Do procedures match the policies?
   * Do they follow legal mandates?

6. Set priorities.
   * Review last year's data.
   * What are the most likely crisis situations in your setting?
   * Ask outside agencies for their assessment of priorities.
   * Consider your "public(s)." What is important to them?
   * Agree to a schedule for developing policies and procedures.

PREPARATION FOR SCHOOL CRISES

Table 2 offers a checklist for preparing a district's school crisis plan. Included are acts of both intentional and nonintentional injury as well as community conditions (e.g., weather, strikes). A district unprepared for such events can find itself in chaos (Trump, 1998); therefore, schools should review this list carefully and determine which crises are likely to take place or have taken place in nearby districts. Next, we turn to the essential elements of a successful crisis plan.

COMPONENTS OF A CRISIS PLAN

Every crisis plan should have these six components:

1. Prevention
2. Early intervention

  3. Crisis intervention
  4. Postvention or ongoing crisis response
  5. Debriefing
  6. Evaluating the response and improving the plan

This section begins with prevention. Whether one is addressing acts of intentional or unintentional injury or death, the guidelines for these six elements are applicable.

Component 1. Prevention

Prevention guidelines tell school staff members, parents, and students how to avert a problem. Critical to this phase is the inclusion of all school staff, including secretaries, bus drivers, groundskeepers, custodians, and security guards. These paraprofessionals often spot visitors and unusual activity before teachers do. Supervision and surveillance are critical and easily learned skills for all school personnel. All employees need to be vigilant about their physical surroundings as well as watchful of those who come and go during the school day. Underscoring the importance of being watchful is research on the prediction of school crime. Studies have shown that violence takes place more often in the "unowned" times and spaces of a school day (Astor, Meyer, & Behre, 1999). These include cafeterias, corridors, restrooms, playgrounds, fields, parking lots, and stairwells. In other words, adult presence and attentiveness are major deterrents to school crime (Lockwood, 1998).

Component 2. Early Intervention

The second section of a crisis plan tells staff and students how to know if there is an imminent problem and what immediate steps to take. For example, school employees should know exactly what to do if a student threatens self-harm, if a faculty member complains of chest pains, or if a teenager threatens to bomb the school. Communications through buildingwide codes or alerts are one example of an early intervention step. *Threat assessment* is another example of an early intervention activity, best performed by a team of trained professionals, including school mental health specialists with specific skills in threat assessment. These skills include (1) identifying the potential perpetrator, or subject; (2) assessing the actual risks; (3) and management of the situation to keep the perpetrator and the potential victim(s) safe. (For an excellent discussion of threat assessment, see Fein, Vossekuil, & Holden (1995).) Clinical interviewing skills are especially helpful in identifying whether a threat is serious. This interview might include taking a weapons history (see Pittel, 1998) or conducting a structured psychiatric interview.

Component 3. Crisis Intervention

Once a crisis has begun, individuals need clear and concise steps for getting both help and advice on what *not* to do. In our crisis team training, the acronym "Be CALM," reminds crisis responders of their tasks:

Before you act, be sure you have the facts and be sure you call for help.
Call out crisis responders with codes or other on-call systems.

<u>C</u>ommunicate so that every responder receives the same updates through briefings.

<u>C</u>oordinate staff—a step that requires advance preparation, a "dispatcher," and preassigned roles.

<u>C</u>ollaborate with *other* agencies, assistance pledged through an interagency leadership council.

<u>A</u>nticipate what could happen in the next hour, 24 hours, and 72 hours.

<u>A</u>ctivate the crisis intervention plan.

<u>A</u>djust the plan accordingly, as the situation changes.

<u>L</u>ook for signs of *things* getting worse or better (e.g., emergence of new crises or restoration of routines).

<u>L</u>isten to your "audiences." These include the public, parents, staff, and students.

<u>M</u>anage the overall crisis, including the media. Designate a single spokesperson.

<u>M</u>aintain the team's mental and physical health. Be sure team members eat nutritional foods, take breaks, and drink plenty of water.

A comprehensive crisis intervention plan includes situation-specific information, with accompanying Be CALM procedures. The situations are those identified as local priorities (e.g., playground injury, suicide threat, angry parent, student with a weapon, bomb threat). A hypothetical example of these procedures to respond to a bomb threat might include the following information. The plan would call for school secretaries to *be sure to get the facts* from the perpetrator of the threat by completing a form next to their telephones. This form would specifically elicit the information needed by police (e.g., date, time, exact words spoken by caller, characteristics of caller's voice, background noises, information about the time and location of the bomb). Secretaries would also know whom to call for help. Other steps in responding to a bomb threat would be (1) *communication* and *collaboration* with law enforcement agencies, the telephone company, school district administration, faculty and staff, and mental health providers; (2) *anticipating* a school closing and activating the school evacuation plan; (3) *listening* to reactions from parents, by contacting key parents such as PTA officers; (4) *managing* the media coverage, by writing a press release and holding daily briefings; and (5) *maintaining* the mental health of crisis responders who return to the building with the bomb squad, by having backup teams take turns. As indicated in this example, the "Be CALM" steps can serve as a procedural checklist for writing crisis plans.

Component 4. Postvention

Guidelines for what to do and not do in the hours, days, and weeks following a crisis constitute a *postvention plan*. Figure 1 provides an overview of the steps in postvention after a sudden death.

During a postvention, mental health specialists meet with students affected by the tragedy and screen those at risk for psychological problems. Students who experience a traumatic event are likely to exhibit signs of *acute stress disorder,* including shock and surprise, helplessness, fear, and horror. Parents and school staff (who may also experience these reactions) need to know that such responses

POSTVENTION IMPLEMENTATION PLAN[1]

Crisis Team Members:

1. _____   5. _____

2. _____   6. _____

3. _____   7. _____

4. _____   8. _____

Plan of Action:

Date:	Time:	Initials:	Responsibility:
_____	_____	_____	1. The school is informed of the death.
_____	_____	_____	2. Factual information is gathered:
_____	_____	_____	⇒ death/cause of death is confirmed by the coroner
_____	_____	_____	⇒ sample coroner's form
_____	_____	_____	3. School informs the superintendent
_____	_____	_____	⇒ postvention plan is initiated with superintendent and building principal
_____	_____	_____	⇒ school coordinator is identified
_____	_____	_____	⇒ school spokesperson is designated
_____	_____	_____	⇒ security is notified
_____	_____	_____	4. School coordinator contacts mental health agency with factual information
_____	_____	_____	⇒ MH states what services will be provided
_____	_____	_____	⇒ MH coordinator is identified
_____	_____	_____	⇒ form for MH is included
_____	_____	_____	5. School coordinator contacts mental health with factual information.
_____	_____	_____	⇒ superintendent approves postvention plan
_____	_____	_____	6. Superintendent contacts mental health coordinator to authorize services.
_____	_____	_____	7. Coordinators examine the contagion effect, if death was a suicide.
_____	_____	_____	⇒ contact with other service providers is made.
_____	_____	_____	⇒ contact with other feeder schools is made.
_____	_____	_____	⇒ sample form
_____	_____	_____	8. School begins to compile a list of students to be individually screened.
_____	_____	_____	⇒ friends of the victim
_____	_____	_____	⇒ siblings of the victim
_____	_____	_____	⇒ students with h/o substance abuse
_____	_____	_____	⇒ students with h/o past attempts
_____	_____	_____	⇒ extracurricular groups
_____	_____	_____	⇒ students with h/o mental health treatment
_____	_____	_____	⇒ sample list is included
_____	_____	_____	9. Coordinators prepare the announcement which is to be read to homeroom classes.
_____	_____	_____	⇒ Sample list is included
_____	_____	_____	10. Faculty contact is made through the initiation of the phone chain.
_____	_____	_____	⇒ teachers are informed of faculty meeting prior to homeroom

Figure 1. *Continued*

_____	_____	_____	11. Meeting is arranged for coordinators and building administration.
_____	_____	_____	⇒ interview rooms are identified
_____	_____	_____	⇒ principal prepares letter to inform parents of the death/postvention: sample
_____	_____	_____	⇒ family contact is identified
_____	_____	_____	12. Meeting is arranged for coordinators and SAP Team.
_____	_____	_____	⇒ SAP assignments are made
_____	_____	_____	⇒ Gatekeeper
_____	_____	_____	⇒ Runners
_____	_____	_____	⇒ Screeners
_____	_____	_____	⇒ Group facilitators
_____	_____	_____	13. Faculty meeting is held before homeroom.
_____	_____	_____	⇒ Principal and coordinators participate in faculty meeting
_____	_____	_____	⇒ Condolences are offered to the faculty
_____	_____	_____	⇒ Facts of the death are reviewed
_____	_____	_____	⇒ Announcement is made to the faculty to be read: sample
_____	_____	_____	14. Letter is mailed by the school to parents.
_____	_____	_____	15. Individual screenings/groups are conducted.
_____	_____	_____	⇒ Individual screening form used
_____	_____	_____	⇒ No recommendation
_____	_____	_____	⇒ School monitor: attendance/academics
_____	_____	_____	⇒ Rescreen
_____	_____	_____	⇒ Referral: scheduled or emergency evaluation
_____	_____	_____	⇒ Continue in treatment
_____	_____	_____	⇒ Parent contact is made by individual screener
_____	_____	_____	⇒ Parents are given resources
_____	_____	_____	16. (Optional) Faculty meeting is arranged for the end of the day.
_____	_____	_____	17. Debriefing with postvention team, SAP team and building administration.
_____	_____	_____	⇒ review of students seen
_____	_____	_____	⇒ Individual recommendations made by mental health coordinator are reviewed
_____	_____	_____	⇒ Identify plan for next day, if needed
_____	_____	_____	18. Arrangements are made for the final debriefing at the end of the postvention.
_____	_____	_____	⇒ Scheduled for 2 weeks to 1 month.
_____	_____	_____	19. Optional parent meeting is held.
_____	_____	_____	20. List of students screened individually/groups and follow-up letters with recommendations are mailed by the mental health coordinator to school principal.
_____	_____	_____	⇒ Sample included
_____	_____	_____	21. Principal mails letter to parents with recommendations.
_____	_____	_____	⇒ Sample included.
_____	_____	_____	22. Final debriefing is held with the postvention team, SAP team, and building administration.
_____	_____	_____	⇒ To review the efficacy of the services.
_____	_____	_____	⇒ To review postvention policy.
_____	_____	_____	⇒ To review students who were given recommendations
_____	_____	_____	⇒ To identify additional training needs.

---

[i] Source: Reprinted with permission from Kerr, Brent, & McKain (1997). Postvention standards guidelines: A guide for a school's response in the aftermath of a sudden death. Third edition. Pittsburgh, PA: University of Pittsburgh, Services for Teens at Risk (STAR Center). Available from the author.

Figure 1.

are (1) normal, (2) should diminish with time, and (3) require additional support if they do not resolve within 4 to 6 weeks. Children and adolescents typically exhibit reactions to trauma including indicators of *shock and surprise,* such as

- being upset with changes in routine
- needing to control what happens
- wanting more frequent communications with parents
- asking questions repeatedly to get information about what is about to happen
- heightened dependency on routines at school and at home
- nervousness; hypervigilance (easily startled)
- less willingness to try unpredictable social situations or new experiences, including academic assignments and tests, sports competitions, public performances
- moodiness, including anger

These reactions make sense when one considers the *unpredictability* of a trauma. The trauma victim, feeling helpless, does not want any more surprises and needs to feel secure and safe. After all, the child or teen exposed to a trauma has experienced a complete and sudden loss of control and power. Accordingly, youth react by expressing their need for *control and order.* These feelings can cause children and teenagers to be

- irritable when not given choices or power in decisions
- "bossy" with family and friends
- critical of others; judgmental; argumentative
- stubborn; insistent on having one's way
- inflexible; focused on self
- "show-offs," engaged in risk-taking behaviors

Mental health specialists can help identify and interpret these reactions for teachers, who may view them as intentional oppositional behaviors. In addition to feelings of helplessness and other reactions to trauma, children may also come to view the future with a greater sense of fear than prior to the traumatic event. This *fearfulness* can result in

- absentmindedness, inability to concentrate
- poor appetite; nervous eating
- being frightened by: darkness, monsters, strangers, "bad guys," reminders of the event
- using alcohol and other drugs to calm one's fears
- anxiety when separated from parents or caregivers
- concerns about own health and that of loved ones
- demands for reassurance and attention

These reactions often result from interrupting thoughts and visual memories about the event, or flashbacks. Youth who have experienced *horror* may also have

- thoughts about death and dying
- disbelief; "numb" feeling; in a daze
- nightmares; difficulty falling asleep; other sleep disturbances
- intrusive thoughts; preoccupation with the event
- fascination with morbid details of the event

- a desire to act out aspects of the event in imaginative play
- sadness

Other signs of acute stress include general anxiety, guilt, withdrawal from others, and not wanting to engage in favorite activities (i.e., anhedonia) (Kerr, 2001).

Schools can alert parents to these signs of stress in children by sending a letter briefly describing the event and then offering a list of common reactions. The letter to the parents (or a written announcement scripted for teachers) may form the basis for a *personal* announcement in a classroom with a familiar teacher. School personnel should avoid using the public address system or a large assembly to inform students about a tragedy. Small groups are preferable over large assemblies, as they provide a situation in which adults can watch for student reactions and offer support. Teachers emotionally affected by the tragedy may require the assistance of a school mental health specialist during these class meetings. If the tragedy involved a teacher, a mental health specialist should remain in that teacher's classroom with the substitute teacher throughout the day.

Depending on the scope of the crisis, the school may need to call in additional crisis responders or mental health specialists to meet either individually or in small groups with students whose needs extend beyond mere classroom discussions. Individual screening of students identified as especially vulnerable (e.g., those with prior psychiatric illnesses, those close to the victim(s), and witnesses) should include a review of symptoms of depression, anxiety, suicidality, and conduct problems (Kerr et al., 1997). These students will require monitoring for several weeks after the crisis and may require referrals to outside agencies. If the crisis remains unresolved (e.g., continuing threats to a building), both staff and students will require ongoing assistance and reassurance. Employees need information on adult signs of acute stress disorder, posttraumatic stress disorder, and resources to which they can turn for support.

Component 5. Debriefing

The fifth phase requires those with specific crisis response to facilitate a session with the crisis responders (and perhaps other employees affected by the trauma). One approach to debriefing is critical incident stress debriefing, or CISD (see Everly, Boyle, & Lating, in press). CISD involves a highly structured, 1- to 2-hour, small group session to allow crisis responders to relate and reflect on their cognitive, behavioral, and emotional responses to the crisis. (For more information, see International Critical Incident Stress Foundation at www.icisf.org.) Mental health specialists often provide some form of CISD for schools, while wisely seeking their own support from skilled debriefers trained through agencies such as the American Red Cross (www.redcross.org) or the National Organization for Victim Assistance (www.try-nova.org).

Whether a school chooses a formal CISD approach or a less formal discussion of what happened, it is important for the crisis response team to spend time reviewing their actions and using their experience to improve future crisis responses. When districts overlook this step, their crisis teams may experience additional stress and burnout (J. Yuhasz, 1983, personal communication).

For example, the staff at the schools affected by the crash of United Flight 93 on September 11, 2001, met after the tragedy to review the emergency responses from various agencies. Participants included emergency management agencies, state and local law enforcement and fire departments, local government, and mental health providers. Through this all-day discussion of what took place, educators and agency personnel were able to identify issues they wanted to work out for any future crises. Facilitating the discussion were several experienced crisis response coordinators who could highlight common concerns and identify resources and strategies for the schools.

Component 6. Evaluating the Response and Improving the Plan

This step ensures that crisis responders learn from their experiences, mistakes, and successes and that they capture information while it is still fresh in their minds. There will be a natural tendency to return to routines and put the stress-inducing crisis behind. However, effective crisis management is an expertise derived of accumulated experience and new lessons. Candidly acknowledging the flaws in a crisis plan is the only way to refine the next response. The crisis response team should meet to review their plan and make necessary modifications to improve it, ultimately with the endorsement of the interagency safety council.

Common Mistakes in Crisis Preparation

Mental health specialists should be aware of common pitfalls in school crisis planning. One is the failure to identify crises that take place *outside* of school, yet have serious consequences for the school staff and students. Consider, for example, how these situations would affect a school:

- A family of four dies in a house fire in plain view of the elementary school.
- A plane crashes in full view of a community soccer team practicing on a local field.
- On her way to pick up her sick child, a third-grader's mother dies in a car accident.

In each of these *community* crises, the school's personnel and students would experience acute stress requiring the support of school mental health staff. Strategies for responding to such *psychological* needs should be included in the postvention section of the plan. These psychological supports might include (1) individual screening of students for acute stress symptoms and other psychological issues, (2) small group "debriefing sessions," (3) support for staff and faculty through the employee assistance program, (4) psychoeducational sessions for parents and community members on traumatic grief and/or the specifics of the event, and (5) CISD for the responders. School mental health specialists need to be familiar with each of these aspects of crisis response.

Policy without procedures (or procedures without supporting policy) is another common mistake. Without *both* policy and specific procedures confusion will arise at the time of a crisis, given the hierarchical and methodical nature of decision making in most school districts. Building-based administrators need policy to back their decisions. School boards want a say in how their "managers" react (see Day & Golench, 1997). A source of conflict in many school crises is the role of outside agency personnel, especially if this role is not delineated in policy and procedures.

Often, schools focus their crisis plans exclusively on one time period (e.g., preventive steps, postvention) or confuse prevention, intervention, postvention steps. For example, some districts have an excellent plan for responding to a suicide (postvention) but no prevention procedures for identifying students at risk for self-harm. Others have formal conflict resolution programs (prevention) but no staff training on how to deescalate an angry student or visitor (intervention).

Another common mistake is to assume that an agency will dispatch one of its employees to a school site on a moment's notice. Most commonly, schools assume this "on-call" service from child protection agencies, local police, and community mental health providers. This misunderstanding can leave a school unprepared during a crisis, when the agency cannot or will not respond rapidly. This is an important issue for interagency safety councils to discuss and define through written interagency agreements or mutually endorsed crisis plans. Mental health specialists may observe that such interagency negotiations are intense and require facilitation, especially if the school and agency have different expectations about how each will respond.

Reliance on one essential person can lead to major delays or confusion at the time of a crisis. Often this essential crisis team member is the school social worker, counselor, nurse, or psychologist. School mental health specialists must guard against single-handedly managing crises or creating dependency among other staff. Teams must face the reality that no one is indispensable and plan for the inevitable absences of important staff. To overcome this dependency, teams should hold "dry runs" in which the essential player is absent. This exercise forces others into the decision-making and coordination roles.

Failure to have alternative communications procedures also causes delays in responding. Schools too often rely on telephone trees and other traditional, "top-down"communications. Working out an on-call schedule with a shared pager is highly preferable to a telephone tree that stops abruptly when one member is absent. Mental health specialists, accustomed to being on-call, can help educators design a workable on-call system.

Overgeneralization from one incident can be avoided by carefully debriefing each crisis response one or two weeks later to identify common themes as well as address unanticipated issues. No two crises are identical, so teams need to review a variety of scenarios to be adequately prepared. We suggest that teams have "dry runs" based on sample vignettes such as those included in this chapter, and that members be preassigned specific duties in a crisis to save time.

Lack of familiarity among crisis responders often leads to additional stress and conflict among the team members. Initial training followed by refresher meetings is essential for effective crisis responses. We have seen chaos emerge when team members do not know one another and cannot work as a cohesive unit.

In addition to meetings and practice exercises, one practical strategy for overcoming conflicts and creating team cohesion is to have every member train with, and carry, the same materials and supplies. These should include

- copy of the crisis plan for each school
- copies of forms that are frequently used (with diskettes for Mac and PC computers found at the school office), such as

- letter(s) to parents including consent for students to be seen by outside school personnel such as someone from the local mental health agency. Unfortunately, a school or district may have more than one loss over a given year. It is suggested that schools have a template for more than one letter. The purpose of this requirement is to save time when a crisis requires fast notification to parents and students. The letter will be different for each crisis, but having the diskettes with basic language already typed is a timesaver.
- announcement to be made to students. This could also be on a diskette, with the outline of an announcement to be completed at the time.
- tracking forms to monitor students to be seen and followed up. The team coordinator should maintain these logs, as it will be necessary to recontact students if additional crises emerge (e.g., a student goes to trial for a shooting), there are students who need more support, or parents have follow-up questions.
- confidential screening form. This form should provide the outline of an interview with items to screen for depression, suicidality, acute stress and posttraumatic stress disorder, homicidality, and other pertinent information (e.g., relationship to the victim, phone number to reach parents).
- grief lecture/support group script. These offer talking points for those leading small group sessions with students affected by the crisis. Students learn the typical signs of traumatic grief, ways to help themselves, and what to do if they need more support or want to get help for a friend.
- copies of frequently used handouts/pamphlets and booklets, including brochures for mental health agencies, employee assistance programs, and school support services.
- phone list(s) including crisis team and faculty, student emergency numbers to reach parents, agency, emergency, and community response numbers, personal numbers (e.g., day-care center, next-door neighbor in the event that the crisis responder needs childcare while working long hours).
- floor plans and maps for schools, so that crisis responders will know how to get there and where they can meet with one another and with students.
- batteries for pagers, phone cards, pens/paper, tissues, nonperishable nourishment, bottled water, and personal medications

In summary, this section has illustrated an interagency approach to crisis plan preparation, with suggestions for avoiding common mistakes. The role of the mental health specialist in preparing crisis plans may be one of administrative coordinator or merely as a well-prepared team responder who assists others in a cohesive and efficient response.

SUMMARY

This chapter has highlighted the steps in (1) identifying, (2) preparing for, and (3) responding to, school crises, including tragedies caused by interpersonal violence. School mental health specialists will discover that crisis responding is both administrative and clinical in nature. Done effectively, it requires advance planning, interagency collaboration, teamwork, clinical expertise, practice, and common sense. The ability to focus a school's attention on the details of crisis preparation—especially the psychological aspects—is as daunting and complex a task as one's clinical treatment of those traumatized. Yet, one could not ask for work more meaningful than serving schools during their darkest and most chaotic hours.

REFERENCES

Astor, R. A., Meyer, H. A., & Behre, W. J. (1999). Unowned places and times: Maps and interviews about violence in high schools. *American Educational Research Journal, 36,* 1, 3–42.

Day, D. M., & Golench, C. A. (1997). Promoting safe schools through policy: Results of a survey of Canadian school boards. *Journal of Educational Administration, 35,* 332–347.

Everly, G. S., Boyle, S., & Lating, J. (1999). The effectiveness of psychological debriefings in vicarious trauma: A meta-analysis. *Stress Medicine, 15*(4), 229–233.

Fein, R. A., Vossekuil, B., & Holden, G. A. (1995). *Threat assessment: An approach to prevent targeted violence.* Series: Research in Action. Washington, DC: National Institute of Justice.

Kerr, M. M. (2001). *Children and trauma: What you can do to help.* Unpublished manuscript. Pittsburgh, PA.

Kerr, M. M., Brent, D. A., & McKain, B. W. (1997). *Postvention standards guidelines: A guide for a school's response in the aftermath of a sudden death* (3rd ed.). Pittsburgh, PA: University of Pittsburgh, Services for Teens at Risk (STAR-Center).

Lockwood, D. (1998). Violence among middle school and high school students: Analysis and implications for prevention. *School Intervention Report, 11,* 1–11.

Pitcher, G. D., & Poland, S. (1992). *Crisis intervention in the schools.* New York: Guilford.

Pittel, E. M. (1998). How to take a weapons history: Interviewing children at risk for violence in school. *Journal of the Academy of Child and Adolescent Psychiatry,* October, 1100–1102.

Poland, S., & McCormick (1999). *Coping with crisis: Lessons learned.* Longmont, CO: Sopris West.

Trump, K. S. (1998). *Practical school security: Basic guidelines for safe and secure schools.* Thousand Oaks, California: Corwin Press, Inc.

U.S. Department of Education and U.S. Department of Justice (1999). *Annual report on school safety.* Washington, DC.

Vossekuil, B., Reddy, M., Fein, R., Borum, R., & Modzeleski, W. (2000). *U.S.S.S. Safe school initiative: An interim report on the prevention of targeted school violence in schools.* Washington, DC: U.S. Secret service, National Threat Assessment Center.

Yuhasz, J. (1993). Personal Communication. Pittsburgh, PA.

23

Achieving Generalization in School-Based Mental Health

STEVEN W. EVANS, JOSHUA LANGBERG, and JEFF WILLIAMS[†]

School-based mental health services present a unique opportunity to improve the effectiveness of mental health care for children. One of the key advantages to school-based mental health services is the opportunity to successfully generalize treatment gains to the settings in which the presenting problems exist (Evans, 1999). This type of service is especially timely, as studies are raising questions about the effectiveness of many clinic-based treatments for children (Weisz et al., 1995). Speculation as to why clinic-based treatments often fail is particularly interesting in light of the fact that laboratory studies consistently document the effectiveness of various treatments (Kazdin & Weisz, 1998).

Many efforts have been made to bridge the gap between the lab and the clinic with the hopes of increasing the effectiveness of the general practice of psychotherapy. Unfortunately, these efforts are unlikely to yield the intended results until the field increases its emphasis on the generalization of treatment gains. The lack of emphasis on generalization has been a limitation in the literature for a long time (Rutter, 1982), yet it is central to the goals of treatment. A review of the child behavior therapy literature revealed that less than 50% of the 904 treatment studies reviewed reported data on generalization (Allen et al., 1991). While methods for achieving generalization are described in the literature (e.g., Evans, Axelrod, & Sapia, 2000; Stokes & Osnes, 1989), there continues to be a lack of emphasis on this critical element of treatment outcome.

The emergence and rapid development of school-based mental health services (Weist, 1997) have afforded the field the opportunity to focus on the generalization

STEVEN W. EVANS, JOSHUA LANGBERG, and JEFF WILLIAMS • James Madison University, Harrisonburg, Virginia 22807.

[†]The authors wish to thank Sherry Serdikoff for her helpful comments and suggestions on previous versions of this chapter.

of treatment. Treatment services provided in schools have a unique opportunity to take advantage of tools for generalization that are largely inaccessible to clinicians working in other settings. Many of the presenting problems that bring youth to mental health clinicians are related to problems occurring at school. Providing treatment in the setting where the presenting problems exist is a step toward diminishing the distinction between the treatment settings and the natural environment. This built-in advantage in the school-based model of care should lead to an increase in the generalization of treatment gains. The greater the integration between the treatment and the natural environment, the fewer barriers exist to achieve generalization. This chapter begins with a review of the literature related to children and treatment generalization. The implications that can be drawn from the literature are then discussed in relation to the practice of school-based mental health.

Definitions of generalization have evolved over the last 75 to 100 years, and a summary of this development is provided by Edelstein (1989). One of the most frequently cited definitions in the recent past was proposed by Stokes and Baer (1977) when they defined generalization as "the occurrence of relevant behavior under different non-training conditions (across subjects, settings, people, behavior and/or time) without the scheduling of the same events in those conditions as had been scheduled in the training conditions" (p. 350). Shortly after proposing this definition, Drabman, Hammer, and Rosenbaum (1979) added greater specificity to the definition by defining 16 classes of generalization and creating a *Generalization Map* that was used to discriminate between the classes. Ten years later in a special issue of *Behavior Therapy* devoted to the topic of generalization, Edelstein proposed that the definition of generalization needs to incorporate the primary role of stimulus control. He differentiated generalization from other similar terms and in particular differentiated generalization from transfer. Edelstein noted that both terms refer to exhibiting behavior in the context of novel or untrained stimuli; however, transfer refers to the occurrence of this process with the need for cognitive mediation and generalization does not. For example, behavior that a person exhibits when angry requires that the individual generate specific cognitions that result in anger. These cognitive appraisals of the environment that provoke the anger mediate the response and differentiate transfer from generalization. Edelstein defined generalization as behavior that is exhibited in response to novel or untrained stimuli without the need for cognitive mediation. In other words, specific external stimuli serve to directly cue the behavior, and the behavior is exhibited as a result of these stimuli and is not mediated by cognition. For the purpose of this chapter, the term generalization is used to refer to both generalization and transfer as defined by Edelstein (1989).

The behavioral literature on children with cognitive handicaps includes a great deal of discussion of generalization. While research has documented several successful methods that effectively train or modify behaviors in individuals with mental retardation, many reports reveal that the investigators have been unable to successfully demonstrate generalization of these behaviors to natural settings. Some success has been reported when using techniques such as self-control interventions, feedback, and behavior modeling (Berg et al., 1995; Foxx et al., 1983, 1986). Nevertheless, much of the research concerning trained behaviors in people with mental retardation has either not been able to conclusively show generalization or did not evaluate the demonstration of these behaviors outside the training setting.

For example, Langhorne et al. (1995) reported that they were able to success-fully demonstrate improvements in the social skill ability of three mildly retarded individuals through the use of a game. Unfortunately, at the completion of training the researchers found that the behaviors of all three individuals had not general-ized to a nontraining, general education setting. The authors concluded that the stimuli present in the training settings were not similar enough to the stimuli operating in the nontraining setting to achieve generalization.

Foxx et al. (1986) suggested that researchers often train behaviors that are not supported by the natural environment. The researchers found that trained social skills in six mentally retarded females did increase in a natural setting when used with other trained peers; however, the skills were not demonstrated when untrained peers were in the natural setting. The peers who had received training supported the learned social behavior of the others, but the untrained peers did not. Foxx et al. suggested that an in-depth analysis of the individual's environment is necessary before determining how to train or modify behavior in a manner that will be maintained in the natural setting. The identification of stimuli in the natural environment that reinforce and cue the desired behavior should be programmed into the training.

Studies that have incorporated the findings and suggestions for programming generalization with mentally retarded individuals have met with some success. For example, Berg et al. (1995) examined generalization across settings, material, and motor responses in four profoundly mentally retarded individuals. The de-sired behavior of ordering food was trained in multiple community settings. This technique, designed to promote generalization, served two main purposes that addressed the findings of prior research. The authors reported that varying the stimuli that cued the desired behavior by training in multiple settings increased the likelihood that their subjects would perform the desired behavior in novel settings when training was removed. Training the behavior in the setting where it is expected to occur develops natural relationships between a variety of stim-uli, the target behavior, and the reinforcement that will persist when training is removed.

Similar difficulties with generalization have been reported in studies us-ing children without cognitive handicaps (Mathur & Rutherford, 1996). Tisdelle and St. Lawrence (1988) attempted to teach problem-solving skills to conduct-disordered adolescents. Once the skills were mastered, the researchers assessed generalization of the trained skills in novel settings. Their results indicated that the adolescents were able to learn the strategies for effective problem solving in the training setting; however, they failed to employ them when the identical situ-ations they were exposed to during the training phase were encountered in their daily life. Herring and Northup (1998) reported similar problems when assessing generalization of social skills in a behaviorally disordered student after the student received social skills training. The investigators concluded that the social skills training was insufficient to promote generalization. Although the student could clearly demonstrate the use of the targeted social skills during individual train-ing sessions, the skills were not displayed during follow-up observations in the child's natural setting (e.g., classroom, recess). Subsequently, the researchers insti-tuted a group contingency strategy, which led to generalization in multiple settings. The subjects and their peers were given a number of "happy faces" during group activities. Each time any student engaged in the negative behavior, the group would lose one happy face. As long as there remained one happy face at the end of the activity, all group members would earn one of a variety of tangible rewards (e.g., pencils, stickers). The group contingency strategy employed by Herring and Northup held both the target student and peers accountable for behaviors exhibited by the group as a unit, resulting in a substantial decrease in complaining and in inappropriate tone of voice.

Christopher, Hansen, and MacMillan (1991) suggested that another reason that social skills training fails to generalize is reputation bias. Cowen et al. (1973) noted that labels that peers attach to target students influence behavior directed toward the target student and maintain a negative social status. Unfortunately, the labeling of peers can remain constant even when behavioral patterns that contributed to the acquisition of the label are no longer manifested (Dodge, 1983). As a result, a reputation bias becomes an obstacle to the generalization of newly learned social skills. As suggested by Kohler and Greenwood (1986), this bias perpetuates the negative social interactions, reducing reciprocal social exchanges that facilitate the link to the natural social contingencies that potentially exist in the child's peer group. In other words, a target child may exhibit the same behavior as that of a popular peer, but due to the reputation bias the target child may receive social punishment for the behavior while a peer may be socially reinforced for the same behavior. To counteract the deleterious effects of reputation bias, Christopher et al. (1991) studied the use of peer helpers. Once peer helpers had been identified, gave consent, and had been trained, the experimenters brought together the socially adept peer helper with the target student. It was explained that the peer helpers had been learning to help other children get more involved with each other and with play activities, and that the peer helper would be spending time with the target child if the target child agreed. By associating a socially skilled and popular peer with the target child, the reputation bias was not only abated but also aided the reaping of natural social "trappings" within the child's environment (Kohler & Greenwood, 1986).

Prompting by agents other than peers, such as teachers and parents, has also been shown to be effective in promoting generalization (Roca & Gross, 1996). Children in the Roca and Gross study were trained to prompt their teachers for praise when they completed their work, answered a question correctly, or achieved some other identified accomplishment in order to elicit social reinforcement for appropriate academic effort or performance. During the process of tapping the natural community of reinforcement available in the classroom, additional functional mediators were established, including teacher verbalization and student modeling.

Peers of the targeted children have been taught to do the same thing. In a recent study reported by Skinner, Cashwell, and Skinner (2000), the authors described an intervention in which peers were trained to report any prosocial behaviors that went unrecognized by the teacher. In this program, the students in the class would report positive peer behaviors rather than their own. This intervention was sparked due to the difficulty educators experience when attempting to notice and praise all instances of prosocial behaviors displayed by their students. The failure to reinforce these incidental positive behaviors may decrease rates of these behaviors, while indirectly teaching students that these types of behaviors are not valued (Skinner et al., 2000). The inclusion of peers in this intervention increased the likelihood that prosocial and appropriate behaviors were recognized and reported for those students who were attempting to use skills learned in a concurrent intervention; thus, generalization of these prosocial behaviors was promoted.

Peers have also been used when treating children with cognitive handicaps. The use of peers to promote social interaction was investigated and found to be successful in a study by Odom et al. (1986). Odom and colleagues taught a single peer and group of three children five social initiations (i.e., play organizing, sharing, assisting, affection, and persistence) by modeling each initiation and having the children practice each with adults. Two handicapped children were grouped either with the single peer or a small group of peers. The trained peers were instructed and prompted by their teacher to use the social initiations strategies learned to encourage play with the handicapped children. Their study demonstrated that both single and multiple peers may be used in peer-initiation interventions to increase the social interactions.

Another method of achieving generalization has been through the use of self-management strategies. Peterson et al. (1999) reported that a programmed generalization strategy involving self-monitoring and teacher-matching of behaviors resulted in a significant improvement in the behavior of 29 students across settings. Self-monitoring consisted of having the students rate their behavior on a scale designed to assess their awareness of progress toward the treatment goals. At the end of the rating period, the students would have their teachers rate them on the same behaviors and provide them with verbal feedback. Once the students were able to obtain "matches" with their teachers at a predetermined level of mastery, the technique was expanded into regular education classrooms. A token reinforcement system was used to promote accurate ratings on behalf of the students, with bonus points given for perfect matches. At the end of the week, the students could spend the points they earned throughout the week to purchase materials (pens, pencils, paperback novels, etc.), game time, computer time, or snacks. Others have reported similar benefits with these techniques (Clees, 1994; Clark & McKenzie, 1989; Gregory, Kehle, & McLoughlin, 1997).

The use of sports as a medium has also been shown to improve maladaptive social interactions and to enhance generalization of trained social skills. Anderson et al. (1987) explored the usefulness of a basketball program serving as the context to strengthen appropriate social skills. By applying the use of a token economy strategy, the students were reinforced during basketball play for proper demonstration of basketball skills, including dribbling, passing, guarding, scoring, and other skills. In addition, they could earn points for prosocial behavior (e.g., cooperative interactions, sharing, cheering for teammates). The results showed that social skills training within the context of a structured sports activity not only increased prosocial behaviors and decreased isolated play behaviors during the training situation, but these skills were also exhibited in the portion of the sports activity without the opportunity to earn points.

The common thread among these successful strategies is connecting the target behaviors with the naturally occurring social contingencies in order to effectively generalize the behavior. While this connection has theoretical appeal, there may be practical problems. For example, the naturally occurring social contingencies have usually been present all along and did not shape the appropriate behaviors prior to the intervention, so they may be insufficient to maintain new behaviors.

In addition, the naturally occurring social contingencies will only be salient if the child grasps the relationship between the behavior and the contingent response. When children do not understand the relationship between the contingent social responses and their own behavior, the responses of others may seem random and unrelated to their own behavior. If the social behavior of others appears unrelated to one's own behavior, the social contingencies that normally shape emerging social skills in children as they develop will have little influence. Children with attention deficit hyperactivity disorder (ADHD) have been described as having an altered sensitivity to reinforcement that can distort their perception of these social contingencies (Douglas, 1983; Kollins, Lane, & Shapiro, 1997; Murray & Kollins, 2000). The cumulative effect of altered sensitivity to reinforcement over the developmental period where social functioning is learned could partially explain the social deficiencies that characterize many youth with ADHD.

The emergence of functional behavioral assessment and functional analysis has addressed some of the generalization obstacles described previously (Gresham, Watson, & Skinner, 2001). The procedures for completing functional assessment and analysis are described elsewhere and are beyond the scope of this chapter (see Ervin et al., 2001; O'Neill et al., 1997; Sterling-Turner, Robinson, & Wilczynski, 2001). While many of the techniques described in the subsequent sections of the chapter overlap with functional assessment and analysis techniques, the focus of this chapter is on generalization procedures that may be used with or without functional assessment or analysis.

Generalization appears to be an allusive goal, but one that is central to the mission of psychosocial treatments. While many descriptions of interventions and treatment manuals do include a discussion of techniques intended to foster generalization, given the complexity of the task and the disproportionate amount of time that it demands, it appears that it frequently receives far too little attention. The shifting of many mental health services out of clinics and hospitals and into schools provides a wonderful opportunity to reemphasize this critical element of care. Schools provide the opportunity to efficiently implement two key strategies that appear to emerge from the literature. First, schools provide clinicians with opportunities to train with diversity. In other words, clinicians provide treatment in settings that closely mimic or are the targets for generalization and therefore can provide training that accurately reflects the variety of cues and responses that are actually present in the target environments. Second, school-based clinicians have the opportunity to manage and assess the social contingencies in the child's environment. Clinicians can identify the naturally occurring social contingencies that will either enhance or inhibit generalization. This includes providing the opportunity for the clinician to assess the reputation bias of a child client. In addition to assessment, schools provide the clinician with the opportunity to influence the social contingencies through the use of teachers, peers, and other school personnel.

TRAIN WITH DIVERSITY

In order to achieve generalization, clinicians have been encouraged to provide training that is specific enough to a situation to make it useful but flexible enough to allow the child receiving the training to confidently respond to the variety of responses that his newly trained behavior may elicit. Specifically, clinicians have been encouraged to train diversely (Stokes & Baer, 1977). In order to identify the variety of situations and responses that will make up the range of diverse training settings and scenarios, the clinician should be aware of the actual situations in the child's natural environment in which the child will be expected to exhibit the target behavior. Based on the variety of settings in which the clinician is expecting the child to exhibit the new behavior and the variety of responses the child might receive when the child does exhibit the new behavior, the clinician should prepare training paradigms. Those situations and responses most likely to be paired with the new behavior should receive the most emphasis and greatest approximation in training. Less likely situations and responses from others should be included in training but receive less attention than the other settings in proportion to their likelihood. Three examples of tools used to achieve diverse training in school-based mental health settings are described in the following.

The first example comes from the Challenging Horizons Program (CHP) at James Madison University which is a school-based mental health program treating middle school students with diagnoses of ADHD (Evans, Axelrod, & Langberg, 2002). Many of the students in the program have a history of responding poorly to provocation. When provoked, they frequently respond impulsively and emotionally to a degree disproportionate to the provoking stimulus. These responses frequently alienate peers and adults. Sports activities create many situations that lead to agitation and are generally less structured than many other activities in the CHP. Students are frequently asked to play positions that they do not want to play, play games that they do not want to play, and run when they do not want to run. In addition, perceived unfairness frequently occurs when fouls are not called as the students believe that they should be called, when students believe that others are being favored by counselors, and when there is the perception that some students are playing either too competitively or too roughly. The agitation that occurs in these fairly unstructured activities frequently leads to anger and inappropriate social behavior.

These characteristics of the recreation activity make it an ideal setting to advance the generalization of skills taught in the program's individual and group settings. Immediately prior to the recreation activity, a counselor reviews specific sports skills and the interpersonal behaviors that are going to be targeted during the activity. This conversation is intended to remind students about the skills they have been learning. During the recreation period, counselors frequently prompt and model the targeted behaviors. Students who exhibit inappropriate behaviors are temporarily pulled out of the activity and individually coached (depending on the behavior, consequences may precede the coaching) by a counselor on the target skills. Some youth have specific contingencies put in place for the recreation period to enhance their learning. The recreation activity produces a wide range of interpersonal situations that call for the child to display the target behaviors and experience a wide diversity of peer responses. The recreation activities allow for the practice of the skills being taught in the program in a supported environment that challenges students with a variety of situations similar to those they experience in their school and home environment.

A second method for generalization used in the CHP targets initiating and maintaining conversations. Many youth referred to the program exhibit social avoidance and withdrawal. (Frequently these are the youth with diagnoses of ADHD predominantly inattentive type.) Skills related to initiating and maintaining conversations are frequently taught and practiced in interpersonal skills groups. After approximating mastery of these skills in a group setting the children in the CHP are given conversation cards by their primary counselors. Initially, these cards list the names of other adults in the CHP as column headings and list specific skills that the child is attempting to achieve as row headings. The child is instructed to initiate conversations with the adults listed on the card by a given time and date. The student has to find the time to complete and initiate these conversations on his/her own (usually during transitions or snack time). Following the conversation the student is to give the card to the adult and ask him/her to complete the ratings for each skill (a Likert scale is provided on the card) and initial the card. Counselors in the program are encouraged to provide verbal feedback to explain the ratings. Primary counselors review the ratings with the student, graph the scores, and develop the next conversation cards. As the student progresses, the names on the conversation cards change from counselors, to other students in the CHP, to students or friends outside of CHP. Peers are not asked to complete the ratings of the skills; however, counselors complete observations in the cafeteria or in other unstructured settings in the school and observe these interactions. The ratings, follow-up conversations, and observations of the conversations are used to ensure that skills have been trained with adequate diversity. Novel responses by peers and adults are integrated into the skills repertoire and practiced with the student. In addition, skills that lead to the greatest social reinforcement are emphasized, while those that are socially discouraged are eliminated. Integrated into this process of revising the skill set is a focus on context. Some social behaviors may be discouraged as a result of a reputation bias, while others may be discouraged as a result of the situation within which the student attempted to demonstrate the new skills. This process results in an expanding skill-set for the students in response to their experiences practicing the skills. Furthermore, it provides a graduated method for practicing and evaluating the skills being taught to increase the likelihood that the student's training has been sufficiently diverse to elicit the social reinforcement available in the child's environment.

Another example of training diversely to ensure generalization was used in an elementary school and provided as part of services by the Bridges for Education Program at Western Psychiatric Institute and Clinic. The procedure involved the use of an art group with a third-grade girl who was referred for problems related to poor peer relations. Similar to the previous example, the student quickly learned a variety of social skills in a series of individual social skills training sessions. In order to ensure that she could demonstrate the skills learned with peers and that these skills would lead to social reinforcement by her peers, it was necessary to create an activity that could be closely monitored to allow for the assessment and the provision of prompts. The student typically isolated herself at recess and would not attempt to practice her skills in this setting. She did enjoy art activities and, as a result, the counselor met with the art teacher to gather some materials and art activities that the student could complete during recess time. Initially, the counselor and the student completed art activities together and practiced the social skills in this context. When the student had achieved a degree of mastery with this activity, the counselor arranged for her to display some of her artwork to her class and the teacher invited up to two other students to participate in this art activity. The targeted student began meeting with the counselor for approximately 10 minutes ahead of the art group to plan the skills she was going to attempt to exhibit during the activity and to prepare for the potential responses of the peers. The skills were not directly discussed during the art group, and the peers were never made aware of the purpose of the activity (other than the art). The counselor did provide subtle prompts during the activity and informally collected data on the behavior of the client and peers. After art group the counselor and the young girl met to evaluate the successes and failures of the social skills. The student's social repertoire was expanded in response to the experiences in this art activity, and this process served as a bridge for her to get to the next step of trying these skills in situations without the counselor. In addition to the benefits pertaining to ensuring adequate diversity of skills, additional benefits emerged from this positive experience with the two peers added to the group. Relationships with these two peers improved, and these two girls provided safe opportunities for the young girl to try her skills in other settings.

The three generalization activities described above served as bridges for the generalization of skills by providing students with relatively safe environments to practice their skills, gauge their effectiveness, and gain confidence in their use. Each of the activities provided the clinician with an opportunity to ensure that skills had been taught with adequate diversity to promote generalization. Skills were modified during these procedures and repertoires broadened. Schools uniquely provide the opportunity to use these tools and include other referred youth as well as nonreferred peers to ensure the diversity of training recommended in the literature.

MANAGE AND EVALUATE CONTINGENCIES

Access to the natural environment including the classrooms, lunchroom, hallways, and other settings is a defining advantage of school-based mental health. Direct access to these settings allows clinicians to observe opportunities unavailable to most clinicians. School-based mental health allows for identification of contingencies operating in the natural environment that are specific to the individual receiving treatment. For example, if a mother reports that her child is calling out in class instead of raising his/her hand and the teacher is frustrated with the child's behavior, a clinician without access to the classroom might assume the individual is calling out in an attempt to receive attention, and consequences for calling out might be recommended. However, observation of the classroom may reveal that most children in the classroom talk out, and the teacher responds to the content of these statements. Approximately once each day the teacher exclaims that students should quit talking out, but she continues to reinforce the behavior through her normal classroom interactions. The consequences recommended by the clinician without access to the classroom would probably have no impact on the behavior of the target child. A school-based clinician could work with the teacher on her overall classroom management strategies and thereby improve the behavior of not only the target child but also the entire class.

One of the keys to the successful generalization of behavior is to ensure that the child exhibiting the new behavior receives enough social reinforcement to maintain it. This reinforcement comes in many obvious and subtle ways including verbal praise and many other indirect routes that probably contain greater saliency than some of the most obvious forms of social reinforcement. These reinforcers include the attention of others, being liked, being pursued to participate in social activities, receiving phone calls, someone choosing to sit near a child in the cafeteria, and conversation in the hallways. The more socially desirable the peer is in delivering the reinforcement to the target child, the greater the saliency of the reinforcer. Clinicians in schools have the opportunity to understand these variables as they relate to a particular child, and in many cases they can influence them.

The first step in attempting to manipulate these social contingencies is to understand them as they relate to the client. Interviews with the student, teachers, and parents along with direct observation (especially in unstructured situations) are the tools most frequently used to assess these contingencies. School-based clinicians have relatively easy access to all of these sources of information. Once these contingencies are understood, then the clinician is challenged to find creative methods for manipulating them.

A special education teacher in an elementary school implemented one such method that was used in the Southwest Allen County Schools outside of Fort Wayne, Indiana. This teacher ran the school's intramural sports program and frequently led popular informal recreation activities during recess. Many of his students tended not to participate in these activities and were frequently ignored or rejected by peers when they did. The teacher modified the procedures for participating in the informal recreation activities by handing out passes to his special education students that were required for admission to this activity. His students could give the passes to whomever they chose. In addition, he frequently made his students captains of teams and highlighted their successes when they participated. The result of these modifications was that some of the most popular and athletic males in the school sought out some of the least popular and least athletic students in order to participate. This intervention alone did not change the social status of these children; however, it did influence the social contingencies as experienced by the special education students and opened up opportunities for additional modifications. While the intervention lacked skill training, investigators have reported improvement in peer attitudes toward a child, and the child's self-perceptions of social efficacy were only found under treatment conditions involving positive peer interactions under superordinate goals and not in traditional skill instruction groups alone (Bierman & Furman, 1984).

Another technique used in the Bridges for Education Program was also used in an elementary school. Many of the students referred for services frequently lost materials and assignments and as a result were frequently unable to complete and turn in work. The counselor worked with these students to develop an organizational system for everything in their desks and book bags. The system was operationalized in a checklist that was taped to the inside of each student's desk. During recess, lunch, or other times when the students were not in the room, the counselor came to the room and checked the desk and book bag against the check-list. He marked the list and left a brief note for the student following his checks. Many students had home and school contingencies in place for successful checks. Initially these checks were at least daily, and the schedule of checking gradually faded to a variable interval schedule at a rate dependent on each student's success. Once on a variable interval schedule, the responsibility for the checks was trans-ferred to the teachers. When a student reached a level of mastery with these checks, the home and school contingencies were transferred to reports of completing and turning in work and ultimately were transferred to grades. This process transfers the contingencies from labor-intensive contingencies that are outside those that occur naturally (daily desk checks) to those that most parents deliver regularly (in response to grades). In addition, the focus of the contingencies shifts from the pro-cess of achieving good grades (keeping things organized) to the product of achiev-ing good grades. Clearly there are other factors that contribute to poor grades be-sides organizational systems; however, this example was included to demonstrate how this process can work with one of the factors.

As a result of systems such as the desk checks, counselors can sensitize teach-ers and parents to the target behaviors. This sensitization can lead to greater mon-itoring which alone is likely to modify the social contingencies. As adults focus on specific behaviors exhibited by children, they are likely to increase their praise and criticism of successes and failures. In addition, many adults will increase their prompting and coaching when counselors are communicating with them regularly about a certain behavior. This specific counselor–parent/counselor–teacher com-munication is one mechanism for modifying social contingencies.

The use of daily or weekly report cards is another tool that can be used to mod-ify contingencies. This technique has been described in the treatment literature for youth with ADHD (Evans, Vallano, & Pelham, 1995) and has been part of the psy-chosocial interventions provided in many treatment outcome studies (e.g., Wells et al., 2000). This technique has been used in elementary and secondary schools and begins with the counselor working with the student, parents, and teachers to identify and operationalize three or four goals. Teachers rate the student's progress on these goals on either a daily or a weekly basis and these ratings go home to par-ents. The student's parents are expected to use privileges and other potential rein-forcers or punishment (e.g., allowance, bedtime, television viewing) contingently based on the teacher ratings. This process results in parents transforming non-contingent privileges and tangibles to contingencies operating to modify school behavior.

Access and influence over the social contingencies in the school environment provides a valuable clinical tool to school-based clinicians for both assessment and intervention. Coupling strong behavioral expertise with strong collaboration and consultation skills will lead to a clinician with tremendous ability to improve the functioning of children and adolescents. All of these interventions require care-ful assessment of contingencies that shape the motivation of students. Hypothesis generation and testing are integral parts of each of the interventions reviewed and others that take similar advantage of the school setting. While creative manipula-tions of the contingencies in an environment that the clinician does not control are a significant challenge to the clinician, it is also an opportunity to greatly enhance the effectiveness of psychosocial interventions.

SUMMARY

Schools provide a unique opportunity to advance the field of psychosocial interventions by enabling clinicians to achieve levels of generalization that cannot be achieved in clinics. The research and clinical techniques described in this chapter refer to specific procedures that lead to generalization of behavior gains. It is important to note that these gains are not achieved by simply locating services within a school, but successful generalization requires the active collaboration of clinicians, educators, and parents, and shared responsibility for interventions. It is also important to note that many of the interventions described in this chapter are facilitated by clinicians but not implemented by them. Teachers, peers, and parents provide many of the naturally occurring social contingencies that children experience every day; therefore, they are central to the implementation of most successful techniques for generalization. The disadvantage of these procedures is that they do not match well with third-party payers' fee schedules; therefore, school-based mental health programs that are funded through third-party payers may have trouble implementing many of these techniques.

Generalization is an area that is critical to advancing our field but still receives little attention in the research literature and graduate training programs. School-based mental health models of care have the opportunity to emphasize this advantage to gain funding leverage and to increase their role in the mental health field. Research and outcome measurements are needed to identify this relative advantage over clinic-based care. Behavior change within treatment sessions has been relatively easy to achieve. It is time for us to increase our focus on behavior change in the hallways, homes, school buses, neighborhoods, and classrooms of children. School-based models of care will greatly enhance our efforts to accomplish this goal.

REFERENCES

Allen, J. S., Jr., Tarnowski, K. J., Simonian, S. J., Elliott, D., & Drabman, R. S. (1991). The generalization map revisited: Assessment of generalized treatment effects in child and adolescent behavior therapy. *Behavior Therapy, 22*, 393–405.

Anderson, C. G., Rush, D., Ayllon, T., & Kandel, H. (1987). Training and generalization of social skills with problem children. *Journal of Child and Adolescent Psychology, 4*(4), 294–298.

Berg, W., Wacker, D., Ebbers, B., Wiggins, B., Fowler, M., & Wilkes, P. (1995). A demonstration of generalization of performance across settings, materials, and motor responses for students with profound mental retardation. *Behavior Modification, 19*, 119–143.

Bierman, K. L., & Furman, W. (1984). The effects of social skills training and peer involvement on the social adjustment of preadolescents. *Child Development, 55*, 151–162.

Brantley, D. C., & Webster, R. E. (1993). Use of an independent group contingency management system in a regular classroom setting. *Psychology in the Schools, 37*(2), 60–66.

Broussard, C., & Northup, J. (1997). The use of functional analysis to develop peer interventions for disruptive classroom behavior. *School Psychology Quarterly, 12*(1), 65–76.

Buehler, R. E., Patterson, G. R., & Furniss, J. M. (1966). The reinforcement of behavior in institutional settings. *Behavior Research and Therapy, 4*, 157–167.

Christopher, J. S., Hansen, D. J., & MacMillan, V. M. (1991). Effectiveness of a peer-helper intervention to increase children's social interactions: Generalization, maintenance, and social validation. *Behavior Modification, 15*(1), 22–50.

Clark, L. A., & McKenzie, H. S. (1989). Effects of self-evaluation training of seriously emotionally disturbed children on the generalization of their classroom rule following and work behavior across settings and teachers. *Behavioral Disorders, 14*(2), 89–98.

Clarke, G., Lewinsohn, P., & Hops, H. (1990). *Leader's manual for adolescent groups: Adolescent coping with depression course.* Retrieved February 8, 2002, from http://www.kpchr.org/.

Clees, T. J. (1994). Self-recording of students' daily schedules of teachers' expectations: Perspectives on reactivity, stimulus control, and generalization. *Exceptionality, 5*(3), 113–129.

Cowen, E. L., Pederson, A., Babigian, H., Izzo, L. D., & Trost, M. A. (1973). Long-term follow-up of early detected vulnerable children. *Journal of Consulting and Clinical Psychology, 41*(3), 438–446.

Davies, S., & Witte, R. (2000). Self-management and peer-monitoring within a group contingency to decrease uncontrolled verbalizations of children with attention-deficit/hyperactivity disorder. *Psychology in the Schools, 37*(2), 135–147.

Dodge, K. A. (1983). Behavioral antecedents of peer social status. *Child Development, 54,* 1386–1399.

Douglas, V. I. (1983). Attentional and cognitive problems. In M. Rutter (Ed.), *Developmental neuropsychiatry* (pp. 280–329). New York: Guilford Press.

Drabman, R. S., Hammer, D., & Rosenbaum, M. S. (1979). Assessing generalization in behavior modification with children: The generalization map. *Behavioral Assessment, 1.*

Edelstein, B. A. (1989). Generalization: Terminological, methodological, and conceptual issues. *Behavior Therapy, 20,* 311–324.

Ervin, R., Radford, P. M., Bertsch, K., Piper, A. L., Ehrhardt, K. E., & Poling, A. (2001). A descriptive analysis and critique of the empirical literature on school-based functional assessment. *School Psychology Review, 30,* 193–210.

Evans, S. W. (1999). Mental health services in schools: Utilization, effectiveness, and consent. *Clinical Psychology Review, 19*(2), 165–178.

Evans, S. W. (in press). *Challenging horizons program: Treatment manual.* Unpublished manuscript.

Evans, S. W., Axelrod, J. L., & Langberg, J. (2002). Efficacy of a school-based treatment program for middle school youth with ADHD: Pilot data. *Behavior Modification.*

Evans, S. W., Axelrod, J. L., & Sapia, J. L. (2000). Effective school-based interventions: Advancing the social skills training paradigm. *Journal of School Health, 70*(5), 191–194.

Evans, S. W., Vallano, G., & Pelham, W. E. (1995). Attention-deficit hyperactivity disorder. In V. B. Van Hasselt & M. Hersen (Eds.), *Handbook of adolescent psychopathology. A guide to diagnosis and treatment* (pp. 589–617). New York: Lexington Books.

Foxx, R. M., McMorrow, M. J., Bittle, R., & Ness, J. (1986). An analysis of social skills generalization in two natural settings. *Journal of Applied Behavior Analysis, 19,* 299–305.

Foxx, R. M., McMorrow, M. J., & Schloss, C. N. (1983). Stacking the deck: Teaching social skills to retarded adults with a modified table game. *Journal of Applied Behavior Analysis, 16,* 157–170.

Gregory, K. M., Kehle, T. J., & McLoughlin, C. S. (1997). Generalization and maintenance of treatment gains using self-management procedures with behaviorally disordered adolescents. *Psychological Reports, 80,* 683–690.

Gresham, F. M., Watson, T. S., & Skinner, C. H. (2001). Functional behavioral assessment: Principles, procedures, and future directions. *School Psychology Review, 30,* 156–172.

Guevremont, D. C., MacMillan, V. M., Shawchuck, C. R., & Hansen, D. J. (1989). A peer-medicated intervention with clinic-referred socially isolated girls: Generalization, maintenance, and social validation. *Behavior Modification, 13*(1), 32–50.

Hatch, J. A. (1987). Peer interaction and the development of social competence. *Child Study Journal, 17*(3), 169–183.

Herring, M., & Northup, J. (1998). The generalization of social skills for a child with behavior disorders in the school setting. *Child and Family Behavior Therapy, 20*(3), 51–66.

Hollinger, J. D. (1987). Social skills for behaviorally disordered children as preparation for mainstreaming: Theory, practice, and new directions. *Remedial and Special Education, 8*(4), 17–27.

Kazdin, A. E., & Weisz, J. R. (1998). Identifying and developing empirically supported child and adolescent treatments. *Journal of Consulting and Clinical Psychology, 66,* 19–36.

Kohler, F. W., & Greenwood, C. R. (1986). Toward a technology of generalization: The identification of natural contingencies of reinforcement. *The Behavior Analyst, 9,* 19–26.

Kollins, S. H., Lane, S. D., & Shapiro, S. K. (1997). Experimental analysis of childhood psychopathology: A laboratory matching analysis of the behavior of children diagnosed with attention-deficit hyperactivity disorder (ADHD). *The Psychological Record, 47,* 25–44.

Langhorne, J., Clees, T. J., Oxford, M., Malone, M., & Ross, G. (1995). Acquisition and generalization of social skills by high school students with mild mental retardation. *Mental Retardation, 33*, 186–196.

Mathur, S. R., & Rutherford, R. B., Jr. (1996). Is social skills training effective for students with emotional or behavioral disorders? Research issues and needs. *Behavioral Disorders, 22*(1), 21–28.

Murray, L. K., & Kollins, S. H. (2000). Effects of methylphenidate on sensitivity to reinforcement in children diagnosed with attention deficit hyperactivity disorder: An application of the matching law. *Journal of Applied Behavior Analysis, 33*, 573–591.

Nevin, A., Johnson, D. W., & Johnson, R. (1982). Effects of group and individual contingencies on academic performance and social relations of special needs students. *The Journal of Social Psychology, 116*, 41–59.

Odom, S. L., Strain, P. S., Karger, M. A., & Smith, J. D. (1986). Using single and multiple peers to promote social interactions of preschool children with handicaps. *Journal of the Division of Early Childhood, 10*, 53–64.

O'Neill, R., Horner, R., Albin, R., Sprague, J., Storey, K., & Newton, J. (1997). *Functional assessment and program development for problem behavior* (2nd ed.). New York: Brooks/Cole.

Peterson, L. D., Young, K. R., West, R. P., & Peterson, M. H. (1999). Effects of student self-management on generalization of student performance to regular classrooms. *Education and Treatment of Children, 22*(3), 357–372.

Roca, J. V., & Gross, A. M. (1996). Report-do-report: Promoting setting and setting-time generalization. *Education and Treatment of Children, 19*(4), 408–424.

Rutter, M. (1982). Psychological therapies in child psychiatry: Issues and prospects. *Psychological Medicine, 12*, 723–740.

Sasso, G. M., Melloy, K. J., & Kavale, K. A. (1990). Generalization, maintenance, and behavioral covariation associated with social skills training through structured learning. *Behavioral Disorder, 16*(1), 9–22.

Skinner, C. H., Cashwell, T. H., & Skinner, A. L. (2000). Increasing tootling: The effects of a peer-monitored group contingency program on students' reports of peer's prosocial behaviors. *Psychology in the Schools, 37*(3), 263–270.

Solomon, R., & Wahler, R. (1973). Peer reinforcement control of classroom problem behavior. *Journal of Applied Behavioral Analysis, 6*, 49–56.

Sterling-Turner, H. E., Robinson, S. L., & Wilczynski, S. M. (2001). Functional assessment of distracting and disruptive behaviors in the school setting. *School Psychology Review, 30*, 211–226.

Stokes, T. F., & Baer, D. M. (1977). An implicit technology of generalization. *Journal of Applied Behavior Analysis, 10*(2), 349–367.

Stokes, T. F., & Osnes, P. G. (1989). An operant pursuit of generalization. *Behavior Therapy, 20*, 337–355.

Tisdelle, D. A., & St. Lawrence, J. S. (1988). Adolescent interpersonal problem-solving skill training: Social validation and generalization. *Behavior Therapy, 19*, 171–182.

Wahler, R. G. (1967). Child–child interactions in free field settings: Some experimental analyses. *Journal of Experimental Child Psychology, 5*, 278–293.

Weiss, B., Catron, T., Harris, V., & Phung, T. M. (1999). The effectiveness of traditional child therapy. *Journal of Consulting and Clinical Psychology, 67*(1), 82–94.

Weist, M. D. (1997). Expanded school mental health services: A national movement in progress. In T. H. Ollendick & R. J. Prinz (Eds.), *Advances in clinical child psychology*. New York: Plenum Press.

Weisz, J. R., Weiss, B., Han, S. S., Granger, D. A., & Morton, T. (1995). Effects of psychotherapy with children and adolescents revisited: A meta-analysis of treatment outcome studies. *Psychological Bulletin, 117*(3), 450–468.

Wells, K. C., Pelham, W. E., Kotkin, R. A., Hoza, B., Abikoff, H. B., Abramowitz, A. J., Arnold, D. S., Cantwell, D., Conners, C. K., DelCarmen, R., Elliott, G., Greenhill, L. L., Hechtman, L., Swanson, J. M., & Schiller, E. (2000). Psychosocial treatment strategies in the MTA study: Rationale, methods, and critical issues in design and implementation. *Journal of Abnormal Child Psychology, 28*(6), 483–505.

24

Cultural Sensitivity, Relevance, and Competence in School Mental Health

MATTHEW R. MOCK

A PERSONAL, CHILDHOOD STORY OF ILLNESS, WELLNESS, AND CULTURAL COMPETENCY

As a young boy, I remember becoming instantly aware of cultural practices in maintaining maximum health in my own Chinese American family. When I came down with the mumps at age 4, my more traditional Chinese mother toted me off to an apothecary in the heart of Chinatown. Standing up on the tip of my toes, barely tall enough to see above the glass counter, I could see bins of carefully laid ginseng root, dried seahorses, preserved plums, and finely pressed leaves. I observed the elder Chinese herbalist carefully placing selected ingredients from wooden bins on different sheets of paper upon which he then wrote directions. In Cantonese, I heard this expert herbalist emphatically tell my mother how to prepare the poultice and then wrap my face when we arrived home to bring down the swelling from the mumps.

Following his every instruction, my mother prepared the salve in a mortar and pestle and carefully applied it to my face and upper body. Born in America and more acculturated than my parents, I remember thinking back then that if there were not something actually curative in the black, pastelike mixture adorning my face for consecutive days, surely the smell and itchy feel of this stuff would make me mentally will myself to get better! I also remember feeling too embarrassed and ashamed to tell any of my neighborhood friends and schoolmates, most of whom were non-Asian, that my parents had ever even thought of this traditional Chinese cure. What would the school nurse say about this folk remedy? How would

MATTHEW R. MOCK • Department of Health and Human Services, Berkeley Mental Health, Family, Youth, and Children's Services, Berkeley, California 94704.

my teacher respond? Would the principal call in social service authorities? Now, several decades later as a practitioner, professor, and father, I have great curiosity about the medicinal elements that made the salve so soothing and able to cure my childhood ailment (Mock, 2000, in press). In some ways, cultural sensitivity, relevancy, and competency in school mental health means looking towards the future. But in other ways it may really mean recovering what we may have known all along but had not put into continuous practice.

THE URGENCY FOR CULTURAL SENSITIVITY, RELEVANCY, AND COMPETENCE IN SCHOOLS

Consistently emerging realities highlight the need to address ethnic and cultural diversity through school mental health programs. The first is the rapidly changing demographics in the United States. As of the year 2000, approximately one-third of the U.S. population is composed of people of color. Demographic projections indicate that within the next decade, there will be no majority group in this country. Students of color are already the majority in some of the largest states (e.g., California, Texas, New York). In fact, ethnic minorities are now the majority in California—representing 51% of the entire state with other states predicted to follow (U.S. Census Bureau, 2001).

Second, the number of individuals in the United States who are foreign-born rose to 19.8 million in 1990. These individuals come from over 100 different countries. There are over 11 million immigrants working in America already, with a steady increase in population anticipated (Hall, 1997; Johnson & Mock, 2000). Latinos in particular are changing the face of California, and this may portend what lies ahead nationwide. Reports have indicated that close to 60% of children aged 5 and under in California are Latino or Hispanic (Hayes-Bautista, 2001).

Third, nationwide, students of color are a steadily growing percentage of the public school population. According to the U.S. Department of Education (1997), percentages of students of color grew from 22% in 1974 to 36% in 1997. The percentages in 1997 were as follows: 64% White, 17% African American, 14% Latino, 4% Asian American and Pacific Islander (AAPI), and 1% Native American. Compared to 1974, Whites decreased by 14%, Native Americans remained the same at 1%, AAPIs increased by 3%, African Americans increased by 2%, and Latinos increased by 8%.

Last, students of color encounter specific risk factors. For one, there are growing racial disparities in school suspensions. In 1974, students of color represented 22% of the population yet 34% of suspensions. Similarly, in 1997, thirty-six percent of students were individuals of color yet comprised 49% of suspensions. Perhaps more alarming is the fact that 29.4% of 16- to 24-year-old students of color were neither enrolled in school nor had completed high school as of October 1996. Even college-qualified students of color are less likely than their White counterparts to go on to attend a 4-year college (Applied Research Center, 2000). In contrast to students, teachers in the United States remain vastly White at 88% of the total work force. In Los Angeles, California, while 70% of enrolled students are Latino—some with limited English skills—only 22% of teachers are Latino. In maximizing learning opportunities for students, linguistic and cultural understanding likely play a positive role (Applied Research Center, 2000). The aforementioned facts contribute to some of the stressors in school settings and emphasize the need for more appropriate cultural and linguistic teaching and interventions.

The need for cultural competence in health and mental health settings, including schools, is clear. In fact, cultural competency is now included in guidelines, service principles, and mandates. In June 1998, President Clinton ordered sweeping protection for all Medicare beneficiaries. These Medicare rules, viewed as stricter than the standards governing commercial health insurance, include the following requirement: "Health plans must provide services in a culturally competent manner to all Medicare patients including those with limited English proficiency or reading skills, diverse cultural and ethnic backgrounds and physical or mental disabilities" (Pear, 1998, p. A1). The American Psychological Association and American Medical Association also have each published comprehensive cultural competence recommendations for all psychologists and physicians (American Psychological Association (APA), 1993).

A WORKING DEFINITION OF CULTURAL COMPETENCY IN SCHOOLS

In their widely cited monograph, Cross et al. (1989) define cultural competence as a set of congruent practice skills, behaviors, attitudes, and policies that come together in ways that enable professionals to work effectively in cross-cultural situations. Hence, culturally competent service delivery in schools would include the following aspects: (1) acknowledges and incorporates at all levels the importance of culture, (2) provides an assessment of cross-cultural relations, (3) is vigilant of the dynamics that result from cultural differences, (4) engages in the expansion of cultural knowledge, and (5) provides an adaptation of services to meet culturally unique needs (Cross et al., 1989). Cultural competency may be viewed as the integration and transformation of knowledge and observations about children, their families, and their specific communities into specific standards, skills, and service approaches that match the child's or family's culture. By adopting culturally competent practices, professionals working in schools can increase the probability that students reach successful outcomes (Johnson & Mock, 2000; Mock, in press).

Cultural competency in school mental health is not a new concept but one with emerging levels of complexity. Different from other concepts of absolute achievement or attainment, cultural competency in schools and in other human service settings is viewed along a continuum—from cultural destructiveness, cultural blindness, cultural precompetence, fundamental cultural competence, and advanced cultural competence, to cultural proficiency (Cross et al., 1989).

While working definitions of cultural competency in community venues have been available for more than a decade, the implementation, measurement, and attainment of cultural competency in clinical practice have been more elusive. It may be argued that cultural competency is a relative concept. That is, unlike other standards to be attained such as licensure or certification, cultural competency is an ongoing process and a dynamic, constantly changing one. In this way, it is possible that a mental health professional working at a school may seem culturally competent at one specific moment but culturally incompetent at another.

A student or family's language, cultural set, or world-view may necessitate the need to implement additional strategies to reach for cultural competency. Cultural competence is not a linear concept so that once a practitioner or service system seemingly attains it, it always remains. In fact, the opposite has been argued: there must be constant efforts to provide and maintain culturally and linguistically responsive and effective mental health services.

Cultural competency imperatives and mandates in school mental health clinical practices can be used to inform and drive the system. Until cultural sensitivity, relevancy of services, and cultural competency are fully understood and embraced, culturally appropriate services may be lacking for increasingly diverse communities within schools. An understanding and appreciation of services that culturally *exclude* contrasted to school-based mental health services that culturally *include* are highly relevant. What follows are a description of both exclusive and inclusive mental health practices and the author's stance of culturally responsive and effective mental health care in schools.

CULTURAL EXCLUSION OR MARGINALIZATION IN SCHOOL MENTAL HEALTH PROGRAMS

School mental health programs that fail to fully address cultural competence often have processes and replicate dynamics that lead to marginalization or exclusion of student consumers and families. While some of these exclusionary processes may seem obvious, sometimes they operate on more subtle levels. Defining and describing some of these processes may elucidate some of the school-based mental health practices that are exclusionary. They fall short of the goal of cultural competency. It should be noted that these processes of exclusion might operate simultaneously and to different degrees.

At one time or another, service providers in schools might all engage in what is referred to as "acts or designs of omission" or "designing services for only a few" (Kunisawa, 1998; Mock, in press). Acts of omission refer to values, items, or actions that are left out, kept separate, or put in a lower status. One high school-based mental health program, served an increasingly culturally and ethnically diverse adolescent student body. When teenagers of different cultural backgrounds came to the health center for counseling, there were few portrayals of them in the waiting room (e.g., posters, handouts, or psychoeducational materials). Beyond just the clinic setting, language also plays a role in client comfort with services. With more diverse families, especially Latino families, there may be a lack of adequate access when there are not specific Spanish-speaking outreach efforts. Having Spanish-speaking capability within school mental health programs can help improve access and level of comfort with services. The same clinic had no bilingual materials visible for students.

Another example of practices that exclude can be found in the following experience. Parents were asked to call a central number within the school system to access mental health services. In the initial assessment, neither cultural nor economic issues were taken into account. In one school district there were fewer inquiries from African American families than had been expected, given their proportion within the population. The interpretation by the school administration was that the African American community did not seem to be interested in obtaining academic support services, including mental health. Therefore, this system was designed only to be accessible to parents who have phone access, were willing to articulate their child's problems in this impersonal way, and were amenable to trust a professional who they could not see. The culturally insensitive conclusion that these students and parents had minimal educational and psychological needs was brought into question by culturally responsive mental health consultants. Recommendations were made to outreach in more community-based settings culturally relevant to the local African American community, including churches, community-based, multiservice programs, and school youth programs. More respectful and relevant information was disseminated in person and in less stigmatizing community settings such as local churches. Groups for grandparents raising their grandchildren were also started at the school.

Mental health professionals may also collude with omissions, marginalizations, and potentially "blaming the victim" through the way they view problems presented by students in school-based mental health settings. One example of this has to do with psychiatric diagnosis using the *Diagnostic and Statistical Manual* (DSM-IV; APA, 1994). In utilizing the DSM-IV multiaxial system, Axis IV requires clinicians to identify psychosocial stressors that contribute to a child's or family's current mental health problem or diagnosis. While racism, oppression, various forms of discrimination, and the cycle of poverty especially for single mothers are certainly stressors, they are grossly underutilized on Axis IV when diagnosing individuals, including children in schools. The author observed one clinician argue that since all minorities face some level of discrimination, there is no need to list the obvious (Mock, 1999). Yet another counselor working in school contended that stressors were only needed to be current ones related to the immediate problem of the child, not enduring conditions. One school administrator even protested that racism or discrimination played little role in students' lives, including education. These are examples of how practitioners may perpetuate "acts of omission" in schools.

Other culturally incompetent acts include processes in which we "take away the voice of the other." The vast majority of Americans began at one time as "strangers from a different shore" (Mock, 1998a; Takaki, 1989). That is, most of our ancestors emigrated from other countries. Processes of assimilation and acculturation lead to questions about who we are and/or what we value. As socialization processes occur in schools, students often feel pressure to conform to a majority standard in the way they speak, dress, and behave (Fine, 1991; Wright, 1998). One's "voice" is central to one's convictions, representation of views, and self-construction. Therefore, a "taking away of voice" can be seen as a metaphor: when a "majority" group is being represented, this is what gets referenced or internalized as preferred, desired, is treated as better than, etc., by those who have "minority" status. Removal of "voice" places the locus of control externally (Sue, 1998). Clinically, especially for children and their families, this often entails a deleterious process of giving up something valued by less-represented individuals.

Practitioners in school-based mental health programs may engage in acts where there is a "pretending we are all the same." While there are relative truisms to this (e.g., all human beings bleed and can feel joy and pain), there are conditions certainly among children and their families in which people are richly different. For example, in early versions of the DSM, there were general diagnostic categories given with no mention of culture. Now in the DSM-IV (APA, 1994), there are provisions for culturally based symptoms and syndromes. For example, there is Chi Gong Psychosis (Chinese), Fallen Awatick (American Indian), and Ataque or Mal de Nervios (Latino).

The preceding have been descriptions of exclusionary or marginalizing acts or processes in school-based mental health programs. They contribute to cultural incompetency, insensitivity, and disrespectfulness. Fortunately there are alternative processes or stances that can contribute to greater cultural sensitivity, relevancy, and effectiveness in outcomes in school-based mental health programs.

CULTURAL INCLUSION, INTEGRATION, AND RESPECTFULNESS IN SCHOOL MENTAL HEALTH PROGRAMS

One initial, basic premise in establishing and providing culturally competent mental health services in schools is that we *all possess culture*. Some of us are more distant from or close to our cultural heritages of origin. Culture defines who we are not just by race, culture, class, sexual orientation, or gender but by faith or spiritual backgrounds, abilities, and disabilities or even if we grew up in rural or urban settings. Some studies (Sue, 1998; Vega et al., 1998) are beginning to indicate that holding on to one's culture—through customs, traditions, roles, and relationships among family members—may actually be a protective factor. Assuming this perspective of culture being connected to survival, if our survival is threatened we either "take flight or fight." In working in schools with children and their families from different cultures, even opening up a conversation about how one's culture has been a source of grounding information or survival leads to many opportunities to talk about identity, family, community, self in relation to others, etc. It can also open up difficult, yet often critical conversations, about experiences of discrimination, unequal treatment, and oppression in schools or in the community.

Practitioners in school mental health programs might also include an understanding of how legacies of oppression may still impact the lives of the children and adolescents served. Collaborations between teachers, administrators, and mental health practitioners can produce educational discussions and therapeutic interventions useful to students. School rivalries of opposing gangs or groups, such as Southeast Asian and Latino, for example, have been deescalated by acknowledging their histories and shared backgrounds. Historical injustices, such as slavery, the Holocaust, Japanese internment, antigay movements, hate crimes against those perceived as Muslim or Middle Eastern, or gay or lesbian, have not gone away. Some psychologists (Boyd-Franklin, 1989; Carter, 1995; Hardy, 1994) have discussed the continual residuals of slavery for African Americans in such processes as psychological homelessness and trying to cope with marginalization, especially among teens through violence or use of drugs. Hardy (1994) describes a cycle among African American teenagers that, if not addressed and interrupted by mental health practitioners, violence may be the final outcome. Subtle and overt racism encountered by African Americans, for example, may be experienced as frustrations or microaggressions at minimum. If these are not allowed expression they may lead to anger. If the anger is not channeled into appropriate outlets there may be heightened or cumulative anger. If this is not given an outlet, the rage with the continued, unattended injustices may be expressed as violence either directed at oneself or at someone else. For young people, especially latency-age children and teenagers, school-based programs may be ideal to proactively address these potentially destructive dynamics. A psychoeducational approach can open meaningful dialogue and serve as a prevention strategy to stop violence. Supporting cultural connectedness may also protect teenagers from societal risks (Vega et al., 1998).

Another important and culturally respectful perspective that a school-based mental health provider might consider in working with students who are culturally different is understanding that multiple oppressions are traumatic and insidious. In her important work on the sequelae of trauma and recovery, Judith Herman (1992) describes some of the impact of traumatic experiences and potential interventions. Racist acts experienced by children whether they are verbal or physical can certainly be argued as being forms of violence along the continuum. However, even though they should be treated as traumatic, verbal epithets even when degrading, disrespectful, and repeated are often not treated as potential forms of violence. Clinicians often try to explore potential roots or the original trauma leading to the current problem presentation. Providers in schools must be willing to look at the trauma of racism, sexism, homophobia, and inequalities that still exist in some schools and surrounding communities. This would be a major contribution to breaking the cycle of inappropriate educational placement or overincarceration of ethnic youth.

In school-based mental health programs, it is important to understand and perhaps even impart a strategy of "bicultural competency." All children and teenagers exist in multiple contexts. For example, some Latino children may come from homes highly Latino in cultural representation. However, in their schools they may find very little of their culture reflected, including lack of classes taught bilingually in Spanish. It may be an important strategy to acknowledge the cultural cues and values in specific contexts. For example, among some minority youth, certain behaviors or manner of dress might be different among one's peers or close circle of friends rather than in front of police or school authorities. With evidence that some authorities might stop certain teenagers who wear certain color clothing or frequent certain areas, adolescents who do not want to be stopped might be helped to understand what portrayed attitudes or perspectives they might adapt in order to avoid such confrontations and stay out of trouble. Schools and school-based mental health programs are fertile grounds for this kind of education and intervention.

As a contribution to community healing, people from all cultures must look deeply into our abilities to share collective grief, shame, and loss. The events of September 2001 certainly underline this. As has been said: "Racism, getting sick wasn't our fault, but getting well is our responsibility" (anonymous source). While racism was not any one of our creations, there must be an understanding of how individuals might perpetuate its existence. For culturally competent mental health practitioners in all settings including schools, this means acknowledging ways people are more privileged or have more power or influence than others. All individuals have been targets of mistreatment to differing degrees and in different ways at one time or another in our lives. In fact, even clinicians may have been unintentional perpetrators of such injustices. There must be an owning of these circumstances or acts and an ability to share sadness and shame in order to move on to a better place and work more effectively with students and families.

Last, in developing culturally inclusive and respectful mental health services in schools, providers might also remember that solutions to problems often emanate from the family and surrounding community. That is, sources of healing are in the children and families served. Many marginalized communities have endured a series of challenges, even assaults, yet they have survived and in ways, have even thrived. Tapping into these sources of resiliency and survival, while being engaged in a process to additionally empower these families or communities, may be the most important sources of culturally competent services in school programs.

CULTURAL COMPETENCY IN SCHOOL MENTAL HEALTH AS A PRACTITIONER STANCE

One major perspective in moving practitioners and mental health systems in schools toward cultural competency is a proposed stance in working with children who are culturally different from oneself. This is a stance with the *power of not knowing* (Mock, in press). It is important to understand what it means to be in a power position in the therapeutic relationship with children and their parents and how to best appreciate this, especially when assisting those often marginalized (Pinderhughes, 1988). Rather than entering into a therapeutic relationship with a child and family in a school setting with a fixed or set knowledge base of any culture, it is more informed for the practitioner to hold any knowledge base in a relative way for comparison. After all, "In some ways we are like some persons, like all persons and like no other persons" (Kluckhohn & Strodtbeck, 1961). Rather than an absolutist "knowing," a practitioner striving toward cultural competency may be more effective in taking a respectful stance of naiveté and curiosity (Dyche & Zayas, 1995).

Children and their parents are often called upon in school settings when their children are not performing up to par academically or when there are attendance and behavioral problems. Given this already "one down" position of families, a stance that conveys respectful inquiry or even humility in cultural knowledge may be engaging. In other words, while school-based therapists have something to impart, entering into a relationship accepting that they first need to be educated about the particular family and its unique cultural nuances can forge a strong working relationship.

Cultural competency and effectiveness in school-based mental health programs also require degrees of establishing credibility and giving (Sue, 1998; Sue & Zane, 1987). Psychotherapists are credible when we are believed and can establish trust and an ability to effect change. Credibility is established through a provider's degrees, track record to help improve a child's academic performance or social skills, or endorsement by others treated. Rather than an amorphous process, ethnic minority children and families may benefit from specific giving of homework, behavioral intervention, direct instruction, realistic hope for improvement, and linkage to other school and community services.

While psychotherapists in schools may possess great knowledge, working with others who are ethnically or culturally diverse may mean facilitating well-timed discussions about differences (Mock, 1999). As stated earlier, the therapeutic relationship in a school may be used as an example of overall power imbalances experienced by the child and family. Anything brought up by students and families in the counseling room can be used as a source of discussion, leading to greater awareness, insight, or needed analysis. When a discourse about differences unfolds this is a clinical opportunity to not just be "politically correct" but to address the issue in a "personally compassionate" (G. Masuda, personal communication, July 15, 1998) or "professionally committed" manner. Mental health practitioners in school settings are often trained and committed to providing services—whether it be psychotherapy, psychological testing, or teacher consultation to improve the human condition. Clearly, parts of the human condition experienced in society are our racial and cultural differences with inequities based in these differences.

For many practitioners, working in school mental health and in the community, adopting a stance of contributing to social justice through cultural competence can have a broad impact (Mock, 1999). On a broad level, practitioners working in schools are recommended to adapt the following practice strategies when striving to reach cultural competency:

- Examine the foundations of education and psychology in relation to dominant forces of race, culture, class, sexual orientation, gender, faith, abilities, etc.
- Critique psychological and related educational research and therapeutic models in relation to cultural factors and biases as they have impacted minority communities.
- Address the significance of acknowledging cultural differences, broadly defined, in the therapeutic relationship with children and families.
- Consider the power of the therapeutic role, how it comes into play in work in the schools, and how it can be made a part of the therapeutic work.

On an individual level, school mental health practitioners may strive to be more culturally sensitive, relevant, and competent through the following committed actions:

- Acknowledge the influences of our own world-view and how we are shaped by our own family backgrounds and society.
- Understand not only the differences in human interaction but also the roles that societal forces embedded in race, culture, class, and power have played in society.
- Adopt a therapeutic stance of informed naiveté, of respect for cultural differences, curiosity, and of humility when working with children and families from different cultural backgrounds.
- Accept children and families as co-collaborators of change within the therapeutic process.
- Be aware of prejudices and stereotypes that can lead to certain impasses and hinder the therapeutic process.

- Appreciate the fact that working toward cultural competency is an ongoing and dynamic process. It entails a continuous, active learning process and consultation.
- Translate conceptual ideas into actual clinical behaviors. Strive to work effectively with all children treated at schools including linguistically or culturally different children.

As providers of mental health services in schools, there is work to be done in the larger institutional context of education. In these schools, mental health practitioners can also take on several challenges in advocating for the inclusion of cultural sensitivity, relevance, and competency. Organizational/agency recommendations for culturally sensitive and competent services include the following:

- Address systemic inequities and flaws in effective education and related mental health concerns with ethnic communities as well as with marginalized or underrepresented groups.
- Promote an inclusive, rather than exclusive, school environment through adopting mission and service statements, developing linguistic and cultural capability, having culturally responsive accessibility, and culturally representative staffing.
- Involve and continue to empower diverse communities through advocacy and accountability.
- Integrate and infuse multicultural efforts throughout the school so that there is a deeper change process within all existing structures and at all levels of the school from administration, to support staff, to clinicians.
- Strive toward cultural competency, knowing that sustained progress must be made through institutionalized changes.

ADDITIONAL SPECIFIC APPLICATIONS OF CULTURAL COMPETENCE IN SCHOOLS

The high dropout rate and academic failure among racial minority children have been longstanding concerns (Boyd-Franklin, 1989; Fine, 1991; Wright, 1998). Debates on black English, social and behavioral problems, motivation, and intelligence of African American children continue. The dropout rates of specific groups, for example, Latinos, especially Latina teenagers, remain a serious problem. Minority students and their parents may feel an increasing sense of alienation and anger toward schools (Boyd-Franklin, 1989; Falicov, 1998; Wright, 1998). One of the potential contributors to the dropout rate among Latinos may be the incompatibility between school and home in primary languages spoken, social values, or even cognitive and relational styles. With at least two sets of cultural expectations or codes to adhere to, there may be conflict or confusion for Latino children in schools (Falicov, 1998; Kiselica et al., 1995). The parents and teachers may experience dissonance in understanding each other. Latino or Asian American families, that place importance on education and family, for example, may need help in both linguistic and conceptual understanding and having a place to confer where respect is at a premium. A bilingual, bicultural therapist can help serve in this capacity and as a positive role model (Kiselica et al., 1995) for the adolescent and their family. This can serve to validate the bicultural experience and can provide opportunities for narratives underlying conflicts.

One of the primary efforts of culturally responsive intervention models in schools is to have mental health staff work actively with families having difficulties in schools. There should be proactive outreach. In the African American community, for example, linking with church groups, community leaders, and youth organizations can help circumvent problems in schools. When African American students, for example, come to the attention of the school for problems in behaviors or learning, it is critical that the students and their parents have a trusted voice to represent their points of view and help them negotiate an otherwise daunting, sometimes overpowering school process. Many schools have a student study or success team (SST) to discuss at-risk, problem students. To have an African American mental health professional as a member of such a school team can facilitate a child's getting back on track by making certain the child's and parents' voices are heard in a strength-based rather than in a pathological way. The process of reaffirming or reclaiming "voice" can make the school process less adversarial and more collaborative. Assisting minority children and families to feel more hopeful, reengaged, and empowered may also mean holding schools or classrooms more accountable (Wright, 1998). Therapists aware of individual development and group dynamics can serve in this key capacity especially if they can reflect the ethnic or linguistic identity of the family.

A *culturally sensitive and responsive* mental health professional has expertise in understanding behaviors in a cultural context with an interpretation that may make a difference between a child in schools being angry and defiant, for example, or more sullen and going through social adjustment. For instance, an elementary school girl was initially thought of as angry and defiant because she would not speak when addressed by her teacher and would turn away from peers. When a culturally responsive therapist was consulted, she found out that the family had emigrated from a Southeast Asian country. There were separation issues among family members still in Southeast Asia and, rather than being defiant, the girl was being more quiet out of respect and deference to authority. In this situation, the cross-cultural therapist had to be aware of not only nationality but also gender roles. Cultural competency in schools can play a key role in issues such as conflict resolution, teacher training, self-esteem building, or group interrelatedness.

A final, glaring example of the need for cultural competence in school interventions is exemplified in dealing with school-related traumas and critical incident stress interventions. Involvement of schools as essential sites for critical incident stress debriefings (CISD) for children and families has been well documented (Figley, 1985; Johnson, 1989; Nadar & Pynoos, 1993). Intensive clinical interventions in all phases of the trauma and aftermath as well as primary and secondary preventative efforts should be adapted to meet the cultural, diverse perspectives of the communities affected. Following the events of September 11, 2001, for example, there were different constructions of the violence, loss, and mourning for families that needed to be taken into account. Given the different faith communities and those associated by stereotyped appearances to the perpetrators of the terrorism, special outreach efforts were made to the Muslim communities and families from the Middle East. Dialogues were sensitively held by culturally representative and aware therapists in those communities to elicit their mental health and safety concerns. Schools for Muslim children became targets of hatred and threats. With many immigrant and refugee students and their families coming from countries in war or conflict, it was important for practitioners to be aware of some of those histories and reeruptions of posttraumatic stress experiences. Schools proved to be excellent sites for interventions. Families were brought together for education and support and were able to draw upon resources of schools and culturally representative mental health teams.

In large-scale situations such as those of the New York City twin towers attack, earthquakes, fires, floods, and mass school shootings, efforts to bring the communities together to process and work through the violence and losses are critical. Given the continuously increasing ethnic, cultural, racial, economic, and spiritual diversity of school communities, cultural competence and sensitivity should be interwoven and acknowledged throughout all clinical strategies including groups, parent involvement, educational outreach and skills building. Schools provide unique environments for culturally responsive interventions to children and families.

THE TRIPLE c-a-r-e MODEL OF CULTURAL COMPETENCY IN SCHOOL MENTAL HEALTH

In summarizing some of the primary elements of cultural competence in a school mental health program, this author proposes a "triple CARE" acronym model. This CARE–CARE–CARE (triple C-A-R-E) acronym model stands for words that have meaning first on the personal level of the provider, second on a professional level, and third on a systems or program level. Each of these must be viewed through a broad but well-understood cultural lens. On a personal level, the mental health practitioner should have the following: Compassion, Awareness, Respectfulness, and Empathy for the other. On a professional level, this same practitioner should culturally strive for the following: Competence, Assessment (of self and child/family) throughout, Responsiveness, and Effectiveness. Finally, on a systems level, school mental health programs should develop culturally competent services that are Coordinated and Committed, Accountable and Accessible, and Reflective and Responsible, and Evolving or Emerging continuously. To have cultural competence addressed in school mental health programs at all three levels provides multiple support with one level feeding back and enriching or supporting the others. It not only will impact the successful operation of clinical services but also may positively influence the school environment and atmosphere.

Adopting the triple C-A-R-E model in school mental health programs can lead to greater success in working with children and their families from diverse cultural and ethnic backgrounds. It can also make a significant contribution to a healthier, more engaging school environment based in equity and fairness. For many mental health practitioners, working in the community such as in school-based settings began through acts of social justice. For many it is also a lifelong process of giving continuously to the communities that originally taught and nurtured.

REFERENCES

American Psychiatric Association (1994). *Diagnostic and statistical manual of mental disorders* (4th ed.), Washington, DC: Author.

American Psychological Association (1993). Guidelines for providers of psychological services to ethnic, linguistic, and culturally diverse populations. *American Psychologist, 48,* 45–48.

Applied Research Center (2000). *Forty-six years after Brown vs. board of ed: Still separate, still unequal.* Oakland, CA: Author.

Boyd-Franklin, N. (1989). *Black families in therapy.* New York: Guilford Press.

California State Department of Mental Health (1997). *Required components for implementation plan: Cultural competence plan requirements* (Revised) (pp. 1–17). Sacramento. CA: Author.

Carter, R. (1995). *The influence of race and racial identity in psychotherapy: Toward a racially inclusive model.* New York: Wiley.

Cross, T. L., Bazron, B. J., Dennis, K. W., Isaacs, M. R., & Benjamin, M. P. (1989). *Towards a culturally competent system of care.* Washington, DC: CAASP Technical Assistance Center.

Dyche, L., & Zayas, L. (1995). The value of curiosity and naivete for the cross cultural therapist, *Family Process, 34,* 389–399.

Falicov, C. (1998). *Latino families in therapy: A guide to multicultural practice.* New York: Guilford Press.

Figley, C. R. (1985). *Trauma and its wake.* New York: Bruner Mazel.

Fine, M. (1991). Invisible flood: Notes on the politics of "dropping out" of an urban public high school. *Equity and choice, 8,* 30–37.

Hall, C. (1997). Cultural malpractice: The growing obsolescence of psychology with the changing U.S. population. *American Psychologist, 52,* 642–651.

Hardy, K. (1994). *Psychological residuals of slavery.* Topeka, KS: Equal Partners Productions.

Hayes-Bautista, D. (November 3, 2001). *California's demographic changes: Implications for building culturally competent delivery systems.* Paper presented at the meeting of the Cultural Competence and Mental Health Summit IX: Cultural Competence: California's Future—Our Mission, Sacramento, CA.

Herman, J. (1992). *Trauma and recovery.* New York: Basic Books.

Johnson, J., & Mock, M. (June 21, 2000). The foundations of cultural competence in mental health. Paper presented at the meeting of the Adult & Children Systems of Care Conference, Santa Clara, CA.

Johnson, K. (1989). *Trauma in the lives of children.* Alameda, CA: Hunter House.

Kiselica, M., Changizi, J., Cureton, V., & Gridley, B. (1995). Counseling children and adolescents in schools: Salient multicultural issues. In J. Ponterotto, J. M. Casas, L. Suzuki, & C. Alexander (Eds.), *Handbook of multicultural counseling.* Thousand Oaks, CA: Sage.

Kluckhohn, F. R., & Strodtbeck, F. L. (1961). *Variations in value orientations.* Evanston, IL: Row: Peterson Publishers.

Kunisawa, B. (1998, November). *Addressing the third wave: The global challenge for the 21st century.* Paper presented at the meeting of the Cultural Competence and Mental Health Summit VI, Bakersfield, CA.

Mock, M. R. (1998a). Breaking barriers: A primary movement for social justice in psychology. In M. Mock, L. Hill, & D. Tucker (Eds.), *Breaking barriers: Psychology in the public interest* (p. 1). Sacramento, CA: California Psychological Association.

Mock, M. R. (1998b). Developing cultural proficiency in clinical practice. In M. Mock, L. Hill, & D. Tucker (Eds.), *Breaking barriers: Psychology in the public interest* (pp. 3–6). Sacramento, CA: California Psychological Association.

Mock, M. R. (1999). Cultural competency: Acts of justice in community mental health. *The Community Psychologist, 32*(1), 38–40.

Mock, M. R. (2000). From illness to wellness: Appreciating our cultural perspectives. *The Journal of NAMI California, 11*(4).

Mock, M. R. (in press). The meaning of cultural competency: Voices of reality, voices of new vision. In R. Hampton & T. Gullotta (Eds.), *Promoting racial, ethnic, religious understanding and reconciliation in the 21st century.* Washington, DC: CWLA Press.

Nadar, K., & Pynoos, R. (1993). School disaster: Planning and initial interventions. *Journal of Social Behavior and Personality, 8*(5), 299–320.

Pear, R. (1998, June 23). Safeguards ordered for Medicare. *San Francisco Chronicle*, pp. A1–A5.

Pinderhughes, E. (1988). *Understanding race, ethnicity and power*. New York: Free Press.

Sue, S. (1998). In search of cultural competence in psychotherapy and counseling. *American Psychologist, 53*(4), 440–448.

Sue, S., & Zane, N. (1987). The role of culture and cultural techniques in psychotherapy: A critique and reformulation. *American Psychologist, 42*, 37–45.

Takaki, R. (1989). *Strangers from a different shore*. Boston, MA: Little, Brown.

U.S. Census Bureau (2001). *Profiles of general demographic characteristics: 2000 census of population and housing*. Washington, DC: Author.

U.S. Department of Education (1997). *Elementary and secondary school civil rights compliance reports*. Washington, DC: Office of Civil Rights.

Vega, W. A., Kolody, B., Aguilar-Gaxiola, S., Alderate, E., Catalano, R., & Carveo-Anduaga, J. (1998). Lifetime prevalence of DSMIII-R psychiatric disorders among urban and rural Mexican-Americans in California. *Archives of General Psychiatry, 17*(3), 1–7.

Wright, M. (1998). *I'm chocolate, you're vanilla: Raising healthy black children in a race-conscious world*. San Francisco: Jossey–Bass.

25

Addressing Unique Ethical and Legal Challenges in Expanded School Mental Health

CHRISTINE A. PRODENTE, MARK A. SANDER,
CHANDRA GRABILL, MARCIA RUBIN,
and NADINE SCHWAB

As the school mental health movement and related prevention efforts have grown, this has paved the way for increased collaboration among educators, school mental health professionals, and community-based practitioners such as clinical psychologists, social workers, psychiatrists, nurses, counselors, and supervised trainees (Flaherty et al., 1998). An emergent aspect of this interdisciplinary approach to mental health care, however, is the lack of clarity about which professional codes and licensing statutes should serve as the guideline for appropriate professional conduct within school mental health programs. In this chapter (as in others in the book), we use the term *expanded school mental health* to refer to school-based programs that involve schools working in partnership with community agencies and programs to provide a full array of mental health care and special education to youth in general (Weist, 1997). Since expanded school mental health providers are located within, but are not necessarily employed by, the school, they must navigate a difficult course through professional ethics codes, state and federal mandates (both health and education), local school board policies, and the policies of their employing agencies. Addressing such issues as client confidentiality and parental consent within the school setting, while maintaining collaborative relationships with the school staff, for example, can be very challenging.

CHRISTINE A. PRODENTE • Partial Hospitalization Program, Medical College of Ohio, Kobacker Center, Toledo, Ohio 43614.   **MARK A. SANDER** • University of Maryland School of Medicine, Baltimore, Maryland 21201. **CHANDRA GRABILL** • Dekalb County Schools, Decatur, Georgia 30032. **MARCIA RUBIN** • American School Health Association, Kent, Ohio 44240.   **NADINE SCHWAB** • Westport Public Schools, Westport, Connecticut 06880.

The goals of this chapter are to (1) identify factors contributing to the confusion regarding the professional obligations of expanded school mental health providers, (2) highlight some of the unique liability and ethical issues related to providing mental health services in the schools, and (3) provide suggestions for addressing these concerns. It is beyond the scope of this chapter to discuss every ethical and legal challenge that may occur when working in school settings. Rather, the chapter will focus on those ethical and legal issues specific to expanded school mental health programs. The chapter is meant to provide a stimulus for further discussion by mental health providers, educators, and policymakers.

CONFUSION REGARDING ETHICAL AND LEGAL OBLIGATIONS

While ethical codes serve to protect the public, and to guide practitioners, at times they are vague and ambiguous (Jacob-Timm & Hartshorne, 1998). Competing ethical principles may apply in a given situation, and ethical guidelines occasionally conflict with state and federal laws (Bersoff, 1994; Bersoff & Koeppl, 1993; Hughes, 1986; Jacob-Timm & Hartshorne, 1998; Kitchener, 1986). Furthermore, ethical codes tend to be reactive and may not address new and emerging ethical issues such as the dilemmas faced by expanded school mental health programs (Bersoff & Koeppl, 1993; Jacob-Timm & Hartshorne, 1998). Professional organizations typically form committees to investigate the ways in which the existing codes relate to emerging issues. Codes may then be revised in response to new ethical concerns, but generally such revisions reflect a drawn-out process.

The progressive growth of expanded school mental health programs has outpaced the rate of development of professional standards and principles uniquely applicable to mental health practice in the schools. While a potential strength of these programs lies within the diversity of provider training backgrounds, the ethical codes and standards of these professionals sometimes fail to adequately address issues specific to practice in the schools. For example, while the American Psychological Association (APA) and the National Association of School Psychologists (NASP) have been at the forefront of outlining ethical guidelines for school-based mental health providers (APA, 1992; NASP, 1997), these guidelines are not uniformly applicable to all mental health providers who work in schools. Furthermore, while the ethical codes established by various professional organizations are seldom in conflict, there may be differences in language and in interpretations of general principles that add to the complexity of the school-based provider's situation (Jacob-Timm & Hartshorne, 1998; Patterson, 1998).

There is also some confusion among educators about the roles of school mental health practitioners, particularly when these practitioners are employees of outside, community agencies. Educators are most familiar with the traditional school psychologist, school social worker, or guidance counselor. These professionals are clearly employees of the school system and their mental health records are school records. As such, federal law, specifically the Family Educational Rights and Privacy Act (FERPA; 20 U.S.C. § 1232g; Regulations at 34 CFR § 99), allows school professionals to share confidential student information internally in the school district without written parental permission, so long as it is of "legitimate educational interest." In other words, although ethical and professional codes may hold professionals to more restrictive confidentiality standards, FERPA states that school psychologists and other school personnel may share confidential student information with teachers, administrators, and other school employees or contracted personnel who provide educational services to the student. "Legitimate educational interest" is rarely well defined in terms of what, why, when, and how much student health and mental health data should be shared. Further, with school district policies being primarily developed by and for educators rather than health and mental health professionals, these policies sometimes lack sufficient detail regarding applicable standards for mental health professionals. Many school district policies were developed prior to the growth of expanded school mental health programs. Therefore, they do not address the unique issues being encountered in the programs, such as informed consent, confidentiality, and the privacy of mental health records.

Federal and state laws and regulations that educators adhere to are different from those of mental health professionals working in the health system and vary from state to state. In fact, the majority of statutory law regulating public schools is enacted at the state level (Jacob-Timm & Hartshorne, 1998), as is the majority of statutory law regulating health care, especially for minors. Nevertheless, many states have inconsistent mandates between their health codes and education codes. For example, many states allow minors to obtain treatment for certain health conditions without parental consent (health code). However, state education laws, as required by FERPA, allow parents access to all of their child's school records (education code), even if the information relates to a student's confidential treatment under state health law. This conflict of laws highlights the fact that "under education law and culture, the legal rights of parents to make decisions for their minor children are upheld almost without qualification." In contrast, in health care, "the legal rights of parents to make decisions for their minor children give way, at least in part, to the right of competent minors to seek, and make their own decisions regarding, certain types of health care" (Schwab & Gelfman, 2001, p. 281). Thus, mental health providers must become familiar with education and health laws and regulations at federal and state levels, as well as with school district policies and procedures, and must recognize and reconcile the conflicts that exist.

UNIQUE ETHICAL AND LEGAL CHALLENGES IN EXPANDED SCHOOL MENTAL HEALTH

These legal and ethical uncertainties foster confusion with regard to informed consent, confidentiality, and record-keeping procedures for documenting client services in schools. Clinicians in expanded school mental health programs must continually balance their obligations to clients, parents, employers, and schools in which they provide services. At times, helping one party (e.g., a student with a drug problem) places the clinician at odds with another party (e.g., a school with a "zero tolerance" policy; see Greenspan & Negron (1994) and Jacob-Timm (1994)). These kinds of pressures occur for school-employed mental health staff and may be exacerbated for clinicians in the school from community agencies, as there is no uniform standard of practice for them.

Informed Consent

Informed consent for mental health services is critical and is one of the most important early discussions to have with a client. The practice mandates of professional organizations that govern the various mental health professionals working in the schools (e.g., American Counseling Association, 1998; APA, 1992; National Association of School Nurses, 1990; National Association of Social Workers, 1993; National Association of School Psychologists, 1997) require that potential clients be fully aware (informed) of the risks and benefits of treatment before they agree (consent) to receive services. However, federal, state, and local statutes and regulations may be inconsistent with respect to whether either the youth or the parent/ guardian is able to provide legal consent for services.

There is growing consensus in the developmental literature that adolescents who have reached the age of 13 years have the same cognitive capacity as adults to provide consent for treatment (Scherer & Reppucci, 1988; Shields & Johnson, 1992). However, states differ regarding the age of consent for mental health treatment. If a troubled 13-year-old *voluntarily* seeks expanded school mental health services without parental consent (perhaps the parent is unavailable, has refused services, or the adolescent feels he would be in danger, if he tells his parent that he is seeking services), the law in many states requires that services be denied (Shields & Johnson, 1992).

Yet, what should a clinician do when there is a child desperately in need of mental health services but parental consent cannot be obtained? There are some situations, for example, in which it is difficult to determine the legal guardian (e.g., child residing with the grandparent while the parent is incarcerated). In cases such as this, it may even be unclear what documentation is required (e.g., is verbal consent ever acceptable?). Clearly, if schools or practitioners take the position that consent can only be given by a formally appointed guardian, as a practical matter, many children will not receive the services that they need (Cohn, Gelfman, & Schwab, 2001, p. 232).

Even in cases in which adolescents can legally consent to treatment, school-based clinicians should strive to involve parents. Caretaker involvement is a critical aspect of delivering mental health services to children (Bickham et al., 1998; Burns, Hoagwood, & Mrazek, 1999; Prout, DeMartino, & Prout, 1999; U.S. Department of Health and Human Services, 1999). However, it is not uncommon for adolescents seeking school mental health services to request that parents not be informed or involved. State laws and regulations vary with regard to the rights of minors to consent for mental health services without parental involvement. For instance, some minors can provide independent consent if they fall into a certain category such as emancipated minors, mature minors, married minors, minor parents, pregnant minors, minors who serve in the military, minors who are living apart from their parents (including runaway and homeless youth), high school graduates, or minors who have reached a specific age (Loxterman, 1996). States often only recognize a few of the minor consent exceptions listed previously and may differ on which of the exceptions they will allow. Even if the school-based clinician learns that the state laws allow mature minors to provide legal consent for mental health services, there is still the question of whether school policies apply to the expanded school mental health clinician. School policies may prohibit the clinician from seeing the student without parental knowledge or consent. Furthermore, if insurance is being billed for mental health services, this may necessitate parental consent as billing forms are typically mailed to parents.

Similarly, it may be unclear whether teacher consultation can be provided without parental consent (Scholten et al., 1993). Even among school-hired mental health professionals, there is disagreement about whether problem solving with either a teacher or an administrator about a specific student without parental consent, even if the name is not identified, is ethical. Some school psychologists believe that they can go into the classroom, observe a student, and engage in a facilitative dialogue with the teacher, as long as they do not interact directly with the student. If school psychologists struggle with these teacher/administrator consultation issues, it is almost certain that expanded school mental health providers, whose roles are not as clearly defined within the school setting, face an even greater challenge. From a practical standpoint, ethical codes prohibiting any form of student-related consultation without parental consent can inhibit informal problem solving and may not be in the best interests of the students (Hughes, 1986; Scholten et al., 1993).

Confidentiality Issues

The confidential nature of a client's communication in therapy is vitally important. Confidentiality promotes trust between the client and therapist (Everstine et al., 1980) and improves the effectiveness of therapy (Gustafson & McNamara, 1987) by encouraging open communication and preventing the improper dissemination of information that might increase likelihood of prejudice, differential treatment, discrimination, harm, or embarrassment (Taylor & Adelman, 1998). Without the assurance of confidentiality, many students either would not seek help or would not be entirely forthcoming (Ford et al., 1997). However, clinicians know that confidentiality is rarely absolute (English, 1995; Taylor & Adelman, 1998). In school-based practice, clinicians typically find that other school personnel (e.g., teachers, principals, special education staff), in trying to help students be more successful, will request confidential information about students (Weist et al., 2001). Thus, expanded school mental health providers must delicately balance the school's and the parents' right to know with the client's rights for privacy.

There are some practical constraints that make it difficult to maintain client confidentiality in the school setting. Client referrals, for instance, are likely to come from administrators, teachers, and other school staff—either individually or through a coordinated schoolwide referral system (e.g., Student Support Team, Child Study Team) aimed at avoiding service duplication. Furthermore, to maintain program viability, it is important that expanded school mental health practitioners provide feedback to school staff (Prodente, Sander, & Weist, in press), i.e., communicate that referrals have been received and acted upon. Additionally, as students transition from class to therapy appointments—using hall passes or by clinician escort—teachers and peers are likely to discover that the student is receiving services. The situation becomes even more complex when group therapies are implemented in schools.

To obtain teacher/administrator support for the student missing class time to attend therapy sessions, it is important for the clinician to collaborate and to share information with school personnel (Prodente et al., in press). Furthermore, providing feedback heightens the educator's understanding of the student's problem behavior and can serve to strengthen the student's support network (Weist et al., 2001). If the clinician does not have written consent from the mature minor or parent, however, the clinician cannot either legally or ethically disclose such information. Clinicians should also realize that sharing privileged information with either teachers or administrators introduces the possibility that this information will become part of the pupil's school record, which is accessible by parents and by a variety of school staff. Yet, tensions and resentment can result when mental health professionals refuse to divulge confidential client information to either educators or administrators who believe that they should have this information (American School Health Association, 1999).

The ethical principles of mental health professional organizations (American Counseling Association, 1988; American Psychological Association, 1992; National Association of Social Workers, 1993; National Association of School Psychologists, 1997) state that clinicians have a clear ethical and legal responsibility to protect clients who are at risk for hurting either themselves or someone else. Expanded school mental health professionals, however, may be unsure as to whether—or to whom within the school—they need to inform when they file a report of suspected abuse, or if a client is a danger to self or others. Even in cases when it is clear that the school administrator must be notified (i.e., the client makes a specific homicidal threat against a fellow student), the question is raised as to how much information should be shared. Thus, it may be challenging to balance the client's right to privacy with school administrators' concerns about student safety and liability (Schill, 1993).

Furthermore, it is unclear what obligation the expanded school mental health provider has to break confidentiality, and make a report to school administrators, when a client violates school policy. While the responsibility of these providers to the school may be clear in certain instances (e.g., a client brings a gun to school), there are many more instances for which there are no clear guidelines. What is the responsibility of the provider, for example, if a student is observed cutting class in the hallway, when a client wears clothing prohibited by the school, if a 16-year-old rape victim reports in session that for protection she is carrying pepper spray, when a client is observed in session with a cell phone, or if a client reports having assaulted a peer who had been verbally harassing her at school? Huey (1986) believes that any clinician working in the school building implicitly agrees to the institution's objectives, principles, and policies. Other providers are unsure if the policies apply to them and are concerned about how enforcing such policies could impact rapport. Cohn et al. (2001) state that students have a right to confidentiality when seeking treatment for substance abuse, for example, but that they do not have a right to confidentiality when committing crimes or violating school rules which are enforced. If the clinician observes the client using drugs on school grounds, for example, this should be treated as a criminal offense, and the clinician should report this violation to school administrators. If, however, the client reports difficulties with drug use during a therapy session and does not specifically request treatment for substance abuse, this information would be maintained in mental health records but would not be reported to administrators. In the unique case of substance use, if the client reveals substance abuse while specifically seeking treatment for this problem, the minor's right to confidentiality is protected under federal law. Yet, practicing clinicians are often unclear about whether they are obligated to report noncriminal offenses that constitute a violation of school policy (e.g., dress code violation).

Recordkeeping

Since school-based mental health providers struggle with their obligations to provide informed consent and to maintain client confidentiality, it follows that confusion would exist with regard to the limits of confidentiality of records in expanded school mental health programs. These programs typically are funded through mixed arrangements, for example, a combination of contracts and fee-for-service revenue (see Evans et al., this work). Because expanded school-based mental health providers tend to be employed by outside agencies, it is often the practice of these professionals to consider treatment records as separate and distinct from educational records. Schools, however, may consider mental health records to be part of the educational record. Thus, programs need to ensure that understandings about client records have been formalized (e.g., in contract language or memoranda of understanding) to avoid confusion and tension between school systems and providers.

The question of whether the expanded school mental health client records are considered part of the students' educational records is of critical importance in light of FERPA, which states that federal funds will not be made available to schools, unless they adhere to the recordkeeping procedures outlined in the law. The law is meant to ensure not only the confidentiality of records, but also the access by parents to their child's school records. According to FERPA, parental consent must be obtained before records are released to outside agencies or individuals. FERPA also states that parents have the right to access their child's school records, to challenge the accuracy of those records, and to have a hearing regarding the accuracy of school records (Jacob-Timm & Hartshorne, 1998).

In guaranteeing parental access to school records, FERPA makes no distinction between students' academic and health records. Furthermore, there are no national guidelines available that take into consideration the ethical standards of school-based mental health practice along with the provisions of FERPA and other relevant federal and state laws (American School Health Association, 1999). Unfortunately, the parental access rights established by FERPA conflict with other federal and state statutes. Whereas in most states minors have the right to seek treatment without parental notification in certain circumstances—such as a minor seeking alcohol/drug treatment or in the case of a mature minor—FERPA gives parents the right to access their child's educational records, including health records, but does not make exception for these conditions (American School Health Association, 1999). Minor consent statutes are based on the idea that minors might not seek treatment if the information is not kept strictly confidential.

A related confidentiality dilemma focuses on the source of referrals for expanded services. If it is the school nurse or counselor who refers a student to the program for treatment, documentation of that referral will be noted in the school health record to which parents are granted access under FERPA (American School Health Association, 1999). A similar conflict arises when expanded school mental health providers seek to enlist the aid of school health professionals to provide follow-up and aftercare for the mature minor or to collaborate in treatment planning. Once this referral information is sent to the school, and it becomes part of the school health record, it will be subject to FERPA guidelines.

Finally, while FERPA protects the confidentiality of a therapist's personal notes, that protection may cease to exist once the content of those notes is shared, even verbally, with other school professionals (e.g., guidance counselor, school psychologist, teacher). Under FERPA, once the school professional documents or shares this information with any other person, it is considered part of the school record, which is accessible by parents (Cheung, Clements, & Pechman, 1997). Thus, the issue of professional collaboration in the school setting is even more complex.

Working with Children with Disabilities

Some unique ethical and legal issues arise when expanded providers treat youth either diagnosed with or suspected of having a disability as defined by the Individuals with Disabilities Education Act (IDEA; 20 U.S.C. §§ 1400, et seq.; Regulations at §§ 300–303). Expanded providers need to become familiar with laws and statutes relevant to children with disabilities, including IDEA and the civil rights provision of Section 504 of the Rehabilitation Act of 1973 (29 U.S.C. § 794; Regulations at 34 C.F.R. § 104). While a comprehensive review of special education and civil rights laws is beyond the scope of this chapter (refer to Gelfman (2001) for further information about applicable laws), it is important that providers understand, refer, and help students access services when appropriate.

Expanded school mental health providers may encounter some difficulty when they provide services to youth who receive special education services. One potential concern relates to the fact that children who receive special education services must have an active Individualized Education Program (IEP). The IEP is a legal document that outlines the special education and related services that a child will receive; these services include specialized instruction as well as related services (e.g., psychological services, special transportation, physical therapy, and health services). Under IDEA, the school is required to provide mental health/psychotherapy services at no cost to the parent, when they are included in the child's IEP (Jacob-Timm & Hartshorne, 1998). Typically, school psychologists, school social workers, or school counselors provide these services. There may be occasions, however, when expanded clinicians are asked to serve as related services providers on the IEP. In essence, the clinician would be acting as a contractual employee of the school—since the school is accountable for the implementation of the IEP. Confidentiality concerns may be raised when expanded school mental health providers are asked to document these IEP-related services in the school records and disclose treatment information at team meetings.

ADDRESSING LEGAL AND ETHICAL CHALLENGES

While the various professional guidelines for mental health providers may be similar in terms of the broad themes or principles addressed (i.e., respect for the dignity of persons, professional competence and responsibility, integrity in professional relationships, and responsibility to community and society) (Jacob-Timm &

Hartshorne, 1998), there are differences in terms of content, scope, language, and emphasis. Thus, in addition to the ethical codes and professional standards established by their mental health association, expanded practitioners would benefit from a greater knowledge of the ethical codes and standards espoused by other mental health professionals working in the school (e.g., American Counseling Association, 1988; American Psychological Association, 1992; American Nurses Association 2001; National Association of Social Workers, 1993; National Association of School Psychologists, 1997). Clinicians would also benefit from interacting regularly with school-based mental health providers belonging to different professional organizations. With this enhanced awareness of diverse ethical codes and standards, providers will be more sensitive to emerging ethical issues as well as to potential barriers to interdisciplinary collaboration.

The ethical principles of professional organizations are often incorporated into the licensing and practice laws of individual states (Baird, 1999). The purpose of such laws is to protect the welfare of persons seeking mental health services. Mental health practitioners who violate the law risk loss of licensure, civil action, and possible criminal prosecution (Bennett et al., 1990; Swenson, 1993). Therefore, it is imperative that practitioners know the current federal and state statutes and case laws (e.g., minor consent laws) in both mental health and education. Unfortunately, the ethical principles of mental health professionals are not typically integrated into local school board policies; thus, providers will need to keep abreast of these regulations as well. It will be particularly important for expanded school mental health programs to clarify, in writing, which policies will and will not apply to their mental health clinician.

Keeping abreast of the current federal and state statutes, case law, and the local school board policies impacting mental health providers is not easy. This information is not typically available in a single resource that is easily accessible. A coordinated effort by professional associations, governmental agencies, and local school boards to develop and regularly update a resource for this purpose is needed. In light of the legal complexity and the relative lack of guidance available, expanded school mental health programs are well advised to seek advice from a competent attorney when aspects of the law or policy are unclear (Jacob-Timm & Hartshorne, 1998). Preferably, the attorney selected should be knowledgeable about both mental health and education law, particularly for both children and adolescents. Recognizing that it can be difficult to find a lawyer specializing in both areas of law, it may be necessary to consult with multiple attorneys.

An ideal time to clarify providers' responsibility to the school is when the expanded school mental health program is in the planning stage (Acosta et al., 2002). When negotiating a contract between the school and the community mental health agency, for example, it will be important to include provisions that are consistent with the ethical codes and standards of the staff who work in the program. Ideally, the contract should specify that the program records are confidential and separate from the pupil's school record. The contract should also specify provider responsibilities with regard to reporting pupil violations of school policy as well as with what information the expanded provider will share with school personnel (e.g., referral feedback, notice of reports filed with child protective services). In the case of an established program, where no written contract or policy exists to address these concerns, it would be a good idea to approach the local school(s) and school board in an effort to develop such a written policy. Once developed, it will be important for practitioners to educate school personnel about the nature of this policy as well as with any other ethical concerns that may impact collaborative involvement.

In areas where current law and policy are either inadequate or in need of revision or clarification, it may be useful for expanded school mental health programs to initiate a dialogue with administrators, mental health professionals, and members of the surrounding community (Acosta et al., 2002). Through ongoing forums and focus groups, programs can identify and problem-solve about the emerging legal and ethical concerns. A related suggestion involves the development of a school-based ethics committee comprised of school personnel, expanded providers, and community representatives (including youth and families) to address ethical issues that are likely to arise within the school.

CONCLUDING COMMENTS

Virtually all mental health staff who work in schools have been challenged by at least some of the ethical and legal complexities described in this chapter. However, these issues are only beginning to be articulated. Clearly, there is a need for diverse staff who work in schools (whether they be hired by the school or a community agency) to come together in open and honest discussions about these and other legal and ethical issues and to involve school and community stakeholders (e.g., students, families, community leaders) in these discussions. This dialogue should occur at multiple levels—within schools, at interagency forums in communities, and at state and national meetings. A national task force to develop preliminary guidelines for the operation of and the negotiation of legal and ethical issues by expanded school mental health programs would be a major step forward.

REFERENCES

Acosta, O., Tashman, N., Prodente, C., & Proescher, E. (2002). Establishing successful school mental health programs: Guidelines and recommendations. In H. Ghuman, M. Weist, & R. Sarles (Eds.), *Providing mental health services to youth where they are: School and other community-based approaches* (pp. 57–74). New York: Brunner-Routledge.

American Counseling Association (1988). *Ethical standards.* Washington, DC: Author.

American Psychological Association (1992). Ethical principles of psychologists and code of conduct. *American Psychologist, 47*(2), 1597–1611.

American School Health Association (1999, October). *Guidelines for protecting confidential student health information.* Author.

Baird, B. N. (1999). *The internship, practicum, and field placement handbook: A guide for the helping professions* (2nd ed.). Englewood Cliffs, NJ: Prentice–Hall.

Bennett, B. E., Bryant, B. K., VandenBos, G. R., & Greenwood, A. (1990). *Professional liability and risk management.* Washington, DC: American Psychological Association.

Bersoff, D. N. (1994). Explicit ambiguity: The 1992 ethics code as an oxymoron. *Professional Psychology: Research and Practice, 25,* 382–387.

Bersoff, D. N., & Koeppl, P. M. (1993). The relation between ethical codes and moral principles. *Ethics and Behavior, 3,* 345–357.

Bickham, N., Pizarro, L., Warner, B., Rosenthal, B., & Weist, M. (1998). Family involvement in expanded school mental health. *Journal of School Health, 68*(10), 425–428.

Burns, B. J., Hoagwood, K., & Mrazek, P. J. (1999). Effective treatment for mental health disorders in children and adolescents. *Clinical Child and Family Psychology Review, 2,* 199–254.

Cheung, O., Clements, B., & Pechman, E. (1997). *Protecting the privacy of student records: Guidelines for education agencies.* Washington, DC: Council of Chief State Officers.

Cohn, S. D., Gelfman, M. H. B., & Schwab, N. C. (2001). Adolescent issues and rights of minors. In N. Schwab & M. Gelfman (Eds.), *Legal issues in school health services: A resource for school administrators, school attorneys, and school nurses* (pp. 231–260). North Branch, MN: Sunrise River Press.

English, A. (1995). The legal framework for minor consent: Introduction. In A. English, M. Mattews, K. Extavour, C. Palamountain, & J. Yang (Eds.), *State minor consent statues: A summary* (pp. 3–7). San Francisco: National Center for Youth Law.

Everstine, L., Everstine, D. S., Heymann, G. M., True, R. H., Frey, D. H., Johnson, H. G., & Seiden, R. H. (1980). Privacy and confidentiality in psychotherapy. *American Psychologist, 35,* 828–840.

Flaherty, L. T., Garrison, E. G., Waxman, R., Uris, P. F., Keys, S. G., Glass-Seigel, M., & Weist, M. D. (1998). Optimizing the roles of school mental health professionals. *Journal of School Health, 68*(10), 420–424.

Ford, C., Millstein, S., Halpern-Felsher, S., & Irwin, C. E. (1997). Influence of physician confidentiality assurances on adolescents' willingness to disclose information and seek future health care. *The Journal of the American Medical Association, 278,* 1029–1034.

Gelfman, M. B. H. (2001). Discrimination in school: § 504, ADA and Title IX; and Special education law. In N. Schwab & M. Gelfman (Eds.), *Legal issues in school health services: A resource for school administrators, school attorneys, and school nurses* (pp. 335–371 and 373–397). North Branch, MN: Sunrise River Press.

Greenspan, S., & Negron, E. (1994). Ethical obligations of special services personnel. *Special Services in the Schools, 8,* 185–209.

Gustafson, K. E., & McNamara, J. R. (1987). Confidentiality with minor clients: Issues and guidelines for therapists. *Professional Psychology: Research and Practice, 18*(5), 503–508.

Huey, W. C. (1986). Ethical concerns in school counseling. *Journal of Counseling and Development, 64,* 321–322.

Hughes, J. N. (1986). Ethical issues in school consultation. *School Psychology Review, 15,* 489–499.

Jacob-Timm, S. (1994). Ethically challenging situations encountered by school psychologists. *Psychology in the Schools, 36*(3), 205–217.

Jacob-Timm, S., & Hartshorne, T. S. (1998). *Ethics and law for school psychologists* (3rd ed.). New York: Wiley.

Kitchener, K. S. (1986). Teaching applied ethics in counselor education: An integration of psychological processes and philosophical analysis. *Journal of Counseling and Development, 64,* 306–310.

Loxterman, J. R. (1996). *A guide to school-based and school-linked health centers: Vol. V. Introduction to legal issues.* A. English (Ed.). Washington, DC: Advocates for Youth.

National Association of School Nurses (1990). *Code of ethics.* Scarborough, ME: Author.

National Association of School Psychologists (1997). Principles for professional ethics. *School Psychology Review, 26*(4), 651–663.

National Association of Social Workers (1993). *Code of ethics.* Washington, DC: Author.

Patterson, T. E. (1998). Ethical school counseling: Managing a balancing act. In L. Palmatier (Ed.), *Crisis counseling for a quality school community: Applying Wm. Glasser's choice theory* (pp. 77–90). Washington, DC: Accelerated Development.

Prodente, C., Sander, M., & Weist, M. (in press). Furthering support for expanded school-based mental health programs. *Children's Services: Social Policy, Research, and Practice.*

Prout, S. M., DeMartino, R. A., & Prout, H. T. (1999). Ethical and legal issues in psychological interventions with children and adolescents. In H. T. Prout & D. T. Brown (Eds.), *Counseling and psychotherapy with children and adolescents: Theory and practice for school and clinical settings* (3rd ed., pp. 26–48). New York: Wiley.

Scherer, D. G., & Reppucci, D. (1988). Adolescents' capacities to provide voluntary informed consent. *Law and Human Behavior, 12,* 123–141.

Schill, K. (1993, Fall). Violence among students: Schools' liability under Section 1983. *School Law Bulletin,* 1–11.

Scholten, T., Pettifor, J., Norrie, B., & Cole, E. (1993). Ethical issues in school psychological consultation: Can every expert consult? *Canadian Journal of School Psychology, 9*(1), 100–109.

Schwab, N. C., & Gelfman, M. H. B. (2001). Confidentiality: Principles and practice. In N. Schwab & M. Gelfman (Eds.), *Legal issues in school health services: A resource for school administrators, school attorneys, and school nurses* (pp. 261–296). North Branch, MN: Sunrise River Press.

Shields, J. M., & Johnson, A. (1992). Collision between law and ethics: Consent for treatment with adolescents. *Bulletin of the American Academy of Psychiatry and Law, 20*(3), 309–323.

Swenson, L. C. (1993). *Psychology and the law for the helping professions.* Pacific Grove, CA: Brooks/Cole.

Tashman, N. A., Weist, M. D., Acosta, O., Bickham, N. L., Grady, M., Nabors, L., & Waxman, R. (1999). Toward the integration of prevention research and expanded school mental health programs. *Children's Services: Social Policy, Research, and Practice, 3*(2), 97–115.

Taylor, L., & Adelman, H. S. (1998). Confidentiality: Competing principles, inevitable dilemmas. *Journal of Educational and Psychological Consultation, 9*(3), 267–275.

U.S. Department of Health and Human Services (1999). *Mental health: A report of the Surgeon General.* Rockville, MD: U.S. Department of Health and Human Services, Substance Abuse and Mental Health Services Administration, Center for Mental Health Services, National Institutes of Health, National Institute of Mental Health.

Weist, M. D. (1997). Expanded school mental health services: A national movement in progress. In T. Ollendick & R. J. Prinz (Eds.), *Advances in clinical child psychology* (Vol. 19, pp. 319–352). New York: Plenum Press.

Weist, M., Proescher, E., Prodente, C., Ambrose, M., & Waxman, R. (2001). Mental health, health, and education staff working together in schools. In I. H. Berkovitz (Ed.), *Child and Adolescent Psychiatric Clinics of North America: School Consultation/Intervention, 10*(1), 33–43. *School Consulation Intervention* (pp. 33–43). Philadelphia: Saunders.

Index